ADRIATIC

About the Author

Caroline Boggis-Rolfe is a writer and lecturer. After receiving a B.A. in Italian from London University, she followed her husband to Berlin in 1969 where he worked for the British Commanders'-in-Chief Mission to the Soviet Forces (BRIXMIS). Their proximity and access to Iron Curtain countries piqued Caroline's interest in the Baltic region, and this led to her first work of history, *The Baltic Story*. Over the past twelve years, Caroline has been a regular visitor to the Baltic as a guest lecturer.

Caroline's new book draws on her Italian degree and experience of living in Italy, where she began to research the long history of the nations of the region. She holds a Master and Doctor of French from UCL.

ADRIATIC

A Two-thousand-year History of the Sea, Lands and Peoples

Caroline Boggis-Rolfe

AMBERLEY

For Nicholas

This edition published 2024

Amberley Publishing
The Hill, Stroud
Gloucestershire, GL5 4EP

www.amberley-books.com

British Library Cataloguing in Publication Data.
A catalogue record for this book is available from the British Library.

ISBN 978 1 3981 1957 4 (paperback)
ISBN 978 1 4456 9506 8 (ebook)

1 2 3 4 5 6 7 8 9 10

Typesetting by SJmagic DESIGN SERVICES, India.
Printed in India.

Contents

Introduction

While for many today the Adriatic is chiefly a favourite holiday destination, particularly popular for its beautiful islands, beaches and coastal towns, this ignores the more significant role that for centuries the region has played in the lives of untold numbers of people. A centre of international relations, a vital crossroads between east and west Europe at the heart of the Roman Empire, it later became the all-important trading route of the Venetians. Besides being a strategic waterway connecting the opposing western-eastern shores, an alternative and often easier passage at a time of poor road communications, in the south it provided a way through the narrow Strait of Otranto into the wider Mediterranean and the seas lying beyond. This book explores how over many centuries the Adriatic became central to the lives and ambitions of a variety of peoples, among them the Goths, the Normans, the Spanish, Albanians, French, British, Austrian-Hungarians, Italians, Germans, and also Slovenians, Croatians, Montenegrins, and all those who in the 20th century were collectively called Yugoslavs. Known as the Roman *Mare Adriaticum*, sometimes in classical times (and on occasion along with the rest of the Mediterranean), it would be referred to as the Adria, the name having been taken possibly from an Etruscan town in the Po delta. Its boundaries, however, were ill-defined, and so later it was usually limited to the shallow area north of the Gargano peninsula, where a submerged ridge separated it off from the waters near Brindisi where they descended to more than 5,000 feet. However, finally, with the Venetians' eventual arrival in Puglia, the whole maritime region east of this to Albania began to be labelled as one sea.

While I was writing this book, the world was hit by the appalling global crisis that soon was to impact on the lives of peoples and societies everywhere: the Coronavirus pandemic. In a startling way this would bring to the fore major concerns regarding public health, poverty, and social discrimination, issues often largely ignored by many people. All this has given us a better insight into the experiences of previous generations, making their stories more relevant to us today. Having been widowed myself during the pandemic, and also having had to live through the extra pain of forced separation during my husband's hospitalisation, I have personally witnessed

7

how this virus has increased our understanding of the horrors of the plague, the bitter experiences of the peoples of the past, whose terrible suffering for the most part without any medicine or help was often further exacerbated by quarantining, isolation, and the continuing fear of probable death from the deadly disease. Alongside the sickness and bereavement, we too have now seen how our own familiar social structure, for all its modernity, has been so easily overturned, broken or irreversibly changed for numbers of people, just as it was so often for our ancestors.

Recently there has also been considerable questioning about the role of history, with arguments levelled both for and against any honouring of some of our famous, but more controversial, predecessors. While some people believe these individuals still deserve to be remembered, others consider they should be removed from all public recognition. Yet the potential whitewashing of the uncomfortable issues of the past that this might create could at the same time risk throwing out the good with the bad. We still listen to the music of the antisemitic Wagner, just as we still appreciate the magnificence of the Colosseum, a structure that is justifiably allowed to stand as a great achievement of mankind, even though it was constructed by a regime that used forced labour and persecuted its enemies or subjects. In this book we find the same paradox in the treatment meted out to the Slavs, the people whose name was to be the origin of the word slavery itself. They would play a role in helping Venice achieve the wealth that enabled it to create the beautiful city that we still so much admire.

In light of this, I would propose that while any analysis of previous times should not attempt to excuse what we now see as unacceptable behaviour, each instance still deserves to be considered in the context of its period. While in the past some people may have chosen to shut their eyes and not question what was happening around them – even Voltaire for one investing for a time in the lucrative triangular slave trade with the colonies – many would only come to realise the full horror and brutality of that particular system once the abolitionists had produced shocking images of what it entailed. Although both the well-being and the employment of still more people were indirectly dependent on the wealth the nation was accumulating by that same inhumane commerce, certain individuals were quite possibly largely unconscious of the degree to which they were beneficiaries of the brutal practices of their own age. Ignorance is no excuse for wrongdoing, but we have to accept that we, as equally flawed human beings, are no doubt making our own mistakes. Even if these things do not appear wrong or contemptible to us, they will most probably shock later generations. To quote Emperor Maximilian of Mexico, 'In the future, men will look back in horror and amazement at some of our actions.' (See p. 279.) Therefore, I believe that we have to approach history with a more open and unprejudiced mind. Even while condemning unreservedly the unacceptable – all intentionally immoral or cruel behaviour – and fully admitting the faults of those who have lived before us, we should still, in the main, be able to acknowledge any good that they may otherwise have achieved.

The long history of the Adriatic region is marked by commercial and political rivalries, conflicts, changing governments, and fluid borders, and so my purpose has been to try and condense this, bringing the whole area together without over-complicating the narrative. This has meant that I have had to omit referencing many places and many people, but while the inclusion of certain individuals might appear arbitrary, I have selected those who, I believe, best represent their time and place. So too, while trying to limit this study to matters of relevance to the Adriatic – and, to a certain extent, the Ionian Sea and its islands – I have had to put restrictions on the material included. This was moderately easy to do when looking at the earlier years of the Venetian Republic, the *Serenissima*'s possessions being largely contained along the eastern shores within a short distance of the coast. It was more difficult, however, in many other cases. While, for example, Venice later branched out onto its mainland *terraferma*, Puglia had in time become included within the Kingdom of Sicily. Similarly, besides gaining various Dalmatian possessions, the Hungarians had gradually extended their reach right up to the Danube and beyond. Therefore, unable always to keep strictly to my set geographical boundaries, I have on occasion been forced to include places considerably further afield – one notable example being Constantinople that was so extensively destroyed by the Venetians and others during the infamous Fourth Crusade. And equally, because people are not stationary, when the lives of some of the more notable individuals have taken them elsewhere, I have had to follow, to Palermo, Rome, Milan, Vienna, Belgrade, Berlin, London, Paris, or wherever. Finally, in every case, I have attempted to keep the narrative from getting too complicated by limiting the number appearing at any particular time, and while I have introduced some figures from outside the region, people like the Holy Roman Emperors, and various foreign dignitaries or invaders, all these appear only when they are particularly relevant to the overall Adriatic story.

This book starts with a Preface that is intended to act as a brief preparatory overview. Here the aim is to try and describe in the simplest possible terms the complicated story of how the Roman Empire gradually extended its reach across the region. As the narrative then moves into the first millennium, we are still restricted by the limited amount of material available, and by the fact that any existing documents tend to be immensely biased for political or personal reasons. Even so, as this is not fiction, I have tried to keep as close as possible to the most verifiable facts in every case, and have intentionally avoided attributing thoughts, words, or deeds to anyone. Nevertheless, the experiences of many of these people were so exceptional that our own imaginations can often give their individual stories a more human face.

As I am covering a vast canvas, stretching across numerous centuries and a wide geographical area, I obviously do not pretend to be an expert on every aspect I have explored. While I have done extensive study, relying heavily on the thorough research of specialists – and I apologise for any misrepresentations of their work or errors that might have slipped in – I have produced this as an introduction to the region, one which I hope will give some people a general picture, and others a starting point to further discoveries of their own. Even though perhaps today chronological studies of any kind are not as popular as they once were, they can still inform our understanding of certain events and attitudes. Past struggles and successes have always motivated for better or worse later generations, and so I believe by looking at such connections, we can often gain a clearer understanding of why things eventually happened in a particular way, and why people thought and behaved as they did.

Originally, I intended to avoid addressing the twentieth century, a period well covered in books and all forms of media, but it then seemed wrong to exclude key figures like Mussolini and Tito entirely. This drew me into the complicated environment of World War II and the struggle between the Allies and the Axis powers, the fascists and the communists, as well as between the various loyalist and dissident groups. It also led me into the troubled years of Yugoslavia before the outbreak of its terrible civil war in the 1990s. While not attempting to deal with all these things in any academic detail, I have tried in the Postscript to untangle part of this complex history and produce a brief summary of the period. However, this then inevitably became a chapter of bloodshed and horror, with atrocities being committed on every side. Such things I would have preferred to leave out of this book, and while I have not wished to describe them too graphically, nor to risk the accusation of casting blame unfairly on one side or another, there is no escaping the fact that the twentieth century was a period of much widespread brutality, and the truth cannot be avoided. As the former Croatian prime minister Zoran Milanović stated in 2015, such terrible events have to be acknowledged and 'heads must not be turned away from them.'[1] However, with the new century having seen the opening up of borders, and peace between the neighbouring nations further strengthened by the EU, the lands surrounding the Adriatic have again become places to be enjoyed. When life returns to some form of normality and travel is more generally permitted again, visitors will once more be able to appreciate not just the beauties of the climate, landscape, and coasts, but also the region's famous towns, cities, monuments and much else, historic treasures that remind us of its rich cultural past.

While in any study of this sort there is a problem over the frequently changing names of places, I have usually adopted those currently in use at the time. This is not always easy as even in the 20th century towns like Zara/Zadar and Cattaro/Kotor were repeatedly being occupied and reoccupied, and so where clarification appears to be necessary, I have added the alternative version in brackets. I also list some of these variations at the end of the book. In the Preface and first section I have used the Roman names of the towns, and although elsewhere I adopt the Italian version of Puglia, here I refer to it as the ancient Roman region of Apulia – a name also given by the Normans to their county and duchy. Yet this Latin term is in itself problematic, because originally it applied only to the northern part of the present-day Pugliese region. The southern area around Taranto, Brindisi, and Otranto in the Salento peninsula was at the time called Calabria – the name now given to the toe of Italy, which was formerly Roman Bruttium. Finally, although I have usually given towns like Marseille, Lyon, and Livorno their local names, I have generally called the famous cities and capitals such as Venice, Turin, Florence, Rome, Paris, and Vienna by the English version we use today – the only exception being Istanbul that until the 20th century was known in the West as Constantinople.

Names of people also present problems. While my methodology may not be very systematic, I have tended to use people's original names in most cases, barring those famous individuals (such as ruling popes, monarchs and emperors). These generally appear in the English version, except for the French kings, Henri II, III, and IV, and Louis-Philippe. And, in the case of Emperor Franz Josef, I have chosen to avoid the rather hybrid German-English alternative. Finally, I give the Holy Roman Empire (later to become the Empire of Austria or Austria-Hungary) and its Emperor capital letters in order to distinguish them from the various others holding a similar title.

As Christian Europe's use of the word 'Turks' was highly derogative, I tend to use this name – instead of the alternative more accurate 'Ottomans' – only when it appears in a particular context, as, for example, in all the Venetian discourse relating to the Battle of Lepanto. The term 'Byzantine' is similarly problematic. Originally derived from the name of the ancient city of Byzantium, it would not become current until the 16th century, when the West then began to use it in an increasingly pejorative way. I have, however, decided that it is sometimes necessary to use this popular shorthand to avoid confusion, first to distinguish more clearly between the eastern (Greek) Roman Empire and the western (Latin) Roman Empire, and second between the remaining (Byzantine) Roman Empire and the Holy Roman Empire of the West.

While originally I much appreciated being able to use the London Library, because of the problems caused by the lockdown, I later turned more and more to the internet, and so among the many websites that I have visited, I particularly want to recognise JSTOR's generosity in giving free access to an exceptional number of papers and articles. Others that I would like to thank are my agent, Tom Cull – who also contributed to the images – and all those at Amberley Publishing who took so much trouble in completing this book. I am also very grateful to my friends Alex and Ingleby Jefferson for their help with my research in Puglia in 2019, to my granddaughter Sophie for her untiring support, my son Edward for his valuable comments and advice regarding certain topics, and to my daughter Dr Camilla Elphick for her academic input concerning some of the other issues that I have raised. Finally, I particularly want to express again my gratitude to my husband for his constant encouragement and helpful advice throughout the time I was writing this book, and for the unfailing interest he showed in my work right to the end.

Preface

Rome's expansion into the lands of the *Mare Adriaticum*

'As Geography without History seemeth a carkasse without motion; so History without Geography wandreth as a Vagrant without a certaine habitation.'

John Smith[2]

When the Romans were gradually beginning to extend their reach, work was started in 312 BC on the construction of the first of their famous roads, the Via Appia. While initially this connected the capital to Capua just north of Neapolis (Naples), within about seventy years it had been continued into Magna Graecia, passing through Tarentum (Taranto) to arrive finally at Brundisium (Brindisi) in 264. Although it was long believed that two vast columns were then put in place at the port to mark the end of the route, more recent research suggests that these were probably erected by an emperor of the second or third centuries of the new era as a way to create a more imposing triumphal entry into his city – an idea that quite possibly the much later Venetians copied in their Piazzetta in Venice. Whoever in fact constructed the impressive Brindisi columns, today only one remains on the site, the other having collapsed in the 1500s. This would continue to lie in ruins until 1666, when it was presented to the people of nearby Lecce, who transported the pieces south and reassembled them in their main square, topping the heavily restored column with a statue of Oronzo, their patron saint credited with saving the city from the recent outbreak of the plague.

By the time the Appian Way had finally reached Brundisium in 264, the road had already helped the Romans bring about the expulsion of the resident Greeks from the south of the Italian peninsula. By 272 BC Rome had begun its colonisation of the region, increasing the area's cultivation of wheat and encouraging the production of oil, so that before long the coastal plains were covered with mile upon mile of olive trees. Although these are still a major feature of the region today, the ancient industry is now seriously threatened by a disease that has become rampant. At the present time, this is particularly true in the more southern parts of

Puglia where the evidence is clear of the appalling damage being caused by the Xylella Fastidiosa outbreak that is sweeping through the region's vast groves. While the desperate landowners are left uncertain as to how they should deal with the catastrophe, opinions are divided on whether to leave the apparently lifeless trees standing in the hopes of some eventual regrowth, or, alternatively, to fell and burn the diseased specimens and replant. As the arguments continue over what should be done, many, whose livelihoods are now reduced to tatters, watch the destruction of the often ancient trees that for generations their families have lovingly tended.

Roman column still standing in Brindisi. (Author)

Meanwhile, during the third century BC, Rome would twice be caught up in war with the Carthaginians, the First Punic War breaking out in 264 over the control of Sicily. Although on its eventual conclusion twenty-three years later the Romans gained possession of the island, soon after the start of the second war in 218 they were again to find themselves under serious threat. Two years later in mid-summer, things finally came to a head when, between present-day Canosa di Puglia and the coastal town of Barletta, the larger Roman army was confronted by the much-feared general Hannibal. Having already won two victories the previous year, he would now at the Battle of Cannae achieve one of the greatest military triumphs of all time. His successful strategy of encirclement and annihilation was to be an example to generals for generations to come, it still inspiring leaders even in the 20th century. With some estimates suggesting that possibly only around a sixth of the Roman army survived the slaughter, the disaster would be not just an appalling shock to those back in Rome, but also lead to widespread desertion by many people who were living in the south. Numbers of towns in the region forgot their previous loyalty to the colonisers, and before long they began to surrender willingly to the Carthaginians. Refusing to agree peace terms with Hannibal, Rome would struggle on until finally, a year after gaining a major victory in North Africa in 202, it was able to bring the war to an end.

Since the time of the First Punic War, Rome had also become militarily involved across the Adriatic, in the Greek region of Illyria, now renamed

Illyricum. Here, concerned about the attacks on their trade and other shipping, in 229 the Romans had taken on those they held responsible for the raids, and after defeating them again ten years later in a third war, in 168 they would force the Illyrians' last king, Gentius, to surrender. With the Romans now in full possession of the king's most southern lands in the region of modern-day Albania, the area had become an independent protectorate. Yet, wanting more, in 156 the victors turned their attention towards the Dalmatians, who had previously declared themselves to be independent of the surrounding Illyrians. Although these would come under attack from the Romans and be forced to pay tribute money, they still managed for almost another two centuries to resist a full takeover by their aggressor. To the north, however, by 177 Rome had already succeeded in taking Istria, and here, on the most southern tip of the peninsula, it would later establish the town of Pola (Pula), which was to become one of its most important cities.

During this same significant period of its growth, near to the coast northwest of Istria, in 181 BC Rome had founded yet another new colony at the town of Aquileia. Already important for being at the end of the ancient Amber Route, in time this would be linked by its various roads to other parts of the growing empire. With these having helped it become a major imperial city, often dubbed *Roma Secunda*, it would be visited over the centuries by various emperors and their wives, and in AD 168 under Marcus Aurelius be turned into a fortress defence against the barbarians. The later Emperor Diocletian had also often chosen to stay in the town, and then, after Christianity had become the official religion, in the 4th century work had started on building the basilica with its impressive mosaic floor. Yet Aquileia's fortunes were about to change and having been besieged by the Goths and sacked by the Huns in the 5th century, it would be finally occupied by the invading Lombards in 568. From that time on, it gradually started to slip from the limelight, its situation being made worse not just by natural disasters, such as earthquake and the rising sea waters, but also by the destructive arguments of the two regional patriarchs. Even so, the vestiges of this town's ancient past remain, and Aquileia is today a recognised UNESCO site of special interest.

The *triumvir* Julius Caesar, the governor of Illyricum, was stationed here in Aquileia during the last years of the Republic in 59-58 BC, in command of three legions. By then, tensions had already started to build up between him and his son-in-law, Pompey, and things became still more strained when Caesar's daughter died in childbirth. Soon after, the situation was made even worse by the death in May 53 of Marcus Licinius Crassus, the third player in the First Triumvirate that had been established seven years before. With Crassus now gone, the rivalries between Caesar and Pompey quickly escalated and the bitter rift between the two men turned into a full-blown civil war.

Fearful of the ambition of Caesar, whose popularity and renown had grown with his recent military successes, and in light of the fact that his

Gallic Wars had ended, Pompey and the Senate now demanded that he should give up his command. Refusing to do so, one night in January 49 BC Caesar slipped out of Ravenna and, having joined his loyal troops camped nearby, he led them across the narrow Rubicon River that marked the boundary between his province of Cisalpine-Gaul and the rest of the country. As any such military invasion was expressly forbidden, this bold action was the equivalent of an act of war and, realising that there was no turning back, Caesar famously declared, 'the die is cast.' Believing Rome to be under threat, Pompey and his followers hurriedly fled the capital and so, on discovering this, Caesar continued to march south. Having gathered additional supporters along the way, he eventually arrived at Brundisium to find his rival among the last fugitives waiting to be shipped across the Adriatic. While these continued to reject all offers of peace, Brundisium remained under siege, but after Pompey had escaped to Dyrrachium (Durrës in Albania) the city finally surrendered.

Although at the time Caesar lacked the fleet he needed to pursue his rival, he was still determined to defeat him. Therefore, when a year later on returning from fighting in France and Spain he finally found enough ships, he immediately set off across the Adriatic and began to lay siege to the enemy's camp near Dyrrachium. Soon both men were constructing opposing defences that stretched for several miles. Caesar's works were still incomplete when at last on 20 May (7 July in the Roman calendar) Pompey decided to break through the remaining gap and mount a full-scale attack. But, as he failed to take full advantage of the situation after Caesar had decided to withdraw, their bitter rivalry was left unresolved. So, the fighting carried on until Pompey's luck eventually began to run out. After having suffered a major defeat at their last meeting on the battlefield in Greece, he fled to Egypt, where before long he was assassinated on the orders of Cleopatra's brother and husband, Ptolemy XIII. While the Egyptian king – who died himself in battle the following year – had hoped by this to ingratiate himself with Caesar, the latter was apparently shocked by the killing. Nonetheless, he was finally rid of his opposite number and so, after punishing those like the people of Pola who had earlier supported Pompey, he was then able to remain in sole power until his own assassination four years later in March 44.

Caesar's great-nephew, Octavian, who was now his officially adopted son, met with Mark Antony and Marcus Lepidus near present-day Bologna in November 43. Here the three men formed the Second Triumvirate, which the next year, following the defeat of Caesar's murderers, would become a virtual joint dictatorship. Although the widowed Mark Antony – entranced like Caesar before him by the Egyptian queen – would soon embark on his own notorious love affair with Cleopatra, in 40 BC he married Octavian's sister, Octavia. This union was intended to re-enforce the alliance recently drawn up at Brundisium, where the men had agreed on the division of their individual areas of control. While Mark Antony was now to take charge of the eastern regions stretching from Dalmatia to the Caspian Sea, Octavian

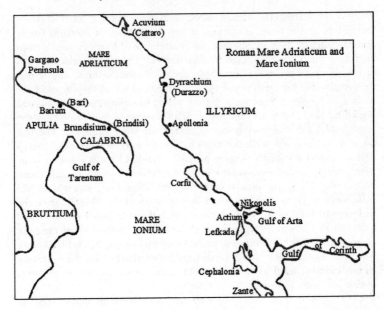

would have the western areas including Gaul and Spain, and Lepidus be chiefly compensated with parts of North Africa.

Three years later Mark Antony and his brother-in-law met again at Tarentum, but by then the tensions between the triumvirs had grown, and in 36 BC Lepidus was finally exiled by Octavian. After that the situation deteriorated still further, the relations between the remaining two ultimately collapsing in 33 when Mark Antony, who had been living permanently for some time in Egypt, divorced his wife and allegedly married his Egyptian mistress. Becoming increasingly concerned that with her support Mark Antony had ambitions for supreme power, at last in 31 Octavian declared war on Cleopatra. At this time Octavian's navy, under the command of Agrippa, was in control of the waters of the Adriatic, so Mark Antony, who still had his eyes on southern Italy, had taken shelter with his ships just south of Corfu in the Ionian Sea. While these were now anchored in the Gulf of Arta (the Ambracian Gulf) his troops were camped on the nearby Actium (Aktio) promontory that today is just outside the Greek town of Preveza.[3] Blockaded on land by Octavian and his army, and from the sea by Agrippa, Mark Antony was cut off from his supplies in Egypt, and so eventually on 2 September he was forced to abandon the safety of the gulf. Despite apparently hoping to slip back home to Egypt unhindered by outrunning, or else defeating, the enemy lying in wait outside, before long both sides found themselves fiercely engaged in the famous Battle of Actium.

During the fighting, despite his possibly bigger fleet, Mark Antony's larger galleys soon proved to be less manoeuvrable than Octavian's craft.

While investigating the winds, tides, and unpredictable local currents facing him at the time, academics at the universities of Poitiers, Patras and Montpellier have shown how the greater size of Mark Antony's ships became a major disadvantage to their crews. 'The wave resistance was increased up to ten times' for those aboard Antony's ships, and it was thus impossible for them to use the ramming tactics that they would have wished to employ.[4] Ever since it took place, questions have been raised regarding the course of the battle, with various other probable (and improbable) explanations being suggested for what occurred, but this latest analysis could well explain why for some reason Mark Antony's fleet remained stationary – quite possibly unable to move – for so long. After coming under vicious attack, the battle began to go against them, whereupon Cleopatra finally withdrew her ships that, laden with the valuable war chests, had been sheltering at the rear. Shortly after she had set sail for Egypt, Mark Antony similarly abandoned the fight and followed in her wake. Already utterly disgraced by the loss of the bulk of his fleet and the subsequent surrender of his troops, he and Cleopatra would then continue to suffer further military setbacks over the following eleven months, until at last they both came to see suicide as the only option left open to them.

Octavian was thus free to assume sole control of his empire and, in commemoration of the Battle of Actium, he had a vast monument built on high ground about three miles north of the gulf from where he could look down on the place of his great naval success. This would be the founding of Nikopolis, his 'victory city', where every five years celebratory games would be held in honour of the triumph. Besides its being visited by several future emperors, the Apostle St Paul also chose to stay here for a while, and by the second century of the new era, Nikopolis, with its fine buildings, had become the capital of the recently established Epirus province. Even so, with the gradual decline of the Roman Empire, in time the city would largely disappear from view. Although later visited by men like Byron and Hobhouse (see chapter 14), it was not until the early 20th century that major excavation work began, raising once more the profile of Nikopolis, now a proposed UNESCO site of special interest.

In the years leading up to this turning point in his career, Octavian had been administering his own areas of control, and near Ravenna he had founded his strategic naval base of Classis (literally 'the fleet'), a port large enough to hold 250 ships. Being close to the city, whose complicated drainage system had probably been introduced by the Etruscans, he set out to connect the two places with a canal, using the fast river flow to help keep the low-lying surroundings healthy and free of disease. Classis would over the following centuries become one of the most important trading ports in the area, and the growing network of waterways in the region provided further useful commercial links across the whole Po basin. Classis and Ravenna would therefore continue to thrive until the 7th and 8th centuries, when eventually their fortunes began to fade as the river started to change its course.

After his successful campaigning in the regions of the eastern Adriatic, Octavian had begun devising new building projects for the area, these including the founding in 34 BC of Slovenia's later capital, Ljubljana, on a site that had been made famous by the legendary Jason and the Golden Fleece. Besides constructing defensive walls around Jadera (Zadar) to control the Dalmatian pirates, he established new colonies at Salona (near present-day Split) and at the former Greek settlement of Buthrotum (Butrint, Albania) on the mainland near Corfu. As his territories had grown, within three decades of making Illyricum a Roman province he had also expanded into the neighbouring lands of the various Pannonian peoples, who at the time inhabited the plain that stretched over the northern region of modern Croatia as far as the Danube. Nonetheless, Octavian still faced challenges, having to deal among other things with a serious revolt by the Dalmatians in AD 6 that only began to come to an end about four years later when the rebels withdrew to their mountain fortresses. Even though the women of Arduba – encouraged by their men – chose to throw themselves and their children to their deaths in the river below rather than face capture, certain groups, such as those at Adetrium (Klis), still managed to hold out until after Octavian's death in AD 14.

Having already assumed the title of *Princeps*, in January 27 BC Octavian was given full recognition by the Senate, who then further honoured him as *Augustus* – the name by which he would be known ever after. He was now recognised as the emperor, and during the four comparatively peaceful decades of his rule, Rome would see a spectacular growth in its power. At the same time, other more tangible records of his reign would start to appear across his empire, vast constructions such as the great theatre at Nikopolis and the arch at Ariminum (Rimini), the latter believed to be the oldest of its kind still standing. Persuaded by his daughter Julia, he also rebuilt the city of Pola that he had earlier ordered to be destroyed in punishment for the people's loyalty to Pompey.

Apart from Pola's Temple of Augustus and its triumphal arches, before long other equally notable examples of ancient Roman architecture had begun to appear around the Adriatic. Augustus's reign had initiated the beginning of an impressive period of building, one that was then taken up by his successors, each of whom sought to find his own way to leave a lasting legacy. The bridge over the Marecchia River in Rimini and the amphitheatre in Verona were both built by the second emperor, Tiberius. Later still, Augustus's earlier timber amphitheatre at Pola was replaced by Claudius, before then being reconstructed under Vespasian. This impressive 'arena', finally completed by Titus in 81, was designed to hold some 5,000 spectators at the gladiatorial games, and over the following centuries it would continue to play a central part in the life of the city. Chosen for the brutal execution of Emperor Constantine's son, and for the dangerous jousts and tournaments of the later Knights Templar, today it is still used for a variety of more peaceful public entertainments. Meanwhile, at the end of the first century, the Emperor Trajan had built a 22-mile-long aqueduct to provide drinking water to Ravenna and had ordered further work done on the port in Ancona, where his triumphal arch still stands. Besides constructing a shorter, alternative extension of the Via Appia to Brundisium along the Via Traiana via Canosa and Barium (Bari), he had also ordered the building of the immensely large amphitheatre in Dyrrachium that is now in much need of restoration. Hadrian's later amphitheatre built at Lecce was also largely forgotten over the years until the start of excavation work at the beginning of the 20th century.

***

By the 3rd century of the new era, Rome was facing a period of economic decline and general unrest, the situation being made worse by the internal and external barbarian threats to the empire. The dynastic succession of its emperors had collapsed and in the half century before the Illyrian ruler Gaius Aurelius Valerius Diocletianus (better known as Diocletian) came to power, some twenty others had for the most part met untimely ends as victims of war, assassination, suicide, or plague. Diocletian had probably been born at Salona in Dalmatia, and although from an undistinguished background, quite possibly being the son of a freed slave, he had risen to prominence serving in the army while engaged in the wars against the Persians. When the eastern emperor, Numerian – joint ruler with his brother since the death of their father the year before – died in 284 in strange circumstances, the prefect Aper was charged, on highly questionable grounds, with responsibility for his death. Using this situation to his own advantage, Diocletian then personally drew his sword and executed the accused man, doing so with the approval of the soldiers, who had already acknowledged him as their emperor. The next year Diocletian went further, going into battle against the other co-emperor, Numerian's brother Carinus. Here the accounts become confused, but regardless of what exactly happened, Carinus died, possibly (according to the unreliable records of the victor who was seeking to destroy his reputation) murdered by a jealous husband. Diocletian was now in sole command. As the empire had, however, grown to be vast and unwieldly, within a year he had decided to divide it up, handing partial control to Maximian – another man from Illyricum – who on becoming a fellow Augustus, began to rule Italy and the entire western region from his base at Mediolanum (Milan). Diocletian, meanwhile, continued to direct his affairs in the east from Nicomedia (Izmit in Turkey). Nevertheless, despite his visiting it only once, Rome still retained its status as the overall capital.

Even these changes were not enough, however, and so in 293, Diocletian promoted two lesser Caesars as well. Constantius I Chlorus would reside in Augusta Treverorum (Trier) and take charge under Maximian of the north-western regions including Gaul. Galerius, acting under Diocletian, was to take control of the eastern shores of the Adriatic from his capital Sirmium (Sremska Mitrovica in Serbia). Yet despite having established this First Tetrarchy, Diocletian still held full authority as the absolute ruler and, with the Senate's privileges having been gradually removed, he was free to

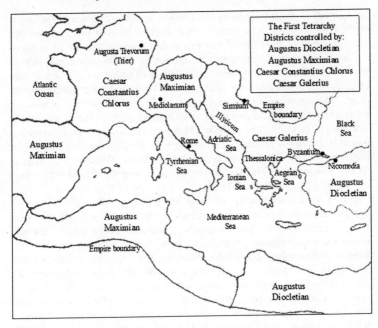

introduce his multiple reforms. An able administrator, during his two decades in power he created a bureaucracy to help carry out his many programmes – these introducing new laws, taxes, and multiple other changes affecting all aspects of everyday life. By increasing the size of his army, not only had he quashed the threats from his outside enemies, but he had also largely curbed the unrest at home, and so his empire enjoyed a period of relative peace. After his departure, much of what he had achieved would begin to crumble as corruption and unrest destroyed large parts of his administrative work, but one notable change would remain. Having wanted to raise his own status, he had introduced new ritual and splendour to his court, imitating many of the practices he had seen while in Persia. After his death, bowing to the emperor and other such customs would be enthusiastically adopted by his successors, and this ceremonial was then to live on, surviving in the Byzantine court for many centuries even after the fall of the Western Empire.

Although he personally was a pagan, calling himself Jovius and seeing himself as chosen by the gods, Diocletian was prepared for most of his rule to leave the Christians largely unmolested, possibly even allowing his much-loved wife and daughter to express their sympathy for some of the new faith's teachings. But while Rome had long tolerated different pantheistic religions, there was some anxiety that the monotheistic preaching of the new sect could threaten the stability of the state. Whether or not this concern played a part in Diocletian's decision, under the persuasion of the intransigent Galerius – now his son-in-law – in 303 he issued the first of his four edicts directly targeting the Christians. When ordering the removal of their possessions and offices, he had declared himself to be against the actual spilling of their blood, but this would soon be ignored by some of the local authorities. Although Constantius in the West adhered only to the first edict and was opposed to the killing of those found guilty of any offences, in the more eastern regions several Christians were brutally put to death. The actual number of victims overall remains uncertain, with some contending that the figures were later exaggerated by those wishing to emphasise 'the cult of the martyrs'. However, the discriminatory measures would be gradually phased out everywhere, first being brought to a close by the same unforgiving Galerius on his deathbed, and then two years later in 313 by Constantine. This finally brought to an end the official persecution of Christians by the Roman Empire.

Just a year after issuing his own edicts, on 1 May 305 Diocletian decided to abdicate, simultaneously persuading Maximian to do the same. A new tetrarchy was then formed with Galerius being one of the two men named as Augustus. Yet, almost immediately, rifts developed as the various individuals jockeyed for position, and although Diocletian and Maximian later tried to resolve the situation, the disputes between the different factions continued. Matters became ever more complicated as other candidates presented themselves as being equally worthy to wear the purple. With most of these eventually suffering violent death, killed in battle, murdered, or becoming suicide victims, finally in 313 just two men took power as Rome's joint rulers. The empire was therefore divided for a time between Valerius Licinius and Constantius' son, but with the defeat of his rival in 324, the latter became the sole ruler – in time famous as 'the Great Constantine' – and within six years he had founded at Byzantium his new eastern capital of Constantinople. By then the already disgraced and humiliated Diocletian had been dead for some years, possibly, according to the accounts that refer to his ill-health and depressed state of mind, having taken his own life.[5] Over the years he had been increasingly threatened by Licinius and Constantine, and he was still alive to witness some of the cruel treatment meted out to his daughter Valeria who, after the death of her husband Galerius, was persecuted by her next suitor and eventually forced into hiding. Fortunately, however, Diocletian most probably would never have known of her death, nor that of her mother, the women killed in 314 by Licinius' men who, having decapitated them both, then threw their bodies into the sea at Thessalonica (Thessaloniki).

Diocletian had chosen to spend his retirement, tending his gardens – not forgetting his famous cabbages – in the magnificent palace he had built for himself in Dalmatia. Overlooking the sea a few miles from Salona, this impressive building, today a famous UNESCO site, now lies at the heart of the Croatian city of Split (formerly Spalato). Constructed on the lines of a military fort, and extending over several acres, it contained – in addition to the resident garrison – temples, private rooms, open spaces, and much else. In the eighteenth century its architecture had so inspired the traveller

Robert Adam that he had drawn on it to develop his neo-classical designs, which had then become the vogue across much of Europe. For more than 200 years the water from Diocletian's approximately 5-mile-long aqueduct would continue to serve the city, and although his tomb would later disappear from the mausoleum where he had been buried, this building would eventually be converted into the cathedral, and his private temple turned into a baptistery. Even though the palace itself would suffer serious damage in the 7th century when the region was attacked by the Avars, still protected by its massive outer walls it became a refuge for the people of nearby Salona. Thus, it took on a character of its own, in time becoming virtually a small city within a city, the palace incorporating the homes and business establishments of its citizens, and as such it still continues to play an intrinsic part in the modern everyday life of Split.

SECTION I

RAVENNA, THE CAPITAL OF THE WEST

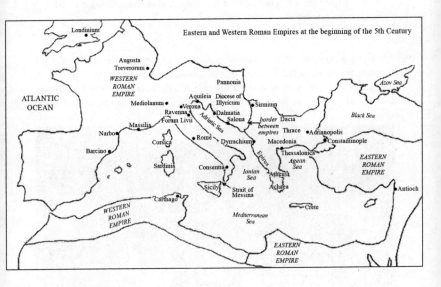

Eastern and Western Roman Empires at the beginning of the 5th Century

Galla Placidia, daughter of Theodosius, last Roman emperor of the East and West

'It is not just that it is more difficult for women to succeed; they get treated much more harshly if ever they mess up.'

Mary Beard[6]

After Diocletian's first division of the old Roman Empire at the end of the 3rd century, the western and eastern regions would alternately reunite and divide, either ruled by one man, or by separate individuals. Finally, in 364 Valentinian I – recently elected as sole emperor – appointed his younger brother, Valens,

Interior walls of the Mausoleum of Galla Placidia, Ravenna. (Author)

the ruler of the East. But in the 370s a series of disasters hit the family. Shortly after Valentinian died from a seizure during a furious altercation, the Goths crossed the Danube into the Roman Empire, and two years later in 378 they achieved a major victory at Adrianople. Apart from this having left the Roman army greatly depleted, the disaster had also seen Valens killed in the heat of the battle. As it was now necessary to replace him, the next year his young nephew Gratian – the new western emperor – decided to promote his general (Flavius) Theodosius to the purple. Having moved back to Spain during the unrest following Emperor Valentinian's unfortunate death, Theodosius was now summoned by Gratian to Sirmium in Pannonia (Sremska Mitrovica, Serbia) to be officially recognised as Augustus of the eastern empire.

On finally dealing with the latest and most pressing threats from the Goths, Gratian went back to Augusta Treverorum (Trier) – one of his three capitals along with Mediolanum (Milan) and Aquileia. In the east, however, Theodosius's movements were still restricted by the on-going challenges he faced from the different clans within his borders. Therefore, despite previous emperors having generally travelled around, spending the greater part of their time at Antioch, he chose to settle at Thessalonica. While here he became seriously ill and believing he was on his deathbed, he was hastily baptised.[7] As this experience had a major impact on him, after his eventual recovery he became even more convinced of the Christian trinitarian teachings that had been officially declared at the Council of Nicaea in 325. The fourth and fifth centuries were a period of much theological dispute, with matters of doctrine being so widely debated that Bishop Gregory of Nyssa famously reported that discussion regarding the articles of faith continued on a day-to-day basis even among the ordinary people in the street – the money-lender, the baker, the bath-attendant apparently pronouncing on the meaning of the divinity. Throughout the period of the Valentinian and Theodosian emperors, arguments would persist over the multiple interpretations of the Christian religion, the various parties arguing the rights of their case while pronouncing against those who contradicted their views.

As in 380 Theodosius was at last able to make his triumphal entry into Constantinople, he began to use the city as the permanent capital of the eastern empire. Through force, and by the cutting off of their supplies, he had now partially eased the situation with the Goths who were living on his lands. But he still faced problems elsewhere. With the continuing shortage of manpower because of the disaster at Adrianople, the empire was now under military threat from the growing numbers of other 'barbarians' who were gathering on its borders.[8] Occasionally, when it appeared to be to their advantage, the various bands of disparate Huns, Rugians and others would join forces. Therefore, faced by this challenge, two years later Theodosius adopted a more practical and pragmatic way to improve relations with those closer to home. He drew up a treaty with the Goths, granting then lands within the empire in exchange for their service as mercenaries. And, even after they had settled there as semi-independent *foederati* under their own rulers, they were still able to practise their Arian faith.

Arianism had been thrown out at the Nicaean council, when its founder Arius had been denounced and exiled for denying that Christ was equal to the Father. Although eventually allowed by Emperor Constantine to return to Constantinople, here in 336, according to popular rumour, Arius had died in very public and humiliating circumstances, in the words of St Ambrose allegedly collapsing in the road 'amid the outgush of his very bowels'.[9] Although this was eventually adopted as the official story, the account had appeared for the first time some twenty years after the event and by then, most probably, it had been grossly exaggerated by the priest's bitter rival Bishop Athanasius. Wanting to revile Arius and demolish his teachings, the bishop had purposely made his original report intentionally salacious. Others had then followed suit, not only moving the scene from the private to the public space but also seeking to add further scatological details. In this way, through emphasising the repellent nature of the affair, and underlining the similarity between Arius's death and that of the arch sinner, Judas Iscariot, critics were able to draw attention to the 'filthiness' of the priest's heresy and the punishable wickedness of its followers.

Over time these increasingly negative representations tapped into the current attitudes that became more established with the devout Theodosius. Under pressure from the Church, shortly after coming to the throne, in 380 he abandoned his earlier more tolerant approach and began to issue a series of increasingly restrictive edicts. These not only banned all pagan worship and sacrifice, but also declared the recently revised Nicene creed to be the official faith of the empire. While Emperor Valens and some other members of the imperial family had embraced Arianism, this and all other so-called heresies were denounced by Theodosius, who, having raised to prominence his own Christian faith, would now establish it at the heart of all the imperial rituals and ceremonial.

Just three years after Theodosius's arrival at Constantinople, the situation in the West changed again, when the 24-year-old Gratian was murdered in Lyon and replaced by the general Magnus Maximus, who had been responsible for his overthrow. Having seized the western throne and established his court at Augusta Treverorum, Maximus declared himself co-emperor with Valentinian II – Gratian's 12-year-old half-brother, resident in Mediolanum. Before long Theodosius decided to make peace with Maximus, but being ever-conscious of the challenges facing his own dynasty, in January 383, in a highly symbolic ceremony at Constantinople, he appointed his five-year-old son Arcadius co-emperor in the East. Following this, he honoured his wife, Aelia Flaccilla, with the title of Augusta, and three years after promoting Arcadius, he raised his second infant son, Honorius, to consul. But while his family's position was now apparently secure, for Theodosius this period of good fortune would be short-lived, ending soon after with the deaths of a much-loved daughter, and then of his wife.

During all this time Theodosius's army was led by Stilicho, a man of Vandal descent, who in 384 had become engaged to the emperor's favourite niece, Serena. Valentinian I and his brother Valens had banned intermarriage

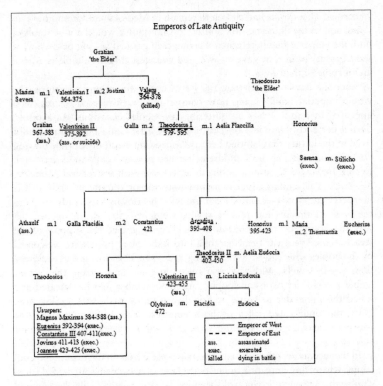

Emperors of Late Antiquity

with the barbarians on pain of death, but periodically in later years the ruling had come to be ignored whenever such relationships were seen to serve a purpose.[10] Three years after Serena's engagement, Theodosius met Galla, the reputedly beautiful sister of Valentinian II, who had now escaped Maximus by fleeing with her family to Thessalonica. Here, to the apparent delight of her scheming mother, she soon attracted the attention of Theodosius, whereupon the older woman reportedly demanded an exchange, her daughter's hand for the overthrow of the hated Maximus. Whether or not this part of the story is strictly true, the couple were soon married, and the following year Theodosius set off to the West, where civil war had now broken out. This would end only after Maximus had been defeated in battle and then executed. While these events allowed the young Valentinian II – helped by his Frankish *magister militum*, Arbogast – to regain his authority in the West, it also enabled Theodosius to appoint his second son Honorius as the future western emperor. Meanwhile, Galla had remained behind in the East and probably sometime between 391-393 she had given birth to a daughter, who was then called (Aelia) Galla Placidia. Having moved to Constantinople from Thessalonica, things had become more difficult for Galla because of the ill-treatment shown to her by her stepson Arcadius. After the overthrow of

Maximus, Theodosius had chosen to remain in Mediolanum for another two years, and so the domestic situation in Constantinople would not be resolved until the emperor finally returned. Having then granted his son possession of the large city palace, he gave his wife and youngest child a suitable residence and income of their own.

Since the days of Diocletian, the status of the emperors had grown, the whole imperial family being now remote and much-revered figures, who appeared in public solely on glittering ceremonial occasions. As a result, during her early years in Constantinople the little Galla Placidia no doubt lived in the luxury that befitted her rank, spending much of her time playing with Serena and Stilicho's children. But her peaceful childhood was soon to end. In May 392, after a public disagreement with his general Arbogast, her uncle Valentinian either committed suicide or – quite possibly – was murdered at Vienne in Gaul. Even though Theodosius was ready to claim the western throne and reunite the two empires, this death opened the way to another usurper, Eugenius, who, having gained the support of the treacherous Arbogast, then marched into Italy. Here both were welcomed by the nobles who had earlier been angered when Theodosius had outlawed their pagan beliefs. With civil war once more on the horizon, the eastern emperor again left Constantinople, and in September 394 he defeated and killed the pretender in battle at Frigidus in the Vipava Valley (Slovenia). Now the undisputed ruler of both empires, Theodosius displayed the usurper's head in triumph, and Arbogast fled the field, later to commit suicide.

In the meantime, other changes had taken place back in the eastern imperial court, where the emperor's young wife (and a new-born son) had died in childbirth. Although Serena had therefore decided to take Galla Placidia and her half-brother Honorius to join their father in Italy, at the start of 395 and just a few months after their arrival in Mediolanum, the 48-year-old Theodosius also died. Following Bishop Ambrose's eulogy and the 40-day lying in state, his body was returned to Constantinople for the funeral. Once the ceremony was over, however, the visiting family found itself no longer welcome at the eastern court, and so, wanting to find a new home, Serena and the children returned to Italy, where they eventually settled in Rome.

Although said to have been a kind man, devoted to his family, Theodosius I had had a quick temper. Five years before his death this had been all too evident when he had ordered reprisals against the people of Thessalonica, who during an uprising had murdered some of the Goths he had placed in command of the town. Although almost immediately he had rescinded his instructions, news of this had been too late to prevent the massacre of possibly thousands of the local citizens. Nonetheless, Theodosius I had been able to maintain the peace in the East, and despite his two costly civil wars, he had on the whole maintained his authority in the West, but because of his premature death, this was about to change. The empire was now broken up once more and the two regions were divided between his young and ineffectual sons. Though the western empire faced serious challenges both in Gaul and along its eastern borders, from this time on it could count less and less on support from Constantinople, where the main concern was now to protect itself from potential problems that might arise in the Balkans. Moreover, as the eastern emperor had begun drawing up his own separate treaties, the different barbarian groups had started to turn their attention instead towards the West, thus adding to the pressures already facing the region. Stilicho, who apparently saw the preservation of the united empire as his responsibility, had remained after Theodosius' death as head of the army, but his position as acting guardian for the 8-year-old western emperor Honorius had been given no official stamp. Similarly, since details of what Theodosius had said on his deathbed were uncertain, there were further complications in the general's relations with the 18-year-old (and poorly prepared) eastern emperor Arcadius.

Theodosius had also left other problems unresolved. Like Gratian before him, he had welcomed the settlement of the Goths and, even though they had later broken their agreement with him, with Stilicho's help he had eventually succeeded in defeating them and calming the situation down. In the immediate aftermath of his death things began to change again as the enfeoffed Goths started to question their loyalties. They had been particularly angered by the apparent lack of concern Theodosius had recently shown for them at Frigidus when he had placed them in the forefront of the fighting. As large numbers of their men had been killed in the action, many now renounced their position as *foederati* and decided to settle in Thrace in the eastern empire, where they would then join those Goths who had just acclaimed Alaric as their king.

Being leader of the combined armies, Stilicho intended to deal with this latest challenge, but because of the shortage of troops, he needed first to recall men from the frontiers where they were defending the borders. However, in the end no attack on the rebellious Goths took place, since Stilicho was rumoured to have been prevented in this by his jealous rival. According to this version of events, the all-powerful eastern Praetorian Prefect of Illyricum, Rufinus, whom Theodosius had appointed guardian of his older son, had persuaded the young Arcadius to recall his army to Constantinople. While this story suggests that there had been an intentional effort to thwart Stilicho's campaign, it appears more probable that the general himself was unwilling to make the situation worse with the loss of yet more men. As a result, he may well have personally called off the action.[11] Whatever the truth, the tensions in the East did not improve even when shortly after – very likely with Stilicho's connivance – Rufinus was brutally murdered. Having been literally butchered to death, he was succeeded by the eunuch Eutropius, who two years later appointed Alaric as *magister militum* of the Prefecture of Illyricum, a promotion that before long would make it easier for the Gothic king to march with his troops into the Western Roman Empire.[12]

That invasion, which finally took place in 401, would increase the alarm of the empire's terrified people, who were already living in dreadful expectation of the end of the world. They had recently witnessed an unusual number of strange events such as comets, eclipses and other natural phenomena that they held to be portents of doom. Having attacked Aquileia, Alaric marched on to Mediolanum, keeping this under siege until Stilicho was at last able to cross the Alps in the spring and come to its rescue. Having also lost a hard-fought battle at Verona – a town of particular importance as it controlled the east-west crossroads and the Alpine passes – the Goths were eventually defeated in northwest Italy and Alaric was persuaded to abandon his invasion. But even though the immediate threat had receded, Emperor Honorius had become greatly concerned and so, besides ordering the strengthening of the old Aurelian walls around Rome, he now left the capital and moved north to Ravenna. This coastal town, partly defended by its surrounding marshes, had the additional attraction of being close to Classis.[13] Even though relations had already started to break down badly between the two imperial brothers, this port could provide, if necessary, an easy escape route to Constantinople. Furthermore, as Ravenna was well placed across the water from Illyricum, Stilicho had chosen it to be his military base, and so it had the added protection of the army.

However, Rome was not forgotten, and although Honorius began to spend more time in the Adriatic town, he still periodically returned to the old capital to celebrate or mark the major events, among these the burial in 404 of his apparently neglected wife. Regardless of his previous treatment, he now had her interred in the mausoleum he had recently created for himself and his family alongside Constantine's large basilica, buildings that would be demolished in the 16th century to make way for the construction of the new St Peter's. While over the previous century Rome had been less visited by the emperors, Honorius would reverse this trend, spending a greater amount of time in the city than his predecessors. But around 408, some six years after his initial move to Ravenna, the Adriatic town became his more permanent capital.

In 400 Stilicho had become consul, and that same year it appears he and his wife Serena may well have suggested that Galla Placidia should marry her childhood companion, their son Eucherius. Although nothing came of this scheme, two years earlier the couple's own daughter Maria had married Emperor Honorius, and then, four years after her death, in 408 she had been replaced by her sister Thermantia. Rumour indicates that both these unfortunate women would be totally ignored by Honorius, with the younger woman suffering still further humiliation when shortly after her marriage she was publicly repudiated in the aftermath of her father's disgrace.

Earlier in that same year, Emperor Arcadius had died in Constantinople, and his eastern throne was now in the hands of his 7-year-old son, Theodosius II.[14] Although Stilicho initially wanted to go to the Byzantine capital to use his influence to reunite the empires, he was soon under considerable pressure from the various barbarian groups threatening on the western emperor's borders. With the situation in Gaul being made still worse by the actions of the latest usurper, Constantine III, the general found himself unable to deal with all these problems at once, and so he grew yet more unpopular. As his enemies had long questioned his motives, accusing him without evidence of having ambitions to gain supreme power, he was now arrested on a charge of treason, and then summarily executed on the orders of Honorius, his son Eucherius suffering a similar fate soon after. Following Stilicho's death, the atmosphere grew yet more febrile as numbers of Goths loyal to the dead man were persecuted and, while the slaughter of men, women and children continued, yet more groups began to turn to Alaric. Having been rebuffed by Honorius, the king of the Goths finally decided to avenge his people and mount a second invasion of the Italian peninsula. In their search for land and food, the invaders moved south down the Adriatic coast to Ancona, before then crossing central Italy to arrive in October outside Rome itself.

As the city came under siege, there would be yet another victim of the growing unrest when Stilicho's widow was arrested and put to death by strangulation. Evidence suggests that not only had Serena begun to overstate her importance – styling herself Augusta – but she had also offended many of the pagan worshippers in Rome. She had angered them by the blatant disrespect she had shown for their gods, and she had even gone so far as to destroy their recently reinstated statue of Victory in the Senate. Although Gratian had banned polytheistic worship, and Theodosius had increasingly ordered obedience to the Nicene creed, in Rome the paganism of old had remained particularly strong. By appeasing their earlier gods, many people still hoped to gain divine intervention against the outside threats that were now confronting them.

The later historian Zosimus includes Galla Placidia among those calling for Serena's death, and this raises a question over the part she played in the affair. While no contemporary record exists giving us precise details, some critics consider that Galla Placidia acted against her cousin out of spite. It is quite possible that she may have grown to dislike the older woman, or even that she was happy to see the removal of a challenge to her own position. This was an age of brutal retaliations and punishments, and Galla Placidia would later prove that she could act with cold-hearted determination when she felt it necessary. Alternatively, might she not as a vulnerable single young woman – who was already deeply unpopular with her jealous half-brother – have seen no option other than to allow others to use her imperial name to enforce their own authority? Whatever the truth, while Galla Placidia has often been condemned for this affair, the extent of her responsibility for Serena's death remains a matter of conjecture.

Meanwhile, as the Goths besieged the city, starvation and disease began to hit. With many citizens, including members of the powerful senatorial families, turning again to their pagan gods, even the pope was prepared quietly to condone the continuation of their worship in private. At last, having been paid sufficient ransom, Alaric called off the assault and took his vast army back north to overwinter in Tuscany. As Honorius still refused to discuss peace terms, however, the next spring the king returned to Rome, and here he persuaded the Senate to appoint a new emperor. The man chosen for this role was the pagan prefect Attalus, who on his election conveniently agreed to convert to the Arian faith of the Goths.

Attalus's reign would be short as Alaric would soon decide to depose him in order to ease his negotiations with Honorius, who had finally agreed to meet him near Ravenna.[15] Before any compromise could be reached, Sarus, a Goth – who supported Honorius and bitterly hated Alaric – launched his own assault on the king. The attacker was killed by Alaric's brother-in-law, but this episode would The attacker was immediately killed by Alaric's brother-in-law, but this episode would later have serious consequences for Galla Placidia herself. An enraged Alaric called off the talks and returned to his siege of Rome, and soon the situation became dire as food supplies began to run out. During this time Galla Placidia was still in the city, but while she did not probably experience the depth of starvation of the general public, some of whom reputedly would resort to cannibalism, even she would have suffered the general hardship in those hot days of August when conditions had soon become unbearable. Eventually, wishing to end the agony, someone – reputedly a rich woman, sympathetic to those who were starving – opened the gates and allowed the enemy to enter the city. Although Alaric immediately rewarded his men with the usual three days of looting, some witnesses would later speak of the remarkable respect the Goths had shown for the holy sites. Rome was so little destroyed that it was possible for the damage to be largely repaired within just a few years.

Galla Placidia was now taken hostage and, having been placed under the protection of Alaric's brother-in-law Athaulf, she joined the Goths as they set off on their march south. Their objective was to reach North Africa, where they hoped to gain possession of the Romans' vast grain stores to feed their large army. While nothing is known about Alaric's first wife, she being probably dead by this time, Galla Placidia had now reputedly become Athaulf's mistress. Although a captive, she was still being shown a certain amount of respect, allowed to travel in some comfort, and also provided with suitable accommodation whenever the long column of travellers eventually came to a stop. Her treatment by the Goths contrasted sharply with that she received from her half-brother, who displayed throughout a scant concern for the well-being of his sister. As he had appeared to care equally little for the damage caused to Rome or the suffering of its people, stories would now be spread ridiculing his apparent misunderstanding of what had happened. His chief anxiety was said to have been for the safety of his missing, much-loved rooster called 'Roma'.

By the time Alaric arrived in Rhegium (Reggio di Calabria) at the southern tip of Italy, the season was getting late, but having found a fleet to transport his followers over the Straits of Messina to Sicily, he was still keen to set out. But as the Goths lacked experience in all nautical matters, they were soon hit by disaster. With a severe storm blowing up as they left harbour, many of the ships were wrecked and scores of the terrified passengers were drowned. Realising the failure of his plans, Alaric gave up any thought of reaching Africa and resigned himself to returning north, but before he had gone far, he died near Consentia (Cosenza). According to the Gothic rites, he was then buried in an unmarked grave in the bed of the temporarily diverted Busento River, the secrecy of the spot then being apparently maintained by the subsequent execution of those who had carried out the ceremony.

Following his death, the Goths chose to replace Alaric with Athaulf. According to the records, by this time he had grown close to Galla Placidia, and she had become equally attracted to him. As she had now come to admire his ideas and appreciate his people, this period was to leave a lasting impression and influence her thinking for the rest of her life. In turn, she was said to have wielded an influence on Athaulf, persuading him not to destroy the Roman state, but rather to try and combine it with that of the Goths. Both their peoples were to be united under Roman law. Later, as the search for new fertile lands continued, she may also have been partly responsible for the king's decision to move west towards her father's former country of Spain.

By 412 this band of Goths, now to be labelled as the Visigoths – in contrast to the Ostrogoths of the east – had left Italy and crossed the Alps into Gaul. Here, the year before their arrival, Honorius had sent his *magister militum* (Flavius) Constantius to Arles to deal with the usurper Constantine III, who was later defeated and sent back with his son to be executed in Ravenna. But with Constantius soon otherwise engaged against another usurper in Africa, a third claimant, Jovinus, appeared in Gaul. Although he had initially backed this man, in time Athaulf had transferred his support to Honorius and so on his orders he had the pretender and his brother executed. At that point, the emperor and the king began to discuss new terms of agreement, Honorius now offering the Goths African grain in exchange for the return of his sister. But while he wanted to marry her to his general Constantius, this idea was swiftly rejected by both Galla Placidia and Athaulf, who quite possibly had already been unofficially married at Forum Livii (Forlì) on their way north through Italy.[16]

Having thus rejected Honorius' plans, Athaulf would first try unsuccessfully to capture the port of Massilia (Marseille), before deciding to lead his followers further west to take Narbo (Narbonne). It was here in January 414 that Galla Placidia and Athaulf were officially married in a sumptuous wedding ceremony conducted according to Roman practices. To mark the occasion, Athaulf presented his bride with fifty silk-clad men laden with two large salvers filled with gold and precious jewels previously taken from Rome – a Gothic custom of bequeathing looted treasure to one's wife. Constantius, however, was furious when he heard the news, and in retaliation he began to block the ports and shut the passes into Italy. As this cut off any further food supplies for the Visigoths, Athaulf moved his people on again, and having finally crossed the Pyrenees, he and his followers reached Spain and settled at Barcino (Barcelona).

While here Galla Placidia gave birth to a son she named after her father Theodosius, but, although destined to become the future ruler of a combined Gothic-Roman state, to his parents' distress, the child died within months. This was a tragedy that his mother appeared never to forget, and although the boy was now buried in Spain, shortly before her own death in 450 she arranged for the child's silver coffin bearing his remains to be interred in the family mausoleum in Rome. This loss was not the end of Galla Placidia's suffering, however, as shortly after the boy's death her husband Athaulf was killed by his own men. In the confusion following his murder, the throne was given to Sigeric, one of those involved in the assassination. As years before his brother Sarus had been struck down by Athaulf following the attack on Alaric, Sigeric was now set on further retaliation and therefore, besides killing the king's daughters from his previous marriage, he also purposely contrived to humiliate his widow. Galla Placidia was forced to walk twelve miles with the other hostages behind her husband's coffin. But, the new ruler's cruelty soon proved to be too much for his own people and so within days he, too, would be assassinated.

Although, unlike Sigeric, the new leader Wallia showed Galla Placidia the respect that was her due, he gradually began to see her as a useful bargaining tool. Having failed in his attempt to cross the Mediterranean and reach the much-needed food supplies in Africa, he decided the time had come to make a deal with Honorius. In return for the Visigoths' military service as *foederati*, and the surrender of Galla Placidia, the emperor would promise to provide Wallia with the necessary grain. This particularly suited Honorius, as he was still determined to marry his half-sister to Constantius. Once the deal had been agreed, she and some of her faithful attendants were returned to Gaul, and then, following her remarriage on 1 January 417, she would finally settle back in Ravenna.

As Constantius's successful military career progressed his status rose, until eventually in February 421 Honorius appointed him co-emperor in the West. But Constantius's rule would be brief as he died seven months later. By that time, however, his wife had given birth to two children, a daughter (Iusta Grata) Honoria, and a son, Valentinian, who became the rightful emperor of the West two years later. But although he had now succeeded his uncle who had just died, by this time other events had already forced Galla Placidia and her children to flee from Ravenna to Constantinople. After years of showing little interest in his sister, on her return to court Honorius had started to display a previously unseen degree of affection for her. As time went by this became ever more apparent, his constant petting and kissing eventually causing gossips to suggest that a possibly incestuous relationship had developed between them. As the rumours grew and tensions increased, Galla Placidia began to realise the danger she was in. Whether or not – as some have suggested – there had also been a major disagreement between the siblings, she had decided to take shelter with her children at the eastern court of her nephew Theodosius II. Yet, because she and her family were still in Constantinople when Honorius died in Ravenna in August 423, another usurper had soon appeared on the scene. Persuaded by the Huns, this man now seized the western throne and became the new Emperor Joannes. As a result, Theodosius II belatedly acknowledged the imperial rights of his five-year-old cousin, then further displaying his support by agreeing to Valentinian's engagement to his infant daughter Licinia Eudoxia.[17] But as Galla Placidia wanted more for her son, she now surrendered her lands in Illyricum, exchanging these with Theodosius in return for his promise to provide the military backing she needed to recover her child's empire.

Around this time, during their travels Galla Placidia and her children were caught in a violent storm that threatened to wreck the ship in which they were sailing. In fear for her life, she prayed to St John the Evangelist for help, vowing that were she to survive she would build a church in his honour at Ravenna. A sincerely devout woman, she later fulfilled her pledge, creating a spectacular building with silver-gilt columns, mosaic floors and walls, and huge chandeliers. Unfortunately, the basilica dedicated to San Giovanni Evangelista would suffer greatly over time, being not only damaged by fire but also subjected to repeated destructive renovations. Among its greatest losses was the removal in 1568 of the magnificent mosaics depicting St John and the storm which, like the rest of the church, had so impressed those who had first seen them when they were created.

Toward the east Galla Placidia built the apse, which rests on two very large columns, incrusted by her with gilded silver. One saw there also the Lord in majesty presenting a book to the Evangelist, underneath which was written St. John the Evangelist. On both sides was the glassy sea, on which two ships were agitated by turbulent storms and powerful winds. In one St. John has come to the aid of Placidia... In the middle of the apse was a most beautiful image of our Lord, seated on a throne and illuminating the whole basilica... It had the following inscription: 'The Empress Galla Placidia with her son the Emperor Placidus Valentinianus and her daughter Iusta Honoria fulfills her vow for her deliverance from the sea.'[18]

This message, remembering the church's founder and the reasons behind the building, is today repeated in the Latin plaque at the back of the church. Yet the removal of the original work would not be the building's only loss, as over time other important mosaics would similarly disappear, in particular those depicting fifteen emperors and other members of the dynasty. Among the people represented were Galla Placidia, her father, two brothers and also probably her dead infant son, lost images that would have given us some idea of how these people appeared. This would not be the last damage done to the basilica, however, since the alterations of the eighteenth century were succeeded by the accidental destruction of the church in the 1940s, when Allied aircraft missed the nearby station that had been their intended target. But this final disaster brought a small compensation. During the restoration work pieces of the 13th-century floor mosaics were found to have survived, today displayed along the walls in the side aisles. Here, besides the depictions of various mythical beasts, there are other images relating to the 4th crusade that were created in celebration of the recent disastrous attacks on Zara (Zadar) and Constantinople. And nearby in the small chapel a few 14th-century frescoes remain that possibly include a work by Giotto.

On arriving back in the Adriatic, half the eastern imperial army, commanded by Ardaburius, was instructed to continue by sea to Ravenna, while Aspar, the general's son, accompanied by Galla Placidia and her children, had orders to proceed up the Dalmatian coast to northern Italy. While Aspar's part of the campaign went according to plan, allowing him to take Aquileia, the same would not be true of his father. Here the invasion failed when further storms hit his fleet and he and others were taken as prisoners back to Ravenna. On Ardaburius's arrival, the usurper Joannes treated him well and granted him free movement around the city. As a result, the general was eventually able to persuade some townspeople to join his cause and with their assistance a message was passed to his son, who then arranged for a rescue party. After being helped to find its way through the surrounding marshes by a local shepherd, this group would succeed in entering the city. No recognition was now shown to Joannes for his earlier good treatment of Ardaburius, and – with the active approval of Galla Placidia – the usurper was arrested, his hand cut off, and in a final intentional public humiliation, he was carried by a donkey to his execution in the hippodrome at Aquileia.

At last, in 425, Valentinian III was officially recognised in Rome as the western emperor, and his sister Honoria was acclaimed as Augusta. But while Galla Placidia had now achieved the position of acting regent, during the next twelve years that she held the role the empire would continue to be challenged by the many barbarian tribes massing on its borders.[19] She also faced difficulties from her generals who had become increasingly embroiled in personal rivalries. Her faithful *magister militum*, Flavius Felix, was challenged by her equally trustworthy Bonifatius, and he in turn was opposed by Aetius. Although the latter had already shown a readiness to interfere in matters of state when ensuring Joannes's earlier seizure of the throne following the defeat of the rebellious Visigoths in Gaul, he had become one of Galla Placidia's most loyal and successful military leaders. But Aetius, too, was jealous of Felix, suspecting that he was plotting against him, and so in 430 he succeeded in getting the general and his wife executed. Adding further to this confusing picture, three years earlier, with equal deviousness, Felix himself had convinced Galla Placidia of Bonifatius' disloyalty, he having instructed him in a forged letter to disobey her orders. For this he had been charged with treason, but after his eventual pardon and return to the fold, it would be the turn of Aetius to be deposed. As within a year the tensions had escalated to such a degree that these two men were at war, in 432 they met at the Battle of Rimini. Here the victorious Bonifatius was mortally wounded, and the defeated Aetius forced to flee to Dalmatia, from where he then sought refuge with the Huns, among whom he had previously spent some time as a hostage.

Two years later, however, Aetius was allowed to return to Ravenna, where, after the ending of the regency in 437, he began to exert his control over the young Valentinian III. Despite the general's efforts the empire was crumbling, threatened by the Goths, Franks, Burgundians, Huns and others. From their base in Spain, the Vandals had finally crossed the Mediterranean and taken the fertile lands of North Africa before going on to capture the major prize of Carthago in 439. These were disasters for the empire, the territorial losses made worse by the resulting reduction of tax revenue. Therefore, as the situation continued to deteriorate and Valentinian looked for new allies, he honoured Attila the Hun with the title of *magister militum*.

In this same period Pope Leo I began to assert the supremacy of Rome over the other bishoprics, emphasising its importance as the site of St Peter's martyrdom and burial. Having always been the seat of senatorial power, the old capital further increased its status in 440 when it was again chosen by Valentinian as an alternative residence. Just a year after his death in 454, however, Rome would suffer untold damage at the hands of the Vandals, who during their two-week sacking of the city would strip it of its greatest treasures. Even so, for the next two decades Rome remained an imperial capital, continuing as such until the empire was officially declared ended.

The year before moving permanently to Rome, the western court was rocked by a scandal, the emperor's sister Honoria being discovered to have embarked on an affair with one of her entourage. While her lover was tortured and put to death, she was engaged to an elderly senator, but determined to avoid her fate the girl now turned to Attila the Hun for help, sending him a message via her eunuch Hyacinthus. On his return this poor man was captured, tortured and, after revealing all the details, executed, whereupon Honoria was quickly married to the senator. Although her ultimate fate is not recorded, her situation was no doubt made worse the next year when Galla Placidia died, her death depriving Honoria of the protection of her mother, who had always tried to defend her from her brother's wrath. Honoria's story was not quite finished, however. Because she had included a ring when appealing to Attila, he now chose to interpret her earlier request as a marriage proposal. Using this as an excuse, in 452 he invaded Valentinian's lands, claiming that he was merely asserting his rights to his 'bride's' share of the empire. He now carried out savage raids on the country, sacking Verona and Vicenza. Aquileia also came under siege for three months, then being left in such a ruined state that it was never again to recover its former standing.

In July 450, shortly after Honoria's affair, Theodosius II died in Constantinople following a riding accident. Within months, his competent sister, Augusta Pulcheria, married the general Marcian and he was declared emperor. This initiated a new period of militarily strong rulers who together helped maintain Roman power in the East, and the survival of the empire for another thousand years. But the situation would soon be very different in the West, where just months after Theodosius II's death, Galla Placidia also died.

While it is likely that the building in Ravenna, popularly known as Galla Placidia's mausoleum, was meant to house the relics of St Laurence, it still contains its original three sarcophagi. These were apparently intended for Galla Placidia, her husband Constantius, and either her brother Honorius or her son Valentinian. Here, until the 16th century an embalmed body was visible through the small hole drilled in the side of the Augusta's tomb, but this was destroyed when some boys accidently set it on fire while inserting a lighted taper through the opening to look inside. There is in fact no evidence to prove that these remains ever belonged to Galla Placidia, who was most probably buried alongside her recently re-interred infant son in the family mausoleum in Rome.[20] Despite critics pointing to the similar lack of historical evidence linking the building itself to her – some actually suggesting that she played no role at all in its construction – it acts nonetheless as a fitting memorial for this exceptional woman. Its plain exterior increases the impact when visitors enter the small interior, where the ceiling and walls are completely covered with mosaics, depicting Christian motifs, naturalistic images of fruit and flowers, and various symmetric patterns and designs. These still glow brightly, their freshness appearing unchanged from when they were created more than 1500 years ago. Influenced by her time in Constantinople, Galla Placidia brought some of the most exceptional examples of Byzantine work to the West, and she helped initiate a new taste in mosaics and art forms that would be continued by those who succeeded her. A devout follower of her Nicene faith, she was responsible for some of the most significant artistic treasures of the late Roman Empire, and although today little of her period remains in Ravenna and elsewhere, her artistic heritage lives on.[21]

Although several Roman women before her had played a significant role in public affairs, Augusta Galla Placidia stands out. Besides being the daughter, wife, sister, and mother of emperors, she became an acting regent for her underage son. In a period when the empire was undergoing a transformation that would increasingly mark it as different from that of the East, for eleven years she was in control of the Western empire's affairs. During this time she had to confront the challenges the West was facing from the growing numbers of barbarians living either within the empire or on its fringes. Her competence in dealing with these things was highlighted after her less capable son Valentinian III came of age. Just a couple of years after her death, Attila had begun his savage assault, and in spite of having now extended Ravenna's city walls, the emperor decided to retreat permanently further south to Rome. Although he would feel more secure the next year when Attila died, he was soon to bring new difficulties on himself by killing the man on whom he most depended. Despite Aetius being now married to his daughter, because of the rumours he had heard Valentinian became convinced of this man's disloyalty, and in a fit of rage in 454 he struck him a fatal blow. This murderous action immediately deprived him of his most successful general, and only a few months later the emperor himself would be assassinated by the dead man's supporters. Thus, just five years after her death, the dynasty that Galla Placidia had hoped to establish came to an end. Although Valentinian's son-in-law Olybrius would be one of the eight men who briefly followed him, in the remaining 21 years of its existence the Western Roman Empire would be ruled by a series of weak men whose unsuitability for the role would undermine its position and ultimately guarantee its collapse.

2

Theodoric the Ostrogoth and the End of the Roman Empire in the West

'After a reign of 37 [*sic.*] years he died, having been a terror to all his enemies, but leaving a deep regret for his loss in the hearts of his subjects.'

Procopius[22]

After a period of upheaval with nine changes of leadership and at least five murders, executions and depositions, finally in 475 the last of the western Roman imperial rulers came to the throne. This teenaged boy, Romulus Augustus – nicknamed because of his diminutive size 'Augustulus' – was brought to power through the machinations of his ambitious father Orestes. Never even recognised by the eastern Roman emperor, he was clearly unfit for the role, and unsurprisingly within a year civil war broke out and he

Theodoric's Senigallia Medallion.

was overthrown. despite his father being killed, Romulus survived and being considered no threat he was removed far away to live out his life in retirement. Although Odoacer, a barbarian of unknown origins, had now become ruler in Ravenna, he accepted the eastern emperor as his overlord, openly acknowledging his own subservient position by returning Romulus's imperial regalia to Constantinople. Meanwhile, the last traces of the Roman Empire of the West lingered on in Dalmatia, where Julius Nepos continued to hold sway after being ousted from Ravenna by Romulus's father. Having fled to his lands across the Adriatic, he was still recognised by the imperial court in Constantinople, and he therefore continued to hold on to the remnants of his power until his own assassination in 480 in Diocletian's palace near Salona. It was at that point that the eastern emperor Zeno officially declared the western empire ended.

Before long, justifying his action by declaring that he was avenging Julius Nepos's death, Odoacer used his new fleet to invade Dalmatia and capture the dead man's lands. This helped him protect his own territories from the pirates infesting the Adriatic and also allowed him to assert his position as the king of Italy. However, in 484, having been drawn into a plot to overthrow the eastern Roman emperor, Odoacer's good fortune began to run out. Angered by his treachery and determined to get rid of him, Emperor Zeno turned for help to someone who had previously been of equally questionable loyalty, the Ostrogoth general Theodoric the Amal. This man's far from straightforward story had begun when his father, formerly an ally of Attila the Hun, had guaranteed his peace with the empire by sending his approximately eight-year-old son to Constantinople, where during his ten years as a hostage he would be introduced to the Byzantine culture that was to have a lasting influence on him. He finally returned home in 469 and, having proved himself on the battlefield, he then succeeded his father as the leader of his people. In 476 he received an appeal for help from Zeno, who, having just recovered the throne that he had lost after only a year in office, would now instruct him to go to war against Theodoric Strabo – 'the Squinter' – the leader of the rival Gothic band who had previously brought about the emperor's overthrow. While he had hoped to weaken the separate barbarian groups by creating dissension between them, in the end Zeno only succeeded in uniting these people against himself. As Theodoric the Amal now joined in the plundering of the imperial lands, he would capture Dyrrachium (Durrës), and bring more havoc to the emperor's Balkan region. And, although with the return of peace the Ostrogoth was declared a patrician and promoted to consul, he still periodically engaged in further acts of rebellion.

In time, however, Zeno became so concerned about the situation in Italy that he again needed help, and in 488 Theodoric was returned to full favour. On being instructed to deal with the rebellious 'tyrant' Odoacer, he had set off west with his large army, which had increased in size with the addition of more Goths from various other groups. After engaging in a series of battles, and suffering defeat at Faenza, Theodoric eventually reached Ravenna. For more than two years it remained under siege, but in 493 the town fell and the

15-year-long reign of Odoacer came to an end. But the king was now to commit a fatal error. Having agreed to make peace on the understanding that he was to receive generous terms, he then accepted an invitation to a banquet, where Theodoric suddenly turned on him and struck him down with his sword. After that he ordered the slaughter of Odoacer's remaining family and supporters. Theodoric's ruthlessness ensured his position and earned him the respect of the Goths, who, greatly impressed by his strength and perceived valour, now declared him to be their king. While we cannot know Zeno's original intentions for his general after he had brought the rebellious region back within his empire, Theodoric's success in Italy had now put him on the path to becoming the imperial ruler of the West. Zeno was never to see the Ostrogoth's rise to power as by the time of Odoacer's murder, he, too, was dead.

Although Theodoric's subjects would recognise him as the new western emperor, he would not receive any official recognition from the East until 497, when Emperor Anastasius I acknowledged him as the King of the Goths and Romans. Yet, even after the return of the western imperial regalia, Theodoric continued to define himself by the republican title of *princeps*. Although, unlike Odoacer, he was eager to adopt the wearing of the purple, showing an active interest in the production of the necessary dye at Hydron (Otranto), he assumed the traditional manners of the earlier Roman rulers. While he appears on the Senigallia Medallion created in 500 to celebrate his reign, he did not put his head on the coins and he avoided the ostentation and public veneration of the Byzantine court. Rather than imposing laws that demanded unquestioning obedience, he chose to issue edicts that merely expressed his wishes. This determined display of modesty raises questions as to his exact status, and we are left in doubt whether he was subservient to the eastern ruler or an equally honoured head of state. While, according to Procopius, he never chose to assume 'either the garb or the name of an emperor of the Romans', he governed his different people 'with all the qualities ... appropriate to one who is an emperor by nature'.[23] Whatever his precise position, the Ostrogoth king reigned over the whole Italian peninsula and wielded his influence over the Visigoths and Vandals. At the height of Theodoric's power his control stretched from Spain to Dalmatia, and from Burgundy to Africa.

As a result of his years spent in Constantinople, Theodoric was probably fluent in Greek and Latin, but there is some uncertainty as to whether he could read and write. Some claim that he was illiterate, their argument based on the grounds that he reportedly used a stencil when signing his name; something, if true, that may have been purely a measure to ensure a precise and well-written signature. Most believe the claim to have been the result of the negative propaganda later spread against him by the Byzantine conquerors of Italy.[24] Regardless of these different views, Theodoric was much admired by his contemporaries for his wisdom and, besides ensuring the good education of his own children, he was recognised for encouraging the spread of learning among his subjects in general.

Although a devout Arian believer, Theodoric guaranteed religious tolerance and equal rights to all. Popular for his new laws, he also gained the people's

favour by improving their daily lives through ensuring a regular provision of grain and a constant supply of drinking water. This had always been a problem for Ravenna, it being surrounded by wide saline marshes, and although the matter had first been resolved four centuries before by Emperor Trajan, his aqueduct was out of service. Having ordered its restoration, Theodoric would further improve life in the city by draining some of the land and laying out new gardens. Among the many new buildings he created was his palace, with an Arian chapel named in honour of Christ the Redeemer. Later re-dedicated on the orders of Emperor Justinian to St Martin in Golden Heaven. In the mid-800s this became known as Sant' Apollinare Nuovo after the saint whose bones had been brought there from his church at Classis. At the end of the 6th century Pope Gregory I purportedly ordered the removal of certain images, and already by that time several important Arian individuals represented had been blacked out, so that today only traces of their former existence remain among the extensive mosaics that still decorate the walls. Disconnected hands on the columns and shadows behind the curtains draw attention to the vanished depictions. Emperor Justin had already outlawed all Arian worship by the time his nephew and successor Justinian conquered Italy, but this later emperor's determined obliteration of these images reveals his intention to wipe from the records all reference to the former 'heretic' rulers. Theodoric was then to be seen as one of the temporary usurpers who had taken power without any rightful claim to authority. In this great church, there is one surviving work that may perhaps date from the period of the building's construction. Although the theory is much contested, some claim that the mosaic portrait with its 19th-century inscription identifying the subject as Emperor Justinian might be an image of Theodoric himself.[25]

Despite the later alterations carried out in the church, Sant' Apollinare Nuovo – today a UNESCO site – still displays its large early mosaics depicting Theodoric's palace and the nearby Classis port, representations of particular interest to historians. These places, along with several Arian churches and much of the early cathedral, are gone, but some of the king's other constructions remain, among them his baptistery – today known as the Battistero degli Ariani to distinguish it from the earlier Battistero degli Ortodossi (or Baptistery of Neon). Although lacking the font and wall ornamentation of its predecessor, this still contains a similar ceiling mosaic of the baptism of Jesus, Christ depicted as a younger, beardless man. It was not just in Ravenna that the ruler carried out his extensive building programme. Elsewhere, work continued on new or restored palaces, aqueducts, and amphitheatres, projects that together with his social improvements and military and political successes were eventually to earn him the title of Theodoric the Great.

Although the king had first set up his court at the Roman city of Mediolanum and nearby Pavia, he had then moved his seat of government to Ravenna, it being no longer vulnerable to sea-borne attack following his agreement with the Vandals. Although the Senate remained in Rome, Theodoric visited the old capital only once, in 500, when he spent five months celebrating his reign. To mark the occasion, he made public donations, held games in the circus and, in an even more significant move, visited the tomb of St Peter, a religious site that was much revered by the Nicene believers, now known as Catholics. And at the same time, having improved relations abroad, he arranged the marriage of his sister to the Vandal king. This was just one of several such contracts; besides his own marriage to the sister of Clovis, King of the Franks, he would find Visigoth and Burgundian husbands for other family members. Understanding the complex nature of such relations, in particular those that linked his people to the Romans, Theodoric famously summed up their mixed aspirations with the comment: 'A poor Roman plays the Goth, a rich Goth the Roman.'[26] While Romans still held the administrative positions, the military was dominated by the Goths, and the more sophisticated of these would imitate qualities that seemed to define the other. They adopted their style, education, and their eloquent language – even though their own Gothic language remained in use until the first half of the sixth century. There was not a total crossover of the cultures, and excessive imitation of Roman ways could become the cause of friction, as Theodoric's own daughter would later find, to her cost. The communities remained separate and with many proudly retaining their own identity, Theodoric himself chose to wear the long hair and the moustache thought to be a particular characteristic of the Goths.[27]

In the early years of the 6th century, Theodoric's empire was riven by the Acacian Schism that had begun in 484. This, the first serious split between the two churches of Rome and Constantinople, had arisen from a dispute over the doctrine that asserted Christ's hypostasis, or two natures – the divine and the human – an article of faith which had been first declared in 451 at the Council of Chalcedon. It was against this background that Theodoric initially set out to create a tolerant relationship with the Christians in the

West, marking his openness to their faith by his visit to St Peter's tomb. But over time riots broke out in Rome and with other tensions starting to develop further afield, things came to a head in 505. With the Byzantines being now militarily engaged with the Persians, Theodoric decided to take Sirmium, which lay just within the eastern border. As a result, fighting broke out between the East and West, and, although this soon came to an end by that time food shortages had increased the unrest in various cities throughout both regions. With relations between the two sides remaining fraught, two years after the start of the troubles, the Byzantine fleet mounted a pirate raid against the southern Italian cities of Sipontum (Siponto) and Tarentum (Taranto). But these were just some of the problems that Theodoric was facing. Already under threat in the northwest from the Burgundians, now he also had to confront the Franks, who had crossed the Loire to defeat the neighbouring Visigoths. However, by sending his army to deal with the problem, Theodoric was ultimately able to reclaim all his lands, including those he held in Spain.

In 519, Pope John I's gentle negotiations helped bring the Acacian Schism to an end, and with that the relations between the eastern and western churches began to recover. Yet Theodoric's other troubles were not over and fresh unrest in the last years of his reign led to riots against the Jews breaking out in Rome and Ravenna. Although the king paid personally for the reconstruction of the synagogues damaged by the mob, his earlier goodwill was now diminishing. Then, when the devout Emperor Justin started to take measures against the Arians in Constantinople, Theodoric's patience finally ran out. Despite his earlier reluctance to enter into Church matters, he now began to target his Catholic subjects at home.[28]

As the tensions increased, and Theodoric became more fearful of an attack by the Byzantines and the Vandals, he ordered 1000 new warships to be built. With his sense of persecution having grown even more acute by this time, he had become suspicious of his own officials. After listening to rumour, he turned against his close adviser, the Roman senator Boethius. Falsely accused of sorcery, Boethius was charged with inciting revolution on the grounds that he had defended Albinus, his fellow senator, who had been suspected of having private dealings with Constantinople.[29] On being declared a traitor, Boethius was condemned to death together with his father-in-law Symmachus, and while he was awaiting his sentence in prison, he wrote his famous work riling against the 'tyranny' of the king. With Boethius already widely famed for his exceptional scholarship, this incisive criticism was ultimately to cause serious damage to Theodoric's reputation for years to come.

Theodoric's growing bitterness would again be manifest when the delegation led by the sickly Pope John I returned from Constantinople. Furious at how little the pontiff had achieved in reversing the measures against the Arians in the East, the king now turned his wrath on the frail old man, imprisoning him in such harsh conditions that he died soon after – he later being honoured as a martyr by the Catholic Church. Although some would argue that Theodoric regretted his brutal actions, others now considered him to have become tyrannical, and as these opinions grew more polarised, a sharp distinction began to form between those who declared him a great leader and the rest who condemned him out of hand. Accordingly, when Theodoric died of dysentery in 526, his opponents soon began to spread stories giving various – often outrageous – reasons for his death. Some claimed he had died of remorse over his treatment of Symmachus and Boethius, others announced that his fearful prediction of dying from a bolt of lightning had come true. His most savage critics went further, linking his manner of death to that suffered by those other traitors, Arius and Judas Iscariot. Theodoric's supposed treachery was soon predicated on the general condemnation of all 'heretical' beliefs. This interpretation would then gradually grow more widely accepted and was repeated for years to come. Alongside the entrance porch to San Zeno's Basilica in Verona, in addition to the scenes from the Bible, twelfth-century bas-reliefs would later depict episodes assumed to have occurred in Theodoric's own life. In addition to showing his defeat of Odoacer, they portray him chasing a deer to his doom – the artist here linking the Ostrogoth to the mythical figure of Dietrich von Bern of medieval Germanic legend. This was just one of such stories that were now attached to the king, another being based on the account of a hermit from the island of Lipari, who had claimed to have seen the elderly ruler mounted on a black stallion riding to his death in the crater of nearby Volcano.[30]

When he died aged 72, Theodoric was nevertheless widely acclaimed as a great leader. Despite the discord at beginning of his long reign and the later instances of rebellion and urban unrest, in the main until 523 he had brought peace to his people. During his 33 years in power he had played a more active role than had the good-natured but rather passive Odoacer before him. Theodoric had improved the country's poor finances, initiated urban renewal, and built or restored houses, churches and ancient monuments. Despite his own dislike of such popular entertainments, he had laid on circuses and games, and he had treated his people with generosity and justice, causing his reign to be remembered by many as a golden age. Therefore, following his death he was respectfully interred in a large mausoleum of white Istrian stone close to a Gothic burial ground just outside Ravenna. This was topped by a massive round monolith that was said by some to have been chosen by the king to give him shelter during the storms that he feared so greatly. Probably damaged while it was being installed, the stone still displays the large crack the rumour-mongers claimed to have been caused by the bolt of lightning that had killed him. Here, in this peaceful spot, he would lie for the next 25 years until the city was conquered by Emperor Justinian's general, Belisarius. At that point, Theodoric's remains were removed and lost. For a time his mausoleum was turned into a church, but today, empty except for his broken porphyry sarcophagus, it has regained its role as the last memorial to Italy's greatest Gothic king.

After Theodoric's death his kingdom passed for a time to his grandson Athalaric, a child aged about eight, whose mother Amalasuntha acted as regent until his death in 534 when she became queen. An intelligent, well-educated woman, she would prove so successful in her dealings with the eastern emperor Justinian that he returned to her some of the lands previously surrendered by Galla Placidia. Yet, growing increasingly unpopular in certain quarters for her overtly Roman ways, within months of her accession Amalasuntha was overthrown and imprisoned by the cousin she had made her joint ruler. Being soon blamed, however, when she was strangled in her bath, he, too, would be murdered by her son-in-law Witigis, who had already inherited the throne. But by this time, Justinian, a former supporter of the dead queen, had responded to her death and sent his generals west, ordering Konstantianos to capture the region of Dalmatia and Belisarius to invade Italy. Ambitious to reunite his lands with those of the former western empire, Justinian's actions marked the start of the Gothic Wars, and for another two to three decades these would continue to ravage the area. Having already defeated the Vandals in North Africa, taken Sicily and Naples and received the submission of the people of Calabria and Puglia, in December 536 Belisarius entered Rome and was acknowledged as the conqueror of the southern Italian regions.

Around the same time, on an exploratory expedition to the Dalmatian capital of Salona, the large army of the Gothic king Witigis had by chance encountered the enemy, and in a vicious battle many would be killed on both sides. Following the bloodbath, the town was abandoned until the arrival of the emperor's large fleet. With the Goths having been forced to withdraw without a fight back to Ravenna, Dalmatia was in the hands of the imperial army, who now controlled all activity across the Adriatic. Nevertheless, back in Rome, Belisarius remained under attack from the Goths, who only abandoned their attempt to regain the city around a year later. There were now mixed fortunes on both sides, but finally in 540 the fighting came to an end. Following his surrender at Ravenna, King Witigis renounced his throne and retired to a comfortable exile in Constantinople.

Despite his success, Belisarius now fell out of favour with Justinian who, suspicious of his general's ambitions, recalled him to Constantinople and charged him with treachery. As this dismissal greatly helped the Goths, their leader Totila was able to recover the lost lands and recapture Rome. Even though three years later in 549 a reinstated Belisarius was able briefly to retake the city, after the general's retirement the Goths again regained possession. Now as his people's recognised king, Totila was to continue his successful campaigning, managing to capture most of Italy before he died of his battle wounds in 552.[31] Yet, within just two years of his death, the eastern emperor had reconquered the peninsula, adding this to his ever-increasing territories that were eventually to extend all the way to Spain. Claiming to be Romulus's successor, from this moment on Justinian was the emperor of both the East and West. Since this meant that Ravenna had lost its earlier status, it would now remain an exarchate, a mere province of the empire, for the next two centuries. However, during the bitter iconoclastic dispute that resulted from Emperor Leo III's order in 726 to remove all Christian images, a riot erupted in Ravenna and the penultimate exarch and his followers were killed.

Despite Constantinople quickly finding a replacement, he, too, would lose his position when the town was forced to surrender in 751 to the Lombards, who three three years later handed it over to the Franks. After another three years Ravenna was passed on again, this time to the pope, after which it remained for the next thousand years within the Papal States almost without interruption.

With Justinian having already ended the rights to free worship he had previously granted, ordering at the same time the seizure of the Goths' religious possessions and the closure or conversion of their Arian churches, Belisarius was soon to bring these measures to bear in the emperor's newly conquered lands.[32] As a result, in Ravenna most of the earlier buildings no longer exist, but in addition to the baptisteries, Sant' Apollinare Nuovo, and the magnificent Archbishop's palace chapel that was built soon after, there still remain two other spectacular 6th-century buildings (today of World Heritage status): the church of Sant' Apollinare in Classe and the famous basilica of San Vitale, both of which were begun around the time of Theodoric's death. The first of these, a few miles outside Ravenna near the port, was the original resting place of St. Apollinaris's bones. As a result of silting up, today the coastline is five miles away from the site but being close to the shore at the time and vulnerable to pirate or foreign attack, it had been thought necessary to move the precious relics to the more secure Sant' Apollinare Nuovo. Nevertheless Sant' Apollinare in Classe is a remarkable building, the apse displaying stunning naturalistic mosaics of the saint in a pastoral setting, standing with rows of sheep in a field of flowers, surrounded by images of other religious figures and various biblical scenes.

Equally remarkable is the large church of San Vitale in the city centre close to the Mausoleum of Galla Placidia. Possibly modelled on the emperor's golden reception hall in Constantinople, its outstanding mosaics cover much of the impressive building. Among these, on the walls in the apse are the two prominent tableaux dating from the time of Belisarius's conquest, created to honour Justinian and his notorious wife Theodora. Both emperor and empress had risen from lowly beginnings, she – according to a not unbiased account – having begun her career as an actress, if not a courtesan, but here the pair are arrayed in full imperial splendour, complete with crowns and even haloes. Neither of them would ever visit the city, but in San Vitale these two, who were responsible for the end of Ravenna as a Roman imperial capital, would in its dying days become timelessly linked to its story.

SECTION II
PUGLIA: THE EARLY MIDDLE AGES

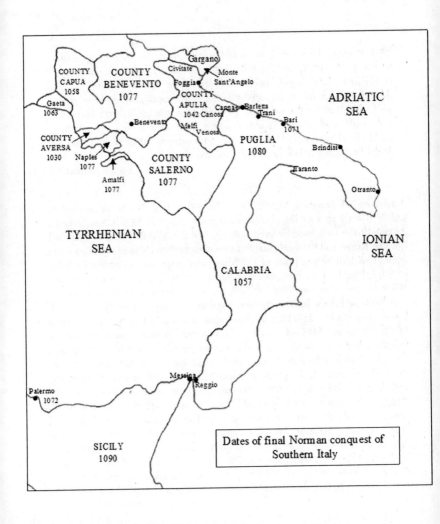

Dates of final Norman conquest of Southern Italy

3

The Norman rulers of southern Italy

'Now Robert, as rumour insisted and many said, was a most exceptional leader, quick-witted, good-looking, courteous in conversation, ready too in repartee, loud-voiced, easily accessible, very tall in stature ... he showed respect to all his subordinates, more especially to those who were well-disposed towards him... For all acknowledge Robert's bravery, remarkable skill in warfare and steadfast spirit; and he was a man who could not be conquered easily but only with extreme difficulty, and after a defeat he seemed to rise again with renewed vigour.'

Anna Komnena[33]

According to accepted legend, in 1015, 40 young Normans arrived in southern Italy to visit the Gargano's famous shrine at Monte Sant'Angelo. As one of the four most revered holy sites of the Middle Ages, this rivalled not just Rome and Compostella, but was even ranked close to the Holy Land itself. This had been a place of Christian pilgrimage since – on the evidence of a local lord – a mysterious event had taken place outside a cave in 490. While he was searching for a lost bull, the man's arrow had turned around in mid-flight and come back to hit him. Even as his story was being questioned, it was capped a few days later by claims that the local bishop had seen a vision of the Archangel Michael guarding the entrance to that same cavern. After this there were two more reports of apparent miracles, a further sighting, and the sudden appearance in the cave of an altar and the saint's own footprint. As a result, within three years, a chapel had been built underground at this now highly venerated site. Over the years, the pilgrims descending down the steep, dark steps to reach it would leave on the walls their miscellaneous miscellaneous votive offerings, a multitude of small images, pictures, dresses, crutches, and other more bizarre or unlikely articles. On my own visit at the end of the 1960s these were still on display but today they are gone, most transferred to the nearby museum. Their removal was part of the renovation of the Sanctuary, which in 2011, together with the rest of the town's historic complex – including the Norman castle – became a UNESCO site dedicated

Hauteville tomb of Robert Guiscard and his brothers at Venosa, Puglia.

to the 'Places of Power' of the Lombards in Italy. The crypt itself, however, remains essentially unaltered, its dark, hushed atmosphere still reflecting the deep spiritual significance that the place has for the numbers of faithful who visit it each year.

It was here at Monte Sant'Angelo that the Norman visitors were said to have met a Lombard called Melus of Bari. Wishing to remove the ruling Greeks who were still in control of much of the Italian peninsula's southern region, this man used the occasion to put his concerns to the visiting pilgrims. On returning home, these same men spread his message to other young Normans eager to find fame, fortune, and above all land. Accordingly, soon after arriving in southern Italy in around 1017, these would become mercenaries in the service of the Lombards.

Descendants from Scandinavian tribes that had first moved south in the sixth century, the Lombards had initially settled in northern Italy, the region of the country that still bears their name. Eventually evicted from these territories by the Franks, they had then established their bases further south. Here, besides their various west coast possessions (including Capua, and Salerno), and the region around Benevento and the Duchy of Spoleto just to the north, they held parts of present-day Puglia. Yet, over time the Lombards found themselves increasingly at odds with the Byzantines, and things would eventually come to a head at Cannae near Barletta, where Hannibal had won his victory over the Romans more than twelve hundred years earlier. Here in 1018, the eastern emperor's vast army finally crushed the enemy, inflicting such a major defeat on the Lombards that their former power in the region would be permanently undermined. Now they would gradually lose all their strongholds, and before long their situation was made no easier by the actions of their earlier comrades in arms. Like many of their contemporaries, the Normans had few loyalties and being concerned only for themselves, they were prepared to give their backing to whatever faction best served their own interests. As a result, within a couple of years of the battle they had begun to offer their services to the other side, and so they were fighting for the Byzantines when in 1021 they met the pope and the Holy Roman Emperor, Henry II, on the battlefield.[34] Benedict VIII, who had been angered by the capture and brutal murder in Bari of one of the Lombards faithful to the papal cause, had started by attacking Capua, Salerno, Naples and Montecassino, but following some initial successes, eventually at Troia, south-west of Foggia, his luck ran out. Here for more than three months the papal-imperial army had tried unsuccessfully to dislodge the Byzantines from their well-defended fortress, but with his own men overcome by sickness, the pope was eventually forced to call off the campaign. This retreat would leave their enemy still in place, but more importantly it would serve to enhance the reputation of the Greeks' latest allies, the Normans. Having soon received land in return for their military service, by the mid-eleventh century the standing of these newcomers had grown. With some of the men now starting to fortify their own towns, Rainulf Drengot had become the Count of Aversa, and Peter the first Count of Trani.

Among the Normans who came to the south, there was also a group of young men from the region of Coutances on the Cotentin Peninsula of northern France. Of the twelve sons of Tancred de Hautville, eight would eventually make a name for themselves in southern Italy. Having arrived in around 1034, one of the earliest to create an impression was William, who, having earned the sobriquet 'the Iron Arm' for his bravery, had by 1042 become Count of Apulia. On his death four years later his title passed to his brother Drogo, Count of Melfi, but following his murder by the Byzantines near Bovino to the south of Troia in 1051, Drogo was succeeded by a third of Tancred's sons, Humphrey. Some five years earlier, the first of their younger half-brothers, Robert 'Guiscard' ('the Crafty') had arrived in the region along with a small band of five knights and a few foot soldiers. An impressively tall, imposing man, with the blue eyes and reddish-blonde hair of many in his family, he would soon be joined by the youngest of Tancred's sons, Roger. But because Drogo had not been prepared to grant him any land, Robert had temporarily taken up service with the Prince of Capua. Here he remained for about a year until he was finally given his own castles in Calabria, where he enriched himself by robbing and pillaging the local people.

When in 1053 Humphrey – now also the Count of Apulia – found himself facing papal attack, Robert came to his assistance, joining his brother at the battle of Civitate near Foggia. Because the current pope, Leo IX, had become fearful of the Normans' growing power, he had marched south with a large force, which by this time included numbers of Lombards, who no doubt were now ruing their earlier invitation to the knights from the north. Despite his bigger army, as the battle approached its end Leo came to realise that he was facing a crushing defeat, so he made a last attempt at reconciliation. After personally approaching the enemy with an offer of peace, he was taken prisoner and for the next nine months he would remain a captive at Benevento. The Normans treated him well as they now wished to repair their relations with the Church and thus improve their own public standing.

As the Normans' power continued to grow, Robert was increasingly making a name for himself, by this time having also added Otranto to his possessions. Already recognised for the courage he had shown at Civitate, after Humphrey died, in 1057 he was chosen by his brothers to be the new count. Two years later further promotion followed in a glittering ceremony at the Norman capital Melfi, where, the recently enthroned pontiff, formally invested his vassal Robert as the duke of Apulia, Calabria and Sicily. Because he had just replaced the antipope Benedict X, Nicholas II was looking for strong allies, and he hoped by granting the Norman this appointment to gain his protection against his own his enemies. Among these was the Holy Roman Emperor, who was particularly hostile to Nicholas's ecclesiastical reforms that had banned imperial interference in papal elections and so asserted the sole responsibility of the Church to appoint the pontiff.

Meanwhile, other highly significant events had taken place. Just a year after the Battle of Civitate, in 1054 the already fraught relations between the eastern and western Christian churches had finally collapsed. From the latest, relatively minor, incident, things had escalated into an ever more bitter disagreement that ultimately resulted in the Great Schism, the split between the Catholic and Orthodox confessions that continues to this day. Although people of the time were unaware of the permanent nature of the breakdown, this divide would be the start of the centuries of growing tensions between the two opposing factions..

When in 1061 the Guiscard made a first unsuccessful attempt with his youngest brother Roger to conquer the island of Sicily, the Byzantine emperor, taking advantage of the duke's absence, renewed his attack on Robert's mainland duchy. Although in the end the Normans defeated the eastern imperial army and captured Brindisi, the Greek presence in Puglia continued. Only in 1071, when Robert succeeded at last in taking Bari after a three-year-long siege, would the last vestiges of Byzantine rule be finally removed from southern Italy. The duke then returned to his campaign in Sicily, and having the next year taken the Saracen city of Palermo, he would over the following decade succeed in capturing Amalfi and defeating the Lombards at Salerno. Thus, over time he gradually increased his hold, so that by the end of the 1070s he had extended his authority over the whole of the southern Italian peninsula. Despite the on-going feuds with some of their fellow countrymen and even certain relations, with Robert's brother Roger ruling as his vassal in Sicily, now Tancred de Hauteville's descendants held sway over most of the region, only Capua remaining in other Norman hands.

Already excommunicated in 1074 for encroaching on the papal fief of Benevento, four years later, following his attack and capture of the town, Robert Guiscard was again issued with a papal indictment by a furious Gregory VII. However, growing more concerned about the intentions of the Holy Roman Emperor Henry IV, the pope eventually lifted this edict and returned Benevento to the duke, whom he now made his vassal. As other tensions with the East were coming to the fore, Robert Guiscard began to turn his attention towards the Greek possessions across the Adriatic. While some would argue that the duke had ambitions to seize the eastern empire for himself, it appears more probable that he was motivated simply by the militaristic desire for conquest. As a warrior he had risen to power, and thanks to his successes in the field he had been able to reward his followers with stolen booty and land. And since by this time all the former Byzantine possessions on the Italian mainland were in his hands, those across the water now appeared to offer more rich pickings. Wanting, however, to excuse his actions, Robert now claimed that he wished to settle the political unrest that had recently developed following the removal of the eastern emperor. Because this man's son was engaged to his own daughter, the duke sought to justify his actions by announcing that he was avenging the insult to his family, and he further strengthened his hand by producing a pretender to act the part of the deposed Emperor Michael.

Ready at last to begin his campaign against the new Greek ruler Alexius I Komnenos, Robert set off across the strait from Otranto, intent on meeting up on the other side with his oldest son. This boy, born to his first wife in Calabria during the 1050s, had grown into a large and well-built man. Although his baptismal name was Christian Marc, he would always be more popularly known as 'Bohemund', a nickname that his father had given him in reference to a mythical giant. A 19th-century investigation of bones found in his tomb at Canosa seem to confirm his exceptional size. Like his father, immensely tall, blonde and good-looking, he would both impress and terrify the people he met, alternately being admired for his charm and feared for his ruthlessness. Now in 1081, having recently taken Valona (Vlorë), he waited down the coast at Buthrotum (Butrint) until Robert Guiscard arrived, and the pair were then able to move on together to capture Corfu. But when they were later establishing a land base for their assault on the region's main port of Dyrrachium, their fleet was hit by two disasters, first a storm and then an attack by the Venetians, who had come to the aid of the Greeks. Although Robert still persisted in laying siege to the city, before long his own army began to suffer from disease and starvation, and so on realising the growing likelihood of his troops deserting, he prevented them from absconding by ordering his remaining ships to be destroyed. Eventually, in October the Greek army arrived to help the besieged city and a fierce battle ensued, which was to cause heavy casualties on both sides. Alexius's army was forced to retreat, and so once again Dyrrachium was left unguarded. Even though it would still attempt to struggle on, four months later its starving people had to surrender, and finally Robert could add this strategic coastal town to his other possessions.

Within two years, the duke was back in Italy, having returned not only to deal with a rebellion in Puglia but also in response to the pope's appeal for help. With their relations having now improved, Gregory was seeking Robert's support against the approaching army of the Holy Roman Emperor. The pontiff was already under siege in Castel Sant'Angelo when in May 1084 the Guiscard eventually reached Rome, but although his arrival would soon force the imperial troops to retreat, his assistance had come at a price. Over the following three days the Norman soldiers subjected the city to such horror and savagery that much of it would be left in ruins. By then Robert Guiscard had already whisked Gregory away to safety at Salerno, where the pontiff was to remain until his death the following year.

After his father's departure, Bohemund had been left to continue his conquests in the Balkan regions, but following his first successes he was finally defeated in Thessaly, and feeling the strains of the long campaign he decided to return to Italy to rest and replenish his army. This allowed the Greeks to recapture some of their former possessions with the help of the Venetians, who were then rewarded with special trading rights in Constantinople. Robert wished to regain these lost areas, and when at the end of the year he and Bohemund re-embarked on their campaign assisted by the people of Ragusa (Dubrovnik), they succeeded once more in retaking Dyrrachium and Corfu. Both men soon became ill. Bohemund returned to Italy and his father decided to follow soon after. Two months after the death of the pope, while still on his way back home, in July Robert died on Cephalonia. Absent at the time, Bohemund was distraught when he heard the news, but because his stepmother Sikelgaita had been able at the last minute to join her husband, she immediately took charge and arranged for the body to be shipped back to Italy. With the ship caught in a storm, the corpse was washed overboard and only recovered with the greatest of difficulty. Once back in Otranto, the internal organs were removed and the battered remains were interred in the Church of the Holy Trinity (or Old Church) at Venosa in the Basilicata region. Built originally on an ancient pagan and early Christian site, this had later been consecrated and given to the Benedictines by Nicholas II in 1059, the year he had confirmed Robert as Duke of Apulia and Calabria. After first putting it into the hands of some monks who had come with him from France, the Guiscard had extended the building and chosen it as the burial place for his family. Here, along with his four brothers, he is remembered on a memorial plaque above the 16th-century tomb that was later created to contain all their bones.[35] This lies in the south aisle of the church, the traditional site for male burials, the north aisle housing the tomb of Bohemund's mother, Robert's first divorced wife, Alberada, who had died some years after him. She had been interred here along with other members of the family, even though her marriage had previously been ended (allegedly) on the grounds of Nicholas II's new laws regarding co-sanguinity. This had been the official reason, although more probably the divorce had taken place because Robert had wanted at the time to contract a new and more politically expedient marriage.[36]

Alberada had been replaced by the eighteen-year-old Sikelgaita, the daughter of the ruler of Salerno, a principality that – as the Lombards' largest possession at the time – stretched over much of southern Italy. Her father, who had previously tried to secure his position by arranging her marriage to one of the Normans, had finally achieved his goal in 1058 when he had gained Robert Guiscard as his son-in-law. Even so, eighteen years later in 1076 Robert had not just seized her family's Lombard lands, but also deposed her brother, the current ruler, before taking the title for himself as the new Prince of Salerno.

A large, imposing woman, renowned for her forceful personality, stamina and courage, Sikelgaita was described by the Byzantine princess Anna Komnena as a formidable sight when, dressed in armour, she joined Robert on campaign. In 1080, while he was engaged in putting down unrest at Taranto, she directed the siege of Trani, and in October the next year was actually present on the battlefield outside Dyrrachium helping her husband when – against her advice – he took on the Greeks. Here she made her name, remembered ever after for her determination to keep up the fight, shaming into action those Normans ready to flee the field with the words: 'How far will ye run? Halt! Be men!'[37] Plunging into the fray herself, she saved the day by her example.

Soon rumours spread questioning the part played by Sikelgaita at the time of Robert's death, however. Some – possibly Bohemund himself – suggested that she had first attempted to poison her stepson, and that it was on her husband's discovery of this that she had murdered him instead. For these charges there is little evidence. But while these stories might be founded on no more than jealous gossip, what remains certain is that Sikelgaita had wished her own child Roger Borsa to replace his father, rather than Bohemund. In preparation for this, already twelve years earlier she had had the boy's rights acknowledged by some of the barons. Whatever eventually happened in 1085, Sikelgaita was able for a time to retain the title *dux* and exert enough power to arrange that her son was ultimately given his father's position as Duke of Apulia. In compensation, Bohemund was granted the Bari-Otranto region and awarded the title Prince of Taranto by the pope. Having achieved her aims, Sikelgaita would then gradually withdraw from the scene until, five years after her husband, she died at Salerno and was buried in the atrium of the abbey at Montecassino.

While Robert Guiscard was alive, he had been the dominant presence in the whole of the south, and with his strong fleet he had also earned the respect of others abroad. But after his younger son succeeded, the situation began to deteriorate as Robert Borsa proved himself unfit for the task. For a while there was civil war between the brothers, but at last, after taking Oria and Otranto, Bohemund agreed to meet Robert Borsa at Venosa. Here, by their father's grave, they agreed a pact that allowed Bohemund to retain his captured towns, and also gain Brindisi, Taranto, and nearby Gallipoli. Even so, the peace did not last long and with the war beginning again, Bohemund took Bari and its surrounding lands. Just three years earlier this city had gained further in significance by the arrival in May 1087 of the remains of St Nicholas. Because the veneration of relics had grown ever since the days of St Ambrose, this had increased the stature of the bishopric of Bari and before long the basilica under construction to house the saint's bones was to become another famous place of pilgrimage.

When the First Crusade was called in 1095, Bohemund became one of its leaders. Having recruited some of the best fighting men to be found in the region, he and his fellow crusaders set sail from Puglia. Although during their march to the Holy Land the troops looted the captured areas, Bohemund's attempts to restrain some of his men's actions would help ease relations when two years later he met the emperor, Alexius Komnenos, in Constantinople. As he now wanted to build bridges with the Byzantines, here Bohemund swore an oath of fealty, but within a year this pledge would prove to be of little significance. Because his own reputation had continued to grow, after capturing Antioch the Norman had declared himself to be the new prince. This had greatly displeased the emperor, who considered that his vassal Bohemund had now abused his status, so when the Norman was captured by the Seljuks in 1100 he refused to help in securing his release. Equally infuriated in his turn and feeling that he was the one who had been betrayed, Bohemund responded, he now – according to the emperor's daughter Anna Komnena – declaring Alexius to be a pagan, and a supporter of the pagans. Four years later, after his eventual release from prison, Bohemund turned his back on the emperor and chose to make his way instead to France where, with the backing of his new father-in-law, the French king, he soon set about raising his own army.

As the pope, among others, may have believed Bohemund to be mounting a crusade against the Muslims, he gave him his blessing. The pontiff had most probably not realised that the Norman's main target was now the Byzantines, but this would soon become apparent when Bohemund sailed not to the Holy Land but across the Adriatic towards the imperial lands on the other side of the Strait of Otranto. With the Venetians again coming to their aid, by the next year the Greeks had forced him to withdraw and accept the strict terms of a new treaty that obliged him to surrender his captured lands and reconfirm his vassal status under the eastern emperor. In 1108 Bohemund therefore left the Balkans and returned to Puglia. While some claimed he was now crushed by his recent humiliation, other evidence suggests that he continued to have ambitions to return to Antioch, and he was still assembling a new army when he died about three years later.[38]

Bohemund was buried at Canosa, a town about 40 miles from Bari, but still within that city's bishopric. Here he would be interred beside the Duomo of San Sabino – a building that had been recently reconstructed at his own expense.[39] Similar with its five domes to the later demolished Church of the Holy Apostles in Constantinople, it followed a style of architecture that was familiar to the well-travelled Norman. The early cathedral, the victim of repeated attack and even earthquake, has been much altered, among its later additions the 18th-century façade. According to the ancient Roman custom of Byzantium, Bohemund's tomb was placed outside the cathedral against the external wall of the south transept. In spite of its earlier neglect and later restoration, it remains a poignant memorial to this knight. Although his sarcophagus has now gone and his burial place is marked only by a plain gravestone, the small building topped with a dome is still fronted by bronze doors etched with his name and image.[40]

Other places in Puglia with links to this man have also survived, among them them the San Giovanni al Sepolchro in Brindisi that he built to be a place of prayer for the Knights Templar, and also somewhere where they could camp before boarding their ships on their way to the Holy Land. Created to resemble the Holy Sepulchre in Jerusalem, this small round building with its ancient Roman columns and Medieval frescos has finally after years of abandonment been carefully restored and become again a peaceful spot reminding us of the aims of its founder. The same is true of the Abbazia di Santa Maria di Cerrate on the way south to Lecce. According to legend, this had been established as a monastery by Bohemund's grandfather, Tancred de Hauteville, and although that particular claim cannot be verified, there is little doubt that it was Bohemund himself who ordered the building's construction. The abbey eventually became a farm – one of the typical *masserie* of this area, complete with defensive walls built during Puglia's later turbulent times. Although it too suffered years of neglect, today its frescos can again be seen, palimpsests displaying the layers of the place's history, some like those in the Brindisi sepulchre now speckled with small holes left by the removal of the later overpainting.

* * *

All this time Count Roger, who had formerly been the vassal of his brother Robert Guiscard, had been bringing his duchy of Sicily to the fore. Earlier, when his nephews were tied up with their disputes, he had also begun to extend his own possessions onto the mainland, and by ruling all his territories with tolerance he had laid the foundations for the glittering court that would come to prominence under his son, also Roger. With this child's older brother having predeceased him, in 1105 the 10-year-old boy had succeeded his father. During his reign of almost a quarter of a century, he managed steadily to advance his position, first inheriting the mainland territories of Roger Borsa's son in 1127, next becoming Duke of Apulia, Calabria and Sicily, and eventually acquiring the full status of monarch. This final promotion he would achieve by taking advantage of the problems that were currently facing the Church. Following the papal election of two candidates in 1130, he had chosen to support the antipope Anacletus II, who in return had agreed to the Norman's coronation on Christmas Day as King Roger II of Sicily. While for the next few years he had to fight – not always successfully – to keep his possessions in Puglia, eighteen months after Anacletus's death, in July 1139 he defeated the papal army of Innocent II. Having been temporarily held captive, this pope would finally concede to Roger's wishes and confirm his position as the Sicilian king. Puglia had now lost its autonomy, and with its boundaries having been officially laid down by the mid-1140s, it had become fully incorporated into Roger's *regno* covering the whole of southern Italy.

On Roger II's death in 1154, the kingdom passed to his son, William I 'the Bad', an unfortunate ruler who not only had to confront the ever-rebellious barons in Puglia but would also be challenged by Adrian IV – the English pope – who wanted to limit Norman influence and bolster the power of the papacy. In addition, William had to face threats from the Emperor Frederick Barbarossa, and also the latest eastern emperor, Manuel I Komnenos. After invading Puglia, the Greeks recaptured the majority of the southern towns, Trani, Andria, Giovinazzo, Bari and Taranto being among those that surrendered. Yet, once he had crushed the rebels at Brindisi in May, the king was able to recover all his lost possessions and the Byzantine emperor's ambitions in the region were finally brought to an end. William's position then became even more secure after he reached an agreement with Pope Adrian at Benevento in June 1156. From then on, despite only narrowly surviving a later plot to kill him and also undergoing a brief period of imprisonment, he would remain on the throne until his death ten years later.

The king's successor, William II, enjoyed a period of peace, but, although he received the favourable epithet of 'the Good', and was later placed by Dante among those in Paradise, in reality he achieved little. Although in 1177 he married Joan, the daughter of Henry II of England, he was still without children when nine years later he declared his aunt Constance to be his heir. The youngest daughter of Roger II, she was now apparently forced to abandon her convent life and marry the future Holy Roman Emperor Henry VI, an arrangement that fitted well with her husband's ambitions. Having already recaptured the former Norman possessions of Dyrrachium, Corfu and Cephalonia from the Greeks, this man was now at peace with the eastern emperor in Constantinople. But following William's death in 1189, the Sicilian barons became fearful of excessive imperial control, and with their concern growing for the country's independence, the next year Roger II's illegitimate grandson, Tancred, mounted a rebellion.

Although described in unflattering terms as a small, ugly man, who had none of the good looks so commonly found among his tall, fair-haired Norman relations, Tancred had soon gathered a large following and, while his aunt Constance was absent from her kingdom, he managed to win over the support of his people. Although he had earlier been among the

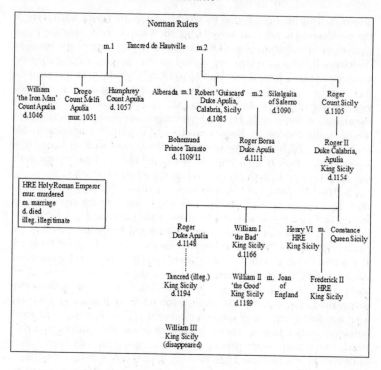

Norman Rulers

Tancred de Hautville m.1 ... m.2

William 'the Iron Man' Count Apulia d.1046

Drogo Count Melfi Apulia mur. 1051

Humphrey Count Apulia d.1057

Alberada m.1 Robert 'Guiscard' Duke Apulia, Calabria, Sicily d.1085 m.2 Sikelgaita of Salerno d.1090

Roger Count Sicily d.1105

Bohemund Prince Taranto d. 1109/11

Roger Borsa Duke Apulia d.1111

Roger II Duke Calabria, Apulia King Sicily d.1154

HRE Holy Roman Emperor
mur. murdered
m. marriage
d. died
illeg. illegitimate

Roger Duke Apulia d.1148

William I 'the Bad' King Sicily d.1166

Henry VI m. Constance HRE Queen Sicily King Sicily

Tancred (illeg.) King Sicily d.1194

William II m. Joan 'the Good' of King Sicily England d.1189

Frederick II HRE King Sicily

William III King Sicily (disappeared)

conspirators who had plotted against his uncle William I, with the backing of Pope Clement III, Tancred now took the throne and was crowned in Palermo. Before long he was facing his own challenges from the English king, Richard the Lionheart, who along with Philip II of France had arrived on the island en route to join the Third Crusade. Demanding the release of his sister, William II's widow Joan, Richard passed his time by sacking Messina until Tancred agreed to his terms. On his handing back Joan's dowry, Tancred received in exchange the Lionheart's support, which he was to retain until the English king's arrest by the duke of Austria in 1192.

In the meantime, Tancred experienced a series of other major setbacks and disasters, not just the invasion by the Holy Roman Emperor's troops, nor the further instances of open rebellion by the barons in Puglia, but far more seriously the threatened end of all his dynastic ambitions. Although he had strengthened the position of his royal house by crowning his son as co-ruler of Sicily, in 1193 this boy died, leaving his devastated father to replace him with his younger brother, another William. While this was only the start of the major catastrophes that were soon to hit the family, Tancred personally would be spared the full horrors that lay ahead as he too was to die two months later. Seeing that the path was now clear, Emperor Henry VI was soon ready to march south to Sicily, where he finally celebrated his own coronation in Palermo on Christmas Day 1194. Although the Hohenstaufens had become the official rulers of southern Italy and their dynasty was apparently secure, Henry was still determined to impress the people with his authority. Before long he began to deal harshly with those who had supported the previous regime. Included among his victims was Tancred's young son, the recently crowned William, who with his mother and sisters – not forgetting to mention tons of looted treasure – was taken captive back to Germany, where, very possibly blinded and castrated, he was eventually to disappear for good. And there would be one more act of brutality that was purposely devised as a stern warning to those who might be tempted to oppose the new Sicilian king. In a determined effort to wipe out all traces of the last of the Norman rulers, Henry ordered Tancred's body to be disinterred and decapitated.

4

The Holy Roman Emperor, Frederick II: 'the Boy from Puglia'

'Things which for centuries everybody had seen and accepted as facts challenged him to curious enquiry.'

Ernst Kantorowicz[41]

On 26 December 1194 at the small town of Jesi, a few miles from Ancona, the future Holy Roman Emperor Frederick II was born to 40-year-old Constance of Sicily. After eight years of childless marriage, news of his

Frederick II.

mother's pregnancy had been met in some quarters with scepticism, gossips suggesting that the baby's father had been a mere butcher. Determined to do all she could to prove her child's legitimacy, when the time came Constance quashed any further rumours by creating a tent in the square and inviting the local women to witness the birth.

The posthumous daughter of the great Norman king, Roger II, Constance had married Henry Hohenstaufen in 1186, five years before he was elected to succeed his father Emperor Frederick Barbarossa – 'Redbeard' – who had been drowned in 1190 while taking part in the First Crusade. Shortly after the couple had been crowned by the recently elected Pope Celestine III in Rome in April 1191, events had rapidly moved on in the Kingdom of Sicily. As a result of Tancred of Lecce's earlier seizure of his aunt's rightful throne, immediately after the coronation the new Emperor had marched south with a large army to regain her crown. But although Henry had been welcomed in the towns through which he had passed along the way, things were to change on his arrival in Naples, where he was met by stiff resistance. Although for the next three months he tried to take the city, after his troops began to be struck down by an epidemic he would be forced to abandon the siege. At that point, Constance was taken captive in Salerno by Tancred and she would then remain his hostage until the next year, when the pope eventually intervened and arranged for her release. In the meantime her husband had been continuing to pursue his private ambitions, and ten months after Tancred's death, the day before his son's birth in Jesi, he had succeeded in becoming the crowned king of Sicily.

A few weeks later, Henry travelled to Foligno and briefly met his infant son before returning with Constance to tend to his affairs. For the time being the child was left in the care of the Duchess of Spoleto. A couple of years later at his baptism, instead of Constantine – the choice of his mother – he was given the names of his grandfathers, Frederick Roger. Although Henry failed to persuade the pope to crown his son, he managed to induce the German princes to elect the boy as their king. By this time the man chosen to be King of the Germans, alternatively known as King of the Romans, had more or less become the accepted heir to the imperial throne. But even though for the moment the child kept his title, the hereditary rights he had also received would soon be removed. However, before long, Frederick's position became even more uncertain. Less than three years after his coronation in Sicily, in September 1197 Henry died aged only thirty-two. Although he was probably the victim of malaria, there were soon whispers of poison, something often suspected as the cause of such unexpected deaths. Although there were certain proven instances of its use, in this case the gossip probably arose because of the dead Emperor's unpopularity. Henry VI was not widely mourned, many Sicilians hating him for the often savage treatment that they, and others, had suffered at his hands during his short time in power. When rebellion had erupted within days of his coronation, among his other punitive measures he had ordered the torture or execution of several nobles. The brutality of their sentences had even appalled the Empress, whose stronger sympathies lay with her fellow Sicilians. By the end of her husband's reign, the unrest that had been developing in the region ever since the death of William the Good had reached such a pitch that it was threatening the security of the Sicilian crown itself.

Constance tried to stabilise things by crowning Frederick as her co-ruler of Sicily. Although in the days shortly before her husband's death, his brother, Philip of Swabia, had set off south to fetch the boy and take him back to Germany, on hearing that the Emperor had died Philip abandoned the plan and returned home immediately. As the situation for the dynasty now looked precarious, made all the more so by the German princes' rejection of Frederick as their king, he decided it was better to secure the Hohenstaufen's position in the north. For that reason Philip accepted his own nomination as ruler, probably – according to most critics – not out of personal ambition, but rather more in order to protect the family's interests. Even though he remained King of the Romans until his untimely death in June 1208, the situation in Germany had by then become still more complicated with the alternative election of Otto of Brunswick, a member of the Welf dynasty. This man, a grandson of Henry II of England, never stopped challenging Philip, and after the latter's murder at Bamberg he continued to press his claims to the throne. The rivalry of these two parties fed the dispute begun over half a century before that in time would escalate into the bitter divisions between the rival Guelfs and Ghibellines that were to ravage much of Italy in the Middle Ages, the former group taking their name from the Italian pronunciation of Welf, and the latter from Waiblingen, a Hohenstaufen possession in Germany.

When Frederick was still only three years old, his mother died on 28 November 1198. As previously she had acknowledged her Sicilian kingdom to be a papal fiefdom and nominated the recently elected Pope Innocent III to be her child's official guardian, the new pontiff had selected his cardinal-priest Cencio Savelli as the child's tutor. The bishop of Troia, Walter of Palearia, continued as regent. These choices were not popular with everyone, and among those who opposed the appointments was Markward of Anweiler, one of Henry VI's followers whom Constance had earlier dismissed. Furious over the removal of his powers, and already in league with the unruly barons in Puglia, in 1200 he mounted a successful invasion of the island. The next year, after he had managed to persuade a court member to give him access to the royal castle in Palermo, he succeeded in kidnapping Frederick and he kept him under his tight control until his own death in 1202, when the child was passed on to the care of another German, William of Capparone. Throughout all this time, in addition to the bitter feuding that continued between the different parties, Sicily itself was being riven by anarchy and unrest, this making the island so vulnerable to foreign attack that Genoese corsairs would be able to capture and hold Syracuse for the next seventeen years.

While Frederick had initially had some more regular education and upbringing, everything appeared to change with the arrival of his German masters. There were stories of how, ignored and uncared-for, he spent much of his early childhood out in the city streets, mixing with the ordinary men and women and on occasion even being fed by them when he was hungry.

As this version of events would seem to be at odds with that which depicts the boy as a virtual prisoner of his new guardians, today some argue that Frederick was always 'closely protected and well observed'.[42] Yet, whether or not the earlier accounts are exaggerated, or even true, there is no doubt that a deep and lasting bond between the king and his Sicilian subjects would form while he was growing up in Palermo. Whatever happened to him during that time, Frederick always remained closely attached to the south of Italy, and it would be here, rather than in his German lands, that he would spend the greater part of his life. His childhood in the multi-cultural city would undoubtedly influence his later development, his early experiences giving him that openness to other beliefs, ideas and patterns of behaviour that would later mark his policies and personal lifestyle. This period in Palermo would also help him to become a highly competent linguist. He was said to be fluent in Arabic, Greek, Latin, Norman French, Provençal, German and the local Sicilian vernacular. Yet, despite his affection for the place, as an adult Frederick would not make the island his base, choosing instead the mainland region of Puglia that, besides being more central to his southern territories, had better access to his foreign neighbours and the distant parts of his empire.

With peace at last agreed between Innocent III and the Germans, the situation improved in Sicily and in 1207 the possibly rather unsympathetic Walter of Palearia returned to retake charge of Frederick. In December the next year, on his fourteenth birthday, the boy officially came of age, and just eight months later he married his first wife, the widowed Constance of Aragon, a woman some eleven years older, who was to arrive with a retinue of 500 knights. While it had been hoped that these might help supress the rebellious nobles, the majority of the men would soon die of the sickness that quickly spread through their ranks. Frederick, however, had already begun to increase his authority. This meant that new tensions were now beginning to develop in his relations with the pope, who had become worried about his own diminishing influence in the region. And, being equally concerned about challenges he was facing from elsewhere, Innocent would therefore decide to go further and in October 1209 he crowned Otto of Brunswick as the new Emperor. Within days, however, the pontiff realised that this man had no intention of honouring the earlier pledges he had given in exchange for the imperial throne. Disregarding his former promises to defend the pope's territorial possessions, Otto quickly invaded the Matildine Lands – territories that had frequently been the cause of dispute ever since Matilda of Canossa's apparently confusing double bequest of her vast estates to both the pope and Emperor Henry V around a century earlier. Otto now marched across the papal lands to capture Barletta, Bari, and a number of other towns in Puglia. His high-handedness would eventually prove too much for the pope and in November 1210 Innocent excommunicated him and began to reaffirm Frederick's position as King of the Romans.

Having regained the pontiff's support, Frederick agreed to crown his oldest son, one-year-old Henry, the king of Sicily, and, having then appointed his wife as the child's regent, in 1212 he set off to reclaim his throne in the north.

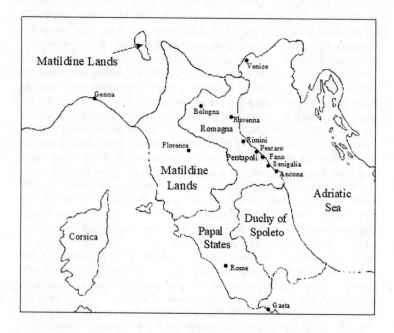

When passing through Rome, he paid the pope homage and reconfirmed his mother's commitment to maintain the separation of the empire from his southern kingdom. After moving on north, he was welcomed by the Genoese, but on leaving their city he was nearly captured by his enemies, only narrowly escaping the clutches of the Guelf-supporting Milanese and their allies by riding over a fast-flowing river. From the loyal town of Cremona he then crossed the Alps to Chur in Switzerland and eventually reached Constance just a few hours before the expected arrival of the Emperor himself. Here, despite the preparations in place to welcome Otto, Frederick used his well-known charm to win over the townspeople, and they, enchanted by the blond young man from the south, gave him the reception that they had intended for his rival. Hailed as the 'Boy from Puglia', he would now continue on his triumphant progress, welcomed all along the way by adoring crowds, until finally in December he received the recognition of the southern German princes and was crowned King of Germany at Mainz.

While Otto still retained the support of the northern German princes and the nominal backing of his English uncle, King John, things would change dramatically for the Emperor in July 1214, when he was decisively beaten by the French at Bouvines in Flanders. Although for the next few years he would hold on to his titles, the tables had now turned and just a year after Otto's defeat, in July Frederick was crowned Emperor in a spectacular ceremony at Aachen (Aix-la-Chapelle), the city where Charlemagne's own coronation had taken place more than 400 years earlier. Swept up in the enthusiasm of the moment, Frederick took an oath, swearing on pain of excommunication to go on a crusade to the Holy Land, a promise he later came much to regret, it continuing to plague him for years to come. Although Innocent III died 12 months later, under his successors this commitment, hastily made, would result in years of discord between the pope and the Emperor. However, for the moment Frederick's future looked rosy, particularly when in 1216 his early tutor Cardinal Cencio Savelli became Pope Honorius III. Although the new pontiff had his own concerns regarding his former charge, four years later in Rome, seven months after appointing his son Henry VII as the king of the Romans, he would personally crown Frederick as the Holy Roman Emperor.

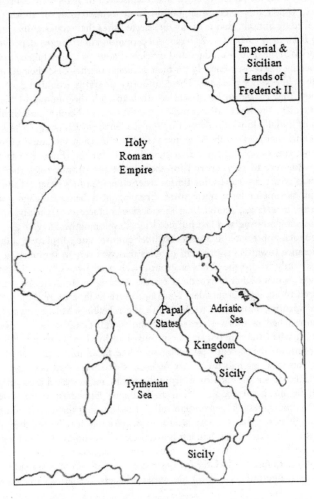

Just as Frederick's kingdom and empire were separate, so was the form of government he chose for the two. In his southern *regno*, which stretched right across to Puglia and north to the region of the Marche, he maintained a tight control, exerting an authority that was denied to him in his imperial lands. Here he began to lay out a new and clearly defined system of laws that would eventually be precisely set down in the constitutions that he established at Melfi in 1231. Believing in his own divinely ordained rights, Frederick saw himself as both God's mediator and the proper successor to the great Roman emperors of the past and so, adopting the role of Augustus, here in his southern kingdom he began to impose his absolute rule. At the same time, he reduced the privileges of his nobles, among other things forbidding them to marry without his permission. He also confiscated their recently constructed castles, which they were then permitted to rebuild only in those places approved by himself, that is to say on selected sites that were significantly far away from their earlier power bases. All promotion in the *regno* depended on Frederick alone, and his judges and officials – now no longer taken from the aristocracy but chosen entirely on their personal merit – held their positions purely at the king's pleasure. Their authority or status would end when in his view they ceased to be of service. To help with the running of his new bureaucracy, Frederick also founded a university at Naples, and although this was initially looked down on by the academics of Padua and elsewhere, in time its merit was fully recognised. Unlike the usual religious centres of learning, this establishment was designed solely for the training of laymen, men who were to be prepared for the new administrative roles that their king was creating. At the same time, Frederick made other practical changes, altering the methods of agriculture, bringing in a better coinage system, imposing new taxes, establishing the local manufacture of various articles such as silk and iron, and last but not least, developing his navy.

Frederick appreciated the value of other cultures and, displaying a degree of tolerance towards his different peoples that was rare at the time, he was always ready to use the skills of groups such as the Jews.[43] But in certain instances, when he felt it expedient for the security of the state, he was not prepared to accept the outsider. Wishing to give Sicily a more national and unified identity, he set out to deal with the rebellious Muslims who were still entrenched in the western part of the island. Gone were the days of Roger II, when the different ethnic groups had lived in harmony. By now, in response to the violent oppression they had faced under the subsequent rulers, the Saracens had turned to violence. Once these had been defeated, in 1222 Frederick expelled them from the island and resettled the estimated 15-20,000 displaced people in Lucera in Puglia. However, again showing an open-mindedness, he gave them full rights, granting them such complete religious freedom that the city would be remarkable for the number of its mosques. As his childhood had left him at ease with peoples of other religions or ethnicities, here he would also create one of his own favourite palaces. While these things would later help feed the negative rumours spread by the popes regarding the question of his spiritual beliefs, Frederick's treatment of the Saracens ensured their undying loyalty, and it would be from their ranks that his faithful bodyguard would be chosen.

With his lands fringed by the papal possessions and those more northern Italian regions that were allied to the pope, Frederick soon set out to strengthen his defences by building a string of fortresses along the border of the *regno*. In addition, he created places for his own pleasure, castles that displayed his wealth and status. Although little remains of the large palace he constructed at Foggia near his favoured hunting forests in the Capitanata, many other similar buildings are still scattered across the region. Among them is the impressive Castel del Monte, which, perched on a hilltop dominating the landscape around Andria, commands a 360-degree view stretching from the distant foothills of the hinterland to the Adriatic coast some fifteen miles away. Possibly inspired by the Dome of the Rock in Jerusalem, this remarkable structure illustrates Frederick's love of mathematical logic, the whole place being constructed in a series of octagonal shapes, including the eight towers with their eight sides. While the exterior appears comparatively stark and unadorned, the interior in Frederick's time was decorated with oriental taste, filled with mosaics, marbles, carpets and tapestries, and even a marble bath for his daily washing – a habit little known in the West at the time. All of these things no longer remain, but the structure itself has withstood the depredations of later generations, those such as the Angevins who sought to demolish this fortress belonging to their predecessors, or even those in search of easy building material. Restored to its former splendour, today it still impresses its visitors just as it did eight hundred years ago.

Apart from displaying his standing, these castles also illustrate the true nature of Frederick's relations with his neighbours. While throughout his reign he sought to protect his territories, successive popes and the northern states would endeavour to restrain his powers, the pontiffs in particular, fearing – not without reason – that the personal union of his kingdom and the imperial territories would threaten the security of their own encircled lands. After the fading of his early understanding with Innocent III, his tensions with the papal see had grown and they would steadily develop following the election in 1227 of Honorius's successor, the octogenarian Gregory IX. A personal friend, admirer, and follower of the deeply spiritual St Francis of Assisi, Gregory was always suspicious of Frederick's beliefs and ambitions. Over the years he would repeatedly switch from limited acceptance to bitter rejection of the Emperor, freely adapting his policy as appeared most propitious at the time. More than once, Gregory would interpret the Emperor's actions in such a way as to find an excuse to condemn and excommunicate him. Before long, these two men were bitter enemies, their mutual antagonism soon becoming the driving force behind their actions. Shortly after his enthronement, the pope announced his first excommunication of Frederick, punishing him for his perceived reluctance to abide by the crusading oath, originally made at his coronation in Aachen, which he had recently repeated at San Germano near Montecassino. When at the last moment Frederick aborted his much-delayed departure to the Holy Land, Gregory insisted on issuing his edict on the grounds that he considered the Emperor's excuses to be falsehoods. Yet, according to his followers, shortly after setting sail from Brindisi Frederick had become seriously ill, suffering from the epidemic that was now raging among his men still crowded into the hot and unhealthy camps. With his health seriously in doubt, Hermann von Salza, the Grand Master of the Teutonic Knights, and the Emperor's other close advisers had persuaded him to turn back.

Having recovered, the next year, although still excommunicated, Frederick finally set off for the Holy Land, and by diplomacy rather than force he succeeded in reaching agreement with the Egyptian sultan Al-Kamil, the nephew of the great Saladin. Being under pressure from his own family at the time, and also threatened by the ever-approaching Mongol hordes, the sultan wanted to avoid further conflict. He therefore agreed to surrender not just Bethlehem and Nazareth, but also Jerusalem, where in March 1229 the Emperor crowned himself the king in the Church of the Holy Sepulchre. Frederick rested his right to this throne on his second marriage to Yolande (Isabella), the daughter of John of Brienne, Jerusalem's former king.[44] Although the previous year the hereditary rights of the poor 16-year-old girl had passed with her death in childbirth to her son Conrad, Frederick had nonetheless claimed her lands for himself. While the holy sites had been gained without the spilling of any blood, and he was now in possession of all Jerusalem bar the two great mosques, Frederick's treaty with Al-Kamil proved unpopular with both Muslims and Christians. The pope, furious that Frederick had taken part in a crusade while still excommunicated, quickly repeated his edict and banned Christian pilgrims from visiting the city. Similarly, the patriarch in Jerusalem issued his own interdict, forbidding the Orthodox faithful from taking part in religious services. Adding further to Frederick's problems, his relations had already soured with his father-in-law, John of Brienne. While this man had been unceremoniously deposed immediately after his daughter's wedding, he had now also been told of the lack of kindness the Emperor had shown to Yolande. According to the gossips, on her arrival in Brindisi for the couple's official marriage in the cathedral, Frederick had ignored his bride, preferring instead to seduce her older cousin. Whatever the truth behind these accounts, John had understandably become enraged, and having joined Frederick's enemies, he was ready to lead the pope's invasion of the *regno*.[45] However, with the papal army eventually being forced to retreat, and the Emperor still lurking on his borders, Gregory IX would at last reluctantly accept defeat and lifted his edict of excommunication. After that, for the next nine years the two sides would continue to maintain their uneasy peace.

Although in Sicily Frederick was now taking steps to reform the government, his rule of the Empire rested on quite another basis. Here he maintained his support by granting considerable rights to the individual rulers of the separate states. Even so, this did not ensure constant loyalty and periodically the princes joined forces with his enemies, even allying themselves occasionally with the Lombard League that had originally been set up in 1167 in opposition to Frederick's grandfather, Frederick Barbarossa.

This was a new, loose association of the northern Italian states that from time to time, according to the particular circumstances, formed their own separate allegiances.

Even closer to home, meanwhile, Frederick was having to face another serious challenge to his authority. Although, against the wishes of the pope, his son Henry had been elected King of the Romans and also regent in the Empire, over the years the younger man had repeatedly contravened or hindered his father's wishes. Besides having stirred up trouble among the Germans with his tough measures, occasionally Henry had also encouraged the League to close the Alpine passes and thereby block the movement of the imperial troops. Although for a while Frederick had tolerated his son's mistakes and intentional show of disrespect, when finally his own position appeared to be in jeopardy, he became more ruthless. Having discovered how Henry had betrayed him by backing the rebels, in 1234 Frederick demanded that he should be excommunicated by the pope. Since at the time Gregory was sheltering from his own rebels at Rieti, and thus dependent on the Emperor's support for his safe return to Rome, he had little option other than concede to this wish. Frederick was still not satisfied, however, and so, having arrested his son and forced him to renounce his throne, he kept him captive until his death. Already a sick man, suffering from leprosy, Henry would die in 1242 when he rode – very possibly intentionally – off a cliff while on his way to a new prison. Despite their differences, Frederick was saddened by the news. He ordered Henry's body to be buried in the cathedral at Cosenza in Calabria.

While in 1235 Frederick replaced Henry in Germany with his younger brother, the Emperor was never again to leave Italy, his later plans to do so being prevented by mounting problems that he was now partly bringing on himself. His own reputation was not helped by his association with men like the notorious and exceptionally cruel Ezzolino da Romano. Having abandoned his former allies in the League, the year after he married Frederick's 13-year-old illegitimate daughter, in November 1237 Ezzolino helped his father-in-law to rout the Milanese at the battle of Cortenuova. After the victory, wanting to add to the humiliation of his prisoners, the triumphant Emperor paraded through the streets of loyal Cremona the precious, highly symbolic *carroccio* that meant so much to the people of Milan. Here, draped with its standards, this carriage was drawn along not by the usual oxen but by an elephant, and – since Frederick was equally enraged with his enemies' allies – chained to the back was the doge's son, Piero Tiepolo. Having run out of patience with all who opposed him, the Emperor then ordered the young man to be hanged at Trani and his body left on display as a further deterrent to the Venetians.

Already unpopular for refusing to consider anything other than an unconditional surrender by the members of the League, within months of Cortenuova the Emperor's reputation would be further traduced by the brutal and depraved Ezzolino, who in 1239 had been appointed the viceroy of the March of Treviso. And as Frederick's problems continued to mount up, following his unsuccessful three-month siege of Brescia, new disagreements began to arise between him and the pope regarding the situation in Sardinia. Because this was a region where the Church had long wanted to extend its influence, Gregory had become deeply concerned by the recent marriage agreement between the Emperor's oldest illegitimate son Enzo and the widowed daughter of William of Cagliari. Fearing that Enzo intended to assert the young woman's claims to parts of the island in order to become King of Sardinia himself, the pope again excommunicated Frederick, and before long the two sides were once more at war. After Enzo, now the newly appointed Imperial Vicar in northern Italy, had been sent to capture the Duchy of Spoleto, the Marche region, and the Romagna, by the end of the year his father had regained control of towns like Ravenna and Faenza, and had even begun to threaten Rome. Here, however, Frederick became nervous of how his invasion of the capital would be seen by the people, and so he then withdrew and moved on to Benevento.

Meanwhile, Gregory was using his indictment to undermine his rival's reputation still further. Publicly railing against the other's perceived heretical beliefs, he strengthened his condemnation by declaring Frederick guilty of the most heinous of crimes. This pronouncement would give voice to the many accusations still laid at the Emperor's door, not least his supposed declaration that Moses, the prophet Mohammed and Jesus Christ had been charlatans. In response to the pope's edict, Frederick issued a series of manifestos and as the personal threats against him grew, he became steadily more tyrannical, treating those who opposed him without mercy. As the war went on, even his loyal, well-governed kingdom in the south began to feel the effects, suffering from increased taxes as the king continued to milk the *regno* to finance his battles against the many northern cities that were beginning to desert him.

Concerned about the deteriorating situation, in 1241 Gregory summoned a council, calling on Church representatives to attend from far and wide. Since he was anxious to prevent this taking place, the Emperor had already blocked all paths through the imperial territories, and he now made preparations to take on the Genoese ships that were going to transport the delegates to Rome. As these approached Civitavecchia, three vessels were sunk, twenty-two more captured, and over a hundred of the churchmen were taken prisoner, their subsequent incarceration in Puglia only increasing Frederick's unpopularity. Undaunted, he marched back to Rome, but once more he hesitated, choosing to defer his entry until he could be welcomed by the people. In the event, this would never happen as in August the old pope died and so, with his arch enemy finally gone, Frederick decided to return once more to his kingdom.

After that there would be two years of uncertainty as the separate factions in the Church were unable to agree on who should be the new pontiff. Although this was temporarily resolved by the election of Celestine IV, his death after just sixteen days made it necessary for the cardinals to reconvene. With these men forced to return to the harsh living conditions intentionally imposed on them to speed up their decisions, the earlier stalemate was soon brought to an end and in 1243 the Genoese candidate was elected as Innocent IV. Having formerly been on good terms with him, Frederick was initially confident that there might at last be an individual on the papal throne with whom he could negotiate. Soon, however, he discovered that once more he was facing an implacable enemy, having in his own words, 'lost the friendship of a cardinal and gained the enmity of a pope'. As their rift grew and the two parties failed to reach agreement on questions like the suzerainty of the Lombard regions, Innocent began to fear that plots were developing against him. Having therefore fled Rome and eventually found refuge in Lyon, in 1245 he officially announced that the Emperor was deposed. Besides also declaring Frederick to be a heretic, guilty of all sorts of crimes and perversions, the pope then went further and gave his backing to a plot to assassinate him. On discovering this, Frederick took his harsh revenge against those whom he believed to be involved; but Innocent's condemnation was to have more serious long-term consequences for the Emperor. As he was soon facing active opposition throughout his imperial territories, new pretenders, backed by the pope, had started to come forward to lay claim to his German throne.

Many of Frederick's former Ghibelline followers had by this time joined the Guelf supporters of the pope, and various cities had also started to change their loyalties. So, when Parma abandoned him, Frederick finally had had enough. Determined to regain the town, in June 1247 he began to put the place under siege. Over time, however, the attackers started to relax their guard, and so when eight months later the Emperor and several of his followers had gone out hunting, the starving people in the city saw their opportunity to take matters into their own hands. Having at last broken out, during the subsequent battle Frederick's nearby encampment was rapidly demolished. A fledgling town, already named Vittoria in expectation of the Emperor's ultimate success, this had been intended as an eventual replacement for Parma. Laid out with well-constructed houses, streets and churches, it had been filled with the typical luxuries of the imperial court – complete with Frederick's retinue of men and women, various animals, and other treasures. As this had been mostly destroyed and many of its people taken captive, the Emperor now had little alternative other than to limp back to Cremona.

Having survived the earlier conspiracy, Frederick once more escaped assassination when his doctor – again apparently encouraged by Innocent – attempted to poison him. While this was a bitter betrayal by a trusted member of his entourage, the Emperor's confidence would be even more shaken when at Cremona in 1249 his closest companion and adviser, Pietro della Vigna, was found guilty of treason. Although most probably engaged in some illegal financial business, the precise charges against him were never clearly laid out. Della Vigna knew the fate that awaited him, and reportedly he chose to end his own life by deliberately crushing his head against his prison walls. This was not the end of Frederick's difficulties, however, as he now found himself unable to bring about the release of his much-loved son Enzo, who by this time was a captive of the Bolognese. While the conditions in which he was kept were not unduly harsh, Enzo was to remain a prisoner for the rest of his life in the Palazzo Nuovo that still stands in Bologna city centre. The last of Frederick's sons, he died in 1272, one year before Rudolf became the first of the Habsburgs to be elected King of Germany.

The frequency with which the various popes had issued edicts of excommunication had diminished their impact. Therefore, at home and abroad men had begun to ignore the indictment of Innocent. Still holed up in Lyon, and without even the support of the French king Louis IX, Innocent was now feeling insecure. Although the situation was therefore finally beginning to improve for the Emperor, before anything was resolved, in December 1250 Frederick died unexpectedly of dysentery in Puglia at Castel Fiorentino – this, by a strange coincidence, fulfilling the prediction he had much feared that he would die in a place connected to flowers. Despite the reports that he had rejected all Christian beliefs, he had chosen to be dressed in the simple clothes of a Cistercian monk and had confessed his sins and received the sacrament on his deathbed. His body was taken back by his Saracen bodyguard for burial in Palermo Cathedral, where it was laid in the impressive sarcophagus that he had earlier moved from Monreale for his interment.

Frederick was a man of contrasts. His court was modelled on the oriental system, a male-dominated environment where in the main his wives and several mistresses played an insignificant role. Although his first wife Constance would act as regent in his absences, women as a whole remained largely hidden from view in what many saw as a virtual eastern harem. His retinue would astound those that witnessed its arrival in their town, the Emperor accompanied by numbers of exotically dressed attendants, Saracen dancers, servant girls and eunuchs, as well as his famous menagerie of animals, including monkeys, camels, various great cats such as lions, leopards and panthers, and even the odd elephant. His love of the exotic first developed as a child in the culturally mixed environment of Palermo had grown during his time in the Middle East. Here, where he had also formed close acquaintances, his diplomatic skills had enabled him to achieve much previously denied to those before him. At the same time, he had greatly impressed foreign dignitaries with his knowledge of their culture, their studies of astrology and other sciences, and also of the Arabic language. He was also fascinated by their mathematics, which he had studied with the renowned Pisan mathematician, Fibonacci. Besides this he had encouraged the use of the new Italian language and shown an equal appreciation of poetry and philosophy. In addition to studying the writings of the famous Hellenists such as Aristotle, whose teachings and ideas he was prepared to question, he had a profound interest in a wide range of other subjects, including anatomy, biology and zoology. And even with this busy programme, Frederick had found the time to produce his own remarkable study on falconry, a work – complete with diagrams and drawings very possibly by his own hand – that is still read today.

Although (in the West at least) the stocky, red-haired Emperor was frequently described as attractive and charming, he could at the same time be undoubtedly cruel, and there were reports of his sudden, unpredictable flashes of temper.[46] His vengefulness would become more pronounced as his reign progressed and he found himself and his empire increasingly threatened by some of the most intransigent of medieval popes. These leaders of the Church would be responsible for destroying his reputation, making him particularly reviled by the faithful who were highly suspicious of his pro-Muslim leanings. While he was convinced of his right to rule as God's representative and was loved and honoured by those of his supporters who believed him to be their long-awaited saviour, many others accused him of holding heretical beliefs. Dante would put him among the heretics in the sixth circle of the *Inferno*. Basing their arguments on the charges first made by Gregory IX in his savage second edict of excommunication, Frederick's critics would repeatedly suggest that he had denied such fundamental Christian beliefs as the immaculate conception and the existence of the afterlife. Much of the negative reporting of the Emperor comes to us through the accounts of his contemporaries, people such as the monk Salimbene, who took great pains to recount his wickedness. While some instances of Frederick's gross misdeeds can be verified, other reports telling of his savage experiments for the advancement of knowledge carried out on living victims remain unproven. While here there might be some exaggeration, certain elements of these charges could be true, and there may have been some investigative research performed on victims for greater knowledge on the workings of the human digestive system. Yet the account of his search for the origin of language, a study carried out by raising children in an environment without speech or human interaction, is similar to stories found levelled against other people elsewhere. Without clear evidence, therefore, these particular cases against Frederick remain open to debate.

Undoubtedly the Emperor took ferocious revenge on those who opposed him, particularly after his second excommunication, which had been responsible for bringing on a rapid collapse of his authority in much of his empire. This, however, points to a possible major difference between him and those who opposed him. While Frederick's ambitions were directed above all towards the good of the state, those of Gregory IX were largely driven by hatred and suspicion. The earlier dispute appeared to be for Frederick a political argument rather than a private vendetta against the Church, and so when the pope died, he ceased his assault on the papal lands. Gregory, however, launched a personal attack on the Emperor, determined in his defamation to emphasise, if not exaggerate, the faults of the individual. While no doubt the pontiff did have reason to fear an all-powerful Emperor whose military might could threaten his papal lands, his anxieties and those of his successor Innocent IV appear to have been provoked as much, if not more, by the intellectual courage of their rival. At a period when faith was expected to rest on the unquestioning acceptance of dogma, Frederick showed a willingness to query that was well in advance of its time. An empiricist, he 'dared to think' in a way that would be openly promoted only centuries after him by those such as Voltaire and Kant. Yet while Frederick condemned the dogmas of the established faith and the corruption of the prelates, he did not reject all religious thinking, his deathbed confession suggesting evidence of a continued spirituality. But the actions of the Church have to be set against the challenges it was facing in this period, when there was the widespread belief that the end of the world was fast approaching. Expecting the second coming of Christ, many of Frederick's adherents believed him to be the longed-for redeemer or messiah sent to save his people. This presented a serious challenge to the pontiffs and to the spiritual and territorial authority of the Catholic Church, and so Innocent IV, who was able to incorporate new regions into the Papal States after Frederick died, would openly express his delight on hearing the news of his death, declaring: 'Let the heavens rejoice and let the Earth be glad.'[47]

However Frederick is judged, he certainly brought to his southern Italian kingdom several years of stability, and by the end of his life he had founded a bureaucratic system of management that would last for centuries to come. Yet, tragically, for the Hohenstaufens personally, the policies he pursued and his lengthy wars and disputes with his neighbours would ultimately undermine their position with the result that within just four years of his death the dynasty had collapsed. Riots soon broke out in Sicily, and as cities elsewhere started to assert their independence, the duke of Anjou, with French and papal support, began his preparations to take over the kingdom. In the meantime, the breakup of Frederick's Empire had also begun. During the following twenty-three-year interregnum, the princedoms in Germany would grow in independence and the ducal states in northern Italy start to take shape. This is the paradox of Frederick's reign. While he was, without doubt, a remarkable figure, acclaimed by a contemporary as *Stupor mundi*, the wonder of the world, he would unknowingly be the last of the famous early Holy Roman Emperors.

There is a clear anomaly in the way that he was reviled and worshipped in equal measure, for some the saviour of his people, for others the embodiment of the antichrist. The Guelf-leaning Giovanni Villani, writing nearly a century later, would condemn him for the way he had abandoned himself 'to all the bodily pleasures ... heedless that there would ever be another life'.[48] The openly prejudicial judgement of the Emperor that Villani shared with his contemporary, Dante's teacher Brunetto Latini, would then extend to the whole family. Accusing Frederick's illegitimate son Manfred of having murdered his father, a charge for which there is no evidence, Latini would graphically describe how shortly before the Emperor's death, Manfred greedily began to seize all he could, and then entered Frederick's sickroom and 'pressed down on the pillow and killed him'.[49]

Leaving all this aside, the sudden illness and death of the previously healthy Emperor caused shock among friend and foe alike. But, contrary to what his critics would have wanted, soon its very unexpectedness allowed myths to develop, and there would be claims of later sightings, and prophecies that Frederick would return and his empire rise again. At the same time, some of the Emperor's considerable achievements would have a more practical and long-lasting influence on the future story of Europe. Following the course set by his grandfather, Roger II, Frederick had brought Arabic and Greek learning to the West, and under his rule there had been developments in many fields, including law, agriculture, mathematics, medicine, scientific empiricism, and the humanities. He had also introduced the training of doctors and had attempted to bring in a general uniformity of weights and measures – something only finally adopted some five hundred years later. Highly intelligent and with an intellect that was exceptional among rulers, through his energy, drive, and open-mindedness he had brought remarkable progress to his country. But even while some historians such as Ernst Kantorowicz see him as a free thinker responsible for introducing various ideas that would manifest themselves during the Renaissance, others believe that his questioning of religious authority was solely a pragmatic response to the challenges he faced from the popes. Either way, Frederick stands out from many of his more faceless medieval contemporaries, appearing as a living being, with the qualities and failings common to humanity. Inevitably much has been lost in the passage of time, and we are left with the few early works written by his first biographers. Their usually biased criticisms, whether extoling or condemning their subject, do not give a fully rounded picture of this exceptional individual, and so without the verified evidence or documented records necessary for reaching an unvarnished truth, Frederick's legacy continues to be subject to debate.

* * *

Following his mother Yolande's death, shortly after his birth in Andria in 1228, the child officially became the King of Jerusalem, even though his father ruled in his place until his majority. And this was just the first of the boy's titles: having been removed from his family and sent to Germany to replace his disgraced brother as the duke of Swabia, two years later in 1237 the nine-year-old had become Conrad IV, King of the Romans and King of Italy. Although in 1245 Innocent IV took away his position as the king of the Germans, Conrad held on to the title for a year until he was overthrown by his former regent, Henry Raspe, who died soon after and was replaced by William of Holland.[50] Although these events led to an absence of imperial rule for some twenty years, in 1252 Conrad left his wife and new-born son Conradin to take up his Sicilian throne. Having landed at Siponto near the Gargano, helped by the Venetians, he then issued his own constitutions at Foggia, and reclaimed his southern lands – now also taking large areas from his half-brother Manfred, whom he had begun to distrust. Although he was soon facing multiple revolts throughout his kingdom, the next year he managed to conquer Naples. This, however, was the end of Conrad's good fortune, he being excommunicated by the pope in April 1254, and then dying just a month later after contracting malaria.

Conrad was the last of the Hohenstaufens to rule in Germany, and the family's days in power were now numbered, but things were still not quite finished for Frederick II's descendants in the *regno*, where Manfred had already assumed control of his young nephew's kingdom. Four years younger than his half-brother Conrad, Manfred had been born at Venosa to his father's mistress, he very possibly being later legitimised after the Emperor had reputedly married his mother, Bianca Lancia, on her deathbed. This would have made her Frederick's fourth wife, replacing Isabella, the daughter of King John of England, who had died at Foggia in 1241. As Manfred was much loved by his father, many of whose intellectual interests he shared, he had received the title of the Prince of Taranto. But by assuming the regency of Conradin he had greatly displeased the boy's official guardian, Innocent IV, and as a result he, too, was excommunicated. Although the two men would later draw up an agreement according to which Puglia was to be put under papal authority, before long the pontiff broke the truce and attacked Naples, forcing Manfred to flee to Lucera where he then joined forces with his father's loyal Saracens. With their help, in 1254 Manfred defeated the papal army at Foggia, the victory coming just days before the ageing Innocent IV died. But any hopes that his successor, Alexander IV, would prove more conciliatory were soon dashed. In his turn, the new pope confirmed Manfred's excommunication and issued a bull against the Saracens who had given him refuge. Alexander then offered the kingdom to Edmund, Earl of Lancaster, the son of Henry III of England. But when Manfred defeated the Englishman the next year, he regained control of the whole *regno* and was acknowledged as Conradin's 'vicar'. These successes had increased his standing among his supporters, and so when rumours were heard of his nephew's death, in 1258 Manfred was crowned King of Sicily in his place. Once again, however, Villani, that arch critic of the Hohenstaufens, presents a darker version of these events. According to him, the king had previously sent his henchmen north to poison the boy and Conradin had only been saved by the actions of his mother, who had allegedly sacrificed one of her other children in his place. Nevertheless, even after the earlier stories of his nephew's death were found to be untrue, Manfred held on to the throne, and two years later he strengthened his position by arranging the marriage of his daughter Constance to Peter of Aragon.

Manfred's position was now secure at home, and having also greatly extended his territories, he had come to be viewed by the northern Italian states and the Ancona Marches as the champion of their Ghibelline cause. As a result, concern had grown in papal circles, and so in 1263 he was again excommunicated by the recently enthroned French pope, Urban IV, who now accused him of embracing the 'rites of the Saracens' and dishonouring the Catholic faith.[51] Offering the kingdom instead to Louis IX's brother in January 1266, Urban crowned Duke Charles of Anjou as the new king of Sicily. A month later, Charles met his rival in battle at Benevento, and it was here that Manfred was killed when, according to his critics, he abandoned all caution and rushed headlong into the thick of the action, proof – as Villani saw it – that 'God deprives of sense him to whom he wishes ill.' Latini represented Manfred's death as the divine punishment of God, who had intentionally taken away his vision and deprived him of 'his sense and his good foresight'.[52] Among his supporters, however, Manfred would become famous for the courageous manner in which he had died. Although, when his body was eventually found on the battlefield, it was buried near the place where he had fallen, later it would be reinterred across the papal border close to the Garigliano River – a spot purposely chosen by the Church to ensure that his remains would eventually be washed away leaving no trace. More significantly for the Hohenstaufens, Manfred's defeat and disappearance had hastened the end of their rule in Italy and opened the way for the arrival of Sicily's Angevin dynasty.[53] As Siponto – where Conrad had first landed – had become silted up after a series of earthquakes, Manfred had created a new port in his name, and here three years after his death Charles would try to draw a line under the past. While the town's great bell, created to summon assistance in times of danger, was removed to the Basilica of San Nicola in Bari – and eventually melted down – in Manfredonia the memory of its Hohenstaufen founder lives on.

The remnants of Frederick's great power now lay in the hands of his 14-year-old grandson, Conradin, who two years after his uncle's death marched into the *regno* to take on the Angevin king. With their meeting at the bloody battle of Tagliacozzo leaving Charles the victor, Conradin was soon fleeing for his life, and his supporters were facing execution or imprisonment. One such prisoner reportedly spent the next thirty-two years locked up in Frederick's Castel del Monte. That would not be the end of Charles's revenge, however, as he had one further humiliation to heap on the young Conradin. In a grotesque finale, having been betrayed and captured, the last Hohenstaufen claimant to the kingdom of Sicily was publicly put to death in Naples, when on 26 October he and five of his followers were taken to the market square on the sea front. Here before a weeping crowd, the young king threw down the gauntlet in a last act of defiance, before he and the others were executed and their bodies cast into the sea. Although some later historians would refer to the cruelty of Charles of Anjou, Villani, the king's contemporary admirer, was more nuanced. But while he saw some higher justice in what had happened, Conradin's death being for him the final stage of divine justice for the sins of Hohenstaufens, even he would admit that in this case Charles had been at fault. In Villani's view, this mistake could possibly explain the reason for the Angevin king's later misfortunes, with him believing that since Charles had 'captured Conradin and his retainers in battle and not by treachery ... it would have been better to have him kept in prison than have him killed'.[54] In fact, the king himself would later display his apparent remorse by building a Carmelite church on the spot where the executions had taken place.

While Conradin and Manfred have no tombs, the Hohenstaufens are remembered throughout southern Italy where their great buildings still stand. And, even though their living dynasty disappeared in Puglia, it did not completely die out in the south for another two and a half centuries. When 14 years after Conradin's death Charles lost the island of Sicily following the disastrous events of Easter 1282, his throne would be given to Manfred's son-in-law, Peter III, thus beginning a period of Aragonese rule that would last until the country's unification with Castile under its famous joint monarchs, Ferdinand and Isabella of Spain.

SECTION III
THE EARLY GROWTH OF VENICE

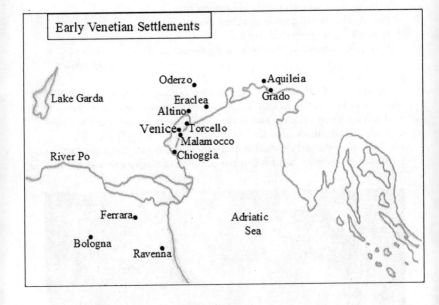

Early Venetian Settlements

Lake Garda

Oderzo

Aquileia

Grado

Eraclea

Altino

Venice

Torcello

Malamocco

Chioggia

River Po

Ferrara

Bologna

Ravenna

Adriatic Sea

5

Traders, crusaders and conquerors

'A ruler of the waters and their powers:
And such she was; – her daughters had their dowers
From spoils of nations, and the exhaustless East
Pour'd in her lap all gems in sparkling showers.
In purple was she robed, and of her feast
Monarchs partook, and deem'd their dignity increas'd.'

Lord Byron[55]

According to a myth developed in the 14th century by the men of Padua, Venice was founded in March 421, when three consuls from the city were said to have set up a trading post in the middle of the lagoon's shallow waters on a high sandbank, or 'rivo alto', later to be known as the Rialto. Whatever the truth, since the early barbarian invasions of the Roman Empire, whenever local men and women had felt threatened they had temporarily taken refuge

Doge Pietro II Orseolo and his son Otto painted by Tintoretto in the Great Council Chamber.

on similar small islands in the region. But even after Venice's supposed founding date those living on the mainland had repeatedly suffered from attack, notably in 452 when the Huns hit the former Roman town of Oderzo, and having sacked and largely destroyed Aquileia, forced its inhabitants to find safety in nearby Grado. With such barbarian threats persisting until the arrival of the Lombard invaders in the latter part of the 6th century, the local people continued periodically to gather for protection in the coastal marshes or lagoons.

Initially surviving on wildfowl, or whatever they could catch from their surrounding waters, within a hundred years Venice's first settlers had begun trading with their neighbours in the northern Italian cities – an early commerce in fish and salt that would be the foundation of the Republic's later wealth. At the same time, as it adjusted to its precarious existence, the place began to take on elements of that democratic character for which it would become famous. While Cassiodorus, Theodoric's prefect in Ravenna, was no doubt exaggerating when he stated in 523 that among the Venetians there was 'no difference between rich and poor', and that there the envy that 'rules the rest of the world' was unknown, his remarks show that already a republican spirit had been born among the Veneti people living in or around the lagoon.[56] Apart from the fact that their lack of territory on the mainland had prevented the growth of individual or private wealth and power such as was found among feudal landowners elsewhere, here the collective need for protection had created an awareness of mutual dependency and a shared sense of loyalty to the community at large. As this developed, step by step there would come into being a complicated form of bureaucracy that gradually assumed the management of its affairs. Although eventually only some would be considered eligible for public office, council members were chosen by ballot in an increasingly complex process that was above all intended to reduce the powers of any one individual. Over the centuries, as an oligarchy began to form, the system's restrictions would extend even to the authority, rights and freedoms of the eventual head of state, the doge.

With its very existence dependent on the sea, before long Venice's maritime strength had come to the attention of others. When in the 530s the eastern Roman emperor Justinian wanted to defeat the last rulers in the West, he turned to the city for naval support. Having a larger fleet, the Venetians could enforce a blockade to help the Greeks capture the imperial capital in Ravenna and bring the old Latin empire to an end. In return for its co-operation, in the following centuries Venice would find itself under the protection of Constantinople, a situation that remained in place until the Franks ousted the Lombards and took control of the whole of the northern Italian region in 804. At that point, having rebelled against the eastern emperor, Venice came under the protection of Charlemagne, who then granted it important new trading rights. Nevertheless, the city's situation was still unsure. Wishing to regain their control, the Byzantines soon invaded the area and within five years they had reached the lagoon and had put Venice under siege. As a result, a decade after it had turned to the Franks, it would be back in the hands of the Greeks, and had officially become a province of their emperor. Even so, its people maintained their own form of independent government, and despite being loyal to the pope, they still managed to balance their relations with both East and West. However, their links to Constantinople would gradually become more tenuous, and over time they grew to see the eastern confession as schismatic and heretical. As their opposition to the Orthodox faith became yet more marked after the Great Schism of 1054 had divided the two Churches, in 1180 the Commune would even permit papal indulgences to be sold in St Mark's Square.[57] Although a little over two decades later, in the aftermath of the disastrous Fourth Crusade, numbers of Greeks came to Venice – and yet more arrived following the fall of Constantinople to the Muslims in 1453 – all these newcomers would face religious restrictions. At first, they were allowed to worship only in the small Church of San Biagio, and even though they were later granted permission to build the larger church of San Giorgio dei Greci, they would still have to wait for almost a century before this building was completed in the mid-1500s.

Earlier, after the Lombard invasions in the 560s, while more refugees from the surrounding regions in Venetia and Istria were beginning to put down roots in the middle of the lagoon, others from Altino had chosen to settle about seven miles away from the Rialto on the little island of Torcello, where in time the Ravenna exarchate would establish a bishopric. Although its first cathedral, dedicated to Santa Maria Assunta in 639, was rebuilt in the 11th century, this would then become famous for the Byzantine architecture and exceptional mosaics that we see today. After arriving on the island, the community had gradually grown in importance and wealth, until its people had become leading traders in several commodities, including the highly important salt.

In the meantime, Venice, too, had become more established. After fleeing the Lombards, in 667 many people from Oderzo had moved to Eraclea (Melidissa) and it was here, according to Venetian tradition, that its first doge Paoluccio Anafesto had been chosen thirty years later. In fact, despite his image appearing in the frieze of portraits eventually painted in the Council Chamber of the Doge's Palace, there is little if any evidence to back this early version of events. Even though documents indicate that a certain Orso from Eraclea would be the first man officially appointed to the role of *dux* more than half a century later, the popular story of Anafesto's election would survive. He was alleged to have been chosen by the local people when he had brought the communities together by proclaiming the unity of the various groups living around the lagoon. Although the role would prove more than a challenge for those supposedly following him, with Orso and three others coming to brutal ends that included blinding and exile, in 810 the situation became even more centralised when the government was again moved from its more recent home at Malamocco to put down roots on the Rialto.

Having settled here, they were ambitious to increase their status. Since the veneration of holy relics established by Bishop Ambrose, churches and towns seeking to increase their importance had joined in the scramble to get hold of anything with a connection to the saints. In 828 some Venetian sailors visiting Alexandria in Egypt managed to get their hands on the remains of St Mark, the gospel writer who had reputedly been martyred in the year 68. With the precious cargo having been smuggled past the Muslims hidden in a barrel of pork, on its arrival in Venice the evangelist was adopted as the city's new patron, replacing the former Greek saint, Theodore. Seeking a worthy place to house their holy relics, the Venetians then began to build a private chapel for the doge in their recently created city square. Modelled on the Church of the Holy Apostles in Constantinople, this was named in the saint's honour, and from that time on, the famous symbolic Lion of Saint Mark would regularly appear on banners, sculptures, and much else wherever the Venetians eventually held sway. Proud of its saint, the city would now begin to see itself on a par with Rome, even having the confidence on occasion to question the primacy of the pope himself.

However, the people around the lagoon of course still faced various challenges. Since the fall of the Roman Empire in the West, the region had been raided by Slavic pirates, based on the Narenta (Neretva) River south of Spalato (Split), who would regularly attack shipping and the coastal towns, Caorle, for one, being hit in 846. Furthermore, after settling permanently on the Rialto, the Venetians had become increasingly unpopular among their commercial rivals on Italy's west coast. Here the merchants of Genoa, Pisa and Amalfi, who viewed the newcomers with apprehension and distrust, had grown increasingly fearful of the competition. Therefore, hoping to disrupt Venice's trade, Naples decided to encourage the Barbary pirates who infested the Tyrrhenian Sea to enter the Adriatic. After these Saracens had laid waste to the region around Ragusa (Dubrovnik), in 878 they arrived at Grado, which had now become the seat of the regional patriarchy. To defend the region from these assaults and to protect their own fleet, the Venetians responded by establishing bases along the shores of Istria and Dalmatia. Yet they, too, were equally ruthless and ambitious. Motivated by a desire to make money, they had now become involved in a practice that was just as brutal as that of their enemies in that they had begun to trade in Christian Slavs sold to non-Christian buyers – a commerce that would be the origin of the word slavery itself. These captive men and women would swell the vast numbers that were simultaneously being taken from Russia, Armenia, Greece, parts of Africa and elsewhere to be shipped to bondage in Morocco, Egypt and other places overseas. Despite the doge's efforts to control it in 870, this would be an on-going lucrative business, and although eventually banned in 960, Venetians would continue to be involved in the trade for some centuries to come. While numbers of the desperate people would over time be employed by Venetian estate owners in Candia (Crete) and Cyprus, closer to home, still at the end of the 14th century a few African slave markets were being held on the Rialto.

With Venice being naturally unproductive because of its location – its imported industries arriving only later – its survival depended above all on trade, and therefore, with so much riding on their business, the merchants could never afford to be choosy when selecting their markets. Even though the eastern emperor had outlawed all commercial activity between the Christians and the Saracens, the traders would continue to be driven by their practical needs. It was thus a significant triumph when by the end of the tenth century, the Venetians gained special commercial rights from Constantinople. Now, as it had once been for the Roman Empire, the Adriatic was again an important highway, providing a direct path to the Venetians' eastern markets. With ports of call from Trieste and Pola to Ragusa and beyond offering welcome rest, replenishment, and shelter for the galley crews, in time there would be an extensive network of coastal stations dotted along the route from Venice to Africa and the east.

Nevertheless, the growing republic was facing other challenges, among these the continuing threat of attack from the Hungarians. To confront this, the city built a surrounding wall and installed a chain to block entry to the main canal, defences that would not be removed until the 12th century. But, besides this, Venice was now struggling with more domestic problems. These came to a head in 976 when a riot broke out in protest at the arrogance and extravagance of the doge, Pietro IV Candiano. With the situation soon spiralling out of control, the mob intentionally set fire to some of the buildings, and as the blaze took hold about 300 houses and several other buildings were destroyed, most significantly the original ducal palace and its chapel. Included among the casualties were Pietro Candiano and his young son, both killed by the people as they tried to escape their home. Needing to find a replacement, the next day the Venetians elected as their doge a member of one of the other influential families, Pietro I Orseolo. During his two years as head of state, besides ordering the immediate rebuilding of the palace, he would personally contribute towards the reconstruction of the ducal chapel – later to become known as the famous Basilica of San Marco. But while Pietro Orseolo used his position to carry out further good works and give generously to the poor, he had no desire to remain in office, and so one night he slipped away without even informing his family of his intentions. Having gone to France, this deeply spiritual man became a Benedictine monk, eventually dying as a hermit nine years after his abdication. Finally, in 1731 Pietro I Orseolo was canonised by Pope Clement VII, and some three decades later his statue was included among those erected on the reconstructed façade of the Church of San Rocco.

After a period of further instability, with another doge soon abdicating through ill health and his illiterate successor facing renewed unrest, in 991 Pietro I Orseolo's son Pietro II was elected. With many of his father's talents, he restored peace at home and promoted further commercial activity abroad with trading partners in Spain and the Middle East. Moreover, besides gaining from the Holy Roman Emperor Otto II the right to the free movement of merchandise down the rivers from the north to the Italian markets, he re-established good relations with the Byzantines. Having helped the Greeks defeat the Saracens who were blockading Bari, in 1004 he received a 'most favoured' status for his city and gained practical benefits for his merchants in the eastern empire. Orseolo's son was offered the Greek emperor's daughter in marriage, Venice would now encounter the customs and manners of the East. While critics sneered at the bride's retinue of eunuchs and condemned her various other 'degenerate' practices, she would be among those Byzantine princesses credited at this time with inaugurating change. Her arrival in the city would introduce Venetians to the exotic silks and scents they soon grew to love, and to foreign practices such as bathing and using a fork.

While civil war was raging in Croatia, Pietro II Orseolo had seen an opportunity of stopping the payment of tribute that Venice was obliged to give the Croatian king. His action led, however, to increased activity by the Narentine pirates, and as the severity of their attacks grew, in 998 the doge decided the time had come to go to war. With his capture of the island of Lissa (Vis), the people of Zara (Zadar) and some other coastal towns turned to the Venetians for protection. Nonetheless, the pirate raids did not stop and so two years later on Ascension Day – the start of the summer sailing season – Orseolo set out again with his fleet. After having been greeted by the men and women of Istria, who were anxious to see an end to the attacks, he continued on to Dalmatia where he decisively defeated the pirates near Zara. In the end all the raiders were crushed and Venice achieved full dominance over the region, extending its reach as far as Ragusa to the south. When eventually the doge returned in triumph to Venice, he received a rapturous welcome and the blessing of the pope. This joyful occasion, to be known as the *Festa della Sensa*, would eventually come to be commemorated in the annual Ascension Day ceremony of the *Sposalizio del Mare*.

Meanwhile, in Croatia, the ruler Svetoslav had been overthrown and replaced by his brothers Gojslav and Krešimir III. When the deposed king turned to the Venetians at Trau (Trogir) for support, he agreed to being taken as a hostage with his son Stjepan (Stephen) back to Venice. Here eight years later Stjepan would marry Orseolo's daughter, and eventually in 1030 he would inherit his uncle Krešimir III's throne. In the meantime, however, while the fighting was still going on in Croatia, Orseolo was making other significant gains. In addition to winning the loyalty of the coastal towns that wanted his protection, he had now expanded the Republic's hold down the eastern shore of the Adriatic, and had started to claim for himself and his successors the titles of 'dux' of Dalmatia and Istria.

In 1006, Orseolo's Greek wife, daughter, and oldest son Giovanni would all die when the plague hit Venice. Having then named his younger child Otto as his heir, and divided his fortune between the state and his family, the doge retired to take up a monastic way of life. Still only forty-eight when he died two years later, Pietro II Orseolo was buried at the now enlarged 9th-century monastery church of San Zaccaria – famous for its relics of Zacharias, the father of St John the Baptist – which would later become the burial place for eight of Venice's heads of state.[58]

Appointed when only sixteen, the youngest of all the doges, Orseolo's son Otto would have a difficult term in office. Just ten years after he had succeeded his father, Venice's relations with Croatia completely collapsed. Having recognised the Byzantine emperor Basil II as his overlord, in 1018 the Croatian king, Krešimir III, attempted to seize his Dalmatian lands back from

Venice. With the people of the coastal towns and islands appealing for his help, Otto felt obliged to invade the region and enforce his possession. Having become unpopular at home for his nepotism, in 1022 he was deposed for the first time and, although soon reinstated, four years later deposed again. Venice was already on bad terms with the Greeks, but now, with Otto having sought refuge in Constantinople, the situation rapidly worsened. Relations between the two cities steadily grew more tense, until finally the emperor removed all commercial privileges from the Venetian traders in his capital. The Holy Roman Emperor in the West soon followed suit, and matters were then made worse by the Croatians attacking Venice's Dalmatian towns, and the Hungarian king showing his support for the ousted Otto. The Venetians therefore decided that they had to invite their deposed doge to return, but their request came too late as Otto was to die in 1032 while he was still in Constantinople.

Although after this there would be no more doges directly succeeding from father to son, twenty-five years later, Pietro II's grandson Petar Krešimir IV would come to power in Croatia.[59] This king, still remembered as one of the country's great rulers, was not just acknowledged by the eastern emperor but also sincerely respected and admired for his military achievements in the West. But, with Petar having been born and raised in Venice after his father's marriage to the doge's daughter, he had adopted Latin ways and his support of the Catholic confession would cause unease among his people, who remained faithful to their eastern Orthodox rites. Regardless of the Schism, however, all Christians would experience the same shock when in 1071 the Seljuk Turks defeated the Byzantines at Manzikert, the Muslims' victory revealing to the West how the balance of power had now shifted in the eastern Mediterranean. But for Petar, there was worse to come. Three years later, when some Normans from Trani and Molfetta invaded and seized various towns such as Zara, Spalato and Trau, he would be captured and then die a prisoner shortly after.

Venice would soon recover its Dalmatian possessions, but for some time its citizens had been concerned about the rise of the Normans and particularly the size of their fleet. They feared the rulers in Puglia might block the trade route into the Adriatic through the narrow Otranto Strait that separated the opposing coasts by only some 45 miles. So a year after Robert Guiscard's invasion of Dalmatia in 1081, the Venetians decided once again to come to the assistance of the Greeks. In return, the Byzantine emperor recognised the Republic's independence and granted it generous new commercial trading rights in the Adriatic, as well as in Constantinople itself. But while this would mark the start of its wider commercial expansion to the east, Venice was less fortunate in its dealings with Bohemund, who still held on to his territories in Epirus and Albania. Despite managing to defeat him at sea near Durazzo (Dyrrachium), and also temporarily recapturing Corfu, the Venetians' earlier successes would ultimately end in disaster. While they were withdrawing their ships for the winter, the enemy's battered fleet mounted an unexpected attack and caused them to suffer such a major defeat that the disgraced Doge Domenico Selvo was removed from office.

On coming to the Croatian throne, Petar Krešimir's successor, Demetrius Zvonimir, had chosen to back the Normans, remaining true to them even after Robert Guiscard's death in 1085. But by the time the king died without an heir four years later, Norman interests were starting to shift in another direction and anarchy had broken out in Croatia once again. As, before long the country was invaded by the Hungarians, the Croatians finally agreed to unite with Hungary in personal union. Following the Hungarian king Coloman's coronation at Biograd in 1102, for more than eight centuries to come the two countries would then remain united.[60] Nonetheless, Venice still had ambitions in the region, and so the doge had pronounced himself Duke of Croatia and reasserted his claims to the Adriatic's eastern shores. As a result, the now infuriated king began to stir up such unrest among the local people that eventually he would succeed in taking back more of the coastal towns.

Despite these various misfortunes and other major setbacks – not least an earthquake in 1084 – the growing Venetian Republic continued on its rise. On the authorities putting an end to violent arguments between the two patriarchs of Aquileia and Grado, the latter was moved with his see to Venice itself. And there were further significant innovations afoot in the city itself, among them the establishment of the famous carnival, and the reconstruction of the ducal chapel. Wanting to make this building worthy of the city's saint, Doge Vitale Faliero ordered all returning traders to bring home stone and other artefacts for its embellishment. But, although these would add to the elaborate decoration being carried out by the skilful Greek artists and mosaicists from Ravenna, one essential element was lacking. Having lost its relics during the riot and subsequent fire in 976, the chapel still remained without the physical presence of its patron saint. In the last days before its final consecration in 1094, lengthy prayers were offered up appealing for a miracle and the request then appeared to be answered when during the Mass a wall collapsed and revealed some hidden remains. On the quick presumption that they were those of St Mark, the final seal of sanctity was given to the spectacular new building, which was soon impressing all who saw it, including the Holy Roman Emperor Henry IV, who visited the following year.

By the end of the century Venice was again defying the wishes of the Byzantine emperor, not least by becoming involved in 1099 in the later stages of the First Crusade, which it had joined in the hopes of gaining a share of the eventual spoils. Among the various treasures it would later gather were the few remains left behind just over a decade earlier when the tomb of St Nicholas at Myra had been raided by the men from Bari. With the city in Puglia having already made him their patron saint, Venice's eventual installation of its own relics in the Church of San Nicolò on the Lido would cause arguments to continue for centuries to come over whose was the genuine article – the debate only being settled when research in the 1950s discovered that both sets of bones had come from the same man.

Since by the beginning of the 12th century Puglia was without the protection of Robert Guiscard and Bohemund, in 1101 on their way home from the crusade the Venetians were able to sack Brindisi. Then as further evidence of their growing naval power, three years later they would establish Venice's great arsenal, which would soon become famous for its remarkable and highly efficient production line. This was capable of turning out in record time large numbers of ships fully equipped and ready for action, and when two centuries later Dante saw it for himself, he would be so struck by the noise and impressive activity of the place that he used it as an image in his *Inferno*:

> One makes his vessel new, and one recaulks
> The ribs of that which many a voyage has made;
> One hammers at the prow, one at the stern,
> This one makes oars, and that one cordage twists,
> Another mends the mainsail and the mizzen...

(Canto XXI)[61]

With the Venetians being ambitious as ever to extend their reach, a few years later Doge Ordelafo Faliero led another invasion of Dalmatia, but after he had briefly captured some of the towns, in 1118 he was killed. Although his successor Domenico Michiel then drew up a temporary truce with the Hungarians that allowed Venice to hold on to Zara and some other possessions, the doge was less successful in his dealings with the new Byzantine emperor John II, who had just removed the trading rights earlier granted to the Venetians. Having therefore made sure that the people of Bari would grant his fleet a safe haven should conflict break out, Domenico Michiel would try to seize Corfu from the Greeks, but he then moved on to the Holy Land where the king of Jerusalem had recently been taken prisoner. While ostensibly the doge had come to help the Christians, he was more motivated by new trading opportunities in the Levant. Here he won a major victory near Ascalon and after ousting the Muslims from Tyre he would go on to have further successes in the eastern Mediterranean, taking some of the Greek islands and destroying Modon (Methoni) in the south of the Peloponnese.

In the meantime, the Hungarians had broken their earlier truce, and, although they had failed to take Zara, they had captured Spalato and Trau. Having responded by raiding the region, in 1125 the doge destroyed Biograd and demolished the great monasteries that Petar Krešimir had earlier founded.[62] After returning home laden with his booty and hostages, and the next year he added the Ionian islands to his other acquisitions. These various achievements meant that when he died in 1130 shortly after abdicating, the inscription on Domenico Michiel's tomb in San Giorgio Maggiore would describe him as the 'terror of the Greeks'. By then, the Byzantine emperor John II had come to realise the damage that was being done to his own city's trade and so seven years after first excluding the Venetians, he allowed them to return to Constantinople.

Throughout this time, however, the Republic had been adding to its influence abroad and Venice itself had been continuing to develop. In spite of disease and other natural disasters such as flooding and repeated earth tremors, the city had grown in size, and by the end of the 12th century the gondola was helping movement around the islands. Trade fairs had started to become regular events, their commercial activities radiating out from a central point around the Rialto. As the merchants took their business further afield, they returned from the north with products such as amber and tin, and from the east with silk and spices, these transactions being assisted by the new banks that in 1167 had begun to offer the first loans. While open spaces were being covered and bridges built to connect the various islands, private homes had started to appear along the sides of the canals. Most significantly of all, the new palace for the doge was under construction. Numerous treasures were being imported, some pillaged, others bought, and yet more acquired as gifts. Three columns were donated by the eastern emperor in 1172 in gratitude for Venice's role in the Second Crusade, and although one of these brought all the way from Constantinople had fallen into the lagoon during unloading, the other two would be erected in the Piazzetta to mark the ceremonial entrance into the city. Here they still frame the landing stage leading from the lagoon to Piazza San Marco, one column topped by the statue of St Mark's lion, the other by St Theodore with his crocodile – a representation of the dragon with which he was often connected. These columns much later became the place of public executions, something that even today discourages Venetians from passing between them.

Even while Venice was awaiting the delivery of these columns, the previous year, Doge Vital II Michiel – the son-in-law of the Norman Bohemund and the third in the family to hold the highest office – found himself embroiled in a particularly serious dispute with the East. For about a century after the arrival of the first resident Venetians, the influence of the foreign traders in Constantinople had been growing, but their increasing high-handedness had made them ever more unpopular. This, and the violent disputes that occasionally had broken out among them and the representatives of the various other Italian merchant cities, had periodically resulted in their arrest or expulsion. As Manuel I Komnenos had already imposed harsh measures to try and control their behaviour and was now demanding the imprisonment of thousands of Venetians, the doge decided the time had come to respond. After ordering an attack on Ancona – the Byzantines' sole remaining port in Italy – Vital Michiel started to make preparations for an assault on Constantinople itself, financing the project by raising taxes from his newly created *sestieri*, the six separate areas that still divide Venice today. But although he then personally led out his fleet to take on the Greeks, his efforts were to end in defeat, and then things were made even worse by his ships returning with the plague. Having been arrested and charged with responsibility for the naval failure, his admiral was soon murdered by the mob, and the equally unpopular doge was killed while fleeing to San Zaccaria.

After Vital Michiel's death, besides a new, more formal system of election being brought in, his successor Sebastiano Ziani would initiate a practice that was to be followed by all subsequent doges. On their inauguration, as they were being carried around Piazza San Marco, they would scatter coins to the crowd – these in time becoming the specially minted *oselle*. Then a few years later Ziani would host an even more significant event, one that marked the end of the bitter dissension that for years had divided the Holy Roman Emperor and the Catholic Church. After a prolonged conflict that had included the election of a rival pope, on Ascension Day 1177 Frederick Barbarossa came to Venice to meet Alexander III, who arrived in the city on a mule. In the great square outside the ducal chapel, Alexander received the homage of his long-time rival, the Emperor according to legend publicly kissing the pope's foot. Today a plaque on the floor of St Mark's Basilica marks the spot where this is said to have taken place. It was during this glittering occasion that the doge was said to have received a papal ring, a bequest that gave rise over the years to the ever more elaborate ceremony of the *Sensa*, the *Sposalizio del Mare* – 'the Marriage of the Sea'. This was the start of the tradition whereby each year the doge, surrounded by scores of brightly decorated craft adorned with banners and other trappings, would board his golden state barge, the *bucintoro*, to be rowed out to the lagoon's edge. Here for the first time, near the island today called the Lido, Ziani threw the golden ring into the water to reaffirm Venice's mystical marriage to the sea.

Soon after another tradition would also be established when the doge and his two guests moved on down to Ancona, one of the five ancient port cities, or Pentapolis, south of Rimini. While for decades there had been disagreements between these two maritime competitors, in 1173 Venice had gone further and assisted the Holy Roman Emperor's third attempt to try and oust the Greeks from the city. Although the subsequent seven-month-long siege would hinder the port's activity, Ancona had been able to hold out and so its trade had started to revive, and piracy had begun once more to threaten the Venetian merchants. It was in order to diffuse these tensions that Ziani and his important guests had now come to visit the city. The pope and Emperor were both presented with umbrellas and a new custom was now born, whereby all future doges would be accompanied by a similar parasol. As Ziani's good relations with the Emperor and the pope had further enhanced the Republic's reputation, besides receiving additional ecclesiastical rights in Dalmatia the Venetians were now given new trading concessions within the Byzantine empire. On top of this, the next year they also took control of the Brenner Pass across the Alps and began to establish themselves more visibly on the Italian mainland.

Although their relations with the Greeks had by this time returned to normal, and the traders in Constantinople had recovered their former commercial rights, within five years the old tensions would resurface. In 1182, as the troubles escalated, widespread violence began to break out in the eastern capital against anyone connected with the Italians. Thousands of men, women and children were butchered, while numerous others were taken to be sold as slaves to the Muslims. This so-called Massacre of the Latins had now seriously poisoned relations between the East and West, and despite the Venetian prisoners being eventually released and the various trading groups allowed to return during the 1190s, the bitterness lingered on. While this antagonism caused both Emperor Frederick Barbarossa and his son Henry to consider for a time attacking Constantinople, it also prepared the ground for the great city's destruction by Venice and the crusaders a few years later.

Meanwhile, other matters were also testing the Republic's patience. With its earlier agreement with Sicily coming to an end, Venice had begun to fear that the agreement between its king William II and the Holy Roman Emperor might have a negative impact on Venetian interests. Already angry with the Sicilians for having attacked the Balkan lands of the Byzantines, with whom they had now drawn up an alliance, the Venetians then became still more enraged on hearing news of the marriage of William's heir Constance to the Emperor's son in 1186. Then, a decade later Venice was to face yet another new challenge from the Pisans. Having entered the Adriatic, these had begun to encourage the people of Zara and Pola (Pula) to rebel against the Venetian Republic, and before the winter had finally forced them to return home, the intruders had actually approached right to the fringes of the lagoon itself.

* * *

When three years after these events, in 1198, Innocent III called for a new crusade to recover the Holy Land, the venture was planned as a French initiative, and so Boniface, the marquis of Montferrat, was appointed its leader. A supporter of the Hohenstaufens, in 1201 he would pay a visit to the court of Philip of Swabia in Germany, where he was then introduced to the king's brother-in-law Alexios Angelos.[63] This man, the son of the blinded and deposed Byzantine emperor Isaac II, had been briefly imprisoned by his uncle who had usurped the throne, and for that reason he had now come looking for Philip's help. Therefore, whether or not his meeting here with Boniface was accidental or by arrangement, some people would later suspect that the eventual assault on Constantinople was never quite as unpremeditated as claimed.

Preparations for the crusade were going ahead, but with all earlier appeals for support from Genoa and Pisa having failed, its organisers had turned to Venice for help in transporting men and animals. After first arriving in the city in 1201 to begin their lengthy negotiations, besides agreeing to pay some 84,000 marks, the Frenchmen eventually promised Venice the rights to half of all the conquests that the crusaders were hoping to make. In return, the knights expected to be provided not just with shipping for some 33,000 men and 4,500 horses, but also to be given additional galley support and a year's worth of provisions. Innocent III, quite possibly aware of the unpredictable nature of the crusaders and the unreliability of the Venetians, included in his own agreement an additional clause insisting that no attack should be made on any Christians encountered along the way. With Egypt having been weakened by its recent unrest and civil war, the pope had come to believe that it would be a convenient first port of call, one that offered a rather easier route to the Holy Land than that taken by the failed Third Crusade. But even though Innocent was now prepared to offer limited trading rights to Venice, since the Republic was already drawing up its own private trade agreement with Egypt it most probably never had any intention of transporting the crusaders in the pope's chosen direction.

Regardless of this misunderstanding, the crusade was already facing other setbacks. By June 1202 – the allotted date for the expedition's departure – the number of combatants gathering in the port was far below what had been expected, and there was little sign that the promised payment would be met. By this time, while some crusaders had decided they would leave from alternative ports, others had already begun to make their own way east. As efforts to raise all the promised funds had failed – with more than a third of the sum still outstanding – there now had to be further further negotiations. A new agreement could only be reached when Venice eventually accepted a lower figure on the proviso that the remaining crusaders would go first to Zara. Repeatedly rebellious, and recently even in league with the Pisans, ever since the time of Pietro II Orseolo this town had been seeking its independence. Furthermore, having signed a pact in 1181 with the Hungarians, Zara considered itself to be theoretically under their control, and so was still actively protesting against the heavy-handed measures the Venetians were trying to impose.

At this time Enrico Dandolo, who had been elected doge about a decade before, was most probably into his late eighties. He was already suffering from serious, if not total, blindness. According to an unverified legend, he had been intentionally blinded during an earlier visit to Constantinople, a story, if true, that could have explained the bitter hatred he later showed for the city. This man would now become instrumental in the way events began to take shape, and having summoned the Venetians to his private chapel, he used his persuasive words and promises of rewards to sway the people to back the proposed crusade. On gaining their support, he then swore to lead the venture himself, and in an intentionally meaningful gesture ratified his promise by sewing a cross onto his ducal cap, the *corno* that was symbolic of his office.

Despite some crusaders being still opposed to the idea, they were eventually worn down by the situation in which they found themselves, the men having been restricted all this time to the island of San Nicolò (the Lido) where in the unhealthy conditions disease had become rife. At last, with the expedition's numbers increased by the addition of Venetian volunteers, in November 1202 409 ships set off, including some 50 galleys and several *palanders* (*huissiers*) which were used for carrying horses. Although the pope, ever suspicious of the Venetians' motives, had given a specific order not to attack the lands of the Catholic Hungarian king, when the fleet eventually arrived at Zara, Dandolo rejected the town's offer to surrender. Instead, he persuaded the crusaders to ignore their spiritual commitments and begin the assault. Five days later the well-defended town fell and the plundering began, the mayhem increased by the attackers fighting among themselves to seize the greatest share of the spoils. As the place was sacked and the people subjected to violence and rape, further fighting broke out as arguments developed between the Venetians and the French crusaders. Appalled when he heard news of the assault on fellow Christians, the pope excommunicated everyone involved and many now abandoned the campaign. Yet, because Innocent still hoped that the crusade might recover possession of the Holy Land, he eventually lifted the interdict from all involved, with the exception of the Venetians, whom he saw as chiefly responsible for the atrocity.

As the army overwintered in Zara, the men began to suffer from the shortage of supplies, but finally on the arrival in January of an envoy sent by Philip of Swabia, a new solution presented itself. The messenger relayed the extravagant promises of Alexios, who had promised to bring his people back to the Catholic Church. Furthermore, the young man had pledged that on the recovery of his father's throne, in addition to the payment of 200,000 marks, he would provide not just additional troops for the continuing crusade but also life-long support for some 500 knights. Although many were opposed to the deal, Dandolo and the French barons were tempted by these offers and finally accepted the proposal. Therefore, despite further defections, towards the end of April the large fleet started out for Constantinople, joined in Corfu a few days later by Dandolo, Boniface of Montferrat, and also Alexios. Here, as others became aware of where they were headed, more threatened to desert, but they were persuaded to remain by the tearful appeals and promises of the leaders, who carefully concealed from the Venetian soldiers news of the interdict that the pope had passed against them. Persuaded to continue, the force of around 10,000 men proceeded on its way, and eventually in June 1203 the crusaders reached the eastern Roman capital. As they sailed past its massive walls, the splendour of the place amazed the newcomers, who were overawed by the city's immense size and its numerous churches and other great buildings. Needing access to supplies and a place to set up their tents, their ships were then anchored on the Asian shore, where the doge and the other leaders took over the emperor's palaces at Chalcedon on the Sea of Marmara and Chrysopolis (Üsküdar) on the Bosphorus.

On 3 July Dandolo took the young Byzantine pretender across the water to show him off to the people of the city. Although Alexios had promised that the local Greeks would support him and be ready to renounce his hated uncle, the people soon made it clear that they did not want to welcome him back. Realising therefore that Constantinople could be taken only by force, two days later troops were ferried across the Bosphorus to the region of Galata, the area on the eastern side of the Golden Horn chiefly occupied by the Genoese traders. Here, any doubts the Byzantines harboured as to their visitors' intentions were soon dispelled when some 80 knights, ignoring the current chivalric practice of declaring their intentions, made their first unprovoked attack. Unprepared to fight, the small force of Greek cavalry that had been sent to protect the region soon fled. The next day the invaders were able to take the Galata Tower and gain control of the city's great chain guarding the harbour where the Byzantine ships lay at anchor. The fleet had become run down during the eight years since the seizure of the throne by the usurper Alexios III, he being the most recent of a series of weak or ineffectual rulers. As he had sold off much of his navy and allowed what remained to deteriorate, when the Venetians finally broke through the chain and entered the sheltered waters of the Golden Horn, they

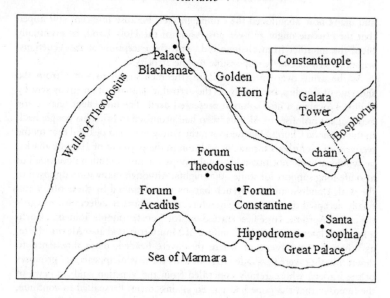

met with little opposition and the Greeks' few remaining largely unserviceable ships were quickly overcome.

Meanwhile, attempts in the north of the city to break through from the landward side at Blachernae had failed. For several days the French crusaders camped beneath the massive defences had vainly tried to batter their way through into the city. On 17 July Dandolo ordered an all-out assault on the lower, less-well defended sea walls overlooking the Golden Horn. Using their maritime skills the Venetians had created covered platforms up on the masts of the sailing ships that they had now lashed together, and from these high points the men were able to fire down on the enemy. But, as the battle raged, the unprotected galleys hung back until the elderly doge personally took charge. Standing at the prow of his own brightly coloured leading craft, he urged his men forward, persuading them to follow him to the very base of the city walls.

In spite of Dandolo's actions, the Venetians eventually had to retire in order to give aid to the knights at Blachernae, who were still being confronted by the emperor's fearless Varangian guard. Unable in the long run to break down their opposition, a general retreat was called, but the damage caused by the Venetians resulted in the outbreak of a fire that continued to consume the city for the next three nights. The day after these events, while a meeting was taking place, it was discovered that Alexios III had secretly fled his city. As a result, the Byzantines released the previously deposed and blinded Isaac, and finally agreed on 1 August to crown his son as co-emperor. With the latter now recognised as Alexios IV, and the crusaders once more at Galata, the Venetians demanded the settlement of the pre-agreed terms that they had been offered. However, not only had the young emperor's financial pledges been unrealistic, but also his promise to persuade the Byzantines to submit to the teaching and authority of the Catholic Church was clearly untenable. Therefore, unable to honour his word, and aware of the danger he was in, Alexios IV plundered some of his city's sacred treasures in an attempt to satisfy, at least partially, his visitors' demands. At the same time, he appealed to Dandolo to postpone his planned departure until the next year. Even though this was unpopular with some of the crusaders, it suited the doge, who did not want to proceed to Egypt and also saw the delay as an opportunity to press for more money from the emperor.

With unrest having begun to take hold in the city, Alexios IV then chose to escape his troubles by setting off with some crusader support to strengthen his hold in his surrounding regions. While he was still away, the Greeks began to wreak their revenge on all the foreign traders resident in the city and although the Venetians were targeted in particular, even the Pisans and others who had remained loyal to the Byzantines were not spared. During this turmoil, Constantinople was again hit by another terrible fire that for the next eight days continued to rage. As this caused yet more untold damage, the bitterness between the Greeks and the crusaders became still more entrenched, and as a result on Alexios IV's return he would find that he had grown even more unpopular. But when his blunt rebuttal of the Venetians' demands for payment were met by a challenge from Dandolo, the Greeks became enraged by the doge's lack of respect for their emperor, and they made two attempts to destroy the crusaders' fleet with fire ships. But as these were then dragged out of harm's way by the experienced Venetian mariners, Alexios was accused by his people of having warned the enemy in advance and feeling against him hardened once more. Things then came to a head on 25 January when a riot broke out and the mob began calling for the removal of both the emperors, they now having found a new, unwilling candidate, Nicholas Kannavos. In desperation, Alexios IV appealed to the crusaders, but two days later Alexios Ducas 'Murtzuphlus' entered his room and declared himself to be the new ruler instead. As the young Alexios IV was soon spirited away and the unfortunate Kannavos quickly dispatched, on 5 February 1204 the savage Ducas was crowned Alexios V. By then the thoroughly demoralised old emperor Isaac Angelos was dead, probably having been strangled a month earlier. The same fate now awaited his son.

With the change of regime, the situation for the crusading party had further deteriorated, the men no longer receiving the necessary supplies they had previously been given by the now-dead Alexios IV. As they had therefore decided to raid imperial territory further afield, Alexios V Ducas set out to meet them in battle, but having been defeated, he was unable to hide the disaster from his people when the Venetians paraded the Greeks' captured banner and sacred icon past the city walls. Although a last attempt was now made to reach agreement, the terms demanded by the Latins were too onerous, and shortly after an unsuccessful attack on the new emperor, the talks ended in failure. As for the ambitious Dandolo, being no longer interested in any truce, he was now determined to take possession of Constantinople and the whole eastern Roman Empire. With all excuse for the crusaders' mission gone, three days after a failed first attempt on 9 April, the final assault began and Alexios V Ducas fled his capital.[64] While the city continued to be ravaged for three more days, the devastation would be increased by yet another outbreak of fire. Among the acts of appalling brutality that now took place, some of the worst atrocities would be committed by the crusaders. Besides taking part in gratuitous destruction, pillage and rape, the men would also intentionally defile many of Constantinople's holy sites, famously bringing horses and mules into Justinian's great basilica and allowing a prostitute to cavort on the patriarch's throne. While the Venetians were more engaged in wholesale plunder, the mindless savagery carried out by all involved would destroy quantities of the city's priceless treasure, and much of Constantinople's ancient historical heritage was wiped out in a senseless frenzy of violence and greed.

At last the mayhem came to an end and the crusader Baldwin of Flanders was crowned as the emperor of the new Empire of Constantinople (sometimes called Empire of Romania). While the Venetians were to stay on until the next year, Dandolo asked Innocent III for permission to return home. As the pope was still ignorant of the details of the assault, he removed his sentence of excommunication on the doge but he refused the old man's request to retire, declaring – possibly out of spite – that he should carry on with the crusade. Ironically, it was in Constantinople, the city he had helped to bring down, that just weeks after fighting alongside Baldwin, Dandolo died in May and was buried in the Hagia Sophia. Today a memorial stone that was later installed on the floor claims to mark the spot, but in 1483 his tomb was destroyed and his body lost when the great church was turned into a mosque by the followers of Islam, the very people he had purportedly been originally sent to defeat. As for Baldwin, after ruling the city and its greatly reduced territorial possessions for a year, he was captured in battle by the Greeks and then killed by their new allies, the Bulgarians. Equally unfortunate was Boniface who, although rewarded with other regions of the former Byzantine empire, was to die in 1207 from wounds received in battle.

Pope Innocent, who had wanted to reunite the two Christian faiths, was at first so delighted to hear of the city's fall that he wrote to Count Baldwin congratulating him on defeating the Greeks, but his pleasure was to be short-lived. Like others, he was appalled when he finally received details of the sacking of Constantinople. Throughout western Europe, there was horror and Venice was soon reviled for the part it had played in the events. Nevertheless, the dividing up of the former empire continued until the following October, when much of the Byzantines' territory was given to the new Latin Empire now controlled by Venice and her allies. By gaining three-eighths of the confiscated lands, and the same amount of Constantinople, the Republic had increased its wealth and further extended its influence into the Mediterranean. This undermined the future of the east Roman Empire, fatally weakening it and thus starting the slow decline that would end with its demise some 150 years later, when it was finally wiped out by the Ottomans. As a result, over the years Dandolo's name would be remembered differently by those who held him responsible for what had happened: in his home city he would be hailed as the 'Lord of a Quarter and Half a Quarter of the Roman Empire', but elsewhere he would become a much-reviled figure. While Innocent III had originally imagined that the Fourth Crusade would be famous for the conquest of the 'infidel', it would instead become infamous for its unwarranted and repeated attacks on its fellow Christian believers.

Paradoxically, Constantinople's fall in 1204 would produce some results that were more positive. Not only would the dispersal of its surviving treasures start the cultural awakening in western Europe that came to fruition in the Renaissance, but also Venice would begin to grow into one of Europe's most beautiful cities. Having, among other things, seized the ancient bronze horses and bronze doors of the basilica, along with much of the ornate work that decorates its Pala d'Oro, from this time on more Greek crafts started to be copied in the city. Their appearance gave birth to a cultural tradition that is particular to Venice, a fusing of eastern and western tastes. In 1253 this was made manifest at the election of the new doge, Renier Zeno, who besides incorporating the trappings of the former Byzantine rulers into his inauguration celebrations and Easter processions, added other similar rituals to the ceremony of the *Sensa* that was now becoming one of Venice's most spectacular events. So as the cultural life of the city continued to develop, from this time on ships returning from the eastern regions would be ordered to bring back increased cargoes of stone for the building work that was replacing the last of the original wooden structures. Lacking the necessary high-quality material with which to cover the facades of the new brick buildings, large quantities of limestone were imported from Istria. Beside other exotic stones from further afield, remnants of older pagan and Christian buildings would also be brought to add to the beauty of the city and make it worthy of its newly acquired position. Now a major player in the Adriatic and beyond, Venice had reached the peak of its maritime power.

6

Competition and conflict in the
Stato da Mar

'... her orderly government, her sound institutions, her exaltation of the worthy, her punishment of evil, the reverence paid to her magistrates, the encouragement of her youth in the paths of virtue and the service of their country. I am forced to believe that come what may, [La Serenissima] will survive until the final dissolution of the elements themselves!'

Henry Wotton[65]

Galleys and Carracks in battle.

Following the breakup of the lands of the old Byzantine empire after the Fourth Crusade's savage attack, the eastern rulers had retreated to the rump of their former possessions in Epirus, Nicaea, and Trebizond on the Black Sea. As the various victors created new principalities, duchies, and lesser kingdoms, Venice seized its own share of the spoils. In addition to its other considerable gains, it now came into possession of the Ionian islands and the Byzantine empire's coastal towns of the eastern Adriatic, before later taking Candia (Crete) as well. Although Durazzo would be lost in 1213, becoming part of the Despotate of Epirus under a new Greek ruler, these ports – along with the Aegean islands where its nobles had been installed as overlords – would all now help in developing Venice's valuable trade routes to the east. Thus it had created the network of overseas possessions that was to be the basis of its profitable *Stato da Mar*. Yet, repeatedly over the next half century, the Venetian Republic – from this period on increasingly to be known as *La Serenissima* – would be forced to defend all these places from its various competitors. Although in the south of the Adriatic the Normans' earlier naval strength had been lost when their later rulers had become preoccupied with affairs elsewhere, Frederick II had already begun to improve his fleet. This was of considerable concern to the Venetians, who feared that the young Emperor's developing trade in Puglia might disrupt their own commercial activities. Therefore, in 1228, while he was involved in his Sixth Crusade, they quickly changed tack and put aside all earlier disputes with their age-old rivals the Genoese. Having improved relations, they now joined Genoa and its allies in the recently re-established Lombard League.

As it still wanted to expand its commercial interests, about a decade later, having defeated Ancona and prevented the Pisans from setting up a merchant centre at Ravenna, the Serenissima would turn its attention to retaking Pola in Istria. At the same time, further to the south, it held on to the recently acquired Ragusa, which in spite of the famine caused by the Tatars' recent ravaging of the area, still continued to be an important trading centre. Venice had also begun to establish bases on the Adriatic's western shores in Puglia, where it was helped by new trading rights received in 1257 from Frederick II's illegitimate son Manfred. While he had possibly planned to strengthen his position by building a navy, his death in battle nine years later had put an end to any such scheme. The loss of their king was disastrous for the Hohenstaufen family, but it was to be of benefit to Venice, since Manfred's Angevin successors were to show little interest in maritime concerns. As a result, before long the Serenissima had not just extended its domination over the whole of the Adriatic but also secured the backing of the lesser coastal towns like Rimini. And two years before Manfred's death, things had also changed in Ancona. Having again attracted the attention of the Serenissima, this city had been forced by its stronger neighbour to impose heavy duties on its incoming goods. With its charges thus becoming four times higher than those demanded by the Venetians, its commercial business had soon been undermined.

Not everything was going Venice's way, however. Just a few years before, in 1261 the Latin empire (formerly Baldwin's Empire of Constantinople)

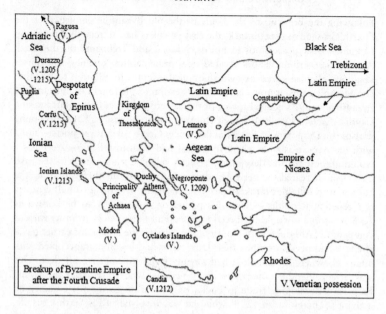

Ragusa (V.)
Adriatic Sea
Durazzo (V.1205 -1215)
Puglia
Despotate of Epirus
Corfu (V.1215)
Ionian Sea
Ionian Islands (V.1215)
Kingdom of Thessalonica
Latin Empire
Black Sea
Trebizond
Latin Empire
Constantinople
Lemnos (V.)
Latin Empire
Aegean Sea
Empire of Nicaea
Duchy Athens
Negroponte (V.1209)
Principality of Achaea
Modon (V.)
Cyclades Islands (V.)
Rhodes
Breakup of Byzantine Empire after the Fourth Crusade
Candia (V.1212)
V. Venetian possession

had crumbled and the Orthodox rulers had at last been able to return from the Empire of Nicaea to reclaim their former capital. Since Michael VIII Palaeologos had not forgotten its role in the disastrous attack on his city half a century before, the Serenissima would now find itself at a disadvantage to the Genoese. While they were granted access to the Black Sea ports, the emperor refused the same rights to the immensely unpopular Venetians, whose remaining traders in Constantinople were now to be brutally attacked. While some were arrested or blinded, many others were forced to flee, and it would be another seven years before they were finally given the same privileges as their Genoese competitors.

With the Black Sea having been opened up to western traders, new opportunities were presenting themselves to the more intrepid merchants. Those wanting to develop commercial links with China and the East were now able to bypass the Arab markets that they had formerly used. With the Mongols having by this time spread across Asia, the year before the Greeks' recovery of Constantinople, two men from the Venetian Republic, Matteo and Niccolò Polo, had set off on a first expedition to the khan. Two decades later these brothers repeated the journey, taking with them Niccolò's young son, Marco. When they returned unexpectedly to Venice fifteen years later in 1295, they were not just unrecognisable, but also immensely rich.

Meanwhile, after his coronation in Rome as King of Sicily, and then his defeat of the Hohenstaufen Conradin at Tagliacozzo, Charles of Anjou had gone even further and claimed the title of King of Albania. Having plans to take the Byzantine throne for himself, in 1271 with his now-improved navy he started to capture towns on the eastern shore of the Adriatic, among them the strategic Durazzo and Valona (Vlorë) around seventy miles to the south. Despite this, Venice was unconcerned, being ready to accept any action on the Angevins' part that might weaken the government in Constantinople and also disadvantage the Genoese. Ten years later at a meeting at Orvieto, the Serenissima drew up plans with Charles for an invasion of the eastern empire. Before this could go ahead, on Easter Monday, April 1282, the so-called Sicilian Vespers broke out in Palermo. Following the abuse of a local woman by an Angevin official, violence erupted, during which those found unable to pronounce a word correctly were identified as the hated foreigners. Condemned by their failure to repeat the shibboleth as required, within weeks thousands had been murdered. Moreover, with Peter of Aragon, the son-in-law of Manfred, having been invited by the locals to come to their aid, Charles now lost possession of Sicily. Even though he died the next year at Foggia, the horrors of the Sicilian Vespers that had begun during his rule would continue to ravage the region for some twenty more years, the opposing sides – and even family members – arguing over their rights to the throne. Finally, in 1302 the former kingdom was divided, the Angevins keeping the Italian mainland (now the Kingdom of Naples), the Aragonese gaining control of the island that was officially called (by its classical name) the Kingdom of Trinacria. (Confusingly, both would at times be referred to as the Kingdom of Sicily.)

Although the Venetians' earlier plans with the Angevins had further soured their relations with Constantinople, in 1283 the Serenissima was able to sign another agreement with Genoa at Cremona. A year later, as a result of a major Genoese victory over the Pisans, the latter's fortunes began to decline, and within a few years Pisa had ceased to be a significant player in the struggle for commercial supremacy at sea. As this left the two main maritime cities of Venice and Genoa in direct competition, their rivalry began to escalate once more and within a decade of their agreement at Cremona they were again at war. While in time their battles spread from the Black Sea to Venice's home waters on the edges of the lagoon at Malamocco, in 1298 the Serenissima faced a new disaster when the Genoese attacked the Dalmatian coast. Here near Curzola (Korčula) – the Adriatic island sometimes claimed as the birthplace of Marco Polo – it suffered such a major defeat that its admiral chose to commit suicide while still at sea. Among those taken prisoner in this battle was Polo himself, who had joined the Venetian fleet just after his return home the year before. During his moderately comfortable three-year-long incarceration in a Genoese prison, he would recount the experiences of his travels to a fellow inmate, and on the latter's retelling of the fabulous tales to an astonished public Marco Polo's fame was soon assured and he was released. The victory at Curzola had, however, left the Genoese weakened and having been unable to take Ragusa, they finally left the area and the two warring sides eventually agreed to make peace.

Having already been damaged commercially by the fall of Acre in 1291 and feeling the effects of its long involvement in the recent war, Venice was now confronting new difficulties in its relationship with Ancona. Here the

Greeks were quietly condoning the actions of their pirates, who were once more plaguing the region. And, as if these problems were not enough, the Venetian Republic was facing other challenges closer to home. Rebellion had broken out against the current doge, Pietro Gradenigo, who had received a cold reception when some years before he had returned to the capital from Capodistria (Koper) to take up his new position. Apparently, because of the lack of enthusiasm shown at his election in 1289, Gradenigo displayed no love for the ordinary people. Recent research has questioned however, the assertion that out of spite he had then excluded them from public office. In reality, during his reign the number of families allowed to join the Great Council was considerably increased, having nearly doubled by the time of his death. While eight years after his election, in 1297 promotion to the nobility and election to the Council was closed off by the establishment of the *Serrata*, the measures introduced to restrict membership to those with previous family connections would in fact only become fully entrenched after Gradenigo had died. It was at that point that the divide between the patricians and the rest of the population would begin to be defined, setting out the first list of names of noble families that eventually would become fixed in the *Libro d'Oro* – the Golden Book.

The full extent of Gradenigo's unpopularity finally became apparent in 1300. Although such events were rare in the Serenissima, there was now an attempt at rebellion when Marino Bocco and his co-conspirators marched to the Piazza to protest at their exclusion from the Council. These men were quickly arrested and publicly hanged, and with that all further protest was rapidly quelled. But, eight years later a similar event occurred. Following Venice's seizure of Ferrara, Clement V excommunicated the entire city, and his edict was soon to have a dire effect on the Serenissima's trade. Its territories were now under attack, and with its army soon defeated, before long the pope's victorious supporters had retaken Ferrara. In addition to having encouraged some of Venice's` landowners to join the bitter Guelf-Ghibelline dispute now raging in the northern Italian states, these disasters had also reignited the unrest in the city itself. With the hated doge even being accused of cowardice during the recent fighting, in June 1310 open rebellion erupted once more.

This latest coup was led by the possibly Guelf-supporting Bajamonte Tiepolo, who wanted to depose the (possibly pro-Ghibelline) Gradenigo and overthrow the government. At the same time, his opposition to the doge was probably partially motivated by a personal grudge. The immediate descendant of two Venetian doges, his father – the people's preferred ducal candidate at the time of Gradenigo's election – had been overlooked because of fears of establishing hereditary family rights to the throne. Bajamonte's conspiracy was bungled, and, with the plotters having apparently been betrayed, when the time came the doge was ready to meet them. While appalling weather had also not helped the rebels, some of the group had been further hindered by the quick thinking of an old woman. From out of her window in the Via della Merceria near the entrance to St Mark's Square, she was said to have thrown a mortar jar that felled the leading protester as he was passing below – a sculpture on the side of her house today still showing her ready to take action. In reward, besides granting her permission to fly a flag on all important occasions, the doge then promised that her rent would never be raised. As for the rebels themselves, although the popular Tiepolo was spared and allowed to go into exile, his two main co-conspirators would be less fortunate, one being killed during the fighting, another executed.

There would be a more long-term result of this apparent threat to the state's security. To help speed up responses in future, the Committee of Public Safety, the later Council of Ten, was now established to spy more closely on the people. Over the years this would become a much-feared organisation, whose tentacles were spread throughout the Venetian empire and beyond. In addition to its espionage network, the council would gain further secret information through encouraging ordinary people to report anonymously on their neighbours by posting their complaints in the mouth of one of Venice's public letter boxes, the *bocche di leone* – the 'mouths of the lion'.

Gradenigo died a year after the rebellion, still reputedly 'so hated by the people' that following his death in August 1311 there had been fear of more trouble. To avoid this and the possible 'violation of his corpse', there had been no elaborate funeral and he was quietly buried instead in the monastery church of San Cipriano on the island of Murano.[66] As further proof of how disastrous his reign had been, no-one was then ready to succeed him, forcing the authorities to select virtually at random an elderly candidate who was to survive in the role for just eleven months.

Even as the city eventually began to return to normal, it was challenged by its neighbours in Padua, where the ruling Scaligeri family threatened to cut Venice off from its mainland trade and its necessary supplies. Yet, as their leader had allowed relations with the other northern states to turn equally sour, in time the Paduans wanted to get rid of him and so they turned to Venice for help. After the Scaligeri were defeated and replaced by the Carrara dynasty, the Serenissima received Treviso and other northern towns in reward, and because these places ensured the Republic's access to the Alpine passes and beyond, more Venetians now began to settle on the Italian mainland.

In the meantime, Venice's merchant fleet had been updated with large galleys that were speedier than the sailing ships formerly used for the transport of goods. Besides the profits gained from the *muda*, the massive convoys that annually returned home laden with valuable merchandise, the city's wealth had been increased by the introduction of valuable new industries, in particular silk-manufacture and glass-blowing. With its rising prosperity, Venice could begin to tend to the wellbeing of the ordinary people, who were now to benefit from charitable guilds, orphanages, hospitals and state-funded doctors. Although most citizens were excluded from the government of the Republic, all could enjoy the comforts and security it offered. Now the Venetians could be proud of their efficiently run state and beautiful city that, with its population of around 120,000, had become one of the largest in Europe.

Just a year before the election of the exceptionally young Andrea Dandolo, the fourth member of his family to become doge, in 1341 work began on the final major alteration of the last ducal palace and its new Council Chamber – a project that would be completed some eight decades later. With the further encouragement of Dandolo, this would begin a building boom lasting into the next century that would see the arrival of Venice's great churches, stone squares – all except for the main Piazza called *campi*, or fields. And, included among the Gothic-style palaces would be the Dandolo palazzo, built towards the end of the century, that is now the Hotel Daniele. A cultured man who had been educated at the famous university of Padua, the new doge would during his eleven years as head of state organise the further embellishment of his great chapel, using the space to emphasise the relationship of Venice's temporal leader to the divine. Although in 1354 he would die prematurely while still in his forties, by then he had left his personal mark on this building, this being particularly evident in the baptistery that he created. Apart from his tomb topped with his effigy, here he also appears in the kneeling figure depicted in the great mosaic crucifixion on the wall above.

Andrea Dandolo was nevertheless fated to reign in a period when Venice was hit by repeated disasters. Apart from the appalling earthquake of 1348 that had been severe enough to drain the Grand Canal and leave hundreds of people dead, other events had occurred soon after which were to be even more catastrophic. In 1333 the khan of the Golden Horde had granted trading rights to the Venetians on the Sea of Azov, and here they had set up an outpost at Tana. Because ten years later these same merchants had become unpopular, after being ousted by the Mongols, they had joined the Genoese on the Black Sea at Caffra (Feodosija, Ukraine). Here their trade would continue until 1346, when both groups came under attack from the Tatars. As the besieged defenders were cowering behind the town walls, the enemy started mysteriously to die. The attackers began to bombard them with the rotting corpses of the dead, and they continued to do so until the whole stinking area became uninhabitable. With that, the assault began to falter and at last some of the merchants were able to escape the horror and flee for home. However, the result of the Tatars' actions would be far more devastating than originally expected. There were probably among the returning ships the first victims of the Black Death that would wipe out much of the population of most of Europe. Although the unfortunate traders would be blamed for their apparent responsibility for importing the disease, they too would now be caught up in the appalling suffering the city was about to undergo. Already reeling from a famine and the recent earthquake, once the epidemic had taken hold, Venice would probably lose around two-thirds of its population. Despite Doge Dandolo's efforts to try and deal with the catastrophe, setting up centres for the obligatory forty days of quarantine and mass burial sites away from the city, hundreds continued to die each day, with fifty noble families included among the masses who would be wiped out for ever.[67]

At last the plague started to abate, but even as it did so, Genoa and Venice began to renew their arguments over their individual rights to the Black Sea trade. With conflict having again broken out, the Genoese captured Negroponte (Euboea) in the Aegean and won another major victory just outside Constantinople. Although the Venetians were then successful in the sea off Sardinia, in 1354 the Genoese re-entered the Adriatic and attacked Lesina (Hvar) and Curzola, before then sailing on to Istria. As if these setbacks were not enough, following the death of Andrea Dandolo Venice was about to experience serious new domestic problems. After a successful career, Marino Faliero, now ambassador to the papal court in Avignon, was informed that he had been elected doge.[68] Already with the backing of the ordinary people, who were angered by their military leaders' failures in the on-going war, just six months later he would become embroiled in a conspiracy to overthrow the nobles. While this was partly motivated by the old man's wish to remove the restrictions of his office, it had also become a personal matter. Following a hot-headed dispute with a young patrician who, jeering at his age, had graphically suggested that he had been cuckolded by his younger wife, the irascible doge had become increasingly determined to get rid of those who had shown him disrespect. Totally unprepared to forgive any who had earlier dishonoured him, he hatched a plot with some of his faithful workers from the *Arsenale* to assassinate all his opposition and seize greater power for himself as the Prince of Venice.

Having got wind of what was planned, when the time came for the rebellion to begin, the Council of Ten was ready to arrest all the conspirators, among them the doge himself. Found guilty of treachery and stripped of his regalia, in April 1355 the 76-year-old was led down the staircase to his execution in the courtyard of the palace. While his co-conspirators were then put to death in more brutal ways, Faliero's body was taken by boat to its unmarked grave in the basilica of Santi Giovanni e Paolo, locally known as San Zanipolo. In time this story would be taken up by various artists; Byron would later search out his tomb and write a play in his name, Donizetti compose an opera, and Delacroix create the painting that now hangs in the Wallace Collection. In Venice, however, Faliero has a more poignant memorial: the absence of his image in the frieze decorating the Council Chamber of the ducal palace. Here, he alone of Venice's doges is not represented, his place taken by a black curtain inscribed with words that recall his execution as a criminal.

Although within days a replacement for Faliero was found, and Venice had soon agreed a peace with the Genoese, the Serenissima still faced problems with its other neighbours. Already threatening the Republic's Dalmatian possessions, the king of Hungary invaded the Friuli region and then besieged Treviso and some other Venetian towns. Although when peace was finally agreed at Zara in 1358 Venice would regain access to the timber-producing forests in Istria and also recover its lost territories on the *terraferma*, there were other terms in this peace agreement that were highly detrimental to the Republic. In addition to having to renounce its patriarchy of Aquileia and hand over certain areas to Padua, it had to surrender to Hungary all of Dalmatia, bar a few coastal towns. Furthermore, although Venice had made a last-minute attempt to satisfy Ragusa with promises of new commercial and city rights particular to it alone, this offer had come too late. After more than a century and a half united with the Venetians, the city now chose to turn its back on the Serenissima and place itself under Hungarian protection. Recognising the commercial benefits of this to himself, in return for small contributions and an acknowledgement of his sovereignty, Ludovik I was content to allow the Balkan republic to retain much of its autonomy. Thus Ragusa would enjoy Hungary's long-distance protection for the next hundred years. Yet, for the Venetians there was one more bitter pill to swallow. The doge now had to renounce the long-held title of the duke of Dalmatia that had first been claimed by his predecessor Pietro II Orseolo over three and a half centuries earlier.

Nonetheless, Venice still impressed its visitors. Although there is little record of Dante's visit in 1321 shortly before his death from malaria in Ravenna, he was clearly amazed by the workings of the *Arsenale*. Later, Petrarch, a Venetian resident for five years after fleeing the plague in Padua, was equally struck by the things he saw in the city. Commenting on the size and majesty of its heavily laden sailing ships, he recorded his impression of the celebrations in June 1364, when the fleet was welcomed on its return from Candia with news that at last a serious revolt on the island had been put down.

> We were interrupted by the unexpected sight of one of those long ships they call galleys, all decorated with green foliage, which was coming into port under oars ... the sailors and some young men crowned with leaves and with joyful faces were waving banners from the bow ... the lookout in the highest tower signalled the arrival and the whole city came running spontaneously.[69]

However, once again there were challenges for Venice on the horizon. Having taken Trieste after a long siege, Venice was soon at war with its former allies, the Carrara family of Padua. More serious still, following another dispute between the Venetians and Genoese over Cyprus, the two maritime states were about to embark on what would be their fourth and most bitter confrontation, the War of Chioggia. The Genoese were backed by Ludovik of Hungary and the cities of Padua and Aquileia, and their fleet was led by their Admiral Pietro Doria. Having picturesquely described how he intended to 'bridle' Venice's beloved bronze horses, he sailed into the Adriatic to begin his attack on the *Stato da Mar*. Although the popular Venetian admiral Vittore Pisani had succeeded in recovering the Dalmatian towns the Hungarians had earlier taken, after being ordered (against his own advice) to take on the Genoese, in May 1379 he suffered a major defeat at Pola. Now blamed for the disaster, on his return he was immediately imprisoned. Within weeks Grado, Caorle and Palestrina had fallen, and by August the garrison at Chioggia had also surrendered to the Genoese, who now, supported from the land by the Carrara family, were able to establish themselves in the town. At that point the Venetian people began to clamour for the release of Pisani, and with the government eventually forced to pardon him, the admiral was at last able to return to service.

Over the next months, the Venetians struggled to improve their defences, blockading entrances to the lagoon, removing posts that marked the channels across its shallow waters, and rebuilding their battered navy. Appeals for help were made to the richest citizens, most of whom were rewarded for their generosity with promotion to the Great Council, something that added thirty new families to the nobility. Yet, even while Pisani's return had strengthened morale, the hardship continued and as the winter set in life became still more difficult for the encircled residents of Chioggia. In mid-December Pisani ratcheted up the problems for the Genoese, cutting off the enemy's supplies by sinking old, heavily laden ships to block the channels that served the town. But Venice too was starving, and so it was hoped that the messengers earlier sent with appeals for help had reached Carlo Zeno, who at the time was engaged elsewhere in the Mediterranean. Just as hopes for his return began to fade, to the general relief Zeno's fleet appeared on the horizon, his arrival on 1 January 1380 at last giving a major boost to the townspeople trapped in Chioggia. Zeno immediately reinforced the blockade of the Genoese and reopened the passage supplying Venetian reinforcements from Ferrara. After that, as the months went on, the two admirals, accompanied by the elderly doge Andrea Contarini, continued to keep up their guard, and in time they began to regain control of the *lidi*. Finally, in June Chioggia surrendered and as the starving people of the town were released, those whose accents proved them to be Genoese were taken prisoner.

Two months later, on his way to Manfredonia after his last engagement against the remaining enemy fleet off Puglia, Pisani died of his wounds. Brought back to Venice, he was then given a hero's burial in San Zanipolo, where today his original statue still stands above his later redecorated tomb. As for Zeno, although honoured for the part he had played in the victory, he would ultimately have a more chequered career. While his eventual burial in Venice in 1418 was well attended by a grateful public, some years before his death he had spent several months in prison on a charge of treachery. Therefore, despite his having once been suggested as a potential doge, unlike Pisani he has no elaborate tomb, and his actual place of burial, Santa Maria della Celestia, would be one of the churches later demolished by Napoleon.

In spite of the triumph at Chioggia, the war would carry on for another year until peace was eventually agreed in Turin in 1381. But here, once again, Venice was forced to hand over some of its territories, including the gulf at Cattaro that was now to be ceded to Hungary. Meanwhile, Trieste, which had surrendered to Aquileia during the war, chose to put itself under the protection of Leopold, the Habsburg duke of Austria, who in his turn then sold Treviso to Francesco Carrara of Padua. This was a town that Venice wanted to regain, but it decided to bide its time and wait for the inevitable breakdown in relations between Francesco and his equally ambitious neighbour, Duke Gian Galeazzo Visconti of Milan. This finally came about in 1388, when Francesco was forced to abdicate. He remained Visconti's prisoner until his death five years later. And, as by that time the Milanese duke had captured Padua and the other Carrara lands from his son, 'Il Novello', Venice was finally able to regain Treviso.

The Serenissima was now recognised as an important independent state, but for Genoese the situation had changed for the worse. As their city continued to be riven during the 1390s by the bitter rivalry that had developed between domestic factions, gradually it would begin to lose its role as a leading player. This was to Venice's advantage. Now unopposed, by the end of the century it had regained Durazzo, Corfu, and a few more possessions in the Aegean. Yet, as the 1300s approached their end, there would be political changes closer to home, the various northern Italian states jockeying for control of the region. As these were seeking to limit the growing power of the Visconti in Milan, Venice pragmatically decided to join the league of the duke's rivals. After helping Il Novello to retake Padua and recover his father's lost lands, it then continued to support the Carrara family until peace was finally signed. The ever-ambitious Il Novello was not content, however, and so besides renewing his arguments with the Milanese he also began to show an undue interest in the territories of the Venetians. Furious, the Serenissima retaliated by capturing Vicenza, and laying siege to the now plague-ridden Padua, which eventually surrendered in November 1405. Il Novello was arrested and, after being charged with trying to overthrow the Venetian Republic, he and one of his sons were taken back to Venice, where both would then be strangled.

With the fall of the Carrara dynasty, the Serenissima had increased its possessions on the *terraferma*, having (among other things) taken control of Padua's famous university. Although by 1407 the Venetians were again briefly at war, now fighting Sigismund, king of Hungary and Croatia over disputed claims to Zara, in 1409 the Republic extended it territories by buying Dalmatia for 100,000 ducats from Ladislaus of Naples. Adding further to their possessions, during the next decade they defeated the patriarch of Aquileia and annexed the town, and here they then began to restore the cathedral that had been so severely damaged during the highly destructive 1348 earthquake.

For the Venetians, there was a negative side to these gains, however. Although by the turn of the century the Serenissima had recovered much of its territory in the Adriatic and Ionian seas, the continual warfare had greatly depleted its navy, and Venice was left with a shortage of manpower. While this had been made worse by the loss of lands that had largely provided the required crews, the problem had been exacerbated by the unwillingness of the young men of the leading Venetian families to work the galleys. Whereas once, apart from the promise of payment and the chance of financial reward, there had been a pride in serving the state in this way, now the more prosperous were focused on building villas and estates on the mainland, where there were alternative ways of increasing their personal fortunes. Apart from this eventually creating a need for chain-gangs to man the boats, the patricians now settled on the *terraferma* were giving less thought to the overseas commercial centres, which were already coming under growing threat from another quarter. The traders' earlier prosperity was being undermined by the rising competition coming from newly discovered ocean routes. On top of this, the Serenissima's movement into the neighbouring mainland regions had added to the concerns of the adjoining states, who had grown suspicious of the incomers' motives.

As Venice turned its eyes landward, others had begun to seek out commercial outlets for themselves in the Adriatic, and by the early 1400s the Viscontis of Milan were eying the region. When in 1423 the Lombard War broke out, the recently elected Doge Francesco Foscari was encouraged to take on the Milanese by his adviser Francesco Carmagnola. Having risen from humble beginnings, Carmagnola had previously been Filippo Maria

Visconti's favourite, but on becoming unpopular at the Milanese court, he had offered his services to the Venetians and then persuaded the doge to go to war. Although he had succeeded in capturing Brescia and Bergamo, in time things began to go wrong for him. After failing in 1431 to bring his army to Cremona in time to help the Venetians' naval attack along the River Po, he was blamed for the eventual defeat. As the authorities were always ruthless towards those believed to have betrayed the Serenissima, after being tortured, the next year Carmagnola was led bound and gagged to his execution between the twin columns in the Piazzetta.

Following his death, a *condottiere* who had served under him, Bartolomeo Colleoni, was employed in his place, and he in his turn would win victories for the Republic at Brescia and then Verona. But, when the Lombard wars came to an end and a tentative peace was agreed with Milan in 1450, he moved to the court of Francesco Sforza, the new duke whose dynasty would now replace that of the Visconti. After losing favour and being briefly imprisoned, Colleoni eventually returned to Venice, where he received a senior appointment in 1455. Immensely proud of his own achievements, at his death twenty years later he left a large bequest to the city together with instructions that a statue be raised in his memory in the Piazza. With such things frowned on by the Republic, individuals never being publicly revered in this way, his beneficiaries – the authorities – resolved the problem by choosing a less significant site outside San Zanipolo, where the statue still stands.

While repeatedly during the 1440s Venice had been fighting its neighbours, the peace with Milan would only be officially confirmed at Lodi in 1454 after the two parties had finally received the horrifying news that Constantinople had fallen the previous year to the Ottomans. For decades, despite repeated visits by the Byzantine emperors appealing for help, the West had continued to pay little attention to the situation in the East. In 1369 John V Palaeologos's failed mission to gain support in exchange for reuniting the two Churches had ended the next year in his own ignominious imprisonment in a debtor's jail in Venice. Similarly, the later urgent appeal for help from John VIII Palaeologos during his visit to the Italian states in the 1430s had achieved no better results. Therefore, with the West having for so long ignored the growing threats to the old east Roman capital, its eventual capture had come as a profound shock to the rest of Christian Europe. The Venetians were particularly appalled by what had happened to their people living in the city, and also – typically – by what had happened to their trade.

> And as [the news] came, a voice shouted out that Constantinople was taken and that everyone over six had been butchered. At once there were great and desperate wailings, cries and groans, everyone beating the palms of their hands, beating their breast with their fists, tearing their hair and their faces, for the death of a father, a son or a brother – or for their property.[70]

Only now would the West wake up at last and realise that there was a need to reunite against the 'infidel' who was challenging the people of Europe.

By this time Doge Francesco Foscari had his own personal problems. During his reign of nearly three and a half decades, the longest term of office of all the doges, Venice had been engaged in repeated costly wars. With his opposition wanting an excuse to depose him, Foscari was now accused of having years before caused the death by poisoning of his rival Admiral Piero Loredan, and as a result he was ordered immediately to step down. This disgrace came on top of another personal tragedy, the death in Candia of his imprisoned son, Jacopo, who had previously been charged with corruption. Crushed by these disasters, just eight days after his abdication Foscari died on 24 October 1457 – a tragic story that was later taken up by several artists, among them the composer Verdi, and again the poet Byron. However, wanting to draw a veil over the recent scandals, the authorities soon chose to emphasise the territorial gains the former doge had brought to Venice and, following his magnificent funeral, his tomb was placed in Santa Maria Gloriosa dei Frari, the great church of the Franciscans that was now reaching completion.[71]

Foscari would leave some major landmarks in the city, among them the remarkable Porta della Carta outside the ducal palace, where he appears above the doorway kneeling before St Mark's lion, holding the open book inscribed with the city's motto of peace: 'Pax tibi Marce, Evangelista meus' (Peace unto you, Mark, my Evangelist). This sculpture – although a 19th-century reconstruction after Napoleon's supporters had damaged the original work – shows how this pairing of saint and doge had become an accepted iconography to symbolise their joint authority. And while Foscari rebuilt his large palace on the Grand Canal (today part of Venice University), other spectacular buildings such as the Ca D'Oro were being completed. This was a period of a new artistic awakening, with many famous names coming to the fore, among them Jacopo Bellini, whose daughter was married to Andrea Mantegna. Having studied under Gentile da Fabriano in Florence, Jacopo had come with his sons, Gentile and Giovanni, to Venice from Padua. Although originally working in tempera, after the arrival of Antonello da Messina in 1473, they began like him to use oil paints, a medium that had recently been discovered by the northern artists. The next year Gentile would be among those involved in the decoration of the hall of the Consiglio Maggiore, but here his works – along with the later ones of his brother and other artists – would eventually be lost in yet another fire that destroyed part of the ducal palace in 1577.

The Serenissima had first taken on the Ottoman fleet in 1415, and after the fall of Constantinople (now the Islamic city of Istanbul) Venice had continued to confront the Muslims as they began to encroach on its territory, one major loss to the Republic being the capture of the strategic island of Negroponte (Euboea) in 1470. Seven years later, the Ottoman threat had even reached the Friuli, after which the Venetians, with their usual pragmatism, agreed to make peace in order to be able to buy new trading rights from the sultan. In 1479 Gentile Bellini set off for the Ottoman court, where the next year he would complete his well-known painting of

Sultan Mehmet II. Yet even while this was happening, the Ottoman fleet was attacking Otranto in Puglia, slaughtering some 800 of its inhabitants, and leaving devastation in its wake. Although the Venetians would again be blamed for this atrocity, accused by their Christian neighbours of not having protected the Italian coastline, they, too, would welcome the news of the sultan's death the following year.

While Giovanni Bellini would leave us the famous portrait of Doge Leonardo Loredan that is today in London's National Gallery, much of his work tended to concentrate on religious subjects and landscapes. Gentile, however, would create pictures depicting contemporary urban views of Venice, ones that give us valuable historic records of the city's important events and celebrations, as well as a clear idea of the architecture and the fashions of the time. Similar images would be produced by Vittore Carpaccio, whose delightful, carefully detailed paintings not only fill the Academia, but are also found in the Scuola di San Giorgio degli Schiavoni, a building bought in 1502 by the brotherhood that had been founded half a century earlier by immigrants from Dalmatia.

For about two decades after Mehmet's death, Venice had easier relations with the East and so it was able to continue its trade and regain Cyprus. But by 1499 tensions had resurfaced and merchants were again being arrested in Istanbul. With the Ottomans once more flexing their muscles, in August the two fleets met, and Venice suffered a major defeat off Cape Zonchio near Navarino in the Ionian Sea. The destruction of a Turkish ship that exploded in a fireball in the heat of the action would become seen as a symbol of the contrast now being drawn between the courageous Muslims and their Christian enemy. The eventual defeat of the Venetians would be blamed not just on bad leadership, but also on the blatant cowardice of those taking part, a disgrace made worse by the surrender of Lepanto and the surrounding area soon after. The sense of humiliation was summed up by one galley captain: 'Everything arose from a lack of love for Christianity and our country, a lack of courage, a lack of discipline, a lack of pride.'[72] Its disgraced Captain General Antonio Grimani was brought back to Venice in chains, and after his trial and brief imprisonment, he was sent into exile for three years on the Adriatic island of Cherso (Cres) just east of Istria. Although Venice was always severe to leaders who failed in their task, these men could sometimes redeem themselves, and so Grimani would succeed over the next two decades in recovering his reputation enough to be eventually elected doge. But a year after the battle of Zonchio, there were further losses, when the sultan's fleet again crushed the Venetians in battle, and took not just their fortress at Navarino (Pylos), but also the even more strategically important Peloponnese town of Modon (Methoni), a Venetian possession since the time of the Fourth Crusade. This loss along with that of the neighbouring Corone (Koroni) would be of grave significance for the Serenissima as both towns were essential ports of call for the merchants on their trade route east. Besides suffering Ottoman attacks across the Friuli right to the doors of Vicenza, in 1501 Venice would also lose Durazzo.

Even though Venice's *Arsenale*, which now covered sixty acres of the city, was according to one visitor able to produce 'ten galleys, fully armed, between the hours of three and nine', the Republic was unable to defend itself against these Ottoman threats.[73] By 1503 it had therefore resigned itself to its losses and agreed to a new peace with the sultan. This came on the heels of another event that would further mark the end of Venice's focus on its *Stato da Mar*. When the city heard that Vasco da Gama had returned safely from his long voyage to India, the news was greeted with horror.

> The whole city ... was dumbfounded and the wisest thought it was the worst news ever heard... Now from this new route the spices of India will be transported to Lisbon, where Hungarians, Germans, the Flemish and the French will look to buy, being able to get them at a better price.[74]

So, from this time onwards, Venice began to turn its attention more towards the mainland and the further development of its *terraferma*.

SECTION IV
THE QUATTROCENTO, A CENTURY OF TURMOIL

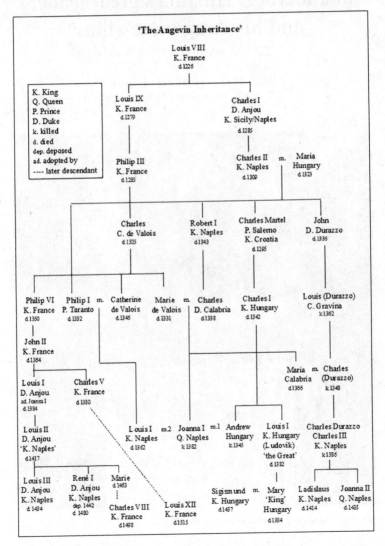

'The Angevin Inheritance'

7

Skanderbeg, Albania's great leader and his Aragonese allies

'I am a friend of virtue, not of fortune.'
Skanderbeg to King Ferdinand I of Naples[75]

Statue of Skanderbeg unveiled in London in 2012.

Before the Aragonese became rulers of Naples, the kingdom had been constantly disputed by the various descendants of Charles, Duke of Anjou, who in 1266 had taken the kingdom of Sicily from the last of the Hohenstaufens. Despite the new king later losing the island and its capital Palermo to Peter of Aragon, the Angevin dynasty would continue to hold on to its throne on the mainland. It was here in 1360 that one of the family's descendants, 15-year-old Charles Durazzo, was sent to live as a hostage at the Neapolitan court of his relative, Joanna I. While this was the result of his father's involvement in a failed rebellion, after the latter's murder in prison the boy was treated with consideration by the queen. Even so, her kindness did not guarantee his long-lasting loyalty, and twenty-one years later when she was overthrown by Pope Urban VI, Charles Durazzo was quite prepared to take her place and accept the throne. He had already sided with another distant Angevin cousin, Louis 'the Great' of Hungary – Ludovik I – who had his own personal reasons for disliking Joanna. Earlier in 1345, his brother Andrew, the queen's first husband, had been killed when a group of murderers had entered his rooms and thrown him out of the window. While there is no evidence verifying the details of what exactly occurred, Ludovik had been convinced of his sister-in-law's responsibility for Andrew's death. Wanting revenge, therefore, three years later in January 1348 he had invaded Joanna's kingdom, claiming the throne for himself and forcing her to flee to Avignon. Here she had remained for the next six months until the arrival of the Black Death had persuaded the Hungarian king to leave her country. Even though he returned briefly two years later, before long he would abandon his campaign and sign a truce with the queen.

Within thirty years of these events the Catholic Church was to find itself confronted by one of the greatest challenges and most serious internal divisions it was ever to face, the so-called Great or Western Schism that had resulted from two popes both claiming to be the rightful heir to St Peter. Having established their separate courts in Rome and Avignon, for the next four decades the rival papacies would give vent to their mutual antagonism. While this rancorous situation was to impinge on the religious and political affairs of most of western Europe, already in 1381, only three years after it had begun, it was a significant element in Joanna's fate as she faced the open challenge of Charles Durazzo. Now as Ludovik's governor of Slavonia, Croatia and Dalmatia, he marched with his Croatian army into Naples, where, with the blessing of the pope in Rome, he arrested the queen and took her throne as the new ruler Charles III. Joanna had already been excommunicated by that same Urban VI in punishment for her support of the antipope Clement VII in Avignon, and so after her murder in prison the next year she was denied a normal Christian burial, and as a final mark of disrespect her body was thrown down a well. For the new Neapolitan king, however, there would be another even more significant event that same year, namely the death of Ludovik, who had been survived by just two daughters. Because Charles was now the oldest living male from the senior Angevin line, he was determined to assert his rights to this second throne as well. But, when four years later he marched north to claim his Hungarian crown, Ludovik's widow Elizabeth had other ideas. Wanting to put her daughter Mary on the throne as the country's new 'king', in February 1386 she ordered an attempt to be made on Charles's life and shortly after this attack, he would die of his injuries.[76] This did little for Mary and her mother, however, as, soon captured by their enemies, they were locked up at Novigrad near Zara, where later Elizabeth would herself be murdered.

A more immediate result of Charles' assassination was the succession in Naples of his nine-year-old son Ladislaus. But a year after inheriting the Neapolitan throne, the boy was deposed by another distant relation, one whose father had formerly been Joanna's adopted son. Having already been crowned by the antipope Clement VII, Louis II, Duke of Anjou, arrived in 1390 to take possession of his kingdom. He never managed to extend his control far beyond the immediate area, and although he held the region surrounding Otranto, he would continue to face on-going opposition in Puglia. In the meantime, the deposed Ladislaus had set his sights on his father's other claims, declaring himself King of Hungary, even though the title now belonged to Mary's husband, Sigismund. With Venetian help, Sigismund had earlier achieved his wife's release from captivity and, although she would die during childbirth eight years later in 1395, he was to continue reigning as King of Hungary and Croatia for more than another four decades.

Before the century was over, the situation changed again in southern Italy. Unable to deal with the challenges, nine years after taking the throne Louis II decided to leave the country, and so in 1400 his ousted rival succeeded in recapturing Naples. But as he was soon faced by the same problems as Louis, not until he had dealt with the rebellion in Puglia was he able to begin attending to matters on other side of the Adriatic. Still determined to assert his rights to his various possessions in Dalmatia, Ladislaus dismissed Sigismund's prior claim and in 1403 at Zara cathedral he was crowned King of Hungary.

Ladislaus's problems at home had not gone away, however, and within three years he was again facing unrest among the nobles in Puglia. After he had partially resolved these difficulties by promising to defend the Papal States – a pledge that he was to ignore before the year was out – his situation would be improved by the opportune death of the rebels' leader, Raimondo Del Balzo Orsini. Although for the next two months this man's wealthy widow continued to hold out against the king at Taranto, on her surrender she agreed to marry Ladislaus and the ceremony then took place in the castle chapel. This was greatly to the king's advantage as he had now gained possession of his wife's vast fortune. Even so, by 1409, despite his successful campaigning in the Papal Lands, he was again so seriously short of money that he decided to sell Dalmatia to Venice.

Just a month earlier, in June, Gregory XII had been elected pope in Rome, but with Benedict XIII still pontiff in Avignon, the on-going struggle between the two rival papacies continued. Because of the damage this was causing to both religious and political affairs, three years later an attempt was made to

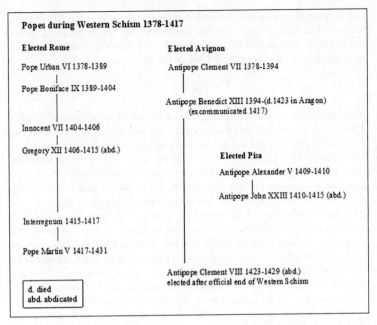

Popes during Western Schism 1378-1417

Elected Rome

Pope Urban VI 1378-1389

Pope Boniface IX 1389-1404

Innocent VII 1404-1406

Gregory XII 1406-1415 (abd.)

Interregnum 1415-1417

Pope Martin V 1417-1431

Elected Avignon

Antipope Clement VII 1378-1394

Antipope Benedict XIII 1394-(d.1423 in Aragon)
(excommunicated 1417)

Elected Pisa

Antipope Alexander V 1409-1410

Antipope John XXIII 1410-1415 (abd.)

Antipope Clement VIII 1423-1429 (abd.)
elected after official end of Western Schism

d. died
abd. abdicated

end the dispute by electing Alexander V to replace both men. Since the solution had depended on their joint abdication, which was not forthcoming, there were now three individuals all claiming to be the true pontiff. More seriously still for the Neapolitan king, because of his earlier support of Gregory, Alexander now excommunicated him and invited Louis II of Anjou back to reclaim his throne. In the event, Alexander died after only a year in office, but he was soon succeeded by the antipope John XXIII, who was equally opposed to Ladislaus. Although the latter was then defeated in battle by Louis, the Angevin soon returned to Provence and by 1412 the situation had again improved for his rival, whose *condottiere* Carlo Malatesta had carried out a successful invasion of the Ancona Marches. As a result, there was a new peace, but with the truce soon collapsing in May 1413, the Neapolitan king then began to turn his sights on Rome. As the attack got under way, the terrified antipope John quit his post and fled the city. Two years later, Gregory – who had already been abandoned by Ladislaus – also agreed to abdicate, and so when eventually the unwilling Benedict XIII was forced to give up his position in 1417, the Great or Western Schism came at last to an end.

Ladislaus was not alive to see the eventual resolution of this saga, having died of some disease in Naples in August 1414. Following his death his throne passed to his sister Joanna II, whose troubled reign would end 21 years later with the succession of René of Anjou, the younger son of Louis. Yet, because Joanna II had earlier proclaimed and then repudiated the rights of the Sicilian king, Alfonso V of Aragon, he was now determined to gain his second crown, and six years later he finally succeeded in ousting his rival. With René having hurriedly fled back home, in 1443 he entered Naples in triumph as Alfonso I, and having thus re-united the divided southern Italian kingdom, he was now to be the first to hold the title of King of the Two Sicilies.

* * *

While the earlier turmoil was going on in Italy, the Byzantine empire had lost Albania where, around two decades after the first arrival of the Ottomans, probably in 1405 Gjergi Kastrioti was born in the north of the country at Krujï. The youngest of a family of nine, he was the son of the Christian nobleman Gjon Kastrioti, a vassal of the sultan. Contemporary records indicate that Gjergi was sent with his three brothers to Adrianople (Edirne) as a hostage when he was aged about nine – although some accounts suggest he was far younger, being just three years old. Alternatively, more recent research proposes that he was probably handed over to Murad II a few years after his brothers, in around 1423, by which time he was in his late teens. Whatever the truth, there is no doubt that while living at the Ottoman court, besides being instructed in the Islamic faith Gjergi received a good education and became fluent in several languages. Eventually, in accordance with the *devirsne* system, he was enrolled in the sultan's army and having proved his ability, he was then dubbed after the great Macedonian general Iskander or S'kander, with the additional 'bey' that signified he was now 'Lord Alexander'. In time, this would morph into 'Skanderbeg', the name by which he became famous in the West. However, the young man's period of military service with the Ottomans would ultimately prove to be to the sultan's disadvantage, it giving Skanderbeg the valuable experience that later served him so well.

In 1428, having been granted Venetian citizenship fifteen years earlier, Skanderbeg's father Gjon would feel obliged to apologise to the Serenissima for his son's actions. Then, within just a couple of years, Gjon Kastrioti went further, personally rebelling against the Ottomans in a failed protest that ultimately resulted in the loss of more of his lands. A second show of resistance would be still more unfortunate, forcing him into exile where he died two years later in 1437. By that time, even though trusted by the sultan, Skanderbeg and his oldest brother had already begun to build up their own relations with Venice and Ragusa. Although in 1440 he was appointed an Ottoman governor in Albania, where he remained on good terms with the local people, there is every likelihood that by this time Skanderbeg had already started to consider regaining his father's lost territories. Despite some historians suggesting that until this moment he had been unaware of his childhood identity, the argument falls down if we accept the recent theory that he had originally been taken hostage at the age of eighteen. In that case, it would appear that Skanderbeg had only been waiting for the right moment to move, and that particular opportunity was to come when he was fighting the Hungarians three years later. Using the pretence that he had been defeated, he deserted with 300 of his men and made his way back to Albania.

Having destroyed the Ottoman garrisons along the way, he eventually arrived at the key fortress of Krujë, which he managed to take by deception. With the all too usual brutality of the times, the defenders were massacred and Skanderbeg reputedly killed the pasha with his own hands, before he then raised his chosen standard – still today the national flag of Albania – and famously declared that rather than having brought liberty to his country, he had found it among the people.

The next year, after he had reconverted to Christianity and regained some of his father's earlier possessions, Skanderbeg was able to use his recent successes to unite his followers. Having inspired them to join in the fight for independence, he brought various rival princes together in the cathedral of the town of Alessio (Lezhë) in Venetian Albania.[77] Here, having formed a league of warlords, he was elected as leader and recognised as the lord of Albania. Stunned by Skanderbeg's betrayal, three months later Sultan Murad II mounted his first attack on his former general. But, despite usually having a larger army, over the coming years all but one of the Ottomans' 25 attempts to crush Skanderbeg would end in defeat. Setting aside the sultan's victory in 1455, in the main the Albanian's force of about 10,000 to 15,000 was to win the day through stealth and guerrilla tactics.

Although until this time the Venetians had been content to see Skanderbeg as a defence against the Ottomans, things were about to change. Shortly after his league had formed, a serious dispute broke out between two of its members who wanted to marry the same woman. When the men appeared at the wedding of Skanderbeg's sister, the situation escalated into a bloody brawl that resulted in the deaths of several guests. While a couple of years later this led to a revenge killing, by that time local feelings had hardened against the princes. As a result, not only had the people invited the Venetians back, but to Skanderbeg's deep regret his mother had decided to hand over her Dagnum (Danjë) fortress. Believing that this was necessary for Albania's defence, her son immediately asked the Venetians for its return, but his request was refused. In spite of Venice's alternative offer of financial compensation, the response did not satisfy Skanderbeg and so in 1447 war broke out. Like the fortress at Dagnum, Durazzo came under siege and before long other towns of Albania Venetia such as Antivari (Bar) and Dulcigno (Ulcinj) were also targeted. The next year the Serenissima put a price on Skanderbeg's head, and the Venetians then allied themselves with his enemy and persuaded the Ottomans to attack him on another front. Angered by what they had done, after defeating the sultan's army Skanderbeg marched straight to the River Drin, where in July he succeeded in routing the Serenissima's army. At the end of a long and bloody battle that left them with losses that were six times higher than those of the Albanians, the Venetians had finally been forced to flee the field. This disaster was then followed by another when around a thousand more of their men became ensnared in a humiliating round-up outside the walls of Scutari (Shkodër). Even so a truce did not come immediately and it would not be until Skanderbeg had again defeated the Ottomans that peace negotiations could begin in October 1448. According to the subsequent agreement, in return for the surrender of some of his land, Skanderbeg received from the Serenissima 1,400 golden ducats and the right to buy salt free of tax at the Venetian town of Durazzo.

Two years later, while those in this town were still honouring the treaty, to the Albanian's fury he discovered that other Venetians were again assisting the Muslims, who were now besieging Krujë. Despite his being able eventually to relieve the city by attacking the Venetian caravans and cutting off the Ottoman supplies, this whole episode had done little for his relations with the Serenissima. No longer trusting the Venetians and having also lost the backing of the other Albanian nobles, Skanderbeg now began to consider strengthening his ties elsewhere. The year before he had sent troops to help the Sicilian king put down a rebellion, and so in 1451 these two men went further and signed a pact. While this confirmed that Skanderbeg was the king's vassal, in return Alfonso had granted him his autonomy and promised to provide him with military support.

By this time, Skanderbeg's remarkable successes against Europe's much-feared Muslim enemy were making him a hero at home and abroad, and his reputation would be further enhanced two years later when just weeks before the fall of Constantinople he won another victory against the Ottomans. With the West becoming increasingly aware of his outstanding contribution to the defence of the Christian world, Ragusa now supported his request to the pope for financial backing, and Calixtus III – although short of money himself –offered him some limited funds. As he needed the Albanian's assistance in his crusade against the 'Turks', he appointed Skanderbeg the Captain General of the Holy See. But this was a step too far for the more pragmatic city of Ragusa, the chief concern of its citizens being for their own security. Therefore, having abandoned the Hungarians and turned to the Muslims in exchange for the payment of tribute money, the republic now received new privileges and the protection of the sultan. Yet Skanderbeg still wished to maintain good relations with his Christian neighbours, and so he formed a new anti-Ottoman alliance with Stefan Branković, the deposed Serbian leader who had fled, on his advice, to Italy. Anxious to improve relations with the Serenissima as well, he decided to surrender the recently captured fortress at Sati (Shati) near Scutari. Even so, before finally handing this site over to the Venetians in 1459, he would take the precaution of destroying the building to prevent it ever being used against him at a later date.

Meanwhile, because Alfonso had died the year before leaving no legitimate children, his kingdom had once again been broken up. While Sicily had been given to Alfonso's brother Juan, the new king of Aragon – the father of Ferdinand II, the later joint ruler of the united Spain – Naples was to pass to Ferdinand I, popularly known as Ferrante, who had been previously recognised as the heir by two earlier popes. Yet as he was only Alfonso's illegitimate son, Calixtus III now saw an opportunity to increase his influence in the region and revive Naples' position as a papal fiefdom by reversing the decisions of his predecessors. But within weeks of Alfonso's death, Calixtus, too, was dead. Therefore, with Ferrante's succession having been confirmed by the new pope Pius II, the coronation took place on 4 February 1459 at the cathedral in the kingdom's second largest city, Barletta. This was not popular, however, with some of the southern barons now wanting instead to see the return of the former claimant, René of Anjou. Therefore, when René's son Jean invaded the next year, rebellion broke out again. As others, too, were eager to unsettle the balance of power in the region for their own ends, the rebels were supported by the *condottiere* Sigismund Pandolfo Malatesta of Rimini. But, on the other side, the pope and the rival mercenaries Federico da Montefeltro and Alessandro Sforza were helping the king. Even though Jean was then defeated in July, Ferrante's problems had not gone away and so he appealed for additional help from Skanderbeg, who immediately honoured his earlier alliance with Alfonso and began to prepare to join the allies.

On receiving the king's request, Skanderbeg sent his nephew with an advance party to relieve the besieged Barletta, and the next year, after agreeing an armistice with the Ottomans, he personally set out to join his men. On his arrival in August, he soon defeated the Angevins at Barletta and Trani, before moving on twelve months later to capture Orsara after a nineteen-day siege. In recognition for what he had achieved, Ferrante granted him and his descendants various possessions at Trani and elsewhere and honoured him with the title of Signore di Monte Sant'Angelo and San Giovanni Rotondo. After this time, as more Albanians began to arrive in Puglia, the Greek language began to be spoken once again, above all in the region around Otranto where vestiges of it still remain.

As the Venetians had become increasingly anxious about Skanderbeg's closeness to the Aragonese – their main rivals in the Adriatic – they had started attempting to stir up discord among the various leaders in Albania. Yet now, with the pope's plans for his crusade against the Ottomans now beginning to take shape, they decided to change tack. Therefore, in 1463 Venice promised further financial reward to Skanderbeg, who, as the campaign's chosen leader, was given the Republic's title of Patrizio Veneto. However, with the pope dying shortly after and the whole affair collapsing, Skanderbeg soon found himself at a great disadvantage. As the sultan had got wind of the crusade, and in particular the Albanian's part in it, the earlier truce agreed between the two parties broke down. While Skanderbeg now received little help from his former allies, his situation was made more complicated by the bitter disputes among the Albanian nobles. Although he visited Venice two years before his death, and in the last months of his life the doge eventually suggested the Christian states might form another alliance to help deal with the increasing threat from the Muslims, he was still involved in his own personal war right until the end of his reign.

The full significance of the role Skanderbeg had played for 25 years almost single-handed in the defence of Europe against the growing Ottoman empire would become apparent in January 1468. Even as the Venetians were proposing to form a united front and Skanderbeg was endeavouring to recreate the league that he had established so successfully over twenty years before, he died at Alessio of malaria. Here he was buried in the church dedicated to St Nicholas, later destroyed, which has now become the site of Skanderbeg's new mausoleum. Following his burial, his widow Andronika (Donika) and 11-year-old son Gjon (Giovanni) fled for safety to Naples, where they were welcomed by Ferrante. Openly declaring that Skanderbeg had been like a father to him, the king gave the refugees lands and shelter in the region of Lecce, and added yet more titles to those Gjon had already inherited.[78] Although Andronika would grow close to the queen over the years, in 1494 with the outbreak of the Italian Wars she decided the time had come to leave the country, and so she was in Spain when she died six years later.

Albania had now lost its military champion, and a decade after Skanderbeg's death Krujë fell to the Ottomans, who two years later took control of the whole country. For a short time after 1481, Skanderbeg's son Gjon would attempt to re-establish himself, and despite the brutal revenge that the Ottomans were now taking on the local people, pockets of resistance continued to keep up the struggle for their country's independence. Yet, by 1500, all resistance was gone. The next year the Venetians ceded Durazzo to the sultan, and with Skanderbeg's grandson abandoning his own attempt at rebellion, many more Albanians started to leave the county. It would not regain its full independence until 1912.

Skanderbeg's fame would live on. Ironically, he would even be remembered – if disrespectfully – by the Ottomans, who when later desecrating his grave reputedly shared out his bones as supposed good luck charms. And, besides becoming a much-loved and revered national figure for the Albanians, he would also be admired abroad. In addition to the respect shown to him over the centuries by men like Spenser, Voltaire, Vivaldi, Byron and Longfellow, his statue can now be found in cities such as Rome, Vienna, and lately even London.

* * *

All this time the Ottomans had been gradually spreading into Europe, their brutal attack in 1480 on Otranto having particularly terrified the people of the Italian peninsula. By the next year, when Ferrante finally succeeded in expelling the invaders, they had taken scores of the townspeople into slavery and murdered many others, the notorious massacre still recalled today by the gruesome display of the victims' skulls behind the altar in the side chapel of the cathedral. But, once again, this was a period of constantly changing loyalties. So, although two years before the assault on Otranto Ferrante had joined the pope in the war against the leaders of Florence, shortly after the murder of Giovanni de Medici in the Pazzi Plot, the surviving brother Lorenzo had visited Naples and agreed to a separate peace with the king. Having equally complicated dealings with his other neighbours, Ferrante had now not only enraged Sixtus IV by ignoring his earlier promises to respect the sovereignty of the Papal States, but had also antagonised the Venetians and their allies by joining forces with Milan and Florence in support of his son-in-law, Duke Ercole I d'Este of Ferrara. Yet, Sixtus, too, would change sides after he became so deeply concerned about

Venice's growing influence in the region that he decided to abandon the Serenissima and revive his alliance with Ferrante.

Following Sixtus's death, his successor Innocent VIII was similarly drawn into the political game-playing, and only a year after his inauguration in 1484 he began to stir up new troubles for Ferrante. Because the pope now encouraged the nobles in the south to take action again against their unloved king, the unrest would continue on and off until the end of the reign, despite the brutal measures Ferrante was taking to try and crush the opposition. Angered by the fact that in the recent papal election he had supported the alternative candidate Rodrigo Borgia – the later Alexander VI – Innocent was particularly antagonistic towards him. Therefore, in 1489, besides taking the extreme measure of excommunicating the king, he declared Charles VIII (the great-grandson of Louis II) to be the rightful ruler of Naples. This would lead to the French invasion and the brutal Italian Wars, which were to ravage the peninsula for the next five years.

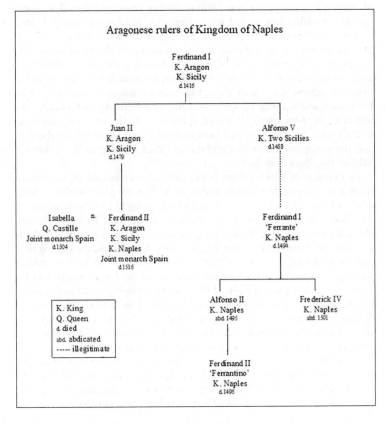

Aragonese rulers of Kingdom of Naples

Ferdinand I
K. Aragon
K. Sicily
d.1416

Juan II
K. Aragon
K. Sicily
d.1479

Alfonso V
K. Two Sicilies
d.1458

Isabella ∞ Ferdinand II
Q. Castille
Joint monarch Spain
d.1504

K. Aragon
K. Sicily
K. Naples
Joint monarch Spain
d.1516

Ferdinand I
'Ferrante'
K. Naples
d.1494

K. King
Q. Queen
d. died
abd. abdicated
----- illegitimate

Alfonso II
K. Naples
abd. 1495

Frederick IV
K. Naples
abd. 1501

Ferdinand II
'Ferrantino'
K. Naples
d.1496

Ferrante's unpopularity stemmed largely from his reputation for cruelty, one contemporary describing him as 'bloody, wicked, inhuman, lascivious [and] gluttonous'.[79] The same source described how the king had impoverished the people of Puglia by buying up their oil and corn to sell at a profit, only then to make them buy it back if the prices fell. After coming into possession of his first wife Isabella Orsini's vast fortune on her death in 1465, he had the means to preside over a cultured court, but his own behaviour was allways quite the reverse. Ferrante apparently took pleasure in various forms of depravity and brutality, much of his enjoyment derived from witnessing the suffering of his victims. One possibly apocryphal or exaggerated story declared that he had even had his enemies mummified and then dressed up so that he might continue looking at them.

When Ferrante died in 1494 aged seventy, he was succeeded by his son Alfonso II. Arguably even more cruel than his father, within thirteen months the new king became so terrified of the invading French force that he abdicated in favour of Charles VIII and retired to a monastery. His son Ferdinand II would fare little better, initially being unable to take up his throne because of the approaching foreign army, and then dying only fourteen months after he had been reinstated. Although he was followed by his uncle Frederick IV, the younger son of Ferrante, the new French King Louis XII was now staking his own claim to the throne of Naples. As the great-grandson of Charles V, brother of Louis I, the duke of Anjou, he asserted his rights to the crown through the tenuous links of the so-called 'Angevin inheritance'. After these had been eventually acknowledged by Ferdinand and Isabella of Spain in 1500 at the Treaty of Granada, the following year Frederick IV would agree to abdicate. By then, according to the treaty, his kingdom had been divided, Naples ceded to the French, and the remaining lands in Calabria and Puglia added to those already held by the Spanish in Sicily.

As instances of violence then began to break out around the country, a particularly memorable episode took place in 1503 on the plains outside Barletta, where a band of local knights took on a similar group of Frenchmen who were stationed at nearby Canosa. Among the latter group was Charles de Torgues, also known as Guy de la Motte, who, like his colleagues, had been brought as a prisoner to Barletta. Here he drunkenly insulted the people, questioning their courage for having submitted to their Spanish rulers. This enraged the men of the town and as the argument grew more heated the French finally issued a challenge, declaring that thirteen of their mounted knights would settle matters by taking on in armed combat a similar number of the Italians. After a day of fighting, the contest concluded with the defeat of the French, among whom there was one casualty. With that pride was restored to the town, where still today a monument boasts its success in the challenge – the *Disfida di Barletta*.

Although this particular episode was resolved, the earlier treaty had now broken down. Elsewhere, therefore, the fighting continued, and it would only be after the Spanish had won two victories – at Cerignola in the region of Foggia and Garigliano north of Naples – that a final peace was reached at

Lyon in July 1504. Here, satisfied at last with their recently taken territories in the north of Italy, the French agreed to surrender Naples and all the south to the joint monarchs Ferdinand and Isabella, whose descendants would then continue to rule southern Italy from Spain almost uninterrupted until the 18th century. However, over the years their appointed viceroys would pay little attention to Puglia and the concerns of its people, and so, becoming increasingly ignored, the region then gradually began to slip out of the limelight.

8

The Papal States and the great *condottieri*

'I am determined to bear it no longer, rather to show with my person against yours that I am a braver man and you a bad one and that you do ill to insult me.'

Sigismondo Pandolfo di Malatesta to Federico da Montefeltro[80]

'Federico da Montefeltro gave himself entirely to his state that the people might be content.'

Vespasiano da Bistici[81]

Sigismondo Pandolfo di Malatesta and Federico da Montefeltro.

During the 15th century, as Italy's city states began to increase in power, the ruling families looked for assistance from the various mercenaries, or *condottieri*, who for a price would contract their services to any who needed them. In addition to being employed by the kings and ruling nobles, for generations these military men had also served the Church, helping the popes to achieve their secular or territorial ambitions. Over the years the Papal States had expanded considerably from their early beginnings in the 4th century, when Emperor Constantine had granted Pope Stephen II lands around Rome. These territories had been further increased four centuries later, when the Franks, having ousted the Lombards from Ravenna, presented that city to the pontiff, along with other vast swathes of land stretching right across central Italy. After this, the so-called Donation of Pippin, the papal possessions had continued to grow. More recently, however, the Church's control over the various neighbouring city states had been considerably undermined by the internal dissension of the Western Schism, and so it was again turning to the *condottieri* for their help. Among the principal soldiers of fortune at this time were the heads of the Malatesta of Rimini and the Montefeltro of Urbino, two dynasties from the Romagna-Marche region, whose long and bitter rivalry is still evident in the numerous extant fortresses they created to protect their borders.

In the 12th century the Malatesta had moved to Rimini, where over time they had begun to hold civic positions, Malatesta della Penna first becoming senior magistrate – the *podestà* –in 1239. For a while the city had been under the control of Emperor Frederick II, but following his defeat at Parma in 1248, Malatesta's son 'da Verucchio' had switched his loyalty to the papacy. Within two decades, he had also given his support to Charles of Anjou when he passed through the Romagna on his way south to seize the Kingdom of Sicily from the last of the Hohenstaufens. During this period there came on the scene various colourful characters whom Dante in the last years before his death in 1321 would include in the first part of the *Divine Comedy*, the 'Inferno'. Malatesta da Verucchio, nicknamed 'Mastin Vecchio' – 'the Old Mastiff' – together with his equally murderous oldest son, the one-eyed Malatestino dell'Occhio, appears among those punished for fraud in Cantos XXVII-XXVIII. The older man, who died in 1312 at the remarkable age of one hundred, was also the father of Paolo, 'Il Bello', who, while employed in Florence, had quite possibly met the poet. After his return home, during the 1280s this same Paolo was famously murdered by his brother, when he was discovered to be having an affair with his sister-in-law Francesca da Polenta, better known as Francesca da Rimini.[82] Both the lovers were killed by her reputedly cruel husband, Giovanni Malatesta – dubbed Gianciotto, 'the cripple' – whom she had been forced to marry by her ambitious family. Francesca's betrothal in 1275, the same year that the Malatesta had helped her relations to take power in Ravenna, had been intended to unite these two dynasties that were fast becoming the most influential in the region. While there is only minimal contemporary reference to Francesca, in *Esposizioni sopra la 'Comedia' di Dante*, completed around half a century later, Boccaccio took up the story, embroidering it to show how the marriage had been conducted by proxy, Paolo acting for his more unappealing brother in order to trick the girl into accepting the proposal. Although Dante had gone into considerably less detail, intentionally leaving much unspecified and open to philosophical debate, when writing the *Commedia dell'Arte* he had actually been living in Ravenna as a guest of Francesca's nephew, the poet Guido Novello da Polenta, a more beneficent member of the family who himself would later be ousted and exiled by his own cousin. For Dante, this personal contact may well have given Francesca's story a particular poignancy, and the tragedy would continue to fascinate for centuries to come, interpreted by numerous painters, sculptors, poets, writers, and composers: Rossetti and Rodin, Keats and D'Annunzio, Rossini and Tchaikovsky, to name but a few.

Despairing of the situation in Italy, above all in the Romagna, Dante placed responsibility for the constant unrest in the country on the various tyrants of Ravenna, Forlì, Faenza, Imola and elsewhere, who 'in their hearts' had never been without war.[83] Even while they remained subjects of their imperial or religious overlords, they had been extending their control, better able to do so by the absence of the popes who were residing far away in Avignon. Viewing with horror the unstable situation that persisted in this region, the Florentine poet would also include many other local leaders in the 'Inferno', among them two from Faenza, Alberigo d'Manfredi (Canto XXX), and Tebaldello d'Zambrasi (Canto XXXII) – the latter the father of Zambrasina, who, after Francesca's murder, had married the murderous Gianciotto. Yet, Dante's most savage criticism remains directed against the Malatesta clan who had finally achieved their ambitions for complete power in 1295. At the end of that year there had been three days of violent unrest in Rimini, during which a full-scale battle had broken out in the streets between the rival factions. When those still supporting the imperial Ghibelline cause at last began to realise that the hoped-for help from Urbino was not going to arrive, 'Mastin Vecchio' affirmed his loyalty to the Guelfs, declared himself ready to make peace, and then departed the city.[84] But this was a deception. Having left behind some of his men, he soon returned and took the unsuspecting pro-Ghibelline Parcitadi by surprise. With his opposition then imprisoned, murdered, or forced to flee, he was finally able to seize full control of Rimini.

Although after that the city was to enjoy a period of comparative peace, the ruthlessness of the Malatesta would continue to show itself in the internecine arguments that plagued the family itself. Over the years, the different contenders for power had no hesitation in inviting their relations to a dinner, only then to murder them, a brutal series of assassinations that eventually resulted in the aptly named Malatesta Guastafamiglia – the family breaker – overthrowing his cousin Ferrantino and becoming the fifth lord of Rimini in 1334. The Malatesta were now officially recognised as the city's hereditary dictators, and nine years later the Emperor appointed them imperial vicars not only of Rimini but also Pesaro and Fano. Under Guastafamiglia's rule the dynasty continued to increase its territory, expanding to places like Ancona and Jesi in the Marche, and even as far as Ascoli lying some 125 miles to the south. The family was equally fortunate a few years later, managing to emerge virtually unscathed from the Black Death. In this it was not alone, however. The Church had actually made capital out of the horrors of the plague. Even while its flock was suffering, its own wealth had continued to grow thanks to the donations of the desperate people, hoping, if not to stave off the disease, at least to save their souls.

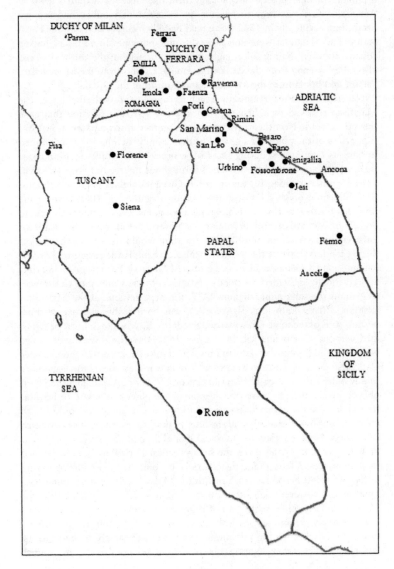

As the Malatesta had grown steadily more unpopular, besides confronting rebellion at home they had faced increased opposition from their neighbours. But now there was worse to come. In 1355 the pope in Avignon sent his army to reclaim the Church's control in the region, and before long its leader Cardinal Albornoz defeated Galeotto Malatesta at Paderno di Ancona, forcing him to make peace and submit to the pope's demands. The family had to surrender a number of their possessions, among them their recently acquired town of Ancona, which was now to become an independent republic under papal protection: eventually in 1532 this would be fully incorporated into the Papal States. The Malatesta were not, however, the only ones to be hit as, having equally attacked the other leading families in the region, the cardinal would also take Ravenna from the da Polenta family, Urbino from the Montefeltro, Faenza and Imolà from the Manfredi, and Forlì from the Ordelaffi.

Nevertheless, after eventually reaching agreement with the pope, the Malatesta received their first papal vicariate – a secular position that gave them the right to elect their own officials – and therefore they were now loyal supporters of the pontiff. As several of their family members then continued to fight as *condottieri*, during the 15th century these would again increase their wealth and extend their control throughout the region. For more than a decade after winning Brescia in 1404, Guastafamiglia's nephew Pandolfo III would hold on to the town, also taking Bergamo in 1408. At the same time, his brother Carlo was making his own gains, even temporarily taking possession of Milan and becoming its governor following the death of Gian Galeazzo Visconti in 1402. His standing would then be further raised during the last years of the Western Schism, when, as the respected Lord of Rimini (and Cesena and Fano), he offered Gregory XII refuge in his city, and personally presented the pope's abdication to the Council of Constance.

Around the same time, in June 1417, the most famous of the Malatesta, Gismondo (later known as Sigismondo), was born in Brescia, one of three bastard sons of the three-times married Pandolfo III. When their libertine father died without a legitimate heir in October 1427, these boys were sent to live with their childless uncle Carlo and his wife. However, as just 23 months later Carlo also died, his position as Lord of Rimini was then passed to Gismondo's saintly older half-brother, 18-year-old Galeotto Roberto. Although he had been obliged by his uncle to marry the illegitimate daughter of the lord of Ferrara, he and his wife had immediately chosen to follow a religious way of life, both continuing to live in chastity, and she finally taking the veil after his early death in October 1432. By then her husband had abdicated and become a tertiary of the Franciscan Order. Even the highly critical Pope Pius II, who loathed the family, would later praise this man's behaviour, describing him as having 'a character that belied his kinship with the Malatesta'.[85] Of more immediate significance, however, Galeotto Roberto had now left his half-brother, the 15-year-old Gismondo, as the lord of Rimini and Fano.

By this time, Gismondo had already earned a reputation for bravery as three years earlier, within just months of his uncle's death, he had proved himself in battle when fighting against one of his relations from another branch of the family. Despite the odds facing them, he and his brothers had held out, defending their city from the combined attack of Carlo II Malatesta of Pesaro, Guidantonio da Montefeltro (Count of Urbino), and Pope Martin V. Although a short time before, this same pope had been on good terms with the lord of Rimini, having agreed with Carlo to an exchange of territories in return for the legitimisation of his nephews, as so often happened in this period, this alliance was to have little meaning. Despite Martin having hosted a peace meeting in Rome between Count Guidantonio and Carlo in 1428, and the latter having been given a warm welcome in Urbino on his way home, the general goodwill had

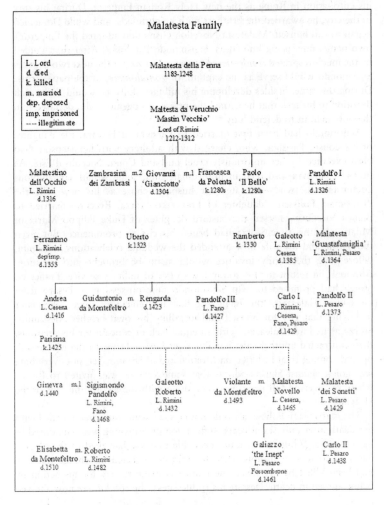

soon evaporated. In addition to the renewal of the age-old Malatesta-Montefeltro feud, the pope had also become embroiled in their dispute, justifying his determination to take possession of Rimini by claiming not to have received the levies that were his due.

The fortunes of Carlo I's nephews would improve when Martin V died in 1431 and the new pope, Eugenius IV, awarded the siblings with a papal *condotta*. Having also confirmed their rights of succession, Galeotto and then Gismondo were officially declared rulers of Rimini, Fano, and Cervia, while their brother Domenico was the lord of Cesena. More promotion would then come the young men's way two years later, when in September the Hungarian king Sigismund passed through Rimini on his way home from his coronation in Rome as the new Holy Roman Emperor. During his stay in the city, he awarded the brothers with knighthoods, and while Domenico began to call himself 'Malatesta Novello', Gismondo adopted the Emperor's own name, now being known as 'Sigismondo Pandolfo'. After that, guided by the much-respected *condottiere* Francesco Sforza, for the next two decades Sigismondo would serve as the captain, or *gonfaloniere*, of the papal army. During this time, besides developing his military skills, he would show such devotion to his task that he earned the praise of Eugenius, who declared him the only man fit to defend Italy.[86]

Sigismondo had been first married to Ginevra of Ferrara, the daughter of his cousin Parisina, who, charged with adultery with her stepson, had been executed by her notoriously cruel husband Count Niccolò d'Este. As in 1440 Ginevra also died in unfortunate and, some would say, dubious circumstances, two years later her husband chose as his new wife the illegitimate Polissena, daughter of Francesco Sforza. Recently married to Bianca Visconti – herself the bastard daughter of Duke Filippo Maria of Milan – by this time Sforza had begun his rise to prominence. But, even though he and his wife now attended the wedding celebrations in Rimini, before long the family loyalties would again be brought into question. Although, in return for his son-in-law's offer of military service, Francesco Sforza had promised to help Sigismondo take possession of Pesaro from his cousin Galeazzo, 'the Inept', he had no reluctance three years later in buying that city for himself and installing his own brother Alessandro Sforza as its lord. Galeazzo, with an equal lack of concern for his relations, then contracted another sale, handing over Fossombrone to the Malatesta's up-and-coming rival Federico da Montefeltro of Urbino. Yet, not everything was going against Sigismondo as that same year he was invited to Rome, where he received full papal honours along with the Sword and Hat of the Holy See.

The marriage to Polissena would not be successful, and when it ended with her death after only seven years, suffocation or drowning were rumoured to be the cause. While it was more probable that she had died of the plague, Sigismondo was so furious when his minister rejected his charge that she had been killed by her lover, the man was made to pay for his action by being starved to death. Despite his ruthlessness, the *condottiere* now showed another side to his character, pouring out his love in romantic poetry to his adored mistress, Isotta degli Atti. Having begun an affair only a year after he had met the 12-year-old girl, by the time the couple finally married sometime around 1457, she was already the mother of their three surviving children. Even though, to her apparent annoyance, he continued to have other mistresses and illegitimate offspring, Sigismondo remained devoted to her. A strong character, she shared his interest in the arts, accompanied him when he went to war, and after his death would for a while play a significant role in helping their son Salustio to run his affairs.

As a successful *condottiere*, Sigismondo had now acquired the wealth that he needed to start beautifying his city, something he saw as an essential way to promote his status. For more than a century Rimini had had its own resident painters, their school having developed as a result of the visit made by Giotto in 1305 while he was on his way to Padua to paint his famous frescos for the Scrovegni Chapel. But this was not enough for Sigismondo. Having spent time in his youth with his highly cultured aunt Elisabetta Gonzaga of Mantua, and also at the sophisticated court in Ferrara, he wished to establish Rimini as one of the great Renaissance centres. He therefore began to alter the Chiesa di San Francesco, the 13th-century Gothic church where his forebears had been interred, and where eventually his own tomb would be placed alongside the new chapel that he was creating. Dedicated to his patron saint, in March 1452 the Capella di San Sigismondo was inaugurated in a glittering ceremony attended by no fewer than six bishops and two abbots.

In the meantime, showing minimal regard for his second wife who was still alive, his mistress Isotta had also applied to the pope for permission for another chapel. This would eventually house her own ornate tomb, proudly displaying the SI monogram first adopted by her later husband, topped with the Malatesta coat-of-arms and supported by the dynasty's symbolic elephants. As more chapels were then added, the sculptor Agostino di Duccio – a student of Donatello – continued to decorate the church's interior, filling it, among other things, with many bas reliefs. These depicted a variety of religious and humanist subjects, among them the prophets and sibyls in the Chapel of Our Lady of the Waters, the signs of the zodiac in the Chapel of the Planets, and the playful *putti* in the Chapel of Childish Games – the burial place for Sigismondo's first two wives and his infant children. Marble had now been brought from Sant'Appolinare in Classe near Ravenna and elsewhere to decorate the interior and encase the whole exterior. At the same time, Sigismondo's Florentine architect Leon Battista Alberti was thinking up further ways to create for his patron a structure that would rival some of the greatest buildings of the time. As shown in a medal produced in 1450, while Alberti's unfinished work had been meant clearly to reference Rimini's ancient Roman monuments, in particular the Arch of Emperor Augustus and the Bridge of Tiberius, it had also been designed to include an upper level and an impressive dome.

Declared in 1809 to be the city cathedral, it was only in that century that the church became known as the Tempio Malatestiano, a title which, besides apparently questioning Sigismondo's religious sincerity, ignores the building's essential purpose as set out in the Greek inscription twice displayed on the exterior wall. This praises the military achievements that had allowed the ruler to build at his own expense this 'temple', dedicated to 'Immortal God and to the City'. Although Pius II was to suggest that Sigismondo had been jealous of his half-brother – possibly even poisoning him – it would appear instead that he had been close to Galeotto Roberto and, rather than wishing to promote himself, had intended to link this building with his dead sibling. As the latter's reputation for sanctity and miracle-working had by this time become a cult among the local people, it would seem according to 20th-century research that Sigismondo, obeying his saintly brother's wishes to be buried outside, may have meant to place his tomb in a central position above the main door.[87]

Despite the ravages of the years and the appalling damage it suffered in the Second World War, this building survives, as does the crucifix by Giotto that was reputedly created during his visit to the city. Besides this, in what may have been a sort of antechamber to Sigismondo's chapel, the *Cella delle Reliquie*, still contains the famous painting dated 1451 by Piero della Francesca. Here, the artist depicts the lord of Rimini kneeling before his personal saint, while a roundel shows an image of his castle in the background.[88] Having frequently been portrayed as yet another example of Sigismondo's pride and self-promotion, some today give this work a different interpretation. This proposes that the fresco was designed to show Sigismondo as the virtuous ruler, a leader who through his generosity and other triumphs has brought glory to both God and his city. As such it would appear to be a humanist message, predating the inscriptions found on the outside of the building.

After the *condottiere*'s excommunication, work on the church would stop, and following his death the building was left unfinished. By that time, he had rebuilt his intentionally spectacular Rimini castle that had been designed by Alberti, probably with some input from Brunelleschi. Even though today only the central part of this building remains, like his other reconstructed fortresses in the surrounding countryside, it is a further testament to Sigismondo's cultural contribution. Some critics question the man's real artistic intent, drawing a negative comparison with his rival Federico da Montefeltro and suggesting that the lord of Rimini was more politically than culturally inspired in his patronage of the great masters. Yet, regardless of his true motives, like many of the Renaissance rulers of this violent and destructive period, he displayed a keen interest in the arts and humanist learning that contrasts starkly with many of his actions. In the same way, his brother Malatesto Novello was leaving his mark on his city, adding to the ancient Cesena Rocca and founding with the support of his wife Violante the Biblioteca Malatestiana that is now on UNESCO's Memory of the World list of places. Apart from its being designed once again by Alberti, and the doorway by Duccio, this building was to be exceptional for another reason. Containing more than 400,000 books, it would become one of the first libraries open to the public.

Even though both these brothers were making improvements to their towns, and the lord of Rimini was generally popular at home for his just rule, Sigismondo Malatesta had by now earned the distrust of others abroad. Having famously declared that he would fight for whosoever would pay him, he was despised for his tendency to switch sides – there being no doubt an element of hypocrisy in the judgement of his critics, who most probably were doing the same thing themselves. Sigismondo was also disliked for his violent temper and his apparently corrupt and devious behaviour. With it already being widely whispered by Federico da Montefeltro and others that he had murdered his first two wives, his reputation was then further demolished in 1450 by the Venetians charging him with the rape of a German noblewoman who was visiting their mainland territory. In his defence, evidence in all these cases is at best scarce, if not non-existent.

Alfonso of Naples had originally hired Sigismondo, but he, too, now had come to loathe him, believing the *condottiere* had betrayed him by changing to the Florentine side during the so-called Tuscan wars that had broken out after the duke of Milan's death. Filippo Maria Visconti had promised his Milanese possessions to the king of the Two Sicilies, but the latter's hopes had been dashed in 1448 when his siege at Piombino had failed. Believing Sigismondo chiefly responsible for this, Alfonso could not forgive him, so when in 1454 the northern Italian states finally came together at Lodi, he insisted on his exclusion from the peace talks. Although Alfonso died shortly after declaring war against him three years later, his son Ferrante then picked up the baton and continued the fight against the hated *condottiere*, who by this time was supporting his Angevin enemy.

Only ten years after Piombino, things became more serious for Sigismondo. Although recently he had been awarded the papal vicariates of Cervia, Rimini, Cesena, Fano, San Leo and various other places – these being the highest titles he was ever to receive – soon after the death of Calixtus III he would be confronted by the trenchant opposition of Pius II, who was to become his implacable enemy. Two years after his election, the new pope excommunicated him and ordered a symbolic burning of his effigy. Repeating the scandalous rumours against Sigismondo, Pius excoriated his personal behaviour and publicly condemned his soul to hell. At the same time he heaped doubt on his religious sincerity and accused him of non-Christian practices, resting his case on the mysterious symbols, astronomical figures, and humanist images that decorated the walls of the great church under construction in Rimini. Rather than being a true Christian temple, this was now declared a place designed for demonic worship.

Around this time Sigismondo received a letter of request from Mehmet II, asking him to send his resident artist Matteo De' Pasti to paint his portrait. This unfortunate man would never reach Constantinople, being stopped by the Venetians in Candia (Crete), where he was found to be carrying Sigismondo's gift for the sultan, an immensely valuable manuscript of military arms and tactics. Arrested and charged with spying, the artist would eventually be released and in 1462 he was able to return to Rimini, but as details of the story became known, Sigismondo's reputation for treachery was again reinforced. As it was now rumoured that among the gifts there had also been an important map of the Adriatic, the lord of Rimini was suspected of giving away secrets that were valuable to the enemy. These accusations were to gain further credence when it was reported that the *condottiere* had declared that if Ferrante should use the services of the Albanian Skanderbeg, he would personally respond by turning to the Ottomans for their assistance.[89] Already defeated by Federico da Montfeltro, opposed by the pope, and now threatened on all sides, in October Sigismondo turned his sights towards Venice. After battling up the Adriatic through a violent storm, he reached the city and offered his services to the doge and the senate. Even though these were concerned about the threat the 'Turks' were posing to their eastern possessions, they were still undecided as to whether or not they should go to war, and so they continued for the following three months to mull over the *condottiere*'s offer of service. By the time they were finally ready to give their approval, the pope had independently begun to plan his own crusade against the Muslims and he was therefore seeking co-operation from the various Italian states and other Christian rulers. Despite Pius being still deeply suspicious of the Serenissima, which he believed to be bent on achieving the 'domination of Italy', he had come to see that he needed the Venetian fleet to transport his army. Therefore he now sent his legate north to persuade the doge to join his campaign.[90]

For their part, the Venetians soon realised that they required the services of Sigismondo, apparently the only mercenary prepared to be involved in this affair. However, no agreement could be reached until the *condottiere* had concurred with the stringent demands of the pope. As well as a payment to the Church, the completion of a three-day fast, a promise to go on pilgrimage to Rome and Jerusalem, and various other similar stipulations, Sigismondo was ordered publicly to renounce his former 'heretical beliefs' and make his confession before a cardinal. After the people of his town had obediently shown their own penitence, on 2 December 1463 his acts of contrition earned him the right to be declared once more Lord of Rimini. Although his confrontation with Pius had now come to an end, to earn the pope's forgiveness he had been forced to give up most of his territory. Backed by Venice, he was able to retain Rimini and its surroundings, but even these small pickings had been left to him on the proviso that they would pass on his death to the pope. The earlier attempts in October by his legitimised son Roberto to hold on to Fano had failed, the town having been ceded to the leader of the papal army. And that was not all, as other Malatesta lands were also gradually being lost. Besides selling Cervia to the Venetians, Sigismondo's brother had agreed that on his death – which occurred just two years later – Cesena would be handed over to the Papal States.

With the Serenissima having officially committed itself to the crusade earlier in the year, and Sigismondo now deemed fit to serve the Republic, the following summer in 1464 the campaign got under way. However, before the Venetian fleet arrived in Ancona to join Pius, the elderly and already sickly pope had died of a fever. Unlike the unwilling doge Cristoforo Moro, he had remained determined to the last to play his part in the crusade, but his death had now brought the project to an end, and the relieved Moro was able to return home to Venice. Even so, acting as the Venetians' captain general, Sigismondo carried on the fight to defend the Serenissima's interests in the commercially profitable Morea (Peleponnese) region, and for some eighteen months he continued to lead the army against the forces of the sultan whom he had earlier befriended. Lacking the necessary military support and supplies, he had achieved only moderate success by the time his hungry and depleted force was finally given permission to return home in April 1466. Here he was recognised for his service against the 'infidel' and given the Golden Rose, but just a year later, fearing that he might be excluded from his own city, he apparently considered a plan to assassinate the new pope who had so recently rewarded him. This would never happen and, although Paul II continued to watch him closely, after the *condottiere* had paid homage and been appointed leader of the papal forces he remained in the pontiff's service until his death two years later at his castle in Rimini.

As had been the case with Emperor Frederick II, the lord of Rimini's reputation was largely demolished by the vitriolic attack of the reigning pope. He had been charged not just with heresy, but also with a variety of the most serious crimes; sodomy, sexual assault and even murder. His nemesis Pius II had seized on the unfounded accusation that he had killed his first two wives and had also claimed that he had caused the death of his older brother. Following the pontiff's demolition of his character, Sigismondo would then remain notorious for centuries to come, still today dubbed the Wolf of Rimini.

This was a particularly turbulent period of Italian history, when the popes frequently changed sides and wreaked their revenge with impunity, and any number of others were engaged in equally ruthless and cruel actions. This in no way excuses Sigismondo of those acts of brutality of which there is strong evidence. While undoubtedly a strong military leader, described by his secretary as 'warlike and ferocious', he was merciless to those who opposed him. In contrast, however, he also had a softer side, as was shown through his devotion to his third wife, his love of romantic poetry, and his patronage of some of the foremost artists of the age. Nevertheless, despite today's more nuanced interpretation of his character, the appalling reputation he gained under Pius II has lingered on down the centuries, the *condottiere* being further denigrated after he was adopted in the 20th century as a symbol of resistance by the fascists. Among these would be Ezra Pound, who first tapped into Sigismondo's story in the early 1920s when he was writing his *Malatesta Cantos*. It has been the misfortune of many famous historic figures – Voltaire among them – to be held as a model by those who wish to use them to help publicise their extremist views. Yet, even though Sigismondo, like others, cannot be held responsible for the actions of subsequent generations, because the blackshirts chose him as their hero, seeing him in Hickman's words as an example of 'fierce strength, artistry, ingenuity, passion, guts, and generosity of spirit', his name has been further destroyed.[91]

In the aftermath of his father's death, Roberto – previously disinherited after his failure to hold Fano – faced competition from his half-brother Salustio and also from his stepmother Isotta. She had the backing of the Venetians, who, because of their earlier alliance with Sigismondo, had gained a stronger presence in Rimini. As this threatened to jeopardise the open access to the Adriatic, others had become concerned, and therefore Roberto sought permission from his godfather, Pope Paul II, to march on the city. While earlier Isotta had requested him to help her defend Rimini from the papal army, Roberto's official purpose was now to secure the lands that had been promised to the Church on Sigismondo's death. Ultimately, however, after taking the town, he refused to give it up, and in this he would be helped by his former enemy, Federico da Montefeltro. Fearing that any papal or Venetian interference might further destabilise the region, Federico had changed sides and was now fighting to maintain Rimini's independence. Therefore, as captain of the League that had formed against the pope, in August 1469 he helped Roberto to defeat the papal army that was besieging the city.

Although Roberto then assumed power, before long this latest Malatesta proved himself to be no better than so many of his family. Murdering Salustio just a year after the victory, three months later in November he killed another half-brother, Valerio – acts that would give several people reason (again without proof) to believe the new lord of Rimini responsible for the later suspicious death of Isotta herself. Nonetheless, with Roberto successfully keeping the peace in his city, for which he was dubbed 'il Magnifico', the pragmatic Federico da Montefeltro continued to maintain contact with his neighbour, and the following April he went further, agreeing to the engagement of Roberto and his daughter Elisabetta. The couple's marriage would finally take place four years later, in June 1475.

Although until the last year of his life, Roberto managed on the whole to uphold good relations with his father-in-law, his obnoxious behaviour eventually earned him such bitter dislike among his nobles that by the time he died he was a hated figure. His equally appalling son, Pandolfo IV Malatesta, would lose the remnants of his people's support, and they finally broke out in revolt when he became involved in a case of rape. Yet, with the Venetians still wishing to use his military skills, he was able with their backing to hold on to his position until 1500, when the new pope's son, Cesare Borgia, arrived on the scene. Now excommunicated, Pandolfo IV sold the city, and, although he briefly regained it, in effect Rimini was lost to the family, eventually becoming fully included into the Papal States in 1528. Then twenty-five years later the Malatesta dynasty itself would be brought to its own humiliating end when Pandolfo's son died in poverty in Reggio Emilia.

* * *

Despite his daughter marrying into the Malatesta clan, Federico da Montefeltro, the most famous of the dynasty's rulers of Urbino, had been one of the main rivals of Roberto's father, Sigismondo. Federico's family had also risen to prominence in the 12th century, when his ancestor Count Montefeltrano I had been among those accompanying Emperor Henry VI on his march south to take possession of his wife's kingdom of Sicily. Already imperial fiefs, ten years after being officially recognised by Pope Honorius III, his two oldest sons,

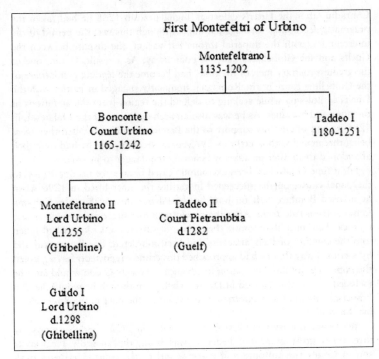

First Montefeltri of Urbino

Montefeltrano I
1135-1202

Bonconte I
Count Urbino
1165-1242

Taddeo I
1180-1251

Montefeltrano II
Lord Urbino
d.1255
(Ghibelline)

Taddeo II
Count Pietrarubbia
d.1282
(Guelf)

Guido I
Lord Urbino
d.1298
(Ghibelline)

Taddeo I and Bonconte I, were invested in 1226 with the County of Urbino. But as they were not accepted by the pro-Guelf people of their city, they then became residents in nearby Rimini, where Malatesta 'della Penna' had just been granted citizenship. Here they remained until finally in 1234 Bonconte was able to take up his role as the first Count of Urbino. But after Frederick II's catastrophic defeat at Parma in 1248, Bonconte's son, Taddeo II, finally abandoned the imperial cause and joined the Guelfs. While this brought him into favour with both the pope and Charles of Anjou, earning him the title of Count of Pietrarubbia, his defection caused a rift within the family. As a result, when the French were invited into the region by the pope in 1282, various relations were to find themselves pitted against each other in the battle that then took place outside the Ghibelline stronghold of Forlì. Consequently, while Taddeo was killed during the defeat, his nephew, Guido I, 'the Elder', emerged triumphant, fighting for the other side. By rounding unexpectedly on the enemy after slyly pretending to surrender the town, he had taken his Guelf opposition by surprise and achieved a major victory.

Guido I had been born in 1223 at the family castle twenty miles from Rimini in San Leo – the town previously known as Mons Feretus, later Monte Feltro, that had been the origin of the dynasty's name. Despite his initial support for Emperor Frederick II's last successor, the unfortunate

Conradin, after the latter's defeat at Tagliacozzo in 1268 he had taken the pragmatic decision to turn against him. Although this was the period of the interregnum, with the imperial throne left vacant, the dispute between the Guelfs and the Ghibellines had not gone away. As a result, Guido, one of the greatest military men of the time, had become the leading *condottiere* of the Ghibelline cause in the Romagna, frequently engaged in battles with the Guelfs of Bologna while seeking to defend the region from the ambitions of the pope and his allies. As he was also an arch opponent of the Malatesta, in 1295 he had offered his support to the Parcitadi of Rimini when they were being threatened with overthrow by 'Mastin Vecchio', and he had only then abandoned them after mistakenly believing the danger to be over.

For a time Guido had been excommunicated because of his opposition to the papal cause, but he succeeded in getting the edict lifted in 1296 when he advised Boniface VIII on how he should oust his rivals – the Colonna family – from Palestrina. After the *condottiere* had suggested a devious ruse to trick them into abandoning their place of safety, the Colonna had fallen into the clutches of their attackers and been murdered. For the cynical and hypocritical way that he had approached this crime – reportedly having asked the pope to grant him absolution in advance – the wily Guido would later be included among the damned in Dante's Hell. Even though he would die as a Franciscan monk, the *condottiere* was placed by the poet in the 8th circle of his 'Inferno'.[92]

Years later at Castello di Petroia near Gubbio in 1422, Guido's supposedly three-times great grandson, Federico was born, the allegedly illegitimate son of Count Guidantonio and a young girl of the court, Elisabetta degli Accomanducci. While Pope Pius II would later go so far as to pronounce the child a changeling, a replacement for the count's dead new-born infant, alternative contemporary accounts focused more on another suggestion. As he was still without an heir, Guidantonio wanted to ensure the succession, and so he had claimed to be the father of his grandson. According to this version of events, Federico was therefore the child of the count's natural daughter, Aura, and the *condottiere* Bernadino degli Ulbaldini who was in his employ. In fact, whatever the truth of the boy's parentage, there was a strong physical likeness between him and the only slightly younger Ottaviano, born to Aura and her husband Bernadino around a year later. These two boys grew up to be very close and would even call each other 'brother'.

To guarantee a truce between their neighbouring dynasties, in 1392 Count Guidantonio married his first wife Rengarda Malatesta, a great-granddaughter of 'Mastin Vecchio' and the aunt of Sigismondo Pandolfo. As she remained childless, however, soon after her death in 1423 her husband remarried, choosing as his new wife Caterina Colonna, the niece of the former bishop of Urbino, who by this time had been elected as Pope Martin V. Although he now legitimised the two-year-old Federico, an extra clause within the papal bull stipulated that this boy would no longer be the heir in the event of another male being born. Since Caterina had lost her first child, Federico was now brought to live at court, but everything was to change three years later when Caterina gave birth to a son. On his stepmother's urging, Federico was moved away to Mercatello sul Metauro, about thirty miles from Pesaro. Here he remained under the more affectionate care of Giovanna Alidosi, until 1433 when the peace signed in Ferrara brought an end to the latest conflict between Venice and Milan. To guarantee this truce, Guidantonio agreed that his putative son should be sent as a hostage to Venice, and here Federico would remain until an outbreak of plague made it necessary for him to move on to the Gonzaga court in Mantua. These experiences would greatly influence his development, this introduction to the rich culture of the two cities awakening his life-long interest in the arts and learning.

Just a year after marrying Giovanna Alidosi's daughter, Gentile, and being knighted by the Emperor, in 1438 the 16-year-old Federico was granted the *condotta* by his father. He then began his military career in the service of the duke of Milan who was now involved in the Lombardy Wars. This roughly thirty-year period of on and off fighting, chiefly between the Venetians and the Milanese, was complicated by the constantly shifting alliances between the neighbouring states and the changing loyalties of the various *condottieri* whom they employed. In line with this, after the defeat of the Visconti duke of Milan, in 1440 Sigismondo Malatesta switched sides and began to support the victorious *condottiere* Francesco Sforza – thus bringing to an end his previous alliance with Urbino and straining relations with his own brother in Cesena. Yet, because an engagement had been arranged between Malatesta Novello and the count of Montefeltro's five-year-old daughter, Violante, these two men still remained true to each other. As the fighting continued, several of the Montefeltro castles were lost, and Federico himself was wounded in battle, but in October 1441 the young *condottiere* succeeded against the odds in retaking the nearly impregnable San Leo fortress. Although, as was often the case, deception and trickery may well have played a part in his success, bolstered by this major achievement, Federico declared that within eight days he and his men would be at the doors of Rimini itself. With Sigismondo now realising that he needed to sue for peace, a truce was drawn up and the Montefeltro were able to recover their lost castles. The following June, relations between the two families were further strengthened by Malatesta Novello marrying at last his 12-year-old bride, although the child would not move to Cesena for another five years. But only eight months later the situation was to change dramatically again, as a result of the death in February of Giudantonio da Montefeltro in Urbino.

The count's second wife Caterina had done all she could to deprive her stepson of his rightful inheritance, which had already been reduced to just a few lands following the birth of her son. It was the younger boy who was now recognised as the new ruler, Oddantonio II, and three months after his father's death he went to Siena, where Pope Eugenius IV ceremoniously appointed him the first duke of Urbino. While some people have suggested the duke as being merely unmotivated, and maybe even naive, his critics portray him much more harshly, depicting him as a degenerate, cruel young man, whom the lord of Rimini had intentionally corrupted in order to unsettle the family's affairs. Although some now question this, for several decades Sigismondo Malatesta would be remembered for the devious role he had allegedly played throughout this time. Federico's court painter Giovanni Santi, for one, would describe how – with his eye on the Montefeltro territories – he had been forever 'like a falcon hovering in anticipation of its prey'.[93] Yet, while his detractors would allege that Sigismondo had attempted to persuade Federico's half-sisters to assassinate him, in the end it was Oddantonio himself who was murdered just a year after becoming duke. Without the valuable *condotta* that had been given to his brother, he had no means to cover the exorbitant expenses that he had incurred by his extravagance. As his only option had been to raise taxes, the people had become angry and eventually a group of nobles had burst into his bedroom and killed him and two of his equally unpopular companions – men thought by some to be Malatesta's agents. This horror was witnessed by his sisters, and it would leave Violante so appalled that she took the vow of chastity she was to keep for the rest of her life. While the duke's body was then reputedly dragged through the streets, the city rose in revolt and the mob broke into the palace and sacked it. At the time Federico was in Pesaro, helping another Malatesta, Galeazzo 'the Inept', whom he was defending from the ambitions of his cousin Sigismondo. Even so, it is not unlikely that he himself had been involved in this conspiracy, and this might partly explain why his relations with his half-sisters were always to remain strained. Nonetheless, he was welcomed back in Urbino where, on agreeing to the concessions demanded by the people, he became their new lord.

Aware of the mistakes of his predecessor and understanding that his position depended on the goodwill of his subjects, Federico immediately set out to win them over, and from this moment on he would present himself as the perfect Christian prince who was dedicated to their wellbeing. Although there would be plots against him during the next two years, over time he succeeded in becoming a much-loved leader. Besides being admired for the way he mixed freely among his people, he was also renowned for his humanity, and for the respectful and considerate way he treated his citizens, paying particular attention to his soldiers' needs. Faced with the dire financial situation he had inherited from Oddantonio, like his brother he would immediately be forced to sell some of the family territories, but he was then able to find a more long-term solution to his financial problems by continuing his highly remunerative career as a *condottiere*. Besides increasing his state coffers, this would also help him to defend the region from the territorial ambitions of his rivals. While Sigismondo Malatesta was his principal adversary, before long he was also being opposed by Eugenius IV, who had become gravely concerned about his continuing military successes. But just a year after excommunicating him in 1446, the pope died, and his successor, Nicholas V, soon absolved Federico, appointing him papal vicar and the official ruler of the Montefeltro territories.

Three years later, while he was taking part in a tournament – an event possibly connected to one of his several amorous affairs – Federico would be seriously wounded, losing his right eye. This accident would greatly affect him, and during a particularly low period in his life, when he was even considering suicide, he would express the impact the loss had had on him. After the death of his much-loved illegitimate son Bonconte in the plague of 1458, Federico wrote a letter to Francesco Sforza linking these two events: 'My Lord, I know that for my sins Our Lord God has taken an eye and now this, who was the light of my life.'[94] The risk of total blindness was something of which he had become all too aware, he having already been threatened with a complete loss of sight five years earlier while he was suffering from malaria. After the accident he would tend to hide his damaged face by choosing to be painted in profile, an unusual pose at the time for such portraits, but one that makes him easily identifiable.[95] But this was not his only highly recognisable feature. Fearing that his impairment would be a serious impediment in battle, he had sought to widen his field of vision by ordering the removal of the bridge of his nose.

During his long and profitable military career, like all the *condottieri*, Federico was in service to a wide variety of employers. Although at the start of his reign, he had helped Francesco Sforza gain control of Pesaro, after his injury he had been replaced by Sigismondo Malatesta, and so on his recovery he had moved on to fight for the Neapolitan kings, Alfonso, and then Ferrante. Although Pius II was now further complicating the situation, not just railing against Sigismondo, but sowing additional discord among the various rulers and their *condottieri*, Federico would lead the Neapolitan-papal army against the Angevins. After that he took on Sigismondo, who was attacking towns in the Marche, and by 1463 he had managed to capture many of the Malatesta possessions that were now added to his fast-expanding territories – by the end of his life, these would be three times their original size.

With Federico now increasingly playing a role in the affairs of others, he would help Galeazzo Sforza defend his claims when his father Francesco died in 1466. Then a year later, at Molinella near Bologna he led the Florentines and their allies against the Venetians and Ercole d'Este of Ferrara. Here, although the battle proved to be inconclusive, his own reputation was further enhanced by Machiavelli describing it somewhat inaccurately as an almost bloodless victory for Federico. Soon after this, because he had become concerned following Sigismondo's death about the increasing papal influence in the Romagna region, he was to help Roberto Malatesta capture and hold Rimini. Since this was a blatant act of disobedience against the pope, war was inevitable, but within months of his victory over the papal army at Mulazzano in August 1469, relations with the Holy See began to recover once more. Roberto was now recognised as ruler of Rimini, Frederico's own position would also begin to improve when Paul II died and Cardinal della Rovere was elected as Sixtus IV. Having been reappointed as his *gonfaloniere* three years later in 1474 the new pope finally invested Federico as the hereditary duke of Urbino.

While the duke had been much influenced during his childhood in Mantua by his tutor Vittorino da Feltre, two years before becoming ruler he had also been inspired by his meeting with San Bernadino, a saint in whose name the duke planned to build the church that was later used for his burial. Besides remaining true to much of his early instruction, both his humanist and devoutly religious thinking, Federico would during his 38-year reign encourage other great scholars and artists to his court. Previously a backwater, it would now become a leading Renaissance centre of learning and the arts. Here he attracted famous names such as Luca della Robbia, Paolo Uccello, Piero della Francesca, and Giovanni Santi – the father of the famous Raffael (Raphael). With Urbino an important stopping place on the route south to Rome, there was now a cultural exchange between it and other cities in both Italy and abroad. This would mean that over the greater part of Federico's near four-decade rule, Urbino enjoyed a golden age. Accordingly, during the later 1460s, the duke introduced a major rebuilding programme. As well as the reconstruction of the city walls following the designs of Leonardo da Vinci, he ordered the creation of an exorbitantly expensive but impressive and comparatively up-to-date palace, which from its dominating position on a hilltop still commands extensive views over the surrounding countryside. Created initially under the direction of Luciano Laurana of Dalmatia and finished by Giorgio Martini, today this is a UNESCO site. Besides its elegant, well-decorated rooms and large kitchens, the architect included a hydraulic system and even a thermal bath, rare luxuries at the time and much appreciated by Federico, who had an obsession with hygiene as a result of his narrow escape from a near fatal infection as a child. But, although this building was mostly finished by the end of the 1470s, after the duke's death his other expensive projects were halted because of a shortage of funds.

During his reign, Federico had become one of the richest rulers in Italy and having begun in 1464 to massively increase his library, before long it would be second in importance only to that of the Vatican. It, too, would eventually go to Rome, when around 25 years after the death of Urbino's last duke, Francesco Maria II della Rovere, it was transferred to the city in 1657 on the orders of Pope Alexander VII. During Federico's time the priceless collection had grown from around hundred to over nine hundred classical and medieval texts written in Latin, Greek, Hebrew, Arabic and Coptic. It included a tri-lingual psalter and an outstanding two-volume Bible – complete with illustrations produced by Lorenzo de' Medici's Florentine miniaturist – that cost the equivalent of an entire palace. The library contained newly copied manuscripts dealing in a variety of subjects from mathematics and astronomy to theology, poetry, philosophy and much else. Printing had rapidly become widespread following its invention some three decades earlier, but even though the first regional press would be set up in 1475 at Caglì, around twenty miles to the south of Urbino, Federico preferred the collection he kept for his personal use to be handwritten. This was housed in his magnificent small *studiolo*, where the marquetry covering the walls included remarkable intarsia images referencing his various cultural and military interests. Above, a sequence of paintings depicted wise or virtuous individuals of both the ancient and contemporary worlds, people that Federico particularly admired, among them the 'most virtuous of teachers', his tutor Vittorino da Feltre. Despite his being a military man absorbed by political and martial affairs, Federico had a genuine interest in cultural and spiritual matters, and it is these two sides of his personality that are reflected in the decorations of his *studiolo*.

His ever-loyal 'brother' Ottaviano Ubaldini was even more of an intellectual. Having also benefited from living in a sophisticated environment during his youth at the court of Filippo Maria Visconti of Milan, he had after his return to Urbino become Federico's right-hand man, taking responsibility for overseeing his numerous cultural projects. The two men shared many interests and responsibilities, and Ottaviano acted not only as friend and adviser but also as tutor to Federico's son, Guidobaldo. This boy had been born when his father was already fifty and, as he was still only ten when the duke died, Ottaviano would become both regent and father-figure. Although he was never ambitious to take power himself, according to Giovanni Santi, Federico had intended that, if the child were to die, Ottaviano should succeed in his place. Guidobaldo survived, however, and, on reaching his majority at sixteen, he would start to establish his own court.

Another person who had particularly influenced Federico had been his adored second wife Battista Sforza, daughter of Alessandro Sforza of Pesaro. He had married her four years after the death of Gentile in 1456, when he was thirty-seven and she just thirteen or fourteen. They appear together in the Uffizi's double portrait painted by Piero della Francesca, who on the invitation of Giovanni Santi had moved to Urbino where he would then produce his famous masterpiece, the *Flagellation of Christ*, now in the city's National Gallery. After losing her mother and spending her early years at the court of her uncle Francesco Sforza, Battista – another highly intelligent and well-educated young woman – had at the age of twelve become the senior female in her home town of Pesaro. Although her marriage to Federico proved to be very happy, tragically, possibly as a result of her numerous pregnancies, she died young, just five months after the birth of her only son Guidobaldo in 1472. As Federico would never fully get over the loss, he chose to remain a widower for the remaining ten years of his life.

Around the time of Battista's death her husband was visited by the Persian ambassador, who had come to Italy seeking an alliance against the Ottomans. Two years later, Sixtus IV further raised Federico's status by agreeing to the marriage of his own nephew Giovanni to the duke's daughter, Giovanna – a match that prepared the way for the later succession to the duchy of the della Rovere family. At the same time Federico received from Ferrante of Naples the Ermine Collar, and from Edward IV of England the Order of the Garter – insignia that he would soon proudly include in the wall decoration of the *studiolo*. Then the following year in June the wedding he had arranged for his daughter Elisabetta (Isabetta) to Roberto Malatesta took place in Rimini, an extravagant event put on to impress the numerous ambassadors from Italy's most senior courts. The ceremony began with a processional entrance through the ancient triumphal arch of Augustus and other similar structures that had been created especially for the occasion. There were besides numerous other Roman-style trappings, including scores of attendants dressed in togas. The elaborate and costly celebrations continued for eight days, the entertainments including jousts and even a mock battle in the main square.

However, by joining forces with Sixtus, Federico was soon to find himself opposing the Florentine rulers. He had been persuaded in return for the papal recognition of his dynasty's rights to support the pope in his ambitions for his own family, Sixtus being determined to ensure the eventual promotion of his nephew Girolamo Riario to the papacy. Therefore, from evidence discovered by Professor Simonetta around twenty years ago, today we know that Federico would now become actively involved in the planning of the Pazzi Plot to assassinate the Medici brothers during the Easter Mass. Although this murderous attack in 1478 would succeed in killing the younger Giuliano, there would be a strange irony in the way things eventually turned out. While Sixtus's ambitions for Riario were never to be achieved, Giuliano's son and his nephew would both eventually become popes. More significantly, as regards Federico, here we find evidence of his hard-headed, unemotional and even devious participation, something for which he, unlike his fellow conspirators, would never have to pay. His involvement forces us to reassess his reputation for humanity, and we have to acknowledge the presence of a different side to his personality. While the faults of his arch rival Sigismondo Malatesta may have been exaggerated, those of Federico appear to have been largely exonerated. When revisiting the opinions of their nearer contemporaries, it is clear that the condemnation by Pius II of the first of the two contrasts sharply with Machiavelli's later highly favourable representation of the second, the writer portraying Federico as epitomising the qualities of the good prince as set out in *Il Principe*. These things underline the difficulty we have today of reaching a fair judgement on past individuals or events.

Again illustrating the changing allegiances of the time, when Ferrara's Salt War with Venice broke out in 1482, Federico, as Ercole I's *condottiere*, took command of the combined army of Milanese, Neapolitan, and Florentine troops, while the Venetians had the support of the Genoese and also the pope – Sixtus wanting to secure his territories in the region and further promote the interests of his nephew Riario. Roberto Malatesta was now fighting against his father-in-law as the Venetian Captain General, and in August he would achieve a major victory against the Neapolitans. His good fortune was to be short-lived, however, because the next month during a period of particularly hot weather he was struck down by malaria. Yet, by then, a similar situation had arisen in Ferrara and Federico was already unwell by the time he heard the news of Roberto's recent victory. Being deeply concerned that his son-in-law might have ambitions to take Urbino itself, the duke immediately insisted on being taken home to his city, but as he became gravely ill during the journey, he was hurriedly returned to Ferrara, where he died shortly after. By a strange irony, his death on 10 September occurred within hours of that of Roberto in Rome.[96]

While on its way back to Urbino, Federico's coffin would rest for the night in the cathedral at Forlì, where despite his recent engagement against the papal forces the duke was shown the full respect that the people still felt to be his due. When at last the cortège reached Urbino, he was laid to rest in the old friary church of San Donato, where his putative 'father', the devout Guidantonio, had been buried in his Franciscan habit nearly forty years before. Here Federico's embalmed corpse was to remain until it could be moved into the nearby friary church of San Bernardino, the building recently constructed by his son as the dynasty's new place of rest. According to the current fashion for such burials, his coffin was suspended on the wall until 1620, when finally it would be to its new position. Here Federico would be left to lie undisturbed in the sepulchre beneath his new baroque tomb across the aisle from that of his son, both monuments surviving to this day, in spite of the alterations and extensive earthquake damage suffered by the church over the years. When the friary was closed on Napoleon's orders in 1810, its most valuable work of art, Piero della Francesca's painting of the Virgin and Child, was removed to the new Brera Gallery in Milan. While critics are still uncertain of the exact origins of this work, Cecil Clough considers that it was created roughly ten years later than many presume, believing it was commissioned after the death of the duke, but 'in association with the building of the Church of San Bernadino', of which it was 'an integral part'.[97] On the other hand, some still argue that it was most probably painted on Federico's own orders, sometime after the major events of 1472, namely his son Guidobaldo's birth and Battista's death. Alternatively, Marilyn Aronberg Lavin connects the painting to events two years later. Pointing to the symbolism that is evident within the picture, she feels we should read the clear message conveyed by the rigid stance of Federico kneeling in the foreground. Appearing unemotionally involved, and cut off from the other figures, he seems to be represented as the dedicated guard of the Christian Church that is symbolised by the enthroned Madonna and Child. According to this theory, the painting was created after the duke had at last overcome the cardinals' fierce opposition to his daughter's marriage to Sixtus's nephew, the work being produced at that time in order to try and reinforce Federico's reputation as the virtuous Christian ruler, ever ready to defend the faith. Whichever way we choose to interpret it, by the end of the 1480s Guidobaldo had chosen this painting to be the altarpiece of the recently completed church.

Described by the author Baldassare Castiglioni as 'the light of Italy', even while he was alive Federico had become recognised as a remarkable man, not only a renowned soldier and intellectual, but also a popular leader who had raised his duchy to prominence. Although he had inherited an impoverished state, through his work as a *condottiere* he had within a few years accumulated vast wealth that soon exceeded that of most other rulers. His highly successful military career had given him the necessary funds to raise Urbino's status and make it one of the most magnificent artistic centres in Italy. Besides his extraordinary collection of works of art, priceless books and other manuscripts, he was responsible for creating palaces, forts and various costly buildings across his lands. Among those of particular note was his summer palace in Gubbio that was to house his second *studiolo*, created shortly after the one in Urbino.[98] After Federico's death, for a while his cultural heritage lived on, Urbino's most famous artist Raffael being born just a year after his death in the house that still displays his early work of the Madonna and Child.

Some of Federico's extravagant projects were too expensive to continue, and among these would be the main city cathedral, which would not be completed until 1604. While his son Guidobaldo would fight for the popes Alexander VI and Julius II and be hired by the Venetians, he was a delicate man and not strong enough to embark fully on the impressively well-paid career of his father. Nevertheless, he and his highly intelligent and well-educated wife, Elisabetta Gonzaga, continued to promote the cultural growth of the city, among other things founding Urbino's university in 1506. Their sophisticated court would become the template for Castiglioni's work describing the ideal courtier, *Il Cortegiano*.

In 1502, unable to defend himself, Guidobaldo briefly lost his state to Cesare Borgia, and although he then recovered it after Pope Alexander's death, six years later he would die aged just thirty-six. Because he and his wife had produced no heir, the city then passed to the family relation they had previously adopted as their son, Francesco Maria della Rovere, the nephew of Pope Julius II. Although the court was moved to Pesaro in 1523, Urbino remained in the hands of the della Rovere family for more than a century, only being fully incorporated into the Papal States in 1631. Nearly 70 years later Clement XI, who had been born in Urbino, was elected pope but, during the following century the city would repeatedly be hit by earthquakes, those of 1741 and 1789 causing particularly serious damage, the latter bringing about the collapse of the cathedral's dome. Although rebuilding work was soon begun, by that time Urbino had become largely forgotten. Yet, while with the end of its Montefeltro dynasty the city had lost its importance and faded from public view, ultimately this neglect would be to its advantage. By remaining largely unchanged until the Risorgimento in 1860, it had retained its Renaissance character comparatively unaltered, and, as a consequence, Urbino is still able to offer us a more complete insight than is usual into the court and city life of six hundred years ago.

SECTION V
THE SFORZA WOMEN

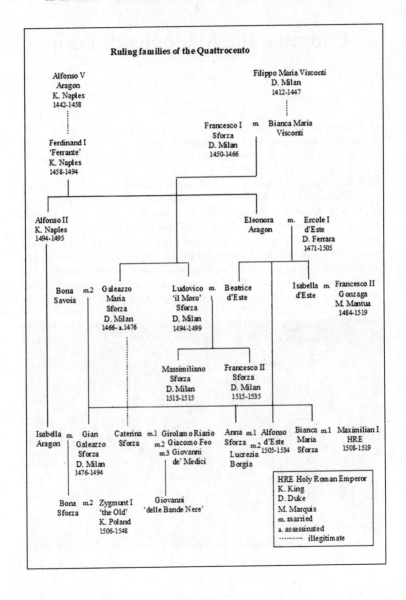

9

Caterina, the Madonna di Forlì

'To promote a woman to bear rule, superiority, dominion, or empire above
any realm, nation, or city, is repugnant to nature.'

John Knox[99]

After Duke Filippo Maria Visconti had died without an heir in 1447, fighting
had broken out among the Milanese, who had burnt his castle and proclaimed
the Golden Ambrosian Republic. This had brought to an end the Visconti
dreams of dividing Italy up with the Aragonese king Alfonso, who had only
recently seized the Neapolitan throne from René, the last of the Angevins. Six
years earlier, Francesco Sforza had risen from his long-held position as the duke's
condottiere to become his son-in-law, but having even more ambitious ideas and
being already the papal vicar of the Marches of Ancona, two years after leading
the Milanese to victory against the Venetians at the Battle of Caravaggio, in

Caterina Sforza (centre right) in the Sistine Chapel fresco by Botticelli.

1450 he had finally succeeded in taking power. Although not recognised by the Holy Roman Emperor, he had now become the first Sforza duke of Milan. Ten years after his death, his son and successor, the brutal Galeazzo Maria – a man renowned for his extravagance, debauchery, and acts of particularly unspeakable savagery – would be murdered in church on 26 December 1476. The perpetrators were soon rounded up, publicly tortured and then executed, but the assassination had left the duchy in the hands of the seven-year-old Gian Galeazzo, and his mother – the regent – Bona of Savoy. While she had soon taken control and restored calm by removing the hated taxes imposed by her dead husband, she would, nonetheless, continue to face serious opposition from his relations. Among these in particular was her brother-in-law, Ludovico, the duke of Bari, famously known as 'Il Moro', possibly because of his dark colouring. While the reasons for this moniker are still the subject of debate, he repeatedly used it himself and, as it was a period when much importance was placed on symbolism, he incorporated this figure into his heraldry.[100] At first Bona tried to keep her ambitious relation at arm's length, even exiling him and his brothers after an attempted coup against her, but eventually, having returned with military backing in September 1479, Ludovico took the reins of government and assumed total power over the duchy. After that, by spreading scandalous rumour, he succeeded in bringing about Bona's fall, ousting her from Milan, confining her at the nearby Castel Abbiategrasso and executing her former adviser. At last, ten years later, when attending her son's marriage, Bona managed to escape to France, and eventually, after Ludovico's own fall, she was able to return to Savoy to die at Fossano in 1503.

Previously, along with her mother-in-law, Bona had cared well not just for her own children but also for her husband's illegitimate offspring, whom she had adopted and treated with equal kindness. Thus a strong and loving bond had been formed, this being particularly apparent in the later letters of the young Caterina, who had been born sometime between 1462-63 to Galeazzo Maria's mistress, Lucrezia Landriani. In addition to her affectionate relationship with Bona and her continuing closeness with her natural mother, this child had also had a deep attachment to her father. She had spent hours in his company and had frequently joined him on his hunts. Besides becoming a very good rider, Caterina had thus been introduced to the more male-dominated pursuits, learning about the bearing of arms and the rudiments of military leadership. At the same time, while being exposed to the sophisticated culture of the sumptuous Milanese court, she had thanks to her stepmother received a good general education and learnt the necessary social skills. Before long, all these experiences would prove valuable, serving her well in the new life that she was soon destined to begin.

Even before her father's death plans had been made for her marriage, and when she was about ten, her engagement had been arranged with Girolamo Riario, one of the six nephews promoted to high office by their uncle, the della Rovere pope, Sixtus IV. Although a man of simple origins, and – according to Macchiavelli – unrefined or 'base' manners, Riario had by this time risen in status, having already been appointed the Captain General of the papal armies, the Count of Bosco, and the papal vicar of Forlì. He was now to receive from the pontiff the title of Count of Imola, the town that Caterina's father had sold for an exorbitant sum to the papacy as part of the marriage agreement. Evidence suggests, however, that in order to cement this contract, Galeazzo Maria accepted yet another of the bridegroom's terms. With no concern for his daughter's exceptionally young age, following the couple's low-key and very private marriage in January 1473, the duke had apparently allowed their union to be immediately consummated. On hearing of this the pope expressed his disapproval, but Galeazzo Maria was said to be delighted that before the groom's subsequent departure that he had 'slept with his wife another time'.[101] Having soon left Milan and his young bride, for the following years Riario would remain in Rome, it being decided that the couple's public religious wedding should be postponed until the child reached the official marriageable age of fourteen. However, just three years later, things were given a greater urgency by the murder of Caterina's father. In the aftermath of her husband's assassination, Bona wanted to secure her stepdaughter's position, and so, as the bridegroom was still absent, she quickly arranged that another marriage by proxy should take place in Milan.

Now at last the time had come for Caterina to set out and join her husband in Rome. During her long fifty-day progress, accompanied by her large retinue, she was received in style at the towns along the way, welcomed above all at Imola. Here all the people turned out to greet the young wife of their still-absent lord, their reception causing Caterina to write to her sister, 'It seemed that even the very stones were delighted by my arrival.'[102] For a time she waited in Imola to be joined by Riario, but as he was further delayed by the discovery of an assassination plot against him, his young bride eventually decided to continue on alone, finally reaching Rome in late May 1477. After a night's rest, she made her triumphal entry into the city, her arrival made all the more splendid by the six thousand horsemen sent to accompany her. She then took part in her third marriage ceremony before the pope at the Vatican, the spectacular occasion followed by a sumptuous wedding feast at her new home in the Campo de' Fiori. Having been immediately welcomed into the highest social circles, she quickly came to love Rome, where she took a keen interest in the major restoration work and re-embellishment that Sixtus IV had now begun. Her intelligence and sophistication impressed the people and her beauty was greatly admired by many, among them Botticelli. Besides including her – while she was pregnant with her third child – in his fresco decorating the new Sistine Chapel, the painter would most probably again use her image for one of the three graces in his famous *Primavera*. The elderly pontiff, too, enjoyed her company, doing so such a degree that before long scurrilous gossips would suggest – without any real evidence – that an even closer relationship had formed between them.

However, the next year, Girolamo Riario, jealous of the powerful Florentine ruling family, became embroiled in the Pazzi Plot to kill the two Medici brothers as the Mass was being celebrated in the great cathedral. Even though Lorenzo il Magnifico was to survive this shocking attack, the same was not true

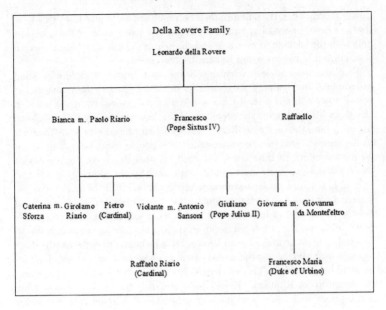

of Riario's reputation, which was seriously damaged following the discovery of his involvement. As he was already so greatly disliked, his cousin Cardinal Giuliano della Rovere, later Pope Julius II, had quite possibly supported the earlier attempt on his life. But even though that same Giuliano had opposed the Pazzi conspiracy, the whole family was now disgraced, especially after evidence appeared indicating that Sixtus himself had been privy to the affair in advance. Even though under torture one of the conspirators later claimed that the pope had been against the actual murder of any individual, this same testimony would imply that the pontiff had been fully aware of the plot.

In what was already a period of deep unrest, annexations and seizures, 1480 would become an especially traumatic year for the pope. As Italy's various rulers were chiefly concerned with their personal ambitions, they failed to present a united front against the on-going Ottoman challenge, so while they were still arguing, in mid-summer the Muslims mounted their first siege of Rhodes. Then, even closer to home, in August they succeeded in invading Puglia, capturing and sacking Otranto and threatening the surrounding area. Their successes would, however, strike such terror into the hearts of people throughout the length of the Italian peninsula that finally at the end of the year Florence agreed to make peace with the pope. And, with the earlier death in February of Forlì's ruler, Pino Ordelaffi, things had now also improved personally for Riario. After the viciously brutal and much hated Ordelaffi had died – possibly having been poisoned by his third wife before being murdered by the mob on his sickbed – his widow had sought shelter for herself and her young son in the Ravaldino fortress. Yet, with the boy dying of unspecified causes shortly after, the situation had become even more unstable. This gave Riario a new opportunity, and being already the papal vicar of Forlì, he was able with the backing of his uncle and the help of Federico da Montefeltro to seize control of the town and become its new count.

To please the Forlivesi, Girolamo Riario soon began an intense building programme, but wanting to remain in Rome he handed the management of the town's affairs over to his wife's uncle, Il Moro, who was now in charge in Milan. But, as the members of the Ordelaffi family still sought to overturn him, the next year Riario made his first official visit with Caterina to the region. Here they were greeted by the people, who were duly struck by the splendour of their court. Amazed by what they saw, the citizens of this modest town were particularly impressed by the glowing jewels and rich fabrics worn by their beautiful young countess. Over the weeks to come Caterina continued to be seen in public but Riario appeared little, remaining mostly out of sight at Imola, where he felt more secure. Jealous of his wife's powerful family, he prevented her from visiting her relations in Milan, but in September he would take her to Venice. Here he hoped to persuade the doge to unite with him against the city of Ferrara, whose duke was preventing him from adding Faenza to his own territories. Having failed in this scheme, on his return to the Romagna, Riario discovered that the Medici were backing a conspiracy to kill him and his wife – Lorenzo il Magnifico having never forgiven him for his part in the earlier Pazzi Plot. Although the guilty were rounded up and executed, the mood in the region had now changed, and among his own people the count's popularity was largely gone.

Girolamo Riario and Caterina returned at the end of the year to Rome, and having been called on to defend the city, he was soon caught up in the continuing bitter rivalry dividing the two great Roman dynasties, the Orsini and the Colonna. Having sided with the former, he would take his bloody revenge on their opponents, wounding and killing members of the Colonna family, destroying their houses and ultimately capping his cruelty by imprisoning, torturing and executing their leader. And, as elsewhere in Italy the political situation remained equally tense, Venice would soon be at war with its neighbour over the essential commodity of salt. Although Alfonso II of Naples sent his army north to help Ferrara, he was soon drawn into a dispute with the pope over right of passage through the papal territories, and so Riario would find himself fighting the Neapolitan army at Campomorto. Here his lack of courage became evident, contrasting vividly with the bravery of his contemporary, Roberto Malatesta, and thus further damaging his reputation. By this time he was unpopular on many fronts: hated by the Romans, out of favour with Sixtus, and disliked by the Manfredi of Faenza and the d'Este of Ferrara. Distrusted by his various neighbours, he was particularly despised by Caterina's uncle Il Moro, who, holding him responsible for the political turmoil that was raging in Italy, openly condemned him for the way he had now ruined the lives of the people he had 'thrown to the wolves'.[103]

The earlier good fortune of the Riario-della Rovere clan ended in August 1484 with the death of Sixtus IV, who had been fading for some time. During the following days of uncertainty, the people's pent-up feelings against this family erupted. While Girolamo Riario remained outside Rome, avoiding the wrath of the Colonna family, Caterina, now seven months pregnant with her fourth child, hurriedly left their country base and rode back to the capital. On coming under attack from the mob, who were intent on sacking her home, she fled for shelter to Castel Sant'Angelo, the massive fortress that had earlier been given to her husband by his uncle. Occupying this in his name and using the soldiers that she – like other great families of the time – kept as her personal guards, she proceeded to mount a stoical defence. Proudly asserting her strength as a descendant of the courageous Sforzas, she held out for twelve days, periodically threatening to fire on the cardinals should they chose to elect a new pope of whom she disapproved. But towards the end of August, on hearing that her husband had submitted to their demands, Caterina conceded that the time had come for all the family to leave Rome. In return for their surrender, besides the promise of financial compensation – which was never forthcoming – Girolamo now received a new military appointment and the official recognition of his hereditary rights in the Romagna.

Having received a less heartfelt welcome when they eventually arrived back in their lands, the couple chose to move into their relatively modest palace in the centre of the more prosperous Forlì. Initially, in an effort to increase his popularity, Girolamo Riario had opted not to raise taxes on the people, but with the loss of Sixtus' financial backing, he found himself unable to meet his expenses and so reversed his earlier policy. This, together with his other harsh measures, increased the ill-feeling that was already mounting against him. Besides an insurrection in the formerly more peaceable Imola, he faced new attempts on his life, which added to the fears that were now beginning to plague him. Although three years after their arrival in the Romagna, in April 1487 Caterina was finally given permission to visit her family in Milan, the next month she had to hurry home on hearing that her husband had become seriously ill. After his eventual recovery, Riario would prolong his convalescence in Imola and continue to leave the running of his affairs to his young wife.

Soon, on her becoming aware of the dangers the family was facing from the troublesome and disobedient castellan of Forlì's Rocca Ravaldino, she was to show her steely side. Having used deception to get this man removed – he then being murdered – she replaced him with her loyal supporter Tommaso Feo. She had now regained control, but although Riario still wanted to leave matters in his wife's hands, because he was no longer feeling secure at Imola, he re-joined her at Forlì. It was here, however, that in April the following year things really came to a head when a group of nobles, angered by the count's actions, hatched a new plot to get rid of him. After they had entered his rooms in the palace, killed several of his supporters, and stabbed Riario repeatedly, they threw his naked body from the balcony onto the square below. By that time crowds had already collected outside, and on becoming aware of the count's death they burst into the palace and began to ransack the place. Meanwhile, Riaro's mutilated corpse remained on the ground to be kicked, spat upon, and subjected to even worse acts of disrespect. Although eventually it was taken to the town's cathedral, here it was barred entry, so the problem of what to do with it then fell to the Franciscans. After they had agreed to accept it, the count's body remained with the brothers until calm was finally restored and the young widow was at last able to find a more fitting place of rest for her husband in the cathedral of Imola.

While this butchery had been going on, Caterina, along with her six children, her sister, and her natural mother, had been sheltering in another part of the palace until, on being taken captive, they were eventually moved into the home of the rebel Orsi family. But the turmoil continued, and so the papal representative of nearby Cesena, Bishop Savelli, was finally invited to come to Forlì and help settle the chaos. As he realised that peace could not be ensured until all the city strongholds had been captured, Caterina was taken to the impregnable and recently strengthened Ravaldino fortress, where it was hoped that she would be able to persuade her castellan to surrender. The plan failed, however, when her apparent appeal to Feo seemed to go unheeded. In reality, the truth was quite the reverse as the castellan, understanding her true motives, was only obeying her earlier orders to stand firm. On Caterina's guards eventually becoming aware of the apparent charade the two were playing, their ploy was abandoned and she was moved with her family into the more secure Porta San Pietro.

The next day there was a re-run of these events, and it was now that an episode occurred for which Caterina would become famous. This time, following her latest secret instructions, Feo offered to surrender the fortress on condition that he could meet Caterina alone for three hours. Theoretically, this would give her enough time to sign the necessary documents clearing his name and exonerating him from failing in his duties. At last, on the understanding that she would leave her children behind as hostages, her captors, confident that she would return, agreed to the terms. But when Caterina, accompanied by just one servant, entered the *rocca* – according to some contemporary reports – she turned at the last minute and having made an obscene gesture towards her enemies, she then had the gates barred. She now refused to come back out, her plan being to delay the action as long as possible so as to allow more time for the hoped-for arrival of support from her uncle in Milan. As soon as her enemies realised that they had been tricked, they tried a new tactic and brought to the walls of the fortress her mother, sister, and two oldest sons, Ottaviano and his younger brother. Caterina was now told that if she did not surrender, the terrified children would be killed. She remained defiant, however, and, refusing to give in to her attackers' demands, she stood proudly on the battlements and scorned their intimidation. Announcing that she was again pregnant, she declared to her enemies that she was still well able to produce more children.

A more scurrilous version of these events was reported by her critic Galeotto Manfredi, an account that was then taken up by Machiavelli in his own later retelling of the story. These men, going further than most, indicated that Caterina had lifted her skirts in order to show she was still able to give birth. While the early documents by other contemporary writers generally concur that she did indeed pronounce herself ready to sacrifice her children, not until two decades after the episode would Machiavelli set out the more salacious details that were to give life to the lasting popular version of events. Comparing this particular account with that appearing in the writer's earlier works, it seems that he had later adjusted the story, either introducing or emphasising the vulgar element reported by Caterina's rival Manfredi.

Machiavelli's apparent antipathy for the countess could no doubt be partly explained by the sense of rebuttal he had felt during his visit to her court as a Florentine representative in 1499. Yet, because he talks of the 'Madonna di Furlì' [*sic.*] more than he does of any other woman, even referring to the respect her valour deserved, it appears that he had a certain admiration for her. He displays an ambivalence, one possibly increasingly felt by men in this period when the appearance of strong and intelligent females was beginning to bring into question the previous social stereotypes of a male-dominated world. Frequent mention appears in contemporary documents of certain Italian women's strength and intelligence, these less prejudiced accounts comparing the females' admirable personal qualities to those of some of their weaker male counterparts. To the displeasure of the Marquis of Mantua, his wife, Isabella d'Este, who in his absence often acted as his regent, was seen by many as a more effective leader. She was an admirer of Caterina, and when the country was under threat of foreign invasion she had remarked that although the French criticised 'the cowardliness of our men', they should remember to 'praise the daring and valor (sic) of the Italian women'.[104] While this apparent tension might partially explain Machiavelli's representation of Caterina as a crude woman lacking any maternal instinct, it ignores the fact that his account demolishes – whether intentionally or not – the fundamental message that she was in fact wishing to transmit. By referring to her ability to procreate, Caterina purposely represented her femininity not as a handicap, but as an advantage over the men who wished to crush her. By claiming to be both pregnant and unconcerned for the welfare of her living children, she could undermine her enemies' main objective, namely their desire to destroy the dynasty by wiping out its heirs. Once her captive children ceased to be bargaining chips, not only was her position strengthened, but also their own lives were made more secure. Accordingly, her brave stance, along with the threat of her uncle's intervention, ensured the hostages' eventual release and the ultimate collapse of the uprising.

During the last days of the siege, support for the Orsi had begun to slip away, some of the townspeople even choosing to take shelter in the fortress alongside Caterina. At last, on 29 April help arrived in the shape of the Milanese army and a small contingent led by Caterina's nephew, Cardinal Raffaele Riario. When the dangers were past, she persuaded the unenthusiastic Milanese leaders to retreat without allowing their men to claim their rights to the victor's plunder. This delighted the relieved people, but even though there had been little love between her and her husband, she then rounded up those she believed responsible for his murder. She executed any who were found guilty of the crime, stripped the assets of their families, and destroyed their houses. Yet once these had been punished, the situation returned to normal and having again asserted her control for the next twelve years Caterina would act as regent for her young son Ottaviano. During this time, fully aware of how the recent improvements at the Rocca Ravaldino had helped her during the assault by her enemies, she carried out various building works. Besides strengthening her fortresses and other defences in Forlì, Imola and elsewhere, she put these strongholds into the hands of her Landriani relations. She then further increased the protection of her family by creating barracks where she could install new mercenaries, soon taking a personal role in the training of the soldiers.

In 1492, following Innocent VIII's death in July, Ottaviano's godfather, the immensely rich Spanish cardinal Rodrigo Borgia, successfully bribed his way to power and was chosen as the new pope, Alexander VI. Although a corrupt and immoral man who used his charm and wealth to pursue a degenerate way of life that had greatly shocked the earlier Pius II and others, he proved himself a highly capable and hardworking administrator. Apart from the fact that this man had been a friend of the Riario family, with another of Caterina's uncles, Ascanio Sforza, now a cardinal, it might have appeared to the countess that she could begin to expect her fortunes to improve. She would soon be disillusioned.

Lorenzo il Magnifico had helped maintain the peace, but after he died in his villa near Florence in April 1492, relations began to break down between Milan and the kingdom of Naples. The situation then further deteriorated when two years later King Ferrante's successor, Alfonso II, came to the throne. Despite this man having been married to Il Moro's sister, his attack on the duchy seemed to be imminent. Although Caterina's half-brother Gian Galeazzo had technically come of age, by this time he had lost all authority in Milan to his powerful uncle Ludovico, and so it was the latter who now appealed to the new French king for help against the Neapolitans. Using Il Moro's invitation as an excuse to reassert his Angevin claims to the Naples crown, Charles VIII marched into Italy. Although Caterina had originally tried to remain neutral and distance herself from the political disputes dividing the country, she now decided to support the Florentine-Neapolitan-papal alliance that opposed the foreign invader. Before long, her hand would be forced again. The expected support from the Neapolitan king did not appear, and so, although she had reinforced her various defences, she was unable to resist the full French onslaught. After Charles' army had destroyed her castle at Mordano, killing all the defenders and raping or abducting the women, Imola and Forlì grew fearful of suffering similar treatment. Therefore, Caterina decided the time had come to agree new terms and allow the French a free path across her territories. As it happened, Charles had by this stage chosen to take an alternative route south, going instead via Tuscany, where the terrified people of Florence decided the time had come to banish their ineffectual ruler, Lorenzo il Magnifico's son, Piero Medici. Having then defeated the Neapolitans, in early 1495 Charles forced the abdication of Alfonso and crowned himself king in Naples. Not content with this, however, he next set his sights on Milan, where, following his nephew's recent death,

Il Moro had become the new duke. Regretting his former alliance, by now Il Moro had joined the new league of northern states, which the next July would finally succeed in driving Charles from the county.

Shortly after Riario's death there had been rumours that Caterina was being courted by Antonio Maria Ordelaffi, one of Riario's former enemies, who had repeatedly tried to overthrow him in order to reclaim his own family rights to Forlì. But although – to the concern of her family and other neighbouring rulers – she had entertained Antonio Maria during the summer months, Caterina had other ideas. Having now taken a lover, Giacomo Feo, the younger brother of Tommaso, she was spending most of her time with him out of sight within the Rocca Ravaldino. Here he had become the castellan, replacing his faithful older sibling, who, despite his earlier good service, had been declared untrustworthy and removed from his post on a charge of indecency. Passionate about her new favourite and overjoyed when he received a knighthood from the Milanese, in 1489 Caterina would celebrate the birth of her seventh child. This was born shortly after the couple had probably had a secret wedding, the marriage being only finally acknowledged by the countess in her will. Before long, however, her new husband had become authoritative, openly asserting his control and showing disrespect towards his wife and her children. After he was seen to slap Ottaviano in public, people began to fear that he intended to take the place of the young count, who had now come of age. Plots against Giacomo and Caterina had already been foiled and most of the perpetrators arrested when in August 1495 Feo was killed, stabbed while he and the family were riding back to the city after a day spent in the countryside. As her husband collapsed dead on the ground, Caterina jumped onto a horse and fled back to the Rocca Ravaldino. Appalled by what she had just seen, her vengeance would know no bounds. Losing all self-control and mad with grief, she punished any she believed implicated in Giacomo's death. Both young and old were subjected to her cruel forms of revenge and, with individuals being thrown down wells, dragged behind horses, burnt, beaten and much else besides, her retribution was now to be far more savage than that following the death of her first husband. Although the people had earlier assumed that Caterina had ordered the assassination to protect her child's rights, before long, to their further shock, there were claims that her own son had played a part in the murder. While to avoid her wrath Ottaviano had first taken refuge with his brother elsewhere in the town, now it was alleged that he had admitted under torture to having been embroiled in the plot. These events and in particular her own almost crazed behaviour would destroy the last remnants of her subjects' good will.

Two years later in September 1497 she secretly married again. Her new husband, from a junior branch of the Medici family, was Giovanni – dubbed 'il Popolano'. Three years earlier, after falling out with his cousins he had been briefly banned from Florence, unable to return until the overthrow of the ruler Piero. Being now truly happy with someone who fully shared her interests, the following April Caterina gave birth to one more child. Initially called Ludovico, he would take his father's name, becoming famous as 'Giovanni dalle Bande Nere', the ancestor of the later Medici grand dukes of Tuscany. Apart from the fact that her earlier financial concerns had been eased by the sale of grain to Florence, this was generally a more secure period for Caterina, but her happiness was to be brief. Three years later, Giovanni died and once more she was a widow.

Now, still overcome by her grief, she had to defend her lands from the Venetians. Worse still, although Pope Alexander VI had earlier suggested the marriage of his illegitimate daughter Lucrezia Borgia to Ottaviano – a proposal that Caterina had turned down – in 1499 his son Cesare had invaded the Romagna. A ruthless man, who had been born to the favourite mistress of his father when he was a cardinal, he and his three siblings had now been openly acknowledged by the pope as his children. On Alexander's election in 1492, the 18-year-old Cesare had been appointed a cardinal, but six years later he had renounced this position following his brother's assassination. Having very possibly been implicated in this crime, after taking over his role as commander of the papal forces Cesare had begun to concentrate fully on his own military career. Besides now carving out important new territory for himself, by offering his service to the new French king, Louis XII, he was to earn the title of Duke of Valence.

When a year after these events, Louis' threatened invasion of Italy finally became a reality, Caterina's earlier protector, Duke Ludovico, fled Milan to seek the protection of her brother-in-law, the Emperor Maximilian I. Despite his eventually returning in February 1500, Il Moro would soon be captured and removed to France, where eight years later he was to die in a dungeon at Loches. For Caterina, her uncle's misfortunes were particularly serious as they left her facing her opposition all alone, having already come under attack two months before his first flight from Milan. While she was acting as regent for her son, who was away on military service with the Florentines, Cesare Borgia (with French backing) began his assault on her towns and various strongholds. After capturing the nearby fortresses at Brisighella, Imola and elsewhere, at the very end of December 1499 he turned his attention to Forlì. Aware that the Forlivesi wanted to avoid further trouble, Caterina decided to leave them free to choose their own fate. Although she now retreated with her followers to the Rocca Ravaldino, because the townspeople were soon to open the gates to Borgia's vast army, before long the fortress was under siege. While the neighbouring states stood back and did nothing, she continued to hold out, waiting in vain for outside help to arrive. As they struggled on under the enemy's heavy fire, Caterina and her supporters would try frantically each night to repair the latest damage done to their defences. Even when the old building began finally to crumble beneath the bombardment of the more modern cannons that Borgia had by this time brought into action, the countess remained determined to make a last desperate stand. Dressed in her breastplate and wielding her sword, she personally joined in the hand-to-hand fighting, declaring: 'If I have to perish, even if I am a woman, I want to perish like a man.'[105]

When on 12 January 1500, after more than three weeks under siege, she was betrayed by some of her fellow defenders, her enemies at last gained access to the *rocca* and Caterina was taken by the French. Feeling duty bound to respect their chivalric laws regarding women prisoners, these would promise to treat her better, but as they were soon forced to hand her over to their commander, Caterina's situation changed for the worse. Angered by the way the countess had humiliated him, Borgia now took his revenge. While accounts vary as to what happened next, some suggesting the reputedly promiscuous prisoner had willingly given herself to her captor, others claim that over the following days Cesare Borgia would repeatedly rape her. While he was absent trying unsuccessfully to take Pesaro from her second cousin Giovanni Sforza, she briefly had a chance of freedom, but before long her captor returned and twelve days after the fall of the *rocca*, she was forced to leave her town and return with him to Rome. Here for a while she was imprisoned in the new Belvedere palace that Innocent VIII had created in the grounds of the Vatican, but after an unsuccessful attempt to escape, she was then moved for greater security to the harsher conditions of Castel Sant'Angelo. This, the very fortress that she had once defended in the name of her family, had now been reinforced by the Borgias, who were its new owners. Although they had renovated the upper rooms with the latest luxuries, the cells remained dank and spartan, and it was here that Caterina was incarcerated. While there was no evidence supporting the rumour, Cesare Borgia sought to excuse her ill-treatment by spreading the story that she had recently attempted to assassinate Alexander VI by sending him a message purposely infected with the plague, an allegation that was then repeated by Machiavelli.

Although eventually released when the French arrived in Rome in 1501, by that time the countess's health had been seriously weakened and having been forced by Alexander VI to hand back her former fiefs, she chose to move to Florence, the city of her much-loved third husband. Here she was reunited with their one child, her adored youngest son, but the boy's Florentine relations were now challenging the claims he had rightfully inherited from his father. She was also being hounded by her uncaring older sons, Ottaviano and Cesare Riario, who were both mainly concerned for their own promotion within the Church.

Two years later, however, the scene changed again. Pope Alexander VI died in August 1503, ending a life tainted by scandal that included reports of orgies and unverified suggestions of incest. Even his death would not be without controversy, as after both he and Cesare became sick during the summer heat in Rome, poison was again mentioned as a possible cause. The younger man survived, but Alexander would suffer a last humiliation as efforts had to be made to stuff his swollen and deteriorating body into a coffin made too small for him. After the brief pontificate of his successor Pius III, who survived for just a matter of days, Girolamo Riario's cousin Cardinal Giuliano della Rovere was eventually elected as Pope Julius II. While this turn of events might have promised to improve the situation for Caterina, she was again to be disappointed. Despite responding to her appeals for the return of her family lands, the new pope would intentionally delay making any further move.

While his father was alive, Cesare Borgia managed to add many Romagnol towns such as Faenza, Cesena, Rimini, Pesaro, and Fano to his possessions, but by the end of 1503 his luck had run out. Although he had briefly taken Urbino and plundered it of much of its fabulous treasure, in the days following Alexander's death, Duke Guidobaldo da Montefeltro had been able to reclaim his city. So, too, Pesaro had been returned to Giovanni Sforza, and after a brief period under occupation San Marino regained its independence. Shortly after he had ceded his remaining possessions to the pope in exchange for his freedom, Cesare was taken prisoner in Naples and sent off to Spain, where eventually in 1507 he would die of his wounds. In the meantime, Antonio Maria Ordelaffi had returned to Forlì to reclaim his old possessions, but he had also died before Julius made public his final decision on the Romagna's contested lands. Therefore, as the pontiff deliberated on the best way to fulfil his own ambitions, Caterina continued to hope, now relying in the absence of support from her sons on the help of her friends. Eventually, however, accepting that she did not have the backing of the people, she renounced all her former claims and the region was returned to the Papal States. She then remained in Tuscany, but, having never fully recovered her health, eight years after her release from Castel Sant'Angelo, in May 1509 she died in Florence. She was still only 46.

Caterina had been genuinely devout, and in the days after Riario's murder her greatest fear had reputedly been the threat of eternal damnation pronounced against her by a priest. During the period of Savonarola's preaching, she had written to the monk for spiritual advice, and during her last years in Florence, besides spending a lot of her time in a nun's cell, she had asked to be buried among the sisters so that they might continue praying for her soul. Her difficulty in life had been to find a role between that of a weak and vulnerable female, and its alternative, a vulgar or despotic virago, flaunting attributes seen as 'rightfully' belonging to a man. According to the situation, she like other women of the period needed to present herself in different ways, sometimes as the dutiful wife or virtuous widow, at others the courageous ruler with the qualities expected of men. For the most part her struggles were conducted without any reliable help, either from her relations or from the Church and the worldly, ambitious popes of the time.

An intelligent woman of spirit, with strong loyalties to her small state, Caterina had endeavoured to do the best for her people. Nonetheless, in spite of the practical and cultural benefits she had brought them and the various religious and secular institutions she had founded, those same people had gradually come to fear her, particularly after her vicious reaction following the death of her second husband, Giacomo Feo. Both at home and abroad, her resilience in the face of danger had earned her a mixed reputation, she being admired and condemned in equal measure. While she was dubbed the Tigress of Forlì or Lioness of Romagna because she was stronger than her husbands, this forceful side of her character would in time give weight to the negative stories told against her. Before long depicted as a predatory female, like so many women of authority and strength, she would become the subject of scandalous gossip, accused of promiscuity. Caterina's interest in alchemy and potions, of which she left more than 450 recipes of her own creation, fed further rumours claiming that she had been involved in witchcraft.

Undoubtedly at times she had lost all sense of proportion and acted with extreme savagery, a crime from which she cannot be exonerated, but here again we must remember that violence was an all too common feature of the period.[106] However, Caterina's actions would always come in for greater investigation and condemnation than that of her male counterparts, and while she saw herself as 'made of the same stuff' as a man, she understood that in reality men would never stop trying to get the better of her purely because she was a female.[107] Without doubt the hypercritical way in which she has often been portrayed has to be viewed in light of this double standard, the attacks against her being particularly vicious because she was a woman, and a young and beautiful one at that. Often let down by her husbands, family members and other allies, and usually forced to act alone, while striving to prevent the overthrow of her small state, she had been forced to become more ruthless. Having thus redefined herself in a less feminine manner, she had not just confused her enemies, but also given rise to the hostile stories that were ultimately to stain her memory. Nonetheless, in the 19th century, during the struggles of Italy's Risorgimento, this woman who proudly proclaimed her descent from the family of Sforza leaders would become for many a symbol of national courage and resistance.

10

Bona, the Polish queen from Bari

'Listen daughter, and behold, and incline your ear, and leave your people behind
… because the king has set his heart upon your beauty, so he is now your Lord.'

Psalm 44, 11-12[108]

The Tigress of Forlì would not be the last of the strong Sforza women as Caterina was followed by another who would show the same determination and resilience. This was her brother's daughter, Bona, named after the child's grandmother who had been banished by Il Moro several years earlier. She was born at the great castle renovated by Ludovico Sforza at Vigevano some 25 miles from Milan

Bona's sepulchre in San Nicola, Bari. (Author)

168

on 2 February 1494, five years after her young father, Gian Galeazzo, had married Isabella of Aragon, the cousin to whom he had been engaged since early childhood. The granddaughter of Ferdinand I – Ferrante – Isabella was a lively, intelligent and beautiful young woman, who had grown up at the sophisticated Neapolitan court. When she was just seven, in 1477 her aunt Eleonora, wife of Duke Ercole of Ferrara and mother of the famous d'Este sisters, had after a five-month visit to her family in Naples finally returned home to assist her husband with his affairs. At that point, to please her father Ferrante, the duchess had agreed to leave behind her younger two-year-old daughter Beatrice, whom the king much adored, and as a result the little girl would continue to be brought up with her cousin. The two remained virtually inseparable until the time came for Isabella to move north for her marriage to Gian Galeazzo.

Soon after her arrival in Milan, Isabella had become well acquainted with the famous court painter, Leonardo da Vinci, whose admiration for the young woman has given rise to the suggestion that she was the subject of the *Mona Lisa* – a work the artist kept with him right until the end of his life. While the 16th-century painter and writer Giorgio Vasari would put forward the idea – still supported by many people – that the sitter was Leonardo's fellow Florentine, Lisa Gherardini, the wife of a silk merchant called Francesco del Giocondo, some art historians have questioned this. Among these is Jerzy Kulski, who backs his case for it being a portrait of Isabella by comparing the painting in the Louvre to the recognised contemporary images of the duchess. He also draws attention to the symbolism that appears in the embroidery on the sitter's dress – the ducal chain of office, and the cross that appears to reference Isabella's hereditary position after 1496 as the honorary Queen of Jerusalem. Responding to the argument that the *Mona Lisa* was created after Leonardo had left Milan, Kulski claims that besides having an exceptionally good visual memory, the artist had previously made several sketches of the duchess.[109]

Whatever the truth, Leonardo had felt real sympathy for the young woman, understanding the extreme difficulties she faced at the Milanese court, where she received little kindness from her new family. Above all she was treated badly by the ambitious Ludovico, who became particularly jealous after the birth of her son in January 1491. Having little support from her ineffectual husband Gian Galeazzo, over the years she would repeatedly appeal to her relations in Naples for help in dealing with his formidable uncle. With the later political changes in the southern kingdom and the break-up of Ferrante's former alliances, Il Moro's ill-treatment of her would only increase as he became more fearful of possible foreign intervention. Denying the duke and duchess the luxuries enjoyed by the rest of the court in Milan, he distanced the young couple from the city, keeping them almost as prisoners at Pavia.

For Isabella, things did not change for the better even when, the same month as her son's birth, her childhood friend Beatrice d'Este arrived in Milan to take part in a double wedding. To cement relations between the two houses of Sforza and d'Este, Ludovico married Beatrice, and her brother Alfonso d'Este married Anna, the sister of Gian Galeazzo. But, although the two cousins and former companions were now even more closely related, the childhood bond between

Isabella and Beatrice would soon be put under strain. Happy at first to be together once again, over time their relationship began to suffer as Il Moro's preferential treatment of his adored wife started to tell. While he showered honours on both Beatrice and their child, granting them precedence over Gian Galeazzo and Isabella, this couple would find themselves being even more side-lined. Not content with this, Ludovico went still further, intentionally allowing the rumour to be spread that the duchess had been planning to poison one of the courtiers. With her life becoming steadily more unbearable, she grew more and more distraught, declaring herself to be 'the most unhappily married woman in the world'.[110]

However, 1494 would prove to be an even more significant year for Isabella. While just a month after her grandfather Ferrante's death in January, Isabella gave birth to her third child, Bona, eight months later, her personal situation was to take another major turn for the worse. As Ludovico wished to reduce the Neapolitan kingdom's power and influence, he had 'invited' – according to Machiavelli – the French to come to Italy and help him. After Charles VIII had arrived in the country and met Il Moro, he would also visit Gian Galeazzo, but, although Isabella had used this opportunity to beg the French king to spare her Neapolitan family, her appeal had fallen on deaf ears. Worse still for her, shortly after the visit, on 21 October her sickly young husband died. While the gossips soon said that he had been poisoned by his uncle, these rumours did nothing to stop Ludovico quickly taking power and, with the backing of Emperor Maximilian, becoming the new duke of Milan.

As Isabella's problems continued to mount, within a few months the French had marched south, first forcing her father Alfonso II to abdicate, and then also removing her brother Ferdinand II – 'Ferrantino' – from his throne. Although Charles was to hold on to the kingdom only briefly, the family's difficulties were still not over as, less than twenty months after being reinstated, Ferdinand died prematurely in 1496. And for Isabella there was more to come. Besides mourning the death of a posthumous daughter, she had now been installed with her other children at the castle in Milan, where she was growing increasingly concerned about the safety of her only son, Francesco. Ludovico Sforza himself was now, however, to suffer a devastating loss as in January 1497, within a few hours of giving birth to a stillborn son, his adored wife Beatrice suddenly became ill and died. Her husband was distraught, and Milan was immediately plunged into public mourning.

Later during that same year, the death also occurred of Ludovico's niece, Anna Sforza, whose wedding ceremony six years earlier had taken place at the same time as his own. This had been an unhappy marriage and, as Anna's husband Alfonso d'Este did not waste time in grieving, he was soon looking for another wife. In 1502 he agreed for political reasons to marry Pope Alexander VI's daughter Lucrezia Borgia. Alfonso d'Este had originally been unwilling to demean the family's famous name by marrying the pontiff's bastard child, a young woman who had already earned a highly dubious reputation for herself. The obvious adoration felt for Lucrezia by her father and brother had given rise to stories of incest, and, although never verified, these had fed the gossip surrounding all the family. It was even whispered that Lucrezia might have earlier given birth to an illegitimate child – one later passed off as her father's natural son. It was well known that she had been an amused spectator at the ribald public entertainments put on by the Borgias and had also been present at their various feasts and orgies. Then, there was also the uncomfortable fact of her two previous marriages: the first to the humiliated Giovanni Sforza of Pisaro, annulled on the improbable grounds of the groom's impotence, and the second brought to a violent end when her husband Alfonso of Aragon – Isabella's half-brother – was murdered, most probably on the orders of the jealous Cesare. Despite these many reasons for opposition to the marriage, the promise of a massive dowry eventually swayed Alfonso d'Este and following the proxy ceremony in Rome, the bride came at last to Ferrara at the end of January 1502. Her arrival was a spectacular affair, and she would please her husband and also the crowd with her beauty and decorum, qualities that subsequently helped her perform her role so successfully that she earned general respect and admiration. Even so, Lucrezia would fail to win the approval of her highly intelligent and virtuous sister-in-law, Isabella d'Este – the older sibling of Il Moro's wife, Beatrice.[111] Already disapproving of the newcomer, before long she would have still more reason to dislike Lucrezia, who would become the mistress of Isabella d'Este's previously devoted husband, Francesco Gonzaga, the marquis of Mantua.

In the years leading up to this, however, there had been more serious concerns for the other Isabella in Milan. Still deeply anxious for the safety of her son, when Il Moro began to find himself under threat from the French, she had finally decided to turn to the new king Louis XII for help. But again she would be deceived. After she had allowed *il duchetto* to be taken to France on the mistaken understanding that he might possibly marry Louis' daughter, she was eventually to discover that he had been sent instead to a monastery. Here he was to remain and, around twelve years later, having never seen his family again, Francesco would die as a result of a riding accident. Before then, however, in 1499 Isabella had finally left Milan and returned south to her former home, but here she was to suffer further loss. The next year her older daughter died, and Bona was now her only surviving child. Adding still further to her stress, as Naples was constantly being threatened by the French, for a while she and her family would have to seek shelter on the island of Ischia.

Nevertheless, just before fleeing Milan in the same year, Il Moro had compensated Isabella for her lost dowry by giving her the rights to the southern possessions of Rossano and Ostuni, as well as the important Pugliese town, Bari. Around three decades earlier this had been bequeathed by Ferrante to Ludovico's father Francesco, the gift being given partly in gratitude for his service, and partly in recognition of the marriage contract between their two children. While that particular wedding would in fact never take place, Eleonora of Aragon having married Alfonso d'Este instead, the duchy of Bari now belonged to Isabella. Two years later, therefore, she and her daughter moved to the city and for the next sixteen years this was to be their home. Here they lived in the old 12th-century castle constructed by Emperor Frederick II to replace the earlier building largely destroyed when the Norman king William I recaptured the city from the Greeks. Since that time the castle had undergone further alterations under the Angevins, and it was now Isabella's turn to give it her own personal touch. Besides strengthening its defences, she surrounded it with gardens and added elegant Renaissance interiors. Nonetheless, on occasion the duchess returned to visit her relations in Naples, and here her talented daughter was said to have impressed the people with her intelligence. However, while after the early death of Isabella's brother 'Ferrantino', her uncle Frederick (Federigo) had succeeded to the throne, in 1501 he was finally was forced to surrender all his lands to his more powerful Aragonese cousin Ferdinand II, the joint ruler of Spain. (See table p.127) Even so, Isabella was still allowed to rule undisturbed as the duchess of Bari, and here she continued to be popular for her practical improvements, good works, and general beautification of the city.

Bona had a happy childhood, during which she received a good education from her tutor and her humanist mother, their combined influence imbuing her with the ideas and practical measures that she would later adopt as an adult. When she was 12 she was also joined by her less fortunate little cousin Rodrigo – the young son of Lucrezia Borgia and Isabella's half-brother, Alfonso of Aragon, who had been murdered three months before the child's birth in 1500. Because two years later Rodrigo was removed from his mother – according to the terms laid down in her marriage agreement with the duke of Ferrara – he was then passed around his different Borgia and Aragonese relations until finally he went to live with his aunt in Bari in 1506. Lucrezia would never see her child again, but, while she was apparently saddened by the news when he died six years later, the unexplained cause of his death would soon allow various myths and conspiracy theories to develop.

For some time, Isabella had been searching unsuccessfully for a suitable husband for her daughter, but all her efforts had ended in failure as one after another the politically expedient betrothals she had planned came to nothing. She had even considered a match for her daughter with the son of her former enemy, Il Moro, seeing this as a way for her child to regain the rights she had inherited from her father, Gian Galeazzo. Just as the situation began to look hopeless, the Emperor Maximilian stepped in. Intent on furthering his own political ends and wanting in particular to build an alliance against the Ottoman threat, he now proposed the girl as a wife for the recently widowed Polish king and grand duke of Lithuania, Sigismund (Zygmunt) 'the Old'. Already in his fifties and still in need of an heir, he finally agreed to a marriage with Bona after all the other candidates suggested to him had dropped out of the running. Although Isabella had difficulty in raising the vast dowry required, by increasing taxes she was eventually able to provide her daughter with quantities of gold, silver, jewellery, clothes, precious fabrics, tapestries, and much else, not forgetting the elaborate marriage bed. At last on the feast of St Nicholas, December 1517, amid great public celebration, the girl's spectacular proxy wedding ceremony and lavish bridal banquet took place in Naples.

The Polish king was anxious not to delay his wife's arrival and so despite the winter weather, about three weeks later Bona, accompanied by Cardinal Ippolito d'Este and a retinue of around 300 followers, set off on her long, carefully planned and at times uncomfortable progress to Poland. After a tearful parting from her mother at Manfredonia in February, she crossed the Adriatic to Lagosta (Lastovo), and then travelled north up the Dalmatian coast, making frequent stops at Lesina (Hvar), Spalato, Zara, Arbe (Rab), Veglia (Krk), Fiume (Rijeka), and other places before reaching Vienna in mid-March. Having eventually arrived at Krakow in April, at last on the 15th, in a formally staged setting, she met her husband for the first time. Accompanied by some 6000 ambassadors, courtiers and other horsemen, the couple then progressed through the streets of the city. Three days later, following the official wedding ceremony, Bona's coronation took place, the event being celebrated by a 70-gun salute and another week of festivities attended by thousands of guests.

In recognition of her new status, besides receiving from the king jewels and other treasures Bona was given several of her own towns, these being intended to provide her with a revenue that would cover the costs of her court. She administered these so well that they later formed the basis of her considerable wealth. Before long the marriage would produce the desired results, the birth of a daughter being followed in August 1520 by the much-wanted son, Sigismund Augustus. Although during the following six years there would be three more daughters, things changed after 1527 when – again pregnant – the queen was attacked by a bear while she was out hunting with her falcon. This disaster would not only cause the death of a premature son but also leave Bona unable to have any more children.

Despite the Emperor's role in arranging this marriage and her mother's dislike of the French, Bona would always be a Francophile. Moreover, because she feared the influence of the Empire on her new country, she had little love for the Habsburgs and their German vassals, who impeded Poland's access to trade on the Baltic. Accordingly, even while she largely ignored her younger daughters, she endeavoured to arrange the marriage of her favourite – the oldest – to the son of the French king, Francis I, a match she saw as possibly opening the way for her descendants to reclaim their rights to the Milanese possessions of their Sforza ancestors. As this plan and similar ones would ultimately fail, in the end the girl was found a Hungarian husband instead.

Meanwhile, the royal couple had a close – if sometimes stormy – relationship, and Bona would continue to advise her rather indecisive husband whenever she could. The couple created an elegant and impressive court, filled with the treasures and works of art that had been purposely collected to display their high standing and the importance of the dynasty as a whole. During his early life in Hungary Sigismund had absorbed much of that country's thinking, and so he had already brought to Poland some Renaissance ideas in the field of music and architecture. His new wife was now to add to this, introducing various aspects of Italian culture and, through her sponsorship of humanists and artists, she would usher in a period that was to become known as the Polish Golden Age. She also passed on to her children many of her interests, most notably her love of tapestries, several of which she had brought from Bari as part of her dowry. These would particularly inspire her son, who would later order more from Flanders, some still on display in Wawel Castle in Warsaw.

Bona would shock the more conservative Poles with her Italian fashions. While clothes would remain important for her even as she became more conventional with age, her husband, remarking on the sheer number of her dresses, considered she had enough for several queens. But by overturning some of the more restrictive Polish practices, she had given women a greater freedom to express themselves in public. She had equally used her influence to introduce several other more significant reforms, these including changes to the law, improvements in agriculture and farming methods, and even bringing new elements into the Polish diet. In the latter case, the queen's responsibility may have been rather exaggerated, as what she personally chose to eat would have probably had little impact on the lives of the ordinary people. Yet, as she genuinely loved the vegetables and fruits she had known during her childhood in the south, on her arrival in Poland she had created gardens in which to grow these things, and so undoubtedly had influenced the tastes of those immediately around her. Her daughter Anna when queen would include some of the dishes of Italy in the sumptuous banquets she laid on to impress her guests. At the same time, Bona brought her stricter ideas of personal cleanliness to Poland, again no doubt influenced by her mother Isabella, who had once engaged Leonardo da Vinci to design a water system for her bath.[112]

More significantly still, Bona had begun to write regularly to Roxelana, the daughter of a Ukrainian priest who had been captured by the Muslims, and in the 1520s become Hurrem Sultan, the favourite wife of Suleiman the Magnificent. These two women would form a close rapport, and through their continued correspondence they would have an influence on the policies of their husbands. Their input would be indirectly of service to both their countries, their friendship helping to maintain the peace between the Polish-Lithuanian Commonwealth and the neighbouring Ottoman empire.

Following the death of her mother Isabella in 1524, possession of Bari once more came into dispute. Bona's rights as the new duchess were now contested by an alternative claim put forward by the son of Il Moro, who questioned his father's earlier right to have ever bequeathed the territory. This problem would only be finally resolved in 1536 when the new Emperor, Charles V, asserted his own claims to the city's castle and Bari's surrounding territories. Although Bona was then granted the duchy for her lifetime, this was only on the condition that all her possessions would ultimately be surrendered after her death.

When the queen's son was only ten, she managed – even though her husband was still alive – to arrange for the boy to be crowned, hoping by doing so to ensure the future of the dynasty. However, together with her sometimes questionable accumulation of wealth, this had increased her unpopularity with the nobles of the *szlachta*.[113] As a result, seven years after the coronation there would be an inconsequential attempt at rebellion against the king's policies. But even after her husband died in 1548, Bona continued to exert her authority, attempting to play a key role in her son's affairs. Already greatly disliked for her forceful character, she would now be accused of a variety of crimes, and as the rumours spread, the so-called Black Legend began to take hold. Despite total lack of evidence, she faced accusations of corruption and witchcraft, as well as charges of immoral behaviour.[114] Having been on bad terms with her first daughter-in-law, Elizabeth, the child of the disliked Habsburgs, it was now whispered that she had murdered her son's second wife, Barbara Radziwiłł. This beautiful daughter of a minor Polish nobleman had married Sigismund Augustus secretly, against the wishes of his mother, who was particularly opposed to the young woman's lower social status and Calvinist upbringing. In spite of the religious tolerance practised in the country, Sigismund the Old and his Italian wife had sought to defend their Catholic faith against Protestant influences. While again there is no evidence to support the charge of murder levelled against Bona – Barbara most probably contracting cancer soon after the wedding – as usual the rumours surrounding such unexplained deaths took hold, and gradually the story gained credence. As by this time Sigismund II was seriously at odds with his mother and she was unwelcome at court, she was now living with her three younger daughters on her estates in Mazovia, where the king continued to keep her under observation. Faced by the breakdown in their relations, as well as her intense unpopularity among the nobles at large, she wanted to return to Puglia. Like so many women of the period, she had spent most of her life in her husband's foreign country, but she had never lost interest in her childhood home, and she was still attached to her Sforza-Aragonese heritage of which she was so proud. For the time being, however, her son opposed the idea, believing that she had some scheme to deprive him of his claims to those same territories in southern Italy.

At last in January 1556, some forty years after she had first left Italy, Bona was finally permitted to return. Having set off south with her large retinue, she arrived in Venice in May. Here she was given a lavish reception before then being transported by galley to Bari to receive an equally impressive welcome from her people. Once she was resettled, she began to buy new properties and reinforce the castle. As part of her programme to strengthen the city's defences against the possibility of an Ottoman attack, she also renovated and raised the harbour and city walls. Furthermore, picking up where her mother had left off, she brought improvements to the people's daily lives, among other things constructing cisterns and wells to provide the public with drinking water – some these still in use during the last century.

Bona's return would not bring her long-term happiness, however. While Emperor Charles V had begun to abdicate his numerous roles, his son, Philip II of Spain, who had already seized many of her possessions, now refused to repay the vast sum of money that she had previously lent him. This was to leave Bona in comparative poverty, and even though her daughter Anna would later receive interest on the loan, for years to come this unpaid debt would continue to rankle with the Poles. But, for the 63-year-old Bona, there was worse to come. Just a year after returning home, she became seriously ill. Even as it became evident that she was dying, Philip persisted in plaguing her, still determined to get possession of her remaining lands, and although she had wished to leave these territories to her son, she was now forced to name the Spanish king as her successor. Despite later trying to alter her will in Sigismund Augustus' favour, she was unable to achieve this before she died on 19 November – allegedly having been poisoned by a member of the court on Philip's orders.

Following her death, Bona was buried in Bari's cathedral, where she remained for more than three decades. As by that time Sigismund II had died without an heir, he was succeeded by his sister, Anna Jagiellon, who was ruling jointly with her husband, Stefan Batory. Ever conscious of her royal status, and having ordered some spectacular tombs for her brother, husband and also herself, she now commissioned a magnificent sepulchre to be made for her mother in Naples. On its arrival in Bari, it was placed in the side aisle of San Nicola, the great basilica built to house the relics of the city's patron saint. So at last in 1589, with Anna having gained the pope's permission, Bona's remains were transferred from the cathedral to this most holy of sites, and here, on the hundredth anniversary of her birth, the former queen of Poland and grand duchess of Lithuania was finally laid to rest.

SECTION VI
THE LAST YEARS OF VENICE'S *TERRAFERMA*

11

Two centuries of art and war

'Venice embraces Italy when others shun her, and upholds her when others abase her.'

Pietro Aretino[115]

Although the sixteenth century opened with an uneasy peace following the Milanese duke Ludovico Sforza's capture and removal to France, the situation throughout the Italian peninsula remained fragile, and before long the region would again be riven by war. Soon after succeeding his second cousin Charles VIII in 1498, Louis XII had begun taking steps to assert the rights that he believed he had inherited from his Visconti grandmother. To prepare the way for his invasion of Italy, after coming to terms with the Holy Roman Emperor he had also reached an understanding with Pope Alexander VI, striking a deal that was of benefit

19th-century depiction of the Battle of Lepanto at the National Maritime Museum of London.

to them both; in addition to Milan, Louis was to receive the annulment of his unwanted marriage, while in return the Borgia family was granted a free hand to seize new territories in the Romagna. After that, in order to prevent another possible conflict breaking out, the French king also approached Venice. Even though at the time the Serenissima had more pressing concerns, its latest unsuccessful war against the Ottomans only coming to an end in 1503, it now agreed with Louis to a sharing out of the lands that he intended to take in Lombardy.

At the same time the French king had also begun to set his sights on the south, and so in November 1500 he signed a treaty at Granada with Ferdinand of Aragon and Isabella of Castile, the three rulers agreeing – with the later approval of the pope – to their joint seizure and division of the Neapolitan kingdom. Accordingly, when the next year, shortly after his succession in Naples, Frederick (Federico) IV was forced to flee and Louis claimed the crown for himself, the Spanish rulers had taken possession of their Aragonese cousin's lands in Calabria and the heel of Italy. This agreement between the French and Spanish monarchs had soon broken down, however, and by 1502 the two sides were again at war. Louis' army then invaded Puglia, but when the French were finally ousted from the south, in January 1504 a new peace was signed at Lyon. With the Second Italian War having therefore come to an end, this treaty confirmed the rights of Louis to hold on to northern Italy and the Spanish monarchs to keep Naples and the south. Although Isabella of Castile died at the end of that year, her husband had now incorporated the whole of the former Kingdom of Sicily into their possessions, and from this time on the Mezzogiorno was to be ruled until the eighteenth century by successive viceroys answerable to Spain.

Meanwhile, following the death of Pope Alexander VI and the fall of his son Cesare Borgia, the political situation had changed elsewhere. Fearful of another invasion, many of the northern Italian rulers had begun to make peaceful approaches to the French. Besides Florence and those cities like Genoa and Pisa that lay to the west, closer to the Adriatic seaboard various places like Bologna and several towns of the Romagna had started to swear allegiance to Louis. Others such as Mantua had soon followed suit, and then later, Ferrara, where – having survived his brothers' plot to overthrow him – in 1505 Lucrezia Borgia's husband Alfonso d'Este had succeeded to the duchy.

The new pope had his own ambitions, however. As towns like Rimini and Faenza, earlier captured by the Borgias, once again placed themselves under Venetian protection, Julius II was determined to recover these possessions and reincorporate them into the Papal States. Despite the Serenissima agreeing to pay the relevant dues and acknowledge papal sovereignty, Julius feared that the Republic meant to extend its territorial hold over the whole region. He therefore devised a way to deal with this threat by combining his own objectives with those of the Holy Roman Emperor Maximilian, who had set his sights on some northern Italian cities. But although he was now persuaded by the pope to invade the area, ultimately his campaign would bring him no benefit as after the defeat of the imperial army at Vicenza in

February 1508, and then further losses along the Venetian-Austrian border to the east, he finally had to agree to make peace.

As Venice had further antagonised the pope by appointing its own bishop in Vicenza, Julius now created his Holy League of Cambrai, a union combining the papal forces with those of the Emperor, the French, and Ferdinand of Spain. While this purported to be an anti-Muslim alliance, in reality it was mainly directed at Venice's defeat. Besides the Spanish desire to oust the Venetians from the southern Italian ports in Puglia, the various parties wanted to dismantle the Republic's *terraferma* and share out the spoils. With war having broken out, in the following weeks Venice would experience a series of disasters, not just the loss of various towns, including Faenza and its recently acquired Rimini, but also a crushing defeat in May at Agnadello east of Milan, a catastrophe caused largely by disagreements among its generals. This left Venice's northern Italian possessions undefended, and so Vicenza, Verona, and Padua – a Venetian town since 1405 – now fell to the French-imperial forces. Adding further to the Serenissima's woes, while Ravenna was then captured by the duke of Ferrara and the papal army, already in April Julius had placed Venice under papal interdict.

For the Serenissima, these serious misfortunes would, however, be partially offset when in July the Venetian general Andrea Gritti came to the aid of the Paduans, enabling them to rise up against their German occupiers and retake control of their city. Although two months later it was again put under siege by the imperial army, Padua managed to hold out and within fifteen days the enemy had retreated. In the meantime, Julius had begun to have a change of heart, and so the next year, having become nervous about the growing power of the French, he lifted his earlier interdict and made peace with the Serenissima. Alfonso d'Este remained loyal to his former allies, however, and after the pope had failed to take Ferrara, at the end of 1510 he would lead his army to attack the duke's Mirandola fortress around 35 miles to the west of the city. Here, throughout the following bitterly cold winter, Julius personally maintained the siege until he was eventually able to force the defenders to surrender. Nonetheless, even though this persuaded neighbouring towns to join the Papal States, before long the pope would again be facing setbacks and defeats. In November he therefore decided to create another Holy League to confront his new French enemy, he now bringing together the Emperor, Ferdinand of Spain, Venice, and even Henry VIII of England.

As the war continued and the French retook towns and cities in the Romagna and the Veneto, the chain of disasters and suffering inflicted on the local people had made them grow increasingly fearful and prone to superstition. When wild stories started to take hold and reports were spread that a 'monstrous' child had been born at Ravenna, many began to see this as a sign of divine displeasure and a forewarning of further horrors to come. Eventually for the Ravennesi, these fears seemed to have come true, as in late March 1512 it would be their turn to come under siege. Things finally came to a head on 11 April when the people heard the news that the Spanish and papal army had been defeated on its way to relieve them. Without any further hope of rescue, they now agreed to surrender and their town was sacked by the French. Yet, because the victors' popular leader had been killed in the fighting, the tables were about to turn and the general's troops were soon defeated by the Swiss. After that, events began to move quickly. Within a month of the capture of Ravenna, the French had been driven out of Italy, and Il Moro's son, Massimiliano Sforza, had retrieved his Milanese duchy.

The following February, much to the distress of the people of Rome, Pope Julius II died. During his pontificate he had greatly embellished their city, overseeing among other things Michelangelo's completion of his paintings for the Sistine Chapel. A more questionable act, however, was Julius's destruction of the ancient church first constructed on the orders of the great emperor Constantine over St Peter's presumed grave. Needing money to help cover the exorbitant sums involved in creating the vast basilica that Bramante had designed to replace it, the pope had promised indulgences to anyone who was prepared to contribute to the cost. This had enabled construction to begin, and work was therefore already under way by the time of the pope's death. He was now replaced by the son of Lorenzo the Magnificent, the young and rich Leo X, who had been elected partly by gaining the backing of his predecessor's nephew, Cardinal Raffaele Riario. Because the latter had been in Florence at the time of the Pazzi Plot, in which he, like his other uncle Girolamo Riario, had been involved, his relations with the Medici family had never been good, but they would soon deteriorate further. As Leo had earned his support by convincing him that he had not long to live, when in 1517 Cardinal Riario eventually began to realise that he had been deceived over the state of the man's health, he became so angry that he apparently became implicated with four other cardinals in an unproven conspiracy to poison the pope. The plot's leader would ultimately be executed, but after his own interrogation and temporary imprisonment, Riario was able – at a cost – to recover his position. However, there were now other far more important issues on the horizon, as within months of these events the papacy would be challenged for the first time by a former monk in Saxony. With Leo's continuing sale of indulgences having greatly increased the criticism of the Church, Martin Luther boldly attacked its very practices, setting out his argument in his famous ninety-five theses. This action started a debate that would soon be the cause of lasting damage to the Vatican's authority, and, unknowingly, Luther had set in train the Reformation and its long history of terrible ferocious religious conflict.

Just a month after Julius II's death, while the War of Cambrai was still continuing, Venice left its former allies to side with the French, doing so once again in the hopes of gaining a share of the much-desired regions in Lombardy. Because this put the Serenissima at odds with its neighbours, following the latest defeat of Louis XII's army at Novara in June, the Republic came under attack, the Spanish taking Padua, mounting a failed bombardment of Venice and routing the Venetian army at La Motta near Vicenza. Nonetheless, the Serenissima would continue skirmishing with its enemies in the north-east region around Trieste until its situation finally began to improve with the arrival of the French in 1515. Earlier in January Francis I had succeeded his cousin (and father-in-law) Louis, and ambitious to regain his lost territories, the new king had confirmed his treaty with Venice and mounted another invasion of Italy. Having with the Venetians' help defeated the Swiss Confederacy and their papal allies at Marignano, a month later in October Francis was able to retake Milan from the young Sforza duke Massimiliano, who, on being forced to sell his lands, then moved to France for the rest of his life. As the War of Cambrai was finally coming to an end, Venice's position had now become more secure. Although the eight years of hostilities had deprived her of her leading maritime role, and her *Stato da Mar* no longer wielded its earlier influence, she had recovered most of her *terraferma*. So, when the new treaty was signed at Noyon the following August, besides officially confirming Francis I as the Milanese ruler, Spain acknowledged the joint French-Venetian control over all of northern Italy east of the Duchy of Savoy. The Serenissima had again become a major player in the affairs of the region.

The same treaty had given Naples to Charles, the grandson of Ferdinand and Isabella, who was now the new Spanish king. The agreement had come with the proviso that he marry a French princess and produce a son, a condition that in fact would never be fulfilled; he eventually chose a Portuguese bride instead. As it happened, already by then the earlier goodwill between him and Francis had collapsed, their relations having broken down following the death of the Holy Roman Emperor three years after the meeting at Noyon. When Charles had been elected to replace his grandfather, the ambitions of the young French king had been frustrated, and as a result the two men had rapidly become implacable enemies. By 1521 they were again at war. Although Venice maintained its loyalty to Francis and denied the imperial army access to its territories, before the end of the year Emperor Charles V had entered Lombardy and expelled the French. With the Sforzas now reinstated in Milan, in November the younger Francesco would replace his older brother Massimiliano and be acknowledged as the new duke.

In spite of the French army losing two more battles in the region, for Francis I the war was not over and he was determined to try and regain his Italian lands. Therefore, in October 1524 he personally led his troops back to Lombardy, but after suffering a major defeat at Pavia in February, he was taken captive and held in Madrid for nearly a year. Although by acknowledging the loss of all his Italian territories he was eventually allowed to return home, he soon ignored the terms of his release and in May formed a separate League of Cognac with Florence and the recently elected Pope Clement VII, as well as Duke Francesco of Milan – who had now abandoned his former imperial champion. Venice was also a signatory of this alliance, but when war broke out again shortly after, it would prove its unwillingness to become involved. Even when in May 1527 Charles' troops invaded Rome and began to sack the city, the Venetians refused to come to the aid of Clement, who was now cowering in Castel Sant'Angelo.[116] The next year the imperial army finally left the city, but as the fighting carried on it brought further suffering to the untold numbers of men, women and children already scarred by these repeated wars. Among the many reported atrocities committed by every side at this time would be the massacre of the people of Molfetta when their town was sacked by the French in July 1529. However, just a month after this act of barbarism, the leaders would meet at Cambrai. Having been persuaded at last by Francis I's mother and the Emperor's aunt to make peace, here the two men eventually agreed to the so-called *Paix des Dames*. While Venice now ceded to the Emperor her remaining possessions in Puglia, and to the pope her recently gained Ravenna and nearby Cervia, Francis renounced his claims in Italy. For his part, Clement consented to conduct Charles's imperial coronation, which – the last of its kind – eventually took place at Bologna in February 1530. And five months later, to reinforce the peace the Emperor's sister was married to the French king.

Meanwhile, further afield there had been other highly significant developments in Europe's relations with the Ottomans. Only three years after crushing the Hungarians at Mohács, in September 1529 Suleiman the Magnificent's army had arrived at Vienna and begun to besiege the Habsburgs' capital. Although its attempt to take the city would ultimately be unsuccessful, this episode had further shaken the confidence of the West. Already throughout this period the feared 'Turks' had been terrorising communities around the Mediterranean as the sultan's corsairs, the Barbarossa brothers, had persisted in their raids on numerous coastal towns and cities. Therefore, with the Ottoman challenge continuing to grow and the threat of invasion becoming steadily more real, Charles V had begun to erect additional strongholds to protect his various possessions or places of interest around the Adriatic. As well as his new castle at Barletta and the reinforced fortress at Brindisi in Puglia, in Dalmatia he had created a fort to defend Venice's important port of Lesina (Hvar) – something that was to prove its worth to the local people before the century was out. Yet, even while their king had been in prison in Madrid, the French had begun to make approaches to the sultan, and some ten years after their first agreement, to the shock of many Christian leaders, by the start of 1536 Francis had signed a full-blown official alliance with the Ottoman Porte.

* * *

The political and diplomatic problems that Venice had faced throughout the first years of the 16th century had caused other tensions to develop at home. As a result, to the embarrassment of the Council of Ten (who later forbade any further mention of it), in 1511 a violent argument had actually broken out in the Senate. Even so, the everyday life of the city had been progressing on several fronts and the cultural scene was now flourishing under the Bellini brothers and Gentile's earlier student, Carpaccio. Besides the careful rebuilding work that had now been completed on the sacred area of the Rialto – destroyed by fire two years earlier – in 1516 Venice appointed its first official historian. That same year, it had brought in another change, but one which was to have a direct and much more long-lasting impact on some of its people. As Venice was always a more open city, showing that greater degree of tolerance towards different ideas and customs so often found among trading people, it was relatively flexible about religious matters. Despite being a Christian city, unlike so much of Europe it accepted followers of other faiths. Ever practical and materialistic in its outlook, it was ready to recognise any who could be of service to the Republic. For that reason it appreciated the valuable contribution of the Jews, recognising the important part they played in the financial and commercial roles that were forbidden to the Christians. Now, therefore, the authorities established for these citizens a special area, the closed-off *ghetto* that in time would give its name to all such places. Declaring that they intended to ensure the Jews' safety, they then imposed a curfew on the residents and ordered them to be locked behind their gates every night. Over the years this small area would become more and more crowded and, as the growing community needed to find additional space, the tenement buildings became taller and taller in an effort to provide sufficient accommodation and enough room for their synagogues. Yet, even while their living conditions grew increasingly congested, and the Jews undoubtedly still faced the racial prejudice described by Shakespeare in *The Merchant of Venice*, here again Venetian pragmatism was evident. The Jews were allowed to practise their religion in private and they were never subjected to the discrimination and pogroms experienced by others elsewhere.

In 1523 Venice would elect a new doge, the former general Andrea Gritti, who had earlier worked as a grain merchant in Istanbul. An exceptionally good linguist, he had acted as the Republic's unofficial representative in the Ottoman city and, despite being for a time imprisoned for spying, he had then played a key role in a peace agreement with the Porte. But while he had won public acclaim for his leadership in the recent Italian war, he was never popular as the head of state, and many questioned the morals of his private life. On his becoming doge, he had immediately made peace with the Holy Roman Emperor, and in exchange for a payment had guaranteed Venice's possession of its previously disputed lands. After that, just as he had done during Charles V's attack on Rome, he would try to distance the Republic as far as possible from all further fighting. This allowed Venice to enjoy another cultural explosion that helped it maintain its reputation as one of the most magnificent cities of the time. During Gritti's 15 years in office he would sponsor many famous artists, being himself painted by the master Titian, who had first trained as a child under the Bellini brothers. After working alongside Giorgione, during his long career Titian would spend time at the courts of Ferrara and Mantua, and be employed by Charles V, Philip II of Spain, the pope, and many other distinguished individuals. When he died of the plague in 1576, he was buried in the Frari, where sixty years before he had made his name with his large painting of the

Assumption of the Virgin that still hangs behind the altar. This great church belonged to the *Scuola Grande dei Frari*, one of the charitable organisations that had gradually been established over the preceding two centuries. By the end of the Republic, there would be over 900 *scuole piccole* for the trade guilds, and, following the promotion of one of them just thirty years before the Serenissima's fall, seven scuole grandi, which were reserved for Venetian citizens who did not belong to the clergy or nobility.

Besides Titian, other great artists were engaged in decorating many of the churches or halls of these *scuole*. The *Scuola Grande di San Rocco* was one of the last of these great organisations to be founded, having been established after an outbreak of the plague in 1478, when a church had been built to house the bones of the saint believed to guard against the dreaded epidemic. With the constant fear of a recurrence of the disease, the people turned more and more to San Rocco, in 1576 adopting him as one of their patron saints. The doge began to honour him in an annual ceremony and as the saint's status grew, so too did the *scuola's* wealth, greatly increased through public donation. Four years after the confraternity completed their new hall next to the church, Jacopo Comin – famously dubbed 'Tintoretto', or the little dyer after his father's profession – would be employed in 1564 to start decorating it, eventually completing the 64 masterpieces that still cover both the upper and lower chambers. Always working at such speed that he had also been given a second nickname, *Il furioso*, he received his first commission from the *scuola* after unfairly trumping his rivals in the competition to paint the church ceiling by presenting the already finished piece when asked only to submit the designs. Fortunately for the *scuola*, in 1806 when Napoleon closed down most of Venice's religious establishments, it – unlike the others – would be allowed to continue its charitable work and keep its art treasures. While a few confraternities would be re-established later, by then most of their buildings had been demolished or converted to other uses, this being the case of one of the earliest, the *Scuola Grande di Santa Maria della Carità*, which, still housing a Titian *Pietà*, is now the Gallerie Dell'Accademia.

In addition to Titian and Tintoretto, other famous artists were also coming to the fore, among them Jacopo Bassano – repeatedly reviled by Titian – and Paolo Veronese. Architects, too, were at work, and with the area in front of the St Mark's Basilica by this time fully laid out, Mauro Coducci was in the process of creating the *Procuratie Vecchie* along the northern side of the square. This building, like the later 'new' wing facing it, was created for the procurators who held a position second only to the doge.[117] Two years after the Florentine-born Jacopo Sansovino arrived in Venice in 1527, where he soon became involved in the on-going alterations of the ducal palace, he was appointed the city's official architect. He became particularly renowned for creating the *Loggetta* at the base of the *campanile* – this largely rebuilt after the collapse of the bell tower in 1902 – the nearby *Zecca* (or Mint), the *Biblioteca Marciana*, and also the church of San Francesco della Vigna, where Doge Gritti would later be buried.

While this cultural movement was taking place in Venice, a similar flowering had been happening elsewhere. Since the early 15th century, the Republic of Ragusa (Dubrovnik) had increased its territory to what was now to be its final size. Although its payment of tribute money to the Hungarians would cease after the latter's disastrous defeat at Mohács, by then Ragusa had secured good relations with the Ottomans through the payment of similar dues. While it had always remained nervous of the Venetians, suspicious of the ambitions of its maritime rivals, there had, nonetheless, been a constant exchange of artistic ideas between the different towns across the Adriatic. When in 1438 the Dalmatian republic wished to provide water to the city, the authorities invited the Neapolitan Onofrio della Cava to create an aqueduct tapping into the supplies lying some twelve kilometres away. He constructed various fountains for the townspeople, among them one solely for the use of the Jews, and two marking each end of the main street, the Paca or – as the Venetians called it – the Stradun. While the Big Onofrio's Fountain would be badly damaged in the earthquake of 1667, the Little Onofrio Fountain still displays the carved stonework added to it by another Italian, Pietro di Martino of Milan. This man would also decorate the capitals of the columns in the Rector's Palace, the residence of the elected head of state during his month-long term of office. Unfortunately, this building would suffer repeatedly over the years from poor restoration work, the numerous earth tremors and quakes, and even a gunpowder explosion in 1463.

Further proof of a shared artistic interest between the Balkan republic and Venice can be found in one of Titian's earliest dated works, the *Madonna and Child in Glory* (now in the Pinacoteca in Ancona) that he painted for one of Ragusa's merchants. Nonetheless, the Dalmatian city already had its own famous artist, Nikola Božidarević, who had probably been born sometime around 1460 in Cattaro (Kotor). Having most likely been first influenced by Carpaccio during the period he had spent in Venice, he was to produce numerous remarkable works before his death in 1517, three years before another earthquake hit Ragusa. Despite the damage done at this time, the destruction was to be considerably less than that caused by the far more catastrophic shock that struck the region almost 150 years later. Then, tragically, most of Božidarević's works would be lost, just four fully verified pieces remaining, three in the Dominican monastery and one at the church of St Mary at Dance. The general devastation was intense, but some of the old buildings still survive, these including the Sponza Palace, and the small votive Church of Our Saviour beside the western gate that was erected after the plague in the same catastrophic year as the 1520 earthquake. These disasters were, however, just some of the trials that Ragusa was facing in this period. By now, the Mediterranean muda or convoy system was declining, and the city's merchants were confronting a more serious threat. They were starting to feel the pressures of the new oceanic trade that had begun to develop after the explorers to the New World and beyond had discovered alternative routes to their distant markets. In this misfortune they were not alone, however, because Venice, too, was feeling the effects. Even so, the Dalmatian republic still feared the Venetians. But being also concerned about attack from other quarters as well– in particular from the Ottomans – in 1538 it began to strengthen the impressive city walls, adding further to its defences with the massive Revelin Fortress.

Earlier, a different political crisis had developed elsewhere as a result of the Hungarian and Croatian king, Louis II, having drowned as he was fleeing the field during his crushing defeat at Mohács in August 1526. As he died without an heir, in November the Hungarian aristocracy had elected in his place his brother-in-law, Ferdinand of Austria – the brother of Emperor Charles V. As a result, within a couple of months part of the archduke's kingdom had broken away and decided to put itself under the protection of the Ottomans. Because the threat of civil war was now looming across the border, on 1 January 1527 a group of Croats came together at here, having accepted that Ferdinand was the monarch of both Hungary and the Slovenian people of Carinthia, they acknowledged him as their own ruler – the king of Royal Croatia. But this was not the end of the region's problems. Seven miles from Spalato stood the fortress of Klis – the Venetian Clissa – a strategic stronghold that had guarded an all-important pass since Roman and Byzantine times. The capital of the medieval Croatian kingdom at the start of the new millennium, more recently this had had to resist repeated attack from the Tatars, and also avoid being sold to the Venetians along with the rest of Dalmatia in 1420. Now this key point of defence on the front line between the Christians and the Muslims was again being threatened by the Ottomans. While for the next five years it would receive minimal support from the pope and nothing from the Venetians or the Croatian king, it would still manage somehow to struggle on. Finally, however, in 1537 Suleiman the Magnificent decided to send his vast army in a last push to capture the fortress. Here the Croat feudal lord Petar Kružić continued to put up a determined defence, he having the backing of the so-called 'fugitive, runaway, deserter' Uskoks, those mainly Christian refugees from the Balkan regions that were now occupied by the sultan. Although they still resorted on occasion to banditry and piracy, because Ferdinand had by this time realised how much he needed the Uskoks' help against the on-going Muslim threat, they had at last begun to receive some support from Trieste.[118] Since the pope also believed he had a claim to Klis, he, too, promised to provide some aid, but all help arrived too late to prevent the place from collapsing under the heavy Muslim attack. With the allies having fled the scene, the Ottomans broke through, and, after beheading Petar Kružić, they took full possession of the fortress.

* * *

When two years earlier in 1535 Francesco II Sforza of Milan had died without an heir, Francis I had again turned his attention towards the duchy, and started to assert the rights of his son Henri d'Orleans. This claim was immediately disputed by Ferdinand of Austria and the region was quickly annexed by the Habsburgs, who gave it to Charles V's son, Philip. In response, the French king secretly drew up a new agreement with the sultan and by March 1536 another Italian War had begun. Although he had not wanted Venice to become entangled in this costly conflict, Doge Gritti could not prevent trouble breaking out among his own merchant traders and before long their disputes escalated, dragging the Venetians into their own battles with the Ottomans. By August 1537 their French allies were attacking the Serenissima's island of Corfu. Even though the next month's extremely wet weather would help the town's fortress to hold out, the danger was not over, and the sultan's fleet still posed a major challenge at the entrance to the Adriatic, where it was again threatening the Serenissima's movement into the wider Mediterranean. Over the following months, the Venetians were defeated in the Ionian Sea, and the nearby mainland town of Preveza was then captured by Barbarossa, who, fresh from his successful raids in Puglia, soon gained total control of the surrounding waters. As a fitting end to a disastrous year, on 28 December 1538 the octogenarian Gritti died, allegedly from overeating. He had tried to maintain the peace, but he had left his country at war and so it would now fall to his unfortunate successor to find a way to bring the fighting to a close. When two years later this was finally achieved, the peace would be agreed only at the cost of Venice accepting humiliating terms. The Serenissima was now compelled to surrender for ever its main Aegean bases, its only remaining presence in the area to be found in a few minor, privately owned possessions. Adding to its problems, for some years, besides coping with the people's increasing unwillingness to man the fleets, it had been facing financial pressures, corruption, and even betrayal. As these things had helped to undermine the security of the state, the Muslims had become so dominant in the region that they were now able to force Venice to accept stringent new restrictions on the activities of its merchants.

Francis I was already in contact with Barbarossa, and even though he was married to Charles's sister he remained determined to defeat his brother-in-law. The truce agreed in 1538 at the end of the earlier Italian war was now forgotten and he had re-established his agreement with the sultan, the 'unholy' alliance that appalled the rest of Christian Europe. The year after the renewal of hostilities, in 1543, he even joined the Ottomans to attack Nice, the possession of the duke of Savoy, the Emperor's ally. Francis was still supplying troops to the sultan for his war in Hungary when he died four years later, and his son Henri II would then take up where he had left off. This foreign policy would be adopted on and off by the French kings until the revolution of the 1790s, and even then, the earlier conditions agreed with the sultan would remain in place until the 20th century.

Although Francis's last Italian War had come to an end in 1546, five years later another conflict was to begin. This would be ongoing when Charles V, exhausted by his many responsibilities, decided to retire from public office. Aware of the impossible challenges he faced as ruler of the vast territories he had inherited from both his mother and father, he divided his Habsburg lands, handing his Spanish throne over to his son Philip II and bequeathing the Empire to his brother, Ferdinand I, who had already been administering its affairs for a quarter of a century. Yet, even though three years later in 1559, the last Italian War finally ended with the Peace of Cateau-Cambresis, for Venice other more serious issues were now looming.[119]

Besides a failed harvest and a severe famine, in September 1569 an enormous explosion in the *Arsenale* halted the ship-building and destroyed parts of the neighbouring area. Then, four months later the peace that the Serenissima had managed to maintain with the Ottoman Empire for the last thirty years finally collapsed. The growing disagreements between the different merchants in Venice and Constantinople had now erupted into a fourth Venetian-Ottoman War, and with the sultan declaring his intention to take possession of Cyprus, in August 1571 the Republic lost this last foothold in the eastern Mediterranean to the Muslims.[120] As a result, Venice was now eager to join a new alliance with the other Christian allies, a Holy League that was to include the pope, the Genoese, various other states, the Knights of Malta, and eventually the previously reticent Spanish king. Although for their planned naval attack the overall leader was to be John of Austria, the illegitimate half-brother of Philip II of Spain, the large Venetian contingent would be led by Sebastiano Venier, a man destined a few years later to become doge. As their combined fleet began to congregate at Messina in Sicily, the 'Turks' continued to enjoy the freedom of the Adriatic, but with the allies' approach they started to retreat to their southern ports in the Ionian Sea. On their way past Lesina they stopped briefly to sack the town, forcing the people gratefully to take shelter in the fort so recently built by Charles V. At last, off Lepanto (Naupactos) at the entrance to the Gulf of Patras, on 7 October 1571 the vast opposing fleets met in a clash of galleys, galleons and galleases – the last such conflict of its kind to make use principally of such vessels.[121]

By the end of the day, the allies had achieved a stunning victory, the league having captured 117 ships and the Ottomans having suffered casualties said to have been four times greater than that of their enemy. As Venice had played a major part in the victory, the city celebrated the achievement not just with various festivities, Masses and *Te Deums*, but also by granting liberty to those 15,000 galley slaves who had played their part in the battle. Before long, various other festivals, memorials and art works would recall the triumph for posterity, among these the inauguration of a yearly procession of thanksgiving and the decoration of the entrance to the Arsenale with sculptures of St Mark's winged lion and Santa Giustina, on whose feast day the battle had occurred. Veronese produced two paintings recording the scene, one still in the ducal palace and the second now in the Accademia. However, despite its having provided more than half of the galleys employed in the battle, Venice received little compensation for its involvement, and it would be granted no territorial gains. Instead, having been deprived of its allies after the Spanish had turned their attention to their affairs elsewhere, two years later in March it found itself forced to sign another treaty with the sultan. Besides this earning the Republic the condemnation of its European neighbours, it also officially confirmed its earlier loss of Cyprus. Although in

1588 the Republic sent ships to assist the Spanish Armada in its attack on England, the reality was that its maritime power had now begun seriously to wane, and after its last notable success at Lepanto, it would begin on that steady decline that would lead to its eventual fall two centuries later.

In 1574, hurrying home to France after abandoning his Polish crown to take up that of his recently deceased brother, Henri III stopped in Venice to be given the usual spectacular welcome.[122] This would be the last major celebration the city would see for some time, as the next year it was again hit by the plague. This outbreak was to last for two years and by the time it was over it had killed more than 50,000 people. While the epidemic continued to rage, few risked going out, other than those struggling to dispose of the dead bodies littering the narrow streets and canals. As numbers of Venetians fled to the mainland in the hope of escaping the infection, still more turned to religion for salvation. When, therefore, the danger was finally past, Andrea Palladio, an architect chiefly resident in Vicenza, was given a new commission. Famous for his style of building that had now become fashionable throughout Europe, he was called on to design a new church of thanksgiving dedicated to the Redeemer. For centuries to come, at the Redentore on the Giudecca a yearly Mass would take place, attended by the doge and other dignitaries. These would make their way to the island over a bridge of boats, a pilgrimage across the wide basin that would continue even after the fall of the Republic, only finally being abandoned for safety reasons with the arrival of larger shipping in the 1970s.

As the horrors of the plague came to an end, another catastrophe hit the city. Just three years after a previous fire had destroyed part of the ducal palace, a second far more serious blaze took hold in December 1577. Now the great Council Chamber and the *Sala dello Scrutinio* were destroyed, along with the priceless works of art by the Bellini brothers, Titian, Tintoretto, Veronese, and others. In spite of initial uncertainty as to what should be done, the palace was quickly restored and Tintoretto and Veronese were called on to redecorate the interior, reproducing the earlier, often imaginary, portraits of the popes, and creating on the walls vast new paintings that represented Venice's moments of glory, among them the Battle of Lepanto. At the same time, work was going on elsewhere, not just in the centre but also out in the countryside on the *terraferma*. Palladio was now designing cool summer retreats for the wealthy Venetians who were eager to escape the heat and disease of the crowded city. Accordingly, the Brenta Canal became one of the most popular places for these new buildings, among them the famous Villa Foscari – later known as 'La Malcontenta' after the unfortunate woman confined there in the 19th century by her husband. In Venice itself, plans were now going ahead to build the latest version of the Rialto bridge. For the first time, this was to be constructed of stone, following the designs of Antonio da Ponte, who, after Palladio's death in 1580, had overseen the completion of his Redentore. This bridge, the fourth such structure to span the Grand Canal at this point, would be finished in 1591, nine years before the architect's nephew

Antonio Contin built another linking the palace to the prison – this dubbed in the 19th century the Bridge of Sighs. Among the other on-going works was Palladio's San Giorgio Maggiore, which, like his spectacular Teatro Olimpico in Vicenza, would be finished by Vicenzo Scamozzi, the designer of the *Procuratie Nuove* that completes the symmetry of St Mark's Square.

Even though Venice's war with the Ottomans was now over, many people still saw the Muslims as a danger, 'the present terror of the world'.[123] But these 'Turks' were not the only ones to be causing fear, as for some time the Uskoks had been creating equal concern to shipping and various coastal communities. Besides having been given official recognition as a military organisation by the Hungarian-Croatian king, Ferdinand I, after the earlier disaster at Klis they had also been granted a new base on the Gulf of Quarnero (Kvarner), near the Venetian-held island of Veglia (Krk). They had settled in the king's vassal town of Senj (Segna), which was not only barely accessible from the land but also particularly well defended by the notoriously treacherous seas in the region. As agriculture and other occupations were not an option here, the Uskoks had taken up ship-building instead, and soon, having created craft suitable for navigating the difficult local waters, they were attacking the Muslims' ships. While the Ottomans were enraged by this and blamed Ferdinand, as Venice had always claimed this sea as its own it would also be held responsible for failing to control the piracy. But as the Venetians' own vessels, islands and towns were occasionally targeted by the Uskoks, so in time they, too, became extremely angry and lodged a complaint with Ferdinand.[124] Yet, even after he became Emperor, he remained unwilling to expel the Uskoks as he still believed them useful for his security. Two years after he died, however, other parties would join in the complaints made against them, and the criticism grew particularly vociferous when in 1566 these corsairs made their first open assault on a Christian ship. This action indicated that they were no longer focused solely on carrying out pirate raids on the Ottoman vessels, and were now openly attacking those from Venice, Ragusa, and other places. Despite the new Emperor then promising to curb the pirates' attacks, they did not stop and even the imperial territory itself would continue to be hit.

Eventually, in July 1593 the peace accord between the Ottoman and Habsburg empires collapsed, and for the next fourteen years in the so-called 'Long War' the Ottomans continued to attack coastal towns, settlements, and also the Uskok bases. In retaliation, besides briefly recapturing Klis and massacring its occupants, the pirates kept up their raids on shipping and towns all round the Adriatic. Throughout this time, the Serenissima tried to maintain its neutrality and remain on the sidelines, but by 1599 its patience had run out and it had begun to take action against Trieste, Fiume (Rijeka), and various places along the Austro-Croat coastline. As a result, the Archduke Ferdinand of the semi-independent Inner-Austria (ruled from Graz) decided the moment had come to make peace, and in 1600 he sent his representative Count Joseph de Rabatta to negotiate with the Serenissima.[125] With tensions now eased, and the Austro-Ottoman War ended, Graz and Venice were happy to let things ride, both parties intentionally ignoring much of the continuing unlawful activity of the Uskoks, until eventually Venice again became so exasperated that in 1611 it renewed its earlier blockades. Even though the Archduke Ferdinand continued trying to control his troublemakers, two years later the Uskoks were reported to be still plundering 'Turk and Christian, Venetian and Austrian alike'.[126] This was a period of much brutality on both sides, and after seizing Carlopago (Karlobag) near the island of Pago (Pag) in May, the Serenissima decapitated some sixty Uskoks, whose their heads were then put on public display.[127] Reputedly the Uskoks responded with comparable violence, murdering the crew of a captured Venetian galley, slaughtering the admiral and allegedly eating his heart. Whatever really happened, with stories like this circulating the hatred of the Uskoks continued to grow. Because before long Venice took further steps to restrict movement from the Austrian ports, in spite of the attempts by the new Emperor to maintain the peace, in 1615 war broke out between the Empire and the Serenissima. In line with the religious divisions now beginning in Europe, the archduke in Graz was supported by Catholic Spain, while Venice, always less obedient to the pope, had the backing of the British and the Dutch. Yet the dispute itself remained localised, and in September 1617, after Venice's blockade of Gradisca in Gorizia was broken, the first moves were taken towards a resolution and by early the next year most of the Uskoks had at last been expelled from Senj.

* * *

Back in Venice, the dreaded Council of Ten had increased its surveillance, watching in particular the behaviour of a growing numbers of Venetian and foreign ruffians who had now appeared, offering – for a fee – to commit any crime. Wishing to contain these and other malefactors, the council was helped in its work by its spy network and also through the information gained from the *bocche di leone* scattered across the towns under Venetian control. Acting on such evidence and believing with good justification that the Republic was threatened with overthrow by a Spanish plot, in 1618 the authorities took more draconian measures, stringing up in the Piazzetta three *bravi* and bringing about the disappearance 300 others thought to be implicated. After this, the Council of Ten would retain its power, becoming still more ruthless as it grew less concerned about its own reputation.

Although Venice contrived to distance itself from the horrors of the Thirty Years War in which much of Europe was now caught up, it became involved in a separate dispute over the claims to Mantua, when following the death of Vincenzo Gonzaga the Serenissima supported the rights of his distant relation Charles, the duke of Nevers, against the Spanish claimant. After the besieged city fell to the imperial army in 1630, Mantua was stripped of its treasures and reduced to such destitution that by the time it was eventually returned to Nevers, hunger and disease had taken their toll. Worse still, the plague had reappeared and, having spread to Venice, tens of thousands more were to die, the epidemic eventually killing about a third of the city's population. So, once more in desperation the Venetians turned to their religion, the authorities now ordering the construction of an impressive new church dedicated to the Virgin. This would be the great Santa Maria della Salute, standing at the end of the Grand Canal that is such a significant landmark in the city today.

With Baldassare Longhena of Venice having won the commission for this immense project, in April 1631 the foundation stone was laid by the unfortunate doge, Niccolò Contarini, a delicate man, whose year in office would end when he died just a few hours after the ceremony. With 1,000,000 wooden piles driven deep into the mud of the lagoon for the foundations, work on building the church could now begin. Only months later in November, the epidemic having at last been declared over, the first of the annual processions of thanksgiving took place, the new doge and other dignitaries crossing the canal on a pontoon bridge of boats put in place for the occasion – another Venetian festival that is still celebrated today. The Salute had only just been consecrated when Longhena died in 1682, and the church's remaining scaffolding would not be removed for another six years; by which time the architect had also created two of the most famous buildings on the Grand Canal, the Rezzonico and Pesaro palaces.

Although during this time Venice had continued to avoid any major conflict close to home, further afield it would again be drawn into a serious dispute. Despite maintaining its peace with the Ottomans, even as places like Manfredonia had come under attack, in 1644 the Serenissima undeservedly became the object of the sultan's fury. Enraged by an assault on one of his ships – that had in fact been carried out by the Knights of Malta – he falsely accused the Venetians of being responsible. As a result, in June 1645 the vast Ottoman fleet landed on Candia (Crete). With the town of Canea (Chania) having soon surrendered, and the Republic's allies having provided only inadequate help, before long the situation on the island looked bleak. Although to raise the funds for the war, senior government positions were offered for sale in Venice, the island capital (today Heraklion) was also soon under siege. Remarkably, for the next 22 years the city struggled on under the assault, but in 1669 this most important colony could hold out no longer and, to the horror of the Venetians, the Captain-General Francesco Morosini was forced to surrender.

In the 1650s six elderly doges died within a five-year period, some having to be replaced after just days in office. But Venice's difficulties would soon be put in the shade by the horrors that Ragusa then suffered in April 1667 when it was hit by the most destructive earthquake it had yet experienced. Following landslides, rockfalls and a tsunami, fires blazed in the city for two to three weeks. Besides the Rector's Palace and numerous other important buildings being destroyed, much of the town was wiped out, and some 5,000-6,000 people were killed. Despite the death of the rector and others in authority and the subsequent chaos that then erupted, steps were quickly taken to rebuild the place. As so little of the former medieval architecture remained, it was decided to reconstruct the city in the now-fashionable baroque style. With regulations dictating the height and design of the houses, there would be a new conformity in the appearance of the town, something particularly evident in the Stradun that cuts through the historic centre. With most of the old buildings gone, the only records of the place's previous appearance now remains in the town's earlier artworks, such as the painting in the Church of St Blaise in which the saint holds a model of old Ragusa in his hands

For Venice, there was now better news, however. Apart from the recapture from the Ottomans of Novigrad in Istria, there were other successes in Dalmatia, with Klis fortress being retaken in 1669 after 132 years of Turkish possession; it was then held by the Venetians until the fall of the Republic. Yet the following period of peace was not to last. While Vienna survived a second assault by the Ottoman army in September 1683 – the city saved at the last minute by the timely arrival of the Polish general Jan Sobieski – in the minds of many of the Christian leaders the Turkish menace had still not gone away. Therefore, the following January, just days after the death of doge Contarini, Venice responded to appeals for help and agreed to join the new league formed with the Russians and others against the Ottomans.

In spite of the harsh criticism he had received for his surrender of Candia, Francesco Morosini had later been exonerated and then become immensely popular as people had begun to hear of his bravery and good leadership during the siege. Although he now wanted to stand for election as doge, it was felt that he would better serve the Republic as head of its fleet, and so another candidate was chosen in his place. Soon after assuming his position as captain-general, Morosini was able to capture the Ionian island of Santa Maura (Lefkada), and he then used this as a base over the next two years while he and his foreign allies continued taking back other towns from the Muslims. Having eventually gained full possession of the Morea (Peloponnese), Morosini moved on to Athens and occupied the city. Here, on 26 September 1687, he gave the command for a mortar to be fired towards the Parthenon. As the ancient temple was still virtually intact, the Ottomans were using it at the time to store their gunpowder, and so the allies' direct hit resulted in a major explosion that destroyed for ever a considerable part of the historic building. While the Swedish General Königsmarck was said to be shocked, Morosini, with the careless disregard often shown for such heedless destruction in the heat of battle, was reported to have declared it a 'lucky' shot. Not content with this, besides then attempting to plunder its treasures – and in the process causing further damage to the temple – before his departure from the port Morosini would two ancient and priceless stone lions, which still proudly guard the entrance to Venice's *Arsenale* today.

While the damage done to the Parthenon would leave a stain on Morosini's reputation, in Venice reports of his triumphs were greeted with wild enthusiasm, and the respect in which the captain-general was held led in 1688 to his election to the highest office. Still unwilling to retire from active service and determined to lead his army, he became the last serving doge to go to war. Morosini's objective was to capture the important Aegean islands of Negroponte (Euboea) and Chios, but his campaigning over the next few years would not go according to plan. The Venetians and their allies suffered defeats and disease, and the doge himself was temporarily forced by sickness to return home. After that Morosini's health began to decline and in January 1694, the year before Chios was finally abandoned, he died at Nauplia (Návplio) in the Peloponnese. After his body had been returned to Venice for a funeral in San Zanipolo, it was interred in Santo Stefano the spot still indicated by a simple plaque on the floor. There would, however, be other more extravagant ways in which he was remembered; besides receiving the honorific *Peloponnesiacus*, he was honoured with a bronze bust and had a triumphal arch erected in his memory in the Doges' Palace. His most poignant memorial, however, is the mummified body in the Museo Correr of his adored cat, from which he always hated to be separated.

For another five years after Morosini's death the war carried on, but eventually, under pressure from its allies, on 7 February 1699 Venice agreed to an end of the hostilities. According to the Treaty of Karlowitz, the Republic retained possession of the Peloponnese, the island of Santa Maura, and also the places it had gained along the Dalmatian coast. At the same time, however, it was forced to renounce its other claims further afield. Therefore, although it now became the acknowledged owner of the Kingdom of Morea, the Serenissima would go into the new century with its influence in the Mediterranean greatly reduced, and the status of its *Stato da Mar* significantly diminished in the eyes of others.

12

The Serenissima's last days of carnival

'Le superflu, chose très nécessaire.'

Voltaire[128]

The eighteenth century would open with two deaths, in Venice that of Doge
Silvestro Valier, who had a fatal seizure after a heated quarrel with his wife,
and in Spain four months later, on 1 November, that of Carlos II. The first of
these events was chiefly of significance for the Venetians, but the second was
to have more widespread consequences. With the disabled Spanish king having
left no heir, finally, after years of waiting, his Bourbon and Habsburg relations
began to assert their rights, and soon their dispute had turned into a bitter
rivalry. Within eight months, Louis XIV's French grandson Philip of Anjou
had taken the throne and the situation had escalated into a full-blown war that
was soon to involve several of the continent's major powers. Yet, even though
their territories were invaded by the opposing armies and their coastal waters

'Il Ridotto', by Francesco Guardi in Ca' Rezzonico, Venice.

filled with foreign fleets, the Venetians again chose to distance themselves from the conflict. Therefore, with the government determinedly pursuing a policy of neutrality for most of the coming century, the people would enjoy the peace that had eluded them throughout most of the previous two hundred years.

When, with the eventual end of the War of Spanish Succession in 1713 Philip V was at last acknowledged as Spain's new king, the Austrian Habsburgs were compensated with Naples and the whole of southern Italy.[129] But even before the fighting was over another major conflict had broken out in the north between Sweden and its neighbouring countries. Nonetheless, having temporarily been forced to withdraw from the fighting, in 1708 the king of Denmark visited Venice with his large entourage. Said in jest to have brought his northern weather with him, he would experience one of the coldest winters suffered by the city on record, the canals and lagoon freezing so that it was actually possible to cross on foot to the mainland. Even so, during his stay Frederik IV enjoyed the opera and other entertainments and in March he attended a regatta that had been especially laid on in his honour. Having been painted by the famous Venetian portraitist Rosalba Carriera and bought a large collection of Murano glass to add to his hosts' extremely valuable parting gifts, by the time he left it was generally agreed that the visit had been a major success.

Soon after, despite its efforts to avoid conflict, Venice briefly found itself again under threat. The Ottoman sultan, determined to regain his lost lands, had now concocted an excuse to go to war and, after taking the last Venetian outposts in the Aegean, had turned his attention to the Peloponnese. By the end of 1715 he had captured all of the Morea and Venice's last remaining small possessions further south in Candia. The next year Corfu, too, came under attack, but after being besieged for months the fortress succeeded in driving the Turkish invaders off. Buoyed by this success, the Venetians then won victories over the Ottomans in the eastern Mediterranean, the Ionian Sea, and up and down the Dalmatian coast. Now finding himself under further pressure from the Emperor's armies, the sultan decided the time had come to sue for peace and after three years of fighting, in 1718 the combatants met at Passorowitz. Here, to its chagrin and humiliation and despite its recent gains, Venice was forced to agree to the surrender of much of its recently won territory. Although in the Aegean it held on to the island of Cerigo (Kythera), and in the Ionian-Adriatic region Preveza and a few other fortresses, this treaty would limit all further expansion of the *Stato da Mar*, which would now remain unchanged until the fall of the Republic in 1797.

Venice, now with a population of around 160,000, had by this time become famous for its many theatres and seven opera houses.[130] Interest in opera had developed considerably during the previous century when Claudio Monteverdi had been *maestro di cappella* at St Mark's Basilica. Born in Cremona, Monteverdi had moved from Mantua to Venice in 1613, and by the time of his death and subsequent burial in the Frari three decades later, the first opera theatre had been open for six years. In this same period the city had begun to be a popular destination for foreigners, Bonny Prince Charlie, for one, visiting in 1737. Above all it had become a favourite destination for the large numbers of young men who were travelling on the Grand Tour. Soon being seen as second only to Rome, by 1740 Venice was already publishing a guidebook listing the attractions that it had on offer. Although it had grown rich over the years, largely thanks to its trade having been restored with the return of peace, now it had also begun to appreciate the profits to be found in tourism.

By this time, in many regards the Signoria showed a greater laxity, but it still imposed strict rules on any behaviour that it considered dangerous to the security of the Republic. Besides clamping down fiercely on any verbal criticism of the state, equally doggedly it sought to curb all excessive display that might raise an individual above his peers. Whatever threatened to disturb the public peace was forbidden, and so anything that could induce rivalry or jealousy was not permitted. Just as the gondoliers had been ordered in 1562 to paint their boats black to prevent unnecessary competition, lavish banquets had been banned. So too, in the final years of the 17th century, after a law was introduced to limit blatant ostentation and extravagance, lace ruffles and certain other fabrics were no longer condoned. In much the same vein, about forty years later, when the Frenchman Charles de Brosses visited in 1739, he was surprised to find how a Venetian noblewoman could wear her fabulous jewels and colourful dresses only for one year after her marriage. Even so, over generations females had found other ways to show themselves off. While some had publicly exposed their breasts – something that had much shocked a visiting late 15th century churchman – several had bleached their hair with urine. Many had also adopted a bizarre fad that had been popular since the 16th century, namely the wearing of the platform-soled zoccoli or chopines, which at times had been as much as eighteen inches high. These had possibly been introduced from the eastern lands with which Venice was at the time trading, but while they might have once had some practical use in protecting the women's hems, for patrician ladies until the early 18th century they had more importantly allowed them to show off the rich materials of their exceptionally long skirts. This impractical fashion meant that in order to maintain their balance when out walking, the wearer needed the support of her attendants, in particular of her personal escort, or cicerone. Even though it was often not clear to what degree – if any – there was a sexual element to this young man's role, his constant presence was viewed even by the woman's husband as a mark of the family's distinction.

In spite of certain restrictions, Venice was now, therefore, a place where there was display of extravagance and a determined pursuit of enjoyment. While in the later 1600s, Amelot de la Houssaie, secretary to the French ambassador, criticised both the decadence of the 'perfidious' Venetians and the cumbersome way the government held its people in thrall, state surveillance was less feared and the general atmosphere had become more relaxed. Despite being a profoundly Catholic city, where the people devoutly followed the Church practices and took part in the multiple ceremonies put on in celebration of feast days, the authorities' approach towards the morality of people's private lives was again marked by that typical Venetian pragmatism. According to the popular mantra, all that was needed was a little Mass in the morning, a little gambling in the afternoon, and a little woman in the evening: *a messetta, bassetta e donnetta.*

No longer would those found guilty of 'transgressive behaviour' be imprisoned, tortured or executed. So as long as the population was contented and happy and its behaviour did not disturb the peace or prosperity of the state, individuals were free to act as they wished. In the words of one of Goldoni's characters in *La Bottega del Caffé*, Venice was a city where it was possible for all to 'live well' and 'enjoy freedom, peace, and joy', provided they knew 'how to be prudent, cautious, careful and honourable'.[131] This balance was reiterated by de Brosses, who, having declared that nowhere else in the world could such liberty and licence be found, summed the situation up with the advice: 'Do not meddle with the government, and you can do just as you want.'[132]

With Venice thus famous at this time for its easy morals, among the places popular for assignations were the *felzi*, those enclosed curtained spaces on the gondolas that were only removed by the fascist government in the 1930s. Here people were guaranteed privacy, the gondolier being expected to show discretion, as any failure on his part to abide by this unwritten rule would earn him the condemnation of his fellows. This licentious situation was partly the result of the bachelor status of many Venetians. Careful as ever about their money, they tended to contract few marriages in an intentional effort to avoid the division of family fortunes or the payment of expensive dowries. So, with the resultingly large number of unmarried men and women, fathers opted to send their single daughters into one of the numerous religious houses. In many of these, sexual freedom was the norm, the nuns receiving their lovers within the convent walls, or slipping out to meet them elsewhere. One such young woman had met Casanova when he was attending Mass at her convent church of Santa Maria degli Angeli, and after they had agreed to a rendezvous on Murano, they had been joined by others with the same intentions.

Since the establishment of the Ospedale della Pietà for foundlings in 1346, Venice had tended to its orphans, and with three more Ospedali Grandi set up in the 16th century the impoverished, homeless, and mortally sick were equally cared for. Over time these establishments would become famous for the quality of music performed by the young women who had been put into the care of the nuns. With life here offering more opportunities for the girls, in time public warnings were issued to those who attempted to place their children in the convent on the false pretence of their being orphaned. While religious zeal might often have been lacking, the musical talent in the Ospedali was now generally recognised, and by the 18th century the singers were attracting large audiences and receiving widespread praise. When the young women sang and played, many would be impressed by the quality of the performance, among them Frederik IV of Denmark, and the Grand Duke and Duchess of Russia – the later Tsar Paul and his wife. Another eager audience member was Jean-Jacques Rousseau, who would express his regret at being unable to see what he initially imagined to be the 'beautiful source' of the 'angelic sound' emanating from behind the grill concealing the women. After eventually contriving a meeting, he was disappointed by their appearance, but nonetheless he would claim that his earlier image still returned whenever he heard their ethereal music. De Brosses, on the other hand, was not disappointed. Also comparing their voices to those of angels, he would recall his pleasure at catching sight of a 'young and pretty nun, dressed in white, with a bunch of pomegranate flowers behind her ear, conducting the orchestra and gracefully beating time with the greatest of precision'.[133]

These girls were trained by professional musical directors, one of whom was Antonio Vivaldi. A sickly man, he was born in Venice in 1678 and had taken orders at the age of fifteen, in time working at the *Ospedale della Pietà* as a priest before becoming *maestro di cappella*. Dubbed 'il prete rosso', the red priest, because of the colour of his hair, here he would spend two long periods teaching and writing new compositions for the women. He was an exceptional violinist, but his music would eventually be rejected as unfashionable by the fickle Venetians, and so having lost favour he decided to go abroad and find work in the courts of other heads of state. By the time of his death in Vienna in 1741, he had composed hundreds of instrumental works and operas.

By the 18th century, the carnival season that had existed ever since the 1100s had been extended, no longer lasting for just the short period before Lent but beginning in October and continuing for several months until Easter.[134] As the celebrations became more extravagant and exuberant with fireworks, bull fights, bull runs, and other entertainments, in 1751 the organisers even went so far as to bring a rhinoceros into the city. Now, famous for its feasting, festivals, and free love, Venice had also become renowned for the exceptional number of its courtesans, of whom apparently there some 12,000 at the end of the 16th century. The city's prostitutes even had their own guild. There was of course a price to pay for this. During their stay, many of the young visitors would contract syphilis, the disease that within a hundred years of first appearing in Europe in the fifteenth century had spread throughout much of the continent's male population.

The right to erect the first public gaming table had been granted to the man responsible for initially raising the two columns in the Piazzetta, and after that the habit had become increasingly popular, with more and more gambling centres gathering around the Rialto. After private houses were given their own licences, the first public ridotto would be officially opened in 1638. While the stakes were soon too high for the average person, by the end of the century these were fashionable meeting places for the richer members of society. With still more being on offer, here the players wore masks, even though this practice had been forbidden to gamblers since 1268. Masks had also been banned for those visiting convents in 1339, and, similarly, following some 'serious incidents', in 1517 they had ceased to be permitted for visitors to the carnival. Yet, around a hundred years later records show that they had become widespread at festival time, and in the ridotto near San Moise they were now customary, as was the obligatory black tricorne hat that was supposed further to guarantee anonymity – a reality on which Montesquieu would throw considerable doubt.[135] While special masks were also originally worn by doctors during the many outbreaks of the plague, their strange, long beaks filled with the herbs intended to stave off the infection, all types and designs had gradually become so emblematic of

Venice that even Voltaire, who never visited the place, would sardonically refer to their wearing in one of his short stories:

> The few public places on show in this city, were filled with men and women who had a double face, that which nature had given them, and a badly painted cardboard face that they had placed on top; as a result the population seemed to be composed of spectres.[136]

By the 18th century everyone, except for the money-changers, wore disguises at carnival time. As masks allowed people from all walks of life to mix freely, patricians, priests and the general public continued to wear them until the Austrians restricted their use to the theatre in 1802. The revellers were expected to take on the role of the character in whose clothes they were dressed – Casanova for one choosing on at least one occasion to be Pierrot, the sad, white-faced, lovelorn clown who appears in the *commedia dell'arte*. As Venetians had little time for tragedy, this early form of burlesque theatre played a big part in their lives, and from it would develop the more modern style of comedy made popular by Goldoni. Born in Venice in 1707, after a fairly rebellious youth spent in Rimini, Pavia, and various towns in the Veneto, he had returned to his native city. Here, after giving up his law practice, he turned to the career he had always wanted to follow, and from this time on he dedicated himself to working in the theatre and writing plays. After abandoning his early attempts at tragedy, he turned to comedy, drawing inspiration from the earlier *commedia dell'arte* and the French playwright Molière. On discarding the masks of the earlier art form, his 250 plays – some written in the Venetian or local dialect, others in the current Tuscan Italian, or French – would focus on the everyday life of real people. This went down well in Venice and for a time Goldoni enjoyed notable success. Eventually, however, having fallen out with his rivals, in particular Carlo Gozzi, in 1761 he moved to France. Here again he became popular, enjoying the sponsorship of the French court, but by the time of his death in Paris in 1793 everything had changed. With the king dead and the Revolution coming to its height, Goldoni was by then a poor man. Over the following years he was largely forgotten in Venice, his works banned for a time by the Austrians, but in 1883 the city erected a statue to him near the Rialto, and later one of the theatres where he had presented his plays was renamed after him.

Perhaps no-one better represents 18th-century Venice than Giacomo Casanova – a multi-talented, highly intelligent, hedonistic man, who, by surviving into old age, would live to witness the tragic collapse of his home city. Having repeatedly fallen foul of the authorities, he would twice have to leave Venice, eventually dying in his early seventies in 1798 in Bohemia, today the Czech Republic. Naturally superstitious, some Venetians would later believe that he had returned to Venice and others that he had even achieved immortality.[137] To modern eyes much of his behaviour appears to be utterly reprehensible, evidence going so far as to suggest his rape of young women, a charge that he would always deny. As a free-thinking libertine, he happily boasted of his multiple seductions and freely admitted that his main aim in life was to 'indulge' his senses. But, even though this is the reason for his notoriety today, among his contemporaries his fame was largely founded on his successful escape in 1757 from the city's prison. For this achievement he was immediately the talk of the town and years later, when allowed to return to Venice, even the authorities were eager to speak to him and learn more of how he had achieved the feat. Prisoners were confined to cells each side of the Rio della Paglia, the small canal that runs beneath the Bridge of Sighs. While some inmates were held in the ground floor 'wells' (*pozzi*) that were subject to flooding, others like Casanova were confined on the upper floor under the lead-covered roof – the so-called 'leads' (*piombi*) – that became stiflingly hot during the summer months. Venice is often depicted as a virtual police state, an idea that Napoleon would later do much to promote. Yet, as Goldoni had indicated, for those who went about their normal business, life was uncomplicated and urban unrest virtually unknown. Despite being critical of many aspects of the Republic – in particular the judicial body of three Inquisitors that had been established in the mid-16th century – even Montesquieu had noted during his visit to Venice in 1728 that 'the people of Venice are the best in the world. There is no-one on guard at the spectacles, and one hears nothing of disorder; one sees no fighting.'[138] So, by the time the Republic fell, there were in fact no prisoners in the *piombi*, and only a few more in the *pozzi*. While here, according to John Julian Norwich, there now were just three murderers still incarcerated, Peter Ackroyd reduces even this number, he believing that there was only one inmate, a man who had been trapped in these appalling conditions for sixteen years.[139] Following a first failed attempt, Casanova had managed against the odds to cut his way out of his cell and climb over the roof tops. After that, he and his fellow inmate – a priest – had made their way into the ducal palace and descended the great stairs to freedom, they thus becoming the only two people ever to escape from Venice's infamous prison.

Born into an acting family, after an early period as a lawyer and then briefly as an unsuccessful *abbé* within the church, Casanova had succeeded in convincing the state to give him a position as an army officer. In time, dissatisfied with this new occupation, and already dismissed from the Church, he chose to become a violin player for the theatre. While continuing to gamble and indulge in tiresome – sometimes tasteless – pranks, he had the good luck to win his way into the circle of a nobleman whose life he had saved by his quick thinking, and a little medical experience. Yet, with the authorities now watching him, in the early 1750s he decided to travel around Europe, drawing further negative attention to himself from the authorities in most places that he visited. On finally returning home, his behaviour caught up with him and in 1755 he was arrested on the grounds of his irreligious and immoral conduct and sentenced to five years imprisonment. This would end fifteen months later with his famous escape, and subsequent flight to France. Now an exile, he assumed a noble name, and began his period of extensive travel, covering vast distances – possibly some 40,000 miles – around Europe, his journeys taking him to Madrid, Paris, and even St Petersburg far to the north. Although eventually able to return to Venice in 1774, nine years later he found himself again unwelcome and once more he had to leave the city. With his youthful good looks and charm by this time fading, he would end his days deep in the Bohemian countryside, where, lonely and hard up, he was working as a nobleman's librarian. Here he was encouraged to tell his story, and so he began with remarkable honesty and no pretence at false modesty to write down all the facts as he saw them. Not seeking to explain or excuse, he produced a typically frank 18th-century Rousseauesque account of both his misdeeds and his achievements. While he is chiefly remembered today as an arch reprobate, this shows him as a genuine lover of the many women in his life, and it also recounts how he met, sometimes advised, and often debated with many of the great names of the age: Frederick the Great, Catherine the Great and Voltaire, among others. And while he had come to know Lorenzo da Ponte, the librettist of Mozart, in Venice, later apparently he had also met the composer, possibly even giving him some suggestions for his opera *Don Giovanni*.

The equally scandalous da Ponte had been born in the ghetto to Jewish parents at Ceneda (today Vittorio Veneto) in March 1749. As his widowed father, wishing to marry a Catholic, had chosen in August 1763 to convert with his three sons to Christianity, all had then changed their names, the oldest boy, Emanuele Conegliano, taking that of the bishop Lorenzo da Ponte who had baptised him. Thanks to this man, the young Lorenzo was belatedly given a good education in the seminary, and here he had learnt to write poetry in both Latin and Italian. After that, having few opportunities open to him he took minor orders and began teaching, before becoming a priest in 1773. Around that same time Lorenzo moved to Venice, where before long he would take up a disreputable lifestyle, spending the greater part of his time gambling and womanising. The next year he and his brother moved to Treviso where they worked as teachers in the seminary, but by 1776 Lorenzo was in trouble, having angered the local authorities by encouraging radical thought among his students and producing inflammatory writings and seditious poetry. Therefore, he now returned to Venice to defend his name. Having already achieved a level of notoriety, here he would continue on his dangerous path, becoming acquainted with men like Casanova and certain other rebellious young noblemen who were calling for reform. After a series of affairs, Lorenzo eventually settled down with a new mistress, by whom he had two children, both of whom were sent before long to the *Ospedale della Pietà*. By 1779 his scandalous behaviour had proved too much for the authorities and he was facing charges of disrespect, irreligious behaviour, and immorality. Having been anonymously accused in the *bocca di leone* of adultery and rape, he was indicted both for living in a brothel and for helping to run it. At that point, finding himself seriously at risk of imprisonment in the *pozzi*, he fled from the city to Gorizia (Görtz). After two years he moved on again to Dresden, where he met Antonio Salieri, who then helped him gain a post as librettist in Vienna. However, on the death of Joseph II in 1792, da Ponte lost his earlier financial support and, distrusted by the new Emperor Leopold, he left the city and went to Trieste where he later married. Although for a time he considered going to France, because of the deteriorating situation in the country he ultimately decided to take Casanova's advice and go to London. Having soon fallen seriously into debt and been repeatedly arrested for his involvement in a dubious business scheme, eventually in 1805 he fled England and joined up with his family in the USA. Here, at last da Ponte was able to create a successful new career for himself, teaching Italian at Columbia College, introducing the people to the works of Mozart and Rossini, and even founding his own opera theatre. Ten years after becoming an American citizen, he died aged 89 in 1838.

Music continued throughout this time to play a central part in the lives of the Venetians. Remarking on their *joie de vivre*, many visitors were struck how song could be heard everywhere, Goldoni commenting on this when returning home in 1734 after a period away. He gave a vivid description of how businesses remained open throughout the night, the well-illuminated public *campi* and other areas thronged with people enjoying themselves. According to the playwright, everyone was singing:

> They sing in the squares, the streets, the canals; the merchants selling their merchandise sing, the workmen leaving their work sing, the gondolier waiting for his master sings. The character of the people is one of cheerfulness.[140]

Many others would be similarly impressed by the musicality of the people, particularly the way the gondoliers sang their barcarolles with interchanging verses taken from the work of the city's famous 16th-century resident, Torquato Tasso. His *La Gerusalemme liberata*, written in the days after the battle of Lepanto, had grown so popular after its translation into the Venetian dialect a century later that it had become part of the gondoliers' repertoire. Byron would write regretfully in *Childe Harold*, 'In Venice Tasso's echoes are no more / And silent rows the songless gondolier,' but even after the fall of the Republic this music would still continue to impress and influence several great visiting composers, men like Chopin, Verdi, and Wagner. The gondoliers' song would also be taken up again during Venice's struggles for independence, and there would be a few more scattered reports of it right to the end of the century.

From the 15th century onwards popular drinking and eating places had started to proliferate, these *bacari* providing wine and small snacks, or *cicchetti*. Reputedly the oldest of these was 'Do Mori' near the Rialto, where Casanova was said to have arranged his first trysts with his many lovers. At the start of the 1600s, Venice opened some of the earliest coffee houses, and within a hundred years many cafés had sprung up, 35 in the Piazza alone. In 1720, about 40 years after the first house had appeared, the famous Florian's opened in the *Procuratie Nuove*. This, the oldest such establishment still in existence, was initially known as 'Alla Venezia Triomfante', but after the Republic's fall the owner thought it expedient to rename it after his uncle. For Goldoni, Casanova and others, including many of the city's foreign visitors, this was a popular meeting place where they could exchange the latest news and gossip.

Even so, care had to be taken regarding discussion of government affairs, the city being still full of spies, Casanova himself having been employed by the authorities in this way for a time. The informants, who came from all walks of life, had the same instructions as the merchants and diplomats working abroad, namely to report on any activity that might harm the state.

As other attitudes became more relaxed, in 1715 the Jesuits who had been expelled around a century earlier while Venice was under papal interdict were allowed to return. With the support of the rich Manin family they now demolished their old church and built the larger and highly ornate Santa Maria Assunta, better known as the Gesuiti. Even more elaborate was the Baroque church of San Moise completed in 1726 to replace the 9th-century building originally dedicated to the Byzantine-canonised prophet of the Old Testament, Moses. This would only narrowly escape demolition 150 years later when its style was described by one of its critics as 'the mad fantasy of the epoch of decadent architecture'.[141] At the same time there were other more practical changes taking place around the city, most notably the introduction in 1732 of public lighting. But, while some praised the state of its streets, others had been less complimentary, and even though St Mark's mosaics were cleaned of their soot and wax twice a year at Christmas and Easter, in the 1780s several visitors commented on the dirtiness of the basilica. In these last years of the Republic a string of important visitors continued to arrive, among them the young Mozart in 1771 and Goethe in 1786.

Less happily for Venice, the Serenissima's protectionist approach to the changing markets was now beginning to play against it. Since the 14th century it had been a centre for luxury goods, its industries producing not only things such as silk and soap but also the precious glass of Murano, the production methods for which would be kept a close secret. It was alleged that in the 17th century, after they had been invited to France to create the mirrors for Louis XIV's *Salle de glaces*, the artisans had been poisoned by the Venetian authorities to prevent them divulging the processes that they had used. Even a century later, in 1745 two others suspected of the same crime were believed to have suffered a comparable fate. Yet the Republic's very conservatism and unwillingness to adapt to the more industrial age was adding to its problems. Since the end of the 1600s, it had been facing outside competition from places able to produce cheaper items and so from that time on, rather than luxury goods, it had been the agricultural products of the *terraferma* that had provided the greater part of the city's income. Even boat construction had been left behind, and despite a large new building being created in the *Arsenale* in 1750, the production of ships had not kept up with modern demands. As a result, its greatly reduced navy was now ill-equipped to withstand an enemy attack. This, however, was far from the minds of most people, lulled into a false sense of security as they enjoyed the benefits of the peace their leaders had achieved by adhering to their policy of neutrality.

Among those who now began taking full advantage of the city's increasing tourism were the new *vedutisti* artists. Seeing a ready market among the 30,000 or more visitors attending the carnival, these were soon setting out to satisfy the foreigners' desire to take home a souvenir. After the first volume of *vedute* was published in 1703, and these painters continued to produce their popular representations and interpretations of Venice, often depicting the elaborate ceremonies, costumes and customs. Several constructed their pictures with the precision of a stage manager, further perfecting the image by adjusting the proportions and lay-out of the buildings and open spaces. Besides those well-known Venetians such as the former set-designer Antonio Canal (dubbed Canaletto), his nephew Bernardo Bellotto, and Francesco Guardi – who also came from a family of artists – there were many others, both Italian and English, who sought to cash in on this vogue. Some created their own original works, while others copied those of the more famous, something that still causes a headache for experts trying to verify a painting's provenance. With large numbers being bought by collectors, many masterpieces of this period are still in foreign hands. The British banker and eventual consul Joseph Smith, who loved the city and made it his home for seventy years, accumulated an exceptional collection of paintings, books and manuscripts that was later sold to George III and would eventually become part of the Royal Collection now held at Windsor and in the British Library. Besides supporting or befriending playwrights and musicians like Goldoni and Vivaldi, Smith also backed various other artists and performers, among them the young *castrato* Farinelli, born to a musical family in Andria in Puglia, who came to Venice to attend the carnival in 1729. Yet, it was not just the *vedutisti* art works that now went abroad, but also the painters themselves, Canaletto, for one, moving with the help of Smith to England for nearly a decade in the 1740s. Similarly, his nephew Bellotto, often confusingly given the same popular name as his uncle, became the guest of the Polish king, spending 16 years in Dresden before moving to Warsaw, where he remained until his death in 1780.

While many artists were focused on city or seascapes, Pietro Longhi concentrated on genre painting, depicting interior scenes showing Venetians enjoying entertainments in their *palazzi* or at the *ridotto*. The city's most renowned artist, Giovanni Battista Tiepolo, became famous for his historical and allegorical subjects and great theatrical frescoes. Pragmatically remarking that it was better for artists to 'please the noble and rich gentlemen' who can make their fortune, instead of those other people who could 'not buy paintings of great value', he succeeded in earning an international reputation, carrying out commissions for royalty and dignitaries abroad.[142]

* * *

As the Republic continued to be ruled by its oligarchy, elsewhere changes had been taking place. In 1731, the ambitious Elizabeth Farnese, the second wife of the Bourbon Philip V of Spain, had succeeded in gaining her father's dukedom of Parma and Piacenza for her fifth son, Charles. Two years later, Europe's next major conflict broke out, and during this War of the Polish Succession Spain found itself ranked alongside France against their common enemy, the Emperor. Therefore, wishing to regain Naples, an imperial possession since 1713 and the end of the War of Spanish Succession, Philip instructed his son to march south and retake the city. Charles achieved this in May, entering Naples just a few days after the Austrians finally left Puglia following their defeat at Bitonto. The next year, after successfully mopping up the last pockets of resistance on the mainland and capturing the island of Sicily, he became king, his coronation as Charles VII of Naples beginning a period of Bourbon rule that would last – with some interruption – well into the next century. Further redistributions of territory were then confirmed three years later when, at the end of the Polish war, Parma was surrendered to the Emperor.[143] Meanwhile, Charles VII had already begun considering how to bring reform to his country. Its general condition was now poor, the situation being particularly bad in Puglia where only a few places, such as Lecce, had not suffered from the years of punishing taxation and neglect. Besides building roads, and initiating measures to increase the region's trade, the king called for improvements to the ports at Brindisi, Bari, and Barletta, also ordering the harbour at Trani (his regional capital) to be dredged to make it suitable for larger craft.[144] While seeking to reduce the influence of the Church, which still held about a third of the land, he tried equally to limit the powers of the landowners who were hampering his efforts to end feudalism.

Twenty-five years later, on his older brother's death in 1759, Charles succeeded to the crown of Spain. As he was forced by the terms agreed at the recent treaties to abdicate his throne in Naples and Sicily, that would now pass to his son, Ferdinand I. While the new king was a weak, not highly intelligent man, whose preferred pastime was hunting, his wife, Maria Carolina of Habsburg – the older sister of Marie Antoinette – was a far stronger character. At her betrothal it had been agreed that, were she to produce a son, she would be able to join the state council, and this would happen nine years later following the birth of the heir. After that, exerting her considerable influence, she had taken a leading role in the running of affairs. Yet, with the king being more approachable, he was obviously more popular when he visited Lecce. He also gained the approval of the tax-payers of Bari a year later, when in 1798 he granted them equal status to the nobles. Similarly, he pleased the peasants in and around Taranto by awarding them their independence from the local Count of Selva, who had previously ordered them to demolish their houses whenever the tax inspector appeared on the scene. As a result of Ferdinand's action, the local town became a 'Royal City' under the jurisdiction of the crown, and although previously called after the count, it was now rechristened Alberobello. Largely undiscovered until the 1960s, this and its neighbouring villages have now become a tourist attraction for their many white conical *trulli* that are built in a style not unlike the round dry-stone shelters found throughout Puglia. Although often extended over the years to accommodate the owners' growing families, as they are still constructed in the traditional style, they continue to give this region its particular distinctive character.

In Venice, as the 18th century was approaching its end, the majority of people continued to enjoy themselves, most of them untroubled by the watchful eye of the state, and largely unconcerned by the Republic's mounting problems. While some hundred years earlier even men such as Monteverdi had found themselves denounced in the *bocca di leone*, and the mouth outside San Moise had still been used in 1779 to charge da Ponte, things were changing. Nine years earlier, Charles Burney had thought these *bocche* defunct and out of service, and was relieved to find some of them full of cobwebs. In the continuing festive atmosphere, Venice was still able to stage elaborate celebrations, and in January 1782 it laid on a spectacular display in the Piazza for the benefit of its Russian imperial visitors, the Grand Duke Paul and the Grand Duchess Maria Feodorovna, who at the time were travelling incognito as the Count and Countess of the North. Even as the storm clouds were gathering and in France the Revolution was tightening its grip, in 1791 work began on the construction of the new Fenice theatre.[145] So in these very last days of the Republic the Spanish playwright Leandro Fernández de Moratín would still find the Venetians contentedly carrying on with their old way of life, working and enjoying themselves, happily leaving affairs in the hands their government. Fewer than twelve weeks before the Republic was finally brought to an end in May 1797, the Venetian ambassador in Paris was told that the carnival had so far gone well and that 'there was almost nothing unpleasant, and everything proceeded joyously.'[146]

It was already clear nevertheless that the authorities were becoming increasingly worried about the moral and social fabric of their city. The reformist Carlo Contarini railed in the Great Council in 1774 about the general disorder of the state, declaring that everything was 'out of control'. Seeking to address the problem, the members decided to close the *ridotto* at San Moise and issue a ban on all gambling – a law the Venetians soon managed to contravene. The problems facing Venice were more deep-rooted, however. Many of the richer families were now causing concern by deserting the city and moving more permanently to their estates and palaces on the *terraferma*. Even Casanova, living abroad by this time, feared the effect this exodus might have. Although membership on the council was offered for sale to some new, wealthy families, few came forward to accept this chance to be promoted to the patriciate. At the same time, those members of the older elite families who had fallen on hard times, the so-called *barnabotti* – men like Carlo Contarini, Georgio Pisani, and Andrea Memmo – had now begun publicly to voice their dissatisfaction. Lorenzo da Ponte had once mixed with these radicals, sharing with Memmo and others those inflammatory verses that had added to his eventual disgrace and exile. While the Inquisitors sought to prevent the exchange of such dangerous ideas in the cafes, Contarini and Pisani took every opportunity to speak out against the corruption and decadence of the state. So, in 1780, with censorship having returned and the Council of Ten having again begun to tighten its surveillance, these two radicals were arrested and imprisoned. While Contarini would die soon after at Cattaro (Kotor), his colleague remained incarcerated for another ten years. Continuing to suffer further periods of house arrest and imprisonment in Brescia, Pisani would not be set entirely free for good until the arrival of the French in 1797.

Soon, however, the call for reform became still louder from the opposite quarter. In May 1784, Andrea Tron, popularly known as *il Paron*, openly condemned the decadent way of life, not of the government, but of the people, whom he held responsible responsible for Venice's decline. A xenophobe and fiercely anti-Jewish, Tron believed the Venetians had allowed themselves to be 'supplanted by foreigners', who, having 'penetrated [to] the guts of the city', were now driving the Republic to its fall. In his opinion, this failure was all the worse for Venice having allowed its valuable trade to pass into these foreign hands. Tron scorned the Venetians for being 'weak and effeminate', and he condemned them for now seeing trade only as a means to support their 'excessive extravagance, mad spectacles, pretentious entertainments and vice'.[147] By turning away from the commercial and industrial interests that had so long sustained and enriched them and made them great, he believed they had abandoned those industries that were so essential to the moral as well as financial well-being of the state.

In Paris the first days of the revolution were now foreshadowing the on-coming disasters which, in addition to overturning life in France and destroying the peace of much of Europe, were ultimately to prove the pessimists right and bring about the end of the Venetian Republic. Just four months before the fall of the Bastille, in March 1789 Doge Paolo Renier died and was replaced by his relation, the immensely rich Lodovico Manin. Despite the grave misgivings of himself and his wife, he dutifully accepted his nomination 'with tears in his eyes'.[148] His inauguration ceremony would be the most expensive ever, the doge making his traditional procession around the Piazza while he scattered at his own expense the obligatory gold and silver coins to the vast crowds gathered to witness the occasion. This was a flamboyant but anachronistic display of Venetian theatre. Yet it would not be quite the last such event; three years later in St Mark's Basilica Manin held a spectacular funeral for his wife. Heartbroken, he then offered to abdicate, but his suggestion was turned down by the Senate.

By this time Venice had allowed its army and navy to become seriously run down, but, although it was still determined to remain detached, this would be no guard against its being drawn inexorably into the wider conflict that was now developing. Already Sardinia had made its first appeal to the Serenissima to join a separate alliance, but this request had been turned down by the Signoria, which was still doggedly clinging to its neutrality. For this it would later be condemned, blamed by the other powers for its failure to help stop Napoleon's rapid rise. However, matters would come to a head a year later. As in 1792, the Emperor and his allies became so terrified by the threatened spread of revolutionary zeal from Paris that they ignored all approaches from the French, finally responding on 20 April by declaring war. Although, for a time further action was stalled as the situation in France grew even more dire with the Terror having taken hold, when eventually the bloodshed ended the new government was able at last to turn its full attention to defeating its enemies. Hoping ultimately to crush the Emperor in his German lands, it now decided to mount a diversionary campaign in his northern Italian territories.[149] Accordingly, after the French won their first battle over the Austrians near Genoa in November 1795, the young 26-year-old Bonaparte was ordered to march east, and the following April he achieved his first victory over the combined Austrian-Sardinian army.

Meanwhile, the French had also begun to toughen their stance against the Serenissima, who had angered them by continuing to offer asylum to a distinguished enemy of their new Republic, the Count of Provence. Although for the last twenty months he had been living under the assumed name of the Count of Lille in the Venetian city of Verona, the previous July he had issued an official declaration proclaiming himself to be the new French king. As Louis XVIII, he pronounced himself the successor to both his executed brother and his young nephew, the latter by this time being widely presumed to be dead. While the Signoria was loath to banish him as the French were demanding, confronted by Napoleon's approaching army it finally agreed to do as asked and, to the shocked disapproval of other foreign royal courts, on 13 April Louis was officially told that he had to leave. He was furious and before departing, in a fit of pique, he demanded not just the withdrawal of his name from the *Libro d'Oro*, but also the return of the gift the Venetians had earlier received of Henri IV's armour – requests still not met when the Republic finally fell. With the Serenissima now bowing to the demands of the French in its desperation to maintain its neutrality, in early June the newly appointed *provveditore generale* of Verona saw no option other than to allow Napoleon's army to enter the city. Left to their own devices, in the coming weeks the Veronese would find themselves being tossed back and forth between their new masters: first under the French, then the Emperor, and then a week later, back again under the French. Although for a time the Senate was worried enough to toy with the idea of recalling not just the army but also the navy from Corfu and its other bases in the Adriatic, it soon returned to its previous inertia and dropped the idea. As the authorities dithered, the French continued to strengthen their hold in Venice's *terraferma*, and soon the Republic's towns were being taken or – like the republican-leaning Brescia – choosing to surrender. Elsewhere too, Napoleon achieved a remarkable number of his goals, having within a month of starting his Italian campaign defeated the Austrians at Lodi, captured Milan, and signed armistices with Sardinia, Parma, and Modena. To these triumphs, in June he added yet another. To the horror of Queen Maria Carolina, who declared that she viewed them as the murderers of her sister, her husband Ferdinand now signed an armistice with the French. Then just a few months later, Napoleon also occupied the papal lands in the Romagna.

By the close of 1796, not only had French warships entered the Adriatic but all Venice's mainland possessions were seriously under threat, the situation for the Serenissima being made worse by its territory being overrun by the two opposing armies. In addition to the French invasion, the Austrians were crossing through the Friuli on their way to defend Mantua, which had been under repeated French attack since July.[150] Venice was too weak to do anything to block the Emperor's path, but Napoleon, wishing to manipulate the situation, declared the Austrians' free passage to be a betrayal of Venice's claimed neutrality. While angrily dismissing their complaints of damage done to their own property by his army, Napoleon continued to bully the Venetians. Even though they attempted to appease him, as the Signoria still remained unwilling to take a side, on three occasions between late August and the end of October it turned down his offer to form an alliance.

On Christmas Day 1796, the Serenissima's most western city, Bergamo – a Venetian possession since 1428 – surrendered to the French and having then become a republic, three months later it was annexed to the larger Cispadana Republic that lay to the south of the River Po in the region of Modena. Like the neighbouring Transpadana Republic that now occupied the former Duchy of Milan, this had been created by Napoleon following his defeat of the Austrians at Bassano. Yet, soon losing their semi-autonomous status, both of these would then be combined into the new Cisalpine Republic that was fully dependent on the Revolutionary French Government.

In early 1797 Napoleon again marched south into the Papal States, and in February at Tolentino he agreed a peace with the pope, who now handed over Bologna, Ferrara, and Ancona. The city of Avignon that had been unlawfully seized six years earlier was also officially declared a French possession. But other matters were of more concern for the Emperor. He had recently lost Mantua, his last city in northern Italy, and his retreating army was being pursued by the French who continued winning victories as they made their way to Trieste, which they reached in late March. Finally waking up to the danger, the Serenissima now instructed its more distant towns and outposts to reinforce their defences. At the same time, the authorities recalled navy personnel from Istria, blocked the lagoon, and increased naval production in the *Arsenale*. All this merely further enraged Napoleon and on 9 April he threatened Venice with war. In a furious letter sent to the doge ordering him to control the militias who were attacking his troops, he declared himself ready to 'deliver' the Venetian people from the 'tyranny' of their masters. This was to leave Venice with no option other than to concede to his demands.

Although there was open opposition to the Venetian government in cities such as Brescia, Bergamo, and Crema, others remained loyal. As a result, while the authorities were attempting to placate Napoleon, events in Verona would make the task still harder. On Easter Monday, 17 April, the people took up arms against their foreign occupiers, and over the next three days there was mayhem in the city as the French attempted to take shelter from the violence. Eventually, reinforcements arrived and with no help coming from Venice, the Veronese were forced to surrender. So on 27 April the Signoria officially handed the city back to the French, who then proceeded to take matters into their own hands, repaying the local people in kind for the brutality they had suffered during this bloody rising. Napoleon, equally eager to avenge the treatment of his men, ordered the city to be robbed of anything of worth, and from this time on he became determined to see the end of the Venetian Republic.

Although the doge had agreed to the earlier humiliating climb-down, within a fortnight it was clear that this would not be enough. With Napoleon having at last forced the Austrians to begin secret peace talks, on 18 April at the Treaty of Leoben the two sides agreed that the French would receive Belgium, Lombardy and Mantua, while the Habsburg Emperor would be given all the Venetian Republic, with the exception of the city itself. Even though at this point Venice was still to remain independent, Napoleon's attitude to it was antagonistic. When writing at this time to the Directory, he tapped into the popular negative propaganda, announcing that his only remaining course was 'to destroy [its] ferocious and sanguinary government and erase the Venetian name from the face of the earth'.[151] He repeatedly portrayed the Republic as a place where the population had long lived in fear under their 'tyrannical' regime – a reputation that was in fact refuted by the majority of its people. Then two days later, another event would add to the tensions that were already escalating. While on the 17th the lagoon had been officially closed to foreign warships, these waters, which had always been so sacrosanct for the Serenissima, were now entered by a French vessel. Whatever might have been the reason for the captain's action, after coming under attack from the shore, his ship was sunk and its few survivors were arrested. Even though this whole affair appears merely to have been an unfortunate mistake, the Senate would again misplay its hand by sending congratulations to those responsible for the sinking. This all added fuel to the fire when just a week after Leoben, on 25 April – St Mark's Day – two envoys arrived at Graz to speak to Napoleon. Here they were subjected to a terrifying slating as the Frenchman raged against the Republic, ordering that it should release all its political prisoners and punish those who had attacked his people. While his earlier idea had been to give Venice territory around Ferrara and Bologna, the Easter Rising in Verona and the recent sinking of the French ship had hardened his resolve. Declaring that his intention was now to abolish the inquisition and the Senate, he roared that he was going to be 'an Attila to the state of Venice'.[152]

Five days later, as the French army was being deployed along the shores of the lagoon itself, Napoleon, who was now based at Palmanova, ordered the Venetians to introduce a new constitution. At the same time, he demanded they pay reparations, if necessary surrendering paintings and other treasures to settle the bill. Although the next day Doge Manin hurriedly instructed the Great Council to agree to these terms, it was already too late because within hours Napoleon had declared war, instructing his commanders to crush the lion of St Mark wherever it appeared.

With the Senate now no longer functioning, on 8 May Manin again proposed his own abdication in the hope that this might improve the situation, but once more his proposal was refused. When the next day the French suggested that he should become President of the planned Provisional Municipality, he turned the offer down, declaring that while they might control his life, only God could direct his religion and his honour. Even so, the doge attempted to appease his enemy by agreeing to Napoleon's harsh terms, among other things cancelling the mobilisation of his troops, ordering home his loyal Dalmatian soldiers, and even arresting the Inquisitors who were so hated by the Jacobins in the city. On 12 May 1797 the Great Council gathered for the last time, its numbers now seriously depleted by the absence of hundreds of its members. Still debating when they heard the shots of the departing Dalmatian soldiers who were firing a last salute to the city, they immediately began to fear that either the French had already arrived, or the mob had begun to rebel. Despite lacking the regulatory quorum of 600 by some 50 members or more, they hurriedly cast their votes, most present choosing to declare the end of the great Serenissima. With this the world's oldest republic, one that had lasted for more than a thousand years, was brought to an end, and, in an undignified finale, all – with the exception of the doge – then beat a hasty retreat out of the back of the building. Although the delegates had been afraid of meeting the crowds gathered outside, for a last time Manin appeared before his people as their doge, his courage being greeted with cries of 'Viva San Marco!' As feared, however, the day ended in violence, when shots had to be fired to quell the unrest caused by loyal Venetians, who were now turning their anger on those known to support the Jacobin cause.

Retiring to his palace, the dignified Manin removed his symbolic *corno* and took off the cap beneath before handing it to his servant with the words: 'No la dopero più' (I shall no longer be using it.) With the French cannons already echoing across the lagoon, three days later before their arrival in the city Manin left the Doge's Palace for the last time, going to stay temporarily with his nephews at Ca' Pesaro. He then moved for the remaining five years of his life to Palazzo Dolfin Manin on the Grand Canal, where, despite being now greatly impoverished, he continued with his charity work. Otherwise, he led a very private, simple existence, keeping out of the public eye and trying to see visitors as little as possible.

Even though advised in the final days before the city fell to take refuge in Zara, unlike many others Manin had resisted the temptation to flee. It had been his misfortune to come to the fore when Venice was already gravely challenged, with both its military and naval strength severely reduced. Manipulated by the wily Napoleon and deceived by the Austrians, he and his cautiously conservative patrician advisers were unable to confront these problems. Instead, when faced with what seemed to be the Serenissima's inevitable destruction, Manin adopted the government's policy of appeasement, seeing it as the only way to protect his fellow citizens from unnecessary suffering. For this, he would be reviled by many, who blamed him for the city's demise. Today there are still those who condemn him for his lack of leadership, his prolonged maintenance of neutrality, and his refusal to join forces with the allies or with Napoleon. Yet while these things no doubt hastened Venice's collapse, as John Julius Norwich has pointed out, there was one beneficial result of this feeble response during the final months before the disaster. The government's quick submission spared the otherwise inevitable war damage the city would have suffered. Although over the coming years much of the fabric of the place would deteriorate through neglect, its essential structures would remain for future generations to appreciate and enjoy.

Dying at the age of seventy-six in October 1802, Manin was buried according to his wishes in the baroque Carmelite church of Santa Maria di Nazareth (or Santa Maria dei Scalzi) on the Grand Canal.[153] Here he would lie surrounded by the works of Tiepolo, the artist he had commissioned at the time of his marriage to decorate his Venetian home. The doge's simple tomb still remains in situ, having survived the damage caused by an Austrian bomb hitting the church on 24 October 1915, but Tiepolo's great ceiling fresco in the nave was less fortunate, and only a few remnants are today on display in the Accademia.

By the end of the century, Venice's previously carefree way of life had disappeared. When, in November 1798, eleven months after the French had handed the city over to the Austrians, da Ponte returned to his home after a 20-year absence, he was profoundly shocked. He was immediately struck on entering the Piazza from the *Mercherie* by the silence and desolation of the place, noting sadly that there were now only seven individuals in the great square that had once been filled with vast crowds.[154] But although it had entered a period of neglect and decay, in time the city would be rediscovered by the new wave of 19th-century visitors, who, by bringing it once more to the attention of the outside world, would start Venice back on its road to recovery.

SECTION VII
CHANGING BORDERS; AND STRANGE ALLIANCES

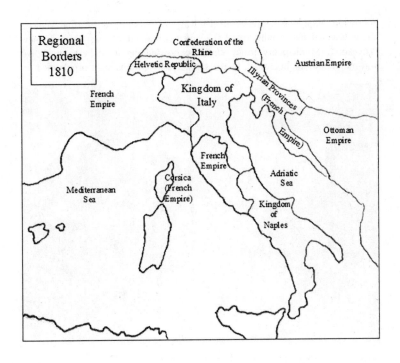

Regional Borders 1810

Confederation of the Rhine

Helvetic Republic

Austrian Empire

French Empire

Kingdom of Italy

Illyrian Provinces (French Empire)

Ottoman Empire

French Empire

Adriatic Sea

Mediterranean Sea

Corsica (French Empire)

Kingdom of Naples

13

Napoleon's expanding empire

Before St. Mark still glow his steeds of brass,
Their gilded collars glittering in the sun;
But is not Doria's menace come to pass?
Are they not bridled? – Venice lost and won,
Her thirteen hundred years of freedom done

George Gordon Byron[155]

Following Napoleon's orders, on 15 May 1797, three days after Venice's Great Council had finally voted the Serenissima out of existence, the new Provisional Municipality took office, acknowledging its debt to its 'great and magnanimous liberator'. In the same sycophantic vein, it proclaimed 'to

Napoleon's removal of the Bronze Horses from Venice.

all Europe that it [owed] its liberty to the glorious French nation and to the immortal Bonaparte'.[156] Within 24 hours of the French arrival, the 60 members of the Municipality had signed the peace treaty and agreed to pay the heavy indemnities that were demanded. They now added to their Jacobin credentials by ordering the destruction of the Serenissima's highly symbolic winged lions, the one with the kneeling Doge Francesco Foscari above the *Porta della Carta* of the ducal palace among those destroyed. Even more notable was the removal from the column in the Piazzetta of the ancient bronze lion that was taken down from its former important position on the Molo and carted off to Paris. Besides abolishing the previous custom in Venice of ending the day officially at 6.00 pm with the ringing of the Angelus, the Municipality introduced France's revolutionary calendar. As this was to replace the one used by the Venetians since medieval times, beginning each year on 1 March, in future the New Year's Day celebrations would be largely forgotten until their revival in 2015. Instead, on 25 May an alternative event took place in the great square outside St Mark's Basilica. Now renamed the Piazza Grande, it was bedecked with banners promoting the new revolutionary laws and extolling the achievements of Bonaparte. As a finale, a ceremonial pyre was then lit and the old Venetian symbols of office – the regalia, the *corno* of the doge, and the Golden Book – were all cast into the flames. As nothing representative of the former Republic was sacrosanct, out on the island of Murano, Doge Pietro Gradenigo's grave was desecrated. Blamed for introducing in 1297 the *Serrata del Maggior Consiglio* that had first restricted the number of ruling patrician families, Gradenigo's remains were now scattered to the winds. Then, with Venice's famous ceremony of the *Sensa* having also been abolished, in early June another festival was laid on to celebrate the new regime. While many Venetians watched on uncertainly from the side lines, a Tree of Liberty, topped with the revolutionary Phrygian cap, was erected in the Piazza. Around this some of the more enthusiastic – and sometimes inappropriately dressed – onlookers danced with abandon, several sporting the symbolic tricolour cockade. One noblewoman reported seeing her aristocratic friend Countess Marini Querini-Benzoni 'throw herself into a frenzied dance around the Liberty Tree … wearing a light Greek tunic, open at the sides all the way to her hip'.[157] Among those joining in the merriment was the poet Ugo Foscolo, originally from Spalato, who was now a member of the Provisional Municipality. An admirer of Napoleon, he was confident that under French influence Venice and the Italian people at large might expect a better future. However, despite never quite losing his faith in his champion, within months he like others would be disabused of his early hopes when Bonaparte's true intentions came to light.

Even though numbers of Venetians for the time being remained optimistic about the future, in reality the writing was on the wall, and before long most of Venice's remaining territories were gone. Although the *Provveditore generale da Mar* had endeavoured to strengthen the defences on the Ionian Islands, here throughout that summer the French would continue to extend their hold. In June, fearful of Corfu falling into the hands of the Russians (who were now equally interested in the area), Napoleon sent a ship under the colours of the new Municipality to take possession of the island and the nearby mainland towns of Preveza and Vonitsa. Although the French were not welcome among the former Venetian nobility and clergy, they were now in control, and before long, just as had happened in Venice, the Tree of Liberty was erected in the centre of Corfu town, and the local *Libro d'Oro* and flag of St Mark burned.

Gradually, the Venetians began to lose confidence in the survival of their independent Municipality, and so they started to turn against the French. Although Napoleon still had no desire to visit the city himself, he decided to appease the people by sending Josephine to Venice as his representative. Previously widowed after the guillotining of her husband during the Revolution, she had married Bonaparte the previous year, just two days before he had embarked on his Italian campaign. On 12 September, after being given the customary welcome on her arrival at the Piazzetta, she was rowed in a gondola up the Grand Canal to Palazzo Pisani Moretta. Here she would stay for the next four days, enjoying the various entertainments that were laid on for her benefit. Besides attending the opera, a ball, and several sumptuous dinners, she visited the basilica, the Doges' Palace (now called the National Palace), and the *Arsenale*. Despite her visit being cut short when Napoleon unexpectedly instructed her to join him, just before leaving she was able to watch the regatta that had been hurriedly arranged at her request. By the time of her departure, Josephine had not only won the affection of the Venetian people with her elegance and natural charm, but she had also encouraged some to believe that she would be able to help their cause by later speaking with her husband.

Such hopes were in vain, however, as only a month later news arrived in the city of the final agreement Napoleon had reached with the Austrians. Whether or not his intention had been to add to the humiliation of the former doge, he had chosen as his headquarters the Manin family home, some twelve miles from Udine at Passariano. Here, when drawing up the Treaty of Campo Formio, he ratified and extended the peace terms that he had agreed at Leoben in mid-April. Wanting to guarantee the peace and ensure his own pre-eminence over his rival French generals, in addition to acknowledging the Austrians' possession of all their new territories east of the River Adige, he also confirmed their right to Venice's former Adriatic possessions from Istria to Budua, just south of Cattaro in Venetian Albania. Even more significantly for the people of Venice, because he had now given the city itself to the Emperor, he had effectively abolished the Provisional Municipality.

Determined to make the most of the little time that remained to him, Napoleon immediately set about stripping Venice of anything of value. Having already, as early as May 1796, declared to the Directory in Paris his intention to rob the Italian museums of their works of art, he had previously seized as much as possible from Parma and Piacenza. Now, therefore, no longer content with his earlier demands, he issued a new order calling for the systematic looting of Venetian treasures. During the second week of December one of the most significant thefts of all was carried out when the four ancient gilt bronze (in reality largely copper) horses were taken down from outside the basilica and trundled off to France. Over the centuries people had recognised the symbolic significance for Venice of these priceless works, even the Genoese Admiral Doria having acknowledged their immense importance to the city when he had famously expressed his determination to 'bridle the horses of St Mark'. The dispirited Venetians now had to watch as these were lowered from their position above the entrance to the basilica and accompanied by a full military parade were sent on their way to Paris. Having arrived in the French capital, they were put on display, a caption justifying their theft. This declared that after their journey from Corinth to Rome, and later from Constantinople to Venice, they had arrived 'at last in a free country'. Much of the loot taken at this time, such as Veronese's great painting of the *Wedding Feast at Cana* stolen from San Giorgio Maggiore, would never come back to the city, but the horses – like the ancient winged lion – would be returned after Napoleon's eventual defeat.

On 9 January 1798, just before the arrival of the Austrians, there would be one more act of intentional destruction, the demolition of the large golden *bucintoro* that Goethe had admired just eleven years earlier. Having been launched in 1729, this was the last of the four recorded state barges built over the centuries to allow the enthroned doge to be rowed out in full splendour on the great ceremonial occasions. Manned by a large crew, with four men to each of its 42 oars, besides the onboard orchestra it had been able to carry around 90 dignitaries. Highly ornate and covered in gold leaf, this spectacular craft was now dragged out into the *bacino*, and on the island of San Giorgio, in full view of the Venetians, much of its wooden structure was broken up and set alight. For three days it continued to burn, after which the ash and remnants containing the melted gold were collected up, packed onto 400 mules, and carted away. Although the remaining hull, loaded with cannon, was later used to help defend the city, after another period as a prison ship, in 1824 it was finally scrapped and only those few small remnants of its glory days now found in the Museo Correr were left. Although not present in the city at the time, Napoleon is usually held responsible for this vandalism. Despite being a ready collector of Venice's treasures and most iconic pieces, the removal of the *bucintoro* presented a greater problem. Not wanting to leave behind any symbol of the great Serenissima, there was now an added urgency to resolve the situation before the imminent arrival of the Austrians. Nonetheless, there is uncertainty as to who actually gave the order for its destruction, some arguing it was the fault of a few unruly radical supporters of the revolutionaries, individuals who elsewhere had already revealed their total disregard for all such priceless works of art. Although recently a scheme was initiated, backed by the French, to reconstruct the *bucintoro*, for the time being a shortage of funds has caused this project to be shelved.

The impoverished authorities of the Municipality, faced with demands for war retributions, had now been reduced to melting down much of the city's gold and silver treasure, but this was of no concern to Napoleon. Determined to leave nothing that might be of service or value to the Austrians, he continued to take as much as he could, and the pillaging persisted right up to the last moment. Before the French departure on 18 January, their final instructions had been to strip the *Arsenale* and dismiss the remaining workers. The place was left in ruins. Eventually, on 21 January the Austrians arrived, marking the occasion three days later with a celebratory reception in the former ducal palace, which – adding to his humiliation – the last doge Manin was called on to attend. Now ruled from Vienna, all Venetians were forced to swear allegiance to the Habsburg Emperor, and before long the precious contents still remaining in some of their libraries were being transported back to the imperial capital.

Despite this, with the return of a conservative, elitist government, during the next seven years the Venetian patricians recovered their social position, several receiving new Austrian ranks and titles in return for service to the crown. Others, like the merchants, were, however, less fortunate. Over the next few years, because the Empire had chosen Trieste as its preferred regional port, Venice would be robbed of its former maritime importance and so it continued to decline. Even so, having lost their faith in the French, initially most Venetians were content to see the Austrians arrive, this being particularly true in Verona, where the people were overjoyed at the departure of the troops who had treated them so harshly over the previous year. But their delight was to be brief. By 1800 the city had been divided between the two foreign powers, and five years later it was again under the sole control of the French.

In the meantime, Napoleon had been extending his influence elsewhere, and a month after the Austrians' arrival in Venice, in February 1798 he had occupied Rome and declared it a republic. Apart from now reiterating his intention to have everything that was beautiful in Italy, he would later recall that it was here that he had first 'realised' that he was 'a superior being', capable of 'performing great things'.[158] However, as he continued to seize more areas, the Austrians were becoming increasingly exasperated by the way he was ignoring the terms agreed at Campo Formio. Therefore, in May 1798 the Habsburg Emperor formed an alliance with the Bourbon king Ferdinand of Naples, who had already been encouraged by his wife and the British envoy, Sir William Hamilton, to abandon the peace that he had agreed two years earlier with Revolutionary France. Accordingly, after Napoleon had been defeated in Egypt in August, the king marched on Rome, and by the end of November he had succeeded in ousting the foreign occupiers and restoring the pope to power. This marked the beginning of the War of the Second Coalition, but Ferdinand's personal victory would be short-lived, as before long he was under threat from the enemy. To the shock of his supporters, he scurried back home to his capital, abandoning his 1000-strong army to face the consequences of his actions. With his troops were routed on 4 December at Civita Castellana, by the 15th the French had recaptured Rome. Because in the meantime rioting had taken hold in Naples, the king had now decided to escape the growing danger by seeking refuge in Sicily. Although initially he was prevented from leaving by his people, just before Christmas he and his family were at last able to make their way secretly out of the palace, and, accompanied by the Hamiltons they fled the city aboard Horatio Nelson's ship. Their voyage south was appalling. For two days they had to battle their way through a violent storm, and by the time they finally arrived in Palermo on 26 December, not only had some of the passengers drowned, but the king and queen's six-year-old son had died purportedly as a result of acute seasickness.

By this time civil war had broken out in Naples between the poorer *lazzaroni* – who were still loyal to the Bourbons – and the more revolutionary nobles and bourgeoisie who wanted reform. The day after the latter had finally announced the end of the monarchy on 21 January 1799, the French arrived and confirmed the new Parthenopean Republic. Yet Ferdinand was still king in Sicily, where he had the backing not only of the British but also the Russians, who by this time had become equally nervous about Napoleon's ambitions. Being determined to drive the French from the strategically important Ionian Islands, they had entered the Mediterranean the previous September and with their new Ottoman allies had succeeded in occupying all the islands, except for Corfu, which would hold out until March.

Previously, in December Napoleon had sent his army into the wider Neapolitan Kingdom, where he had gradually begun to occupy the Abruzzo, Molise and Puglia, regions where there were still some groups loyal to the Bourbon king. Ferdinand had previously appealed to his bands of supporters to rise *en masse* in his defence, but by abandoning his army and then fleeing Naples, he had caused their numbers to start melting away. With several towns having begun to desert him, by the beginning of February the citizens of Bari were welcoming the newly created Parthenopean Republic. As proud 'defenders of the revered Tree of Liberty', over the following months they would continue to back the new regime. Likewise, in Barletta, those not wearing the revolutionary cockade had been subjected to ill-treatment and so by early January even the priests and monks had started to adopt the custom. Besides the more traditional and religious people in the countryside, who remained true to the monarchy, there were nevertheless some town dwellers who openly resisted the republican movement. Therefore, when the 'democratisers' began to arrive from Naples and impose new taxes, some of the ordinary citizens, finding themselves to be no better off, started to rise up against their oppressive pro-Jacobin overlords. As a result, trouble was building up in Molfetta, Bisceglie, Andria, and elsewhere. The same thing was happening in Trani, where following their recent defeat numbers of monarchist soldiers had arrived in search of refuge. Here the situation was to grow even more tense after news reached the town on 3 February of the establishment of the Parthenopean Republic. The pro-republican authorities immediately responded by hoisting a tricolour on the cathedral and ordering the singing of the *Te Deum*. The next day a Tree of Liberty was raised in the square, but within 24 hours this was cut down and those responsible had been arrested and imprisoned in the castle. Violence had now erupted and for weeks there was to be on-going bloodshed as the opposition continued to defy the authorities. Even when they heard on 25 March that, after falling to the French, Andria had been sacked and many of its people massacred, those loyal to the king still held out. The diary entry of the Commander of the Civic Guard in nearby Barletta summed up the horrors that the region was now experiencing: 'Oh what times we live in, when everything is mixed with anxiety and terror!'[159] Eventually, on 28 March the French arrived. in Trani and, although for another three days the besieged defenders held out – still defiantly flying the Bourbon flag – in the end they were forced to surrender. The victors then took their revenge, setting the town on fire, destroying several of the buildings, raping nuns and other women, and murdering more than a thousand of the local people.

However, as the French were facing similar unrest further north in Lombardy, the Veneto, the Marche and elsewhere, realising that they needed to deal with these problems, they now evacuated their southern areas. With the soldiers having before their departure robbed even those places that had formerly welcomed them, the local people had finally lost faith in the Parthenopean Republic and from this time on they began to wish for the return of the Bourbons. On 14 May, the same day that Barletta sent a message of submission to the king's representative at Bari, three Russian ships sailed into the harbour, their fleet having arrived in Bari and Brindisi the previous month. With the nobles having pulled down the Tree of Liberty, the town welcomed these newcomers who were promising to protect the area and maintain the peace. Although they soon earned the people's admiration for their good discipline, within a week most of the Russians had left the town, but their place was then taken by their Ottoman allies. Meanwhile, because Napoleon had removed his forces from the south to deal with the latest coalition forming against him, Naples had been left exposed and therefore by the end of April it had fallen to the combined forces of the British, the Russians, and Ferdinand's Sicilian army. So finally, a month after the Parthenopean Republic was officially abolished on 15 June, the king returned and reclaimed his Neapolitan throne.

Already in Sicily, as their position had grown more assured, the royal couple had become set on taking revenge on everyone who had betrayed them. Originally a supporter of reform, Maria Carolina had tried to improve the condition of the poor in Naples, and she had even accepted some of the early aims of the French revolutionaries. But she had grown more reactionary as events in France had then descended into the bloody mayhem that would include the execution of her much-loved sister, Marie Antoinette. In her determination to distance her husband's kingdom from Spain, the queen had long shown her preference for the British, and now, helped by her close friendship with Emma Hamilton, she persuaded Nelson to assist in the punishment of those who had deserted their king. Within days of the fall of the Parthenopean Republic, Ferdinand had placed the British admiral in charge of affairs in Naples. Despite an earlier armistice promised by the monarch's military commander Cardinal Ruffo, and the favourable surrender terms previously agreed by the junior naval officer Captain Foote, Nelson now held a court-martial on board his ship to try the nobleman the queen had most particularly singled out for retribution. Prince Francesco Caracciolo had formerly served in the British navy, and he had also accompanied Ferdinand to Sicily, but on returning to manage his Neapolitan estates he had been drawn into the republican cause. Having been given no chance to defend himself, he was found guilty of abandoning the Bourbons. On 30 June 1799, he was hanged from the yardarm of the *Minerva* and his body was thrown into the sea. Following this, the bloodshed really began as thousands of trials, numerous imprisonments, life sentences, deportations, and more than a hundred executions took place. With

Charles James Fox in the British Parliament loudly condemning the atrocities, Nelson's apologists would attempt to clear his name, denouncing what they saw as the falsehoods levelled against their hero. Still half a century later, Royal Naval Commander Miles, writing in the 1840s, would argue that Nelson had performed his 'most unpleasant duty ... as became a British admiral intrusted by the King of Naples with the command of his fleet, and the honour and protection of his crown and country'.[160]

Haunted by a fear of a repetition of the revolutionary events recently seen in France, the royal family wished to make an example of those who had deserted them. Although pardons were later extended to some of those who had been convicted, the queen was now blamed by many for the savage punishments that had taken place, so she decided to escape the criticism by going abroad. Together with her younger children she went to Vienna to visit Emperor Francis – who was both her nephew and her son-in-law – and here she remained for a couple of years, not returning until the Second Coalition came to an end with the temporary peace agreed at Lunéville between the Empire and France.

After the earlier Treaty of Campo Formio, the French troops should have withdrawn from Ancona and returned the region to papal control, but that was something Napoleon was not prepared to do. Wanting to protect his route to Rome, he had left his men in situ and had then backed the Adriatic city when it had proclaimed itself a republic in November 1797, just four months before it merged with the recently created Roman Republic. But, as opposition had soon grown in the Marche to the French, they were still tackling this problem when on 17 May 1799 the Russian-Turkish fleet arrived off-shore. Initially, the French were given a temporary reprieve as during an attack in June about 20 miles to the north-west at Senigallia, a military blunder had caused damage to the Russians' own ships, forcing them to withdraw to make the necessary repairs. Nonetheless, by the end of the same month the fighting had renewed, and the situation became serious for the French when on 29 September the Austrians arrived to add their weight to the assault. As Ancona was now Napoleon's last Italian foothold on the Adriatic, for three months his men put up a stout defence, but when eventually the Austrians captured their floating batteries, they were finally forced leave the area. For the allies, however, this success was soon undermined. By promptly raising their own flag and asserting their possession of the town, the Austrians so enraged Tsar Paul that he swiftly withdrew from the coalition.

When the French had taken Rome and founded the new republic in February 1798, Pope Pius VI had refused to renounce his temporal authority. As a result, he had been taken prisoner and transported back to France, where the next year, soon after arriving at Valence he died on 29 August. This had created a problem for the Church, the political situation having left the cardinals uncertain as to where they should gather for the papal election. Having eventually sought the Emperor's permission for the conclave to meet in Venice, after three months spent at the monastery of San Giorgio Maggiore, here in March 1800 they finally elected the Bishop of Imola as the new pontiff, Pius VII. Since he had already earned the Habsburg Emperor's displeasure by calling for greater liberty for the people, his inauguration was a small affair, the missing tiara being substituted with a fake, and the ceremony itself taking place quietly on the island across the water from the centre of the city. As the Roman Republic had fallen the previous year following the French departure, the new pope would now turn down the Emperor's suggestion that he take up residence in Vienna. Wanting instead to return to his old capital, with the Austrians' help he then sailed south to Pesaro, from where he made his way overland to Rome. Here his arrival in July came a month after the new French Consulate had restored the Papal States.

In the same weeks as the pope's inauguration, just a year after the capture of Corfu, a new agreement concerning the Ionian Islands was drawn up between the Ottomans and the Russians. Although by this time the tsar was at odds with the British, they would also be represented at the Treaty of Constantinople that now created the Septinsular Republic, 'The State of the Seven United Islands' that was to be protected from the French by resident Russian and Ottoman garrisons. While officially the islands were to remain autonomous, in reality the situation dashed the hopes of those who had wanted greater independence. Despite having never previously been included in the Ottoman Empire, they were now given vassal status and had to pay dues to the sultan. Regardless of this, at the beginning of January 1801 the Septinsular Republic raised its national flag – still displaying the Lion of St Mark – and then introduced its new constitution. But, there were remaining tensions. After the French had left, the former ruling classes regained their positions of authority, and this reactionary oligarchy firmly rejected the recent revolutionary changes. As a result, plots began to develop and violence to break out. As uprisings continued to erupt on the different islands, appeals for assistance were made to the Russians and others, with Zante (Zakynthos), for one, believing it would be preferable to be ruled by the British with whom it had long traded. Finally answering these calls for help to remove the unpopular and undemocratic government, in March 1802 the Royal Navy sailed into Corfu.

That same month, Britain's war with France came to an end with the signing of a treaty at Amiens. Although this peace would not last long, the British agreed to give up Malta, and the French promised to renounce the privileges in the Abruzzo and Puglia that they had received from Ferdinand the previous year. This meant they had to surrender their rights of access to Pescara, Brindisi, Otranto and other such places that were out-of-bounds for the British and the Ottomans.[161] At the same time, as back on the Ionian Islands calm was gradually being restored, and the situation was starting to settle down, in December the next year another more democratic constitution would be drawn up. This would limit the powers of the nobility, defend the rights of the people, and increase the federal independence of the different islands.

Despite his setbacks, throughout this time Napoleon had been steadily on the rise. On the 18eme Brumaire (9 November 1799) he had taken part in the coup that resulted in the fall of the France Directory. In addition to confirming the title he had already claimed for himself as First Consul, this put him at the head of the new, more authoritarian government. Then, seven months later, he had further strengthened his hand at Marengo in Piedmont, where he had achieved a major victory over the Emperor, who – because of the debacle at Ancona – had by then lost his former Russian support.[162] This crushing defeat would mean that at the Treaty of Lunéville in February 1801 the Austrians had to surrender their rights to Verona, this now being incorporated into the Cisalpine Republic. Although later in the year this was renamed the Italian Republic and Napoleon was made its president, he was still not satisfied. Having already declared France an empire, on 2 December 1804 he went further. In a magnificent ceremony at Notre Dame in Paris, in the presence of the pope, he took the crown into his own hands and, placing it on his head, pronounced himself the hereditary emperor of the French.

Although the Habsburgs had enjoyed four years of peace, this spurred them once more into action, and the next year, wishing to regain his former possessions in northern Italy, Francis II joined the allies of the Third Coalition. But by the end of the year, his situation had changed and, following his defeat at Ulm in October, he had been forced to flee his capital. Thus, on 13 November, a triumphant Napoleon entered Vienna with his now bedraggled troops, their poor condition and behaviour amazing the conquered Viennese who watched their arrival. One observer reported:

> Many [wore] blouses of peasants or shepherds' animal skin. Some have a more bizarre appearance [with] long pieces of meat or ham from their belts. Others march with bottles of wine. Their poverty does not obstruct them to [light] their pipes with Viennese banknotes.[163]

With the Austrian troops leaving Trieste five days later to help their allies in the north, the way was left clear for an advance party of the French to arrive in the city from Gorizia. When Napoleon's marshal Masséna joined them early the next month, he was welcomed with cannon fire, and by the time of his departure two days later he had installed a provisional government. Besides that, he had set up the supervision of merchandise arriving and leaving the port, and had placed a further blockade on the already besieged Venice. But soon far worse was to come for the allies. On the very day that the French were taking Fiume in a bloody struggle, the people heard of the routing of the combined Austro-Russian army at Austerlitz. Forced now to make peace, on 26 December 1805 at Pressburg (Bratislava), Francis agreed not only to give up his southern German states and all his possessions in Italy but also the former Venetian lands in Dalmatia and Albania.

In addition to this, the Emperor lost Venice, which from this time on would be just a *département* of France. Yet, because this city had now become a free port for everyone except the British, it was soon to be the turn of Trieste and its traders to suffer. When the representatives of its provisional government were now summoned to Ljubliana, to their utter shock, they were informed by Masséna that Napoleon insisted on their immediate settlement of a pre-agreed payment. Worse still, this had been increased to six million francs. Although threatened that a default on their part would result in the sack of their city, the fact remained that the amount was way beyond what they could afford. Napoleon was adamant, however, and the matter would only be finally settled by the taxation of the merchants and the loan of further millions from Vienna. With part of this money being used to buy the compliance of Masséna and his colleagues, eventually, to the immense relief of the people, the French would leave their city on 4 March 1806.

Just the previous month Napoleon had visited Venice, staying at the time with one of his long-time supporters, the nobleman Alvise Pisani, who had become a member of the Provisional Municipality after the Serenissima's fall. As by this time he was struggling to pay his debts, he sold his magnificent 18th-century villa at Stra on the Brenta Canal to the emperor, who later passed it on to his viceroy. A month after this visit, Napoleon proclaimed the recently created Italian Republic to be the new Kingdom of Italy, and as his brother Joseph and some of his other relations had refused to take on the role, he declared himself to be its king. Therefore, in the *duomo* in Milan on 26 May, he placed the ancient Iron Crown of Lombardy on his own head. Despite his leaving the region within weeks by that time he had appointed as his viceroy his adopted stepson Eugène de Beauharnais, who in his role as the Prince of Venice would continue carrying out Napoleon's reforms. Although over time the mood among the people would change as they faced the mounting costs, in these early days there was some relief to see the return of the French. While a few of the claims of Austrian neglect may have been exaggerated to please their new masters, the Venetians began to see various changes and improvements taking place in the city. Not least among these was the much-needed restoration of the *Arsenale*. Before long, this great dockyard was again in action, building numbers of new warships ready to support the French fleet in its battle for control of the Adriatic.

In the meantime, other important events had taken place in Naples. Contrary to the terms of their Treaty of Amiens with the British – agreements that both parties had broken – the French still occupied Bari, Brindisi, and Taranto. Therefore, in September 1805 Ferdinand made another separate agreement with Napoleon, this time promising his own neutrality in return for the French leaving his ports. But, again, following the main army's departure from the south, Ferdinand would go back on his word and to Napoleon's fury he would join the allies, inviting the British and Russians to Naples. This would be of little help to the king, however, as within two months of Nelson's victory at Trafalgar on 21 October, the allies' luck had deserted them. Already facing the threat of being left with just his small and ineffectual army in Puglia for protection, Ferdinand made things still worse for himself by offending the Russians and the British. Realising at last the danger he was facing, in January 1806 he fled his capital for the second time, returning once more to Palermo. Three days after the invading French army had crossed into his kingdom, Maria Carolina, together with her son, followed suit, leaving Naples for the last time to join her husband in Sicily. Here, he had originally refused the British permission to land, but confronted by the impossibility of his situation, he had at last conceded to their wishes, and they were now to continue occupying Sicily until the fall of Napoleon.

A month after Ferdinand's flight, on 15 February Joseph Bonaparte, Napoleon's older brother, was given a triumphant welcome in Naples, where the next month he would be proclaimed as its new king – beginning the nine-year period during which the region was a client state of France. The occupying French troops would on occasion treat with appalling brutality those believed to be still loyal to the Bourbons – a document recently found hidden among the papers of a parish priest in the Abruzzo graphically recording the massacre of the people of Aquila. Joseph, however, tried to control these crimes, punishing those found to be guilty. A follower of Enlightenment principles, he endeavoured to improve the lives of his people. For the same reason, after staying at Lecce during a ceremonial visit to Puglia in 1807, he attempted to dismantle the feudalism that still existed in the region. This had grown considerably during the period when its Spanish monarchs had sought to manage their affairs by rewarding the elite and limiting the rights of the masses. Yet, even after he had produced a new law in 1808 to control the practice, he was still to be frustrated in his aims by bandit groups in certain areas, who continued to benefit from the system. To help deal with his opposition, that same year Joseph also transferred the regional administration from Trani – 'the most obstinate' of the rebellious cities – to the more loyal Bari. However, his measures to try and improve things for his people and his generally moderate treatment led Napoleon to distrust him, and in July, against his will, he was forced to abdicate in favour of his brother-in-law. Joseph was now instructed to become King of Spain, while Marshal Murat took his place in Naples as Joachim I.

Napoleon was determined to control the whole of the Adriatic in order to prevent the other powers from hindering his freedom of movement. By February 1806 – just two months after the Treaty of Pressburg – the French occupied Dalmatia as far south as the Narenta River between Spalato and Ragusa. As the Russians viewed Cattaro as an essential base from where to maintain their position with the Ottomans, within weeks they sent their fleet into the Bocche and took over the town.[164] Now ensconced in the gulf and in possession of the island of Curzola (Korčula), they and their allies, the Montenegrins, were threatening to block Napoleon's path into the Balkans. As this was one of his prime objectives, the French emperor sent his troops to take over the Republic of Ragusa and in May 1806 the army's commander was able to gain entry by feigning to have come in peace. The next month the Russians and Montenegrins responded by sailing to nearby Cavtat and then, until the arrival of more French troops, for around two and a half weeks they continued to besiege Ragusa, bombing, burning, sacking, and even murdering the local people. Finally, in August Marshal Auguste de Marmont arrived and having joined the defenders in the city he took charge, forcing the citizens to pay their dues and closing many of the monasteries – something that would soon help feed the popular image of the French as 'irreligious Jacobins'.

With Napoleon having now invaded much of Francis II's territories, by July 1806 he had gained enough power to persuade the Emperor to create a new Confederation of the Rhine from his lands within the confines of the Holy Roman Empire. Although this seriously undermined Francis's position, he had already two years earlier seen the writing on the wall and so had raised Austria to imperial status. Therefore, after abdicating his former role, and declaring his ancient Holy Roman Empire ended, he began to style himself Francis I, the Emperor of Austria – adding this to his other titles as King of Hungary, Bohemia, Lombardy-Venetia, Croatia and Dalmatia.

Yet this was just one of the changes taking place, as the next year, besides the sultan deserting his former ally and declaring war on Russia, the Ionian senate announced the end of its neutrality with France. More importantly, however, Napoleon was continuing to achieve remarkable successes on the battlefield, and following his defeat of the Russians at Friedland, in July the tsar agreed to meet him for peace talks at Tilsit. Here the two men drew up a scheme to divide Europe between them, and, when sharing out the spoils, Alexander I was promised rich pickings in the north, while Napoleon claimed Cattaro and the Bocche, as well as the islands of Curzola and Brazza (Brač). Even so, for the French emperor this was not enough, and just a month later – in a move contrary to the recent peace terms – he sent his troops to Corfu and annexed it to his empire. Here, however, the subsequent British blockade caused such immense hardship to the people that they were soon anxious to see the French depart.

* * *

In November 1807, a year after regaining the city, Napoleon decided to visit Venice. Having already issued in the previous months a multitude of instructions for change, he now spent the ten days of his stay in a hectic round of activities. As he wanted to create his own palace in the Piazza opposite the basilica, one of his first moves was to order Sansovino's church of San Geminiano to be demolished.[165] The new building, known the *Ala Napoleonica*, today housing the Museo Correr, was intended to connect the two separate wings of the *Procuratie*, the *Nuovo* and the *Vecchie*. Besides being heavily decorated throughout with frescos, paintings, medallions, and much else, it eventually included a grand staircase, loggia, throne room, and a ballroom, the latter completed only in 1838. Although most of the work was done within six years, when a large bronze 'N' was added to the classical sculptures adorning the outside,Napoleon would never return to Venice to see the finished palace. In the meantime, just as this building's construction had been made possible by the earlier clearing of the site, his decree issued in July 1806 had ordered numerous other demolition or alteration works to be carried out around the city. Besides the four churches in the Castello *sestiere* that had been razed to create the public gardens, many other religious buildings had also been shut down or converted to different secular uses. In addition to the official closure of the *scuole*, and the 34 convents or monasteries and 18 churches that had already gone, others would continue to disappear, and among the famous *Ospedali Grandi*, only the *Pietà* would hold out until the 1840s. Wanting to emphasise the end of the Serenissima, the emperor instructed the doges' private chapel to be given the role that had formerly belonged to San Pietro di Castello, and on receiving many of its treasures the Basilica di San Marco became the city's new cathedral.

During his short visit, Napoleon worked tirelessly, inspecting existing projects, proposing new ones, and checking the sea walls. Having personally experienced the *acqua alta*, he was conscious of the risks of flooding that Venice faced. So, even though the people continued to see more loot being packed off to Paris and the Italian kingdom's capital in Milan, at the same time they began to benefit from some of the improvements the emperor was introducing. Besides ordering the gate to the ghetto to be broken down and its 2000 Jews emancipated, he would, among other things, ban torture and the branding of orphans. He also stopped burials taking place in the city, instructing these to be performed instead on the island of San Cristoforo. As this site soon became too full, an order was then given calling for the draining of the canal that separated it from the neighbouring San Michele, where eventually a larger cemetery was created in 1812.

Elsewhere still more serious changes were taking place. Just two years after its French takeover, on 31 January 1808 Ragusa's Senate was abolished and the 450-year-old republic came to an end. Napoleon having now appointed Marshal Auguste de Marmont its hereditary duke, it was incorporated into the Kingdom of Italy. Two months after the annexation of Ragusa, the Marche towns of Ancona, Fermo, and Macerata, together with Urbino, were similarly added to the kingdom. However, the following year, Napoleon was to be still more brazen when in the early hours of 6 July his troops entered the pope's palace in Rome. Having kidnapped Pius VII, they took him north to Savona and then removed him, like his predecessor, to France. As this action had effectively abolished the Papal States, these were now incorporated into the French Empire.

During this time, war had begun again between the Austrians and the French, and so in April 1809 Marmont left Ragusa to join his emperor, taking with him his much-admired Croat soldiers, whom Napoleon himself had declared 'the best corps in his army'.[166] The marshal's departure enabled the Austrians – with their own Croatian units – to re-enter the county and take Sebenico (Šibenik), Trau (Trogir) and Spalato, although Zara, the besieged provincial capital of Dalmatia, would manage to hold out.[167] Then, in July, after the Austrians had been defeated at Wagram, Napoleon marched on to nearby Vienna, and in October the War of the Fifth Coalition was officially brought to an end with the Treaty of Schönbrunn. In addition to losing Trieste, Francis I now had to surrender his territories in Istria, Gorizia, parts of Croatia, Dalmatia, and most of Slovenia. And, more seriously still, the loss of all his possessions on the Adriatic had finally allowed Napoleon to achieve his ambition of cutting the Austrians off entirely from the Mediterranean. While in Zagreb there was already a faction of Jacobin support, a Tree of Liberty having first appeared there as early as 1794, these newly acquired lands, along with Ragusa and Cattaro, would now be included in the French empire as the autonomous Illyrian Provinces – their name derived from that of the region as part of the ancient Roman Empire.

Marmont, the first governor-general of Dalmatia, genuinely loved Ragusa, even at the time of its takeover expressing his personal reservations over the suffering being caused to 'this little country that used to enjoy the greatest happiness, whose inhabitants are gentle, industrious, and intelligent: an oasis

Disputed
Adriatic coastal regions
during Napoleonic Wars

of civilisation in the middle of barbarism'.[168] So even as he introduced the Code Napoleon, and further removed the identity of the Croatians and their neighbours by making French the official language, he appreciated the difficulties of devising a regime suitable for the very different groups of people under his jurisdiction. He therefore still encouraged the non-official use of Croatian, and even took the trouble to learn the language himself. During his two years in office, he introduced reforms for which he is still remembered in the region, among them the reduction of feudalism, the improvement of education, and the building of roads. But Napoleon was growing less interested in the area, and so when Marmont was transferred to a new command in Portugal in 1811 the region would again begin to backslide. In spite of the Austrians allowing much of its French system of rule to remain in place after their takeover in 1814, because the subsequent prefects did so little for the place, from then on the country would progressively become more impoverished.

Ragusa's fleet had now been incorporated into the French navy, which had already been growing considerably with the arrival of new warships from the boatyards of Venice and elsewhere. But the British had also been stepping up their activities, taking the Ionian Islands of Zante, Cephalonia and Cerigo (Kythera) in October 1809, and then successfully forcing the French garrison to leave Santa Maura (Lefkada) the following April. Only Paxos and Corfu would hold out, not falling for another three or four years. Movement in the area was not just affected by the British blockade, but also by pirates. By 1810 a market for smuggled goods had been established on Lissa (Vis), the island having also taken over much of Ragusa's former trade. As three years earlier this same island had been captured by the British, it had now become an important base from where the Royal Navy could sail out to seize foreign shipping and attack the coastal regions still in enemy hands.[169] For that reason, on 22 October 1810 the French frigates *Corona*, *Favorita*, and the smaller *Belladona*, all flying the British flag to deceive the defenders – a popular *ruse de guerre* at the time – stealthily made their way into the harbour. While the British would later dispute their account, claiming to have lost only eight vessels in total, according to the *capitaine de vaisseau* Bernard Dubourdieu the French captured several craft, burnt numbers of others, and took many prisoners.

With the attempt to take Lissa having, however, proved unsuccessful, five months later the French launched another assault. Having sailed from Ancona, on 13 March 1811 the large force, again under Dubourdieu, reached the island. Now facing unequal odds, just before the battle began the British Captain William Hoste encouraged his smaller fleet with the signal 'Remember Nelson'. However, the fighting had hardly started when the *Favorita* was hit and Dubourdieu and most of his officers were killed. As the captain's flagship ran on to the rocks, the confusion spread and most of the French vessels were captured, among them the *Corona* and the *Belladona*. For the British this was a decisive victory, but for the French there was more in store as, after escaping to Parenzo (Poreč) in Istria, the French supply ship would be destroyed at the harbour entrance.

The disaster at Lissa fatally undermined French naval dominance in the region, but worse was still to come. In February 1812 the long-awaited *Téméraire*-class ship of the line *Rivoli* was at last able to leave the Venetian boatyards, but during her maiden voyage to Pola she was drawn into battle and after being badly damaged, she was captured by the British. Now with their depleted fleet the French were unable to protect their various Adriatic possessions, and so Fiume, Trieste, and numerous other ports and towns were subjected to repeated raids. Besides targeting Napoleon's Kingdom of Italy, Istria, Croatia, and the Dalmatian coast, the British also hit the sea's western shores, striking regions around Venice, the Marche, the Tremiti Islands, and Puglia. Meanwhile, in addition to tackling a revolt in the region of the Bocca, the French were now having to deal with a rebellion that the neighbouring Montenegrins had stirred up in Budva. Moreover, just as Napoleon's rule of the area was approaching its end, elsewhere he was about to face his greatest challenge, the ill-fated Russian campaign.

For Napoleon's governors the posting in Illyria appeared little more than a sentence of exile, and in February 1813 Marshal Jean-Andoche Junot's appointment had increased his feeling of despondency. Besides the public shaming he had received from Napoleon, who had apparently wanted to shift onto him responsibility for some of the disasters of the Russian invasion, the marshal had among his 27 battle wounds received some serious head injuries. His behaviour now became truly bizarre. A few months after his arrival in the sumptuous Governor's Palace in Ljubljana, Junot gave a ball, and here, to the shock of his 400 distinguished guest, although bedecked with his multiple decorations, he appeared totally naked. After years of loyal service and physical suffering, he had become utterly disillusioned by Napoleon's apparent rejection of him. Therefore, he was now hastily recalled to France, where he died soon afterwards of wounds suffered while apparently attempting to take his own life. Junot would be briefly replaced by Joseph Fouché, a devious man who throughout his life would repeatedly change his loyalties, backing whichever party he thought the most expedient. Leaving after just a month in office, he would rob the Provinces of their treasure, and he soon deserted Napoleon for the Bourbons. Eventually distrusted by all sides, he died an exile in Trieste in 1820.

From early 1813, in addition to Fiume and Rovigno (Rovinj) the British began taking a series of Adriatic islands and ports along the Illyrian coast, and in February the French would start retreating from the south. However, as the well-defended Ragusa and Cattaro were still among the garrisons they held, so in October Captain Hoste was ordered to enter the Bocche and capture the fortress. On arriving at the gulf, he and Captain Harper in his brig-sloop negotiated the tricky currents of the inlet and after having captured the enemy's ships and fortifications that were blocking their path, they moved on to try and take the remaining well-fortified French garrison. Being unable at this time to achieve the main objective, Hoste would leave Harper to keep up the blockade, while he captured the now-abandoned Spalato before finally sailing on to Ragusa. As the local people had earlier rebelled against their occupiers in June, here the British were hoping to inspire them to further action by appealing to them 'to recall the old glory and to fight for the freedom of their homeland'.[170] Despite Hoste's personal lack of respect for the Ragusans' 'undisciplined troops', after his arrival at Cavtat he gave them further encouragement by lowering the Union Jack, raising their flag of St Blaise, and ordering a twenty-one-gun salute. By this time, everyone was expecting the imminent arrival of the Austrians, who, having again declared war against the French in August, had with the help of the British taken Trieste and invaded the Illyrian Provinces. Eventually, tired of waiting for them, however, Hoste finally decided to leave and on 13 December he returned to the Bocche.

Here at Cattaro the French commander intended to make a last stand, and so his garrison retreated to the mountain-top fort of San Giovanni above the town. Having re-joined Harper, Hoste now ordered the two ships' cannon to be dragged up the steep slopes of the neighbouring Mount Theodore overlooking the fortress. After days of struggling to the top through appalling weather, on Christmas Day the men were at last ready to begin firing on the enemy below, keeping up the heavy bombardment until 5 January, when Hoste was able to report back that the French commander had surrendered. Since the enemy was now defeated and the Austrians had not yet arrived, Hoste handed Cattaro over to the local people, and to the neighbouring Montenegrins, who had been helping them since the previous September. This action on his part, like his earlier recognition of Ragusa as an independent republic, would be very unpopular with Hoste's superiors, the British ambassador in Vienna, Lord Aberdeen, later condemning him for disobeying his earlier orders to give the area to the Emperor alone.

Having taken Cattaro, on 19 January Hoste returned to Ragusa, where two weeks earlier the Austrians had at last arrived. He now assisted the attackers by once again ordering his ship's cannon to be dragged to strategic points above the town. Eventually worn down by the heavy barrage, the French commander declared that he was ready to surrender and, the day after the truce was signed on 28 January, the British, the Ragusan insurgents and the Austrians were able to enter the town. Here they then raised their three standards. However, despite having ostensibly come to help the people, in reality the Austrians had been seeking to take the place for themselves, so two days later, following the departure of the Royal Navy, they removed the Ragusan flag and asserted their claim to the former republic. Proving that possession was indeed nine-tenths of the law, they continued to hold on to it, refusing, contrary to the terms later agreed at the Congress of Vienna, to give Ragusa back the independence it had been guaranteed. Instead, the city was to remain a crown possession of the Habsburgs until the end of the dynasty.[171]

Soon after the surrender of Ragusa, with the end now in sight for the French, in a final poignant gesture the last French warship in the area, the *Uranie*, was set on fire by its crew at Brindisi on 3 February 1814. Two months later Napoleon abdicated and was exiled to Elba and, following the signing of the Treaty of Paris at the end of May, the fighting seemed at last to be over. Although the British would then leave the Dalmatian islands that they had previously occupied, the next year the independent United States of the Ionian Islands were declared a British protectorate. In much the same way, during the redrawing of the borders by the allies at Vienna, Francis I's interests had not been forgotten. In addition to asserting his right to lands in Dalmatia, the Council confirmed his possession of the new Kingdom of Illyria that comprised parts of Austria, as well as Istria and much of Croatia. Furthermore, the Emperor gained the northern Italian territories that were now to be designated the Kingdom of Lombardy-Venetia.

Since the beginning of the decade, the Neapolitan royal family had experienced their own changes of fortune. In 1810, having divorced Josephine because she was no longer likely to bear a child, Napoleon had married Emperor Francis's daughter, the granddaughter of Maria Carolina of Naples. The celebration had taken place in Paris, attended by a large Illyrian delegation sent by Marshal Marmont. Although not present herself, the queen, who had loathed Napoleon for years, declared when reading of the wedding that the only thing missing to complete her misery was to have become 'the devil's grandmother'.[172] The marriage underlined not just the status the French emperor had now gained but also the weakness of his Habsburg counterpart. Francis I had been forced to embrace the upstart from the same Revolution that had murdered his own aunt. But his Neapolitan relations had been living for some time in Sicily under the protection of the British, and so already by 1813 they had seen a loss of their personal standing. Having, therefore, accepted that he was out of favour, Ferdinand decided unofficially to abdicate and designate his son as the regent, a decision that was finally to make Maria Carolina's position untenable. As she had also become extremely unpopular with the British, her attitude towards them having considerably cooled over the years, their minister persuaded her husband to advise her to leave the island and return to Austria. Forced to avoid the war zones by taking an extremely circuitous route via Constantinople and Odessa, she was still on her way back to Vienna when she heard of Napoleon's defeat in October at Leipzig. She did not, however, live to see his ultimate fall, dying of a stroke in her home near Vienna in September 1814 while he was still on Elba. . The political situation would further improve for Ferdinand the following year when, following Murat's defeat, the Austrians re-entered Naples on 23 May. He was then able at last to regain his throne, and seven months later he officially reunited his monarchies, thus re-establishing the former Kingdom of the Two Sicilies.

Murat's colourful career had taken him from being the son of an innkeeper, to the crowned monarch who had replaced his brother-in-law Joseph on the throne of Naples. Having begun his rise to power after marrying Napoleon's sister Caroline in 1800, a year after proving his bravery at Marengo, he had then driven the Neapolitans from the Papal States and participated at the signing of the armistice with the king. Following his appointment as a marshal of the French Empire, he had ousted the British from Capri, and despite then failing to achieve Napoleon's aim of capturing Sicily, had again proved his bravery at Borodino in 1812 during the invasion of Russia. During the disastrous retreat from Moscow, he had remained with the army until the following January. Having, however, strongly disapproved of the way the emperor had left his men to return to Paris, on eventually returning to Naples, Murat would try for a time to reach a new agreement with the Austrians and the British. Although he dropped the idea when Napoleon asked him in August to re-join his cause, following the French defeat at Leipzig, he had finally lost all faith in his brother-in-law and left him for good. Hoping to hold on to Naples, once more he turned to the British and their allies, but since Napoleon's abdication they were indifferent. Their attitude would only change after the emperor's escape from Elba, but by that time Murat had decided to go it alone. As its former king, he was now determined to achieve independence for his country within a unified Italy.

Having, declared war against the Austrians on 15 March, he led his army north through the Papal States and, having forced the pope to flee to Genoa, then established his base at Ancona, before moving on to Rimini. Here, on the 30th, he made his proclamation to the Italians, encouraging them to rise up against the Habsburgs whose significant presence had been re-established by the Congress of Vienna in Lombardy, Tuscany and the Duchy of Modena. In spite of his troops having some success during April, in May his luck started to run out. The day after his general was defeated near Senigallia, on 2 May Murat personally met the Austrians at Tolentino in the Marche, where at the end of two days of fighting he was forced to retreat. Matters were then made worse for him, first by the Anglo-Austrian fleet capturing his remaining garrison in Ancona on the 5th, and then by the news that Louis XVIII had already returned to Paris on the 3rd. Realising the hopelessness of his situation, Murat fled in disguise to Corsica. Although he soon made a new approach to Napoleon, he was quickly rebuffed, and so he was still at Lyon when he heard of his brother-in-law's final defeat at Waterloo in June. As he still wanted to recover Naples, he now refused the Austrian Emperor's offer of asylum and returned to the south. He was in Calabria, therefore, sheltering from a storm at Pizzo, when eventually he was recognised and arrested by supporters of King Ferdinand and, after a summary trial, was executed by firing squad on 13 October.

As king, Murat had sought to make life better for his people, achieving among other things the completion of Ferdinand's original plans to create a new city in Bari and the definitive end of feudalism. After their return, the Bourbons continued with the development of roads and ports in this part of their kingdom, but with the departure of the French, Puglia and the neighbouring regions were essentially forgotten and from this time onwards the area would began to slip out of sight. Murat followed the practices and policies of his brother-in-law, but in this he had not been alone, the same being true of all those governments under Napoleon's influence. While the French emperor's rule had introduced several changes of lasting value to his conquered territories – among them improvements in education, law, and human justice – these things had come at a tremendous cost to the people. Far more disastrous even than the damage they had endured from his blatant pillaging and destruction of their lands, had been the appalling loss of life they had suffered because of his immense ambition. In addition to the deaths of those killed defending their homes and towns, vast numbers of men had died when forced into military service, many of these taken from the confiscated lands that Napoleon had always viewed as a valuable source of manpower. Millions of others across Europe would perish as they were caught up in his wars. From the Kingdom of Italy alone, when called on to support his stepfather, Eugène Beauharnais had taken 27,000 troops with him on the disastrous invasion of Russia from which so many never returned.

Although by the end of 1813 the British and the Austrian siege of Venice had left the people sick and starving, following Napoleon's abdication and the French withdrawal the situation had generally begun to improve. On 19 April, amid great celebrations, the Austrians returned to the once-more illuminated city, and the occasion was marked by a regatta. A further line was later drawn under the years of French occupation with the hasty removal of two unwanted reminders: the 'N' adorning the emperor's palace, and the vast statue of Napoleon that the grateful Chamber of Commerce had erected on his birthday in August 1811 in the Piazzetta outside the Doges' Palace. The latter still continues to arouse strong feelings, as became apparent after the *Comité français pour la Sauvegarde de Venise* donated it to Venice in 2002. Bitterly, opposed to the statue being put on display in the Loggia at the Museo Correr, a group of individuals then brought a show case against Napoleon, who was ultimately found to have been guilty of war crimes.

In the months after Waterloo, an issue of more importance to the city had been the recovery of its two most treasured emblems. In April 1816 the Serenissima's much-restored winged lion – badly damaged during its earlier removal – was at last put back on its column in the Piazzetta, and four months earlier, on 13 December, a magnificent ceremony had celebrated the return of the famous bronze horses. So now, once again, these were installed in their former position over the front porch of the Basilica di San Marco.[173]

14

Ali Pasha, the 'Lion of Ioannina', and Lord Byron

In marble-paved pavilion, where a spring
Of living water from the centre rose,
Whose bubbling did a genial freshness fling,
And soft voluptuous couches breathed repose,
Ali reclined, a man of war and woes;
Yet in his lineaments ye cannot trace,
While Gentleness her milder radiance throws
Along that aged venerable face,
The deeds that lurk beneath, and stain him with disgrace.

George Gordon Byron[174]

Ali Pasha with his wife Kyra Vassiliki.

Preveza, in the Ionian Sea close to the island of Santa Maura, had over the last 300 years been repeatedly contested by the Venetians and the Ottomans. But, after the fall of the Serenissima, like Venice's other former possessions in the region this coastal town had been ceded to France. Yet, although its small garrison of around 550 men had been welcomed by the local people, only a year later it had found itself in extreme danger. With Napoleon having turned his attention to affairs further afield in Egypt, the sultan's local governor Ali Pasha had taken the opportunity to mount an attack on this useful port that he had wanted for so long to possess. As the combined force of the French and other local defenders was now greatly outnumbered by an army of some 7000, unsurprisingly the assault soon turned into a rout. And worse was to come. Ignoring his earlier promise of leniency, after having around 200 people murdered or taken prisoner, the pasha had instructed the surviving French to carry the piles of decapitated heads back to his capital, Ioannina. As a further refinement of cruelty, these same men had earlier been forced to skin and salt the skulls of their colleagues, a process intended to preserve the remains for later display before the sultan in Istanbul. While this would confirm Ali's reputation abroad as a cruel and ruthless tyrant, he had now taken control of Preveza and was able to turn his attention to making further gains in the region.

The grandson of an Albanian chieftain who had died in the 1716 siege of Corfu, Ali Pasha came from a family with a violent past. While he was still a boy, his father – who had gained power by killing his cousin – was himself murdered, and this had left the child in the care of his forceful mother, a woman capable of leading her people into battle. Having grown up under her influence and in an area renowned for brigandage, unsurprisingly Ali became a bandit, spending his early years fighting both his rivals and his Ottoman overlord. In the 1780s, however, he began to support the sultan, who, having recognised Ali's military skills during the Turkish war with Russia, now hoped to ensure his loyalty by acknowledging his growing authority in the region. Accordingly, he appointed Ali *dervendji-pasha*, the chief of police or governor of the passes, thus making him responsible for policing the western part of Romelia – the Ottoman lands of southeast Europe. After that, with his own army Ali had gradually taken over the region of Delvina, become pasha of Trikana and Ioannina, and finally received the senior Ottoman rank of vizier, with the title of *Aslan* – the 'Lion'. While he controlled the Epirus region between Macedonia and the sea, today part of southern Albania and northern Greece, because his sons had later gained control of the Morea and Avalona (Valona, Vlorë) on the Strait of Otranto, Ali's influence would eventually be felt over most of the Greek mainland.

Once in power, Ali had begun to introduce practical changes to his lands, upgrading the roads, building fortifications, helping trade, improving agriculture, and encouraging the educational and cultural life of his capital. In 1803 the British diplomat William Hamilton would report back that Ali had 'established the most perfect tranquillity, and security of Persons and Property throughout his dominions, whose Inhabitants, Greeks and

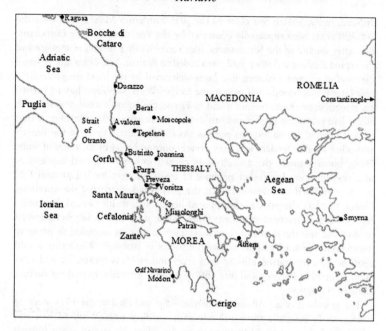

Turks, are richer, happier, more contented, and less oppressed, than in any other part of European Turkey.'[175] Similarly, Byron's companion Hobhouse, by then Lord Broughton, would later recognise the extent of the pasha's achievements, although in his case the compliment came with a telling caveat that questioned Ali's underlying motivation:

> He has built bridges over the rivers, raised causeways across the marshes, laid out frequent roads, adorned the country and the towns with new buildings, and by many wholesome regulations has acted the part of the good and great prince, without perhaps a single other motive than that of his own aggrandisement.[176]

Despite being brought up in the Islamic faith, Ali showed little genuine religious conviction, telling the Russian consul in 1806 that he was no 'fanatic' Muslim, and at the end of his life going so far – when facing challenges from the Ottoman government – as to suggest to the Greeks that he had converted to Christianity.[177] But even though his flexible attitude toward religious belief allowed him to tolerate other faiths whenever they served his purpose, in 1788 his troops destroyed the important trading town and much revered cultural centre of Moscopole, leaving only the few remarkable 18th-century Orthodox churches that still stand today. Nonetheless, in 1813 he commissioned the construction of an Orthodox monastery at Kolikontasi near Berat, a building dedicated to the martyred St Cosmas of Aetolia. In this case, however, there may have been another reason for this show of respect.

Just a few years before the holy man's murder in 1779, on meeting the pasha he had predicted that one day Ali would become the conquering ruler of all Albania.

Although highly educated and often charming, Ali was a man of stark contradictions, maintaining his power by multiple acts of appalling brutality. Usually unforgiving of any opposition and apparently unwilling to forget a grudge, he left his enemies in dread of his vengeance, one such notable case being the destruction of the town of Gardiki in 1812 and the murder of 600 of its people in retaliation for their brutal treatment of his mother and sister fifty years earlier. Similarly, when fighting in 1803 alongside the sultan in his war against the Greeks, Ali had been determined to quash the ambitions of the rebellious Orthodox Souliotes who were seeking to maintain their independence. As he took their various mountain strongholds, the terror his merciless reputation struck in the hearts of his captives would result in an appalling event. The majority refused to surrender, and even though some moved to the Morea, the island of Corfu, or the town of Parga, others had retreated to Zalongo, around 15 miles north of Preveza. Here, facing inevitable capture and probable death, about sixty of their women, fearing the expected abuse and brutality that would follow, decided to join hands in a traditional dance and song, and then, clutching their children, one by one they threw themselves over the edge of the 700-metre-high rock into the valley below. This tragedy would soon be famous throughout Europe, the story growing with the retelling, becoming not just part of Greek nationalist legend but also the subject of Western literature, music, and art. On a painting tour in the region in 1859, Edward Lear would be among those to visit the area, where a monument erected in 1961 now dominates the landscape as a memorial to the suicidal Dance of Zalongo. This, together with another later episode during which 130 women were said to have chosen to avoid their fate by drowning themselves, would reinforce the West's preconceptions of the typically brutal oriental despot.

Among the further tales spread of Ali's atrocities was the story of how he had punished some unfaithful women by tying them in sacks and throwing them into the lake at Ioannina. While one version of this suggests the victims to have been of members of his harem, individuals he apparently no longer found appealing, another is based on the true account of the Greek woman Euphrosyne (or Kyra Frosini), whose relationship with Ali's son caused such jealousy with the latter's wife that the pasha ordered her to be drowned along with some other females. Although the pasha's apologists were to explain this as just punishment for her immoral behaviour, her admirers, on the other hand, would see it as an act of virtuous self-sacrifice that she had committed in order to avoid the lecherous advances of Ali himself. In this latter guise Euphrosyne would later be revered as another martyr in the fight for Greek independence. But while there is little doubt of the pasha's brutality given his bragging to Byron in 1809 that in his time he had personally killed 30,000 people, this extravagant boast only adds to the complexity of his character. Evidence points to how Ali made use of his fearsome reputation. Being aware of the preconceptions of people abroad, he would manipulate the way he was seen in the West, purposely representing himself as the cruel oriental autocrat.[178]

Jack Morier, the British representative who had grown up in Smyrna and was one of the first sent to visit him in 1804, would find an additional reason for Ali's brutality. Having explained his heavy taxation of the Greeks as being a necessary measure to deal with financial 'deficiency', rather than an act of extortion, Morier – echoing Hamilton – claimed that in return the people enjoyed 'a security which at present is unknown to most of the wretched inhabitants of Roumelia'. He then continued:

> There, the weakness of the Government has reduced most of the male population to have recourse to robbery & plunder for subsistence; here indeed the nature of the country which is wholly mountainous, & the fierce disposition of the inhabitants makes them follow the same course. In endeavouring to subdue them, Ali Pasha has a double object in view, that of insuring the safety of the peaceable part of his subjects; and in the next place of forcing those turbulent people to a more pacific mode of life... I firmly believe that the fierce nature of the people he is endeavouring to reduce into order, rather than his own disposition obliges him sometimes to be cruel. The shocking inhumanities committed by the bands of robbers upon his subjects, compel him to make as cruel examples of them, & sometimes he prevents further disorders by taking those very offenders into his pay.[179]

Occupying the geographical region dividing the Ottoman and Christian European nations at a time when the area was of particular interest to the different empire builders of the West, Ali responded by becoming a central player in their rivalries, alternately opposing or befriending them as he saw fit. Although he was not alone in this, France, Austria, Russia, and the Ottomans switching allegiances with equal insouciance during the troubled years of the Napoleonic wars, his deviousness and his readiness to negotiate simultaneously with opposing factions meant he was distrusted by all. He was not just viewed with suspicion by the powers of Europe but also by his Ottoman neighbours, and he was accused by both East and West of falling too much into the opposite camp. In fact, Ali was playing the various parties at their own game, and he was not the polarised figure of their imaginations. This blending of the two cultures was even evident in the style of his court. While European visitors remarked on the oriental trappings, complete with the seraglio, harem, fountains, cushions, and other 'exotic' luxuries, they also noted the chandeliers and precious artefacts from Italy and elsewhere, Byron and Disraeli being just two of his many visitors to be struck by the vast Goblin carpet in his palace.

Wanting to benefit from the collapse of the Venetian Republic's hold over the eastern coastal regions of the Adriatic and Ionian seas, after the Treaty of Campo Formio Ali initially decided to ally himself to Napoleon. He even wrote to him to congratulate him on his achievements and to assure him of his friendship. For a time, the Frenchman's occupation of the Ionian Islands had suited the Albanian, who hoped it might lead to further territorial gains for himself. But things had then changed when the recently allied Russians and Ottomans became involved in the area. At that point, having lost confidence in Napoleon, Ali decided to switch sides and began to support the British, who in return acknowledged his possession of Preveza, Butrint, and Vonitza. Grateful that they had liberated the Ionian Islands, in January 1800 Ali personally sent a sword, a gun, and a silver pitcher to Admiral Nelson. Fully realising the significance of this new relationship, three years later in a letter to the British resident, Spiridion Foresti, Nelson wrote: 'I am really much interested for Ali Pacha; for he has always been a stanch [sic.] friend to the English, and most particularly kind to me; and if I should ever go to Corfu, I shall certainly, if he is within a few days' reach, go and see him.'[180]

The admiral had no illusions as to the regional ambitions of Napoleon, seeing him as 'not very scrupulous in the honourable means of accomplishing his darling object'.[181] He was above all convinced that the Frenchman was determined to achieve, with or without Russian help, the end of the Ottoman Empire. With the evidence indicating that the Balkan region had now become more important to him than the whole of Italy, it appeared to Napoleon's enemies that his interest in Ali Pasha and the Greeks most probably hinged on a conviction that by granting the latter independence, he might be able to take possession of the Morea. That was something the British wanted at all costs to prevent, Nelson, for one, stressing that such an outcome would inevitably mean a 'farewell' to India.[182] The scene was now set for the collapse of the short-lived peace between Britain and France, and by May 1803 the two countries were back at war. As their contest in the Adriatic and Ionian seas steadily intensified, Nelson became still more convinced of the need to secure the pasha as an ally. Therefore, when writing to Henry Addington, he spoke of Ali's 'good disposition', and how he might be 'made most useful' to the British. He considered it had been a grave mistake to have failed to send him some relatively inexpensive gifts costing 'a few hundred pounds which would have made him ours for ever'.[183] The admiral warned that if they were not careful the Albanian might be lured into the French camp. He was right in believing Ali had been offended at not receiving the things that he had expected, but by early the next year the pasha was again writing to Nelson, requesting on this occasion to be sent two artillery officers, 'a vessel', and some 'shot and shells'.[184] Since Ali had become anxious that the tsar's alliance with the sultan might lead to a reduction of his own powers, it was apparent that he intended to use these items against the Russians, but Nelson stressed, nonetheless, that the pasha's demands should be met to ensure his continuing support. With good relations being still maintained, before long Jack Morier, the British Consul-General in Albania, was able to report that the Albanian was eager for a closer alliance and along with the free entry to his ports and the possibility of additional manpower, he was also promising open access to his forests – this being a particularly tempting offer as the Royal Navy needed a constant supply of timber for shipbuilding. Shortly after, however, these negotiations would be halted when the British decided to side with the tsar, who was once again at war with the Ottomans. Ali reacted to this latest development by reconsidering his personal relations with Napoleon, hoping that a new agreement with the French might ultimately improve his chances of gaining Parga, the coastal town lying across the water from Paxos that was so essential for the security of his own lands. This had been in French hands since the fall of the Venetian Republic in 1797.

The situation in the region would be overturned again, however, by the treaty drawn up at Tilsit in 1807, which had seen the tsar finally agreeing to cede Parga, the Ionian Islands and Cattaro to the French.[185] This proved too much for Ali and once more he changed sides, on this occasion largely swayed by the British representative William Martin Leake whom he had met secretly one night on the beach near Preveza. Here, apparently following instructions, Leake had allowed him to believe that, after it had recaptured the islands and also Parga, Britain would be prepared to hand these possessions over to Ali, a misunderstanding that over the following years would drive the Albanian's determination to get what he considered his due. For the moment, however, good relations between the two sides were strengthened, and two years later the pasha would play a part in the treaty ending the recent outbreak of British-Ottoman hostility. At the same time, the Royal Navy agreed to protect Ali's ships that were taking grain to his famine-struck people in the south of the Gulf of Arta. It was against this background that, at the end of the year, the young British aristocrat Lord Byron and his travelling companion John 'Cam' Hobhouse made their famous visit to the Albanian's court.

Born of his father's second marriage, George Gordon Byron was the son of the profligate 'Mad Jack', a bankrupt who had soon abandoned his family to live abroad, remaining in France until his death. Having dissipated his second wife's fortune, his Scottish widow then moved back with her 3-year-old child to the more affordable Aberdeen, and here she remained until 1798. At that point, her son, now aged ten, inherited the title of the sixth Baron of Rochdale from his mad great-uncle, 'the Wicked Lord'. However, besides the barony, Byron inherited his predecessor's debts and so when he and his mother moved to Nottinghamshire, they found his extensive estates to be utterly dilapidated and stripped of most of their valuables. Nevertheless, she managed to send the boy to a crammer in Dulwich and later on to Harrow, from where he finally went up to Cambridge. Showing his maverick streak and the arrogance of a young aristocrat, on being told that dogs were not allowed he was reputed to have chosen to keep a pet bear – a foretaste of that passion for animals that later resulted in the strange menagerie that he kept in his palazzo in Venice. Although an avid reader who had already begun writing poetry in the fashion of his contemporaries, he did the minimum of work, passing most of his time gambling, spending extravagantly, piling up still more exorbitant debts, and debauchery. Hobhouse, one of his many male friends at this time, would later write in his diary that 'irregularities' in conduct were not new to Byron when he arrived at the university, he having 'nothing to learn in the way of depravity either of mind or body when he came from Harrow'.[186]

Two years after leaving Cambridge, in 1809 these two young men set off on their Grand Tour, they like others at the time choosing to avoid the previously popular destinations in France and Italy now embroiled in the Napoleonic wars. Tempted instead by the exotic pleasures they hoped to find in the east, they had set their sights on Persia, a country free as they believed from the rigid morality of the British. Accordingly, fantasising about the delights they expected to find on their travels, Byron would declare in his letter to Henry Drury that 'Hobhouse further hopes to indemnify himself in Turkey for a life of exemplary chastity at home by letting out his "fayre Body" to the whole Divan.'[187] From Portugal they crossed through Spain to Gibraltar, before finally sailing to Malta. Here, as the two young gentlemen filled their time being entertained by local society, they also took lessons in Arabic, which they hoped to be able to use at some point later in their travels. This, however, they soon gave up, since by then they had been persuaded to change their plans. Possibly encouraged by that same Spiridion Foresti, the former assistant British Consul on the Ionian Islands, who had moved to Malta after the Treaty of Tilsit, they now considered a new destination. Wanting to further British interests, Foresti encouraged them to explore Albania, promising them they would be given introductions to Ali Pasha. Therefore, ignoring those who suggested they should continue on to Constantinople, on 19 September the two young men took Foresti's advice and set sail for the Ionian Sea. Just days later the British fleet followed in their wake, on its way to the islands that – with the exception of Santa Maura and Corfu – it was soon to capture. While Foresti's motives may have been to use Byron and Hobhouse to win further backing from Ali, by the time the pair met the pasha these first successes had already been achieved. This would only increase the pleasure with which the Albanian greeted his guests, he (according to Hobhouse) indicating his preference for the British over the French and Russians, who had protected those whom he described as 'runaway robbers'.

The earlier journey from Malta had not been without incident. Having taken passage aboard a privateer, during their week at sea Bryon and Hobhouse's eyes would be opened to the maritime rules of the time. Before their arrival at Patras, any vessels encountered thought to belong to the enemy were attacked and robbed of their cargo. On eventually reaching the mainland, the ship continued up the coast, sailing past the site of Mark Antony's disastrous battle at Actium before arriving at Preveza, where the two young men visited the still largely uncovered remains of Emperor Augustus's Nikopolis. However, as news of their arrival had been passed from Patras to the British resident Leake at Ioannina, the pasha was now expecting them, and so without any further delay Byron and Hobhouse set off to meet him.

Having travelled mostly by Pony Express, exchanging their mounts along the way, they arrived at Ioannina on 5 October. On entering the capital they were greeted by the sight of a man's arm and part of his body hanging from a tree, something which Hobhouse with notable understatement said, made 'no pleasant impression', it leaving them both 'feeling a little sick'.[188] While the victim was a priest who had been tortured and then torn to death for his opposition to the ruler, the remains were explained as being as those of a felon, and, whether or not the visitors ever learned the truth they soon put the matter to one side and began eagerly to look forward to their meeting. The pasha, however, was temporarily delayed, being away fighting one of his rivals, and so the two young men spent the next few days benefiting from his hospitality. Besides visiting Ali's son in his nearby palace, they passed their time shooting, riding, attending the odd local festival, and ordering new Albanian costumes for themselves.

Eventually, their meeting was rearranged to take place some miles to the north at Tepelenë. By this time the party included not just Byron's servant and a few other attendants, but also eight janissaries the pasha had provided for their protection as they travelled through the wild and treacherous mountainous country. Their journey was made even worse by the appalling weather they experienced, but although Byron was lost for a time during a storm, finally after eight days they reached their destination. Although little remains today of Ali's sumptuous palace and its surroundings, the two men were immediately impressed. The next day, dressed suitably for their meeting, Byron wearing for the occasion 'a full suit of staff uniform, with a very magnificent sabre, etc.', they were finally ushered into Ali's presence.[189] The pasha was equally enthusiastic and eager to meet his visitors, particularly the young nobleman, whose importance he may have overestimated. Perhaps thanks to the consuls, he seemed to have gained the impression that Byron was someone of special significance, possibly even the nephew of George III himself. And, with his good looks, the youthful aristocrat may have had a further appeal for the elderly ruler, who in addition to his vast harem of some 300 women, was said to have had in his seraglio a similar number of young men and boys, his Ganymedes. Hobhouse described how Ali had looked 'leeringly' at his friend, inviting him to visit again on his own, but although Byron was well-known for his bisexuality, there is no proof that there was any intimacy between him and the pasha.

The young man was now intrigued by Albania, and so attracted to its culture that later back in England he would commission Thomas Philips to paint him in the country's national dress. Struck by these new insights, Byron began at once to record what he had seen, using his experiences to start composing his poem, *Childe Harold's Pilgrimage*. Byron wrote to his mother telling her of the luxuries, refinements and other splendours of the court and, despite the possibly naïve response of both young men to certain aspects, here he shows himself fully aware of the paradoxes in Ali's personality:

> ... his manner is very kind and at the same time he possesses that dignity which I find universal amongst the Turks. He has the appearance of anything but his real character, for he is a remorseless tyrant, guilty of the most horrible cruelties, very brave and so good a general, that they call him the Mahometan Bonaparte.[190]

While appreciating the complexity of his character, here he links the eastern despot with Napoleon, who was now terrorising much of Europe. Although respected and maybe revered by his enemies for his military brilliance, he was equally loathed for his ruthless determination – the 'bogeyman' with whom British parents threatened their recalcitrant children. According to the poet Robert Southey, Byron again alluded to the Frenchman's paradoxical character when in 1814 he asked whether Bonaparte was not 'a great man in his villainy'.[191] But, although now fascinated by his Albanian host, as the years passed the poet seems to have come to realise that in this adventure he had most probably been manipulated by Foresti, dangled as it were like a dainty morsel before the pasha to advance the political game. Whatever the truth, later in his life he would not wish to discuss this episode, significantly, perhaps cryptically telling a friend there was no need to return his borrowed Albanian costume as it reminded him of two things that he did not 'wish to remember'.[192]

After a few days the young men returned to Ioannina and on 3 November they left the capital with an escort provided by the pasha. While sailing from Preveza in one of his boats, they were caught in a fierce gale and swept north, only narrowly escaping death as the vessel threatened to break up. As the incompetence of the terrified captain led Byron and Hobhouse to abandon ship at the first opportunity, they then had to make their way back south overland, passing French-held Parga and the tragic site of Zalongo to arrive once more at Preveza. Eventually, having used a variety of means of transport, together with their escort they reached Missolonghi, this being Byron's first visit to the coastal town on the Gulf of Patras where he would die 15 years later. After two days they were on their way again, going via Patras to fetch their mail, then Delphi, Athens, Smyrna (Izmir), and finally Constantinople, where they abandoned their plans to visit Persia and at last made their way home.

The turning point in Byron's career came after his return to England with the publication of the first two cantos of *Childe Harold's Pilgrimage* in 1812. With some exaggeration, since there had been a certain amount of pre-publication marketing revealing the identity of the poet, Byron wrote: 'I awoke one morning and found myself famous.'[193] The public loved his exotic descriptions derived from the places he had seen on his travels, and these would inspire many of his readers to start wanting to explore the still largely unvisited eastern Mediterranean for themselves. However, during his next few years in England, while he was growing ever more famous for his poetry, Byron was becoming equally notorious for his romantic affairs. In addition to his various brief encounters, he was soon involved in a passionate and stormy relationship with Lady Caroline Lamb, who then famously described him as 'mad, bad, and dangerous'. But even worse for his reputation was the fact that he was now suspected of having a relationship with his half-sister Augusta Leigh, who around this same time gave birth to a daughter. To calm the gossip, therefore, Byron decided to marry Annabella Milbanke in January 1815, and eleven months later a daughter Ada was born. However, just a year after the marriage his wife left him on grounds of his unreasonable behaviour, cruelty, drunkenness, and continuing infidelity, and by the following March their separation was official. Riddled by debts, mired in scandal, and badly shaken by the break-up of his marriage, Byron now returned to an idea he had flippantly considered some years before, namely to leave the country for good. This he finally did on 25 April 1816, and after his departure he would never again see his only legitimate daughter – the later famous Ada Lovelace who became renowned for her role with Charles Babbage in the early development of the computer.

With the Napoleonic wars at last over, Byron was able this time to travel across Europe, going via Belgium and Germany to arrive eventually in May at Lake Geneva. Here Percy Bysshe Shelley, although not yet divorced, had also arrived with his future wife Mary Godwin and her stepsister, Claire Clairmont. Having pursued Byron in England and briefly become his lover, Claire now found an excuse to renew their relationship by arranging to introduce the poets to one another. With Byron soon renting the Villa Diodati, and Shelley a smaller house nearby, over the following weeks of that exceptionally wet summer the two groups began to spend much time together. When on one occasion Byron suggested they amuse themselves by writing ghost stories, only Mary and one other completed the challenge, but this no doubt would later give her the inspiration for her Frankenstein. Claire, however, continued to plague Byron, and he, never serious about her, now wanted to be rid of this woman whom he found so tiresome and demanding. By August she was clearly pregnant as a result of their affair in England, but he was refusing to be alone with her and was relieved when at the end of the month she finally left with the Shelleys. He would not see her again before she gave birth the following January to a daughter, a child initially called Alba. By that time Byron had also left Geneva, and in October he was reunited with Hobhouse in Milan. Here, over the next three weeks, the poet was frequently entertained by Ludovico di Breme, a highly educated man he had recently met in Geneva, who was an ordained member of the Council of State of the Kingdom of Italy. In that role, he had built up a close rapport with the Armenian monks in Venice, who had appealed to him for help when faced by Napoleon's draconian measures against religious organisations. Besides inspiring Byron's interest in their order, di Breme most probably also arranged an introduction for him with the monk, who would later become his language instructor in Venice.

Before leaving Milan, Byron would commit one last mischievous act, reputedly pilfering a souvenir from the Ambrosiana Museum. Describing to his friend Moore how he had been shown the 'beautiful love letters' written by Lucretia Borgia to Cardinal Bembo, he then boasted how behind the caretaker's back, he had secretly taken a single strand of her long, golden hair. Although this story would later be exaggerated, requiring much of it to be refuted, such apparent disregard by Byron for others' treasures could appear to be in character with an alleged episode that had earlier occurred while he was on his Grand Tour. Byron had then reputedly scratched his name on some of the ancient Greek ruins. Today the faint example of his and Hobhouse's handiwork in the Gymnasium at Delphi receives little attention, but that at Sounion has become a matter of debate, with Lawrence Durrell arguing that 'it is not in his hand and nothing like his signature' and so 'it is fair to suppose that Byron would not have indulged in such sacrilege by himself.'[194] Were he responsible for any such defacing of the antiquities, it would certainly sit badly alongside his much-repeated condemnation of Lord Elgin. Horrified by the damage the earl had recently done to Athens' ancient monuments by his removal of the famous Parthenon sculptures – several of which were subsequently lost in the process during a storm off Kythera – in *Childe Harold* Byron clearly points his finger at the unnamed Scottish aristocrat:

> Dull is the eye that will not weep to see
> Thy walls defaced, thy mouldering shrines removed
> By British hands, which it had best behoved
> To guard those relics ne'er to be restored.[195]

The last consignment of these marbles had been brought back in 1811 by a ship on which, by a strange irony, the poet himself was travelling home. Elgin had sold these by an Act of Parliament to the British Government, and they had then been put into the British Museum. While some people pinned their hopes on their staying there only until the Greeks had gained their independence, others insisted that it was a safer place for them and they should remain in their new home. Already the issue was beginning to cause debate. To demolish the stand of those who justified Elgin's actions on the grounds that he had been protecting the artefacts from further deterioration or demolition, many drew attention to the appalling harm done to the sculptures and their surroundings at the time of their removal. Further complicating the argument, with the ending of the Napoleonic Wars, the steady repatriation of much of the French emperor's booty had begun, and so there was now a general move afoot to see all confiscated treasures restored to their former owners.

On 10 November 1816, Byron arrived in Venice, and here he began his study of the Armenian language. Initially he was rowed across daily to the island of San Lazzaro degli Armeni, doing so for about seven weeks until he was temporarily stopped by becoming ill. With his usual flippancy he wrote to a friend, 'I am studying daily, at an Armenian monastery, the Armenian language. I found that my mind wanted something craggy to break upon; and this – as the most difficult thing I could discover here for an amusement – I have chosen, to torture me into attention.'[196] In exchange for his lessons, he paid the printing costs of the first Armenian-English grammar, written by his teacher Father Pascal Aucher. But, writing to Moore he also claimed he had another role in this. 'In the mornings I go over in my gondola to babble Armenian with the friars of the convent of St. Lazarus, and to help one of them in correcting the English of an English and Armenian grammar which he is publishing.'[197] While two years later in an appendix to another grammar book Aucher anonymously published Byron's own translations – only being reprinted under his name in the 1870s – it is hard to judge exactly how much of the passages were his own work, as they appear to depend to some considerable extent on earlier Italian translations. Byron, nevertheless, claimed that he had personally 'compiled the major part of [the] two Armenian & English grammars'.[198] Whatever the truth, he continued to visit the monk for two years, until eventually he fell out with his teacher, who described him as not just moody and hot-tempered, but also a lightweight who preferred to spend his time enjoying other pleasures. Their disagreement finally came to a head after Aucher removed from his book the preface written by Byron condemning the sultan. Even though the younger man later apologised for his reaction and uncontrolled response at the time, after this the two would never meet again. Aucher, however, would finally give his pupil some credit in the preface to his 1821 dictionary.

A few months after arriving in Venice, at the end of April Byron went on a visit to Rome with his friend Hobhouse. He was delighted by what he saw, spending his days riding around the city, and also going out to see other sights in the surrounding countryside. Before leaving, however, he was 'determined' to witness a different and 'more horrible' event that he believed he should see. He watched the public execution of three criminals, which, despite his initial revulsion, he later said he had found 'more impressive than the vulgar and ungentlemanly dirty' method of hanging that was carried out in England. The next day he set off back to Venice to arrive home on 28 May, explaining his reason to Hobhouse for not following him to Naples by saying that it was a city where there were too many English people, whom he preferred to hate 'at a distance'.[199]

During his first two years in Venice he stayed in the Frezzaria district in the centre of the city, where he had soon engaged in a long affair with his landlord's wife, Marianna Segati. Although he was always generous to the poor, he followed a notoriously extravagant lifestyle, complete with numbers of servants, a stable of horses on the Lido and other expensive trappings. Besides attending some of the salons of the foremost Venetians, he spent the summer months of 1817 staying with Hobhouse out at Villa Foscarini on the Brenta, where the two enjoyed pursuing their separate assignations – something that no doubt partly explained the reported 'frenzies' of Marianna. While in January 1818 Hobhouse returned to England, by March Byron's affair with his mistress was over and he was already involved with a young baker's wife, a poor, simple girl called Margherita Cogni, better known as *La Fornarina*. Around the beginning of June they both moved into Palazzo Mocenigo on the Grand Canal, he paying an exorbitant sum for the privilege of living in such a magnificent location. He soon began to fill the palace with a collection of exotic birds and animals. He now enjoyed a particularly wild period, entertaining numerous women to the fury of his latest mistress, who, after returning briefly to her irate husband, had by the end of the summer firmly reinstalled herself – although uninvited – with her lover. Despite initially having amused Byron with her wit, *La Fornarina's* tantrums and interference began to annoy him, and he eventually asked her to leave, whereupon she responded with a dramatic gesture by throwing herself into the Grand Canal. Although she was hurriedly rescued, this latest ploy did not work and she finally had to accept that his affections had moved on.

Possibly from an accident at birth, Byron had developed a twisted foot that according to Hobhouse, besides giving him pain, made him particularly sensitive. In the opinion of Jan Morris his resulting limp may also explain why he was reluctant to appear in St Mark's Square when it was still light, being aware of how the more superstitious Venetians feared people with a disability. Concerned about his appearance and wanting to disguise his lameness, he refused to wear a splint. As he was equally insecure over the matter of his weight, which fluctuated between nine and a half to about fourteen stone, he developed an eating disorder. Consequently, he turned to drastic measures, regularly half-starving himself, sometimes bingeing, constantly measuring himself, and often engaging in extreme exercise. Apart from his daily riding on the Lido, he would often swim from the island to his palace on the Grand Canal, occasionally challenging others to compete with him, only then to win. As a result of this, in the early 20th century a race called the Lord Byron Cup was inaugurated, only finally suspended for reasons of health and safety in the 1950s. Over the years he was to carry out similar feats, most famously swimming across the Hellespont and later the harbour in Genoa.

Shelley, perhaps somewhat hypocritically, disapproved of Byron's liaisons, being particularly shocked by his friend's affairs with low-born Italians, women he considered as 'the most contemptible of all that exist under the moon; the most ignorant the most disgusting, the most bigotted [*sic.*], the most filthy'. While he considered it particularly vile that Byron mixed with women from the lowest rung of society, ones who had been found in the streets for him by his *gondoliere*, there was a further aspect to these relationships that especially appalled him. His friend followed the local custom that required him first to bargain with the girls' parents, Shelley believed his behaviour had shown itself as beneath that expected of 'an Englishman'.[200] When he visited him in October 1818, however, he was struck by how well he appeared: 'I saw Lord Byron, and really hardly knew him again; he is changed into the liveliest and happiest looking man I ever met.'[201] But now the little Alba was causing some embarrassment to the Shelleys, the situation not being helped by rumours suggesting incorrectly that she was the result of a relationship between Percy himself and his sister-in-law. Claire finally agreed, therefore, to hand her much-loved daughter over to Byron, whom she presumed would be better able to provide for the child. Having at last, therefore, accepted his responsibility, before long he had changed the little girl's name to Allegra, and was boasting to friends of her prettiness and intelligence.

Over ten days in February 1819 Emperor Francis I made a second visit to Venice, but a more dramatic event was to occur the next month. Byron later recounted to Hobhouse how an elephant had been brought to the city for the carnival, only for the poor, terrified animal to escape from its handlers, one of whom it trampled to death in the process. Having bolted from the Riva degli Schiavoni, it tore through the streets, crashing into a woman's house on the way. The police rushed in pursuit, firing their guns in a hopeless effort to stop it until at last the animal was cornered inside the church of Sant'Antonin (near Santa Zaccaria). Here having done untold damage, it was eventually killed by a cannon that had been brought hurriedly to the scene from the *Arsenale* – the patriarch's permission having first, bizarrely, been sought in case the animal might be 'seeking sanctuary'. The elephant's skeleton would eventually find its way to Padua University, where it remains today. The story would later be picked up by various writers, chief among them the Venetian Pietro Buratti. Having already mocked the earlier French occupation, he now used the story as a metaphor to criticise the Austrians in a long, coarse satirical poem that ultimately landed him with a month-long prison sentence.

Shortly after this excitement, in April Byron met Teresa, the wife of Count Guiccioli from Ravenna, a young woman whom he had just briefly seen the previous year shortly after her marriage. Despite his reputation, she was soon devoted to him, and he would become far more closely attached to her than he had been to her predecessors. Her arrival on the scene spelt the end for *La Fornarina* and eventually, after Teresa had returned to Ravenna, Byron also left Venice to re-join her on Christmas Eve 1819. In accordance with the Venetian custom, her elderly husband accepted the poet's presence as her 'cavalier servente', and, as he was equally happy to accept Byron's generosity, before long he would even invite him to stay in his house. In spite of the disapproval of Teresa's father, Byron accepted this offer, and in January he moved in with her, along with his illegitimate daughter Allegra and his sundry collection of animals. Not wanting to live any longer in Venice and wishing now to give up his former extravagant lifestyle, in June he cancelled his rental contract on Palazzo Mocenigo. As his landlady was intractable, she demanded he give her the full payment, but because some of Byron's money was ultimately found to be missing, it would be the unfortunate British Consul who was forced to settle the difference. Meanwhile, back in Ravenna, by July things had come to a head and Teresa was asking the pope for a separation from her husband. Once this was granted, her other family members began to accept Byron, and before long they had begun to introduce him to the local group of Carbonari dissidents.

Meanwhile, in Albania, with the renewal of peace after the end of the Napoleonic Wars, the Ottoman Porte started to pay more attention to the pasha. The octogenarian Ali was growing increasing unmanageable, even finally declaring his independence in 1820. As he was also seeking the Greeks' support by backing their similar demands, the infuriated sultan stripped him of his title as pasha and declared him to be an enemy of the Ottoman empire. Being also abandoned shortly after by his own sons, in early 1822 Ali eventually agreed to capitulate at Ioannina, doing this in the expectation of receiving a promised pardon. He had been deceived, and just two days later on the orders of Mahmud II he was assassinated. The exact details of his death are uncertain, and while it appears that his orders to blow up the palace at the last minute rather than surrender were not carried out, the most repeated version of events asserts that he was shot through the floor while sheltering in the island monastery of St Panteleimon, which he had built out in the lake for his favourite wife, Kyra Vasilike. A Greek Orthodox, who at the age of twelve had first attracted Ali's attention when she had begged him to spare her rebel father's life, this woman had been much loved by the pasha, but in the end she had probably betrayed him. Quite possibly she had allowed him to be captured in return for the promise of an amnesty for the Christian citizens in the town. After Ali's head had been displayed for three days on a silver platter, his widow was forced to accompany it back to Istanbul where it was presented to the sultan. Eventually, however, she was allowed to return to the newly independent Greece, where in 1834 she died at Aitoliko near Missolonghi.

* * *

Byron hated the damp winter weather of Ravenna, even contrasting it unfavourably with the climate of London. While he visited Dante's tomb, he did not display interest in the town's other treasures, claiming that he would not fall into the same temptation as most tourists. In the fifth canto of *Don Juan* written at this time he mocks the way every 'fool' tends to describe in detail everything he sees: 'While Nature, tortured twenty thousand ways, / Resigns herself with exemplary patience / To guide-books, rhymes, tours, sketches, illustrations.'[202] This may partly explain the absence of descriptions of the magnificent mosaics of Ravenna, or of those in the interior of St Mark's in Venice. Nevertheless, as interest in Byzantine art was beginning to be revived in the West, according to some critics, its impact is detectable in Byron's writing.[203] At the same time, however, it is difficult to assess precisely the poet's interest in pictorial art as a whole, as with his usual cynicism he tended to dismiss the value of paintings. In his letter to his half-sister Augusta he praised the places that he had visited in Milan, such as the cathedral, theatre, and library, but then offhandedly remarked that he knew nothing about the galleries, 'except as far as liking one picture out of a thousand'. Similarly, when returning from Rome in 1817 he had told Murray that, as he was anxious to get back to Venice, he had not stopped in Florence, where in fact he 'had already seen the galleries and other sights' –implying, as it were, that he had 'done' these things.[204] Yet, although belonging to the Papal States and ruled from Rome, Ravenna still displayed its former links to Byzantium, and so here Byron witnessed that complex crossover of cultures and relationships that he had so often explored between the Occidental and Oriental worlds.

Because of their liberal views, in July 1821 Teresa's father, Count Gamba, and her brother Piero were banished from Ravenna and sent into exile, and by the mid-summer she had joined them in Florence. Byron remained behind and shortly after she had left, on 6 August Shelley arrived to spend ten days with him. Struck again by how much his friend had changed and glad that he had 'got rid of all those melancholy and degraded habits which he indulged at Venice', he remarked on how his host appeared to be happy and in love with his new mistress who was 'a lady of rank'. Shelley then described some of the more unusual details of his stay:

Lord Byron gets up at *two*. I get up, quite contrary to my usual custom ... at 12. After breakfast we sit talking till six. From six to eight we gallop through the pine forests which divide Ravenna from the sea; we then come home and dine, and sit up gossiping till six in the morning. I don't suppose this will kill me in a week or fortnight, but I shall try it no longer. Lord B.'s establishment consists, besides servants, of ten horses, eight enormous dogs, three monkeys, five cats, an eagle, a crow, and a falcon; and all these, except the horses, walk about the house, which every now and then resounds with their unarbitrated quarrels, as if they were the masters of it... After I have sealed my letter, I find that my enumeration of the animals in this Circean Palace was defective, and that in a material point. I have just met on the grand staircase five peacocks, two guinea hens, and an Egyptian crane. I wonder who all these animals were before they were changed into these shapes.[205]

After leaving Ravenna, Shelley went to visit Allegra, to whom he had earlier become much attached while she was staying in his house. By now the little girl was living in a convent at Bagno Cavallo where she had been sent on 1 March 1821 by her father, who believed this would be better and safer for the child. Having already been frequently farmed out to friends and moved from one household to another, the 4-year-old Allegra had become spoilt and rather difficult to handle, and Teresa thought she would benefit from living with the nuns. For his part, rather than sending her to an English boarding school, Byron preferred to give his daughter a Catholic upbringing in an Italian environment, thinking that this would provide her with a better start in life. While Shelley and his wife Mary, both non-believers, had grown anxious about the little girl, Claire, besides being worried about her becoming ill in a cold convent, was furious that Byron had gone against his earlier agreement to keep the child always with him. Although the nuns apparently treated her well and were fond of her, her mother's fears were soon proved right as just over a year later the child caught a fever and died on 20 April 1822. Shelley, already depressed, was shattered by the news, and Claire would never forgive Byron. But he was already suffering from remorse. While he had ignored Shelley's advice and for four months not visited Allegra when she had asked him to do so, he was now left heartbroken by the loss of the little daughter he had only just come to fully appreciate. He wrote: 'While she lived, her existence never seemed necessary to my happiness; but no sooner did I lose her, than it appeared to me as if I could not live without her.'[206] While Byron was still grieving, three months after her death he was hit with another disaster when on 8 July Shelley was drowned with a companion in a sailing accident off Livorno. By this time the bond uniting the two men had virtually broken, because Shelley had grown to suspect his former friend of spreading the earlier rumour of his scandalous relationship with his sister-in-law Claire. Yet a month after Shelley's death at the spot on the beach where his body had been recovered and temporarily buried, Byron took part in a cremation ceremony, finding some relief from his distress by swimming out to sea while the pyre continued to burn.

* * *

Holding them partly responsible for Venice's final loss of independence, Byron believed that the English should be ashamed of having stood back while the great Serenissima had been brought to its knees. Hinting that a similar fate might await the British, in *Childe Harold* he warns, 'in the fall / of Venice, think of thine'.[207] This cautionary message would later be reiterated by John Ruskin, who, drawing a comparison between Tyre, Venice, and England, suggests a similar outcome: 'Of the first of these three great powers, only the memory remains; of the second, the ruin; the third, which inherits their greatness, if it forget their example, may be led through prouder eminence to less pitied destruction.'[208] Viewing the British as complicit in Venice's takeover by the Austrians after the Congress of Vienna, Byron had previously gone even further, declaring to his wife, Lady Byron: 'The English terrier will meddle of course in anything that will keep down freedom – or prop up their own villainy.'[209] But his attack was also directed at the new imperial masters, who had regained control in Venice about a year and a half before his arrival in the city. Although he had already attracted the attention of the Austrians in Milan and his activities were always carefully watched, he still continued to show an arrogant disregard for the authorities. Accordingly, in his letter to John Murray in October 1820 he sarcastically decried their heavy-handedness, disparagingly labelling the Austrians as 'Huns':

Of the state of things here it would be difficult and not very prudent to speak at large, the Huns opening all letters: I wonder if they can read them when they have opened them? If so, they may see, in my most legible hand, that I think them damned scoundrels and barbarians, their emperor a fool, and themselves more fools than he.[210]

While Byron here gives the suggestion that he is untouchable, in reality he had already felt the censor's hand, his first cantos of *Don Juan* having been placed on the list of works banned for reasons of immorality and irreligious content. But even more serious was his brazen vilification of the new regime, which he condemns in the fourth canto of *Childe Harold*: '... now the Austrian reigns – / An Emperor tramples where an Emperor knelt; / Kingdoms are shrunk to provinces, and chains / Clank over sceptred cities.'[211] Intrigued since his arrival in Venice by the story of the executed doge, he now used it for his play *Marino Faliero*, which, like *The Prophecy of Dante*, would address political themes and dare to call on the Italians to unite. With his situation becoming increasingly precarious, in November 1821, following Shelley's advice, Byron moved to Pisa to join his mistress and his friends, now leaving Ravenna where he had drawn further unwelcome attention to himself by becoming leader of the local band of the Carbonari.

The Carbonari had come to the fore in the Kingdom of Naples during the reign of Murat, but their exact origins are unknown. Individual sects of young men, bound together by oaths of loyalty, were thought to have formed independently in several countries, apparently taking their name from their occupation; when hiding from the authorities in the woods they had become charcoal burners. By the beginning of the 19th century in Naples their association had grown to around 200,000, the membership embracing all strata of society. For a time, they had accepted the French king because their main objective was to achieve liberal reform, but when Murat became more authoritarian they began to revolt against him. Even Queen Maria Carolina was then thought to have backed the Carbonari. Similarly, during the earlier period of Joseph Bonaparte's reign Ferdinand I had looked to them for support, but after he was restored to power as King of the Two Sicilies, he had begun with the help of the Austrians to try and re-impose his absolute rule. As a result, in Naples in July 1820, having declared themselves enemies of his tyrannical and unconstitutional authority, the Carbonari rose up in revolt. A similar uprising in Sicily was fiercely repressed and the earlier constitutional rights that the people had gained under the British were removed, but in the capital on the mainland the rebellion succeeded and the king was forced to declare a new constitution. As this horrified Europe's more conservative rulers, the next year the Austrians marched south to defeat the Neapolitan army, and after dismissing the Parliament and crushing the liberal factions they took control of the city, then holding it for the next six years.

The rebels' earlier achievement in 1820 encouraged them to take their message to Turin, where they hoped to bring about the establishment of another constitutional government. In this they were soon disappointed, their objective being undermined by the abdication of the Sardinian king Victor Emanuel I. He was replaced by his more resolute brother Charles Felix (Carlo Felice), who chose to side with the Austrians, so the Carbonari were soon excommunicated and arrested. A decade later their movement would play a part in the country's political affairs, but for the time being all calls for liberal reform in Italy had been quashed. Byron, bitterly disappointed in 1821 when he heard that the rising in Naples had failed, sarcastically summed up his feelings in a letter to Thomas Moore: 'As a very pretty woman said to me a few nights ago, with the tears in her eyes, as she sat at the harpsichord, "Alas! the Italians must now return to making operas." I fear *that* and macaroni are their *forte*, and motley their only wear.'[212] Despairing of the Italians' lack of determination, when writing to Shelley he linked it in a way to his own increasing apathy: 'As I grow older, the indifference – not to life, for we love it by instinct – but to the stimuli of life, increases. Besides, this late failure of the Italians has latterly disappointed me for many reasons – some public, some personal.'[213] He still wanted to fight for the cause of liberty, and for a time he had even considered going to Spain or South America. Before long, however, he began to turn his attention towards the developing situation in Greece where the War of Independence had broken out in March that year. He had already developed a first interest in the Greeks during his Grand Tour and had frequently displayed his liberal thinking in other ways: as a Whig member of the House of Lords, by his involvement with the Armenians, and through his membership of the Carbonari. Flattered when approached by the newly formed London Greek Committee, an organisation to which his friend Hobhouse belonged, he agreed to join their fight for the country's independence.

After tearful goodbyes from Teresa, despite his obvious foreboding and growing doubts about the whole enterprise, Byron was ready to depart. His fears were increased when on their first abortive attempt to leave Genoa a storm damaged their ship and forced them to return to harbour. According to Teresa's brother, this increased Byron's melancholy, who saw it as a bad omen. On 14 January 1823, accompanied by Piero Gamba, he finally succeeded in setting sail, and his spirits then began to lift. Travelling in his usual flamboyant style, besides his collection of impressive uniforms and a variety of weapons, he took five horses, eight servants, and his black groom, who, he believed, would increase his 'dignity in the East'.[214] On 4 August he arrived on the British-held island of Cephalonia and, while he fended off demands from the various different Greek factions eager to claim him as their own, Byron began to build up his small army, engaging the resident Souliotes and other mercenaries in what was to become his 'Byron brigade'.[215] Having personally paid £4,000 towards refitting the ships they needed for their transport, by the end of the year they were ready to set off again. Despite the short distance to the mainland, the journey would take eight days as they tried to avoid contact with the Ottoman fleet and, only after narrowly escaping attack were they at last able to reach Missolonghi on 5 January 1824.

Here, dressed in a scarlet uniform ordered for the occasion, Byron was welcomed by a military parade and gun salute, and having established his headquarters he joined forces with some of the local Greeks. Although he was sympathetic towards his Souliotes, who had suffered so much, infuriated at not having received their pay they now began to cause trouble. Even though he realised that they were all too ready to cheat him with false expense claims for non-existent family members, he again dipped into his own finances, giving them £6,000 of his own. Only too aware of the extent of his difficulties, Byron compared his own situation to that of Ali Pasha when he wryly commented to the Greek captains: 'Is it not likely that we shall now have to put up with the same thing?'[216] While his generosity would increase his reputation for being immensely wealthy, in fact he was short of money and so he now sold his estate in Northamptonshire to find the funds for the wages of the new officers he was hoping to try and encourage to join the cause. Some two years earlier, in May 1822, men from all over Europe had been enrolled in the newly formed Battalion of Philhellenes, but in the intervening period interest in the cause had begun to fade, and numbers were dwindling. For that reason Byron's actions were now invaluable, his presence alone helping to reverse the trend and persuade new volunteers to join the fight.

Yet Byron was soon irritated by the rivalries and disputes between the different Greek groups and the foreigners, and on losing patience with the hot-headed Souliotes he decided to dismiss them. At the same time, although more practical support would eventually appear with the arrival of equipment from the London Greek Committee, he was annoyed by the delays and postponements that were causing such serious shortages for his army. Because of these things, he was losing hope in the venture, and on his 36th birthday in January he expressed a poignant premonition of what lay ahead. In a poem created to mark the occasion he wrote: 'If thou regret'st they youth, *why live?* / The land of honourable death / Is here:– up to the Field, and give / Away thy breath!'[217] Just a month later he suffered a fit and although he recovered, his disillusion was visibly increasing, saying to the captains, 'We have wasted these two months on all this. I am tired of it.'[218] Over the following weeks Byron's health declined and having eventually caught a cold that turned into a fever, his condition was made worse by the doctors. By insisting on bleeding their patient four times, they not only made him weaker but also most probably caused him to develop blood poisoning, with the inevitable result that only three months after his arrival in the country, on 19 April 1824 he died. His last words were 'Poor Greece'. His body was then taken back to England in the very ship that had finally arrived in Zante with the much-needed funds sent by the English and Spanish. As this money was held up on the island, leaving the frustrated Philhellenes waiting impatiently for its release, support for the movement again began to crumble. As the different factions continued to argue, and men to die, others started to return home to their own countries. Even though Byron's enterprise had proved to be unsuccessful and Missolonghi itself would fall to the Ottomans two years later, with their eventual defeat at the naval battle of nearby Navarino in October 1827 the tables would finally turn. In 1830 the Greek independence for which Byron had fought was at last recognised.

In England many were shocked on hearing of his death, Tennyson, for one, weeping at the news, and even though Byron had not wanted his body to be repatriated, crowds of mourners still gathered to pay their respects. As the Dean of Westminster was not prepared, however, to give the poet a burial on grounds of his controversial past, he was then interred instead at the Byron family church of Hucknall in Northamptonshire. But although he had been refused official recognition at home, in 1881 the people of Missolonghi honoured him with their own monument, just one of many such memorials found today in Greece, where he is still remembered with affection. Even though he had not personally achieved his goal, he had earned the gratitude of the Greeks for bringing their struggle to the attention of the West, and, for paying for this with his life. Many in Britain, however, saw it as shameful that he was not given equal respect in his country of birth and so, after repeated appeals, in 1969 Westminster Abbey finally agreed to right this wrong and a plaque was placed in Poets' Corner, alongside the various memorials honouring his former companion Shelley and the other great names of English literature.

1. The old walls of Diocletian's Palace in Split. (Courtesy of LBM1948 under Creative Commons 4.0)

2. Mosaic in Sant'Apollinare Nuovo, Ravenna, showing the facade of Theodoric's palace, with the disjointed hands and arms of the obliterated images still visible on some of the columns. (Author's collection)

3. Theodoric's mausoleum in Ravenna. (Author's collection)

4. Mosaics in San Vitale, Ravenna, built during the time of Justinian, possibly on the lines of the emperor's reception hall in Constantinople. (Author's collection)

5. The underground crypt at Monte Sant'Angelo where the Lombard Melus of Bari was believed to have met the first group of Norman knights to visit Puglia. (Author's collection)

6. San Nicola, Bari, the basilica built to house the bones of the city's patron saint. (Author's collection)

7. The Abbazia di Santa Maria di Cerrate near Brindisi that was closely linked to Bohemund, and possibly even his grandfather, Tancred de Hauteville. (Author's collection)

8. The interior of the Abbazia di Santa Maria di Cerrate. (Author's collection)

9. The interior of San Giovanni al Sepolcro at Brindisi which Bohemund built as a place of shelter for the Knights who were on their way to the Holy Land. (Author's collection)

10. Bohemund's tomb at Canosa. (Author's collection)

11. Frederick II's Castel del Monte in Puglia. (Author's collection)

12. Plaque marking the location of the remains of Frederick's wives Yolande of Brienne and Isabella of England at Andria Cathedral. (Author's collection)

13. Palazzo Nuovo, Bologna, where Frederick II's son Enzo was imprisoned for over two decades until his death. (Author's collection)

14. Federico da Montefeltro's Palazzo Ducale in Urbino. (Courtesy of VlRan under Creative Commons 4.0)

15. Federico's Studiolo in the Palazzo Ducale. (Courtesy of Fabrizio Garrisi)

16. Fresco by Piero della Francesca depicting Sigismondo Pandolfo Malatesta in the Tempio Malatestiano. (Courtesy of Henry Townsend)

Above: 17. Bari Castle, the childhood home of Bona Sforza. (Author's collection)

Left: 18. The cathedral at Ostuni, 'the 'White City' that was given to Bona's mother by Il Moro. (Author's collection)

Below left: 19. The view from the fortress built by Emperor Charles V at Lesina (Hvar), where the local people sheltered from the Ottomans on their way to the Battle of Lepanto. (Courtesy of Tom Cull)

20. The triumphal Porta Napoli at Lecce built at the time of Emperor Charles V, displaying his imperial arms. (Author's collection)

21. Trani in Puglia where the local people attempted to hold out against the French, and where the Tree of Liberty was then erected in the square. (Author's collection)

Left: 22. The side chapel in Otranto Cathedral where the skulls and remains of those massacred by the Ottomans in 1480 remain on display. (Author's collection)

Below: 23. Aerial view of Dubrovnik showing the old town that, divided by the Stradun, is encircled by its massive walls. (Courtesy of Chensiyuan under Creative Commons 4.0)

Bottom: 24. Klis Fortress near Split where the Uskoks tried to hold out against the Ottomans. (Courtesy of Bernard Gagnon under Creative Commons 4.0)

25. Looking towards the Piazzetta in Venice – the traditional point of arrival marked by the two ancient columns. The Zecca and Biblioteca Marciana are on the left, the Doge's palace on the right, and the Campanile and the Basilica di San Marco are in the background. (Author's collection)

26. The *Arsenale*, showing the Lion of St Mark above the entrance and, on the left, Morosini's lion, which he stole after his destruction of the Parthenon. (Author's collection)

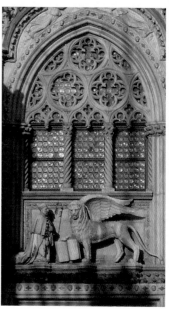

Above left: 27. The Bocca di Leone where secret denunciations could be posted by the public. (Author's collection)

Above right: 28. The Porta della Carta, with the statue of Doge Foscari and St Mark's lion that had to be restored after it was damaged by the Napoleonic French. (Author's collection)

29. San Giorgio Maggiore with its basilica designed by Palladio. Pope Pius VII was elected and crowned on the island and just offshore the last Bucintoro was destroyed by the French. (Author's collection)

30. The great Basilica di Santa Maria della Salute on the Grand Canal, built as a votive offering during the seventeenth-century outbreak of the plague. (Author's collection)

31. The Piazza di San Marco seen from the Piazzetta dei Leoncini, looking towards the Ala Napoleonica, Napoleon's Palace, that today houses the Museo Correr. (Courtesy of Jean-Pol Grandmont)

32. The tomb of Daniele Manin in the Piazzetta dei Leoncini, alongside the north wall of St Mark's Basilica. (Author's collection)

33. The much-loved Miramar Castle built by Emperor Maximilian outside Trieste that was later frequently visited by his sister-in-law, Empress Elizabeth of Austria.

Above: 34. The Achilleion that Empress Elizabeth built for herself in Corfu, but which she seldom visited. (Courtesy of Marc Ryckaert under Creative Commons 3.0)

Below: 35. The Villa Pisani neat Stra where Hitler and Mussolini had their heated meeting in 1934. (Courtesy of Gianfranco Zanovello under Creative Commons 4.0)

Above: 36. Looking down on Kotor in the 'Bocche di Cattaro' from the mountains of Montenegro. (Courtesy of Diego Delso under Creative Commons 4.0)

Below: 37. The Piazza Grande in Trieste that after the fall of the Habsburgs was renamed the Piazza Unità d'Italia. (Courtesy of Diego Delso under Creative Commons 4.0)

SECTION VIII
REVOLUTION AND REJECTION

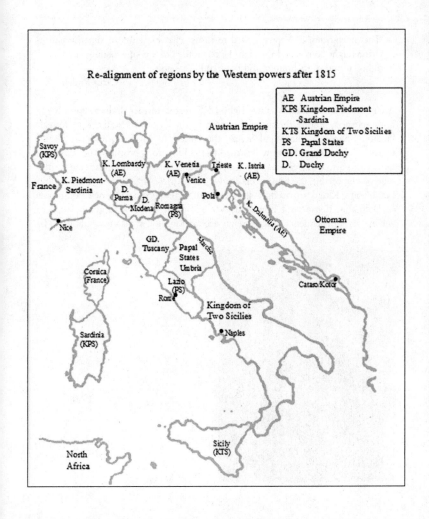

Re-alignment of regions by the Western powers after 1815

AE Austrian Empire
KPS Kingdom Piedmont
    -Sardinia
KTS Kingdom of Two Sicilies
PS Papal States
GD. Grand Duchy
D. Duchy

Savoy (KPS)

France

K. Piedmont-Sardinia

Nice

Corsica (France)

Sardinia (KPS)

K. Lombardy (AE)

D. Parma

D. Modena

Romagna (PS)

GD. Tuscany

Papal States

Umbria

Lazio (PS)

Rome

Austrian Empire

K. Venetia (AE)

Venice

Trieste

K. Istria (AE)

Pola

K. Dalmatia (AE)

Marche

Ottoman Empire

Cataro Kotor

Kingdom of Two Sicilies

Naples

Sicily (KTS)

North Africa

15

Venice's fight for independence and the unification of Italy

'The martyrdom of Venice served to show what extremes of superhuman virtue might be reached through the patriotism of a people confident of its rights, proud of its honour and powerful in its unity.'

Carlo Radelli[219]

After the Congress of Vienna 1814-1815, eight former Italian states were re-established, among them the Kingdom of the Two Sicilies, the Kingdom of Piedmont-Sardinia, the Papal States, the Duchy of Modena, and the Grand Duchy of Tuscany – this now returned to the Emperor's brother. And while the Duchy of Parma was given to the Emperor's daughter Marie-Louise (the former wife of Napoleon), the Empire claimed for itself those regions previously within Napoleon's Kingdom of Italy that were now to become the new kingdoms of Dalmatia, Illyria, and Lombardy-Venetia. Thus Venice had again failed to achieve its independence from foreign occupation. Yet, it was now about to be

Daniele Manin.

struck by more immediate problems as, towards the end of 1816, following a series of bad harvests, the whole region would be hit by famine. Already suffering from pellagra because of their inadequate diets, in desperation many of the poor rural people moved into the cities, only for their misery to be compounded as typhus took hold. Soon sickness and poverty were widespread. Even before this, however, Venice had experienced extreme starvation, with some of its citizens dying during the six months that it had struggled to survive under the British naval blockade and the repeated Austrian attacks from the mainland. While both foreign powers had briefly occupied the city after its eventual fall in the spring of 1814, before long things had changed again. For some time the Austrians had been in charge of most of Venetia, and so, following Napoleon's abdication at Fontainbleau in April, they had assumed full control – finally establishing their government in the city five months later. By that time the formerly beautiful capital of the Serenissima had been reduced to such a state of dilapidation that when Chancellor Metternich visited it with the Emperor in December the following year, he would describe the place as resembling 'one vast ruin'.[220]

On taking possession of the *Arsenale*, Emperor Francis I sold the Venetian battleships to Napoleon's former allies the Danes, and for the next 15 years Venice would be sidelined, its role as a major commercial and military port having now been transferred to Trieste. Although in their relief to see an end of the years of fighting the people of Venetia had initially accepted the Austrians' arrival, like their neighbours in Lombardy they were soon obliged to accept the continued compulsory conscription of their young men, this being made worse by the fact that the period of military service under the French was now doubled from four to eight years. Other measures would be equally unpopular, not least the increased taxes that the impoverished Austrians had started to raise in an effort to recover their shattered finances after years of prolonged warfare. Furthermore, determined to ensure the general peace and security, the authorities had begun to tighten censorship and surveillance, and, in addition to banning secret or masonic societies, over time they would bring in increasingly petty rules and regulations. Among these would be the outlawing of Calabrian-style hats that were thought to show an affiliation to the causes of the rebellious people in the south. Yet, despite in 1818 designating his younger brother, Archduke Ranieri, as the new kingdom's viceroy, the cautious Francis I was still unwilling to make any radical or sudden changes. Therefore, while giving local appointments to Austrians, Hungarians and other members of the Empire, he also retained several men who had previously served in the French administration. Since most of Venice's former ruling families had already left the city, they were absent from its government, but on the Venetian *terraferma* patricians supporting the new regime were able to keep their positions. This helped maintain the peace and for more than two decades to come the unrest and violent movements for change seen in other places would be largely unknown in this region. Today therefore, some question the Austrian reputation for oppression during this time. While there would be instances of extreme brutality during the subsequent wars of independence, at this moment the people continued to live relatively untroubled under their new imperial masters. Stories to the contrary, quite probably largely exaggerated, appear to belong to the negative propaganda that was spread in order to promote Italian patriotism.[221]

Elsewhere, however, during the 1820s and 1830s feelings were hardening against the conservative governments that had been restored with the fall of Napoleon. The first calls for Italian unity were now being heard as the Risorgimento – the movement for Italy to 'rise again' – began to take shape. When, in the wake of the 1820 revolt against the rule of Ferdinand I in Naples, the Carbonari campaign had spread to the regions in the north, Venice had not been involved, but it would too witness the effects of such events. Following an attempted uprising that had been crushed in October in Milan, the writer Silvio Pellico and his fellow conspirators were brought to Venice, where, after their brief incarceration in the *piombi* they were moved to Murano before being taken to begin their long prison sentences deep in the Austrian Empire at Brno in Moravia (today the Czech Republic).

After that, for a while the situation settled down, the tensions easing further when in November 1830 Ferdinand II, a man initially thought to promise a brighter future, succeeded to the throne of the Two Sicilies. Already that year, however, a more dramatic event had occurred, as, following the July revolution in Paris, Charles X had been overthrown and his supposedly more liberal distant cousin Louis-Philippe had become King of the French. But a matter of more significance for the Venetians was the fact that their city had at last been granted free-port status, the Austrian Emperor having now extended to the whole of Venice the special rights that had been granted solely to San Giorgio Maggiore in 1808. At the same time, although much of the commercial business remained in Trieste and Fiume (Rijeka), the increase of military activity had now enabled Venice to start growing again into one of the busiest ports in the region.

But a new disaster was on the horizon as soon the whole of Europe would be hit for the first time by a cholera epidemic arriving from Asia. After striking major cities like Paris, Berlin, and Vienna in 1831, it would then spread further afield, eventually reaching across the Atlantic to America. By the time it finally petered out six years later, this had caused the death of tens of thousands, its victims including the exiled former French king Charles X, who had recently died and been buried in Gorizia (Görz).[222] The dread of this disease had further exacerbated the people's uncertainties, the epidemic adding fuel to the fire among the already superstitious and rebellious people in Sicily, who once more had begun rioting.

Among those who at this time were calling for change were the followers of *La Giovane Italia*, men whose professed aims were 'to constitute Italy as a Nation, One, Independent, Free and Republican'.[223] In July 1831 the 'Young Italy' party had been founded by Giuseppe Mazzini, a former member of the Carbonari, who was determined to improve the education of the people. The struggle to bring the 'brotherhood of Italians' together into one nation, whatever the cost, was a price he believed worth paying as in his view: 'Ideas ripen quickly when nourished by the blood of martyrs.'[224] Briefly imprisoned in Savona for being implicated in a failed plot in Turin, after a short stay in Geneva, he had moved abroad, thus escaping the fate of his fellow conspirators, twelve of whom were executed, while another had opted for suicide. From Marseille he had then written in June 1831 to Charles Albert of Savoy, who two months before had succeeded his distant cousin Charles Felix (Carlo Felice) in Piedmont-Sardinia. Mazzini told the king that while the Italian people demanded 'laws and liberty, independence and union', in reality they had no 'name or country' and continued to live 'divided, dismembered, and oppressed'. Applying further moral pressure on the king, he then declared that they were waiting to see whether he would be 'the greatest of men, or 'the last of Italian tyrants'.[225] Even though initially Charles Albert was believed to be more liberal than his predecessor, he rejected the call for constitutional change and refused to head a national movement to oust the Austrians from northern Italy. While these had also become the objectives of the rebellious people in the papal lands of the Romagna, similar ideas had now begun to infiltrate Venice, where Daniele Manin, a young Venetian lawyer educated at Padua University, had joined a small group advocating reform.[226]

Born in Venice near the Frari in 1804 during the first period of Austrian rule, Manin was descended through his father from a Jewish family that had converted to Catholicism. As was the practice at the time, it had taken the name of its sponsor, the brother of the city's last doge Ludovico Manin. Small, short-sighted, and with poor health, Daniele modestly decried his own abilities, humbly remarking: 'When exaltation is lacking, I feel myself below average; I feel incapable of doing what ordinary men do with ease.'[227] Yet he was highly intelligent and, against the odds, he would rise to prominence, eventually becoming Venice's popular leader in its struggles for independence.

During 1831, while Venice still remained calm, Manin would be mainly engaged in the long, rancorous dispute over the route for the proposed railway line connecting to Milan – the argument finally being resolved when his preferred option ultimately won the day, passing through Treviglio rather than Bergamo twelve miles to the north. That same year, however, rebellion again erupted in various places across the Italian peninsula. Failed revolutions broke out not just in Parma, and Modena – where for a time the duke was deposed – but also in towns such as Bologna, Ferrara, Ravenna, Forlì and Ancona that lay within the Papal States. Here only Lazio would remain unaffected by the troubles occurring elsewhere. In response to the appeal for help from the new pope Gregory XVI, the Austrians began to intervene in putting down the insurrections, but even this did not stop men like Giuseppe Garibaldi from joining *La Giovane Italia* in 1832. Within two years, however, he, too, had been sentenced to death for his involvement in yet another failed coup against Charles Albert's autocratic rule. Having therefore fled to France, he would later move to South America. In spite of these dangers, Mazzini was now busy forming a new organisation called 'Young Europe'. Following his expulsion from Switzerland, he was briefly arrested in Paris, but by early 1837 he had finally settled in London where he would become a close associate of several key figures such as Charles Dickens. In the meantime, however, the situation had become more tense throughout all Italy, and so that same year Ferdinand II would dash the

Sicilians' hopes for reform by taking harsh measures to suppress their calls for a constitution. Similarly, three years earlier, in Venice the Austrians had grown so suspicious of Manin's 'unsound' political ideas that they had put him on their list of possible subversives.

In the interim, on 2 March 1835 Emperor Francis had died and been succeeded by his disabled son, Ferdinand I. Even though for several years there had been concern over the latter's suitability as the heir, his father had insisted on upholding the archduke's hereditary rights. Having been advised 'not to alter' anything, Ferdinand continued on Francis' cautious path and so the Empire continued to stagnate. Nevertheless, while the new Emperor's epilepsy and other learning difficulties were largely misunderstood at the time, and they still tend to be exaggerated today, he spoke five languages, was a good musician, and was genuinely interested in the arts. Just as later, following his retirement, he would become popular in Prague, he would charm the Venetians when shortly after his coronation in Milan in October 1838 he was welcomed to the city. Besides winning the people over with his naturalness and good nature, he honoured their great artist Titian by commissioning the long-overdue memorial to him in the Frari. Yet, even while this paid tribute to the famous Venetian master, the memorial also glorified the foreign occupiers. Despite being topped with the Lion of Venice, here the famous symbol of St

Rulers during the Risorgimento		
Habsburgs Austrian Empire	Bourbons Kingdom of the Two Sicilies	House of Savoy Kingdom of Sardinia
Francis I (1792-1835)		Victor Emmanuel I (1802-21)
	Ferdinand I (1816-25)	
		Charles Felix (1821-31)
	Francis I (1825-30)	
	Ferdinand II (1830-59)	
Ferdinand I (1835-48)		Charles Albert (1831-49)
Franz Josef (1848-1916)		Victor Emmanuel II (1849-61) King of Italy (1861-78)
	Francis II (1859-61)	

Mark was united with that of the Habsburgs, the animal represented not with the usual book, but with a shield bearing the arms of the imperial family.

Before long, however, the call for independence would again grow louder and soon two sons of Baron Francesco Bandiera, a Venetian vice-admiral in service to the Austrians, would be swept up in the Risorgimento movement. Against his own wishes, Mazzini had been the inspiration for a revolt that had taken place in Bologna in 1843, and it was this uprising that had spurred the brothers Attilio and Emilio into action. Despite following their father into the imperial navy, they had already founded a group called *Esperia*, whose aim was to bring about the independence of Italy. One of their plans had been to capture a ship to bombard Messina in order to achieve the overthrow of the autocratic Bourbon government in the south. As their schemes were discovered and the authorities became aware of their political leanings, both young men were issued with arrest warrants. So, in April 1844 the 24-year-old Emilio left his family in Venice for the last time, going via Trieste to join his older brother and their companion Domenico Moro in Corfu. From here, along with another 20 or so members of their group, the young men set sail for Calabria, where they arrived on 16 June. As a local uprising had been brutally suppressed just three months earlier, they were expecting to receive the backing of the local people, but this was unforthcoming and they would soon be betrayed by one of their colleagues. Having been captured and taken to Cosenza, they were tried and condemned to death. Only days after their arrival, on 25 July eleven of the group were taken out to face the firing squad. Reportedly dying proclaiming 'Viva Italia', their youthful good looks and remarkable bravery soon earned them widespread sympathy and admiration, and they would become famous heroes of the Risorgimento. Even though four years later, in the midst of the revolutions of 1848, orders were given for their remains to be thrown into the river, these were in fact secreted away. As a result, in 1866, after the final departure of the Austrians from the Veneto, the Bandiera brothers – now revered as martyrs – were at last given a funeral in their home city of Venice and then interred in the church of Santi Giovanni e Paolo. At the time of their death, however, the fallout from their enterprise would spread even as far as London, where a scandal began to take shape after a Member of Parliament, Thomas Slingsby Duncombe, revealed on 14 June that Mazzini's correspondence had been opened. This had allowed the contents of one of his letters from Emilio Bandiera to be reported to the Austrians. When news of the brothers' execution later reached England, the story was taken up in the press and, with the government coming under severe criticism, it was then held partly to blame for the tragic outcome.

In spite of the disaster in Calabria, attempts to overthrow other authorities continued, and as a result the various administrations further tightened their control. Since 1816 the Papal States had been separated into delegations, with those administered by a cardinal – Bologna, Ferrara, Ravenna, and Forlì – being designated 'Legations', and it was in these regions that, two years after an insurrection in Ravenna, in September 1845 another uprising was harshly repressed in Rimini. Two months earlier on 29 July, during a demonstration in

Hungarian Zagreb, 13 Croat nationalists had been shot by the imperial army. A year later in Venice, where the surveillance of Manin had become more thorough over the previous decade, a break-in at his office appeared to have been carried out on official orders. Even so, the future seemed at last to be more promising for those wanting change as, following the death of Gregory XVI, the more liberal bishop of Imola was elected in his place as Pope Pius IX. Having immediately granted a generous amnesty to his political prisoners, before long the new pontiff would be seen as the champion of the reformist movement, with 'Viva Pio Nono' becoming a popular revolutionary cry.

Change was now in evidence everywhere, and new innovations were appearing even in Venice itself. Much to the dislike of John Ruskin – who considered it put this 'paradise of cities' on a par with Birmingham – gas lighting had arrived on 19 August 1843. Even more importantly, eight months earlier on 12 December the first part of the long-disputed rail line to Milan had opened at Marghera, and work had also begun on building the two-mile long railway bridge that, supported on over 200 arches, was to cross the lagoon. Following its official opening on 11 January 1846, Venice became connected to the mainland for the first time and the previous memorable arrival by gondola that took some four hours to the delight of so many visitors had thus been reduced to a practical journey of just a few minutes. Effie Ruskin would later tell her mother that this 'completely destroys your first impressions of Venice'.[228] Six years later, to the further regret of Effie's husband John, the modernising programme was completed with the building of the terminus on the site of the demolished church of Santa Lucia in the north-west of the city. As this had removed the traditional point of entry at the Piazzetta, Ruskin would now liken the new approach by train to the arrival in 'Liverpool at the end of the dockyard wall'.[229]

In line with these various changes, in June 1847 Manin welcomed to Venice the British Member of Parliament, Richard Cobden, who was travelling around Europe expounding the virtues of free trade. Northern Italy was gradually moving into a more modern age, and since 1839 a series of scientific congresses had taken place across the region. Just three months after Cobden's visit, the ninth of these was held in Venice. Even though the authorities then closed it down early because of concerns about its overtones of nationalism, the Austrians in their own way were still trying to make the city more up-to-date. Despite having picked up where their French predecessors had left off – demolishing several more churches and removing various art treasures back to Vienna – they were attempting to modernise Venice's layout, creating extra bridges, filling in canals, and constructing new streets and walkways. They had already reopened the Fenice theatre in January 1837, a year after it had burnt down, and had started work on the Patriarchal Palace that would finally be completed in 1850 alongside the great basilica in the Piazza dei Leoncini. Furthermore, water buses had begun to row the public up and down the Grand Canal, and hotels had started to open or reopen to accommodate the foreigners who were slowly reappearing. Turner, an early visitor in 1819, returned for the third time in 1840. So too, the coffee houses had again become popular meeting places in the Piazza, the Caffè Quadri being a favourite haunt for the Austrians, who gathered here to talk with their friends and listen to their national band music. Many Venetians would, however, pointedly choose to go to Florian's instead, from where, in a small gesture of defiance, they then attempted to drown out with their own rousing tunes the sounds coming from across the square.

* * *

By the 1840s, attitudes in Venice had begun to harden significantly as a result of the repeated failure of the harvests. Because of a poor yield in 1845, the following year the crops were hit by blight, a disaster that caused wheat and maize prices to double. For the Venetians, things then became even more difficult in March 1847, when their request for increased trading rights was refused by Emperor Ferdinand. He was already faced by other problems in Lombardy-Venetia, where his ineffectual government was failing to prevent the export of some of the much-needed foodstuffs from Venice and elsewhere. As a result, before long widespread starvation had become an all too real threat, the full extent of the people's suffering being laid bare in one report from Treviso:

> The cities were full of poor begging for bread, and were invaded by great hordes of peasants, human carcasses with sunken eyes, who could hardly stagger along with the aid of a stick, and who pleaded for something to eat in faint voices and with a deadened gaze... The countryside did not present a less terrible or mournful appearance.[230]

While this situation led to further instances of unrest around the country, in the regions to the south of Lombardy-Venetia, where some of the meagre supplies were filtered into the stricken lands on the border, maize prices were rising still higher. With riots then erupting in the papal lands of the Romagna and the Marche, in July 1847 the Austrians – against the wishes of the pope – increased the size of their garrison in Ferrara. As the tensions increased and more revolts in Calabria and Sicily broke out in September, various rulers started to consider reform. By the end of the year Manin had begun to call for change in Venice, but in Milan the people had gone even further, boycotting gambling and the smoking of tobacco in order to deprive the Austrians of the relevant taxes raised on both activities. But for the Milanese this was just the start, and things would reach boiling point on the first day of 1848, when violence finally erupted, leaving five dead and several more wounded.

As pressures throughout the region continued to increase, a week later on 8 January Manin wrote to the civil governor in Venice, the Hungarian Count Palffy, to draw attention to the Austrians' failure to abide by the promises they had made in 1815. His call for an end to their abuses of power proved too much for the authorities, and on the 18th he was arrested along with his colleague, Niccolò Tommaseo, the Dalmatian-born writer from Sebenico. Although at his trial Manin praised the Empire for its achievements, he was still calling for reform, and so, charged with treason, the two men were confined in the prison alongside the Doges' Palace.

Six days before Manin and Tommaseo's arrest, more upheaval had hit the Two Sicilies, when on the king's birthday, 12 January 1848, rebellion had again broken out in Palermo. With similar events soon taking place elsewhere around the kingdom, and the pope refusing to allow the Austrians to cross his lands to help the Bourbons, on the 29th King Ferdinand II promised a constitution. The news was greeted with enthusiasm in Venice, and there would be general delight when Pius IX publicly blessed Italy on 10 February. The febrile situation in Europe was, however, about to escalate further, as on the 24th there was another revolution in Paris that brought about the abdication of King Louis-Philippe, this being followed the next day by the declaration of the Second French Republic.[231] Shaken by what he saw happening elsewhere, in Tuscany the Grand Duke Leopold had already on the 17th introduced a constitution, and then on 4 March Charles Albert issued his own *Statuto*. Even though this affirmed his personal overall authority, besides establishing a bi-cameral parliament in the Sardinian kingdom, it promised religious tolerance and other liberal reforms. By now, however, unrest was also spreading to Vienna, and on 13 March, after 27 years as chancellor, Metternich was forced to resign. Although the Emperor tried to calm the situation by proposing his own constitution, the troubles persisted, and so finally in May he was forced to flee with his family to Innsbruck, from where he then continued to offer further concessions. These events would mark the start of the notorious year of revolutions that would engulf Europe, and above all the Austrian Empire, which was soon to see numerous rebellions breaking out all across its lands.

With violent demonstrations having taken place in Padua in February, early on the morning of 18 March things again came to a head in Milan, where the people began vociferously demanding control of their government. After five days of fighting in the streets, the famous *Cinque Giornate* finally ended on the 22nd when Field Marshal Radetzky decided to withdraw from the city. As the Sardinian King Charles Albert had now mustered his troops on the border, seemingly ready to support the rebels, the experienced old military commander retreated with his Austrian army to the defensive Quadrilateral area that was protected by the four fortresses of Mantua, Legnago, Peschiera, and Verona. At Verona – where the regional viceroy Ranieri was also sheltering at the time – the troops would suffer abuse from the local people, but Radetzky's retreat was to be only temporary. With the republicans soon surrendering control of Milan to the pro-monarchist faction, the city's earlier success failed to bring about any long-term reform.

Nevertheless, for the moment Radetzky's climbdown was seen as a victory, and immediately following the recent uprising by the Milanese, Verdi, on his way home from Paris, would triumphantly write to his librettist: 'Honour to these heroes! Honour to all Italy, which in this moment is truly great! The hour has sounded … of its liberation.'[232] Like the pope, Verdi had now become a figurehead for the revolutionaries, and his chorus of the Hebrew Slaves in *Nabucco*, premiered at La Scala six years earlier, was soon taken up as the unofficial anthem for those supporting a unified Italy, free from its foreign occupiers.

By this time the situation had also begun to change in Venice. On 9 March a court hearing declared the case against Manin and Tommaseo to be 'not proven', but the two men were still confined when the next day a rally took place in St Mark's Square. But things were now moving apace, and on the 16th, after news had been received reporting the state of affairs in Vienna, Palffy's wife and Napoleon's former marshal Marmont, the Duke of Ragusa, would be the target of public scorn, a show of disrespect that left both deeply shaken.[233] With the arrival from Trieste early the next day of further information confirming that the Emperor was ready to grant a constitution and give greater rights to the people, a cry immediately went up for the release of Manin and Tommaseo. Nervously, Palffy conceded, although, when signing the relevant document, he mistakenly wrote down the name of the last doge Ludovico Manin rather than that of Daniele.

Finally the two men emerged from their prison and, welcomed by the crowds of supporters who had gathered on the Riva, they were carried in triumph into the Piazza that was now awash with tricolour flags and other symbols of revolution. Here, calling on them to remain calm, Manin appealed to the people: 'Do not forget that there can be no true liberty (and that liberty cannot last) where there is no order. You must be jealous guardians of order if you hope to preserve freedom.'[234] Nonetheless, the next day the mood became uglier and, with open confrontation breaking out between those who supported the latest events and those who were against, in the subsequent violence eight or nine protesters lost their lives. The anarchy that Manin so dreaded seemed to be a real possibility, the people having already forgotten the appeal that he had made the day before.

To prevent things from deteriorating further, a civic guard was now formed, this ultimately comprising some 2,000 men – a number ten times greater than that previously agreed to by the unenthusiastic governor. While Manin himself joined the volunteers, the guard would be led by Angelo Mengaldo, one of those whom Byron had once challenged to a swimming race from the Lido. But while these men helped stabilise the situation, Manin was still concerned that the arsenal might get backup from Vienna. Therefore, after receiving warning that such a thing was about to happen, on the evening of the 21st he summoned a meeting at his own house. Although those present agreed a plan of action to deal with the problem the next morning, this was soon pre-empted by other events. Early on the 22nd the *arsenalotti* independently rose up against their tyrannical commanding officer Captain Giovanni Marinovich, a man originally from the pro-Venetian Bocche di Cattaro, who had remained true, nonetheless, to the ruling Austrian authorities. As he was loathed by the roughly 1,500 men under his command, they now took their revenge and beat him to death as he tried to escape. On hearing that the place was in mutiny, Manin, his young son and numbers of volunteers hurried to the scene. Here, once they had succeeded in quelling the violence, they persuaded the Italians serving in the imperial Wimpffen regiment to lay down their arms and join the revolutionaries, and soon some 4,000 other troops stationed around the city had followed their example.

That evening Mengaldo and a few representatives from the municipality, among them the mayor Correr and the lawyer Giovanni Francesco Avesani, went to meet Palffy in the *Procuratie Nuove* in order to receive his capitulation.

While the governor stalled, Manin arrived in the Piazza just outside and here he was soon surrounded by an adoring crowd of his supporters. Jumping onto a table outside Florian's, then began to address the people, declaring that they now needed to form a new republican government dedicated to bringing about a united Italy. As the shouts of 'Viva la Repubblica' became louder, Palffy, still unwilling to be held responsible for any decisions, handed over power to the local military governor, the Hungarian count, Ferdinand Zichy. When finally at 6.30 Zichy signed the document confirming the resignation of the imperial authorities, Avesani became head of the temporary government. The next day, however, he was persuaded to step aside and allow Mengaldo to declare Manin, the popular choice of the people, to be the provisional president of the new Repubblica di San Marco.

With the fort at Marghera having now surrendered, soon other garrisons would begin to follow suit, the Austrians moving either to join Radetzky at Verona, or alternatively to Trieste. Similarly, Palffy and Zichy left Venice, but, although the Italian captain of their ship had been instructed by Manin to go via Pola, the two Hungarians had then persuaded him to go directly to Trieste. This would make it possible for them to warn others of the events taking place in Venice, thereby enabling the Austrian fleet to take action and prevent those in the southern Istrian port from going to the aid of the revolutionaries. By losing Pola's naval support in this way, Manin's government had committed the first of the serious errors that ultimately would cost the new republic dear.

Nonetheless, as reports of the revolution in Venice spread to other communities further afield, these began forcing the Austrian authorities to hand over control. As elsewhere, the news was greeted with joy in the Serenissima's most southern Dalmatian town where, despite its annexation by the Empire in 1815, the people had not forgotten the almost four hundred years that Cattaro la Veneziana had been the capital of Albania Venetia. Here at the beginning of the 1400s, when its people were seeking protection from their neighbours, the Venetians had been more than happy to establish their own settlement. As a result, living under the auspices of the Serenissima, the town had never fallen to the Ottomans, and, reaping the benefits of its position on the important commercial overland and sea routes to Constantinople, its trade had continued steadily to flourish. With the majority still retaining their Venetian culture and speaking the *Veneto da mar* dialect, most of the people held on to their old loyalties. Therefore, regardless of the constitution they were being offered by the Austrians, on 23 March, as the streets were filled with large crowds voicing their support for the revolution, the municipality voted to be reunited with Venice. In fact, Cattaro's resistance was soon to be suppressed because the neighbouring Montenegrin ruler, anxious about the situation developing across the border, now declared that he was ready to use force if necessary to put an end to the unrest.

During the early euphoric days of the revolution, when Manin had expected to receive outside support – in particular from the French – there was initially a degree of naivety in the way the inexperienced government directed its affairs. Although wanting to pursue liberal reform, the preponderantly bourgeois administration feared unrest among the working classes, and so it had mistakenly allowed Italian troops serving in the imperial forces to return home with their arms. Even though some of these would later join the revolutionary cause, the departure of so many in these early days would ultimately deprive Venice of much needed manpower and weapons. Having gone back to their villages, many Italian conscripts would later be reticent to return, they being little encouraged by the way the new government was tending to concentrate on affairs in the city alone. As the authorities failed to pay enough attention to the towns and rural areas, these regions would often see an increased shortage of necessary supplies, and as a result the local men were further deterred from enrolling in the defence of Venice itself. On the other hand, soon after the last of their troops had left the city on 26 March, the Austrian soldiers had joined their compatriots, and so they had swelled the numbers of those who before long would be marching into northern Italy. Having depended on the poor advice of his elderly military advisers, Manin would discover only too late his mistake in not having raised an army to protect Venice and its surroundings. Now, however, there had been another serious turn of events elsewhere. As only hours after Radetzky's retreat from Milan, on 23 March the Sardinian king Charles Albert of Savoy had declared war on Austria, two days later his troops had started to cross the border into Lombardy-Venetia and the First Italian War of Independence had begun.

The new Venetian Republic's failure to raise the people to arms in its defence had left Friuli open to invasion by the Emperor's Irish-born general Laval Nugent, who had begun mustering his forces at Gorizia. Living in Croatia and a friend of its people, Nugent had previously served Ferdinand I of the Two Sicilies, and while fighting against the French in the Napoleonic Wars he had played a key role in the defeat of Murat and the liberation of Rome. Now, under his leadership, on 17 April the Austrian army crossed the Isonzo river into Venetia and gradually reasserted its control over the region until on the 23rd it re-entered Udine (see map p.257). As a result, six days later Pope Pius issued his Allocution, a statement of intent in which he purposely distanced himself from the violence. Declaring that his role was that of a peacemaker, he refused to become embroiled in the fight against the Austrians, and turned down the suggestion that he should become head of an Italian republic. Instead, admitting his own inability to restrain others from their engagement in the conflict, he insisted that the faithful should accept the authority of their sovereign masters. The outcome of this was that many soldiers of the papal army earlier taken north without Pius's permission, now began to return home, leaving just a few behind with their leader, Giovanni Durando. He, however, would later be blamed when, after some initial successes at Goito and Peschiera, on 8 May the patriots were defeated by Nugent at the Battle of Cornuda. Durando was held largely responsible for this disaster because he had failed through a misunderstanding to come as promised to the Sardinians' support. As a result of this major setback, four days later Venice agreed to join with Lombardy, and on the 29th the Milanese went even further and voted for their region to join with Piedmont.

Although shortly before, on 24 May Nugent had met up with Radetzky at Verona, the Austrians still faced stiff opposition. Just a day after Vicenza had been put under heavy bombardment, the Piedmontese army would achieve some military success, but by 10 June Vicenza was again under attack, and following its surrender Durando was forced to withdraw from all future action. By then the town had suffered considerable damage, not only from enemy fire but also because of the mindless violence that had followed its surrender. Among other things, the painting of *The Banquet of St Gregory* by Veronese hanging in the monastery of the Madonna of Monte Berico was slashed into 32 pieces – an act of senseless vandalism that the young Emperor Franz Josef would later personally seek to put right by paying for its restoration. Within days of the fall of Vicenza, after weeks of heavy bombardment Treviso finally succumbed, and shortly after Padua did the same. With Palmanova following suit ten days later, by the end of June only Venice and Osoppo in the Friuli region remained standing.[235] Meanwhile, the strict naval blockade had so enraged the British and German residents of Trieste that there, too, the Venetian-Piedmontese-Neapolitan allies were forced to withdraw, and so by August the city had once more become a neutral port.

Faced by this worsening situation, on 4 July – following the example of Milan and other Venetian towns on the mainland – the assembly in Venice voted for its own fusion with the kingdom of Piedmont. Manin accepted this democratic decision, but, declaring he was a republican, he then resigned. The Austrians were now camped across the lagoon on the mainland and, with the threat of an assault appearing to be more likely, soon Piedmontese soldiers had begun to arrive in the city to help keep order. Venice was already overrun with foreign volunteers, but these newcomers were not welcome, and the situation became even more tense when on 7 August three of their commissioners arrived to play a role in government affairs. In the meantime, their king had been hit by his own disasters. Despite another victory at Governolo, on 24 July, around 20 kilometres south-west of Verona at Custoza, Charles Albert had suffered a major defeat. Within three days he was considering a truce and, although he refused the first terms offered, on receiving Radetzky's more generous proposal, on 9 August he signed the Salasco Armistice. According to the terms, besides abandoning Milan, he was now obliged to withdraw from Lombardy-Venetia and leave the whole region once more in the hands of the Austrians.

When on 11 August people in Venice heard news of this Armistice, and how the king had accepted the surrender of their city to the Emperor, crowds gathered once more outside the *Procuratie,* the *Nuove* and *Vecchie.* Since the Piedmontese commissioners had been given no instructions, they were still unwilling to make any unauthorised concessions, and so tensions were escalating when at last Manin arrived on the scene. Here he addressed the crowd from the balcony overlooking the Piazza and, declaring 'Governo io', he proclaimed that he personally would take full control for the next 48 hours. With the commissioners having then left the city along with the Sardinian fleet, Manin became the recognised head of a triumvirate that also included the more conservative Colonel Cavedalis, and the cautious Admiral

Graziani. Yet, even though he was in charge, he now re-emphasised that his provisional government belonged to no one party, and its sole objective still remained a determination to bring about the overthrow of the Austrians.

* * *

The political convictions of those involved in the Risorgimento varied widely, their differences eventually undermining the cause of the reformers and delaying the achievement of their goals for several years. While Tommaseo wished to create a federation of states that were under the leadership of the pope, Avesani was among those who preferred them to be united under the umbrella of a constitutional monarchy. Meanwhile, Manin, who was primarily concerned for Venice's independence, wanted, like Mazzini, to see separate secular republics within a united Italy. Yet, because he was still fearful of the people's tendency to rebellion, he gradually became more restrictive in his measures, and so by August he was actually forbidding any open political discussion. Thus Manin's republican zeal became diluted over time, and as the situation gradually developed he would even slowly come round to the idea of a fusion of the northern states united under the Sardinian crown. As for Charles Albert, he primarily wanted to promote his dynasty and maintain the power of the House of Savoy. Besides wishing to protect it against its neighbours, his declared intention was to increase the size of his territories by 'stripping the artichoke', in other words taking bit by bit the adjoining lands. Yet, although he was a good soldier, he was an indecisive administrator and his hesitation in dealing with the current situation would ultimately leave the Venetians without the support that they needed.

Over the previous months, the Neapolitan king, faced by his own problems, had played little part in the events in northern Italy. Following a revolt in March, his earlier promised constitution had been rejected by the Sicilian parliament, which had on 13 April 1848 announced that Ferdinand II was deposed and the Bourbon monarchy had been replaced by a provisional government. But following the pope's Allocution later in the month, the Austrians had been able to cross the papal lands and come the aid of the king. He was further helped by most of his troops having obeyed orders and returned from the north, and so, having by July regained full control of his mainland territory, within two months he would begin to concentrate on his rebellious subjects in Sicily.

Meanwhile the war continued in the north, with the last fortress loyal to the Venetians at Osoppo finally surrendering on 13 October. But that same month Vienna would see another uprising and, before it could be brought to an end on the 31st, the imperial family had been forced to flee the city once more. And just a month later, an equally dramatic event occurred in Rome. The pope was still in favour with his people and among the reformists at large, but, although Mazzini – who had now returned to Milan – declared him the most powerful man in Europe, Pius IX's fortunes were about to take a turn for the worse. On 15 November the pontiff's prime minister, Pelegrino Rossi, a man who had become unpopular for his illiberal reforms, was assassinated in the city. Then, with his Swiss Guard having been disarmed, the pope himself was taken prisoner. He had never had any ambitions for territorial expansion, but as he wanted to maintain his spiritual authority and was still determined to avoid violence, the next day he refused to declare war on Austria. Even though he was still seen by many as the champion of Italian independence, having now proved himself unwilling to give the movement his active support, on the night of 24 November he fled Rome in disguise and took up refuge in Gaeta. While here he set up his own government, and he was still appealing to the French president Louis-Napoleon for help when on 9 February 1849 a new Constitutional Assembly was elected in Rome.[236] Even though Pius threatened to excommunicate its members, a republic having been declared, the next month Mazzini was invited to be its leading Triumvir.

Shortly before this, events in the Austrian Empire had brought about another major change. Following the latest threat to the Habsburg dynasty, on 2 December 1848 Emperor Ferdinand had been persuaded to step down, and the throne had been passed to his young nephew, Franz Josef. This was then followed by a similar change of leadership in Piedmont. Although Charles Albert had lost the backing of both the pope and Ferdinand of the Two Sicilies, a little over a week after rejecting the truce that he had earlier agreed, on 20 March – with his parliament's approval – he again declared war on the Austrians. Yet, only three days later, around 50 kilometres west of Milan at Novara, he was defeated by Radetzky. Even as the Piedmontese began discussing the terms they hoped to get from the Austrians, that same evening Charles Albert declared his intention to abdicate. Wanting to protect his dynasty, shortly after he moved abroad to Portugal, where he died a few months later. Having been replaced by his son, the day after the disaster at Novara, the new king, Victor Emmanuel II, had signed an armistice demanding, among other things, the withdrawal of his fleet from the Adriatic, and so once again Venice had been abandoned.

Throughout this time unrest had been brewing elsewhere, and Brescia would now be among those who were to suffer. At the end of a fierce 10-day-long demonstration in early 1849, the town was sacked and about a thousand of its citizens were slaughtered. Soon after it was Genoa's turn to endure a week of violence that was only to come to an end when the Sardinian army arrived and bombed the area. And, in the meantime, civil war continued in Hungary, where the revolutionaries were demanding their own republic.[237] Sicily, too, had seen weeks of turbulence, but here finally in March Ferdinand II regained control. After he had dissolved parliament and reclaimed his absolute powers, he had begun to impose harsh measures, among them the heavy bombardment of Messina that would earn him the nickname 'Re Bomba'. Therefore, gradually the country was reduced to such an appalling state that on a later visit Gladstone would describe the conditions there as 'awful'.

During this time several cities in the Papal States had chosen to give their allegiance to the new Roman republic, and so the Austrians, who supported the pope, had therefore responded by occupying the Romagna, taking Ferrara, and temporarily putting Bologna and Ancona under siege. Other Christian states were also now beginning to give their backing to Pius, and in April the French president sent troops to Rome to try and take it from the republican defenders who continued to hold out. Having recently returned to Italy to take part in the battles in Lombardy, Garibaldi would eventually arrive at the end of May with his 'Italian Legion' of roughly 1,000 well-trained men to help those in the capital. Joined two days later by the Bersaglieri from Lombardy, the combined force then defeated the French, but – while the negotiations were still in progress – the Neapolitan and Austrian armies arrived and began to mount a siege. With a truce finally called at the end of June, Mazzini fled again to Marseille and Garibaldi retreated to San Marino before then escaping to New York. After Rome's surrender, on 3 July the French marched into the city, but, still unwilling to come back from Gaeta, Pius would not return until the following April, when he finally declared an end to his former constitution. Having reinstated the ghetto, he moved for greater security out of the Quirinal into the Vatican, which was now to become the permanent residence of all future popes. After that, in spite of his concerns about the French, Pius would continue to rely on their support until their final departure in 1870.

* * *

A month after the surrender of Mazzini and his republicans in Rome, on 22 August 1849 the First War of Italian Independence was declared over. With the Grand Duke Leopold now recalled to Florence and Parma put under Austrian protection, the Habsburgs had at last regained control of most of northern Italy. But even after Charles Albert's crushing defeat at Novara in March, Venice was determined to hold out. Having on 2 April gained the assembly's agreement that the city should continue to resist, Manin again took control, and for the next five months he would direct the city's stoical attempt to stand against the full force of the Austrian Empire. With the city already under blockade, on 4 May Radetzky began to attack the fortress at Marghera. For over three weeks this stood up against the onslaught, until finally, with all further resistance impossible, on the 26th the defenders quietly slipped away. By this time the new railway viaduct had suffered serious damage from the bombing, and Venice itself would soon come under similar attack, an enormous explosion occurring on 19 June when the powder magazine blew up. A month later on 12 July the Austrians started releasing hot air balloons that were carrying bombs, but, because the wind direction changed, they failed to reach their target. Equally fortunate for Venice was the limited range of the artillery fire that, having begun on the 28th, was to cause only marginal damage in a few small areas. Throughout the next month, as the heavy assault continued, the local people would nonetheless continue to show their courage, lining the balconies and roof tops to watch as the bombs rained down. Some of the Austrian cannons and cannon balls now adorn the Hotel San Fantin near the Fenice, where a plaque erected above the entrance 20 years after the event recalls this last heroic stand by the city.

However, the hardship was growing worse. Although attempts were made to get supplies from elsewhere, and initially there was some success when a raid on the Austrian troops produced loads of food as well as 200 cows, already by July starvation was beginning to appear and soon cholera began again to take hold. Therefore, by the time Venice finally capitulated, 2,788 people had died. Faced with the inevitable, on 22 August, Manin had convinced the assembly that the time had come to surrender, and early the next morning those defending the broken railway bridge were told to lay down their arms. With the Austrians already starting to arrive in the city, at 2.00 pm on the 24th Manin signed the document that declared the end of the Provisional Government. Finally on the 28th the republic officially came to an end, but already, three days earlier, following his arrest, Manin had left Venice along with his family and 39 others. Adding to his distress, on his arrival in Marseille his wife died, but he then moved on with his daughter to Paris, where he, too, would die eight years later on 22 September 1857. His dream of an independent Venetian republic within a united Italy had failed because the various national patriots had not been prepared to act in unison. So, while Manin had at the end declared his support for Victor Emmanuel II, the city he loved would remain under foreign rule for almost another decade after his death.

Soon the more intrepid travellers were returning and in November 1849, just three months after the ending of the siege, Ruskin arrived with his wife Effie to stay at the Danieli. While he was passionate about Venice's early architecture, considering the Doges' Palace to be the most beautiful building in the world, he had already been shocked on his previous visit four years earlier by the insensitive over-restoration that had taken place around the city. Now, finding the place still littered with the evidence of the assault suffered under the recent siege, he was even more appalled by its general state of disrepair. Nonetheless, like several visitors, the Ruskins chose to mix with the Austrians, enjoying the company of one officer in particular who would join them on their day trips to the islands and elsewhere. The Lido was still more or less unchanged, but here the first bathing huts would soon appear. New iron bridges were being constructed over the Grand Canal, in 1854 the Ponte dell' Accademia, and in 1858 the Ponte delgi Scalzi – both later replaced in the 1930s.

In March 1851 Franz Josef arrived on his first visit to Venice, but the antipathy of the Venetians was apparent, the same being true among the people of Lombardy when the young Emperor returned to northern Italy later the same year. He was still in the country in October when the discovery of a conspiracy resulted in an execution taking place in Venice. This was just one of the various arrests, lengthy trials, and death sentences occurring around this time, the five celebrated Belfiore martyrs who were hanged near Mantua being among the victims. Rather than controlling the opposition, this harsh justice would increase the people's antagonism towards the Austrians. Yet, even though the drive for independence was becoming more pronounced, Manin would have little response when, just a year before his death, he attended the 1856 Congress of Paris and spoke with Count Cavour about Italian unification. The Piedmontese prime minister still thought the idea to be a fantasy.

In the meantime, the dangers facing the rulers had not gone away. Three years earlier, a Hungarian had attempted to kill the Emperor in Vienna, and

King Ferdinand II would escape assassination the following December. Likewise, two years later in January 1858, Napoleon III was targeted by a member of the Carbonari, they having become disillusioned by his failure to support Italian unity. But, although these dissidents felt that he had betrayed their cause, in fact – in spite of the attack – the French emperor was still sympathetic to their movement, and less than six months later he would form an alliance with Piedmont-Sardinia. In July he and Cavour secretly drew up the Agreements of Plombières that were designed to bring about the expulsion of Austrian troops from the whole Italian peninsula. In the meantime, wanting to manipulate the Emperor into taking action in the north, the Piedmontese and French had mobilised their troops along the Sardinian border, and by 29 April 1859 the ploy had succeeded in persuading Franz Josef to declare war. This would be a brief conflict lasting for just two-and-a half months, with the Austrians suffering defeats at Magenta and Solferino, and then again at Varese and Como. When regretfully the Emperor, who was already under pressure from the revolution in Hungary, finally called for an armistice, he agreed on 11 July to surrender most of Lombardy to Napoleon III. The next year the French emperor handed this region over to the Sardinians in exchange for Savoy and also – to the displeasure of Garibaldi, a Niçois by birth – the city of Nice.

With the Habsburgs still holding on to part of Lombardy and Venetia, Venice had gained no advantage from the peace. But the treaty of 1859 had ushered in change elsewhere. Although the idea of Victor Emmanuel invading the papal territories, as suggested by Florence's new revolutionary government, had soon been dropped, from this time on various Italian states would start joining the kingdom of Sardinia, and 'Viva Verdi' – the acronym invented at the end of 1858 standing for 'Vittore Emmanuele Re d'Italia' – was soon to become the battle cry. At last, the possibility of a united Italy seemed to be plausible.

While these things were happening in the north, in the Two Sicilies, following the premature death of the king, the situation was also undergoing change. On 22 May 1859, three months after his wedding in Bari to Marie Sophie of Bavaria, Francis II succeeded to the throne. During his short rule, this spiritually devout man would put forward various projects for the benefit of his country, among them plans for railway lines, water works, drainage schemes, and town planning, as well as better education and the reduction of taxes. Soon events would overtake him, however. A month after his accession, on 7 June a mutiny broke out within his Swiss Guard, and because the general in charge responded by shooting the protesters, the king immediately became unpopular. As the opposition now grew, he steadily became more reactionary. Already opposed to an invasion of the Papal States, against the advice of his prime minister he was unwilling to accept Cavour's proposal to join an alliance with the Kingdom of Sardinia. For him, this decision was to prove disastrous. Although the French emperor was feigning to distance himself from the affair, he was now giving his tacit approval to Cavour's latest proposals to further the movement for Italian unity by invading Sicily. As the British were equally ready to support this idea, before long they were providing the financial support that was largely to go towards bribing the Neapolitan officers to join the cause.

After his return to Italy six years before, Garibaldi had taken part in the recent war against the Austrians, and he was now chosen to lead the campaign. Having set sail from near Genoa on 6 May 1860, he arrived at Marsala five days later, and by the end of the month he had captured Palermo. As the Royal Navy, lying at sea just off the coast of Naples, continued to turn a deaf ear to the loyalists' appeals for help, King Francis II made a desperate effort to calm the situation by granting his country a constitution. Yet, despite Victor Emmanuel II beginning openly to support the campaign, the Neapolitan king still refused to send his large army south, continuing to do nothing to defeat the 'red shirts' even after Garibaldi had crossed the straits into Calabria. At last, wishing to avoid the bloodshed that Palermo had seen, just a day before Garibaldi reached Naples on 7 September, he and his wife abandoned nearly all their possessions and fled the capital.

As the Piedmontese marched north, they would defeat the Neapolitan loyalist army at Volturno on 1 October, and having then attacked various strongholds they eventually arrived in early November at the heavily fortified Gaeta, where the royal couple had taken shelter. Although the place was soon under siege, the king refused to capitulate, and the fortress continued to hold out until the situation became so dire that it was forced to surrender on 13 February 1861. By that time many of the defenders were dead, some having succumbed to typhus, scores of others being casualties of a vast explosion of the powder magazine just days earlier, and still more killed by enemy action even as the final negotiations were being drawn up. During the siege, the courage of the young king and queen had earned them widespread admiration, their stoicism being recognised even by their detractors. She, the equally beautiful but more resilient younger sister of the famous Austrian Empress Elizabeth, would become popularly known as 'the heroine of Gaeta', later being praised for her courage by the poet D'Annunzio among others. Forced at last to abandon their kingdom, they sailed to Rome, where they were welcomed as the pope's honoured guests and given accommodation in Palazzo Farnese. However, having become disenchanted with her marriage, the queen now became involved in a love affair that resulted in her fleeing back to her family in Bavaria at the end of 1862 to give birth to a daughter in secret. The scandal was immediately hushed up and the child was given away, but, after the queen had confessed all to her husband, the couple's relationship improved. In time their only child was born, a little girl who then tragically died at three months old. The next year her parents' suffering was further increased when the major political changes of 1870 forced them once again to leave their home. From then on, they were constantly on the move, spending periods in Paris, Austria, and Bavaria, until Francis's death in 1894. Despite his failings, he had been an honourable man, who, faced by tragedy, had earlier summed up the reasons for his actions:

I preferred to leave Naples, my own house, my beloved capital city, not to expose it to the horror of a bombing, such as later happened in Capua and Ancona. I believed, in good faith, that the King of Piedmont who maintained he was my brother and my friend and disapproved of Garibaldi's invasion, who negotiated with my Government a close alliance for the true interests of Italy – would not break all agreements and infringe all laws to invade my peaceful dominions without reason or war declarations. If these are my faults, I prefer my misfortune to the triumph of my enemies.[238]

Following Francis's defeat, Garibaldi ordered a plebiscite that declared 99% of the people to have come out in favour of handing the whole southern region over to the Sardinian king. This was a highly suspect result, made still more questionable not just by the fact that some 78% of the population was illiterate, but also in light of the cold reception Victor Emmanuel would receive when he and Garibaldi triumphantly rode into Naples on 7 November 1860. In the previous months, Francis had not been alone in facing insurmountable challenges. However, in the previous months, while Francis had been facing his challenges, the pope had been in equal difficulty. After the Piedmontese troops crossed onto his lands, in September his papal army and its foreign volunteers suffered defeats at Castelfidardo in the Marche, and then at Ancona, and these disasters had sufficiently emboldened Victor Emmanuel II for him to claim possession of all the former papal states, with the exception of Lazio and the city of Rome. The next year, just three months before the death of Cavour, on 17 March 1861 the Kingdom of Italy was officially declared, and Victor Emmanuel II became its first king.

Although on his second visit to Naples, Victor Emmanuel would receive a much warmer welcome than before, the situation in the south was still unstable. Even as the House of Savoy would continue until its fall in the 1940s to denigrate the Bourbons, under its own watch poverty and brigandage would persist in the lands of the former Kingdom of the Two Sicilies. As a downside of the abolition of feudalism by the French, there had been a rise of a new class of landowners, who in their turn had begun exploiting the local peasants. Lawlessness was therefore still rife, and to try and deal with this the new government would over the next five years carry out some 5,000 executions in an effort to quell the unrest. At the same time there was some suspicion of those considered to be subversives. Revered by Abraham Lincoln and feted on his visit to England in April 1864, Garibaldi had been instrumental in bringing about the new status quo, but he was still viewed with some fear by the more conservative elements back in Italy. Suspect too were those thought to support radical ideas, most significantly Mazzini, who having been implicated in the recent attempt on the French emperor's life, was found guilty the next year in Paris. Periodically, there was also popular resistance to the authorities' measures, as was the case when details of a secret clause in the 1864 September Convention became public knowledge. According to this, Emperor Napoleon and Victor Emmanuel had agreed to the transferral of his capital the next year to Florence. The people of Turin were furious at their own city's loss of status, but in spite of the subsequent riots that caused the deaths of 30 people, the move went ahead. Nevertheless, in 1871 Florence, too, had to surrender its position when the capital was officially established in Rome, just as Cavour had always intended.

By this time, however, there had been other important political changes in the new Italy. In June 1866, while Emperor Franz Josef was engaged in his own separate conflict with Prussia, the Italian kingdom – now allied with his enemy – used the opportunity to declare war on Austria, thus beginning the Third War of Independence. Despite the courage shown by the Italians, four days later in the Second Battle of Custoza, they suffered a serious defeat, which was then followed on 20 July by another major setback when the Austrians won an important naval victory near the Dalmatian island of Lissa. Yet, while this battle was significant for being fought for the first time between ironclads, it would in fact be the last Austrian success in the war. By early August peace negotiations were under way, and, three days after Garibaldi had been ordered to withdraw from the Trentino, on 12 August the Third War of Independence came to an end.[239] At the Treaty of Vienna early the next month, the Emperor, unwilling to face the humiliation of surrendering Lombardy-Venetia to Italy, handed it over instead to the French, who then passed it on to the Italians. Therefore, the day after the Austrian's final departure, on 19 October 1866 Venice became part of Italy, the agreement ratified on the 21st and 22nd by another plebiscite that – again somewhat questionably – declared the almost unanimous approval of the people.

To mark this important change, on 7 November Victor Emanuel came to the city for a week's visit, arriving in the impressively carved and gilded boat with its 18 oars that had been created for such occasions in the *Arsenale* in the early days of the Austrians' final occupation. The king's statue marking this occasion now stands on the Riva degli Schiavoni, displaying around its base the symbols of the city's fall and recovery, Manin's own name inscribed on the robes of the figurative bronze of Venice itself. And, bringing further closure, a year after the return of the Bandiera brothers' remains, in 1868 Manin's coffin was also brought home. Having been received by Mengaldo, it was taken in a magnificent funeral procession of gondolas down the Grand Canal to St Mark's Square. Here, however, for whatever reason – religious, political, or other – the clergy refused to allow Manin's final interment to take place in the cathedral. Therefore, his supporters chose instead to place him as close to it as possible, positioning his tomb behind its railing in Piazzetta dei Leoncini, immediately alongside the basilica's north wall. So Manin still lies within yards of that great Piazza where he had so often addressed his adoring crowds of followers during the difficult days when the Repubblica di San Marco was struggling for its survival.

16

Dreams and disillusionment: Austria's Archduke Maximilian and the Empress Elizabeth

'I am dying in the knowledge of having wanted to achieve the right thing.'
Maximilian farewell letter to his mother, Archduchess Sophie, 16 June 1867[240]

'Our dreams are always fairer when they are not realised.'
Empress Elizabeth of Austria[241]

With the abdication of the disabled Ferdinand I in December 1848, two months after the imperial family had fled for the second time from Vienna, his nephew the 18-year-old Franz Josef was declared ruler in his place. While they were sheltering at Olmütz (Olomouc) in Moravia, the young man's forceful mother, the Archduchess Sophie of the Wittelsbach family from Bavaria, had taken matters into her own hands. Believing her eldest son's youth might promise

The Imperial family of Austria-Hungary in 1861.

a new start for the Empire, she had persuaded his father, the unimpressive Archduke Franz Karl, to renounce his own claims. This unexpected change of circumstances took many of the family by surprise, and it would ultimately alter the relationship between Sophie's children. After the birth of a second son in 1832, the two oldest siblings had been close friends throughout their childhood, but now there was a marked change in the relationship between the brothers. With the younger (Ferdinand) Maximilian – nicknamed Max or Maxi by the family – appeared brighter and more imaginative, as well as more intellectually and artistically inclined, from the time of Franz Josef's accession, the boys' youthful rivalry would begin to develop into something more serious. While the new Emperor grew increasingly fearful of being outshone by his charismatic brother, Maximilian became resentful of the injustice of the primogeniture system that had relegated him to a secondary role. Over the years to come he would rue his lack of an equally elevated position, periodically grumbling at being denied some meaningful employment. For his part, Franz Josef had soon become concerned by the perceived liberal tendencies of Maximilian, who was openly voicing his disapproval of the draconian punishments heaped on the rebels in Venetia and elsewhere. Opposing his brother's strong stand regarding Hungarian efforts to gain greater freedom, the archduke wrote in his diary:

> We call our age the Age of Enlightenment, but there are cities in Europe where, in the future, men will look back in horror and amazement at the injustice of tribunals, which in a spirit of vengeance condemned to death those whose only crime lay in wanting something different to the arbitrary rule of governments which placed themselves above the law.[242]

Yet, while this displays an awareness of the moral arguments against the Emperor's policies and his own rejection of brutality and injustice, Maximilian was immensely proud of his Habsburg heritage and he would never question the family's right to rule. Furthermore, even though his views have to be understood in light of the thinking of the period, some of his remarks appear to contradict his seemingly more tolerant attitude. His description of the people he encountered during a visit to Palermo in 1852 on one of his frequent trips around the Mediterranean displays the limits of his openness to other ideas and cultures. His comments reveal the extent to which his own mindset was characterised by a paternalistic sense of superiority. Remarking on the 'incredible [...] characteristic differences' to be found between people from the different parts of the world, he sums up:

> In the northern I include the manners of the British, Danes, Swedes etc. and partly ourselves; in the southern prevails the distasteful, flawed ... nature of the Italians, Spanish and most of the French etc. – The north is affiliated with calmness, etiquette, strict discipline ... the south with yelling, bonhomie and comedy; the northern sailor possesses ... bravery and has a fresh and clean appearance; the southern seaman has momentary bravery ... but otherwise he is slavish and low, and his unshaven face is neglected and savage.[243]

Within two years of coming to the throne Franz Josef had considered it best to distance his brother from the court in Vienna, and so in 1850 he had sent Maximilian to join the navy in Trieste. This was something that had always appealed to the archduke, and on becoming the commander-in-chief four years later he would set out at exorbitant cost to improve and update the Austrian fleet. Besides creating a new dockyard and arsenal at Pola capable of producing modern iron-clad vessels to replace the wooden sailing ships, he also established an Imperial Naval Academy for the training of officers at Fiume. As for years the navy had been chiefly manned by Venetians or Dalmatians, in 1858 he strengthened the men's ties to the Empire by ordering German to be used as the official language of command. Even though the local people remained opposed to the Austrian presence in the area, before long Maximilian had raised the navy's morale and won the support and loyalty of those in his service. During this time, while he was constantly on his travels in the Mediterranean and elsewhere, he also sent a scientific expedition to circumnavigate the world.

Franz Josef may have had an additional good reason to send his brother away from court in Vienna. In April 1854, having fallen instantly in love with his cousin, the younger sister of his intended bride, the Emperor married 16-year-old Elizabeth of Bavaria, popularly known in the family as Sisi. When the following year Maximilian briefly made one of his rare visits back to Vienna, she and her brother-in-law would find that they shared several interests in common. Along with their similar passion for beauty and adventure, both had inherited the extravagant artistic taste so often found among their Wittelsbach relations. Besides inspiring her with stories of the Mediterranean, he now thrilled her with descriptions of the palace he was planning to build just outside Trieste. When compared to her dutiful, adoring, but possibly dull husband, whose chief interest was in the military, Maximilian appeared to shine, his cultured and idealistic personality being in tune with hers so much more than that of his brother.

In 1856 the Crimean War ended, and as Austria had chosen to remain apart from the conflict it was now viewed with some suspicion abroad, reviled by the tsar – who felt the Emperor had betrayed him – and distrusted by the British and the French. Nonetheless, Maximilian was sent to Paris to attend the conference that marked the end of the hostilities. Here, initially, he would again reveal his prejudice against those outside his own social circles, dismissing the new French emperor as a *parvenu*, and scoffing at the court members who in his view were 'distinguished by their disgusting dress and tasteless behaviour'.[244] Later, however, he became more impressed by Napoleon III, and with the French emperor and empress then coming to view him in an increasingly favourable way, the foundations were laid for the unfortunate relationship that would ultimately bring about Maximilian's disastrous end.

Later that year in November, as part of their official tour of northern Italy, Franz Josef and his new wife paid an official visit to Trieste. The cold reception received there would be repeated when they moved on to Venice for a further two-month stay. Despite the welcome from Field Marshal Radetzky, and the glittering reception and other spectacular events laid on for their benefit, the city continued to make the imperial couple feel extremely unwelcome. With the failed assassination of Franz Josef having occurred less than four years before, the imperial couple had good reason to feel nervous, and Sisi immediately hated the place. But, while at first the Venetians refused to accept the official invitations, by 3 December the mood had changed considerably after she had persuaded her husband to soften his measures against the local people. Even so, after their departure, although Padua would receive them warmly, their reception would again be cold in Vicenza, cool in Verona, and decidedly unfriendly when they finally arrived on 1 March 1857 in Milan. Here, opposition to the Austrians was still being encouraged by the Piedmontese, even though the Emperor had already begun to take steps to try and ease the situation. He had hoped to placate the Italians by retiring the 90-year-old Radetzky and replacing him with his more liberal younger brother. As Maximilian's future father-in-law had further encouraged this appointment by requesting the Emperor to give his sibling a position 'worthy of his high birth', on 28 January 1857 the archduke became the new Governor-General of Lombardy-Venetia.[245]

Because his engagement to his first cousin Maria Amalia, the daughter of ex-king Pedro I of Brazil, had ended with her death from tuberculosis in February 1853, Maximilian had by this time become engaged to his second cousin, Princess Charlotte, the daughter of Leopold I of the Belgians. According to her mother-in-law, she was a clever, pretty young woman, and she was also someone with immense determination and ambition, characteristics that were to play a significant role in the couple's decisions in the years to come. Maximilian, too, was now impressing people, and in June, just a month before his marriage, Queen Victoria wrote to her uncle Leopold expressing how struck she and the Prince Consort had been by him during his recent visit to England. She wrote: 'I cannot say how much we like the Archduke; he is charming, so clever, natural, kind and amiable, so *English* in his feelings and likings, and so anxious for the best understanding between Austria and England.'[246] In the same vein, Prince Albert would add his own praise, describing their cousin's fiancé as 'very *anglomâne*'.[247]

Maximilian and Charlotte were good linguists, both being, among other things, fluent Italian speakers. While they now lived and entertained in style in their main palace in Monza, they would go out of their way to flatter and charm the people. Besides inviting the nobility and other local gentry to their lavish receptions and balls, they awarded them with honours and positions. But, although popular in themselves, as representatives of the ruling Austrian government, the young couple were still viewed with suspicion. Maximilian was, moreover, hampered by his very restricted authority, his powers being considerably fewer than those previously held by Radetzky, who had been unfettered by the centralist government that was now established in Vienna. Furthermore, deprived of the military command that the old field marshal had enjoyed, Maximilian would find himself powerless when demonstrations began to erupt in Milan and Venice in the aftermath of the attempt on Napoleon III's life in January 1858 in Paris. That event had held particular significance for the Italians as the perpetrator Felice Orsini was one of their own, not just a fighter for the end of all foreign occupation, but also now a much-revered martyr of the movement for independence. With the Austrian government then becoming still more reactionary and the Emperor overriding all Maximilian's proposals for reform, the archduke and his wife were openly insulted when they appeared in public, people even hissing at Charlotte when she was in Venice. Having therefore sent her away for a time to Belgium, in a letter to his mother, Maximilian showed his increasing disillusion: 'I should long ago have left this land of misery, where one has to act as the representative of a weak and inactive government, which one tries in vain to defend.'[248] While this again displays the struggle between his personal feelings, and his loyalty to the Habsburg dynasty, his older brother's opinion was less nuanced. For Franz Josef the archduke had now overstepped his brief to act purely as a figurehead. Considering that he was meddling in the local political affairs, the Emperor took away his naval command, and then in April removed him from the position he had held for two years as governor. The Lombards were delighted by the change of administration, since they had feared that the archduke's reforms might weaken the support for independence among the Italians. For the same reason, the Sardinian prime minister, Cavour, a confessed admirer of Maximilian's 'wise reforms', openly ridiculed the Emperor's decision, seeing the archduke's dismissal as another nail in Franz Josef's coffin.

There was now, however, another matter of more immediate concern for the Emperor, as two days after removing his brother from office, on 26 April 1859 Austria was again at war. Because Maximilian had been prevented from strengthening the Venetian defences, the large French navy was able to mount a blockade of Venice and trap the Austrian fleet inside the lagoon. But there was worse to come. Within weeks the Emperor had suffered such major defeats at Magenta and Solferino that he had been left with no option other than to call for a truce. Therefore, with the brief Second Italian War of Independence having come to an end, in July at Villafranca near Verona, Franz Josef was finally forced to surrender most of Lombardy. However, as he had been allowed to retain Venetia, he still held on to Venice whose independence he was determined to prevent. He was equally opposed to any suggestion of the governorship being given to Maximilian, whom he continued to see as being too liberal. But very probably there was another reason for the Emperor's refusal to give his brother further recognition. While Franz Josef's own poor leadership as military commander at Solferino had led to calls for his abdication, at the same time there had been other voices heard in Vienna crying out, 'Long live Archduke Max'.

Following Maximilian's dismissal, he and Charlotte chose to buy with her considerable dowry a place where they could spend their summer vacations. Enamoured with the Mediterranean, they built a villa in a former monastery just offshore from Ragusa on Lacroma (Lokrum) – a site that had been discovered by the archduke during a visit made to honour the memory of the sailors who had been killed nearby when their warship *Triton* had exploded. But although famous as the place where Richard the Lionheart had survived a shipwreck on his way home from the Third Crusade, today the place has another more dubious reputation. Said to have been cursed in 1798 by the departing Benedictine monks, expelled after centuries of living on the island, all those later connected to it had appeared to suffer sudden death or misfortune. Nevertheless, for a few years this was a favourite holiday retreat for the archduke and his wife, he enjoying laying out paths and terraces, collecting new species for his botanical gardens, and filling the place with exotic birds such as parrots and peacocks. For their more permanent base, however, the couple chose a spot overlooking the sea about two and a half miles north-west of Trieste, where before his marriage the archduke had begun drawing up plans for his official residence. Although after four years the work on this palace of Miramar was unfinished, Maximilian and his wife moved into their new home in 1860. The building would prove to be outrageously expensive, the overall cost being increased by the archduke having to import not just additional granite, but also the soil needed for the extensive gardens that meant so much to him. These he filled with his carefully chosen plants, here again indulging his passion for the study of flora and fauna – a hobby he would follow until the end of his life. Later in Mexico, when writing to the Confederate President Jefferson Davies on the matter of slavery, something to which he was always strongly opposed, he concluded the letter by saying that while 'engaged in scientific and cultural pursuits', he was 'currently doing entomological research on the many splendid varieties of butterfly found in our beautiful Mexico'.[249] And, equally significantly, if not poignantly, in his last letter to his lawyer on 18 June 1867, just before his death, he would ask that his butterfly collection be sent to Europe. Now, however, he described Miramar as his 'fairy-tale castle', his refuge, comparable, as he saw it, to Diocletian's retreat at Spalato. Here again was a place where the young couple could find peace away from the troubles of the world. With its combination of Gothic and other various architectural styles, this castle reflected the vogue for romantic building that was now sweeping Europe, tapping into a fashion followed by the Prussian king, Victoria and Albert in Britain, and Maximilian's Wittelsbach relatives. While his private rooms reflected his naval interest by being decorated as though on-board ship, besides the later additions of the throne room and the Mexican coats of arms, Maximilian filled it with references to the Habsburgs. By exhibiting multiple portraits and a remarkable family tree, the archduke stressed the family's God-given right to rule, and his own place within the imperial dynasty.

Shortly after his dismissal from his role in Lombardy-Venetia, Maximilian made a long overseas trip. After travelling first to Madeira with his wife, he then carried on alone to see his cousin the Brazilian emperor, this once again giving him the opportunity to indulge his interest in nature by visiting the rainforests. Here, apart from perhaps contracting syphilis, a possible cause for the couple remaining childless, he was shocked by the country's continued use of slavery. Horrified as he had been the previous year when witnessing it at Smyrna, he now questioned the immorality of the practice. Speaking as a devout Catholic, he asked: 'Is religion not a mockery when a white man arrogates the right to treat men who, like himself, are born in the image of the creator, as if they were beasts of burden, or bales of goods?'[250]

On eventually returning to Trieste, Maximilian would be approached for the first time by representatives from Mexico. By the close of 1860, with the final defeat and overthrow of the conservative, pro-clerical faction, this country's civil war – the War of Reform – had come to an end. Mexico City was now back in the hands of the Liberals, and their leader, the previously exiled Benito Juárez, would soon be elected as the constitutional president. By this time, many of the opposition had fled to Europe, and among the exiles living in Paris were some who had started to float the idea of Maximilian becoming their new emperor. With the historic Habsburg connections to Mexico, originating at the time of the joint rulers Ferdinand and Isabella, and later passed down through their Spanish descendants, the dynasty remained in the frame among those who wished to see a return to monarchist rule in their country. While this proposal appealed to Napoleon III, Maximilian was also drawn to the idea. For several months throughout 1861 the archduke continued to mull it over, until he eventually expressed in private his willingness to accept the role, 'on the condition that France and England would support him with their moral and material guarantee, both on land and sea'.[251]

In October that same year, French, British, and Spanish representatives had come together at the London Convention to discuss how they could perhaps recover the vast sums they were owed by the Mexicans. The previous July, President Juárez had put the repayment of these loans on hold after he had discovered the dire financial state that his country was in. America was now caught up in the horrors of its own civil war and so, not being represented at the convention, it would take no part in the final decisions. The other delegates decided, however, that the time had come to take action and, determined to recover the money that was due, before the end of the year they had sent troops across the Atlantic to seize the customs houses at Vera Cruz.

By this time, Napoleon III was convinced of the benefit to French interests that would most probably be gained by the archduke becoming the new Mexican emperor. As a useful ally, if not a French puppet, Maximilian might be able to help France maintain its influence in the Americas. As for the archduke himself, he was still toying with the idea when he met Franz Josef in Venice on New Year's Eve. Yet, by then the London Convention's earlier plans were about to undergo a major change. Soon after their arrival in Mexico, the British and Spanish started to be concerned about Napoleon's true ambitions, and so by the following April both these parties had decided to withdraw. The French, who had already received a hostile welcome, were now on their own and at Puebla on 5 May 1862 they were to suffer a humiliating defeat. News of this disaster temporarily put Maximilian off the whole Mexican project, but by June he was again expressing his interest in the plan to Napoleon, who within months was sending additional forces to Mexico. With the British becoming increasingly fearful that his growing interference in the region could eventually threaten their own commercial interests, in early 1863 they came up with another proposal. They now suggested that the Austrian archduke might prefer to accept the crown of

Otto, the recently deposed King of Greece. Despite the backing of his father-in-law Leopold, who saw this as a wiser option than the Mexican throne, Maximilian swiftly turned the offer down, not just offended at the thought of replacing his ousted Bavarian cousin, but also believing it beneath him to accept a throne that had already been rejected by several other candidates.[252]

In the intervening months, the situation had improved for the French, they having at last captured Puebla in May, and then a month later occupied the capital, Mexico City. During this time the Americans continued to be out of the picture, still too tied up in their civil war to protest actively against any non-adherence to the Monroe doctrine laid down some 40 years earlier. This had stipulated that European powers should distance themselves from all political interference in the region. Nonetheless, the conservative provisional Mexican government, which had set itself up in opposition to President Juárez and the Liberals, now sent some of its representatives to meet Maximilian and make him a firmer offer. On arriving at Miramar on 3 October 1863, they presented him with their invitation. Allegedly issued in the name of the people, this requested the archduke to become emperor of their new Second Mexican Empire.

On now deciding to accept the proposal, Maximilian declared that he would take on the position as a constitutional monarch, but only on the proviso that a referendum was called and he received the approval of the majority. He also required the continued backing of the three European powers, Britain, Spain, and France, but on this issue he was less precise – something that later greatly displeased Franz Josef who believed an agreed shared responsibility would have reduced the influence of the French in the region. In the event, however, the British and the Spanish chose for their own political ends to distance themselves from the whole affair, so ultimately Maximilian would be left reliant on French support alone. For the moment, however, Franz Josef was satisfied to see his brother being taken thousands of miles away from his own Empire, believing that the increased distance would help remove the danger of the archduke ever becoming a focus for the opposition. At the same time, by his insistence that it should be a purely personal matter between Maximilian and the Mexicans, he hoped to prevent his Empire from becoming beholden to the French, and possibly later being called on to repay them for the part they had played.

With this project allegedly gaining approval from the Mexican public, at last it could go ahead. Yet the plebiscite that had returned the required mandate was far from democratic, and the result was deeply flawed. Many people and several areas were excluded from taking part in the ballot, and others were openly intimidated by the French into voting for the new emperor. While Maximilian is generally thought not to have been made aware of the truth of this, one American critic, Foster – an advocate of Benito Juárez and the republican government – would allege in 1911 that a Mexican had in fact stayed behind and 'warned [Maximilian] that he was not the choice of the nation and so therefore it would not receive him'.[253] Whether or not this was the case, Maximilian was still convincing himself that he was wanted by the people, later asserting this on 28 May when writing from Vera Cruz to Queen Victoria – his 'Sweetest Cousin Vic':

I am aware that there have been meetings between your ministers and Franz Josef designed to discourage my acceptance of this role, and probably all of this was done with what you and your advisers believe to be the best interests of the whole family. Please understand, dear Vickie, that a plebiscite was held here to demonstrate the firm desire of these people to sweep away the economically and spiritually unsound republican form of government and institute a constitutional monarchy to protect and defend them from the anarchy and chaos of the predecessor regime![254]

Queen Victoria and Franz Josef were not the only ones to have misgivings about the role that Maximilian was about to take on. The American consul in Trieste foresaw the dangers the archduke faced, and the Austrian ambassador in Paris went further, writing: 'How many cannon shots will be needed to put him on the throne, and how many more to keep him there?'[255] Over the previous four decades of violent unrest, revolutions, and civil war, Mexico had seen the fall of some fifty different governments. As Archduchess Sophie and Charlotte's grandmother, Marie Amélie (the exiled former Queen of France), grew more anxious, even the French emperor began to have doubts. But the French empress Eugenie was highly in favour of the idea, and the Belgian king also continued to support it. Leopold's daughter Charlotte was even more enthusiastic and convinced of the good her husband would be able to achieve. An intelligent, energetic woman, she had found life boring at Miramar, and was keen to have a purpose in life. Maximilian was equally satisfied to have a role at last, declaring: 'Out of the blue the Mexican crown was offered to me and with it the opportunity to end in an honourable and lawful manner my unemployed existence forever.'[256]

Making his farewell journey around Europe, he followed up his triumphant visit to Paris with a rather less spectacular stay in England, where, despite the affection that he was shown, he received no more practical or financial backing. The situation then grew darker when in March Maximilian went to Vienna. Here, on the Foreign Minister presenting him with the Act of Renunciation, he became aware for the first time of the harsh terms the government was now placing on him as a result of recent events. The previous year the question of the succession had been brought sharply into focus by the Emperor's heir, young Rudolf, becoming so seriously ill that there had been very real fears that his claim to the throne was about to pass directly to his uncle. To avoid any risk of the Empire falling into foreign hands, the new act now stated that Maximilian's acceptance of the Mexican crown was contingent on his renouncing all his rights as Archduke of Austria. While he and his mother were appalled by this, she trying unsuccessfully to change Franz Josef's mind, after a bitter row between the brothers Maximilian left Vienna and returned to Miramar. Here, having decided the price was too high, on 27 March he once more refused to accept the Mexican crown.

When he was warned by telegram of the developing situation, the French emperor became concerned for his own position and so immediately wrote to Maximilian. Appealing to the archduke's sense of honour, he called on him to abide by his earlier commitment. Nevertheless, Maximilian saw through this, since he had now come to suspect that Napoleon was using him solely to achieve his private objective, namely 'to dominate Mexico without appearing to do so in the eyes of Europe'.[257] However, even though he had personally grown uncertain about what lay ahead, Maximilian finally succumbed to the French emperor's moral blackmail and once more he changed his mind. Yet, despite again begging his brother to soften the terms in the Act of Renunciation, and to add a secret clause promising a restoration of his rights should he have to leave Mexico, but his appeals came to nothing. As he was himself under pressure from his government, Franz Josef stubbornly refused to give in. Instead, besides offering the vague possibility that Maximilian might be found some suitable position in the future should the need arrive, he promised to pay his brother's outstanding debts on Miramar. He then sweetened the deal by promising a small annual subsidy and offering to provide 6000 soldiers and 300 sailors to assist him in Mexico.

As the stalemate continued, with the Emperor refusing to make any further concessions, Charlotte went to Vienna to appeal directly to her brother-in-law, but her visit was to no avail. Although Empress Elizabeth had never been on good terms with her, and had never understood Maximilian's attraction to the Mexican venture, sensing the difficulties that lay ahead for the couple, she like others now showed sympathy for Charlotte. Many felt that there was little likelihood of the affair ending well. Franz Josef was determined, however, to resolve the impasse, and so on 9 April 1864 he and his other brothers, together with various senior ministers and representatives from the Austrian Empire, came to Trieste to talk privately with Maximilian at Miramar.[258] After a long, difficult two-hour meeting spent closeted together, the archduke at last reluctantly agreed to sign the 'Family Pact', something he soon came to regret. While still only in the mid-Atlantic he would refute the document's legality, claiming, somewhat falsely, that, besides not seeing it until the last moment, he had added his signature only under duress.

By this time tensions were high, and the visit ended when the brothers finally parted at the station, where with tears in their eyes they embraced each other for the last time. Even though neither knew what lay ahead because of the political uncertainty in Mexico, and the physical distance that was soon to separate them, both were no doubt aware of the possibility that they would never meet again. Also conscious of this was Maximilian's mother, who before his departure sent him her blessings, writing: 'Farewell for the last time on your native soil, where alas we may see you no more.'[259]

The day after Franz Josef's departure, the delayed ceremony went ahead in a room at Miramar before the group of Mexican delegates. While this marked the beginning of Maximilian's reign, it was to be his only official ceremony, since the coronation that he planned for 10 June in Mexico would never take place. While now affirming that he had the support of the French, he also acknowledged the eventual withdrawal of their main force, agreeing at the same time to the payment of the salaries and expenses of the volunteers who remained. Still more unfortunately, Maximilian guaranteed his empire's repayment of its debts – a pledge within the 'Convention of Miramar' that would soon prove to be impossible and result in the bankruptcy of his new country. Yet, with the Mexican flag flying over the palace and celebratory gun salutes, the day ended with a *Te Deum*. At that point, exhausted after the strains he had recently been under, Maximilian appeared to suffer some sort of mental or physical collapse, and he retired with his doctor to the pavilion. For the next three days, Charlotte took his place, presiding in his stead at the court functions that continued to be held. At last on the 14th, having sufficiently recovered, the new Mexican emperor was ready to leave his beloved Miramar. The Trieste harbour was filled with small boats, and the shore crowded with spectators who had come to see his departure. To a hundred-gun salute, the new emperor with tears in his eyes set sail on the Austrian warship *Novara*. After rounding the heel and toe of Italy the couple arrived in Rome, where they were welcomed by the deposed King Frances II of the Two Sicilies and his wife – Sisi's sister, Queen Maria. The pope also received them in style, blessing them and wishing them well for their future. As the Church in Mexico had lost its authority in the 1850s with the overthrow of the previous conservative government, Pius IX now hoped that with the young emperor's help it would be able re-establish its influence in the country.

After two days in Rome, Maximilian and Charlotte set off from the port at Civitavecchia, and over the next six weeks as they crossed the Atlantic they passed their time devising the complicated rules of etiquette they believed necessary for their Mexican imperial court. Having received a gun salute on Queen Victoria's orders at Gibraltar, and another at Cadiz, they eventually reached Vera Cruz at the end of May. As the town had been the centre of the separate Liberal Party government during the recent War of Reform, here their reception was cool, and the people's obvious indifference to their arrival would now give Maximilian and Charlotte their first glimpse of the problems that lay ahead. The situation improved considerably, however, as they went inland towards the more conservative cities where Maximilian was pleased to report that 'a mass of people came from the surrounding mountains and villages' to see them.[260] Over the months to come, this would be the way he would seek to portray the situation in his empire, and for the next couple of years he would continue relaying a rosy picture to conceal the truth from his relations back home.

Despite his claimed intention to become the constitutional emperor, Maximilian soon discovered the impossibility of achieving this. Although by the end of 1864 his Second Mexican Empire had been recognised by more than ten foreign nations, in the country itself he was still struggling to steer a path between the different factions. In addition to satisfying the various ethnic groups, he had to try and retain the support of the conservatives who had chosen him to be their ruler. Furthermore, besides attempting to appease the Liberals who opposed him, he had to deal with the anger of the Church that had soon become enraged by his refusal to return its confiscated lands, and by his demand for tolerance of other religions. As if this was not enough, guerrilla action was still ongoing. To the monarchists' surprise, the northern Unionist Americans had finally defeated the Confederate states in the south, and so the republicans of the United States were once again able to support the rebel Mexican leader Juárez, who by now was extending his influence over large parts of the country. So, having already declared a temporary postponement of his constitution, on 3 October 1865 Maximilian went further and unadvisedly issued a decree that pronounced the arbitrary punishment of any armed individual who was involved in subversive action. Because instant execution could now be carried out on anyone without prior court martial, the French troops began to deal savagely with the opposition, and by doing so they again hardened attitudes against the emperor.

Things then became even more serious for Maximilian on 15 January 1866, when Napoleon III went back on his word by announcing that he had decided to withdraw his troops, who were ordered to depart by March the next year. This move would allow the Liberals to gain control of still more areas, Maximilian's situation was then made worse after the additional volunteer troops that he had hoped to receive from Europe were forbidden to set sail by the Austrian government. By this time, Franz Josef had been threatened by the USA that such an action would lead to war. So, already, by mid-1866, the situation in Mexico had become so grim for Maximilian that many were suggesting he should abdicate. As he hesitated, Charlotte decided to return to Europe to appeal on his behalf for more support. Still driven by her ambition to uphold his position, before she left on 9 July 1866, she forcefully called on her husband not to give up, declaring: 'Abdication is only excusable in old men and idiots... From the moment one assumes responsibility for the destiny of a nation, one does so at one's own risk and is not at liberty to abandon it.'[261] She would never see Maximilian again.

On her arrival the next month, Charlotte intentionally avoided visiting her brother, who had now succeeded their father as Leopold II of Belgium. She also shunned her Austrian in-laws, since these had greatly angered her and Maximilian by their unwillingness to provide military backup. Therefore, on 8 August she went directly to Paris, where she was eventually able to see a rather unwilling Napoleon III at St Cloud. Even so, she was unable to change his mind, as he, too, was now determined not to antagonise the United States government. Therefore, obviously distressed, Charlotte returned to Trieste, gaining some small pleasure on the way back in seeing how in northern Italy numbers of people had turned out to greet her. As the construction work was still ongoing at Miramar, on her arrival home she decided to stay in the estate's smaller *castelletto*, where for a time she spent her days peacefully looking out over the bay where her husband's former naval fleet now lay at anchor.

After resting at Miramar for three weeks, she went south to Rome to speak with the pope, whom she then met on 30 September. Here her demands were once more refused, and this latest rejection would finally prove too much for her state of mind. Before the papal audience had ended she had suffered such a serious mental collapse that a doctor had to be called. As she now did not want to let the pope out of her sight, Pius IX was eventually forced to resolve the situation by making a previously unimagined concession; he permitted her to stay the night in the Vatican. Although the next day Charlotte was transferred to a hotel, because she was now convinced that there were people who wanted to kill her she refused all food and would only drink water that she had herself taken from the city's fountains. Whatever the reason for her paranoia, this would probably encourage the later unverified rumours that her illness and eventual death had been caused by her having been poisoned while in Mexico. At last on 8 October she left Rome for Ancona, from where she then sailed back to Trieste.

Her brother Leopold II of the Belgians, who had ordered Charlotte's return to Miramar, now arranged for her to be seen by senior doctors, and after they had declared her mental state to be incurable, the king had her removed permanently to a castle near Brussels. By this time Maximilian had been told of her illness, breaking down on being informed that she had been visited by the director of the Insane Asylum. Wanting to see his wife, and realising that all hope of help from Europe was now gone, he decided the time had come for his ministers to vote on the question of his abdication. But with the greater part of the country in the hands of the Liberals, those belonging to the more conservative element were anxious for their own future security. Since some, therefore, voted for him to remain – at least for a time – and only two members of the council called for his immediate resignation, Maximilian agreed temporarily to drop the idea. As the imperial family in Austria was still largely ignorant of the deteriorating situation in Mexico, even his mother Archduchess Sophie now encouraged him to stay. Writing to him at Christmas, she urged: 'I am *bound* to want you to stay in Mexico as long as it is possible and can be done with honour.'[262] So, when the last of the French sailed away in February 1867, Maximilian refused to take up the offer of a place on board.

Having finally decided to go to war against the Liberals, the emperor now moved to Querétaro. This soon came under siege, and during the next 72 days as the defence held out, Maximilian continued to show such courage that he impressed all those around him. With his relief force defeated on 10 April while defending Mexico City, before long the diminished army was unable to prevent the capital falling to the Liberals. Although these now began slaughtering anyone caught carrying messages to the emperor, he still refused to countenance similar behaviour on his side, and only when their inevitable defeat at Querétaro became apparent did he and his generals begin to plan their escape. They hoped to reach Vera Cruz, where there was a possibility of finding a ship to take them to Europe, but, before the idea could go any further, at 4.am on 14 May Maximilian was awoken to find that the Liberals had entered the city. How they had gained access is still open to question, but whether it was accomplished through an act of betrayal, as several believed, or by their own skills, the emperor was now forced to raise the flag of surrender.

He had initially believed that his captors would allow him to return to Europe, and even when the situation began to appear so serious that some of his supporters attempted to bribe them to allow him to get away, Maximilian remained determined to stay on. But although he still relied on his lawyers to arrange his release, a month after being charged, on 13 June he and two of his generals were summoned to court for trial. Having been unwell for some time, the emperor now produced a certificate declaring that he was too ill to attend, here his real purpose being to avoid having to acknowledge the court's authority, a degradation that he deemed unworthy of a Habsburg. However, by eleven the next evening all three defendants had been found guilty and condemned to death.

In the last days, Franz Josef had become so concerned that he had begun to make his own moves to achieve the release of his brother. As news of Maximilian's capture reached him, he even appealed to the US ambassador to intervene. Other rulers also did their best, the Prussian minister, for one, trying – somewhat ironically – to strengthen Maximilian's case with the new republican government in Mexico by drawing attention to the emperor's close family connections with the great ruling houses of Europe. He wrote:

> My sovereign, his Majesty the King of Prussia, and all the monarchs of Europe, united by the ties of blood with the prince prisoner ... his brother the Emperor of Austria, his cousin the Queen of Great Britain, his brother-in-law the King of Belgium, and also his cousin the Queen of Spain and the Kings of Italy and Sweden, will readily come to an understanding to give to his Excellency Don Benito Juárez every assurance that no one of the three prisoners shall return to tread on Mexican territory.[263]

Going still further, Franz Josef would also offer the guarantee that he had earlier refused his brother, assuring the Mexicans that he would 'at once re-establish Prince Maximilian in all his rights of succession as Archduke of Austria, upon Maximilian's release and renouncing forever all projects in Mexico'.

But this was all too late. Already, just days after their trial, at 7.00 am on Wednesday 19 June the three prisoners had been shot. In the last hours before his death, Maximilian had again proved his courage, helping to lift the spirits of his men. Years earlier, when facing the inevitable failure of his schemes in Lombardy-Venetia, he had written to his mother: 'I am not one to turn away in time of danger. Where there is a fire I shall help to the last moment, even though I have to stand in the midst of flames.'[264] Now having reaffirmed how his aim had always been to do the right thing, he asked that she should be told that he had fulfilled his duty 'as a soldier and ... a Christian'.[265] His last words when facing the firing squad had been in Spanish: 'I forgive everybody. I pray that one may also forgive me, and I wish that my blood, which is now to be shed, may be for the good of the country – 'Viva Mexico! Viva Independencia!'[266]

The news when it eventually reached Europe left everyone shocked, many finding it hard to believe that the young emperor's venture had ended so tragically after just three and a half years. His mother aged considerably on hearing of the execution of her favourite son, utterly grief-stricken by the death of her 'darling Max'.[267] Although Archduchess Sophie, like others in the family, would hold the French emperor responsible for the whole fiasco, the genuinely distressed Empress Eugenie and her husband would not be deterred from coming to Salzburg to offer their condolences. But it was not only the Habsburgs who blamed Napoleon III. The republican Edouard Manet started painting almost immediately his three versions of the execution, and to those who saw the works, the suggestion of the emperor's guilt was apparent.[268] While, with artistic licence, the artist showed Maximilian in the middle of the three men – a position that he had in fact intentionally surrendered as a final mark of respect and gratitude for his general Miramón – even more significantly, after gaining further information, Manet would in the later works present the executioners not in Mexican dress, but in uniforms more similar to those of the French.

Because of her fragile mental state, Charlotte was not told what had happened. She would remain for the rest of her life in Belgium, expecting to see again the husband she was to outlive by 60 years. Following six weeks of delays, Maximilian's body was at last released as a result of Franz Josef's further humiliating climbdown, having been forced to ask 'President' Juárez for the remains of the 'Archduke'. The body was then returned to Trieste in the *Novara*, the same frigate that had taken the young emperor and empress to Mexico three years earlier. After that, the coffin was transported by train to Vienna, where it was interred in the Habsburgs' family vault in the Capuchin Church. In Mexico, Maximilian would not be completely forgotten. Here, another memorial chapel was later erected in his honour on the spot where he and his two companions had died.

Maximilian and Charlotte had taken on the imperial enterprise with some naivety, little appreciating or acknowledging the deep-rooted problems that faced them. Although eventually he would come to realise how he had been first manipulated and then let down by Napoleon III and some of his Mexican supporters, there was initially an element of *folie de grandeur* in the approach of the young couple, their desire for status shown by their determination to maintain the strict etiquette of the European courts. They had believed they might be able to do some good, and both had made a considerable effort to prepare themselves for the task ahead, learning Spanish and studying the history, geography and much else of the country. But as Maximilian had been eager to obtain a rank equal to that of his brother, this had no doubt played a major role in his accepting the crown. His desire for status was made manifest in a moment of unguarded honesty five months after his arrival in Mexico. With the tensions between the brothers still high, on 17 September, 1864 he had written to Franz Josef:

I believe we must be very clear with each other from this point forward, as befits out new equality. When I left Trieste for Vera Cruz, it was I, not Charlotte or anyone else, who insisted on renouncing any claims to the Hapsburg Throne. I am at least of your rank and must insist that you treat me with respect in your correspondence. As our map, a copy of which I am including with this letter, reveals in true detail, our territory is now larger than the Austrian Empire by some forty thousand hectares… In your next letter, please remember the rule of decorum Hapsburgs respect and cherish. Please address Us by Our true Mexican names, for in addition to renouncing claims to an Austrian or Belgian throne, We choose to speak and be spoken to in the language of Our people, Spanish![269]

Showing to what degree the relationship between the brothers had soured, while he addresses the Austrian Emperor in a familiar way as Brother Franz, he then signs off this letter using the full titles of himself and his wife – the formality here in stark contradiction to how he usually ends his correspondence. Yet the other side of Maximilian had soon shown itself, admitting when writing to his younger brother Karl Ludwig – who was staying at the time at Miramar – that he understood if Franz Josef had been made angry by his comments. Acknowledging that he had been childish, he apologises for the offence he has caused, and confesses that he and 'Carlotta' had taken their duties 'perhaps a trifle too seriously'.[270]

Maximilian's desire to uphold his honour, together with his unwillingness to admit to his earlier foolhardiness in pursuing his unrealistic ambitions, gave him the strength to stay at his post to the end. While Franz Josef offered too late to return his titles and rights, after signing the Family Pact the younger brother had had little option other than to stay in Mexico, where he would eventually face his end with a bravery that was admired even by his enemies. However, despite the evidence of those who witnessed the execution, in time conspiracy theories would grow up around his death. Throughout the centuries such stories have become all too common in cases where a person of note has died in mysterious or unexpected circumstances. For a time at least one of Tsar Nicholas II's murdered children was believed to have survived, while still today some claim that the body buried at Gorizia of Marie Antoinette's daughter Marie-Thérèse is that of another woman.[271] As it has often been near impossible to prove or disprove many such stories, the myths relating to them tend to linger on, and this is the case with Maximilian. When his badly embalmed body was returned to Europe, Archduchess Sophie was said to have remarked it was not that of her son. This comment, so like that made in similar circumstances by Tsar Alexander I's mother, would (as in that case) help feed the rumours, further strengthened by Maximilian's coffin, contrary to the usual practice, remaining closed during his burial in Vienna. Some suggest that a substitute body was found to replace him and that the firing squad had used blank shots. This argument has been recently strengthened by further research that has claimed that the person resembling him, who later appeared on the scene in San Salvador, was indeed the former emperor. Tina Schwenk argues, however, that not only would such a conspiracy have been difficult to arrange in the time, but also that it would have been extremely risky for Juárez to grant Maximilian an amnesty. To sum up, therefore, although Maximilian's mother – despite her earlier comment – would later appear convinced enough of its identity to ask to be buried beside the body brought back from Mexico, the case is not closed, and this debate will not end until there is analysis of the remains that now lie in the Habsburg vault in Vienna.[272]

* * *

Although Franz Josef would be deeply shocked by the death of his brother, over the years to come he and other family members would often stay in Maximilian's former homes. Charlotte was now too ill ever to return from

Belgium, but the Empress Elizabeth is recorded as staying at Miramar at least fourteen times over the remaining years of her life as she increasingly spent her time travelling around Europe and further afield. Within two years of her marriage, she found herself at odds with her mother-in-law, her aunt Archduchess Sophie, who despite having suffered herself from loneliness and disillusion in the early years of her own marriage, could not understand the younger woman's inability to face up to her role. By August 1858 Sisi had given birth to three children, Sophie who had died aged two, Gisela born in 1856, and then two years later the heir, Rudolf. However, after Franz Josef returned in 1859 from that disastrous campaign in Italy that had seen his personal defeat at Solferino and the surrender of most of Lombardy, for whatever reason the marriage had begun to disintegrate. Whether or not, as is often suggested, this was the result of the Emperor having contracted syphilis, the couple's relationship now became more distant. Even though he still worshipped his wife, she became increasingly unstable and self-obsessed. She was focused principally on her appearance, almost fanatically concerned about her exceptionally long hair, and equally preoccupied with her remarkable figure, which she strove to keep in shape by various methods. Besides virtually starving herself, and going on rapid, extended walks that left her attendants utterly exhausted, she installed gym equipment in the palace for her daily exercise. Already shy by nature, and hating the rigid court life in Vienna, the political situation around Europe soon added to her pressures. Among other things, her own sister and brother-in-law were in considerable danger, both still trapped in the besieged city of Gaeta where they had taken refuge. Eventually, all these strains proved too much for the Empress and by the end of the next year she had suffered a mental breakdown.

As concerns grew for Sisi's health, in November 1860 it was finally agreed to allow her to fulfil her wish to get away for a time. On being lent the use of one of Queen Victoria's private yachts, she set sail for Madeira, a place she had been inspired to visit ever since hearing about it from Maximilian. At first it enchanted her, but within a month she grew bored and although she remained on the island throughout the winter, she was soon looking forward to going home. The following April, while on her way back she stopped at Corfu and, having immediately fallen in love with the place, she became determined to return. On this particular occasion, she could stay only briefly, being due the next day to meet her husband who had come to join her at Lacroma. After that the imperial couple continued together up the coast to Trieste, where they then stayed at Miramar as guests of Maximilian and his wife. The visit was not a great success, a natural rivalry having soon developed between the two young women who were so different in character, one beautiful, neurotic and totally self-absorbed, the other intelligent, dutiful, and dedicated to furthering the career of her husband.

For a time Empress Elizabeth's health seemed to improve, but before long she declined again, and being supposedly too ill to go to the wedding in June of her younger sister Mathilde, that same month she convinced the doctors that what she really needed was to return to Corfu.[273] Here, because he was made responsible for finding her some suitable accommodation, the unfortunate High Commissioner was forced for a time to move out of his own house. Three years later, on the final departure of the British in May 1864, he would have to surrender this for good, and with the Ionian Islands now part of Greece, his former home, renamed Mon Repos, became King George I's summer retreat – the birthplace in 1921 of his grandson, Prince Philip. During Sisi's 1861 journey to Corfu, however, she had been accompanied by Maximilian, who had been struck by the 'miraculous' way that she had quickly recovered. But when a court representative then came to persuade her to go back to Vienna, she refused to listen, and her eating disorder returned. Therefore, by the time her older sister had been sent to talk to her, her health had once more become a matter of concern and she was showing signs of suffering from serious anaemia. Finally in October she agreed at last to be reunited with her family, and after Franz Josef had joined her in Corfu, arrangements were made for her to spend that winter with her children in Venice, where it would be easier for the Emperor to visit them occasionally. Here, even though her rooms in Napoleon's former palace were purposely redesigned according to her own taste, during the following dank, dreary months, she would again become depressed as she dwelt on the negative memories of her first visit to Venice with her husband five years before. Yet, regardless of this and her poor opinion of the Italians, she remained in the city for the next seven months, and she even returned again briefly the next year.

This would be the pattern of Empress Elizabeth's life from now on, and although she would frequently charm many of those around her, earning the love and respect of patients and others she visited in hospitals, her behaviour overall was inconsistent. She was to spend some of her happiest moments in Hungary, where she became deeply involved with the people, learning their language, closely befriending the leader Count Andrássy, and (controversially) supporting the Magyar cause. By exerting her influence on her devoted husband, she would in time be largely responsible for persuading him to recognise the Hungarians' rights, and then to establish the new Dual Monarchy. But otherwise, she showed no interest in his Empire, and having little concern for him or her children, she was to be only truly content when she was abroad. Later, during the 1870s she would stay for weeks in England and Ireland where, as she indulged in her passion for hunting, all her health problems would apparently disappear. An exceptional horsewoman, she spent hours in the saddle, showing such reckless courage that she amazed those riding out with her.

During 1866, while his wife was still travelling around Europe the Emperor was contending with the problems now heralding the break-up of his empire. Unsurprisingly, given her personal interest and involvement in the affairs of Hungary, the next year Sisi returned to join him for their coronation ceremony in Budapest, this occurring just a few days before Maximilian's execution in Mexico. Although before long she was off again, travelling back to Corfu, nine months after the coronation, in April 1868 she returned to Hungary to give birth to her last daughter. This event soon became the subject of gossip as rumours began to swirl suggesting that the baby's real father was the Hungarian prime minister Count Andrássy. There was never any evidence to back these stories up, and while the child was increasingly said to resemble Franz Josef, she herself would later emphasise her German blood and express her dislike of the count. However, from the start the little (Marie) Valerie was to be Sisi's special and much-adored child, being entirely looked after by her besotted mother who showed her the maternal affection the older siblings had never known. Those children had been brought up by their grandmother, who at the time had thought her immature daughter-in-law to be unsuited to care for them, something that had soon become another cause of friction between the two women. Yet, when Archduchess Sophie died four years after Valerie's birth, once again Sisi would show her softer side, remaining at the bedside to the end and expressing remorse after her mother-in-law's death.

When in May 1881 the crown prince Rudolf married his Belgian cousin Stéphanie, the couple chose to spend part of their honeymoon at Lacroma, this having now returned to the family's possession after a brief interruption. The next year they stayed again in one of Maximilian's former homes, when they joined the Emperor and Empress at Miramar during an official visit in September to Trieste. Like her aunt Charlotte, Stéphanie was to have a difficult relationship with Sisi, but by the time she gave birth to her only child in 1883 she was facing a more serious problem, as her marriage with Rudolf had already begun to fail. She was alone therefore when she returned to Miramar two years later. Things finally came to their dramatic conclusion, however, in January 1889, when her husband and Marie Vetsera were discovered dead in his hunting lodge at Mayerling – Rudolf having apparently shot his young mistress before killing himself in a suicide pact. As this threatened to become a major scandal, the affair was hushed up and, after the dead woman had been hurriedly spirited away to be buried privately, the archduke was interred in the Capuchin crypt alongside his ancestors in Vienna. Initially, Sisi rose again to the occasion, choosing on hearing the news to break it herself to her husband, but within a day she had once more retreated, and having apparently never fully recovered from the shock, for the rest of her life she would continue to dress in mourning.

Although Empress Elizabeth had enjoyed her visits to Lacroma to see her son, after the tragedy at Mayerling she wanted to sell it, but its reputation for bringing bad luck was discouraging any potential buyers. In the end Franz Josef would temporarily solve the problem by sponsoring the Dominicans to take it over. Meanwhile, still greatly enamoured with the Mediterranean, Sisi continued to spend much of her time cruising around in her yacht, the similarly named *Miramare*. As she had also wanted her own home in Corfu, the year before Rudolf's death work had begun on her new villa overlooking the sea that, designed in the style of ancient Greece, was to be named the Achilleon. By the time it was finished, however, the restless Empress had lost interest in the property and she would return to it only periodically. After her last visit in 1896, the villa would then remain abandoned until the Kaiser bought it in 1907.

After Rudolf's death, Sisi was almost constantly on the move and in 1894 she made a trip to the South of France, where she then met Eugenie, the former French empress, a woman who had once been equally renowned for her beauty.

The meeting was more poignant for another reason, however, Elizabeth coming face-to-face with the woman who had played such a role in the fatal venture of her brother-in-law. But that earlier tragedy in Mexico, and the equally shocking death of Rudolf were soon to be followed by more family disasters, soon adding to the many concerns already troubling the Emperor. In 1896, Franz Josef's younger brother Archduke Karl Ludwig, the Habsburg heir since the terrible events at Mayerling, died from typhoid. This had now left the succession in the hands of his son Franz Ferdinand, a man already deeply attached to a woman who was considered to be unfit to be an imperial bride. The Emperor viewed this relationship with horror, he considering that such a union would put the Habsburg dynasty in question. Yet before some form of resolution could be found, Franz Josef was to suffer his greatest personal tragedy of all.

While Empress Elizabeth was staying on Lake Geneva in September 1898, an Italian anarchist, who was looking for any royal person he might kill, came across her by chance. As she was about to board the ferry to return home after a day out, he stabbed her through the heart. Initially, she was just shaken and unaware of the seriousness of what had happened, but, having walked on, within a few minutes she dropped dead on the ground. On his hearing the news, Franz Josef was heard to wail: 'Is nothing to be spared me on this earth?'[274] Yet, while he was crushed by the loss, his wife, who had a horror of growing older, had been spared the difficulties and indignities of extreme old age, and her unexpected, and also dramatic and tragic death, may have been just the way the romantically inclined Empress would have wished to die.

Sisi in many ways resembled her other Wittelsbach relations, having that idealistic family trait with its leaning towards fanciful projects and dreams. She embodied a complex mixture of characteristics, being at times amusing, kind, and sweet-tempered, at others cold, distant and selfish. As many, including her own nearest relatives had soon come to realise, she was highly unsuited to take on the challenge before her, apparently little appreciating the role that was facing her when as a 15-year-old she was first swept up in the Emperor's whirlwind romance. Unsympathetic to her husband's enormous problems of state and unsupportive of him in his role, she always tended to see herself as a victim. Often appearing to wallow in her unhappiness, when expressing her sympathy for her eccentric cousin Ludwig II of Bavaria, she tellingly compared his way of looking at things with her own similar 'tendency to melancholy and a love of solitude'.[275] Although undoubtedly she often suffered from real depression and was continually subject to her eating disorders, she tended when it suited her to use these things as an excuse to satisfy her various whims. While she was intelligent, and often generous, she was also spoilt and too self-absorbed, and so she repeatedly failed where she could so easily have succeeded. Time and again she abandoned her husband and children to follow her own course. Like her cousin and brother-in-law, Maximilian, she had flair and imagination, but although both these individuals would be disappointed in their dreams, he was ready to accept his failures and when confronted by the reality of his situation he had been able to turn his mistaken ambitions around and make them serve as an example for the good of others.

SECTION IX
PATH TO THE GREAT WAR

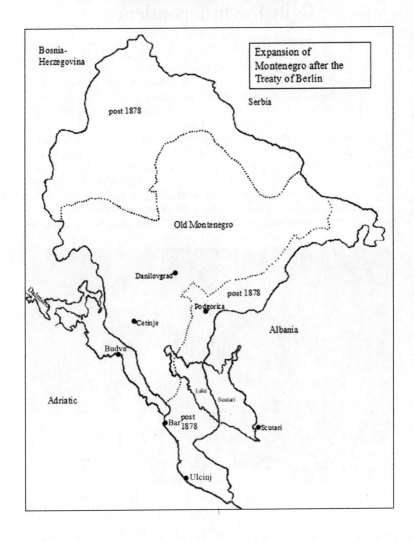

Bosnia-Herzegovina

Serbia

Expansion of
Montenegro after the
Treaty of Berlin

post 1878

Old Montenegro

Dalmatia

Danilovgrad

post 1878

Podgorica

Cetinje

Albania

Budva

Adriatic

Lake
Scutari

Bar post
1878

Scutari

Ulcinj

17

Assassinations, opposition, and the fight for independence

'For the first time in the history of the Eastern Question, the small states have acquired a position of such independence of the Great Powers that they feel able to act completely without them and even to take them in tow.'

A French diplomat in 1912[276]

While engaged in his disastrous war with the Prussians in 1870, Napoleon III had withdrawn his soldiers from Rome, thus leaving the way open for the Piedmontese army to march through the old gates of Porta Pia and take control of the city on 20 September 1870 – a day still celebrated there and in street names all around Italy. Without the support of the French, Pope Pius IX could do nothing other than retreat to the security of the Vatican, and, although threatening Victor Emmanuel II with excommunication, he

Archduke Franz Ferdinand and his wife just before their assassination in Sarajevo.

was unable to prevent the king's confiscation of the remainder of his lands. While it would not be until 1929 that a final resolution was found to the 'Rome Question', from this time on the former papal states were no more, and the Church territories that had once extended over the whole of central Italy were reduced to the Vatican alone. With the exception of the Trentino and the South Tyrol (Alto Adige), which were annexed in 1919 – both in the 1970s gaining their autonomy – the country was at last fully united, and the state capital was returned to its ancient home in Rome.

The second half of the 19th century had also been a period of much uncertainty for the countries of the eastern Adriatic, with perhaps a couple of exceptions. Although in 1868, a year after the founding of the Austrian-Hungarian dual monarchy, the Empire established the new autonomous Kingdom of Croatia-Slavonia, according to the terms of the Hungarian-Croatian Compromise, Budapest would still elect the governor and receive more than half of the region's taxes.[277] And in Cattaro the situation was not dissimilar. After a frequent change of ownership during the early years of the century, since the Paris Peace Congress of 1814 it had been under the Habsburgs, remaining as such until the fall of the dynasty in 1918.

Contrary to this, however, throughout the greater part of the 19th century there had been on-going instability in much of the rest of the Balkans, with Montenegro among those caught up in the uncertainty. Having reputedly taken its name from the great Mount Lovćen or *Crna Gora* (Black Mountain) overlooking the Bocche, like the neighbouring Cattaro, in medieval times this had been part of the Serbian empire. While by the early 1500s some parts of the region had fallen chiefly under the control of the prince-bishops, other areas had been occupied in 1496 by the Ottomans. Yet, despite the sultan maintaining his hold for nearly 400 years, Montenegro had established such good relations with the European powers that its leader Danilo, the sixth of his dynasty to rule, would visit Vienna and also St Petersburg. While his apparent purpose for going to the Russian capital had been to receive his religious appointment as *vladika*, when he returned home in 1852, it would be he – rather than an older brother – who became the new secular ruler, as the Prince of Montenegro. But, although his rise to power had come about largely because he had received the support of the Russian Emperor Nicholas I, Danilo would not return the favour to the tsar when the Crimean War broke out soon after. Having under his wife's influence become a Francophile, he did not want to take sides against the French. Therefore, despite having become engaged in his own war against the 'Turks', he continued for the whole period to maintain Montenegro's distance from the larger Russian conflict. So, when the European powers finally met to discuss peace in Paris, they ignored his wishes and refused to acknowledge his country's independence. Nevertheless, Danilo would achieve much of what he wanted just two years later in 1858, after he had won a major victory over the Ottomans and his brother Mirko had captured their impressive arsenal of weapons. With the borders now clearly delineated between Montenegro and the sultan's lands, the status quo was finally acknowledged by the other foreign heads of state. But even though the prince had begun taking steps to modernise his country, he had

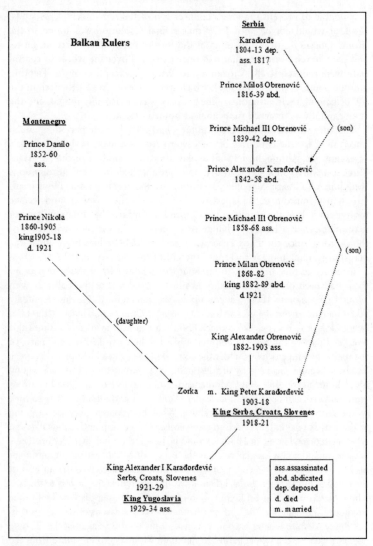

Balkan Rulers

Serbia

Karađorđe
1804-13 dep.
ass. 1817

Prince Miloš Obrenović
1816-39 abd.

Prince Michael III Obrenović
1839-42 dep.

(son)

Prince Alexander Karađorđević
1842-58 abd.

Montenegro

Prince Danilo
1852-60
ass.

Prince Nikola
1860-1905
king 1905-18
d. 1921

Prince Michael III Obrenović
1858-68 ass.

Prince Milan Obrenović
1868-82
king 1882-89 abd.
d. 1921

(son)

(daughter)

King Alexander Obrenović
1882-1903 ass.

Zorka   m. King Peter Karađorđević
1903-18
King Serbs, Croats, Slovenes
1918-21

King Alexander I Karađorđević
Serbs, Croats, Slovenes
1921-29
King Yugoslavia
1929-34 ass.

ass. assassinated
abd. abdicated
dep. deposed
d. died
m. married

grown unpopular at large, partly for having earlier deserted Russia, and partly for the cruel way he had set about enforcing his own authority. Therefore, besides having lost favour in certain quarters abroad, he had inspired particular hatred at home among the Bjelopavlici people, who were especially angered by the way he had rewarded their enemies. Having also lost the loyalty of the senate and his brother Mirko, plots had now begun to take shape to remove him. As a result, Danilo would be shot by an exiled Montenegrin while he was boarding a ship at Cattaro in August 1860, dying two days later.

Danilo was succeeded by his nephew, Mirko's son, Nikola Petrović-Njegoš, who, having grown up in Trieste with the family of his aunt, had later attended the famous Lycée Louis-le-grand in Paris. Here he had joined the United Serbian Youth, but after the organisation was banned by the Austro-Hungarians he had formed his own group, the Association for Serb Unification and Liberation. Nikola was still in Paris when his uncle was murdered, and so that same month, before the situation could get out of hand, he hurried home to Montenegro to become the ruling prince. On returning to Paris in 1867, he met Napoleon III, and the next year he was welcomed by Alexander II in Russia. As the tsar's wife, Empress Maria Alexandrovna, also took an interest in the visitor, in 1869 she founded a boarding school for girls in the Montenegrin capital Cetinje (Tsetinye), a move that was particularly significant at a time when the education of females in the country was considered of little importance. But Nikola's family would soon become more personally linked with the Russian imperial household. With the prince having enrolled his daughters at the famous Smolny Institute in St Petersburg, in time these would be introduced into the court and eventually Princess Militiza and Princess Anastasia (Stana) would marry three of the Romanovs who were particularly close to the emperor: Melitza married Grand Duke Peter Nikolaevich, and Stana, having divorced the cousin of Tsar Alexander II, became the second wife of Grand Duke Peter's brother – the famous, immensely tall, Russian commander-in-chief, Grand Duke Nicholas Nikolaevich. More significantly still, both women would over time become extremely close to the last imperial empress Alexandra, an unfortunate relationship that ultimately was to have a dramatic effect on later events. The two sisters exerted a negative influence on the tsaritsa, not just inspiring her interest in the mystical cults that were of interest to them, but also introducing her to the *strannik* Rasputin. As the troubled empress became more and more dependent on this extraordinary figure and the situation began to spiral out of control, the two so-called 'Black Duchesses' would earn the dislike of many at court. Even though they, too, would eventually be rejected by Alexandra when they began to question her excessive reliance on the holy man, these two women would be held largely responsible for having first encouraged her erratic behaviour. Yet, while they may have played a part in the tragedy that then unfolded, the sisters would ultimately escape the horrors of the Bolshevik revolution, both dying in exile abroad. And in a further twist, having fled the country with Nicholas Nikolaevich on the ship carrying the dowager empress Maria Feodorovna to safety, after the presumed death of the tsar and his family, Stana's husband would become one of the claimants to the Russian throne itself. Outliving him, she would die in Antibes in 1935, eleven years before one of her younger sisters, Elena, the wife of Victor Emmanuel III of Italy, was also exiled from her home.

During his time as ruler, the father of these women had brought beneficial changes to Montenegro, improving education, updating the roads, enlarging the army, and reforming the administration. Always eager to include Herzegovina within his own territory, in 1862 he had gone to war to support the country's rebels against their Ottoman overlords. Although Montenegro was for a time similarly overrun, in the final treaty, despite having to acknowledge his continuing vassal status, he still managed to hold on to his recently expanded borders. Having by now built up good relations with the major European powers, he was then able to maintain the peace until 1876, when he again took on the Ottomans. This time, having been more successful, the Montenegrins earned widespread admiration abroad, and therefore when the European leaders met two years later to redraw the map of the Balkans, Nikola would more than double his territories. Although the Treaty of Berlin had reduced the lands promised to him a few months earlier at San Stefano, besides receiving the towns of Podgorica, Ulcinj and nearby Antivari – now renamed Bar – he had at last fulfilled a Montenegrin ambition and gained access to the Adriatic.[278]

With the Congress of Berlin having recognised his country's independence, Nikola was now to become an honoured guest at the major courts of Europe, also visiting Queen Victoria in 1898. Despite introducing a constitution in 1905, he continued to hold sole power, and then five years later further increased his status by becoming the first king of Montenegro. Although in the meantime his relations with Austria-Hungary had again become more strained, following the assassination of the last of the Obrenović rulers across the border, he had drawn closer to the neighbouring Serbs.

In spite of Serbia not being an Adriatic country, over the hundred years before the First World War it had grown more and more linked to its western Balkan neighbours, and so its complicated and troubled story has to be included here. Its particularly turbulent 19th-century history had begun when the First Serb Uprising against the Ottomans had led to the rise of Karađorđe – 'Black George'. Yet, four years after being deposed, in 1817 this man was murdered in Austria, most probably killed by the agents of Miloš Obrenović, who had then personally bolstered his own position by sending the head of his rival as a token to the sultan. Now the acting ruler, in 1829 Miloš would be recognised as the hereditary prince. But the violence that had brought him to prominence did not end, and the unrest would persist for several years to come as his family continued to fight Karađorđe's descendants. During the time that they held power, the Obrenović family chiefly allied themselves to the Austrian-Hungarians, while their enemies chose to look towards Russia instead. Even so, 11 years after Alexander Karađorđević had at last been able to retake control in 1842, he – like the neighbouring Danilo of Montenegro – opted to remain neutral when the Crimean War broke out. Although at the time this did not directly affect Alexander's relationship with Russia, after the tsar had suffered his own major defeat, he would be little able to help when in 1858 the opposition forced the Serbian ruler to abdicate. With Alexander now exiled, the rival Obrenović family could return to power. But the bloodshed was not over and so, despite Prince Michael III Obrenović endeavouring to introduce a more enlightened rule, ten years later he, too, was murdered, his place then being taken by his 14-year-old cousin Milan Obrenović.

Like his Montenegrin neighbour, Milan had been sent to the Lycée Louis-le-grand in Paris and he, too, was abroad when he heard the news of his predecessor's assassination. While he would only take full control when he came of age in 1872, during his regency a constitution was introduced, and with the Karađorđević family now excluded, the Obrenović dynasty had again claimed its hereditary rights. Once he was fully in charge, Milan would soon become unpopular for his autocratic rule and his close links with Austria. And his problems were made still worse by his unsuccessful marriage to his second cousin Natalia Keshko, the daughter of a Moldavian colonel enrolled in the tsar's army. The couple soon proved to be incompatible, he being notoriously unfaithful and she keeping up her close ties with the less popular Russians.[279] Although after their separation they finally divorced in 1888, over the years to come they would continue competing for control of their son, repeatedly dragging him into their disputes.

Other, more serious, challenges would face Milan in 1876 when, a year after the Serbs' rebellion against the sultan in Bosnia- Herzegovina, he was pushed against his wishes into declaring war. Ultimately, however, his country was greatly to gain as in the treaties of 1878 the Ottomans had to acknowledge the loss of their lands, and Serbia, like Montenegro, finally achieved its independence. But, even though four years later Austria backed the official declaration of Milan as the Serbian king, he still faced opposition at home. While that same year he survived an assassination attempt in Belgrade, this would be just one attack among some other more questionable incidents that included an unexplained bomb, and the possibly intentional collapse of a privy floor that nearly resulted in his drowning in the cesspit below. Whatever was behind these incidents, Milan had generally lost favour as a result of his expensive programme of modernisation that had required the raising of higher taxes, and a greater demand for military service. Relations had also become more fraught with his Montenegrin neighbour, following the marriage in 1883 of another of Nikola's daughters, Zorka, to the exiled Peter, from the rival Karađorđević family.[280] Despite managing to put down a peasant uprising at home, two years later Milan found himself still more unpopular when Serbia became involved in an unsuccessful war with Bulgaria. Although in an effort to improve his reputation he introduced a more liberal constitution, just a couple of months later, in March 1889, he suddenly declared that he was abdicating and, now renouncing his nationality, he moved to Paris, leaving his 12-year-old son Alexander to take his place as the king of Serbia.

During the boy's regency, the Radical Party was able to adopt its more pro-Russian stance and in 1891 Alexander Obrenović personally paid a visit to the tsar. Yet, as the young king was impatient, two years later, before he had come of age, Alexander announced that he was ready to assume full power, and with that he then imprisoned the regents with whom he did not agree. Early the next year Milan broke the previous agreement and returned to help his son, and then, despite the Radical minister Nikola Pašić resigning in protest, he continued to encourage Alexander to follow an ever more reactionary path. Although he would have to leave the country briefly after falling out with his son, by 1897, Milan, in his new role as commander-in-chief, was initiating further reforms in the army. In the meantime, however, even though at the beginning of the year Austria-Hungary and Russia had met at St Petersburg, both sides coming together ostensibly in an effort to maintain the peace in the Balkans, the tsar had been privately attempting to strengthen his personal ties to the individual countries in the region. As he still suspected Milan of being responsible for the on-going tensions, and even of possibly of being an agent of the Austrians, Nicholas II viewed him warily. But, as Milan was equally unpopular on many fronts at home, on 6 July 1899 he would survive another unsuccessful attempt to assassinate him. Although his son responded by imprisoning the Radicals whom he believed to be implicated in this crime, soon after there would be a complete breakdown in his relations with his father. Choosing a moment when Milan was conveniently abroad in the process of arranging Alexander's betrothal, the king publicly announced that he intended to marry his mistress Draga Mašin. His father was appalled, but a few months later while he was still in Vienna, he died suddenly, aged 46.

The tsar had been much concerned by Milan's recent negotiations to arrange Alexander's engagement to the German princess of Schaumburg-Lippe, as he had feared that this match might upset Russia's own interests in the Balkans. Now, encouraged by Draga's pro-Russian leanings, Nicholas II would publicly voice his support for the marriage, even agreeing to act as best man by proxy at the wedding that took place in August. As by this time Alexander had become reliant on Romanov support, he agreed to offer an amnesty to those pro-Russian Radicals suspected of having been involved in the recently attempted assassination of his father.[281] But Milan had not been alone in disapproving of his son's choice of bride, and while the king's mother was equally opposed, the government went so far as to resign in protest. Apart from Draga being considered socially unsuitable as a former lady-in-waiting to her prospective mother-in-law, there were other reasons why she was viewed as unfit. A widow with an allegedly disreputable, promiscuous past, she was ten or twelve years older than her husband, and doubts over her ability to produce the necessary heir would be increased nine months later by her having a false pregnancy.

Although in 1901, in an effort to increase his popularity, Alexander had presented his own liberal constitution, introducing a two-house system of government, this had not stopped him from losing favour at home. And soon he was facing comparable problems in his dealings with those abroad. Because the risk of a closer Serbian alliance with the Habsburg emperor had diminished following the death of his more pro-Austrian father, his relations with the Russians had also begun to cool. Wishing to ease tensions in his foreign affairs, the tsar was now planning to reduce his involvement in Serbian matters and he had therefore taken a decision – one that was later to prove fatal to the royal couple – to cut down on the protection that he had been giving them. Besides Nicholas II wishing to avoid complicating unnecessarily the delicate international situation, several members of the imperial Russian court were reluctant to have anything to do with the allegedly disreputable queen, the two Black Duchesses being strongly opposed to meeting her. So, despite Nikola of Montenegro and Prince Ferdinand of Bulgaria having already received an invitation, to Alexander's profound displeasure, in 1902 his promised visit to St Petersburg was repeatedly postponed. As this delay had continued, he had begun to make approaches to Vienna, a move that was unpopular with many Serbs, who had always disliked the closeness of the Obrenović family to Austria-Hungary.

In addition to the dislike felt for the queen, there was now growing opposition to Alexander himself. His reputation was not helped when in April 1903 he temporarily suspended the constitution for just long enough for him to be able to enact his own measures and install his personally chosen candidates in positions of authority. Further argument was also now developing over the nomination of the couple's heir, since as yet no child had been born. Even as some suggested the position should be given to a distant relation – namely Nikola's son, Prince Mirko of Montenegro – the king's own choice appeared to be his wife's arrogant and unappealing brother. For all these reasons, therefore, a conspiracy to rid Serbia of its king had begun to take shape, Draga's own former brother-in-law being among the various plotters. After two failed attempts, in the early hours of 11 June 1903 the conspirators were successful when, at the end of some two hours of searching the palace, they discovered Alexander and Draga hiding in a wardrobe in their bedroom. After the couple had been shot multiple times, their abused and butchered bodies were thrown from the upper floor windows onto a manure heap below. With the king having no brothers or sons, this slaughter brought the Obrenović line to an end, but even so the assassins were not content. Wanting to ensure that no surviving claimants or supporters remained, the prime minister and a senior army general were among those now killed, and two of the queen's brothers were later shot by a firing squad. Four days after this atrocity, dubbed the May Overthrow, the exiled Karađorđević family was called back to power by parliament, and the son of the earlier deposed Prince Alexander was declared to be the new ruler, Peter I.

Having gone into exile abroad with his father, Peter had been educated in Geneva, Paris, and later Metz, and here he had picked up many of the liberal ideas that later he would try to adopt in his own country. Besides being briefly taken prisoner during France's war with the Prussians, Peter had fought on the side of the Bosnians in their war with the Ottomans. He had been seriously threatened by Milan Obrenović and the Austro-Hungarians, who had pronounced a death sentence on him in absentia. Much to their concern, in 1883, six years before the weddings of the Black Duchesses in Russia, Peter had gone to Montenegro for his own marriage to the ruler's oldest daughter, Princess Zorka. This was a particular threat to the Obrenović family, who were aware that King Nikola and his son-in-law had for a time been actually considering how to bring about their overthrow. Then, adding yet another layer of complexity to the international situation, in March 1890 the new young Kaiser dismissed his chancellor Bismarck, the man who up to this moment had been chiefly responsible for maintaining the dialogue between the three great central European empires. But of more significance to Peter personally, that same month, his young wife Zorka died in childbirth, and so in 1894 he decided to leave Cetinje and move to Geneva. He was still there five years later when he received an invitation from the tsar for his two surviving sons to go and be educated in St Petersburg.

* * *

Although the Habsburgs still ruled over Austria-Hungary, by the end of the 19th century the virtually uninterrupted hold on power that the family had enjoyed for generations was being increasingly challenged. In particular, its involvement in the political uncertainties of the Balkan region were adding to the difficulties confronting the elderly Franz Josef, who would mark his seventieth birthday in August 1900. But Italy, too, was facing serious instability, as a month earlier, King Umberto I had been murdered in Monza.[282] While he had never been on good terms with his father, soon after coming to the throne in 1878 he had also lost favour with his people, so ten months after his succession a first attempt was made on his life. Four years later, Umberto had become even more unpopular by his decision to join the Triple Alliance with Germany and Italy's age-old enemy Austria-Hungary. But although he was now trying to raise his standing by increasing military spending, he had done little to address the problems of poverty and the poor education that still existed in the south. A badly read and unintellectual man himself, Umberto gave these matters little thought, preferring to protect his own position by not antagonising the local criminal organisations. Thus the Mafia, Camorra, and other such bands were allowed to remain in control in the Mezzogiorno. Nevertheless, in a further move intended to raise the status of his country, the king had then set out to increase his colonial territories overseas. But, by taking possession of Eritrea and Somalia, his imperial aspirations would only ultimately succeed in dragging his country into new conflicts abroad, and, with his army suffering a humbling defeat in Abyssinia (Ethiopia) in March 1896, the next year a second unsuccessful attempt had been made on his life. Despite Umberto once more surviving the attack, his enemies were soon plotting again, now spurred into further action after the disastrous and bloody events that took place in May 1898. With two thousand demonstrators taking to the streets in Bari in protest at the rising bread prices, and the rioters then destroying the police station and customs house, further unrest would soon be erupting in several other towns across the kingdom. But the situation grew even more serious when the workers in Milan came out on strike. Here things soon escalated and as the violence took hold in the main piazza, before long scores – if not hundreds – of demonstrators had been killed or wounded. Because Umberto soon approved the draconian measures of the authorities who would not only imprison 1,500 of the protesters, but also tighten the laws and restrict the freedom of the press, his opposition was spurred once more into action. With the plotters eventually succeeding on 29 July 1900 in assassinating the king, his throne then passed to his son Victor Emmanuel III.

Like the Italians, the Serbians soon replaced their murdered king, the coronation of Peter Karađorđević being celebrated in Belgrade in September 1904. He had been shocked by the bloody circumstances of Alexander and Draga's deaths, but, although not personally involved in the couple's assassination, he had been aware that there were plans afoot for him to supplant the king. Yet, while many Serbs now welcomed Peter, believing that he might achieve union among the Slavs, some of the army mutinied in protest at their colleagues' slaughter of Alexander. Abroad there were similar reservations, particularly as Peter's tenuous position made him unwilling to punish the perpetrators. Appalled by the brutality of the recent assassination and questioning whether the new king had played a role in it, the British and Dutch maintained a boycott. Others (including Franz Josef and the Russian tsar), not only delayed in recognising his accession, but also openly expressed their disgust. While for their part, the Austrian-Hungarians were particularly concerned to have lost the influence they had earlier had with the Obrenović rulers, within three years they were to become involved in a serious dispute with the Serbs over another matter. Wishing to avoid the former Austrian trade sanctions and dues, Peter discovered an alternative outlet for the large quantity of his country's pork, and, although the resulting 'Pig War' would eventually resolve itself within a couple of years, by that time the situation in the Balkans had become even more uncertain.

As in early summer of 1908 the Young Turk movement had begun threatening to overturn the Ottoman government, on 5 October Emperor Franz Josef had decided to go ahead and complete his annexation of Bosnia and Herzegovina. While at the Congress of Berlin thirty years before there had been consensus over the redrawing of the borders of the Balkan countries, among the terms there had been one dubious clause that was all too likely to give rise to later argument. This stated that Bosnia and Herzegovina, although remaining under Ottoman possession, should be occupied and administered by the Austrian-Hungarians. The official statement declared:

> In order to assure the maintenance of the new political state of affairs, as well as freedom and security of communications, Austria-Hungary reserves the right of keeping garrisons and having military and commercial roads in the whole of this part of the ancient vilayet of Bosnia.[283]

The Emperor had become fearful that the calls for reform might lead to greater demands for democracy and independence in Bosnia, something that could ultimately lead to the piecemeal break up of his empire. Although at the time the Foreign Minister, Count Andrássy, had hinted that this agreement was to be only provisional, in reality it was a decision that would add to the complex layers of political tension that eventually erupted so disastrously in the next century. For a while the Croats were delighted by the annexation, hoping, as it proved fruitlessly, that they and the Bosnian Muslims might at last be united, soon an international crisis threatened to break out. In February 1909, in return for financial compensation and the removal of the Austro-Hungarian garrisons, the Ottomans accepted the new situation. The next month Russia reluctantly did the same, the tsar being in no position to take a stronger stance since he was still suffering the effects of his disastrous Japanese war. As this episode in Bosnia had hardened Nicholas II's resolve to oppose any similar repetition in the future, one more element had been put in place in the build-up to the Great War that was to erupt five years later. Meanwhile the Serbs had initially been equally opposed to the Habsburg Emperor's actions, but they too had eventually come round to accepting the status quo – after which Montenegro had followed suit.

While the Balkan situation was now relatively settled, events elsewhere were still moving on apace, with the Ottoman empire increasingly coming under attack. In 1911 Italy would find an excuse to claim Libya and take it from the sultan, and in Albania, two years after a previous rebellion, in 1912 there would be further trouble when those loyal to the old regime took up arms against the Young Turks. With the sultan being tied up by these affairs, in October Nikola of Montenegro used the opportunity to cross the Albanian border. Although the country had been under Ottoman rule ever since 1479, after its partitioning at the Congress of Berlin part of Albania's territory had been ceded to Montenegro, and the king now wanted to add to his possessions in the country. Before long, Serbia and Greece, both members of the Balkan League that he had recently joined, mounted their own attacks elsewhere in the region and thus the First Balkan War had now begun. Soon joined by Serbian troops, Nikola started a six-month-long siege of Scutari (Shkodra), a city with particular significance as until the famous battle of Kosovo of 1389 it had been the Serbian capital. With its people dying in their thousands under the heavy assault, a month after the start of the war the Albanians declared their independence. As the brutal conflict continued, a group of ambassadors representing Austria-Hungary, Russia, Italy, Germany, France, and Britain met in London to try and find a way to end the bloodshed. At last, early the next year the Serbs agreed to leave their colleagues and withdraw from Scutari, but although an international naval blockade had been placed on all the coastal ports occupied by the Montenegrins, after the end of the siege it would still take another three months before a resolution to the crisis was finally reached in July 1913.

Besides being determined to prevent the Serbians extending their borders to the Adriatic, the Austrian-Hungarians were against any reduction in the size of Albania, and they particularly wanted the more Catholic Scutari to remain within the county. Therefore, much to the displeasure of Nikola, who at the cost of some 6,000 of his men had finally taken the place and declared it to be his capital, the Montenegrins were instructed to surrender the town. With little concern for the local population, who with the realignment of the borders would find themselves living on foreign soil, the ambassadors awarded over half of the country to Montenegro, Serbia and Greece. In compensation for its losses, however, the new Albania was declared a principality, and the immensely ambitious Essad Pasha Toptani, the head of the self-acclaimed Republic of Central Albania based in Durazzo (Durrës) was persuaded to surrender his control. He then agreed to serve as a minister for a time in the government of the newly elected Prussian-born Wilhelm of Wied. Yet, despite the people receiving this German prince as their king, his reign in the country would be short-lived. Having already had to negotiate a revolution and rebellion, seven months after first agreeing to accept the throne, in September 1914 Wilhelm was forced to flee abroad. Even though he would later return to service in the German army, he still felt bound at this time to honour the Albanian neutrality he had earlier sworn to uphold, and so, refusing to join the Austrian-Hungarians in the Great War that had just begun, he chose exile in Venice instead.

Although the First Balkan War had come to an end in May 1913 with the sultan's defeat, the Bulgarians had soon become dissatisfied with their personal gains, and a month later they began a second war against their former allies in the Balkan League. As this resulted just six weeks later in its defeat, Bulgaria had to accept the new borders and the virtual doubling of Serbia's territory. But of greater significance to the entire region, these two conflicts finally brought the power of the Ottoman empire in Europe to an end. Serbia, among others, celebrated this success, but by June the next year its ageing king was so exhausted that he decided to hand his authority over to his son, Alexander, who was now to act as his regent. Fondly known by his people as the Old King and the Liberator, Peter had brought a golden age to Serbia, introducing a variety of liberal measures to help improve and modernise his country. By strengthening Serbia's ties with France and Russia, he had increased his popularity among his people, many of whom had hated the Obrenović dependency on Austria-Hungary. Ironically, however, this same policy added to that complex mixture of alliances that was ultimately to lead to the horrors of the First World War. The build-up to the global disaster had begun.

The same month as Peter's abdication, Emperor Franz Josef's nephew Archduke Franz Ferdinand, the Inspector General of the Armed Forces since 1913, was sent to represent his uncle at a military inspection in Bosnia. The archduke, the recognised heir to the imperial throne since the death of his father 18 years before, was to be accompanied on this occasion by his morganatic wife, Sophie, a former lady-in-waiting who had later been given the title of the Duchess of Hohenberg. Although from a Bohemian aristocratic family, she had been considered unsuitable as a Habsburg bride, but in 1900 she had finally been allowed to marry Franz Ferdinand on the condition that she was given no imperial title or status, and that their children would never be heirs to the throne. The archduke was devoted to Sophie and eager for her to receive public recognition, something which on this occasion she would be given since she was allowed officially to accompany her husband on the military inspection. As she had previously told her son, she was already concerned for Franz Ferdinand's safety, and so she had personally chosen to be with him. Initially the visit went well, and, after they had inspected the military manoeuvres, the couple arrived by train at Sarajevo. Since the Austro-Hungarian annexation in 1908 this Bosnian city had been developed and modernised, but the programme for better education and communication had allowed the increased infiltration of Serbian nationalism. In this traditional land, where the Habsburg Empire had still not abolished all feudalism among the peasantry, feelings had grown among the local people against the occupiers. Here, concentrating on schemes that were chiefly beneficial to the Austrians, the Habsburgs had continued to run the country in much the same way as the Ottomans had before them. At the same time, the autocratic Hungarians, who tended to be disparaging of the Balkan people, had refused to countenance the growing movement towards a union of the southern Slavs. In 1873, Count Andrássy, for one, had described them as 'wild Indians who could only be treated like unbroken horses, to whom corn should be offered with one hand while they are threatened with a whip in the other.'[284] Against this background, over time separatist organisations had begun to form. As a result, in the few years immediately before the archduke's visit there had been several assassination attempts against senior officials in both Croatia and Bosnia-Herzegovina. Among these had been the unsuccessful attack on the Bosnian governor that had resulted in the suicide of the plotter, Bogdan Žerajić, a man who had subsequently become a major inspiration to Gavrilo Princip, Franz Ferdinand's eventual murderer.

The archduke had never been popular with his uncle Franz Josef. Quick-tempered and rather lacking in charisma, Franz Ferdinand is often remembered for his unfettered passion for shooting and big-game hunting. Yet he was not unintelligent and, tending to be more liberal in his views, was considering how he might bring reform to the Balkans once he was Emperor. Having long been aware of the unfair treatment meted out to the Slavs, especially by the Hungarians, whom he particularly did not like, he was now apparently thinking about establishing a third Slavic kingdom within an imperial federation. While such ideas were strongly opposed by his uncle, ironically they were also unpopular among those who wanted full independence.

Among those most bitterly opposed to the Austrian-Hungarians was Dragutin Dimitrijević, popularly dubbed 'Apis', a man who had previously taken part in the brutal assassination of Alexander Obrenović and Draga.[285] On that occasion he had been seriously wounded when shot three times, but having later been pardoned by King Peter, in 1911 he had founded his own terrorist organisation, Unification or Death, also to be known as 'The Black Hand'. Two years after a plan to assassinate Franz Josef had failed, Apis began to consider the Emperor's nephew as an alternative target. Although by this time he was head of Serbia's Military Intelligence, Apis was acting independently of the government, and according to his later claim, he was personally responsible for ordering the assassination to go ahead. Before long he had started to support the small group of anarchists known as Young Bosnia, a gathering of students and young labourers, who came chiefly from the non-affluent or working classes. Three of its members, including Gavrilo Princip, had previously moved to find employment in Serbia, and it was here that they had begun their training in the techniques that were needed to carry out the assassination. However, when they were at last ready to go home and join the rest of their group, the Serbian caretaker prime minister Pašić got wind that something was afoot. Fearful that any plot would result in war breaking out with Austria-Hungary, he attempted to stop the men from returning to Bosnia, but his instructions were not followed and the trio was successfully smuggled back over the border to Sarajevo. Here, having been joined by three more local young men, they would be guided by the slightly older Bosnian, Danilo Ilić. As the final plans began to come together, Ilić and Apis appeared to have had doubts and they may even have tried to abort the whole affair, but it was too late. The event had now gained further meaning for the conspirators by the fact that it was due to take place on 28 June, which, according to the Julian calendar, was the Orthodox feast of St Vitus or Vidovdan, the same date as that great 14th-century battle of Kosovo that was so important to the Slavs.

When at last the day came, and the convoy of cars was finally on its way to the town hall for the imperial couple's official welcome, the first two assassins lost their nerve and failed to act. Although the third, Nedeljko Čabrinović, threw his bomb and wounded around twenty people, it missed its intended target by bouncing off the folded roof of the car that had been purposely opened to allow the archduke and his wife to be seen. Unhurt, although badly shaken, the couple were then driven at speed to the town hall, travelling too fast for the remaining three attackers placed along the route to be able to act. Having been calmed down by his wife, the furious Franz Ferdinand continued with his speech to the mayor and the other dignitaries, after which a change of programme was quickly devised enabling the imperial guests to go directly to the hospital to see those who had been wounded in the earlier attack. This alteration in the plans was not, however, passed on to the drivers of the cars, and so on their way back the front of the convoy mistakenly turned right just by the Latin Bridge. By a stroke of extreme bad fortune, when the archduke's chauffeur stopped to reverse out of the road, Princip had already moved to a new position nearby, and making the most of his opportunity he stepped forward and shot the couple at point blank range. Sophie died before reaching the governor's official residence, her husband soon after, having in his last moments begged her not to die for the sake of their children.

After their coffins had been ceremoniously processed through the streets of Sarajevo, the couple were returned by ship to Trieste, and then transported by train to Vienna, where many turned out to pay their respects. Yet, because of their morganatic marriage, in a last petty, unfeeling gesture they were given no official salute, and their funeral on 3 July was small and private, all foreign representatives and even their young children being kept away. In defiance of this, however, numbers of aristocrats chose to walk behind the coffins as they were taken to the station on their way to their final interment. This would take place in the archduke's private Artstetten castle near Melk, some hundred kilometres distant from the usual family crypt in Vienna. While Franz Josef's first response had been one of horror, and his youngest daughter Valerie had found him shaken by the news and much concerned for 'the poor children', he had shown considerably less feeling for the murdered couple themselves. Always disapproving of his nephew's marriage, and having grave doubts about his politics, the Emperor – a stickler for what he saw as his duty – had reportedly then said that the archduke's death had given him 'a relief from a great worry'.[286]

While the assassination may have been relatively welcome for the Emperor, the immediate aftermath would be disastrous for the Serbs living in the Austro-Hungarian Empire. They now came under attack and in the subsequent pogroms many would have their houses and businesses destroyed. Even though there was no clear evidence that the Serbian government itself had been involved in the murder of his nephew, and regardless of whether the prime minister had known or perhaps tried to warn Vienna of the attack – something that he now denied – Franz Josef was nevertheless determined to make Serbia pay fully for what had happened. All but one of the conspirators were captured in Bosnia and, after their trial in Sarajevo in October, three (including Danilo Ilić) were hanged. While the three companions who had travelled from Belgrade escaped execution on grounds of their youth, before the end of the war – which they had now set in train – both Princip and his colleague Čabrinović would die of tuberculosis while serving their twenty-year prison sentences.

Holding the Serbs responsible for the assassination, on 23 July Franz Josef sent Belgrade an ultimatum. Even though this contained a number of stringent demands, he insisted on having an answer within two days. Most of his government had favoured making the conditions so severe as to be unacceptable, since a refusal would give the Empire an excuse to declare war and finally deal with its 'Serb problem' for good and all. The answer the Emperor received was not, however, as expected. Wanting to calm the fast developing situation, Pašić appeared to accept all the terms, with the exception of just two more minor clauses that allowed the Austrian police to carry out investigations on Serbian soil. The British Foreign Secretary, who had been struck by the 'formidable' nature of the ultimatum, suggested that the reply was 'satisfactory', while the Kaiser, having changed his mind, also declared it to be fair. The earlier German offer of a 'blank cheque' promising support to the Austrian-Hungarians was no longer on the table, since Kaiser Wilhelm's preferred short, localised war had already ceased to be an option. Franz Josef, however, was intractable. Pronouncing the response as inadequate, he rejected further discussion and, having declared war on Serbia on 28 July, he mounted a first attack on Belgrade the next day. As he had determinedly refused all further negotiation, he lost much of the sympathy initially felt for him abroad in the immediate aftermath of the archduke's assassination, and now in many people's eyes Austria-Hungary was the aggressor. The Emperor's decision to go to war was disastrous, not just for the Empire that he had served for so long, but also for the world. While during the month immediately after Sarajevo Franz Josef had havered over what to do, the other powers had begun mobilising their armies. Therefore, by late July, what might have been a comparatively small regional affair was about to escalate into a global conflict. As the tsar was determined to avoid a similar loss of face to that of 1908 with the Austrian-Hungarians, he had soon announced his backing of the Serbs, while Franz Josef and his Croatian subjects were still depending on the Empire's long-standing alliance with Germany. Thus, as these and various other earlier agreements came into play, within a week of the Emperor's declaration all the major powers had become involved in the war. With Montenegro having been the first to proclaim its readiness to join the conflict, just nine days after announcing its support of the Serbians, on 8 August its artillery batteries would begin firing from Mount Lovćen on to the Austro-Hungarian naval base situated at Cattaro below.[287]

In the days and weeks after the archduke's murder, while the imperial soldiers were committing appalling atrocities against those Serbs living in the Empire, in Bosnia-Herzegovina thousands more were being arrested and expelled on the orders of Oskar Potiorek, the local governor. He had been in the same car as the archduke and his wife at the time of the assassination, and, according to Princip's own statement, had been the assassin's other intended target rather than the duchess. Having little love, therefore, for the Serbs, Potiorek would continue with his punitive regime after he was put in military command on 12 August. In this role, however, he soon proved to be ineffective, and following two humiliating defeats at the hands of the smaller, poorly equipped but experienced enemy, he was dismissed. But, after these initial successes, in October 1915 the tables began to turn for the Serbs, who would now come under the combined attack of the Austrian-Hungarians, Germans, and Bulgarians. By the following month, the army and some civilians were in flight, and their country had been taken over and divided up between the Empire and Bulgaria.

* * *

Although the Italians had joined the defensive Triple Alliance in 1882, having never been consulted by the Emperor before his declaration of war on Serbia, Italy initially remained uninvolved in the fighting. Having eventually decided in March 1915 to approach the British, French and Russian Triple Entente, on 26 April 1915 the Entente responded with the secret Treaty of London. The Italians were now promised that in return for their participation on the allied side in the conflict they would receive all of Dalmatia when the war was over. The offer came only ten days after Austria had turned down Italy's proposal that in exchange for maintaining its neutrality, it would regain its historical lands in the Trentino, Gorizia, Dalmatia, and Albania. This humiliating rejection, together with the widespread pro-war movement that had taken hold in Italy, finally persuaded those in government who were against military involvement to step aside. With numerous demonstrations now calling for the ending of neutrality, on 23 May the country declared war. Immediately, the next day the Austro-Hungarian fleet responded by bombing Ancona and Manfredonia, and within the month the Italians had become fully engaged in the action that was to bring them such hardship over the next three years.

Meanwhile, despite its neutrality, the ill-defined region of Albania had become an area of particular significance to the other nations, who were now seeking to keep this strategically located and recently divided country within their own spheres of interest. With the Serbs and Montenegrins still occupying the north and the Greeks having taken control of the southern autonomous Republic of Northern Epirus, not wanting to be left out of the land-grab the

Italians had decided to make a move in the same direction. So, ambitious to secure the Strait of Otranto and keep the Greeks at bay, in October 1914, even before entering the war, they took the coastal island of Sazan, and then two months later the nearby Valona (Vlorë). Yet, with the Serbs, Montenegrins and Italians being driven from the region the next year, by early 1916 the Austrian-Hungarians had occupied most of central and northern Albania and Kosovo. But, within a few months, the pendulum had swung back again. So by the autumn the Italians had regained control of the south of the country, and in December the French had established an autonomous Albanian Republic around Korçë to the east. While early the next year the Austrian-Hungarians

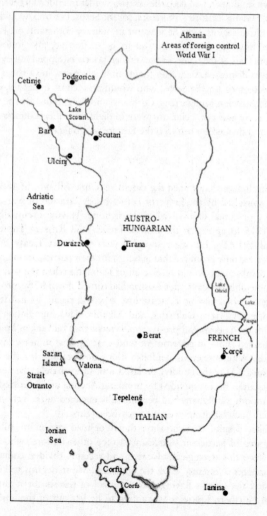

responded by proclaiming the north to be an independent Albanian state under their protection, the southern region was declared a protectorate of the Italians, who, after two weeks of heavy bombardment, would recapture Durazzo (Durrës) on 16 October 1918. This success was followed by others, with Tirana, Scutari, and the former Montenegrin towns of Ulcinj and Bar all falling to the Italians, and so when at last the Armistice was agreed in December, even though some territory remained in the hands of the Serbs, French and Greeks, Italy held the bulk of the Albanian region.

Throughout this time, the Italians had been most engaged in the area of Lombardy-Venetia. Having primarily joined the war to regain the Italian-speaking areas that they saw as rightfully their own, just a month after entering the conflict in June 1915 they had begun a series of assaults in the regions close to the Austrian front around the River Isonzo near Gorizia and Trieste. Here, in difficult physical conditions, over the coming months they would have their share of success, but in reality little if anything was achieved of lasting effect and even though Italy's losses would ultimately be the greater, during the protracted campaign both sides were to suffer serious casualties. When in early 1916 Milan came under bombardment, the fighting continued to the east, and five more battles would take place that same year. Even the death of old Franz Josef on 21 November brought little change to the course of the war. Although his successor, his great-nephew Charles, sought to end the fighting by secretly trying to negotiate an agreement with the French and the British, his attempts ultimately failed, chiefly because a consensus could not be reached over the on-going matter of the Italian irredentist claims. The following year, despite repeated violence in Milan, the tenth battle of Isonzo would marginally favour the Italians, but then the scene began to change as the revolution and military collapse in Russia enabled the Central Powers to begin concentrating their forces elsewhere. By this time the Habsburg Empire was nervous for its own preservation, and so, having called for some backup from the Germans, it was now determined to achieve a final defeat of its Italian enemy.

On 24 October 1917 the Austrian-Hungarians and their German allies began their massive assault on the long Italian north-eastern front. This, the Twelfth Battle of the Isonzo, lasted for nearly four weeks and would eventually spread over a wide region. It began in the lightly defended central section a few miles from the front near Caporetto (today Kobarid in Slovenia), a border town on the river's west bank whose name would become infamous for the disastrous rout that followed. Already exhausted having just achieved a hard-won victory in the 11th battle, the Italian defenders would now find themselves paying the price for their senior commanders' mistakes. In addition to the latter's inadequate preparations and failure to provide good intelligence, poor instructions had been given to the guards who had been ordered to defend at all costs the mountain-top fortifications just across the river. This had left the valleys below free for the enemy to pass unchallenged. As the men stationed back at Caporetto attempted to keep up their defence, without any warning they were quickly surrounded by the Germans who, having crossed lower down the river, now approached unseen

Northern Italian Rivers

from the south. The weather was appalling, the fog and freezing rain adding to the general confusion, and before long the roads were choked with those trying to escape the slaughter. As a result of a mistaken order, the Italians had now blown up the nearby Eiffel bridge, thus leaving many of their colleagues trapped on the other side of the river. Lacking clear leadership and poorly equipped, there was little the outnumbered defenders could do and, by the end of the day, some 20,000 men had been taken prisoner and the rest of the worn-down and dispirited troops had begun to retreat. During the long withdrawal some 300,000 of the mainly inexperienced or irregular soldiers would disappear, having already become demoralised by the harsh discipline of the Chief of General Staff, Cadorna. However, after making a first attempt to establish a new front along the banks of the Tagliamento, the remaining survivors withdrew to the River Piave where they arrived at last on 9 November. Having abandoned the extensive lands in the Friuli region for which they had fought so long, they were now over a hundred kilometres west of their former front, and their new line of defence was within striking distance of Venice and Treviso. Meanwhile, Cadorna, having abandoned his headquarters at Udine four days after the defeat at Caporetto, had already been dismissed.

The German and Austro-Hungarian success had, however, come at a price. Since their armies had over-stretched their supply lines, over the following weeks they, too, began to suffer. Despite the food, wine and other provisions they seized along the way, the now poorly nourished troops were reaching the point of exhaustion. As a result, the situation soon returned to its previous stalemate. But while for the Austrian-Hungarians and Germans the victory had come at a great cost, having resulted in tens of thousands of casualties, for the Italians the catastrophic defeat had caused a far greater shock to both the troops and the population at large. As the situation had been made worse by the vast numbers of the starving displaced local people – estimates suggesting that between some 400,000 and 600,000 had been forced to leave their homes – Caporetto would be a humiliation felt by the country for years to come. Despite the documented instances of individual courage, and the resistance shown by the soldiers at the Piave and in the later fighting in the Trentino, those responsible for the disaster tried to shift the blame by spreading false or exaggerated accounts of the troops' undisciplined behaviour. In this way those in command undermined their own national identity, their remarks making Caporetto a cruel and unfair metaphor for the poor character and ability of the Italian soldier, who was soon to become the subject of ridicule abroad. In spite of the damage done to their own reputation, in order to serve their own purposes, those seeking power in Italy repeated the negative reports and used the catastrophe as a way to attack their opposition. Thus, in their hands, during the difficult inter-war years to come, the disaster became a political weapon in the domestic propaganda campaigns of those wishing to overturn the status quo.

Although all the parties were now exhausted and battle-weary, when the fighting was renewed the following June the situation for the Italians began to improve. At last, exactly a year after their terrible defeat at Caporetto, with the partial help of their British and French allies, they achieved a major victory at Vittorio Veneto. Begun on 24 October to the north of Treviso, and then taking place across a wide area of the Trentino region, this did not end until early November, by which time the old Austro-Hungarian Empire had reached the point of collapse. For some time there had been growing frustration among its demoralised people, and early in the year strikes had taken place at the Istrian port of Pola. Soon after [,] in February, a mutiny broke out at the important naval base at Cattaro, where for three days the red flag had continued to fly until the uprising was suppressed, at which point, four sailors were court-martialled and executed. Yet, the dissension continued elsewhere, coming to a head even as the battle of Vittorio Veneto was still raging. The Czechs and the South Slavs now finally demanded to leave the Empire, and just days after Croatia had been declared a third imperial kingdom, on 29 October 1918, it renounced this position and joined its neighbours in the new state of Serbs, Croats, and Slovenes. More significantly still, on the 31st the Dual Monarchy came to an end with the Hungarians announcing their departure. The allies were now pushing steadily into Macedonia, and, with Serbia, Montenegro and Albania looking towards their liberation, when the battle at Vittorio Veneto came at last to an end, the defeated Austrians called for a halt to the fighting and an armistice was signed at Villa Giusti near Padua on 3 November. The old Habsburg Empire was on its knees, so when eight days later Germany also surrendered, Emperor Charles officially renounced all his 'participation in the administration of the State'. Yet, as he believed he could still keep his throne, he intentionally avoided the word abdication and remained in the country until March. At that point the British, who wanted to avoid a repeat of their earlier failure (with the Romanovs) to intervene, took him into exile on Madeira, and a month later the Austrian parliament finally banished the Habsburgs from the country.

While during the war King Peter of Serbia had played a less visible role, he had still on occasion sought to inspire his troops, never more so than during the Great Retreat. In the depth of winter at the end of 1915, as his army and thousands of other citizens were forced to withdraw through Montenegro and Albania, this elderly man, who was so sick that he had to be carried on a litter, had continued to encourage his people as they made their way through the mountainous terrain to the sea. Over half of the refugees died on the route, estimates suggesting that during the march around 160,000 civilians and nearly 80,000 military personnel would succumb to the bitter cold, disease, aerial bombardment, and other attack. Remembering the atrocities they had suffered at the hands of the Serbs and Montenegrins during the Balkan Wars, some Albanians would use this opportunity to take their revenge, but eventually the king and the other exhausted and starving survivors reached the coast. At last, from Valona, Durazzo, and San Giovanni di Medua (Shëngjin) to the north, they and their several thousand Austro-Hungarian prisoners – many now suffering from cholera – would be taken to safety by the allies who had belatedly come to their aid. During the vast, chaotic evacuation to the Ionian Islands and elsewhere, many would die, some being lost to attack while waiting at the ports, others during their transit at sea, but by the end of February the exodus was largely complete. According to an official British document, only some 16,000 horses and the 10,000 men who looked after them had been left behind. Peter was now safe on Corfu, and from here until the last months of the war he would continue to head his exiled Serbian government. During this time his prime minister Pašić tried to improve the country's reputation abroad by getting rid of the Black Hand, and in September 1916 he ordered the arrest of Apis. Despite this man's recent promotion, he was now accused – on what was apparently false evidence – of having attempted to murder the regent, Prince Alexander. Although he would be posthumously exonerated in 1953, at his trial in June, Apis and two others were found guilty of treason and executed by the firing squad. As for Peter, a year after being given the new title of King of the Serbs, Croats and Slovenes, in 1919 he returned to Belgrade, where he was to die two years later.

After the Serbian defeat in 1915, the dangers had increased for Montenegro. Even though King Nikola had protected the Serbs' retreat during the Orthodox Christmas when he had taken on and defeated the larger army of the Dual Monarchy at Mojkovac, by then his country had been invaded and was facing serious difficulties. With allied shipping being constantly threatened by the German submarines that were patrolling the Adriatic, aid coming from Brindisi was being interrupted. Similarly, French supplies were being prevented by the imperial naval blockade from reaching Bar. But the situation was about to become still worse as, just days after its recent defeat, the enemy succeeded in taking both Mount Lovćen and Cetinje, and these latest disasters would then finally persuade the king to try and make peace. However, with the Austrian-Hungarians demanding that Montenegro surrender all the lands that they now held, Nikola found the terms too harsh, and so, after refusing to sign, on 19 January he fled to Italy. From there, he urged his people to keep up their resistance, encouraging them to try and join the Serbian exiles in Corfu, but within days the commander-in-chief, who had been left behind to deal with the problems on his own, decided that he had no option other than to agree to the armistice that the king had earlier rejected. With the remains of the army laying down its arms, on 25 January 1916 Montenegro dropped out of the war.

Regardless of this, for the next two years as he directed his government-in-exile from France, Nikola tried to continue negotiating with the European powers, his aim being not just to ensure the future independence of Montenegro but also the expansion of its territory. Despite the important role his army had played early on in the war, he had now lost respect by abandoning his country and leaving his troops without clear instructions or leadership. Besides being accused of having deserted his allies and attempting to make peace with the Habsburg Emperor, many had long been suspicious of his ambitions to extend his territories at their expense, the Serbs in particular being wary of his desire to become the overall leader of the Slavs. For these various reasons Nikola was no longer trusted both at home and abroad. Therefore, in November 1918 at Podgorica he was deposed by the National Assembly and within a month Montenegro had been united with Serbia. The Serbian minister in London had for some time seen the writing on the wall, having neatly summed up the situation the previous April: 'Since 1904 the old skilful King has lost the rudder of his ship which he "skilfully" steered from 1860 onwards. Since then his ship has drifted without a rudder, without a mast. It has not been entirely wracked as yet, but the end is near.'[288]

As a result of his mistakes, Nikola had lost out to the very neighbour for whose cause he had joined the war, and from now on his country was to be part of the new Kingdom of Serbs, Croats and Slovenes. Having grown out of the declaration signed by Pašić and the President of the Yugoslav Committee at Corfu in July the previous year, this was to be ruled by the Karađorđević dynasty and – according to the declaration – it was now to comprise 'all the territory where our nation lives in compact masses and without discontinuity'. Granting all its citizens the same rights, the new kingdom was to include Bosnia and Herzegovina, Macedonia, Montenegro, and Kotor. But, as these other member states were not specifically named, there was cause for deep unrest in certain quarters. Several people, angered by their loss of recognition, saw themselves represented as subservient to Serbia. So, the next year at Christmas a group of Montenegrin loyalists, 'the Greens', mounted a rebellion in the hopes of reinstating Nikola as their king, but the attempt failed. Having, therefore, remained abroad, in time he was joined by several of his exiled relations and acquaintances in the south of France, where surrounded by his family he would die in Antibes in 1921.

The last European monarch to lead his army into battle, Nikola was the only man to hold the title of King of Montenegro. Yet, although he had lost his throne, because he had never abdicated, until the end of his life he would always insist that he was still the country's ruler. This was not quite the end of the story, however. When his Serbian rival died just five months after him, Nikola's grandson came to power as Alexander I Karađorđević, and so he, the son of Peter of Serbia and Zorka of Montenegro, was to unite the two dynasties. Eight years after he became ruler of the Serbs, Croats, and Slovenes, the state was renamed and at that point Alexander achieved what his grandfather Nikola had always wanted; he became king of the united land of the Southern Slavs that was now to be known as Yugoslavia.

18

Italy's dictators: D'Annunzio and Mussolini

'Italians want a greater Italy, by conquest not by purchase, not shamefully
but through blood and glory.'

Gabriele D'Annunzio[289]

The First World War had cost Italy dear, and the human price paid for the
country's defeat of its enemies was now summed up in Gabrielle D'Annunzio's
article for *Le Figaro*: 'This victory cost us a million dead and maimed soldiers,
and another million injured and weakened people.'[290] To distract from the
serious economic trouble and political uncertainty they were now facing, many
Italians were eager to reclaim the irredentist territories that three years earlier
they had been promised by the Treaty of London as reward for their joining

Mussolini and
D'Annunzio
meeting in 1929.

the Allies. So, having already retaken Udine, and captured Trieste, by the end of the war they were laying claim to various towns along the eastern Adriatic shore. While Spalato – since 1909 officially called Split – had never been included in the earlier agreement, and it was now to be under international occupation, even here the Italian-speaking minority was proudly flying the flag and claiming the place as its own. By the time the French reached the town, there was growing unrest among its larger Croatian population, and similar trouble was also breaking out in Trogir (formerly Trau) and the neighbouring areas. As the bitter disagreements continued, there were periodic outbreaks of violence, with one incident at Split in July 1920 being so serious that there were several casualties and three people killed, among them the Italian naval captain of the cruiser, *Puglia*. This troubled situation in Dalmatia was just one of the many disappointments the Italians were now experiencing, since it had quickly become apparent that the generous promises given at London would not be honoured at the Paris Conference.

When in September 1919 the Treaty of Saint-Germain was finally concluded between Italy and Austria, besides losing much of its territory the latter saw the official dissolution of the monarchy and the disbanding of its navy. Even so, for the Italians, the terms agreed were highly unsatisfactory. Although their country received the South Tirol (Alto Adige), the Trentino, Istria, and Gorizia, as well as Trieste, an Austrian city since 1866 that was now to be the capital of their new region of Venezia-Giulia, in the final agreement much else that they had been promised was missing. Apart from the fact that the American president distrusted the Italians, he also wished to respect the self-determination of Europe's different ethnic groups. Therefore, to Italy's immense fury, supported by the French premier Clemenceau, Woodrow Wilson opposed the country's demands to receive its former Dalmatian lands. The Italian delegates walked out of the conference in protest as these regions were ultimately assigned instead to the Serbs, Croats and Slovenes. The discussion continued, however, over the tricky question of Fiume (Rijeka), a town not mentioned in the London Treaty, where over the years the situation had become particularly complicated. A free port since the early eighteenth century, three years after the Habsburgs had given it to Croatia, in 1779 it was annexed to Hungary, and then, following brief periods under Napoleonic France and later Austria, it was returned to the Hungarians in the 1820s. As resistance to this had soon grown among its Croatian citizens, in 1868 (by somewhat devious means) a resolution had been found. An intentional discrepancy was included in the agreement's two final documents, the one produced in the Croatian language omitting the clause that specified the town as belonging to the Hungarian crown – a detail purposely kept hidden from Emperor Franz Josef. While for the moment this particular issue was settled, around this time many bourgeois Italians moved to Fiume, and their arrival would add to its complex ethnic mix. Even though these latest incomers helped the place to develop into an important, more modern regional city, the tensions between the different communities continued to grow. Shortly after a group of Italian patriots had thrown a bomb at the Municipal Palace in 1913, some Hungarians threw another in response. Although Fiume was still a semi-autonomous state within Hungary, many of the Hungarian citizens had already decided to emigrate to the USA, estimates suggesting that in the early 1900s some 20-30,000 had left. Despite the Italians being still greatly outnumbered by the Croats in the suburbs, the opposite was true in the city centre, and so two months before the end of the Great War, in October 1918, the city's National Council declared Fiume to be part of Italy, a declaration that would soon bring the threat of further serious unrest. With Rome responding by sending a warship into the area and a separate Serb contingent appearing shortly after, the French, British and Americans arrived to help calm things down. Therefore, by mid-November, despite the continuing heavy presence of Italian soldiers in the city, Fiume was under the joint control of the foreign powers.

The failure of the Allies in 1919 to honour their earlier pledges soon became a cause of deep ill-feeling among the Italians, who felt they had not been sufficiently rewarded for their part in helping win the war. Wanting to be recognised, and appalled by what Gabriele D'Annunzio defined as their 'mutilated victory', many like him condemned the Versailles peace treaties and added their voice to the irredentist movement. The eastern Adriatic was declared by many to be geographically linked to Italy, and D'Annunzio loudly asserted that the region had been part of the Italian heritage since the time of the Roman Emperor Augustus. Determined to reclaim his country's lost lands, within months of the peace he would take action and make his famous, dramatic stand, asserting Italy's rights to its former territories around the Adriatic and elsewhere.

Born into a bourgeois family at the Adriatic town of Pescara in 1863, D'Annunzio soon showed his precocious talent as a poet, and within ten years of publishing his first volume when he was only 16, he had become famous throughout Italy. He largely achieved this by manipulating his image, using methods that were not always strictly honest, on one occasion even spreading a rumour of his own death. During his long and varied career as a journalist, poet, dramatist, and writer of short stories and novels, he would be much admired for his literary style at home and abroad, admired by men such as James Joyce and Osbert Sitwell. At the same time, however, because the content of his writing had become increasingly sensual and salacious, in certain quarters he would earn severe disapproval, not least from the pope. Condemning such works as perverse and immoral, Pius X placed them on the Index of Forbidden Books – a ruling Mussolini would overturn in the late 1920s as a favour to the poet. D'Annunzio, the arch-self-publicist, was always supremely self-confident. On being nominated to parliament in 1897 he declared that 'The world must be convinced that I am capable of everything.'[291] Although at that time he was supportive of the conservatives, three years later he abandoned them and crossed the floor to join the socialists, explaining his change of sides in his usual grandiloquent way, declaring that being 'beyond right and left', and 'beyond good and evil', he was 'going towards life'.[292]

Having remained a (rather uninvolved) member of parliament for just one term, and having then joined the masons, in 1910 he decided to leave Italy when the enormous debts he had built up by his extraordinarily extravagant and louche lifestyle finally caught up with him. Hounded by his creditors and forced to sell everything, including his much-loved dogs and horses, he moved to France and on 28 March settled into a hotel in the rue de Rivoli in Paris. Having now been much influenced by the Decadent, Symbolist and Aesthetic movements of the *fin-du-siècle*, here he would mix with some of the period's great literary names, men such as Proust, Barrès, and Gide. He would also become well acquainted with musicians, collaborating with Mascagni and Debussy to produce libretti. In addition to being impressed by the thinking of Nietzsche, during his five years in France he would also come under the influence of the right-wing anti-parliamentarians, among them the traditionalist monarchist Charles Maurras who later became leader of the far-right *Action Française* movement.

In the spring of 1915, D'Annunzio returned to Italy where he received a rapturous welcome when he gave an oration at a ceremony at Quarto near Genoa. This was to mark the unveiling on 4 May of a monument commemorating the famous departure for Sicily by Garibaldi and his 'Thousand' followers. Being an avid proponent of Italy's entry into the war that was now raging, he had already begun producing poems and short pieces in favour of intervention. As his article, 'La très amère Adriatique' – published in *Le Figaro* a month earlier – had shown, his argument rested on the claim that Italy's 'divine and human' right to the Adriatic region was derived from 'Venice's moral and material heritage'. Drawing on his skills as a political orator to rally the masses, and feeding off the general discontent felt by the Italian people at this time, he used his speech to whip up their sense of patriotism, his words, according to one Irish witness, spreading 'like olive oil on the surface of the sea'.[293] Appealing to their pride in their past, and reigniting their desire to recover Italy's former territorial possessions, he manipulated his audience, inspiring in them a will to fight for the national cause. Adopting the language of the Sermon on the Mount, he summoned his fellow Italians to arms, declaring, 'Blessed are they who return with victories, for they shall see the new face of Rome.'[294] As he would so often do in the future, here he used the filter of art to portray the savagery and squalor of war, as something of beauty. Revered now as 'the Bard' (*Il Vate*), D'Annunzio would be soon repeating these themes. After he had addressed his adoring public, he marched with them to the Capitol Hill and rang the bell of the Campidoglio as a call to action. The Italian government had already approached the Allies, but as Italy was at war with Austria-Hungary within days of these events many would come to see the poet as personally responsible for the country having finally committed itself to engage in the conflict.[295]

A proud patriot, eager for his country to be recognised as one of Europe's major nations, D'Annunzio had for some time wanted Italy to join forces with the French against the Central Powers and, being 'a man of action', unlike his successor Mussolini, he was now impatient to take on the Austrian-Hungarians. Having developed a fascination for the recent discovery of powered flight, and despite being by now in his early fifties, he immediately volunteered to join the Italian air corps. He would later become a highly decorated war hero, who along with numerous other medals and awards, would receive the British Military Cross. His reputation was further enhanced by the many injuries he received, among them the loss of his right eye, and a severe head-wound that he suffered when crashing into the sea off Grado in January 1916. Three years later, as *commandante* at Fiume, he flaunted these battle scars to promote his image as the poet-hero, presenting himself as a much 'maimed soldier of the war'.[296] He also made his name by other heroic escapades that were of his own choosing, his various dangerous feats at Trieste, Pola, and Cattaro becoming of such concern to the Dual Monarchy that it actually put a price on his head.

One of D'Annunzio's most flamboyant acts of bravado took place on 10-11 February 1918. Despite his age and tendency to suffer from seasickness, he volunteered to take part with 29 others in three small motorboats, known as MAS (*motorscafi armati siluranti*), on a daring raid against the Austrian fleet. Accompanied by three larger naval ships and

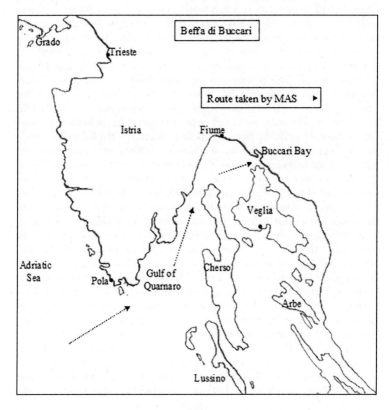

towed by torpedo boats, they set off from the Giudecca in Venice – the spot marked today by a memorial in the church of the Redentore – and after around 14 hours they arrived in the enemy waters of the Gulf of Quarnaro (Kvarner) to the east of the Istrian peninsula. After passing the island of Cherso (Cres), they eventually reached the narrow, well-defended entrance into Buccari (Bakar) Bay, where their escorts finally left them. Now using their own electric motors, they made their way under darkness up the waterway towards the town that lay at its north-western end, around five kilometres from the mouth of the inlet. Thought to be virtually impossible to attack, this was considered a safe anchorage for the Austro-Hungarian ships. While the men were fully aware that they might never return, D'Annunzio had been particularly attracted by the challenge, seeing it as an heroic way to undermine the confidence of the enemy. Ever true to his self-portrayal as the poet-hero, he approached the whole affair with his usual swagger, having during the uncomfortable crossing of the Adriatic stylishly dined on fine food and wine, served complete with tablecloth, glasses and china plates.

On arrival, however, things did not go quite to plan. Instead of finding the expected warships, the men discovered the Austrian fleet to be little more than a small group of merchant vessels. Similarly, the assault itself did not live up to expectations, as the only torpedo that exploded caused no significant damage, and the remaining five got caught in the protective nets. Yet the raid was not a disaster. Despite the efforts to trap them, all the participants survived and returned safely to Ancona, and the venture had given a much-needed boost to Italian morale. This became even more true when it was heard that before leaving the bay, D'Annunzio had thrown overboard three bottles, each tied with the Italian tricolour and carrying his handwritten message that mocked the Austrians for supposedly cowering nervously in port. Later publishing the story in his inimitable style, he made the 'Beffa di Buccari' – the Bakar Mockery – and its accompanying *Canzone di Quarnaro* symbols of Italian resistance. Glorifying the courage of all those who took part, the repeated opening lines of his song described the 30 men going together to their fate, their number soon increased to 31 when joined on board by the figure of Death itself: 'Siamo trenta d'una sorte, / e trentuno con la morte.' Here, too, he tapped into the irredentist ambitions of so many Italians, the *canzone* listing those places 'far and wide' that, belonging to the very body and blood of Italy, deserved rightfully to be returned to the country.[297] Soon popular with its patriotic message, rousing rhythm, and the supposed repeated war cries of Achilles, 'Eia, Eia, Eia, Alala', the song's lyrics would later be adapted to become the fascist chant used to welcome Mussolini wherever he arrived. The actions of D'Annunzio and his colleagues had achieved their main aim by raising the country's spirits in the dark days following the disaster at Caporetto, and the poet now took the boats' acronym and reinterpreted it as his motto, *Memento Audere Sempre* (Remember Always to Dare). But for him, this was still not enough and within a few months he would take on yet another heroic escapade. On 9 August 1918 D'Annunzio led his small squadron on what was an exceptionally long distance at the time, the eight planes completing the 700-mile round trip from Venice to Vienna and back, solely in order to drop tens of thousands of propaganda leaflets onto the people in the Austrian capital below.

These extravagant demonstrations of his courage and daring would stand D'Annunzio in particularly good stead when the details of the peace terms became known. Without its redeemed lands, in his view, Italy would have endured its pain for nothing, and so redemption linked to suffering would now become a central theme in the poet's discourse. Thus, in 1919, despite being all too aware of the price Italy had paid in the conflict, rather than seeing the war as being over, he pronounced that only now was it 'reaching its climax'.[298] While already on 25 April D'Annunzio had addressed a vast crowd of Venetians in St Mark's Square calling for the re-opening of Italy's ports in Dalmatia and also at Fiume, after the Treaty of Saint-Germain he became even more determined to recover the irredentist lands. That same year Italian patriots joined the *Legione Fiumana*, which had been formed by a member of the *Arditi*, Giovanni (Nino) Host-Venturi, who was now to become largely responsible for D'Annunzio's involvement in their cause. On the captain's instigation, a group of officers visited Venice to ask the poet to lead the legionaries in the effort to reclaim their town. Only two days after the final declaration of the peace terms, on 12 September – even though he was seriously unwell with a fever at the time – D'Annunzio set off from the village in Friuli that would give its name to this latest mission, the so-called March of Ronchi. Here, just over a hundred kilometres from Fiume, he joined a body of 200 disillusioned and troublesome Italian grenadiers. These had been previously expelled from the city garrison for their unruly and violent treatment of various citizens and their outright brutality against the occupying colonial troops of the French. Intentionally linking his action with Garibaldi's symbolic march, D'Annunzio now set off in his red Fiat Tipo 4 accompanied by a small convoy of army trucks carrying his motley band of ex-soldiers, nationalists, *Arditi* troops, and sundry others. Obeying orders, on the route an Italian general tried to block his path, but D'Annunzio, presenting his highly decorated chest and demanding to be shot, won such admiration for his show of courage that he was allowed to pass. Joined along the way by new volunteers, he was in command of roughly 2,500 men by the time he reached Fiume. Having previously told the legionaries that he must be welcomed on his arrival, the Italian patriots turned out in force to greet him, thus acknowledging his takeover and Italy's annexation of the city. Before long the British, Americans, and French decided to leave, and soon news of the successful *Impresa di Fiume* was resounding around Europe. Yet even though the Allies had withdrawn, the project did not receive the approval of the nervous government in Rome. Fresh from the Versailles treaties, it wanted to see an end to the whole affair, and so it sent the Italian navy to impose a partial blockade, hoping that this might persuade the poet to surrender the town. But besides being determined to resist outside pressure, D'Annunzio wished to maintain the heroic, embattled image of his city. Despite there still being no serious shortages at this time, he immediately began to stop passing merchant ships, confiscating not just their supplies of food but their armaments as well. Among the various things he seized would be the weapons that the Italian ship *Persia* was taking to the White Armies fighting in the Russian Civil War. Similarly, he authorised raids in the local area, with one of the more amusing instances – which no doubt much annoyed those involved – being the seizure of 46 fine Italian cavalry horsesthat later, in response to demands for their return, were replaced with a collection of broken-down old specimens. A month after his takeover of Fiume, D'Annunzio visited nearby Zara to affirm his support of the town. Then the following spring, having proclaimed his opposition to the great powers and their League of Nations, he declared his determination to form a new League of Fiume that was intended to help separatist groups such as the Irish and the Catalans. In the end this came to nothing.[299]

Besides wanting to recover the lands that had once belonged to Pax Romana, D'Annunzio espoused the idea of a *stirpe dominatrice*, namely a racial stock destined to rule. Accordingly, during his time in control, his Slav citizens would suffer abuse from the *Arditi* and his other extremist supporters. Even so, Fiume soon attracted a wide mix of people from different walks of life and political persuasions, Futurists, Bolsheviks, fascist-leaning Syndicalists, as well as naturists. Here there was an absence of any rules that imposed limits or restrictions on drink, drugs, and sexual behaviour, and in this hedonistic, libertine atmosphere D'Annunzio became – like many of his young *Arditi* supporters – a cocaine user. Nevertheless, he remained for the time being immensely popular among the Italian-speaking community, and with his government relying on a personality cult, the regime soon developed a neo-pagan character of its own. D'Annunzio had become a figure of worship, a god-like saviour, adored by women and emulated by men, many of whom adopted his style of dress and copied his appearance by shaving their heads. A natural showman, he gave daily speeches from the balcony of the governor's palace, addressing the vast crowds amassed in the central square below. He peppered his oratory with poetic terminology and classical references that, although probably little understood by the majority, appealed to their emotions. The public now held the key to his success, and it was their unquestioning love and admiration that enabled him to hold on to his position. Realising this co-dependence, D'Annunzio resorted to a verbal exchange with his audience that consisted of rhetorical questions requiring unthinking answers, a verbal interplay he had taken from Greek classical times. Like some present-day populist leaders, he resorted to simple 'sound-bites' or catchphrases that the public then repeated in unison whenever prompted. Having thus been lulled into compliance by their feeling of participation, and by the simplicity of the message they were being given, the people contentedly continued to give him their full approval. At the same time, being conscious of how he might further promote his message through the medium of the arts, D'Annunzio proceeded to lay on frequent public ceremonies, spectacles, and concerts. Through making all culture, and in particular music, an essential part of his programme, he now contrived to present Fiume as a work of art, the ideal aesthetic and political state that lived contentedly under the guidance of its heroic poet leader.

A social climber, D'Annunzio had elevated his position not just through his short-lived marriage to an aristocrat but also by his multiple liaisons with a variety of society women. They continued to find him attractive, even though he was a small, unprepossessing, balding man with bad teeth and breath. Boasting that he had enjoyed over a thousand affairs, he included among his conquests the famous actress Eleonora Duse, for whom he had written some of his plays. Despite the financial support she gave him, he would ultimately reject her, replacing her with new mistresses and giving her roles to younger women. Always profligate and ready to indulge every extravagant whim, during his later retirement he would spend a fortune on his house and possessions. Claiming that he had a 'need for the superfluous', he was said on one occasion to have bought twenty-two dogs and eight horses.[300] Obsessed by his appearance and taking inordinate care over his clothes, he enjoyed being photographed, more than once posing naked or near naked.

As by December 1919 the Rome government had become keener to prevent Fiume becoming incorporated into the Serb, Croat, and Slovenian kingdom, it had begun to talk of the city's possible annexation to Italy. Yet, this approach was still too timid for D'Annunzio. A year after taking over Fiume, helped by the syndicalist Alceste De Ambris, in September 1920 he brought in a new constitution and rechristened the state as the Italian Regency of Carnaro. He would now present himself as the regent, who through his heroism as 'a soldier, a volunteer, [and] a wounded veteran of the war' had won the people's support and become their *duce*.[301] The *Carta del Carnaro* – otherwise known as 'The Enduring Will of the People' – would not just extol the 'heroic courage' of the people and glorify their work ethic, but also introduce various progressive measures that were far in advance of those found elsewhere. The charter gave new benefits to all Fiume's citizens, and apart from granting female suffrage and equal rights, it enshrined free expression, a minimum wage, old age pensions, financial help for the unemployed, universal healthcare, and primary education. While the various skills and professions were now divided into nine corporations, in accordance with D'Annunzio's more esoteric leanings there was also a tenth category that was more obscure. Defined as being 'dedicated to the mysterious forces of the people in labour and on the rise' and created in honour 'of the truly new man', this was established for 'the freedom of the spirit over the painful anxiety and the sweat of blood'.[302]

Although D'Annunzio's small independent state, complete with its own flag displaying the classical and masonic symbol of rebirth, would only ever be recognised by Lenin, it would establish its own currency and postage system. When Osbert Sitwell visited the city a month before the regime's fall, he was struck by the size of its navy, the large harbour being full, not only of the Italian ships that had joined the cause in the early days of the leader's takeover, but also the pirated vessels the state had since seized. Fiume was now defended by an army that comprised a mixture of romantic patriots, Futurists, and regular soldiers. The state had now adopted *Giovinezza*, the anthem praising youth that was sung by D'Annunzio's loyal *Arditi* storm troopers. These young men, who chose to go to war unarmed except for the grenades in their pockets and the daggers carried between their teeth, had come to represent the dark side of the Fiume experiment. Besides the brutality they showed to any who opposed them, in particular the Slavs, their black shirts and straight-armed salute would be just two of their characteristics later taken up by the fascist regimes of Mussolini and Hitler.

As food, medicine, and other commodities became scarcer during 1920, there was less willingness to welcome visiting outsiders, and orders even went out that babies should be sent for adoption in Italy, the ridiculous absurd excuse being that they might in some way transmit the ideas of Fiume to the peninsula. The initial euphoria was now starting to fade as people became more discontented, and divisions and violent disputes increased between the various groups of legionaries. But things became even more tense when on 12 November the Italian prime minister, Giovanni Giolitti, signed the Treaty of Rapallo with the Serbs, Croats and Slovenes. Despite the opposition of the Soviets, who accused the Italians of stealing their neighbours' lands, the treaty granted Italy all of Istria, Zara and the islands of Cherso, Lussino, Lagosta and the remote mid-Adriatic Pelagosa. More importantly for the people of the *Reggenza di Carnaro*, it also declared Fiume to be a free city. Although many Slavs and Austrians now left for good, despite the worsening situation their places were soon taken by southern Italians. As immigration to America had recently become more difficult, they were now coming to the region looking for a better way of life. Throughout this time, D'Annunzio continued to encourage those remaining to stand firm, calling on them to defend their 'City of Holocaust'. In these last months, he once more presented the hardships as a necessary, sacrificial element of the heroic enterprise, declaring: 'After a year of hard tests, we are confirmed in our truth and exalted in our confession.'[303] Again speaking as the poet-hero, he glorified the hardship, reiterating his message that suffering was something of beauty. During his short visit in November 1920, Osbert Sitwell saw how the regent related to his people, encouraging them by going out onto the balcony whenever he felt called on to acknowledge them. While it is often hard to understand his appeal, Sitwell would remark that despite his physical unattractiveness, within a few seconds of meeting D'Annunzio he had become aware of his 'extraordinary charm ... which had enabled him on many occasions to change mobs of enemies into furious partisans'.[304]

Faced by D'Annunzio's intransigence, a month after the signing of the Treaty of Rapallo, Giolitti was ready to take a tougher stand. Having chosen Christmas Eve when there was less chance of the affair being reported in the press, he ordered the Italian navy to begin its bombardment of Fiume's harbour, and two days later D'Annunzio's palace would come under particularly heavy attack. By the time the assault, dubbed the *Natale di sangue* ('Christmas of Blood') came to an end on the 29th, fifty-four people were dead. At that point, D'Annunzio, who was among the injured, agreed to an amnesty, thus accepting that after nearly 16 months his ambitious project was over. Following his departure on 18 January, Fiume would then remain in the hands of the Italian army.

Having at last settled under house arrest at Gardone Riviera on Lake Garda, D'Annunzio would be visited at his villa in April by Mussolini, but the next year he missed what promised to be a rather more unusual meeting with both Mussolini and Francesco Nitti – the former prime minister who loathed fascism, and whom D'Annunzio had publicly mocked and reviled for years. The poet was absent, however, as two days earlier on 13 August 1922 he had suffered a serious injury after falling out of a first-floor window. No definite explanation was ever given for the accident, although there would be various rumours suggesting that he had been pushed either by a jealous lover, or by a supporter of the equally jealous Mussolini. The latter was now on the rise, his position being assured on 28 October by the March on Rome. Although Mussolini did not reach the capital himself until the next day, and then by the rather more comfortable means of the sleeper train, from this moment on he was in authority, his position confirmed when the king appointed him prime minister.

Although early on Mussolini had been impressed by D'Annunzio, and had supported his takeover of Fiume, at the same time he had been nervous of appearing too involved in the affair. Therefore, when the poet had written to him from the city just four days after his success to proclaim his own achievement, he had excoriated the younger man for the weakness that both he and the Rome government had shown. As Mussolini was the editor of *Il Popolo d'Italia*, he now published the letter in the paper, but only after he had carefully removed all the charges against himself. He had literally cut out the poet's accusations that, 'trembling with fear' and 'prattling away', he had failed personally to keep his earlier promises and done nothing.[305] Besides ordering Mussolini to shake himself out of his endless slumbering, D'Annunzio had drawn attention to the contrast between them both by claiming that he – the famous man of action – had not slept for seven nights.

Even now with the Fiume period over, Mussolini was no less fearful that his famous predecessor would outshine him, so on his own appointment to premier, he immediately asked D'Annunzio not to oppose him: 'I do not ask you to line up at our side, though this would avail us greatly; but we are sure that you will not set yourself against this marvellous youth which is fighting for your and for our Italy.'[306] Anxious to keep him out of the limelight, from now on Mussolini would attempt to sideline this potential rival, keeping him as far away as possible from the political centre. Aware of D'Annunzio's loyal following, he still made a show of honouring him, rewarding him generously for the rest of his life with an annual salary of a million lira. Although he constantly gave him gifts and extravagant favours, he would allegedly explain his reasons for doing so with the comment: 'When you are saddled with a rotten tooth you have two possibilities open to you: either you pull out the tooth or else you fill it with gold. With d'Annunzio I have chosen the latter treatment.'[307] Accordingly, the poet was now able to pour vast sums into the decoration of his home, cramming it full of a heterogeneous collection of objects. He indulged his other passions, too, spending a fortune on his clothes, and following his prurient and decadent lifestyle of sex and drugs – the inscription in the 'Relic Room' of his house notably excluding lust and greed from the seven deadly sins.

With his original villa and its grounds having grown in size and ostentation, D'Annunzio's estate at Gardone eventually extended to ten hectares, encompassing an amphitheatre, mausoleum, and First World War museum that included mementos of his various exploits, including his aeroplane for the flight to Vienna, and the MAS in which he had sailed to Buccari Bay. Also included was the prow presented to him by Mussolini of that same cruiser *Puglia* that years earlier had been engaged in the violent unrest at Split. After the property had been renamed *Il Vittoriale degli Italiani*, D'Annunzio would decide on 22 December 1923 to bequeath it to the people of Italy. The following year Mussolini declared it a national monument, and then in May 1925 he stayed here for two to three days. D'Annunzio was also recognised by the king, who in March 1924 honoured him as the Prince of Montenevoso, the title taken from the mountainous area north of Fiume. Having increased his pro-monarchist leanings while living in France, D'Annunzio was a supporter of Victor Emmanuel III, and, despite his diminutive size, he revered him as a warrior leader. This would be very different from the attitude of Mussolini, who although scarcely four inches taller, was less flattering, describing him as 'too small a man for an Italy which is on the road to greatness'.[308]

In his poems D'Annunzio depicted the contrast between the Latins and the Teutons, emphasising what he saw as the cultural superiority of the former. He was therefore horrified when Mussolini, who had originally felt the same way, began to change his loyalties. Exchanging nearly 600 letters with him over the years, during the 1930s D'Annunzio would attempt to dissuade the Italian leader from drawing closer to the Germans. Trying to prevent his collaboration with Hitler, in 1937 D'Annunzio met him for one last time at Verona station when the Italian was on his way back from his state visit to the Führer. The poet would not live to see the tragic outcome of this period, however, as five months later on 1 March 1938 he died in his sleep of a stroke. Four days later, after a simple funeral in the local church, his open coffin was placed under guard on the *Puglia* at *Il Vittoriale*, and as a further show of respect cannons were fired over the lake to mark his passing. With D'Annunzio dead – the man whose popularity had threatened to rival his own – Mussolini was now fully prepared to honour him, and so he and his son-in-law Count Galeazzo Ciano joined the mourners behind the gun carriage that took the poet to his grave in the extravagant marble mausoleum that he had created for himself.

Alongside his other political and artistic interests, D'Annunzio had also adopted much of the anti-democratic thinking of Nietzsche. He had seen himself as the Superman, the dictator who embodied the qualities of charisma and power. A complex character, he had embraced the extreme doctrines of both the right and the left, melding the two to present himself as the popular leader who held his authority through the will of the people. Although politically he had not been up to the task that he had set himself, much of his thinking would be taken up by the later right-wing totalitarian regimes. Even though he never became a member of the official Fascist party, D'Annunzio would frequently be labelled the 'John the Baptist' of the movement, and Sitwell would describe fascism as the 'child of Fiume'.[309] Equally, the poet himself had emphasised his role in its early development. Although Mussolini denied all responsibility for the house arrest that he was under at the time, when in January 1923 D'Annunzio appealed to him for help in bringing it to an end, he would use this same argument to try to strengthen his hand by claiming: 'In the so-called [*detto*] "fascist" movement has not the best been generated by my spirit? Today's national revanche was announced by me – a good forty years ago, alas – and was promoted by the Leader of Ronchi.'[310] Indeed, even while he was always bitterly opposed to Mussolini's growing closeness to Hitler and the rising Nazi party, the two later regimes would in time adopt many of the poet's ideas and mannerisms, their leaders using his way of addressing large crowds, and whipping up their passions and loyalties by their emotive rhetoric. Writing a few years later, Sitwell would explore the difficulty for those from the more northern countries to appreciate or understand the popularity of this poetic and bombastic style of speaking, acknowledging that before long it appeared outdated, if not ridiculous. Addressing this paradox as it related to D'Annunzio, Sitwell concluded: 'In his discourse there was not a little to northern ears of absurdity, but through it ran the hypnotic thread of his eloquence.'[311]

* * *

By the time of D'Annunzio's death, Benito Mussolini had been in sole power for some 14 years, having come a long way since his birth in the Romagna village of Dovia di Predappio near Forlì in 1883. The intelligent but disobedient child of a blacksmith and a schoolteacher, he was often in trouble at school, occasionally playing truant, and at times being expelled for his unruly and even violent behaviour. This side of his character would remain with him, and as an adult he would take part in duels. He had grown up in a simple household, his Catholic mother struggling to make ends meet, while his socialist father was periodically embroiled in political activities, even being imprisoned for a time after taking part in a riot. Influenced by him, Benito had approved of Umberto I's assassination in 1900, and during his early career he would support left-wing movements and oppositional groups that frequently brought him to the attention of the authorities. To avoid military service, in 1902 he moved to Switzerland, where the next year he would be charged with desertion. Following a brief stay in prison, he was allowed to return to Italy to re-join the Bersaglieri, and on the completion of his military service, he became a teacher in a primary school. Over the next few years, he was frequently on the move – from time to time being sent again to prison – and working temporarily with the socialist press in Trento until he was expelled by the Austrians. After his return to Forlì, in 1911 Mussolini received another prison sentence for organising a strike in opposition to the Italian war in Libya, but he had now earned a name for himself and so the next year he was appointed editor of the socialist newspaper *Avanti*. In this role he would continue to promote the party's anti-military and anti-colonial policies.

In the decades after the *Risorgimento* Italy had been struggling to find its feet, and since the start of the new century the country had seen multiple strikes and much unrest. Although in 1914 things were made worse by a particularly bad harvest, destitution had always threatened the *braccianti*, the peasants whose sole means of survival depended on working for the often-absentee landowners found in the Po valley or on the large *latifondi* estates in the south. As a result, being faced by such hardship, since 1900 nearly a million Italians had emigrated. After becoming prime minister for the fourth time in March 1911, the Liberal politician Giolitti had endeavoured to bring about domestic reform, but much of the country still remained very backward, with about a third of Italy's population illiterate. Things were even worse in the Mezzogiorno, where the figure was about twice that number. This reinforced the sense of superiority felt by the northerners towards those in the south, their arrogance increasing the antagonism between the regions that prevented national cohesion. As the stresses increased, there were many strikes and disturbances, violence breaking out in the Romagna and Marche, and demonstrations in Milan and elsewhere. But the international situation was now causing increasing concern, and by mid-summer of 1914 is was clear that Europe was heading towards a war that would soon engulf the whole continent. In Italy this further increased the tensions and exacerbated the disagreements, with a heated dispute between those who wanted to join the conflict and those who were against.

Just as D'Annunzio had done years before, Mussolini now had no hesitation in gradually reversing his political loyalties, and so, in spite of having written a column headlined 'Down with the War' on 26 July 1914, three months later on 18 October he would produce another article, this time entitled, 'From absolute neutrality to an active neutrality'. As he was now openly calling for Italy's intervention in the Great War, he was reviled by many of his fellow socialists and was dismissed from his post with *Avanti*. But within a month he had opened a new newspaper, *Il Popolo d'Italia*, and, besides taking part in the public demonstrations in favour of Italy's military engagement, he formed the *Fascio Rivoluzionario d'Azione Internazionalista*, a revolutionary body whose members were now to be labelled as Fascists. This organisation was based on the late 19th-century *fasci* workers' groups that had grown up across Italy and were particularly prominent in Sicily until the movement was brutally suppressed in the 1890s. Although Mussolini had now created his own *fascio* to support Italy's entry into the war, by December he had gone urther and was actively rejecting Marxism to promote his form of nationalist socialism. A few weeks before Italy finally made its declaration, on 11 April 1915 he was again arrested in Rome for trying to stir up support for the country's intervention in the on-going conflict. By May, however, his wish had come true and, although there might have been some hesitation on his part, in August he was called up and sent to join the Bersaglieri in the trenches at the battles of the Isonzo. Here he made corporal, and although he would later exaggerate some of the danger he had been in, he served with the regiment until he was badly wounded and invalided out in February 1917. After six months in hospital, he returned to his role as editor of *Il Popolo d'Italia*, and with the encouragement and financial backing of the British Security Service, he continued to publish propaganda in favour of the war.

As by the end of war Mussolini had lost all faith in socialism and become openly opposed to the PSI, the *Partito Socialista Italiano*, in March 1919 he formed the *Fasci Italiani di Combattimento*. Being determined to promote his cause in any way that he could, like D'Annunzio before him, he linked his programme to the country's glorious ancient Roman past, adopting the classical symbol of the *fasces*, a bundle of rods bound together for strength, and tied to an axe to denote the authority of the magistrate. Later in October – much to his fury – he failed dismally to be elected to parliament as the candidate at Forlì, but, despite his then being arrested for keeping arms in his office, two years later he would finally achieve his goal – this time his success being partly due to the fact that he had pragmatically distanced himself from D'Annunzio. Although in September 1920 he had expressed his approval of the *Reggenza di Carnaro* and had briefly seemed to support the suggestion that its leader should not only take over Trieste and the Romagna, but also declare Italy a republic, since then Mussolini had emphasised his separation from the poet.

Mussolini was now also taking advantage of the growing unrest of the *Biennio Rosso*, the two-year period during which Italy was beset by hundreds of workers' strikes, armed attacks, and even murders. Presenting himself as the alternative to this feared extreme left-wing movement, he sent the *squadristi*, his paramilitary squads, to take on the protesters. After declaring in *Il Popolo d'Italia* in July 1921 that Bolshevism was dead, in November he would rename his party as the National Fascist Party, the PNF (*Partito Nazionale Fascista*). This was just the beginning. Within a year various towns had been taken over by Mussolini's much-feared blackshirts, men who were all too ready to use violence against any organisation, group or individual who opposed them. The situation finally reached tipping point on 28 October, when some 30,000 of these marched on Rome to demand the resignation of the latest Liberal prime minister Luigi Facta. He immediately suggested calling out the military, but because of the king's refusal to give his consent, he resigned. Still terrified of civil war, Victor Emmanuel now caved in and after summoning Mussolini from Milan he offered him the leadership. Although the new premier was only 39 and lacking any experience in government, in the king's mind he was now the best option, a strong leader who, besides bringing an end to Italy's troubles, might also help prevent the risk of a communist takeover – something now focussing the minds of many rulers throughout Europe and the wider world.

Victor Emmanuel III was primarily a constitutional monarch, a pedantic man who, like his near contemporary George V, enjoyed his bourgeois homelife. A strict, unaffectionate father who was obsessed by details of protocol, he was happiest when like the British king he could spend hours on his much-loved private collection – coins for him, stamps for George. He, too, would be supported by his wife, having married Elena, the fifth daughter of Nikola of Montenegro, in 1896, the year her father had celebrated the bicentenary of his dynasty. Over time she had become very popular with the people for her charity work and care of the sick, being much admired for her concern for the victims of the devastating earthquake in Messina in 1908, and also for her nursing of the wounded during the Great War. While to her mother's distress, she had converted from Orthodoxy to Catholicism at the time of her marriage, her good works had also earned her praise from the pope. Her husband, on the other hand, was not religious, and as well as having no time for soldiers or diplomats, he enjoyed his nickname *mangiapreti* (the priest-eater). Now, and for the next two and a half decades, he would support the Fascists, particularly relying on Mussolini, whom he saw as the best person to support the monarchy and the status quo. For his part, Mussolini had little respect for Victor Emmanuel, but in this period he still showed him due deference, since he, like the king, was aware of how their positions rested on a mutual co-existence and collaboration.

Although Mussolini began by creating a coalition government, before long he would turn this into a dictatorship, and by early 1923 his blackshirts had become officially the MVSN (*Milizia Volontaria per la Sicurezza Nazionale*). In January of that same year, he had begun his so-called pacification of Libya, which, since its invasion in September 1911 and the successful annexation of Tripoli and Cyrenaica the following year, had come to be seen as Italy's southern 'fourth shore' of the Mediterranean.[312] With unrest having grown in this region in the intervening years, and reports of massacres and other atrocities, Mussolini decided to embark on the Second Senussi War, a bloody conflict that would last for nine years. Eight months after starting this costly campaign, on 31 August he also ordered his army to bombard and invade Corfu. This was an act of retaliation for a border dispute with the Greeks in Albania, an episode that three days before had resulted in the death of a general, three other Italians and one Albanian. Although in the ensuing assault sixteen of the islanders were killed, the League of Nations was unable to the settle the matter, and the 'Corfu Crisis' would only be finally resolved after the Greeks had apologised, paid indemnities, and officially recognised the Italian flag. Satisfied at last, Mussolini ordered his troops to leave the island.

In the meantime, at home, to stifle any criticism of his regime, towards the end of the year the press laws had begun to be tightened. And at the same time Mussolini started to take other measures to increase his political control, most notably by gaining parliament's approval in November 1923 for the Acerbo Law. As this established that two-thirds of parliamentary seats would in future be given to the party that won at least 25% of the national votes, the premier had prepared the way for the next election. Accordingly, when this took place the following April, his power was increased. The result was immediately met, however, with vociferous opposition, in particular from one of Mussolini's most outspoken critics, Giacomo Matteotti, a leading Socialist member of parliament, who excoriated the Fascists and their brutal regime. Having furiously condemned the outcome of the election, within days of his speech, on 10 June Matteotti was seized from outside his house in Rome. After being bundled into a car and whisked away, he disappeared until eventually on 16 August his battered body was found around 15 miles from the city. As the evidence pointed to his having been tortured and murdered by a gang of the *squadristi*, many parliamentary deputies resigned in protest, and for a time a serious political crisis threatened. While debates still continue as to whether or not Mussolini was personally implicated in the assassination, for the moment the future of fascism hung in the balance. Even while he declared that his intention was to rule through fear, by this time the prime minister appeared to be so lacking in confidence that 156 blackshirts were sent from Bologna to help him. After they had succeeded in whipping up support among the Romans, other public demonstrations of loyalty began to take place in towns and cities around the country, and so by the end of 1924 Mussolini's position was reaffirmed.

Earlier in the year, on 27 January, he had persuaded the Kingdom of the Serbs, Croats, and Slovenes to sign the Treaty of Rome, an agreement that to the delight of Mussolini was to see the end of the Free State of Fiume that had been created four years earlier at Rapallo. Although the suburb of Sušak with its mainly Croat population was now within the neighbouring kingdom, at last the new borders had placed Fiume itself on Italian soil. As a further concession to the Slavs, Mussolini guaranteed freedom of language and culture to any who still remained in the city centre. Even though, in reality, this pledge was all too soon forgotten, a year later in July at the Treaty of Nettuno Italy's possession of Fiume was confirmed, and here again Mussolini would make further demands. While he insisted that any Italians who wished to move to Dalmatia should be free to do so, this was so immensely unpopular with the Croats that the relevant clause would not be ratified for another three years.

Still feeling threatened by the very real possibility of the collapse of the party, and also subject to his personal doubts, Mussolini listened to the advice of his blackshirts and decided to take further action. Therefore, while he was addressing the Chamber on 3 January 1925, he announced that he was now assuming sole control. Even so, because this was not enough for his MVSN, and so on 24 December they persuaded him to pronounce himself the official Head of Government. This marked the start of Mussolini's 20-year rule, the *ventennio*, during which Italy was to become a police state. As the authority of parliament had been removed, from this time onwards the only limit to the leader's totalitarian power lay with the Grand Council of Fascism, a body that could be summoned only by himself.

Nevertheless, from the start of November 1925, there began a series of plots to assassinate Mussolini. The first, which was prevented before it could take place, was perhaps a fake, contrived to give him an excuse to tighten his grip, but this would be followed within months by two attacks in Rome in April and September. Another occurred in October 1926 in Bologna, but here again questions remain over who was responsible, some proposing that it might have been fabricated to allow the establishment of the secret police soon after. Although other plots would be discovered later, from this time on the increased surveillance would succeed in preventing further assassination attempts. As throughout this time, Mussolini's regime was steadily tightening its hold, his PNF the only party legally allowed to exist, unsurprisingly in the elections of 24 March 1929, it would win over 98% of the vote.

That same year the Roman Question had been finally resolved with the Lateran Treaty agreeing to the Church being financially compensated for its lost lands. With the official recognition of the Vatican City's independence, Mussolini, who had now earned the praise of of the pope, would mark the agreement by calling for one of his flamboyant urban redevelopments. Demolishing everything in its way, in 1936 he constructed the Via della Conciliazione, a triumphal route leading from the Tiber to St Peter's Basilica. This was in line with his on-going determination to draw attention to Italy's ancient Roman past, and part of his ambition to create a 'Third Rome'. Two years earlier he had removed more of the city's historic buildings to open the Via dei Fori Imperiali. Having broken a path through the ancient forums, he had connected the Colosseum to his palace in Piazza Venezia, passing by the vast memorial that had been inaugurated in honour of Victor Emmanuel II in 1911. These roads were only some of the major projects Mussolini now ordered to promote his regime, and besides other schemes in the city centre, outside the ancient walls he laid out a new route to EUR, a Futurist suburb combining the ancient with the modern that took its name from his projected World Fair of 1942, the *Esposizione Universale di Roma*. In the event, the fair was never take place, the country being by then deeply embroiled in the Second World War.

During this period, besides a drop in wages, there had been a general fall in the standard of living, but despite his own experience of hardship Mussolini's concern for the poorer people was minimal, showing his lack of feeling by remarking: 'Fortunately the Italian people were not accustomed to eating much and therefore feel the privation less acutely than others.'[313] Regardless of this, in 1932 he celebrated the tenth anniversary of Fascist rule, and from this time on he would always be officially addressed as *Il Duce*, adopting as his own the title previously accorded to D'Annunzio and also at times to Garibaldi. This again allowed him to reassert his connection to the ancient Roman *dux*, or leader, and slogans now began to appear announcing that *Il Duce* was always right.

In spite of the admiration Hitler had earlier felt for the Italian leader, because his own standing had grown after his appointment as German chancellor in 1933, the relationship between the two men had started to change. When they met for the first time the next year on 14 June near Venice at Stra, the event would not be a success. To the visitor's obvious discomfort, his own poor turnout was shown up by the *Duce* who appeared in full uniform, surrounded by numbers of his smartly dressed officials and supporters. Knowing only

German himself, Hitler felt outshone by Mussolini's ability to speak other languages – a skill the Italian was always keen to display. During their talks at Villa Pisani, attendants heard the pair shouting at each other as the two men bitterly disagreed over the question of Austria, Mussolini being strongly opposed to Hitler's wish to annex the country, whose rights the Italian had promised to defend. The *Duce*, who described his guest as 'a mad little clown', was also against his promotion of antisemitism, a policy that Mussolini viewed as 'a German vice', and one which, until the following year, would be officially rejected in Italy. Nonetheless, he had long shown evidence of his own racist thinking against various groups. In the 1920s and 1930s, Mussolini had brought in racial laws against the Jews in Trieste, and although he had implemented some visible improvements in Venezia-Giulia, wherever there were minorities in the region, he had introduced various oppressive measures, such as the outlawing of the Slavs' language and the Italianisation of their family names and places. His deep prejudice against these people had already been made clear in September 1920, when he had declared to his audience in Pola: 'When dealing with such a race as Slavic – inferior and barbarian – we must not pursue the carrot, but the stick policy.' He had then gone on to add that in order to confirm the country's borders, one might 'easily sacrifice 500,000 barbaric Slavs for 50,000 Italians'.[314] Such thinking was not out of character for Mussolini, since he, like D'Annunzio, believed in a superior *stirpe*, whose cultural development gave them a right to rule. He was already promoting the idea of Italy's need to gain essential *spazio vitale*, in other words to acquire in its historic regions the extra space that was needed for the Italian population, now hoping to increase this by urging women to have more children. A similar mindset justified all colonialism, whether in the eastern Adriatic or Africa. So he now introduced particularly stringent laws in Libya, where, in addition to handing over all confiscated land to the Italian colonialists and outlawing mixed marriages, he demanded that any resistance be brutally punished by the authorities. Accordingly, they had responded with murderous attacks and the imprisonment of offenders in new concentration camps. And, worse still, after his conquest of Abyssinia in the 1930s, Mussolini was personally to order the extermination of thousands of Ethiopians.

A month after the meeting at Stra, the Nazis murdered Dollfuss, the Austrian chancellor who had condemned them and banned them from the country. While evidence of Hitler's direct responsibility for the crime was only finally discovered by Kurt Bauer in 2013, many had already suspected it. Since Dollfuss had previously formed an alliance with him, Mussolini immediately reacted by sending his troops to the Brenner Pass to demonstrate his support of Austria, and as a result he was hailed for having secured the peace. He declared that 'if necessary I was prepared to go to war to stop the *Anschluss*', and for the moment he would continue to stand up to Hitler – doing so even after the latter had seized full power as Führer in August.[315] The next year Mussolini would join the British in opposing the rearmament that Germany had now begun in defiance of the terms agreed at the Treaty of Versailles.

* * *

By this time, new tensions had been building up across the Adriatic, following the assassination of the Yugoslav king, Alexander I Karađorđević, in 1934. A nephew of Victor Emmanuel III, he had grown up with his exiled father Peter in Geneva before completing his education in Russia and becoming an imperial page at the tsar's court. He had returned home in 1909 when a scandal forced the resignation of his older brother, who had killed his valet in a fit of rage. Having replaced him as the new crown prince, during the first of the Balkan Wars Alexander would contribute to the defeat of the Ottomans, and in the second conflict he had joined the Montenegrin, Greek and Romanian armies in fighting the Bulgarians. Declared regent on his father's abdication in 1914, following the assassination of Archduke Ferdinand by the Black Hand, he had tried to confront the challenges that were facing him by creating his own rival group, the White Hand. But as this was a time of multiple political assassinations – eight years before his Italian cousin Crown Prince Umberto narrowly escaped being shot in 1929 – he, too, would survive when a bomb was thrown at his carriage. Although he had sworn that same day to uphold the Serbian constitution, and ever since the country's unification had attempted to bring together the diverse lands and many differing ethnic groups formerly within the Austrian and Ottoman empires, the antipathy among the king's subjects still persisted.

In June 1928, the Croatian Peasant Party leader Stjepan Radić was mortally wounded in Parliament by the Serb nationalist Puniša Račić. To deal with the mounting pressures, the next year on 6 January Alexander dissolved parliament and abolished the constitution. Having established a dictatorship, he declared that his country was in future to be known as Yugoslavia. By this time some Croatians, bitter enemies of the Serbs and Orthodox Christians, had joined forces, and they were now creating a new, independent nationalist *Ustaša* movement. For most of the 1930s, Mussolini would support this racist, fascist organisation in order to divide and weaken the country further. Openly opposed to the government in Belgrade, in 1934 the *Ustaše* would be implicated in the dramatic turn of events in Marseille. While Alexander was driving through the city on a state visit to France, a Bulgarian belonging to a Macedonian revolutionary group shot the king and his chauffeur dead, also mortally wounding the French Foreign Minister Louis Barthou. Still only in his forties, Alexander left a young son of eleven, and so for the next seven years this boy, now Peter II, would be guided by his father's cousin Paul, the acting regent.

A year after Alexander's assassination, on 2 October 1935 Mussolini ordered the invasion of Abyssinia, thus starting the two-year-long second Italo-Ethiopian war was to drain Italy's treasury. Despite the sanctions imposed by the League of Nations, the following May the region of Italian East Africa – combining Eritrea, Somalia and Abyssinia – was proclaimed as the Empire of Ethiopia, and Victor Emmanuel III was declared its emperor. But Mussolini was eager to increase his country's international standing still further, and so following the start of the Spanish Civil War in July 1936 he offered his help to General Franco. This was followed three months later by his agreeing on 25 October to join with Germany in an alliance that he now personally labelled the Axis. The next year, shortly before his last meeting with D'Annunzio, the *Duce* made an official visit to Munich and Berlin. On this occasion Hitler was determined to impress his guest, and so, as well as the tours of armaments factories and parades of serried ranks of troops, he made sure that throughout the stay Mussolini would see the vast crowds of the Führer's cheering supporters. Struck by what he had witnessed, two months later in November 1937, the *Duce* confirmed his pact with Germany and Japan and withdrew Italy from the League of Nations.

Eager to curry favour with the Führer, Mussolini now started to bring in new measures against the Jews, among other things outlawing marriages between them and non-Jews. Not only was this antisemitic policy against the wishes of the king, but it would also cause many Italians to start to question the path their leader was taking them down. The *Duce* was still trying to prove his international authority, but since their meeting at Stra the balance between the two dictators had tipped in Hitler's favour, and therefore when the Führer marched without warning into Austria the following March, Mussolini forgot his earlier promise to the Austrians and made no attempt to prevent the *Anschluss*. Nonetheless, when the Munich Conference met in September 1938 to discuss the crisis caused by Hitler's invasion of the Sudetenland, the Italian leader would play a key role in the proceedings, appearing for one last time to impress Hitler himself.

Although he still hoped to maintain the peace, before long the *Duce* had his own ambitious objective in mind, namely the occupation of Albania. The year after the end of the first World War, the Italians had surrendered the southern region of the country to the Greeks, and, although holding on to Sazan Island, on 3 September 1920 they had also evacuated nearby Valona. Yet, as they had received in return a mandate in the central regions of the country, Mussolini was now encouraged to put aside his former pledges of support for its ruler, King Zog. Fourteen years earlier the Albanian Parliament had been overthrown, and with the rule of Prince Wied officially ended, a republic had been declared. But even though the new president, the former tribal chief Ahmed Zogu, had been helped to his position by the Slavs, by 1928 they were threatening his borders and so he had responded by declaring himself the new monarch. Soon realising his vulnerability, he had then written to Mussolini to swear his allegiance, and in June he had signed an Italo-Albanian alliance. So, for the following years Albania, as an Italian protectorate, had benefited from new development programmes and a steady flow of Italian aid. Besides having raised Mussolini's international profile, this had extended his influence in the area. Now, with his commanding position on both shores of the narrow Strait of Otranto, he had ensured his control over the entrance to the Adriatic. In addition to the thousands of Italians who had settled in Albania and begun establishing their own schools and businesses, many other Albanians from Kosovo had also moved to the country in these last years before the Second World War. However, as in in March 1937 Yugoslavia signed an agreement with the *Duce*, from then on, despite his earlier claim that Italy's sole objective had been 'to preserve and to respect the independent status' of Albania, Mussolini began to plan for a takeover of the country.[316] Wanting to find an excuse for his actions, he therefore presented impossible demands to King Zog, who, realising the danger facing him, on 7 April 1939 fled with his family to Greece. Just two hours later the Italians landed and within five days Albania had fallen.

Within weeks, on 22 May, despite the concerns of Victor Emmanuel, who had always been against the alliance, the Pact of Steel officially confirmed the earlier agreement between Hitler and Mussolini, but by this time the man who had once modelled himself on the *Duce*, even imitating his Fascist salute, was calling the tune. Mussolini was now copying Hitler, even imitating the German goose-step with his own similar *passo romano*, which he had been practising privately in his rooms. Even so, when the war broke out in September, over the following weeks the *Duce* frequently changed his mind, undecided whether or not to become involved in the fighting. At last, three months after their meeting at the Brenner Pass in March 1940, on 10 June Mussolini declared from the balcony of Palazzo Venezia in Rome that Italy was at war with the Allies. Tightening the bonds with Hitler still further, on 27 September the *Duce* enrolled in the Tripartite Pact with Germany and Japan, this being joined soon after by Hungary, Romania, and Slovakia. By this time he had abandoned his original idea of attacking Yugoslavia and had switched his attention elsewhere. Having been persuaded by his advisers that it would improve his image at home, on 28 October he ordered his troops to invade Greece instead. This came as a surprise even to Hitler, but as Mussolini's generals had feared, the campaign ended in disaster, the Italians being pushed back into Albania within days. Then, just a fortnight later, on the night of 11/12 November, Italy's humiliation was deepened further when 21 British Swordfish biplanes attacked the port of Taranto. Having taken off from the deck of HMS *Illustrious* on a round trip of 170 miles, they had then succeeded in causing such major damage to the Italian ships sheltering in the harbour that the battle fleet was put out of action for months to come.[317]

Problems for Yugoslavia were also now about to increase. In March, shortly after Bulgaria had joined the Tripartite Pact, on the 25th the regent Paul regretfully signed an agreement with the Axis powers. When, however, two days later he was removed from office by a group of officers, appalled by what he had done, Hitler became so infuriated that he ordered the country to be invaded. By mid-April, Germans, Hungarians, and Italians had crossed the border, and with Mussolini's troops having then taken Split, Dubrovnik, Kotor, Kosovo and much of Macedonia, they were eventually able to join forces with their colleagues stationed in Albania.

In spite of these recent successes, Victor Emmanuel was now facing his own opposition. Like so many of his family, he had already survived one attempt on his life in Rome, when in 1912 an anarchist had tried to shoot him and his wife while they were on their way to Mass at the Pantheon. Now, two years after becoming King of Albania, during a state visit to the country in May 1941, he would again narrowly escape assassination when one of King Zog's supporters shot at him while he was driving with the local prime minister through Tirana. Although the 19-year-old Vasil Laçi was in fact protesting against the fascist regime, after his arrest and execution, there were none of the usual roundups or acts of retaliation. As the authorities were unwilling to draw attention to their own unpopularity, they chose instead to represent the young man as someone with a grudge against the prime minister.[318]

Although the writing was now on the wall for the Italians, Victor Emmanuel continued to back Mussolini, refusing to listen when he was warned that his chief minister was mismanaging the war. For his part, the *Duce* had become increasingly disrespectful of the king, even declaring: 'I shall get rid of him. The course of history can be changed in a night.'[319] Yet, although the public were fed false news, the loss of Libya in 1942 could not be kept from them and by early 1943, following the defeat of the Italian army by the Soviets in Russia, Mussolini was becoming visibly depressed. For some time he had been subject to frequent changes of mood and outbursts of rage, even turning against those closest to him, such as his mistress. While his erratic behaviour and his increasing indecisiveness were possibly caused by syphilis, people had started to notice how unwell he was looking. Suffering from a duodenal ulcer, he had lost almost three stone, and although the public was told that he always working, he would at times be found lying slumped asleep on his desk.

On 15 May the king finally sent the *Duce* a message saying that Italy must seek an armistice, but although there were various attempts to reach agreement with the British, these all came to nothing. By July the situation was fast developing, and nine days after the Allied landing in Sicily, on the 19th Rome was bombed for the first time. With the Germans now facing their own disasters, opposition to Mussolini had come to a head. Having passed a vote of no confidence in the leader, on the 24th the Italian Grand Council of Fascism returned the command of the armed forces to the king. The next day Mussolini was summoned by Victor Emmanuel, and to his complete surprise he was then dismissed from office and arrested. Although his replacement Pietro Badoglio and the king now secretly opened negotiations with the Allies, as the new prime minister was unwilling to surrender, he delayed the outcome with his unrealistic demands. This meant that ultimately Italy would lose its advantage over the Germans, the continuing uncertainty allowing Hitler to send more troops into the country. At last, however, five days after the signing of a short version of the agreement in Sicily, an armistice was announced on 8 September 1943.

As Prince Umberto, had never been on good terms with his father, he had not been told of the plans, and although he wished to stay in the capital he was now ordered by Victor Emmanuel to join the other members of the family as they left the city. Together with the government and many senior officers, they fled that same night from Rome in the so-called 'fuga (flight) di Pescara'. On reaching the Adriatic coast, the situation became even more chaotic as others attempted to join the embarkation for Brindisi that then took place from Ortona. Still today, a highly critical plaque relays the sense of disaffection felt at this time for the king who had 'betrayed' the people to fascism and caused 'the ruin of Italy'.[320] This stern condemnation – later erected at the port by the partisans – would reflect the strong feelings of the local people, whose town lay so close to the Gustav line dividing the two separate areas of occupation. Just three months after the evacuation, this would become the site of a bloody battle between the Canadians and Germans.

On 10 September, the day after the king had set sail from Ortona, those who had been left to guard Rome surrendered. The city then began its nine months under German occupation, during which the people were to face the daily risk of deportation, persecution, and retaliation. Among those caught up in this was Victor Emmanuel's second daughter, who had returned to the capital from abroad to join her children. Two weeks after the king's flight from Rome, on 23 September she was arrested on orders of the Gestapo. Later sent to Buchenwald, she would die the next year as a result of injuries she had received during an Allied bombing raid of a factory in the camp. And, in the chaos of the days immediately following the armistice, an equally cruel fate awaited those Italians stationed abroad on military service. Now finding themselves confronted by their former comrades in arms, on the Ionian island of Cephalonia about 5,200 Italian soldiers would be massacred by the Wehrmacht.[321]

While most of the Italian royal family remained in Brindisi, on 29 September 1943 Badoglio went to Malta to meet with the Allies. Here he signed the Long Armistice, a more detailed document that included for the first time reference to Italy's surrender – the word later being deleted – and a demand for the suppression of everything that related to fascism. After yet more confusion, on 13 October Italy finally declared war on Germany, and in November Victor Emmanuel publicly renounced his titles as Emperor of Ethiopia and King of Albania. Meanwhile, his opposition was growing and so on 13 January 1944 a gathering of representatives from different political wings met in Bari, where it was decided that Victor Emmanuel should abdicate to rid Italy of its fascist past. Unable to agree on who or what should replace him, the issue was then shelved, the matter being postponed until the country was finally liberated.

Although the king was always dismissive of his son, he was anxious to preserve the dynasty, so under pressure from the British, on 10 April 1944 he handed much of his power over to Umberto, who would receive full authority on 4 June when Rome was recaptured and the German occupiers were finally expelled. When at last two years later a referendum was called to clarify the situation, on 9 May 1946 Victor Emmanuel agreed to abdicate in the hopes that by doing so his son would have a greater chance of winning the popular vote. In the event, however, Umberto – subsequently dubbed the *Re di Maggio* – would reign for just 34 days, being rejected in the plebiscite of 2 June when 54% of the electorate supported the end of the monarchy. On the 12th the ruling House of Savoy was officially abolished. Victor Emmanuel died the next year in Egypt, and in 1948 Italy established a new constitution. This was designed not only to block the return of a totalitarian regime such as that which had brought it to its knees, but also to bar male royal heirs from the country – a stipulation that would remain in force until 2002. Umberto spent most of his exile in Portugal, eventually dying in Geneva in 1983. He was then interred nearby at the ancient burial site of the House of Savoy at Hautecombe

Abbey in France. Finally, in 2017 the remains of his parents were returned to Italy, where they were laid to rest in the Santuario di Vicoforte, east of Cuneo.

Following Victor Emmanuel's announcement of an armistice with the Allies on 8 September 1943, Mussolini was confined at the Hotel Campo on the Gran Sasso in central Italy, 50 miles west of Pescara. On 12 September, German paratroopers rescued him and after a meeting with Hitler he was made head of the *Repubblica Sociale Italiana*, a puppet state established by the Germans in the Italian regions not yet captured north of the Gustav Line. This was popularly dubbed the Salò Republic after the village north-west of Verona where Mussolini was staying at the time. Besides taking over the north-east Italian regions in the Alto Adige, Trentino, and Venezia-Giulia (the OZAV), and Istria and Fiume (the OZAK), the Germans had by this time further extended their influence down into Dalmatia as far as Kotor and Albania – the only exception being Zara and its surrounding enclave that was able to remain within the Italian Social Republic until it was captured by Yugoslav Partisans in October the next year.

During this period Mussolini was living with his wife and family at Gargnano on Lake Garda, about eight miles from D'Annunzio's former home *Il Vittoriale*, and here he spent time taking revenge on the royal family, among other things encouraging the spread of lurid details about the homosexual lifestyle of Umberto.[322] Despite the establishment of the new republic, Mussolini was now wholly dependent on Hitler, and having therefore become increasingly despondent, he began to turn against those who had earlier supported him. Believing they had betrayed him, he allowed the execution of certain party members, including his son-in-law Count Ciano. With the Allies having advanced by September 1944 to a line north of Ravenna and just short of La Spezia, early the next year he was aware that the end was in sight. Always a superstitious man, during an interview he gave at this time he declared: 'My star has fallen. I have no fight left in me. I work and I try, yet know that all is but a farce.'[323] Yet, even though his doctor would describe him as being 'in a state of complete moral and physical collapse, and absolutely devoid of energy and intelligence', within weeks, following another visit to Hitler, he was again in high spirits, declaring, 'We've won the war.'[324]

Finally, in April 1945, realising the end had come, Mussolini tried to flee to Switzerland with his mistress Clara Petacci – the last of the women in his complicated private life. Recently it has been confirmed that in 1914 Mussolini had married Ida Daiser, who had then given birth to a boy the next year. However, having been abandoned by her husband and then sent to a mental hospital, she would be written out of history by the Fascists. So too, her equally unhappy son was to be confined to an asylum in Venice before being murdered in 1942. Mussolini's second wife, Rachele Guidi, was more fortunate. A local peasant girl, who had become his lover within months of his marriage to Ida, she had eventually married him in a civil wedding in December 1915. Although she would ultimately have five children, the last being born in 1929, throughout the marriage she had had to accept her husband's repeated affairs. Despite the fact that he seldom bathed, and his treatment of them was often rough and extremely perfunctory, many women had been attracted to him. But his relationship with his little 'Claretta' was different. Twenty-eight years younger than Mussolini, she had worshipped him since her adolescence, and after their first meeting in 1933, the two had become closer. Having left her husband, she became devoted to the *Duce*, often spending hours each day waiting in Palazzo Venezia until he was ready to see her. In spite of the scandal that developed when the public learned of their affair, and the attempts Mussolini then made in 1943 to finish it, she would remain at his side to the end, refusing to abandon him and turning down any last chance of escape.

Having previously gone to Milan – against German instructions – on 25 April 1945 Mussolini finally left the city. Although on arrival in Como he wrote a last apologetic and affectionate letter to his wife, he would soon be joined in Menaggio by Claretta. His intention was now to cross the border with the retreating Germans, thus escaping via Switzerland to safety in Spain, but the couple would get no further than the lakeside village of Dongo. Here, despite being dressed as a German, Mussolini was recognised by the partisans and, appearing resigned and exhausted, he then offered no further resistance. Having been taken some 20 kilometres south, on the day before the signing of the German surrender in Italy at Caserta, and just two days before Hitler committed suicide with Eva Braun, on 28 April 1945 Mussolini and Clara were shot outside Villa Belmonte in the hamlet of Giulino di Mezzegra. The same day fifteen others would be executed to the north at Dongo, and Clara's brother, Marcello, was shot when plunging into the lake in a desperate effort to escape. On the 29th all the dead were taken to Milan, and here at Piazzale Loreto, the site chosen by the Fascists for an earlier execution of fifteen partisans, the bodies of Mussolini and his mistress were strung up by their ankles for general display.

Eventually removed from its unmarked grave by his loyal supporters, on 31 August 1957 Mussolini's body was returned for reburial at his birthplace at Predappio in the Romagna, an event attended by thousands of his followers. Despite the post-war official dissolution of the Fascist party, this village that had become renowned following Mussolini's visit to it soon after the March on Rome, is still today a site of pilgrimage for those – often dressed in black – who espouse the far right of politics. Although the main street, originally called after the *Duce*, was later renamed in memory of his opponent, the murdered Matteotti, there are still on sale souvenirs recalling the Fascist regime, as well as images of present-day demagogue leaders. Thus, the complex issues Predappio raises revisit the arguments put forward in Germany at the end of the war, when it was decided that Hitler's Berlin bunker and his mountain retreat, the Berghof at Berchtesgaden, should be destroyed to prevent their becoming pilgrimage sites for his followers.[325]

Mussolini had brought about his own fall, his alignment to Hitler and the Nazi's brutal regime having lost him the support of the majority of Italians, many of whom had once seen him as a man of promise. But even as he had over time become a figure of ridicule, mocked for his posturing and bombast, he had continued to instil fear in his people. Over the years, as he had grown more suspicious of others and increasingly cruel towards those who opposed him, he had become more unpredictable, often rapidly changing his policies on an impulse. The war correspondent, Paolo Monelli, who met him for the last time in 1942, would sum up the tragedy:

> Italy's entry into the war was due to the whim of one over-excited brain, to the personal grudges and spites of one individual, and to the state of mind induced in him by a physical disease.[326]

The workings of Mussolini's capricious nature would bring disaster to his country, and ultimately cause his own demise. Having for a time been confident of his own greatness, in the late 1930s he had declared himself infallible and, despite his months of indecision and wavering over whether or not to join the war, he had told Ciano that he was politically 'much more intelligent than Hitler'.[327] With his growing hubris he had come to ignore the tenuous nature of his position as leader, a reality that would only become fully apparent to him when he was summarily dismissed by the very king whom he had earlier scorned. Victor Emmanuel was also brought down by the failure of the *Duce* and his party, and for his long support of fascism, he and his family would pay the price. On the other hand, D'Annunzio, after the collapse of his Fiume project, would be able to retire to live out his extravagant fantasies. Having never actually become a signed-up Fascist, and remaining always opposed to the Nazis, he would continue after his death to be honoured by many as Italy's poet-hero, and it is as such that no small number visiting *Il Vittoriale* still think of him today. The opposite, however, would be the case for those whom he had influenced, first Mussolini, and through him indirectly, Hitler. Both these dictators who had followed in D'Annunzio's wake would be remembered by the majority of people for the ruinous state to which they had reduced their countries, and the years of suffering that they had brought to so many far and wide.

Old conflicts, new boundaries

'We are part of the general European mess, we do not have the complete and final decision as to our destiny. We are caught in the dynamics of the international politics of the great powers.'

Louis Adamic[328]

Division of Yugoslavia in World War II

Tito with the Partisans.

Although Yugoslavia had sought to remain neutral, within two years of war being declared in September 1939 it had been drawn into the conflict. In the eyes of the Allies, Serbia had come out of the First World War with its reputation largely intact, it alone among the Balkan countries having attempted to maintain its resistance to the Austro-Hungarian-German occupation. Yet, despite its praise for 'valiant little Serbia', Britain's approach to Yugoslavia during the last years of the decade had been inconsistent and erratic. In truth, London's overriding concern had been for the protection of its own interests in Greece. The Special Operations Executive (SOE) had largely ignored the Croat, Slovene and other small resistance groups that might later have proved to be of help. Instead, the undercover agents had concentrated mainly on building up contacts with the Serbs, who on the whole held the elite positions in the country. At the same time, matters had been made considerably more difficult for Belgrade by the disagreements between the different British ministries over the realities of the situation on the ground. Although these had long been supportive of Yugoslavia's neutrality, there had been opposition from certain quarters to any suggestion of further strengthening its position. Some departments had been against providing it with sufficient military material and other necessary supplies for fear that these things might fall into Axis hands. As the situation then began to unwind, and Yugoslavia's non-involvement ceased to be an option, in a last-ditch effort to keep it on side London would make a pledge that when peace came the kingdom would receive Istria and possibly other territories claimed by the Italians. But, the British offers had come too late for the regent, Prince Paul. With the pressure mounting on him, this Oxford-educated Anglophile, so long seen as Britain's 'trump card' in the Balkans, finally abandoned his former policy of strict neutrality. After his latest meeting with Hitler, on 25 March 1941, his ministers in Vienna signed the Tripartite Pact. Although he had for some time distrusted the Führer, being convinced since his first visit to Berlin in 1939 that he was an evil man, Paul had now decided that this was necessary, agreeing to the pact on the understanding that it would allow his country to remain uninvolved in the war. However, with his motives already seen as suspect by some peasants and others, who believed – with little or no evidence – that he was not only personally ambitious but also supportive of the Axis powers, the regent now became deeply unpopular and his people were soon filling the streets of Belgrade, Split and other such towns, chanting, 'Better the grave than a slave, better a war than the pact'.[329]

Just two days later, Paul was deposed in a *coup d'état* that, although led by a group of Serbian Air Force officers, had the endorsement of Britain, which was now hoping to 'salvage something from the wreckage of her Balkan policy'.[330] Although the regent was closely connected by marriage to the Greek and British royal families – his wife being the sister of Princess Marina of Kent and a first cousin of Prince Philip – Churchill and the British press soon joined the Serbs in vilifying him as a Nazi sympathiser, and within a matter of hours he had been forced to leave his country. Denied asylum in Britain, the whole family was deported, going via Greece and Egypt to Kenya. Here, for the next three years, the family was kept under house arrest until at last it was allowed to move to a new home in Johannesburg. Still barred from returning to Yugoslavia, in 1949 Paul and his wife finally settled in Paris, where they both remained until their deaths. Their daughter never gave up trying to rehabilitate them, and in 2012, a year after her father had at last been exonerated of all the charges of treachery that the post-war Communist regime had publicly pronounced against him, the bodies of both her parents and her brother were returned for reburial in Serbia.

As a result of Paul's overthrow, although still technically underage, his 17-year-old cousin Peter II was – with wide public support – recognised as the new king. While Churchill was pleased by this turn of events, Hitler was incandescent with rage and he immediately swore to destroy Yugoslavia. Following the Führer's orders, on 6 April 1941 the bombing of Belgrade began and, with thousands of the citizens soon dead or wounded, just days later the German, Hungarian and Italian invasion of the country had begun. Following the announcement of Yugoslavia's capitulation on 17 April, Peter II was forced to flee. Rescued by a British flying boat, four days later he arrived in London. Here he joined the RAF and over the next few years, besides completing his education at Cambridge University, he led his government-in-exile in Egypt and England. During this time he fully backed the Allies' war programme, on one occasion actually writing his name on a bomb intended for German-occupied Belgrade.

Previously, in August 1939, as the result of a Serb-Croat agreement (*Sporazum*), a new Croatian *banovina* had been created, a province – including the greater part of Dalmatia, Herzegovina, and Slavonia – that had been granted its own governor and home rule. These concessions led to Prince Paul receiving a warm welcome on his first visit. Although defence and foreign affairs remained with the government in Belgrade, Vladimir 'Vladko' Maček, the popular leader of the pro-independence Croatian Peasant Party (HSS) became deputy prime minister in the Yugoslavian National Assembly. Here he served alongside the new Serbian premier, Dragiša Cvetković of the Radical Union party (YRU). However, following the invasion, Maček refused to co-operate with the Germans, and so on his retirement, control of Croatia had fallen into the hands of the already established pro-independence *Ustaša* – 'Uprising' – party. Like the communists, these Croatian pro-fascists wished to see the disintegration of Yugoslavia, and this had been in the forefront in their minds when they had become involved in Alexander I's assassination in Marseille in 1934. Many held Mussolini responsible for that particular crime, which was in fact just one of the organisation's activities to receive backing and financial support from the *Duce* over time. During the war, as the violence began to take greater hold throughout Yugoslavia, under their leader Ante Pavelić, the *Ustaše* would begin to behave with such barbarity that even Mussolini's military leaders were appalled by their actions. Many would come to see these ultranationalists as even more brutal than the Nazis with whom they collaborated. When not massacring entire Serb villages, they either deported the people or forced them to convert to Catholicism. These policies would later prove to be counterproductive, so in April 1942 a Croatian Orthodox Church was founded and other mitigating measures were introduced as a way to pacify the Serbian population. Although the *Ustaše* showed some tolerance for the Muslims as well, they continued to target the Roma and the Jews, and besides the roughly 2000 people they killed every day, during the time they were in power they sent some 40,000 more to die in the concentration camps.

In the meantime, Mussolini had hardened his racist views, moving on from his earlier strict measures against intermarriage and the mixing of black and white communities in the colonies to adopting some of the ideas of his neighbours. In 1938 he had introduced his new racial discrimination laws, announcing these on 15 September in the multicultural setting of Trieste, where the Slavs, Croats and Slovenes had long had claims to the city and surrounding region. Even as Mussolini told his audience that the 'Jewish problem' was only one aspect of the racial 'phenomenon' that he was now addressing, his latest measures were designed to be particularly punitive towards the Jews, confiscating their properties and removing their rights.[331] Although the primary purpose behind *Duce*'s laws was less extreme than that of the Final Solution of the Nazis and the genocide practised by the *Ustaše*, he tapped, nonetheless, into some of their tropes. In his desire to bring together his disparate people whose nation had been united for less than a hundred years, he was seeking to give the population a new shared identity, and as a way to achieve this, he contrasted the stereotypical Jew – the allegedly weak Other of the antisemites – with his idealised Italian. He recreated the latter as the virile *uomo fascista*, a man always ready and proud to defend his country.

Without doubt, Mussolini was totally indifferent to the terrible treatment being meted out by his neighbouring German and Croatian allies. Daniel Carpi describes one notable occasion when he was presented with a memorandum requiring the approval of the transport of 'several thousand' Jews across Italian-occupied territory in Yugoslavia. While it had been hinted to the *Duce* that they were being taken to their 'physical dispersion and elimination' in the east, he gave his approval, merely initialling the paper with the comment 'no opposition' ('nulla osta').[332] Nonetheless, as long as he was in power, some had more chance of escaping the *Ustaše* in these safer occupied regions, where even though the Croat fascists still had a few concentration camps of their own, most were in Italian hands. As some individuals went into hiding, others were interned in southern Italy, or else out on the islands in places such as Curzola (Korčula). Among the thousands of Slovenes and other Croats who were also impounded, those at Arbe (Rab) would later claim that they were kept in conditions that were even worse than the ones imposed on the Jews – the latter apparently having been shown a little more respect by the Italians than their greatly despised Slav neighbours. Although in these camps the general death rate from disease and starvation was high, most of the prisoners who did not later fall into the hands of the Nazis after 1943 were able to survive, and a number then joined the Partisans.

On Holocaust Remembrance Day in 2013, while praising Mussolini's achievements, Silvio Berlusconi described the *Duce*'s racial laws as his 'worst mistake', the Italian prime minister's remarks on this occasion echoing the tone of the controversial comments he had made ten years earlier to Nicholas Farrell and Boris Johnson for *The Spectator*. Declaring the fascist regime to have been a 'benign dictatorship', Berlusconi argued that 'Mussolini did not murder anyone. Mussolini sent people on holiday to confine them.'[333] Although these statements were both shocking and inaccurate, only after the *Duce* had been dismissed by the king in 1943 would the one extermination camp on Italian soil be set up, to the south of Trieste at Risiera di San Sabba (Rižarna in Slovenia). Mussolini's racist views would begin to moderate a little at the end of his life, but even so, it has to be acknowledged that it was while he was titular head of the Nazis' puppet state of the *Repubblica di Salò* that the deportations began. At that point, besides the remaining 204 elderly and sick internees taken from Arbe to Auschwitz, a further 7-8,000 Jews would be transported to Germany never to return.

Following the German invasion of Yugoslavia, the *Ustaše* were rewarded for rejecting their monarch by the Führer, who officially declared in April 1941 Croatia to be an independent kingdom, the NDH (Nezavisna Država Hrvatska) – the sole Yugoslavian region to be granted a degree of autonomy. While in reality this was only another puppet state, during Pavelić's visit to

Rome the next month, the Duke of Spoleto, Aimone, the cousin of Victor Emmanuel III, was named as its new king. Although he accepted the throne as Tomislav II, because he would never actually visit the country he remains a contentious figure, accused by some of being a playboy with little interest in Croatia, but admired by others who declare him an honest man, dedicated to the country's independence. However, in addition to the opposition that soon grew to the handing over to Italy of the NDH's Dalmatian coastal regions, by the end of 1942 a bloody civil war had broken out in the whole of Yugoslavia. Therefore, sixteen months after he had succeeded his older brother as the Duke of Aosta, and just six days after Mussolini had been removed from power, on 31 July 1943 Tomislav abdicated.

By this time, besides having taken southern Slovenia, Italy still held Zadar, Split, Dubrovnik, Kotor, and certain islands such as Lastovo and Vis. Again called by their Italian names, these were now designated as parts of Mussolini's new Governorate of Dalmatia. In addition, between 1941-43, as well as occupying all the Ionian Islands with the exception of Cythera, the *Duce* had incorporated Kosovo and much of Macedonia into Victor Emmanuel's kingdom of Albania. While the king had wanted to avoid becoming more embroiled in the Dalmatian region, foreseeing the problems that this might present, he had been encouraged by his Montenegrin wife to take control of the country, and so he had now become involved in its affairs as well.

After the first World War, Italy had taken longer than the other Allies to recognise Montenegro's loss of independence, and it had only acknowledged its incorporation into the Kingdom of the Serbs, Croats, and Slovenes in 1920. As throughout this time King Nikola had continued to assert that he was still its king, he was succeeded on 1 March 1921 by his son Danilo, but with the latter's abdication six days later the crown had supposedly passed to his nephew, Michael. Nonetheless, on coming of age eight years later, Michael declared the end of his royal dynasty, and, in addition to acknowledging Montenegro's union with Yugoslavia, he then continued to swear loyalty to his cousin, the exiled king Peter II. The Montenegrin-born Italian queen Elena had other ideas, however, and, having persuaded her husband to restore the throne to her nephew, Victor Emmanuel agreed that Mussolini's son-in-law Count Ciano should go to France with the German Foreign Minister von Ribbentrop and offer Michael the crown of his restored kingdom. But as this had been a protectorate of Italy under the watch of the Axis powers since 1941, Michael – still loyal to Peter – turned the proposal down, and as a result he was taken prisoner and held in confinement in Germany. In 1943 Elena was able to arrange his release, but as he was soon recaptured he would remain for the rest of the war with his wife in an internment camp in Czechoslovakia. That same year in September Montenegro also fell to the Nazis, and it remained in their hands until the German retreat at the end of 1944, when Tito declared the country a republic within the Democratic Federal Republic of Yugoslavia. Having at last been released, Michael moved in 1947 to Belgrade, where for a time he gave his support to the new government, briefly working in Tito's foreign ministry. But, on becoming disenchanted with the Communist regime, Michael ultimately chose to return to France, where he died in 1986.

* * *

Josip Broz, first referred to as 'Tito' in the 1930s, was born to a Croatian peasant and his Slovene wife in the village of Kumrovec near Zagreb in May 1892, most probably the seventh of the couple's fifteen children. As Croatia was still within the Austro-Hungarian Empire at the time, during the First World War he fought in the imperial army against the Serbs and, after being badly wounded, he had been taken captive in Russia. On escaping from prison, he had remained in the country, and during the Civil War had served for a time with the Red Army. When at last, in 1920 he returned with his young Russian wife to Croatia, he joined the new Communist Party of Yugoslavia, the KPJ.[334] Although the next year, following the assassination of the minister of the interior, the party was banned and forced to go undercover, Tito was becoming increasingly involved with the Comintern, the Communist International that had been formed in 1919. As this was now hoping to increase the spread of communism by breaking up Yugoslavia, before very long Tito would draw attention to himself and be arrested as an agitator. Imprisoned for five years, he was not released until March 1934, by which time his wife had already returned to Russia. The marriage would later be dissolved. Because Tito was soon fully active in helping the KPJ to grow and had become a member of the committee, he often went back to Russia to continue his work alongside the Comintern. But by 1937 those communists suspected of having Trotskyist leanings had been caught up in Stalin's paranoia,

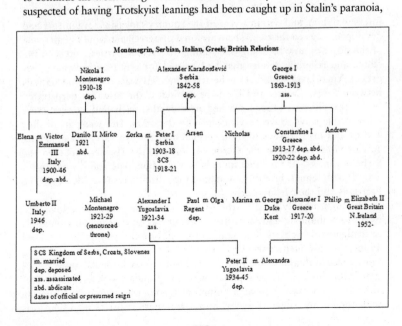

the Soviet leader carrying out a massive purge of any whose loyalty he doubted. But, although around 800 of Tito's Yugoslav colleagues were arrested in Moscow at this time, and he also was in danger, ultimately he avoided the same fate. Whether or not he had survived by playing a part in their disappearance – as some suggest – he would in fact later benefit from their removal, being chosen to fill the place of the head of his party who had earlier vanished. Even though Tito's position would not be fully assured until November two years later, during August 1937 he became the interim secretary and the *de facto* party leader, and in this role he would later visit Paris, where volunteers were being sought to join the Republican cause in the Spanish Civil War.

After Hitler had abandoned Stalin, breaking their former non-aggression pact to invade the Soviet Union in June 1941, the Comintern changed tack and began to see a united Yugoslavia as a useful bulwark against the Nazis. To help in their effort to drive the Germans from the country, Tito – as he was now officially known – became leader of the Partisans. The Allies ignored him, however, preferring to rely on the exiled king's monarchist supporter, Draža Mihajlović. Nicknamed 'the eagle of Yugoslavia', he was the leader of the royalist and mainly Serbian *Četniks* ('the Ravna Gora Movement') – the Yugoslav Army in the Fatherland. After the German invasion, Mihajlović had fled to Bosnia, and from there he would now continue to support the exiled Peter and his government against the opposition at home.

The situation in Yugoslavia had been growing steadily more complex as the separate groups with their different cultures and languages were drawn into the fight: the communists, fascists, Partisans, *Četniks* and *Ustaše*. After two meetings with Tito, Mihajlović turned down the offer of joining forces with him, and within a year of the country's invasion, arguments had developed between the two. Their personal disagreement would be just one of the disputes now breaking out among the various parties, and with the ethnic and religious divides that had existed for centuries becoming ever deeper, Yugoslavia would soon be riven by civil war. As age-old hatreds between Serbs, Croats, and Bosnians exploded, the brutality perpetrated by all the different groups reached new depths, each finding ever more unspeakable ways to wreak vengeance on the other. Tito was part of this, and he and his Partisans would continue over time to carry out appalling acts of violence against the Germans, Italians, the *Ustaše*, and even the Serbian *Četniks*. At the same time, however, Mihajlović and his men were acting with equal brutality, slaughtering Croatians and Muslims, the Partisans and their fellow Serbs.

Although initially feted by the Allies for his resistance to the invaders, by 1943 Mihajlović had fallen from favour. Because of his unwillingness to instigate any activity that would result in brutal reprisals, he was seen as increasingly ineffective. Tito, who had no such qualms, was proving more successful, and so the British had begun to back the Partisans rather than Mihajlović. This new policy was not popular with everyone, but, although some saw Tito as a communist who was secretly negotiating with the enemy, others believed him a true nationalist, a man who was

Old conflicts, new boundaries

fighting for his country. In the latter category was Churchill who, being under serious pressure himself, had put aside his bitter opposition to communism and begun to put his faith in the Partisans. Possibly guided by false intelligence, he ignored the negative reports, not just of their brutality, but also of Tito's apparent preparedness to negotiate with anyone whom he saw as serving his ultimate purpose. Ready to use any means to arrive at an eventual communist takeover of his country, he was quite prepared to talk with both Hitler and Stalin.

With Churchill now wanting to link up more closely with the Partisans, in May 1943 the British Colonel F.W. Deakin from SOE was parachuted into Montenegro on an exploratory mission with a small group of fellow officers. His objective was to make first contact and discover exactly what Tito was achieving in his fight against the enemy. A further meeting took place between the Partisans and Brigadier Fitzroy Maclean in September and within weeks an SOE mission was set up in Macedonia. By the end of November British aircraft from southern Italy had begun making air drops of arms and other supplies. By this time Tito was in Bosnia, attending the second meeting of the Anti-Fascist Council for the People's Liberation of Yugoslavia (AVNOJ), a body founded twelve months earlier. Now appointed prime minister of its National Committee for the Liberation of Yugoslavia and given the title of marshal, Tito as head of the unofficial government presented his proposed structure for the county after the war. Although he insisted Peter II could not return, as the final decision regarding the king's future was deferred, for the time being the fate of the monarchy remained hanging in the balance.

Meanwhile, Stalin, Churchill, and Roosevelt come together for their first meeting on 28 November 1943 in Tehran, where, to the surprise of the Soviet leader, the British prime minister declared his support of the Partisans. Having told Peter of this, on 8 January Churchill wrote to the marshal for the first time, thanking him for his assistance and promising him the help of the three major allied powers. Having eventually informed the British Parliament of his new stance in February, three months later Churchill went further and ordered his liaison officers to stop working alongside Mihailović.

By this time President Roosevelt had been won over, and although initially unsure of Churchill's latest policy he gave his approval to Tito, who, by his willingness to accept people of all political persuasions into his ranks, had now gathered a large National Liberation Army that was achieving notable success. As, however, the Germans had become aware of his importance to the Allied cause, in February they tried to have the marshal assassinated, and so in early June 1944 the British moved him and the AVNOJ to safety, taking them first to Bari and then to the island of Vis off the Dalmatian coast. While here, on 17 June, the prime minister of King Peter's government-in-exile, Ivan Šubašić, signed a new agreement, and two months later Tito and the British premier had a face-to-face meeting in Naples. However, to Churchill's immense fury, on 18 September the marshal secretly left Vis again to visit Stalin in Moscow. Here the two communist leaders would come to

359

an understanding regarding the upcoming Belgrade Offensive, now agreeing on how far during the invasion of Yugoslavia the Soviet forces should be permitted to go, and how long afterwards they would remain in the country.

With Churchill having put increasing pressure on the young king, on 29 August 1944 Peter finally broke all ties with Mihajlović and the pro-monarchist *Četniks*. Two weeks later he went further, and, while appealing to the Yugoslavs to support national unity, he asked them to acknowledge Tito as the leader of the military, and himself as the head of a new, mutually acceptable cabinet. On 1 November in Belgrade this coalition was affirmed in a draft agreement that promised the continuation of the people's democratic rights until a plebiscite could eventually be held. The Provisional Government of the Democratic Federal Yugoslavia would not, however, be finally established until 7 March 1945, and in the interim the monarch's authority continued slowly to be eroded. His position was not helped by the British who earlier, in an attempt to maintain their influence in the face of greater Soviet intervention, had agreed to Tito's stipulation that Peter should remain in exile. Even though still king in name, he was to surrender his position in Yugoslavia into the hands of a regency. Having immediately voiced his objection to this idea, Peter attempted to sack his prime minister for concurring with the plan without his approval, but, unable to stand up to Churchill, in the end he had been forced to accept the situation and reappoint Šubašić as his premier.

As he had officially abandoned Mihajlović, the British prime minister had now become a much-hated figure in certain quarters, being particularly loathed by the *Četniks*, who considered his backing of Tito an act of betrayal that had given tacit approval to the steady increase of Stalin's influence in the region. More significantly still, with the loss of their much-needed support from the Allies, Mihajlović and his *Četniks* had drifted towards the Axis powers, some already having collaborated with the Italians. Others were now equally ready to give their full backing to the Germans, seeing this as their only way to resist a post-war communist takeover and the fall of their king. Nonetheless, the Partisans were able in October 1944 to follow the Soviets into Belgrade, where Tito began to establish his own government. In the meantime, because the marshal had convinced the Allies that a military base was stationed at Zadar, this had undergone 11 months of heavy and repeated Anglo-American bombing raids. These attacks had caused massive damage to the town and its historic centre and the deaths of many of the resident Italians; the exact toll is not known, estimates varying from a thousand to anything between three and five times that number. It would finally fall to the Partisans on 31 October. The next month Kotor was also liberated from the Germans. Now in retreat, many of their former supporters fell into enemy hands, some being lynched while others were sent to internment camps. Meanwhile, further north, vast numbers would be caught up in the bloody maelstrom of these weeks, many choosing in May 1945 to surrender to the British at Bleiburg and elsewhere along the southern Austrian border. While again some were removed to detention camps, the less fortunate were handed over to Tito and his Partisans, who proceeded to take their revenge on anyone thought to have supported the fascists.

All around Europe reprisals, arrests and killings now became the order of the day. The Allies were soon having to deal with the long columns of desperate people who were arriving at their bases. Shocked and terrified refugees were adding to the chaos that had already been caused by the thousands of soldiers who had laid down their arms. As all these people were fleeing in fear from the approaching Soviets. before long the British and Americans were overwhelmed by the situation that was facing them. However, they now found a solution to some of their problems in the exchange programme that Churchill and a less enthusiastic Roosevelt had drawn up at Yalta. According to this agreement, all Stalin's supposed citizens were to be surrendered to him, even those who had left the country years earlier after the fall of the tsar and before the establishment of the Soviet Union. The Cossacks, having been persecuted at home, had hoped to improve their lot by opting to fight for Hitler, but even though it was obvious that Stalin would be set on retribution, the British held firm to the earlier agreement.

By this time, unaware of what was in store, the Cossacks from Yugoslavia, many accompanied by their wives and children, had crossed northern Italy and arrived in Austria, where in early May they then surrendered to the British. While they were housed in an internment camp they were treated well, and some of the men would even build up good relations with their guards or fellow officers. Before the month was out, however, the situation had changed, and several people had started to sound the alarm. Among these was the Cossacks' own German commander, who now tried without success to warn the Allies of what lay ahead if his men should be handed over to Stalin. Having received no positive response to his appeal for asylum, he then chose to remain with his men, a decision for which he would ultimately pay with his life. The British were now driven by their concern that if they failed to do as Stalin wished, he would retaliate by delaying the release of their own POWs, something that was sure to prove highly unpopular with the war-weary public at home.[335] The Americans were equally anxious about this in the areas that they controlled, the US Ambassador Averell Harriman spelling out the problem: 'Eisenhower and his staff were fearful that if they did not send back the Soviet Prisoners, the Russians might seize upon one pretext or another to hold up the return of American prisoners from Eastern Europe.'[336] Thirty years after the end of the war these events caused an uproar when they became public knowledge, the scandal leading to a debate in the House of Lords. Some of the speakers, however, sought to give a more nuanced interpretation of what had occurred in 1945. Drawing on their own experiences as serving officers at the time, they stressed not just the chaos and shortage of food and shelter for all the displaced people, but also the uncertainty that was still felt as to the outcome of the war itself. Until Hiroshima and Nagasaki it was generally expected that the fighting would continue for maybe another two years, and so all decisions had therefore been made without what Hugh Trevor Roper described as 'the comfortable after-wisdom of the historian'.[337] Even so, although the authorities were undoubtedly faced by immense logistical problems over the management of the massed crowds of migrants, questions are still asked as to why the British kept to the earlier agreement with Stalin, while they allowed certain other groups to escape their repatriation back to Russia or Yugoslavia. Whatever the reason for this, all appeals to the British to save the Cossacks from their fate remained unanswered and, despite the distress of many of those who were detailed to carry out the orders, the deportations went ahead. With the scene made worse by some committing suicide, and others being taken away by their new captors and executed on the spot, now the remaining 40,000 or so men, women and children were crowded onto trucks and trains and taken back to the Soviet Union, where the majority would ultimately face death or years of hard labour. While this was the cause of deep shame to the British and acknowledged as such in the 1976 debate, the veterans in the Lords, who acknowledged that grave mistakes had been made and that the screening of the deportees had been poorly carried out, still held that the repatriations were among the many 'very unpalatable decisions' that have to be taken in war.

As the end approached in 1944, many Četniks fled in fear of reprisal. While some were then taken from Gorizia to a year of internment in Forlì, many others were to face a far worse fate, among them their leader Draža Mihajlović. Initially he had tried to play a more cautious game, preserving his forces in the hope that after the possible liberation of his country the Allies might be able to help him in the defeat of his various enemies. As the situation deteriorated, he like some of his men had approached the Italians and Germans, and on realising at last that no invasion was going to take place, in the autumn of 1944 he had unsuccessfully called for a general uprising. As the following May he was defeated by the Partisans at Drina, he then accepted that further resistance was impossible and went into hiding. Eventually captured the following March, three months later he was among a group of men tried for war crimes in Belgrade and, found guilty, he and nine others were then executed on 17 July by firing squad.

Mihajlović was posthumously awarded the Legion of Merit by President Bush in 2005, in recognition of the part he had played in rescuing 500 American airmen during the war – something that had been kept quiet during the period of Communist rule. Ten years after this, Mihajlović was also cleared of the charge of collaboration by Serbia's highest court of appeal, but he still remains a highly controversial figure, particularly among the Croats who hold him responsible for the massacre of their people. There are others who claim that besides trying to save his country and its king, he had dedicated himself to fighting against both totalitarian regimes. Lacking the unsentimental pragmatism of Churchill, Tito and others, men who had been prepared to work with whosoever served their purpose at the time, Mihajlović had hesitated when choosing his alliances. So, although towards the end there had been a possibility that he might be evacuated to safety by the British, he had ultimately been caught between the two rival factions. With the situation becoming even more complex and confusing in the last months of 1944, the Četniks had engaged at different times in fighting the Germans, Ustaše, and their allies, as well as the Soviets and the Partisans. As he had tried to find a way through this mayhem, Mihajlović would make a last-ditch effort to prevent a communist takeover of Yugoslavia by turning to those same enemies who had earlier invaded his country. For this, and for the violence of some of his actions, many would never forgive him.

During the eight months since it had been set up on 7 March 1945, the provisional government had tightened its hold, the communists gradually removing the rights and freedoms that had been promised to the people. After holding a 3rd meeting of the AVNOJ in August 1945, a rigged election had taken place, whose result had been made still more questionable by the opposition refusing to stand. Within days of its overwhelming victory, on 29 November the new government officially deposed Peter II. A year before these events, contrary to advice, the Yugoslav king had chosen to marry in London his much-loved third cousin, Princess Alexandra of Greece and Denmark, the Greek king's posthumous daughter of a morganatic marriage, whose own complicated childhood had been troubled by political unrest and years in exile. The Serbs were shocked by Peter's marriage, considering such a celebration to be highly unsuitable when his country was undergoing the horrors of the war. Forced after the end of the hostilities to remain for ever exiled from Yugoslavia, their lives would then be blighted by poverty, bankruptcy, alcoholism, depression, ill-health, and the mentally fragile queen's repeated attempted suicides. By the time of his death in November 1970, the 47-year-old Peter was living alone in America, where his remains would stay until 2013, when they were returned to Serbia. Having in fact never abdicated, he was then given a state funeral in the capital, before he and his previously estranged wife were finally interred together in the royal family's crypt at Oplenac to the south of Belgrade.

* * *

In February 1945 the British agreed with Tito that Venezia-Giulia should be divided into separate zones, which were then to be occupied individually by the Anglo-Americans and the Yugoslavs. While America was still loath to become involved in a scheme that it believed Churchill had thought up purely to serve British interests, Britain's own concerns were growing. With Tito later claiming to have 'put that old fox Churchill in the bag', by early 1945 the prime minister was seriously worried about the marshal's ambitions, convinced that the Partisan leader wished to take complete control of Venezia-Giulia.[338] While Tito rested his claim to the region on the British promises made in 1941 to the regent Paul, both he and Churchill were set on getting hold of Trieste, which since the Italian Armistice in 1943 had been under German occupation within the *Repubblica di Salò*. Accordingly, on 27 April Churchill wrote to President Truman, declaring that the 'great thing is to be there before Tito's guerrillas … The actual status of Trieste can be determined at leisure.'[339] With both sides realising the importance of possession, Tito was determined to beat his rivals to the city, and on May Day 1945 his troops arrived and took the place over. To the astonishment and confusion of the British soldiers stationed at Venice, they were now hurriedly marched east to deal with their former allies and put a stop to these events. Nonetheless, Field Marshal Alexander, the Supreme Allied Commander in the Mediterranean, remained strongly opposed to Churchill's suggestion that force should be used against the Partisans, and so, when the New Zealanders arrived shortly after the Yugoslavs, their hands would then be tied. Therefore, on 5 May, when Tito's soldiers fired on a peaceful march taking place in the city, they were forced to obey orders and – in Churchill's words – go against 'their sense of justice' and give 'tacit acquiescence to the misdeed'.[340] For the same reason, although the remaining Germans had previously held out just long enough to surrender to these allied troops, the Anzacs were now instructed to hand their prisoners over to the Partisans.

This was the beginning of the tense period of the so-called Forty Days of occupation that continued until 12 June 1945, only coming to an end three days after an Anglo-American-Yugoslav agreement was reached in Belgrade. It was during this interim, while the Yugoslavs were taking over much of Istria as well as cities like Fiume and Gorizia, that so many would suffer throughout the region. Those believed guilty of any association with the former regimes now found themselves in grave danger. In addition to the members of the pro-fascist *Ustaše* and Slovenian *Domobranci* Home Guard, many more Croats, Slovenes, Bosnians and others were among the tens of thousands of people to die, the evidence of their slaughter being brought to light with the discovery in 1999 of a mass grave of 15,000 victims at Tezno in Slovenia – just one of the scores of hidden burial sites that are still scattered across the country.[341] While the exact figure can never be known, it is certain that untold numbers of innocent victims were among those brutally murdered, many of them being cast to their deaths in the *foibe* pits and crevasses that litter the region. As a result, there would be an exodus of roughly 230,000 people over the following year, with 350,000 or more choosing to leave over the next two decades. These, mainly Italians, but also a few Croats and Slovenes, all had the one intention of getting as far away as possible from the Partisans, some even leaving their homes in western Venezia-Giulia to find safety further from the border. But, for both practical and political reasons, the refugees were not always welcome in their new homes. In a country battered and impoverished by years of war, many of the locals were averse to supporting these migrants, and when the suggestion was made of establishing a new Pola on the Gargano, it was quickly dropped, partly for fear that the expense would give rise to local unrest. Although until comparatively recently few people would dare to speak of the horrors that they had witnessed, the victims of this period are today remembered in some cities like Bari and Brindisi, where squares and streets are named after the 'martyrs' of the *foibe*.

At last the immediate political situation would be settled when the opposing sides met in Belgrade and agreed to share the provisional administration of Venezia-Giulia, the British and Americans given charge of the smaller western part labelled as Zone A and the Yugoslavs the eastern, Zone B. The two sectors were separated by the Morgan Line that was named after one of Field Marshal Alexander's officers who had been responsible for drawing it up. According to this plan, the Yugoslavs would leave the areas up to the River Isonzo they had recently occupied, and they would also surrender

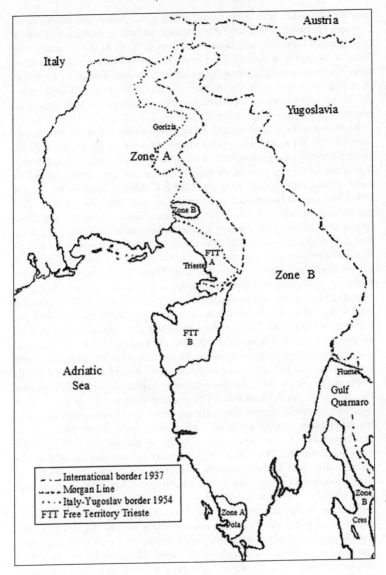

the captured Istrian town of Pola that was now to become a small separate enclave belonging to Zone A. This division of the region as a whole would mean, however, that Italy was obliged to surrender its claims to roughly 3,000 square miles, from where again the local people would soon be leaving in their droves. At the same time, it was proposed that Trieste should be a separate free state under international military occupation, but on this score arguments would continue until the next year, and the situation would not be fully resolved until the peace meeting in Paris in April. In the meantime, the tensions continued to increase, and it was only a month later that Churchill made his famous speech, telling his American audience that an Iron Curtain stretching from Stettin on the Baltic to Trieste had descended on Europe. As the premier's remarks indicated, the Adriatic town had now become a potential flash point in the new Cold War.

By this time the US, which had previously put its trust in the agreements drawn up at Yalta, had also grown extremely wary of Tito's true motives. Having become deeply concerned about his connections with Stalin, America now feared that the two men's rapport might aid the further spread of communism. Despite aid from the UNRRA (United Nations Relief and Rehabilitation Administration) continuing to pour into his country, Tito did nothing to help ease these tensions, instead encouraging the spread of propaganda accusing the Allies of aggressive behaviour. Although the British and Americans responded with their own detrimental reports of what he was doing, it now appeared that the marshal wanted to portray Yugoslavia as standing up to the two superpowers, the Soviet Union and the USA. With instances of illegal crossings of the border adding to the general unease, by August 1946 bad feelings between Tito and the Americans had escalated to such a pitch that two US planes were shot down. While those aboard the first were interned, all those on the second had died, and so for a few days an international crisis loomed. Even after the eventual release of the crew and the payment of partial indemnities by the Yugoslavs, the situation would remain strained. Tito continued to justify what had happened on grounds of the pilots' illegal entry into his country's airspace, and his relations with the Americans would continue to be extremely poor for another year or two. The marshal's eagerness to play a part on the international stage had not gone down particularly well in the Soviet Union either. Although the two communist leaders had signed a treaty of friendship in 1945, Stalin was concerned that Yugoslavia might step out of line and cause a serious confrontation with the other powers, something that he was anxious to avoid since his own country was not yet strong enough to deal with the opposition as he wished.

After further peace talks in Paris in February 1947, during which the Italians had given up their Dodecanese islands in the Aegean and their colonial possessions in Africa, Italy signed a separate treaty with Yugoslavia agreeing to a newly drawn border in the north. This would now run a short distance to the west of the former Morgan Line, along a route suggested by the French. After two years under the Allies' control, Gorizia – which now found itself right on the border – was to be mostly returned to Italy, some of its outer urban regions remaining in Yugoslavia, where the next year work would begin on constructing a new town, Nova Gorica. In September the independent Free Territory of Trieste (FTT) was created, a new independent state under the United Nations, which was to be temporarily administered by the Anglo-Americans in Zone A and the Yugoslavs in Zone B until a governor was appointed.

Following the Paris treaties, along with Istria, Dalmatia, and other former Italian possessions such as Rijeka (Fiume) and Zadar, Pola (Pula), too, was handed over to the Yugoslavs. Having already suffered so much in the war, living under the Nazis, experiencing repeated, heavy Allied bombardment and surviving two periods of particularly brutal Partisan occupation, the city looked on its future with renewed horror. On the very day the agreement was signed in February, shortly before the start of the official ceremony an Italian nationalist, Maria Pasquinelli, stepped forward and shot dead the commander of the British garrison, Brigadier Robert de Winton. With the people's fear then continuing to increase, by the time of the final hand-over in September, the mass exodus had grown to such proportions that the place was largely deserted, there possibly being only some four thousand Italian citizens still left in the city. While many of the refugees had carried with them the bones or ashes of their dead relations, before leaving scores of people had also taken as a memento a stone from the great Roman arena, the symbol for them of Pola's long Italian heritage.

With no acceptable candidate having been found, the initial plan for the Security Council to appoint a governor of the FTT had failed. Therefore, in March 1948 Britain, the US, and France came up with an alternative idea, now issuing a Tripartite declaration that, with the approval of the Soviets, offered the whole of the Free Territory to the Italians. Within months this, too, would be quietly shelved when the developing rift between Tito and Stalin came to a head and it was realised that more co-operation was needed between Italy and Yugoslavia to resist Soviet pressure. Despite the Allies' earlier concerns about the two communist leaders' closeness, by June relations between them had completely broken down, and on the 29th the Soviet press announced that the Communist Party of Yugoslavia had been expelled from Cominform, the organisation founded the year before to bring together the various pro-communist countries. Later, in 1956, under President Khrushchev Cominform would be disbanded to improve relations with Yugoslavia, but for the time being Stalin was so angry that he would regularly attempt to have Tito assassinated, doing this so often that the Yugoslav eventually wrote mockingly to the Soviet leader, demanding: 'Stop sending people to kill me. If you don't stop sending killers, I'll send one to Moscow, and I won't have to send a second.'[342] In Yugoslavia the after-effect of this disagreement was disastrous for the convinced Stalinists who had come to fill the vacancies in the skilled labour force created by the Italian exodus. From the moment of the falling-out with Moscow, these people would be at risk of arrest, imprisonment and even death, as the marshal began to take measures against anyone who stood against him. During his time in power, Tito sent thousands of the opposition into detention camps, one of the worst being Goli Otok, a barren island lying just off the coast of Rab. Despite the humanitarian concerns this raised, in 1951 the USA, hoping to prevent

Yugoslavia from falling to the Soviets, agreed to a new aid programme, and for the next eight years it would provide Tito with food as well as arms.

In March 1952 in Allied-controlled Trieste, riots broke out as the irredentists began demanding the immediate return of the region to Italy. Over fifty people were injured, and within days further similar demonstrations with thousands of protestors were also taking place in Naples and Rome. The following year tensions increased again as Tito, recently appointed President of the Federal People's Republic of Yugoslavia, became more belligerent and began to threaten to annex Zone B. With the international position having changed after Stalin's death in March, and the Trieste situation continuing to grow ever more fraught, by early October the Allies had had enough of the mandate they had only originally accepted as a temporary commitment. They now announced that they wanted to hand the responsibility of Zone A of the FTT over to the Italians. This was of little satisfaction to anyone, many expecting the Allies' quick departure to lead to renewed fighting between Italy and Yugoslavia, because the Italians wanted to claim the land promised in the Tripartite Declaration of 1948 and the Yugoslavs were set on preventing the takeover of Zone B. The first week of November saw more riots in Trieste, leaving at least six people dead after the British opened fire, but by the following February talks had begun in London and on 31 May the Memorandum of Understanding was signed. When this was eventually confirmed by the US, Britain, Yugoslavia and Italy on 5 October 1954, it was agreed that the Free Territory of Trieste (FTT) would be abolished. So with the Allied military government coming to an end, Zone A, together with Trieste, was handed over to Italy, while Zone B – now increased by a few metres on its southern border – remained under Yugoslavian administration.

For the next two decades, this situation would not be entirely resolved as the tensions between the superpowers continued to build. However, although Italy had refused to ratify the Memorandum, with the Mediterranean becoming a more unstable area during this period of the Cold War, within a year of the London talks Rome had reached further agreement with the Yugoslavs. From this time on, in addition to permitting freer movement between the zones, there would be increased commercial exchange over the border. This crossing point continued to grow in significance, especially after 1957 when Italy became a member of the newly created EEC. Being now more open to foreign capitalist trade, Yugoslavia wished to benefit from the Common Market through its association with the Italians, and after the two countries had signed a further pact in 1964, it drew up yet another agreement with the EEC in 1970. At this time Italy still officially claimed its right to Zone B of the FTT – something which so irritated Tito that he cancelled his visit to Rome at the last minute – but with pressures between the superpowers steadily escalating in the Mediterranean, and the improving climate of the European *détente*, relations between Italy and Yugoslavia continued to strengthen. The northern republics of Slovenia and Croatia, in particular, saw the advantage that this situation brought to trade and to their developing industries near the border. Encouraged by these things, in 1975 they ratified their earlier agreement with Italy at Osimo near Ancona. Even so, this same treaty was greeted with large demonstrations in Trieste, where in addition to protesting against the surrender of their claims to Zone B, many Italians feared that a free-trade zone would negatively impact on the easy working relationship they had with the neighbouring communities, an understanding that allowed them to cross the border for work, shopping, or leisure. More seriously for Yugoslavia, however, the economic and industrial advantages gained by Slovenia and Croatia increased the discrepancies between the various republics, over time exacerbating internal jealousies and ultimately threatening the unity of the country.

When he was nearly sixty, Tito married again, choosing as his third or possibly fourth wife, Jovanka, a woman more than thirty years younger. Having, in 1963, after the introduction of another constitution, been made President of the newly named Socialist Federal Republic of Yugoslavia, he continued to follow his luxurious lifestyle, staying around the country in his numerous scattered villas, castles, palaces and hunting lodges, some of which were the former residences of the Karađorđević royal family.[343] Besides liking to entertain heads of state and the famous celebrities of the day – Liz Taylor and Richard Burton among them – Tito much enjoyed sailing. In March 1953 he caused some concern to the British political establishment by unexpectedly accepting an invitation to London and arriving in Greenwich on his impressive yacht, a vast vessel today moored in Rijeka, where there are now some ambitious plans to carry out its much-needed restoration. After the introduction of a new constitution in 1974, when he was declared president for life, Tito would start to step back from some of his responsibilities, but he would continue to hold office right up to the time of his death on 4 May 1980, days before his 88th birthday. He was given a spectacular funeral that was attended by numerous members of foreign royal families and political heads of state, the various guests representing altogether more than 120 different countries.

During his time in power Tito had ruled in his own style, at times combining his communist beliefs with his more liberal reforms, mixing the brutal punishment and persecution of any who chose to oppose him with a general opening up of his country. Although those in search of work were granted greater freedom to travel, the same was not true for everyone, but as tourists were allowed to visit Yugoslavia, people came into contact with the latest Western ideas, and this would lead in turn to a generally higher standard of living than that found in other communist countries. Today certain older people still look back on that period with a degree of nostalgia, a number regretting the disappearance of the Yugoslavia they knew, somewhere that for a time had been one of Europe's larger and more influential countries. When it was already a member of the United Nations, in 1961 Tito had invited leaders from India, Egypt, Ghana, and Indonesia to Belgrade to join his new Movement of Non-Aligned countries, which had been created expressly to be an alternative to the two major western and eastern blocs.

In 2020 his grandson, speaking on France 24, recalled how Tito had told him shortly before he died that he regretted the 'mistake' he had made in weakening the bonds between Yugoslavia's separate federal republics. This had allowed the growth of their political divisions and rivalries and increased nationalist demands. Fearful of this, at the start of the 1970s he had begun to block any further attempt at economic reform. Yet, by having earlier permitted greater federalisation alongside his conflicting policy of increased centralisation, he had already created a situation that would leave his country after his death in a vulnerable state. Its problems were made worse by ever-rising inflation and continuing financial downturn, and so it would not take much to set things alight. The spark came with the fall of the Berlin Wall, and the resultant collapse of communism all around Europe. Therefore, within two years, and just over a decade after Tito's death the country was riven by a series of destructive and bloody civil wars that caused the deaths of over 130,000 people and ultimately saw the fragmentation of Yugoslavia itself. Today, however, the former republics have regained their independence, and – with Croatia and Slovenia now members of the EU club of democratic nations, and Montenegro and Serbia both applying to join – the people of these countries are able to look towards a brighter and more peaceful future.

* * *

During the Second World War, when Albania was liberated by the National Liberation Movement led by the communist Enver Hoxha, many of those opposed to the regime were put to death or imprisoned, but with King Zog having been officially deposed in January 1946, the next year the country's independence would be recognised by Italy in the Paris Treaty. Yet, despite the accord also agreed between Albania and Yugoslavia, by the time of the Tito-Stalin split in 1948, relations between the two countries had broken down with the government in Tirana now adopting a strict Stalinist agenda. Already in 1939 the USA had broken off diplomatic relations following the Italian invasion, and there had been a similar falling out with the British after two of their destroyers had been blown up by mines in the waters off Corfu in 1946. Yet, by 1968 Albania would also be in disagreement with the Soviet Union, it believing that Moscow's policies were now too liberal. So shortly after the Soviet invasion of Czechoslovakia, it had withdrawn from the Warsaw Pact. Although for the next two decades Albanians would have to live in one of the strictest of totalitarian states, the people being kept completely cut off from the outside world, after 1989 and the steady collapse of communism around Europe, their country was finally forced to adapt, and from then on it started to move towards a more democratic form of government. A member of NATO since 2014, and now applying like its neighbours to join the EU, over recent years Albania has also begun to be a more popular destination for foreign tourists.

* * *

Having voted for a republic on 2 June 1946, Italy would initially struggle to find a way through its political and financial problems. Yet, over the next three decades it enjoyed a significant recovery, and, having joined the European Common Market in 1957 as a founding member, it continued to increase its tourism and expand its various industries, becoming at the same time particularly famous around the world for the production of luxury goods. From as far back as 1906 work had begun in the south on the construction of the *Acquedotto Pugliese* that, extending for over 2000 kilometres, had been finally completed in 1939. Despite the considerable work done during the fascist regime on land improvement, Mussolini's measures had been of little or no benefit to the poor, but further plans for the development of the southern regions had begun with the setting up in 1950 of the *Cassa per il Mezzogiorno*. Although questions remain over the waste, ineffectiveness and non-completion of some of the fund's projects, in its early years, before it was financed by northern or foreign investment companies, it would bring notable change, upgrading roads, water supplies, drainage systems, industries, and land management. One of its most notable projects was the improvement of the lives of those housed in the *sassi*. Much to the shame of many Italians, in the 1950s in the Basilicata town of Matera alone there were still approximately 15,000 of these cave-dwellers, whose homes lacked the most basic of facilities. This was also a period of large-scale movement from the countryside to the cities, many young men in particular emigrating north to find work. Despite having begun its economic reform in the 1960s, alongside the two oil crises and international recessions of the 1970s and 1980s, Italy had its own serious domestic problems, among these the terrorist activities of the Red Brigade, and the severe Friuli earthquake in 1976.[344] But at the same time, relations with the northern Yugoslavian republics were helped by the signing of the Osimo Treaty, and although partially drawn into the tragic events of the Yugoslavian wars, the development of this partnership would be marked in 2007 by a highly symbolic event. Three years after becoming a member of the EU, Slovenia was included in the Schengen Area, and with its border controls with Italy now ceasing to exist, amid much celebration, the last physical barrier between the two countries was removed.

While 2020-21 has been an incredibly difficult period for people all around the world, Italy, the first country in Europe to witness the full horror of the Covid pandemic, would experience some of the most extensive suffering during those early weeks. Soon following in the footsteps of the Italians there would be untold numbers of others in Europe and elsewhere who found themselves facing life-changing challenges, comparable in many ways to those confronted in the wars by their parents and grandparents. Businesses failed, livelihoods were overturned, families broken, and sickness and death became all too common. Yet, although the immediate future remains uncertain for everyone, in the Adriatic region people are beginning to see the first signs of a return to a situation that will allow everyone to enjoy life again in this exceptionally beautiful, historic and fascinating part of the world.

Place names

<table>
<tr><td>Former place names</td><td>Modern equivalents</td></tr>
<tr><td>Actium</td><td>Arte</td></tr>
<tr><td>Antivari</td><td>Bar</td></tr>
<tr><td>Arbe</td><td>Rab</td></tr>
<tr><td>Avalona or Valona</td><td>Vlorë</td></tr>
<tr><td>Brazza</td><td>Brač</td></tr>
<tr><td>Brundisium</td><td>Brindisi</td></tr>
<tr><td>Buthrōtum</td><td>Butrint</td></tr>
<tr><td>Capodistria</td><td>Koper</td></tr>
<tr><td>Cerigo</td><td>Kythera</td></tr>
<tr><td>Cherso</td><td>Cres</td></tr>
<tr><td>Curzola</td><td>Korčula</td></tr>
<tr><td>Dulcigno</td><td>Ulcinj</td></tr>
<tr><td>Dyrrachium or Durazzo</td><td>Durrës</td></tr>
<tr><td>Fiume</td><td>Rijeka</td></tr>
<tr><td>Gorizia</td><td>Görtz</td></tr>
<tr><td>Lacroma</td><td>Lokrum</td></tr>
<tr><td>Lagosta</td><td>Lastovo</td></tr>
<tr><td>Lesina</td><td>Hvar</td></tr>
<tr><td>Lissa</td><td>Vis</td></tr>
<tr><td>Lussino</td><td>Lošinj</td></tr>
<tr><td>Moscopole</td><td>Moschopolis, Voskopojë</td></tr>
<tr><td>Narenta</td><td>Neretva</td></tr>
<tr><td>Parenzo</td><td>Poreč</td></tr>
<tr><td>Pelagosa</td><td>Palagruža</td></tr>
<tr><td>Pola</td><td>Pula</td></tr>
<tr><td>Ragusa</td><td>Dubrovnik</td></tr>
<tr><td>Rovigno</td><td>Rovinj</td></tr>
<tr><td>Santa Maura</td><td>Lefkada, Lefkas</td></tr>
<tr><td>Scutari</td><td>Shkodër</td></tr>
<tr><td>Sebenico</td><td>Šibenik</td></tr>
<tr><td>Spalato</td><td>Split</td></tr>
<tr><td>Trau</td><td>Trogir</td></tr>
<tr><td>Veglia</td><td>Krk</td></tr>
<tr><td>Zante</td><td>Zakynthos</td></tr>
<tr><td>Zara</td><td>Zadar</td></tr>
</table>

Timeline

312 BC Work starts on constructing the Via Appia

272 BC Rome begins its greater colonisation of Magna Grecia

264 BC Via Appia reaches Brundisium (Brindisi): start of First Punic War

241 BC End of First Punic War

229 BC First Roman defeat of Illyrians

219 BC Second Roman defeat of Illyrians

218 BC Start of Second Punic War: two years later Battle of Cannae

202 BC Roman victory over Carthaginians: peace the next year

181 BC Romans found colony at Aquileia

177 BC Romans take Istria

168 BC Romans defeat Illyrian king Gentius and take most of his lands; Marcus Aurelius fortifies Aquileia against barbarians

156 BC Romans attack Dalmatians

60 BC First Triumvirate of Pompey, Julius Caesar, and Marcus Licinius Crassus

59 BC Julius Caesar is commander of legions in Aquileia

53 BC Marcus Licinius Crassus dies

49 BC Julius Caesar crosses Rubicon: next year defeats Pompey, who is later assassinated

47 BC Ptolemy XIII dies in battle: Cleopatra ruler of Egypt

44 BC Julius Caesar assassinated

43 BC Second Triumvirate of Octavian, Mark Antony, and Marcus Lepidus

40 BC Mark Antony marries Octavia, sister of Octavian

37 BC Agreement between Mark Antony and Octavian at Tarentum: Lepidus exiled next year

34 BC Octavian founds new city at Ljubljana

33 BC Mark Antony divorces wife and allegedly marries Cleopatra

31 BC Octavian declares war: Battle of Actium, Mark Antony and Cleopatra defeated

27 BC Illyricum becomes Roman province: Octavian is acclaimed Augustus

6 CE Dalmatians revolt

14 Emperor Augustus dies

81 Enlarged Pola (Pula) arena completed by Emperor Titus

284 Death of eastern Emperor Numerian: Diocletian kills prefect and is acclaimed emperor

285 Death western Emperor Carinus, Diocletian divides rule with Maximian

293 Diocletian creates First Tetrarchy with Maximian (Augustus), and Caesars Constantius Chlorus and Galerius

303 Diocletian issues first edict against the Christians

305 Diocletian and Maximian abdicate: formation of new tetrarchy

311 Galerius issues edict of toleration on deathbed

313 Constantine issues edict of toleration: end of official persecution of Christians; Roman Empire divided between Constantine and Licinius

324 Constantine defeats Licinius and becomes sole ruler

325 Council of Nicaea

330 Constantine founds eastern capital, Constantinople

336 Arius dies

364 Valentinian I appoints brother Valens emperor of East

376 Valentinian dies, replaced by Gratian: Goths cross Danube

378 Battle of Adrianople, Goths defeat Romans, co-emperor Valens dies

379 Western Emperor Gratian appoints Theodosius Emperor of the East

380 Theodosius moves to Constantinople: passes edicts against 'heretical' beliefs

383 Maximus overthrows Gratian, becomes co-emperor of West; Theodosius makes son Arcadius co-emperor in the East.

Timeline

384 Vandal Stilicho becomes engaged to Theodosius' niece Serena

387 Theodosius marries Galla (mother of Galla Placidia)

388 Theodosius fights in civil war in Western Empire

392 Co-emperor Valentinian II dies, replaced by usurper Eugenius

394 Theodosius kills Eugenius in battle and becomes ruler of both empires

395 Theodosius dies: East and West empires divided between his sons: Rufinus murdered

396 Galla Placidia arrives with Serena in Rome

401 Alaric and Goths invade Western Roman Empire

408 Honorius begins to use Ravenna as his permanent capital; Arcadius dies in Constantinople, Theodosius II succeeds in East; Stilicho executed, Serena strangled; Alaric invades and besieges Rome

410 Goths sack Rome, Galla Placidia taken hostage

412 Galla Placidia and Visigoths enter Gaul

414 Galla Placidia officially marries Goths' king, Athaulf, who is murdered the next year

417 Galla Placidia marries Constantius

421 Honorius appoints Constantius co-emperor, who then dies seven months later; Traditional date of the founding of Venice

423 Honorius dies: Galla Placidia's son Valentinian rightful emperor in the West

425 Usurper Joannes executed at Aquileia: Valentinian III recognised as emperor in Rome

437 End of Galla Placidia's regency

439 Vandals capture Carthage

449 Honoria sends message with a ring to Attila the Hun

450 Emperor Theodosius II dies in Constantinople: Galla Placidia dies in Rome

451 Council of Chalcedon raises question of Christ's hypostasis

452 Attila the Hun invades Western Empire: Aquileia destroyed: Attila dies the next year

454 Valentinian kills Aetius: Valentinian assassinated: Vandals sack Rome the next year

474 After a year on the throne, Eastern Emperor Zeno overthrown

475 Romulus Augustus becomes Roman emperor of the West: Zeno recovers eastern throne

476 Romulus Augustus deposed: barbarian Odoacer ruler in Ravenna; Theodoric the Amal comes to aid of eastern Emperor Zeno

480 Julius Nepos assassinated in Dalmatia: Zeno declares end of Western Roman Empire

484 Acacian Schism between Western and Eastern Roman Empires

488 Emperor Zeno sends Theodoric against Odoacer in Italy

490 Theodoric besieges Ravenna. First alleged miracle reported at Monte Sant'Angelo

493 Theodoric takes Ravenna, kills Odoacer, and Goths declare him king

497 Eastern Emperor Anastasius I acknowledges Theodoric king of Goths and Romans

500 Theodoric celebrates ten years as ruler and visits Rome

505 Theodoric takes Sirmium: fighting between East and West Empires

507 Byzantines raid Siponto and Taranto

519 Pope John I helps end Acacian Schism

523 Emperor Justin passes edict against Arians

526 Theodoric dies

527 Eastern Roman Emperor Justin dies, nephew Justinian succeeds

530s Emperor Justinian sends Belisarius to defeat the West

534 Theodoric's daughter Amalasuntha becomes queen

535 Start of Gothic War: Justinian orders closure of Arian churches

536 Witigis becomes king of the Ostrogoths

540 End of Gothic War: King Witigis renounces throne

546 Totila, King of Ostrogoths, sacks Rome

552 Totila dies

554 Justinian conquers Italian peninsula: declares himself emperor of East and West; Ravenna becomes an exarchate

568 Lombards take Aquileia

639 First cathedral built on Torcello

667 People of Oderzo flee Lombards to Eraclea

Timeline

690s First Venetian doge allegedly elected at Eraclea

726 Eastern emperor orders removal of Christian images: First Iconclastic Controversy

751 Ravenna falls to Lombards

754 Ravenna given to Franks

756 Donation of Pippin: next year Ravenna given to pope and included in Papal States

800 Charlemagne, King of the Franks, crowned Roman Emperor

804 Venice rebels against eastern emperor, and comes under Charlemagne's protection

810 Venetians settle on Rialto

814 Venice becomes province of eastern emperor

828 Venetian sailors steal relics of St Mark from Alexandria

846 Caorle raided by Narentine pirates

878 Saracen pirates raid Grado

960 Venice bans slave trade, but the practice continues

976 Doge Pietro Candiano killed by mob: ducal palace destroyed; Pietro Orseolo I becomes doge: abdicates two years later

991 Election of Doge Pietro II Orseolo

998 Doge Orseolo goes to war against pirates in Adriatic

1000 Doge sails out on Ascension Day: defeats pirates: Venetians dominant in the Adriatic

1004 Venice receives 'most favoured' status from Byzantines

1006 Plague hits Venice, Pietro II Orseolo retires, son Otto takes over

1015 Forty Norman knights allegedly arrive in southern Italy to visit Monte Sant'Angelo

1017 Normans begin to settle in southern Italy: soon engaged by Lombards

1018 Eastern Roman emperor's army defeats Lombards and Normans at Cannae; Croatian king, Krešimir III, tries to win back lands from Venice

1021 Normans fight for Byzantines against pope and Holy Roman Emperor near Troia

1022 Otto Orseolo II deposed for the first time

1026 Otto Orseolo II deposed for a second time: flees to Constantinople

1030 Stephen (Stjepan) – son-in-law of Doge Pietro II Orseolo succeeds as King of Croatia

1032 Deposed doge Otto Orseolo dies while still in Constantinople

1034 First of Tancred de Hautville's sons arrive in southern Italy

1042 William 'the Iron Arm' becomes Count of Apulia

1053 Battle of Civitate near Foggia: Normans take the pope prisoner

1054 Great Schism divides Catholic and Orthodox Churches

1057 Robert Guiscard becomes Count of Apulia

1058 Robert Guiscard marries his 2nd wife, Sikelgaita of Salerno

1059 Robert Guiscard appointed Duke of Apulia, Calabria and Sicily by Pope Nicholas II

1061 Robert Guiscard fails to take Sicily with his brother Roger

1071 After 3-year siege, Normans capture Bari: Greek rule ends in southern Italy; Normans take Sicily the next year. Battle of Manzikert, Byzantines defeated by Seljuks

1073 Sikelgaita gets barons to acknowledge rights of her son, Roger Borsa

1074 Robert Guiscard excommunicated

1074/5 King Petar Krešimir of Croatia dies in captivity: the Normans take his towns

1076 Robert Guiscard deposes Lombard brother-in-law: becomes Prince of Salerno

1078 Robert Guiscard again excommunicated for attacking Benevento

1080 Sikelgaita leads siege of Trani

1081 Robert Guiscard sails to Valona, joins Bohemund at Butrint: takes Corfu; Normans besiege Dyrrachium, where Sikelgaita spurs Normans to victory

1082 Venetian-Byzantine treaty: Eastern emperor grants greater trading rights; Normans take Dyrrachium from Venetians

1084 Robert Guiscard helps rescue pope from Emperor: Normans leave Rome in ruins; Robert returns to campaigning with Bohemund. Earthquake felt in Venice

1085 May, Pope Gregory VII dies at Salerno: July, Robert Guiscard dies at Cephalonia; Roger Borsa becomes Duke of Apulia

1087 Relics of St Nicholas arrive in Bari

1089 Death of Demetrius Zvonimir: civil war and eventual collapse of Croatian monarchy

1094 St Mark's basilica consecrated in Venice, after miraculous discovery of missing relics

1095 First Crusade: Bohemund leaves for Holy Land: Emperor Henry IV visits Venice

Timeline

1097 Bohemund meets Emperor Alexius Komnenos and swears oath of fealty

1099 Venice joins First Crusade

1100 Bohemund captured by Seljuks. Next year Venetians sack Brindisi

1102 Personal union of Croatia and Hungary

1104 Bohemund released: marries daughter of French king; Hungarian king captures some of Venice's coastal towns. Venice *Arsenale* founded

1105 Count Roger of Sicily dies: 10-year-old son Roger replaces him

1108 Bohemund retreats to Puglia: confirms vassal status to eastern emperor

1116 Doge Ordelafo Faliero recaptures Zara

1118 Temporary truce agreed between Venetians and Hungarians

1125 Doge Domenico Michiel, 'terror of the Greeks', destroys Biograd

1127 Roger of Sicily becomes Duke Calabria and Apulia: inherits lands of Roger Borsa's son

1130 Christmas Day, Roger II crowned first King of Sicily

1154 Roger II dies, succeeded by son, William I 'the Bad'

1156 Byzantines retake Trani and Bari and other towns: William I defeats rebels

1166 William 'the Bad dies', succeeded by William II 'the Good'

1167 Lombard League first formed. First banks offering public loans set up in Venice

1171 Eastern emperor orders imprisonment of thousands of Venetian merchants; Doge establishes Venice's *sestieri* to pay for the war with the Greeks; Naval failure of doge leads to his assassination

1172 Eastern emperor gives Venice three columns: two are erected in the *Piazzetta*

1173 Venice joins the Holy Roman Emperor to try and oust the Greeks from Ancona

1177 Ascension Day, Frederick Barbarossa visits Venice: pays homage to the pope; William 'the Good' marries Henry II of England's daughter Joan

1180 Indulgences sold in Venice

1181 Zara signs pact with Hungary

1182 Massacre of Latins in Constantinople

1186 Constance of Sicily marries Henry Hohenstaufen

1189 William 'the Good' dies. Start of the Third Crusade

1190 Tancred is crowned King of Sicily: Richard 'Lionheart' sacks Messina; Emperor Frederick Barbarossa is drowned: his son is elected Emperor Henry VI; Henry crowned emperor in Rome the next year

1194 Tancred, King of Sicily dies: Henry VI crowned King of Sicily: Frederick II is born

1195 Pisans enter Adriatic

1197 September Henry VI dies: brother Philip returns to Germany, leaving Frederick behind

1198 Pope Innocent III calls for a new crusade: November, Empress Constance dies

1201 Boniface meets Alexios Angelos with Philip of Swabia; French knights arrive in Venice to request help with their crusade

1202 November, Fourth Crusade leaves Venice and attacks Zara

1203 April, Fourth crusade leaves Zara: June, arrives at Constantinople

1204 Crusaders destroy Constantinople: breakup of Byzantine empire: Venice gains Ragusa

1208 Philip Hohenstaufen, King of the Germans, murdered in Bamberg

1209 October Pope Innocent III crowns Otto of Brunswick as Holy Roman Emperor

1210 Innocent excommunicates Emperor Otto

1212 Frederick claims German possessions: pays homage to pope; December, Frederick crowned King of Germany at Mainz

1214 Emperor Otto IV defeated at Bouvines

1215 July, Frederick II crowned Holy Roman Emperor at Aachen (Aix-la-Chapelle)

1216 Frederick's former tutor become Pope Honorius III

1220 November Honorius III crowns Frederick Holy Roman Emperor in Rome

1222 Frederick II expels Saracens from Sicily, establishes them at Lucera in Puglia

1227 Gregory IX elected pope

1228 Frederick II leads Sixth Crusade. Venetians join Genoese in Lombard League

1229 Frederick II crowned King of Jerusalem

1231 Frederick II issues Constitutions of Melfi

1234 Frederick II demands pope to excommunicate his son Henry; Bonconte I Montefeltro assumes role as Count of Urbino

Timeline

1237 9-year-old Conrad IV elected King of Germany (Romans) and King of Italy; Frederick routs Milanese at Cortenuova

1239 Malatesta della Penna becomes *podestà* in Rimini

1241 Pope Gregory summons council in Rome: Frederick captures churchmen: pope dies

1242 Frederick's son Henry killed in riding accident while still a captive

1243 Innocent IV elected pope

1245 Innocent IV deposes Frederick II: start of imperial interregnum that lasts until 1312

1247 Frederick II begins siege of Parma that ends in a disaster for him the next year

1249 Pietro della Vigna found guilty of treason

1250 December, Frederick II dies, son Conrad becomes King of Sicily

1254 Conrad dies of malaria: Manfred defeats papal army at Foggia; Innocent IV dies, Alexander IV elected pope

1257 Manfred grants Venice trading rights in Puglia: next year he is crowned King of Sicily

1261 Baldwin's Empire of Constantinople falls and the Byzantines regain control

1264 Venice removes Ancona from commercial competition

1266 Urban IV crowns Charles of Anjou king of Sicily: Manfred killed at Battle Benevento

1268 Conradin defeated Battle of Tagliacozzo: executed in Naples; Venice bans gamblers from wearing masks

1271 Charles of Anjou, King of Sicily, captures Durazzo and Valona

1272 Enzo, last of Frederick II's sons dies in Bologna

1273 Rudolf becomes first Habsburg elected as King of Germany

1275 Da Polenta family take power in Ravenna: Francesca (da Rimini) betrothed

1282 Sicilian Vespers break out in Palermo: Charles loses Sicilian throne

1283 Venice in agreement with Genoese, who next year defeat Pisans: start of Pisa's decline

1291 Fall of Acre

1295 Marco Polo returns from travels: Mastin Vecchio Malatesta seizes control of Rimini

1297 Establishment of *Serrata* in Venice

1298 Battle of Curzola (Korčula), Marco Polo taken prisoner by Genoese

1300 Revolt in Venice

1302 Kingdom of Sicily divided

1305 Giotto visits Rimini on way to paint Scrovegni Chapel in Padua

1309 Venice excommunicated by Pope Clement V

1310 Bajamonte Tiepolo's rebellion in Venice; Founding Committee of Public Safety, later Council of Ten: first draft of Libro d'Oro

1321 Dante visits Venice, shortly before dying from malaria in Ravenna

1333 Venice granted trading rights in Sea of Azov

1334 Malatesta Guastafamiglia overthrows cousin: becomes 5th Lord of Rimini

1335 Permanent establishment of Council of Ten

1341 Work begins on building of last ducal palace in Venice

1343 The Malatesta become imperial vicars of Rimini, Pesaro, and Fano

1346 Tatars attack Venetians and Genoese at Caffra on Black Sea: first evidence of plague; Louis of Anjou (Ludovik of Hungary) encourages Zara to rebel; Venice founds *Ospedale della Pietà* for foundlings

1348 Severe earthquake hits Venice and Friuli: Black Death arrives in Europe

1354 Genoese fleet re-enters Adriatic: Doge Andrea Dandolo dies

1355 Doge Marino Faliero executed. Cardinal Albornoz sent to reclaim lands in Italy

1358 Treaty of Zara, Venice loses Dalmatia to Hungary: Doge drops title Duke of Dalmatia; Hungary also gains Ragusa as vassal state

1364 Petrarch sees return of Venetian fleet after suppressing revolt in Candia (Crete)

1369 After long siege Venice takes Trieste: start of War of Chioggia with Genoa

1378 Start of papal Western Schism

1379 Admiral Vittore Pisani defeated at Pola and imprisoned: Chioggia falls to Genoese

1380 Admiral Carlo Zeno comes to the rescue: Chioggia surrenders to Venetians

1381 Venice and Genoa agree peace at Turin. Charles Durazzo seizes Neapolitan throne; Joanna I deposed and murdered the next year

1386 Charles III of Naples dies following an attack on his life; Ladislaus becomes King of Naples: next year deposed by Louis II, Duke of Anjou

Timeline

1389 Battle of Kosovo

1390 Louis II arrives in Neapolitan kingdom: Ladislaus declares himself King of Hungary

1400 Ladislaus regains Naples

1402 Gian Galeazzo Visconti dies suddenly: Carlo Malatesta temporarily governor of Milan

1403 Venice defeats Genoese fleet: Ladislaus crowned King of Hungary in Zara

1404 Pandolfo III Maltesta captures Brescia

1405 Venice captures Padua and arrests 'Il Novello': end of Carrara dynasty

1407 Venice at war with Sigismund of Hungary and Croatia over possession of Zara

1409 Ladislaus of Naples, as king of Hungary and Croatia sells Dalmatia to the Venetians

1415 Venice takes on the Ottoman fleet

1417 End Western Schism: Carlo Malatesta presents Pope Gregory XII's abdication; Sigismondo Malatesta born at Brescia

1422 Federico da Montefeltro born

1423 Start of Lombard War

1427 Pandolfo III dies, illegitimate sons go to live with Carlo Malatesta

1428 Peace meeting of Carlo Malatesta, Guidantonio da Montefeltro, and Martin V in Rome

1429 September, Carlo I Malatesta of Rimini dies: Galeotto Roberto becomes Lord of Rimini

1431 Pope Martin V dies: Eugenius IV becomes pope

1432 Galeotto Roberto Malatesta dies: Gismondo (Sigismondo Pandolfo) is Lord of Rimini

1433 HRE Sigismund visits Rimini: Gismondo takes his name as Sigismondo Pandolfo; his brother Domenico becomes Malatesta Novello; Venice and Milan agree to peace at Ferrara

1435 Joanna II of Naples dies

1438 Federico da Montefeltro marries for the first time, and receives his first *condotta*

1440 Skanderbeg appointed Ottoman governor in Albania

1441 Francesco Sforza marries Bianca Maria Visconti; Federico da Montefeltro recaptures San Leo fortress

1442 Francesco Sforza's illegitimate daughter becomes Sigismondo Malatesta's second wife; Violante da Montefeltro marries Malatesta Novello; Alfonso ousts René of Anjou and becomes king in Naples

1443 Guidantonio da Montefeltro dies and succeeded by Oddantonio II; Skanderbeg deserts from Ottoman army; Eugenius IV recognises Alfonso I as King of Two Sicilies: Ferrante legitimised

1444 Oddantonio murdered and Federico da Montefeltro becomes the lord of Urbino

1447 Duke Filippo Maria Visconti dies: Milanese Golden Ambrosian Republic created; Skanderbeg at war with Venetians: Violante moves to join husband at Cesena

1448 July, Venetians routed by Skanderbeg and defeated by Francesco Sforza in September; peace agreed three months later

1450 Venetians join Ottomans against Skanderbeg, who allies with Alfonso of Two Sicilies; Peace brings tentative end to Lombard Wars, confirmed five years later at Lodi; Francesco Sforza becomes duke of Milan

1451 Skanderbeg becomes Alfonso's vassal; Presumed date of Piero della Francesca's painting of Sigismondo Malatesta

1452 Inauguration of Capella di Sigismondo in Rimini

1453 Constantinople falls to Ottomans

1454 Peace of Lodi ends Wars of Lombardi

1457 Doge Francesco Foscari abdicates. Alfonso I declares war on Sigismondo Malatesta

1458 Pius II elected. Alfonso I of Sicily dies and kingdom again divided

1459 Ferrante crowned in Barletta

1460 Skanderbeg relieves Barletta under siege from Angevins; Pius II excommunicates Sigismondo Malatesta

1462 Sigismondo sails to Venice

1463 Senigallia and Fano surrender to Federico Montefeltro and his territory is increased; Cervia sold to Venice: Rector's palace in Ragusa damaged by gunpowder explosion; December, Sigismondo confesses 'heretical beliefs'

1464 Pius II dies in Ancona as crusade begins to get under way

1465 Malatesta Novello dies, Cesena incorporated into Papal States

1466 Sigismondo Pandolfo returns from Morea, awarded Golden Rose by pope; Francesco Sforza dies, succeeded by Galeazzo Maria: Skanderbeg visits Venice

1468 January, Skanderbeg dies: October, Sigismondo Malatesta dies

1469 Roberto Malatesta captures and holds Rimini against pope, helped by Federico

Timeline

1470 Ottomans capture Venice's island of Negroponte (Euboea) in Aegean

1472 Federico da Montefeltro's son Guidobaldo born: wife Battista dies

1473 Painting in oils arrives in Venice: Private marriage Caterina Sforza and Girolamo Riario

1474 Sixtus IV's nephew Giovanni della Rovere marries Federico da Montefeltro's daughter

1475 Federico da Montefeltro's daughter Elisabetta marries Roberto Malatesta

1476 Galeazzo Maria, Duke of Milan, murdered

1477 Caterina Sforza publicly marries Girolamo Riario in Rome

1478 Pazzi Plot in Florence kills the younger Medici brother

1479 Gentile Bellini goes to Ottoman court to paint Sultan Mehmet II; 'Il Moro' seizes control in Milan: Albania comes under Ottoman rule

1480 Ottoman fleet attacks Otranto in Puglia, massacring 800 people; Girolamo Riario takes control of Forlì and becomes count

1482 Roberto Malatesta victory at Campomorto, Girolamo Riario displays cowardice; September, Federico da Montefeltro and Roberto Malatesta die

1483 Raphael Santi born in Urbino

1484 Sixtus IV dies: Caterina Sforza defends Castel Sant' Angelo: Riarios leave Rome

1488 Girolamo Riario murdered: Caterina Sforza makes stand in Ravaldino fortress

1489 Pope Innocent III excommunicates Ferrante and declares Charles VIII King of Naples

1492 April, Lorenzo Il Magnifico dies in Florence: August, Alexander VI elected pope

1494 January, King Ferrante dies Alfonso II succeeds: Bona Sforza born; October, Il Moro invites French king to Italy: Italian Wars break out; Gian Galeazzo Maria Sforza dies: Ludovico, Il Moro becomes Duke of Milan

1495 Charles VIII crowned in Naples: retreats to France: Giacomo Feo murdered in Forlì

1497 Il Moro's wife Beatrice dies: Anna wife of Alfonso d'Este dies

1498 French king Charles VIII dies and succeeded by Louis XII

1499 Cesare Borgia invades the Romagna: Venetian merchants arrested in Istanbul; Venice suffers major defeat of Cape Zonchio in Ionian Sea: Lepanto surrenders; Il Moro flees Milan, Louis XII takes possession, Isabella finally leaves city

1500 Caterina Sforza surrenders to Borgia: he buys Rimini from Pandolfo IV Malatesta; Treaty of Granada signed by Ferdinand and Isabella

1501 Neapolitan king Frederick IV abdicates: Venice loses Durazzo to Ottomans

1502 Renewal of Spanish-French war, French invade Puglia: Cesare Borgia captures Urbino; Alfonso d'Este marries Lucrezia Borgia

1503 Venice agrees peace with the sultan: the *Disfida di Barletta*; Alexander VI dies: after brief pontificate of Pius III, replaced by Julius II; Vasco da Gama returns from voyage rounding Cape of Good Hope to India

1504 Treaty of Lyon: French agree to Spanish takeover of Naples and south of Italy; Isabella of Castile, Queen of Spain, dies

1505 Lucrezia Borgia's husband, Alfonso d'Este, duke of Ferrara after surviving plot

1508 Guidobaldo da Montefeltro dies and Urbino passes to Francesco della Rovere; Defeat of the imperial army: Julius II forms League of Cambrai

1509 Venice loses terraferma towns to League: city excommunicated: Caterina Sforza dies

1510 Julius II lifts interdict, makes peace with Serenissima: pope besieges Mirandola

1511 Julius II creates Holy League against French

1512 Ravenna taken by French: month later French driven from Italy

1513 Julius II dies, replaced by Medici pope, Leo X; Venetians ally with French: after Louis XII's defeat at Novara, *terraferma* under attack

1514 Rialto burns down and is rebuilt

1515 French king Francis I, invades Italy, and with backing of Venetians, takes Milan

1516 Treaty of Noyon, French possessions confirmed in northern Italy, Spanish in the south; Venice establishes the ghetto

1517 Plot discovered to assassinate Leo X: Martin Luther presents 95 theses; Bona Sforza's proxy wedding in Naples

1518 Bona Sforza arrives in Poland and meets her husband

1519 Charles V elected Holy Roman Emperor after death of grandfather, Maximilian I

1520 Plague and earthquake hit Ragusa

1521 Emperor Charles V expels French from Milan and reinstates the Sforzas

1525 Francis I defeated by Charles V in Battle of Pavia

1526 Charles V captures Rome, Clement VII shelters in Castel Sant'Angelo; Hungarians crushed by Ottomans at Mohács: Louis II of Croatia and Hungary drowned

1527 Charles V's brother, Ferdinand becomes King of Royal Croatia

1529 July, French sack of Molfetta: August, Treaty of Cambrai, Paix des Dames; Francis I renounces claims in Italy: Rimini included in Papal States; September, Ottomans start to besiege Vienna

Timeline

1530 Charles V crowned Emperor by pope at Bologna

1532 Ancona fully included in Papal States

1535 After Francesco II Sforza's death, Duchy of Milan given to future Philip II of Spain

1536 Francis I signs 'unholy' alliance with the Ottomans

1537 Start of 3rd Venetian-Ottoman War: Klis fortress captured by the Muslims

1538 New defensive work begun to protect Ragusa

1540 Venetian-Ottoman War ends with Serenissima forced to sign humiliating peace

1543 Francis I joins the Ottomans to attack Nice

1547 Francis I dies

1556 Bona Sforza finally leaves Poland and returns to Italy: Charles V decides to abdicate

1559 Treaty of Cateau-Cambresis ends the last Italian War

1562 Gondoliers ordered to paint boats black

1564 Tintoretto starts painting pictures for Scuola di San Rocco

1569 Large explosion in Venice *Arsenale*

1570 End of Venice's 30-year-long peace with Ottomans: start of 4th Venetian-Ottoman War

1571 Venetians lose Cyprus to Muslims: October, Battle of Lepanto, Turkish fleet defeated

1573 Venice signs another treaty with Ottomans

1574 French king Henri III given spectacular reception in Venice

1575 Venice again hit by plague: Titian dies of plague next year

1577 Doge's Palace partly destroyed

1580 Founding of Lipizzana stud

1591 Rialto Bridge completed

1592 Start of the 'Long War' with the Ottomans

1597 Muslims fail to take Bocche di Cataro

1600 Bridge of Sighs built

1613 Monteverdi moves from Mantua to Venice, where he remains for next three decades

1615 Uskoks continue their violence: Uskok war starts between the Emperor and Venice

1618 Council of Ten reacts fiercely to threats of Spanish Plot

1620 Manfredonia attacked by Ottomans

1630 Plague returns to Venice: plans go ahead to build Santa Maria della Salute

1631 Foundation stone laid for Santa Maria della Salute; death of Urbino's last duke, Francesco Maria II della Rovere

1638 First public *ridotto* opens in Venice

1645 Venice's island of Candia (Crete) comes under sultan's attack

1666 Brindisi column arrives in Lecce

1667 Ragusa hit by catastrophic earthquake

1669 Candia finally surrenders, but Klis recaptured by Venetians

1678 Vivaldi born in Venice

1683 Vienna nearly falls to Ottomans

1687 Venetians blow up Parthenon

1688 Morosini elected doge

1699 Treaty of Karlowitz: Venice granted Morea, but overseas territories further reduced

1700 Death of Carlos II of Spain, leading to start of War of Spanish Succession next year

1707 Carlo Goldoni born in Venice

1713 End Spanish War of Succession: Naples and southern Italy given to Austrian Habsburgs

1715 Jesuits allowed to return to Venice: Venetians and Ottomans at war

1716 Siege of Corfu

1718 Venice makes peace with Ottomans: Treaty of Passorowitz

1720 Florian's opens as 'Alla Venezia Triomfante' in St Mark's Square

1728 Montesquieu visits Venice

1729 Last *bucintoro* launched in Venice

1731 Elizabeth Farnese's son Charles becomes duke of Parma and Piacenza

1732 Street lighting introduced in Venice

Timeline

1733 Charles, Duke of Parma, captures Naples, becoming King of Naples next year

1737 Bonnie Prince Charlie visits Venice

1741 Earthquake hits Urbino

1746 Canaletto moves to England for nearly a decade

1757 Casanova escapes from *piombi* in Venice

1759 Charles abdicates to become king of Spain: son Ferdinand succeeds as king of Naples

1761 Goldoni moves to France

1771 Mozart visits Venice

1774 Contarini complains in Great Council about disorder: *ridotto* closed in Venice

1779 Da Ponte denounced in *bocca di leone* and flees Venice; Croatian port, Fiume, annexed to Hungary

1780 *Barnabotti* Contarini and Pisani arrested

1782 Grand Duke Paul and his wife Maria Feodorovna visit Venice

1783 Casanova again has to leave Venice

1784 Andrea Tron '*il Paron*' openly condemns Venetian people's decadent way of life

1786 Goethe visits Venice

1789 March, Lodovico Manin becomes Venice's last doge; July, Bastille stormed: start of French Revolution: earthquake hits Urbino

1791 Rebuilding of Fenice theatre: Venetians refuse alliance with Kingdom of Sardinia

1792 Emperor at war with French

1793 Louis VVI guillotined: Goldoni dies in Paris

1795 Louis XVIII issues Declaration of Verona asserting position as French king; French defeat Austrians near Genoa

1796 April, Napoleon defeats Austrian-Sardinians: Louis XVIII ordered to leave Verona; more victories by Napoleon, French warships in Adriatic: Bergamo surrenders to French

1797 April Napoleon threatens Venice with war: Easter Rising in Verona: Treaty Leoben; Napoleon says he 'Attila to the state of Venice': Venice officially surrenders Verona; May, Napoleon declares war on Venice: Great Council votes end of Serenissima; Provisional Municipality set up in Venice: June, French take Corfu; September, Josephine, visits Venice: Ancona becomes republic; October, Treaty Campo Formio, Venice ceded to Austrians; December, Napoleon takes the Bronze Horses and other treasures

1798 January, *bucintoro* destroyed days before Austrians arrive; February, French occupy Rome and declare it a republic: republic joined by Ancona; Pius VI taken prisoner: May, Emperor makes alliance with Ferdinand of Naples; French ousted from Rome: August, Napoleon defeated in battle of Nile; October, Ali Pasha, attacks French garrison at Preveza, massacres scores of people; November, Neapolitans oust French from Rome, start of War of Second Coalition; December, Neapolitan army defeated, French return to Rome: king flees to Palermo

1799 January, French arrive in Naples, declaration of Parthenopean Republic; March, Corfu falls to Russian-Ottoman alliance: massacre after French arrive Trani; April, French leave Naples, Parthenopean Republic falls the next month; June, Nelson courtmartials Caracciolo, punishes rebels: July, king returns to Naples; August, Pius VI dies in France; September, French leave Rome, Neapolitan army arrives, end of Roman Republic; November, 18th Brumaire coup, Napoleon seizes power: French surrender Ancona

1800 March, Pius VII elected in Venice: creation Septinsular Republic of Ionian Islands; June, Napoleon victory Marengo: Pius regains his Papal States: returns to Rome

1801 January, Septinsular Republic announces constitution; February, Treaty Lunéville, Austrians surrender Verona: included in Cisalpine Republic

1802 Doge Manin dies in Venice: British help restore peace at Corfu; French-British Treaty of Amiens: Cisalpine Republic becomes Italian Republic

1803 Souliote women commit suicide in Dance of Zalongo: French-British peace ends

1804 December, Napoleon crowns himself emperor of the French

1805 Third Coalition: October, Austrians defeated at Ulm, Francis flees Vienna; November, Napoleon enters Vienna, French take Trieste: December, Battle Austerlitz; French take Fiume: Treaty Pressburg: Emperor surrenders Venice and other possessions

1806 January, Ferdinand flees Naples for second time: Joseph Bonaparte arrives in Naples; Joseph becomes king in March: French occupy Dalmatia; Russians arrive in Bocche di Cattaro, and take Curzola: French leave Trieste; May, Napoleon becomes King of Italy: appoints stepson viceroy: French enter Ragusa; August, end of Holy Roman Empire: Francis II becomes Austrian Emperor Francis I

1807 July, Treaty Tilsit: Napoleon annexes Corfu in August: Royal Navy capture Lissa (Vis); November, Napoleon visits Venice and closes down most religious establishments

1808 January, end of Ragusan republic, now included in Kingdom of Italy; July, Joseph Bonaparte abdicates: August, Murat becomes king Joachim I of Naples

1809 July, French kidnap Pius VII, Papal States incorporated into French Empire; Austrians defeated at Wagram: October, Napoleon enters Vienna; Treaty Schönbrunn: end of Fifth Coalition: creation of Illyrian Provinces; October, British capture Ionian Islands: Byron and Hobhouse visit Ali Pasha

Timeline

1810 April, now divorced, Napoleon marries Emperor Francis' daughter Marie-Louise; October, first French assault on British naval base at Lissa

1811 March, second raid on Lissa ends in French disaster

1812 February, Rivoli lost on maiden voyage; Byron publishes his first two cantos of Childe Harold's Pilgrimage; June, Napoleon embarks on his Russian campaign

1813 British capture Adriatic islands and ports, French begin retreat from Balkans; June, Maria-Carolina leaves Sicily: August, Austria declares war on France; October, Hoste makes first attempt to take Cattaro, captures Spalato; November, Hoste raises Ragusan flag: Christmas Day, assault on Cattaro fortress

1814 January, French garrison Cattaro surrenders: within four weeks also Ragusa falls; February, French set fire to their ship in Brindisi; Venice blockaded by British and under Austrian attack; April, Napoleon abdicates and exiled to Elba: Austrians return to Venice; May, Treaty Paris, British leave Adriatic islands; June, Ferdinand regains Naples throne: Austrians, take control of Venice; Congress of Vienna gathers: September, Maria-Carolina dies in Vienna

1815 Napoleon escapes Elba, but defeated at Waterloo, banished to Santa Helena; Ionian Islands a British protectorate: Congress of Vienna redraws map of Europe; Official recognition of Kingdom of Two Sicilies: October, Murat shot in Calabria; December, Emperor and Metternich visit Venice: bronze horses return to the city

1816 Ferdinand of Naples become Ferdinand I of the Two Sicilies; April, Byron leaves England: famine hits Venetia: November, Byron arrives Venice

1817 Murder of Karađorđe, and rise of Miloš Obrenović of Serbia

1818 Emperor Francis I appoints brother, Archduke Ranieri, viceroy in Venetia

1819 Turner visits Venice: December, Byron joins his mistress Teresa in Ravenna

1820 July, Byron invited to join Ravenna's Carbonari group: Naples Carbonari revolt; Victor Emmanuel I of Sardinia abdicates: Ali Pasha declares independence

1821 Austrians march on Naples, take control of the city: start of War of Greek Independence

1822 Ali Pasha forced to surrender army; Byron distraught by daughter Allegra's death: later shocked by Shelley's drowning

1823 January, Byron leaves Genoa on way to fight for Greeks; Monroe Doctrine calls for non-European intervention in Americas

1824 January, Byron arrives at Missolonghi where he dies in April

1826 Ottomans defeated at Navarino

1829 Miloš Obrenović becomes hereditary prince of Serbia

1830 February, Greek independence recognised: July Revolution Paris, Charles X deposed; November, Ferdinand II becomes King of the Two Sicilies

1831 Cholera hits Europe for first time: dispute over route of Venice-Milan railway line; unrest in northern Italian states: April, Charles Albert king of Piedmont-Sardinia; July, Giuseppe Mazzini founds the Young Italy party, Giovane Italia

1832 Garibaldi joins the Young Italy party

1834 Austrians put Daniele Manin on list of subversives

1835 March, Francis I dies and disabled son Ferdinand I becomes Austrian Emperor

1836 Garibaldi goes to South America: ex-king Charles X dies of cholera, buried at Gorizia

1837 Mazzini settles in London: Ferdinand II introduces harsher measures in Sicily

1838 New Emperor Ferdinand I visits Venice: commissions Titian memorial in Frari

1840 Turner returns to Venice for third time

1842 La Scala premier Verdi's Nabucco: chorus Hebrew Slaves later Risorgimento anthem; Alexander Karađorđević retakes control in Serbia

1843 Gas lighting arrives in Venice: insurrection in Rimini

1844 July, Bandiera brothers are shot and become martyrs of Risorgimento

1845 July, Croatian nationalists shot in Zagreb: September, uprising repressed in Rimini

1846 January, rail bridge opens across lagoon to Venice: June, Pius IX becomes pope; Daniele Manin's office broken into

1847 Widespread starvation Venetia: Austrians increase garrison in Ferrara in Papal States; Richard Cobden visits Venice three months before Ninth Scientific Congress; Milanese boycott gambling and smoking in protest against Austrian taxes

1848 Year of Revolutions: New Years Day, violence breaks out in Milan; January, rebellion in Sicily: new constitution: Manin and Tommaseo arrested in Venice; February, Pius IX blesses Italy: demonstration in Padua: revolution in Paris; Louis-Philippe abdicates, start Second French Republic; March, Charles Albert of Sardinia-Piedmont issues Statuto: Cinque Giornate in Milan; Radetzky retreats to Quadrilateral: Venetians demand release of Manin and Tommaseo; Arsenale mutiny: Provisional Republic San Marco: start First Italian War Dependence; Charles Albert invades Lombardy-Venetia: Metternich resigns; April, Ferdinand II of Naples deposed: Austrians march into Venetia, re-enter Udine; Pope Pius issues his Allocation; May, Austrian victory Cornuda: Venice joins Lombardy, Milan fuses with Piedmont; Emperor and family flee: June, surrender of Vicenza, Treviso, Padua, and Palmanova; Venice-Piedmont fusion, Manin resigns: Piedmontese commissioners arrive in Venice; Charles Albert signs Salasco Armistice, surrenders Lombardy-Venetia to Austrians; Manin, takes charge in Venice as head of triumvirate; October, Austrians take last Venetian-held fortress at Osoppo; imperial family again flee an uprising in Vienna; November, papal prime minister murdered, Pius taken prisoner: Pius flees Rome; December, Emperor Ferdinand II resigns, replaced by his nephew Franz Josef

Timeline

1849 February, Roman Republic established; March, Charles Albert declares war on Austrians: after defeat, he abdicates; Victor Emmanuel II agrees to new armistice: Venice abandoned by allies; April, Marghera and Venice come under siege: July, French re-enter Rome; August, Venice surrenders: end of First Italian War of Independence; November, Ruskin returns to Venice with his wife

1850 Pope Pius returns from Gaeta to Rome, re-establishes ghetto, moves to Vatican; Franz Josef sends brother Maximilian to head navy at Trieste

1851 Franz Josef visits Venice: Marie-Thérèse, Louis XVI's daughter, dies: buried at Gorizia

1852 Danilo becomes Prince of Montenegro

1853 October, start of Crimean War: Hungarian tries to assassinate Franz Josef in Vienna

1854 April, Franz Josef marries Elizabeth of Bavaria; iron Ponte dell'Accademia built in Venice

1855 Last of Belfiore martyrs executed

1856 February, end of Crimean War, followed by Congress of Paris next month; Franz Josef and wife visit Venice: attempted assassination of Ferdinand II of Naples

1857 Archduke Maximilian appointed Governor General Lombardy-Venetia; Daniele Manin dies in Paris

1858 January, attempted assassination of Napoleon III who allies with Piedmont-Sardinia; Alexander Karađorđević forced to abdicate: Obrenović family returns to power; Danilo effectively achieves Montenegro's independence by defeating Ottomans

1859 February, Francis, heir to Two Sicilies, marries Marie Sophie of Bavaria in Bari; April, Maximilian removed from position as Governor General of Lombardy-Venetia; Emperor declares war on Victor Emmanuel II: Second Italian War of Independence; May, Ferdinand II dies, son Francis II succeeds; June, Austrians suffer defeats at Magenta and Solferino; July, end Second Italian War Independence: Austria surrenders most of Lombardy

1860 Maximilian and Charlotte move into Miramar: Garibaldi leaves Genoa for Sicily; August, Danilo of Montenegro assassinated, nephew Nikola Petrović-Njegoš succeeds; November, Nikola marries: Garibaldi and Victor Emmanuel II enter Naples; Empress Elizabeth spends winter in Madeira; December, Liberals defeat their opposition and retake Mexico City

1861 Maximilian first approached with offer from the Mexicans; February, Francis II, King of Naples, surrenders at Gaeta; March, Victor Emmanuel II becomes King of Italy: Juárez elected president in Mexico; April, start of American Civil War: Empress Elizabeth spends winter in Venice; December, Spanish, British, and French troops arrive at Vera Cruz

1862 April, British and Spanish withdraw from Mexico: May, French defeated at Puebla

Adriatic

1863 May, French occupy Puebla, and Mexico City a month later; October, Mexican representatives meet Maximilian at Miramar: he accepts the throne

1864 Garibaldi feted in England: Maximilian sees Act Renunciation: renounces crown; April, Emperor visits Maximilian and persuades him to accept 'Family Pact'; Maximilian becomes Mexican emperor at Miramar; May, Ionian Islands become Greek, British leave; Maximilian and Charlotte arrive at Vera Cruz, and Mexico City a month later; September Convention agrees to transfer new capital of Italy to Florence

1865 April, end of American Civil War; October, Maximilian issues decree pronouncing arbitrary punishment of insurrection

1866 January, Napoleon III announces withdrawal of troops from Mexico; June, Italy declares war on Austria at start of 7-week Austro-Prussian War; July, Austrian naval victory at Vis: Charlotte leaves Mexico; August, Charlotte arrives in France: end of Third Italian War of Independence; October, Venice becomes part of Italy, but Austrians keep Trieste; September, Charlotte meets pope and suffers complete mental collapse; November, Victor Emmanuel II visits Venice

1867 February, last of the French leave Mexico: May, Maximilian captured; Founding of Austrian-Hungarian Empire: imperial coronation in Budapest; June, Emperor Maximilian shot: Bandiera brothers' remains returned to Venice

1868 Daniele Manin's body returned for burial in Venice; autonomous Kingdom of Croatia-Slavonia created: Nikola of Montenegro meets tsar; assassination of Michael III Obrenović, his nephew Milan succeeds

1870 Franco-Prussian War: Piedmontese army enters Rome: Papal States abolished

1871 Rome officially becomes capital of Italy

1872 Milan Obrenović comes of age

1875 Serbs' rebellion against sultan in Bosnia-Herzegovina

1876 Nikola of Montenegro again takes on Ottomans: Serbs join the war

1878 Treaties of San Stefano and Berlin redraw boundaries of Balkan states; Montenegro greatly expands territories: Montenegro and Serbia gain independence; Umberto I succeeds in Italy, ten months before the first attack on his life

1882 Milan Obrenović declared King of Serbia; signing of Triple Alliance by Germany, Austria-Hungary and Italy

1883 Zorka of Montenegro marries exiled Peter Karađorđević

1888 Work starts on Empress Elizabeth's villa, Achilleon, in Corfu

1889 Archduke Rudolf commits suicide with mistress at Mayerling; Milan Obrenović introduces constitution: abdicates,12-year-old Alexander succeeds:

Nikola of Montenegro's daughters the 'Black Duchesses' marry in Russia

1890 March, Kaiser dismisses his chancellor, Bismarck: Zorka dies

1891 King Alexander Obrenović of Serbia visits tsar of Russia

1893 Alexander Obrenović assumes full power and next year his father returns to help him

1896 March, humiliating defeat of Italians in Abyssinia; Crown Prince Victor Emmanuel marries Nikola of Montenegro's daughter, Elena; Austrian heir Karl Ludwig dies, succeeded by his son Franz Ferdinand

1897 Agreement signed in St Petersburg with Austria-Hungary over Balkan question; D'Annunzio becomes member of parliament: assassination attempt on Umberto I

1898 May, violent unrest begins in Italy: Nikola of Montenegro visits Queen Victoria; September, Empress Elizabeth (Sisi) murdered

1899 Failed assassination of Milan Obrenović: Tsar invites Peter Karađorđević's sons

1900 February, Milan Obrenović dies: July, Umberto I assassinated on third attempt; Alexander Obrenović of Serbia marries Draga Mašin:

Franz Ferdinand of Austria finally permitted to have morganatic marriage

1901 King Alexander Obrenović issues liberal constitution

1903 April, Alexander Obrenović temporarily suspends constitution; June, May Overthrow, Alexander and Draga murdered; Peter Karađorđević becomes King of Serbia

1904 September, Peter Karađorđević's coronation in Belgrade

1905 Nikola of Montenegro introduces a constitution

1906 Start of 'Pig War' between Serbia and Austrian-Hungarians; Work starts on 2000 kilometre Acquedotto Pugliese to help land reform in south

1908 Young Turks threaten Ottoman Empire: Franz Josef annexes Bosnia-Herzegovina

1909 February, Ottomans accept Austro-Hungarian annexation of Bosnia-Herzegovina; Russians do the same the next month

1910 Nikola Petrović-Njegoš becomes first king of Montenegro; Gabrielle D'Annunzio moves to Paris: rebellion in Albania

1911 Italy invades Libya, annexing Tripoli and Cyrenaica next year; Giolitti becomes Italian prime minister for the fourth time; Work starts on Victor Emmanuel monument in Rome

1912 Trouble in Albania: October, Nikola of Montenegro invades: start of First Balkan War; November, Albanians declare independence: Ambassadors' meeting in London

1913 May, end of First Balkan War, a month before start of Second Balkan War; Albania declared principality: end of Ottoman Empire in Europe: bombs in Fiume

1914 February, Wilhelm of Wied king of Albania: June, Peter of Serbia hands power to son; July, Archduke assassinated in Sarajevo, Franz Josef sends ultimatum: declares war; September, King Wilhelm flees Albania and it becomes a republic; October, three months after writing 'Down with war', Mussolini calls for intervention:

1915 March, Italy approaches Allies' Triple Entente: April, Treaty London offers terms; May, D'Annunzio returns to Italy: calls people to arms: Italy joins Allies in war; Start of Battles of Isonzo: Austrian bomb damages Santa Maria di Nazareth in Venice; November, Serbia overrun by enemy: Serbs flee in Great Retreat

1916 January, Montenegro quits war: D'Annunzio injured in plane crash off Grado; Milan bombed: August, Italy declares war on Germany: November, Franz Josef dies

1917 February, Mussolini invalided out of the army: October, Caporetto disaster

1918 February, D'Annunzio takes part in MAS raid on Buccari Bay; August, D'Annunzio flies over Vienna: Italian victory at Vittorio Veneto; October, break up of Empire: end of Dual Monarchy: Fiume declared part of Italy; November, Austrian armistice: Fiume put under French, British and American control; Germany surrenders: Peter becomes King of the Serbs, Croats and Slovenes; November, National Assembly deposes Nikola, and Serbia and Montenegro unite

1919 March, Mussolini forms Fasci Italiani di Combattimento; April, Habsburgs banished from Austria: D'Annunzio addresses crowd in Venice; September, Saint-Germain Treaty of Italians and Austrians: end of Habsburg monarchy; D'Annunzio leads March of Ronchi to Fiume; Mussolini loses election to Chamber Deputies: Italy annexes Trentino and Alto Adige; Austria cedes Istria, Gorizia and Trieste (capital of Venezia-Giulia)

1920 Violence in Split, Italian naval captain of *Puglia* killed; Tito returns to Croatia from Russia and joins Communist Party, KPJ; September, D'Annunzio declares Italian Regency of Carnaro; Mussolini denigrates Slavs: Treaty of Rapallo: declaration of Free State of Fiume; Italy acknowledges Montenegro's inclusion in Serb, Croat, Slovene kingdom; November, Osbert Sitwell visits Fiume: December, Natale de sangue in Fiume

1921 D'Annunzio leaves Fiume: King Nikola dies: April, Mussolini visits D'Annunzio; June, bomb thrown at Alexander Karađorđević, two months before his succession; July, Mussolini declares in *Il Popolo d'Italia* Bolshevism is dead; November, Mussolini founds Partito Nazionale Fascista

1922 August, D'Annunzio misses meeting with Mussolini and Nitti; October, Mussolini in power after March on Rome: king appoints him prime minister

1923 Mussolini's blackshirts officially become the MVSN; January, beginning of 'Pacification of Libya': start of Second Senussi War; Italian annexation Dodecanese Islands: August invasion of Corfu: brief 'Corfu Crisis'; November, Acerbo Law alters electoral system: D'Annunzio gives Il Vittoriale to state

Timeline

1924 January, Treaty Rome signed by Italy, and Serbs, Croats, and Slovenes; April, elections increase Mussolini's control: June, Matteotti kidnapped, later murdered; blackshirts arrive in Rome to whip up support for Mussolini; Victor Emmanuel III gives D'Annunzio title of Prince of Montenevoso

1925 January, Mussolini announces to Chamber he is taking sole control; July, new Treaty of Nettuno between Italy, Slavs, Croats, and Slovenes; Mussolini stays with D'Annunzio: November, plots start against Mussolini; December, Mussolini officially becomes Head of Government

1928 Albanian president, Ahmed Zogu, becomes King Zog: signs alliance with Mussolini

1929 January, Alexander I Karađorđević dissolves parliament and becomes dictator; Kingdom of Serbs, Croats, and Slovenes becomes Yugoslavia; March, Mussolini's National Fascist Party wins over 98% of votes; 'Rome Question' resolved: failed assassination of Prince Umberto; Croatian Ustaša movement founded

1932 Mussolini starts to be officially addressed as Il Duce:

1933 Hitler becomes German Chancellor: Mussolini first meets Clara Petacci

1934 March, Tito released after five years in prison for being an agitator; June, Hitler meets Mussolini at Stra: July, Nazis murder Austrian Chancellor Dollfuss; August, Hitler has full power as Führer: Alexander I Karađorđević assassinated

1935 Mussolini starts Second Italo-Ethiopian War

1936 May, Italian Empire of Ethiopia declared: July, start of Spanish Civil War; October, Mussolini joins the Axis Pact: creates Via della Conciliazione in Rome

1937 Stalin's purge in Russia: March, Yugoslavia signs agreement with Mussolini; August, Tito becomes interim secretary and de facto leader of his party; October, D'Annunzio meets Mussolini on returning from Hitler; November, Mussolini withdraws from League of Nations

1938 March, D'Annunzio dies: Mussolini attends burial: German Anschluss; September, Mussolini introduces racial laws at Trieste: attends Munich Conference

1939 April, King Zog flees Albania: Italians invade: Victor Emmanuel III King of Albania; May, confirmation of Hitler and Mussolini's Pact of Steel; August, Serb-Croat agreement (Sporazum): November, Tito officially leader of party

1940 March, Hitler and Mussolini meet at Brenner Pass: June, Italy at war with Allies; September, Italy joins Tripartite Pact with Germany and Japan; October, Italy invades Greece: November, British air attack on Italian fleet at Taranto

1941 March, Yugoslav regent, Paul meets Hitler: signs Tripartite Pact: Paul exiled; April, Yugoslavia invaded: country capitulates: Peter II flees; Hitler declares Croatia independent kingdom, NDH: Montenegro protectorate of Axis; May, Victor Emmanuel III survives assassination attempt in Albania

1942 Italians lose Libya, start to suffer serious losses in Russia: Civil War in Yugoslavia

1943 Mihajlović loses Allies' support: SOE parachuted into Montenegro to contact Partisans; May, Italian king first instructs Duce to seek an armistice; July, Allies land in Sicily, start invasion of Italian peninsula; Grand Council Fascism pass no confidence in Mussolini: next day dismissed by king; July, Tomislav II of Croatia abdicates: September, Italian armistice announced; royal family flees: Rome falls: massacre on Cephalonia: Long Armistice signed Malta; Germans rescue Mussolini: Mussolini made head of Repubblica Sociale Italiana; Montenegro falls to the Nazis: October, Italy declares war on Germany; November, Victor Emmanuel renounces titles of Emperor Ethiopia and King Albania; Tito, prime minister of National Committee for Liberation of Yugoslavia, now Marshal; December, fierce fighting along Gustav Line

1944 January, Churchill writes to Tito: April, Victor Emmanuel hands much of power to son; June, Rome recaptured: British move Tito to safety at Bari, then Vis: agreement signed; August, Tito and Churchill meet in Naples: Peter II breaks with Četniks; September, Tito visits Stalin: agreement over Belgrade Offensive; October, Partisans follow Soviets into Belgrade: Tito establishes government; Partisans capture Zara after months of Allied bombing: November, Kotor liberated

1945 February, British agree with Tito to division of Venezia-Giulia; March, Provisional Government of Democratic Federal Yugoslavia established; April, Tito and Stalin sign treaty of friendship: 27 April Germans surrender; 28 April Mussolini shot: 30 April, Hitler commits suicide; May, Tito's troops arrive at Trieste: beginning of forty days of occupation; surrender at Bleiburg: British hand Cossacks over to Soviets; Mihajlović defeated by Partisans at Drina, goes into hiding; June, Anglo-American-British agreement at Belgrade; November, election in Yugoslavia, Peter II deposed

1946 January, King Zog of Albania officially deposed: April, Paris Trieste situation resolved; May, Victor Emmanuel abdicates, son Umberto II: Churchill's 'Iron Curtain' speech; June, referendum votes for Italian republic: July, Mihajlović executed for treason; August, two US planes shot down over Yugoslavia

1947 February, commander of British garrison in Pola (Pula) shot; September, independent Free Territory Trieste (FTT) created: final handover of Pola

1948 June, Communist Party of Yugoslavia expelled from Cominform

1950 Setting up of *Cassa per il Mezzogiorno*

1951 USA provides new aid programme for Yugoslavia

1952 Italian irredentist riots in Trieste, followed by similar protests in Naples and Rome

1953 Tito, President Federal People's Republic of Yugoslavia: threatens Zone B: Stalin dies; October, Allies want to surrender responsibilities in Trieste: riots in city next month

1954 February, start of talks in London: May, Memorandum of Understanding signed; October, Free Territory of Trieste (FTT) comes to an end

Timeline

1957 Mussolini's body reburied at Predappio in Romagna: Italy founder member of EEC

1961 Tito creates Movement of Non-Aligned Countries

1963 Tito made President of the Socialist Federal Republic of Yugoslavia

1968 Falling out between Soviet Union and Albania: Albania withdraws from Warsaw Pact

1970 Peter II of Yugoslavia dies: peace talks Paris: Italo-Yugoslav treaty agrees new borders

1974 Tito declared president for life: next year Osimo Treaty signed by Italy and Yugoslavia

1976 Friuli earthquake kills around 1,000 people

1980 Tito dies

1989 Fall of Berlin Wall

1991 Start of civil war in Yugoslavia

2007 Border between Italy and Slovenia removed three years after Slovenia joins EU

2013 Remains of Peter II returned to Serbia for state funeral

2014 Albania joins NATO

2015 Ten years after receiving American Legion of Merit, Mihajlović rehabilitated

Endnotes

1. Quoted from 'Tezno massacre', en.wikipedia.org.
2. In Captain John Smith, *The generall historie of Virginia, New England and the Summer Isles, together with The true travels, adventures and observations, and A sea grammar – Volume 1, Chapter XII. The Arrivall of the third Supply*, published 1624, virginiaplaces.org
3. Today this Aktio promontory has the more mundane honour of being the site of Preveza airport.
4. See Johan Fourdrinoy et al., 'Conclusions', 5 in 'The Naval Battle of Actium and the myth of the ship-holder: the effect of bathymetry', arxiv.org
5. In addition to the discussion over the cause of Diocletian's death, the actual date continues to be a matter of dispute, it variously being given as occurring sometime between 311 and 316. See Mats Waltré, 'When did Diocletian die? Ancient Evidence for an Old Problem', www.matswaltre.se/pdf/Diocletian.pdf
6. Mary Beard, *Women and Power: A Manifesto*, p.96.
7. In this period it was customary to leave baptism until the end of one's life in the hopes of dying washed of all one's sins.
8. The term 'barbarian' originally signified the outsider, but over the years the definition became less clear cut, particularly after the undefeated Goths were integrated into Roman service and then in time promoted to the position of rulers. The later Western ruler Theodoric, himself an Ostrogoth, would refer to the Franks as barbarians.
9. St Ambrose intentionally linked Arius to Judas Iscariot, comparing the story of his death with that of the apostle as recounted in Acts I, 18. According to St Ambrose, 'Arius in his teaching showed himself like unto Judas, being visited with like punishment.' See Philip Schaff (editor) Nicene *and Post-Nicene Fathers*: Second Series, Volume X, Chapter XIX, paragraphs 123-24.
10. To name a few of such cases of intermarriage, apart from Galla Placidia's later marriage to a Goth, the Eastern Emperor Acadius would in time marry Eudoxia, the daughter of a Frankish general, and Valentinian III's daughter Eudocia became the wife of the Vandal Huneric.
11. Williams and Friell set out the arguments of this case, see *Theodosius the Empire at Bay*, p.146.
12. The Praetorian Prefecture of Illyricum, named after the early Roman province, had been established in different guises during the 4th century, and at the same time it had extended to incorporate lands to the east and south, with Macedonia and

Achaia among those included. As a result, after Theodosius's death and the division of his empire, this area would be disputed. Because the West still claimed possession of the westernmost parts, these were incorporated within the Prefecture of Italy as the Diocese of Illyricum or Pannonia. Most of this region, barring Dalmatia, was finally handed over to the eastern emperor by Galla Placidia in 425.

13. Andrew Gillett points out that the defensive role of Ravenna's surrounding waters has been exaggerated by modern historians. In his view, these would have made it more vulnerable to being cut off from supplies during a siege. See 'Rome, Ravenna and the Last Western Emperors', pp.160-161, jstor.org

14. Theodosius II had been declared co-emperor six years earlier.

15. Attalus remained with the Goths until they later arrived in Gaul, where, having then been abandoned, he was captured by Constantius and sent back to Honorius. After his public humiliation and partial mutilation – the loss of two fingers – he was exiled to the Aeolean (Lipari) islands.

16. Details of Galla Placidia's life are often obscure. Bjomlie has drawn attention to how we must treat with caution propagandist and inaccurate accounts by people like the contemporary writer, John Malalas. He asserted without any doubt that 'Galla Placidia did not marry Alaric's successor Athaulf, rather she remained a virgin until her marriage to the patrician Constantius'. *Politics and Tradition*, p.120

17. The marriage would eventually take place in October 437, the year Valintinian came of age and assumed full power.

18. The contemporary account of Rossi, in Ian Wood, 'Theoderic's Monuments in Ravenna', in *The Ostrogoths: From the Migration Period to the Sixth Century: An Ethnographic Perspective*, p.258.

19. According to an early chronicler this position gave her the power she wanted. 'Placidia had been advanced to the royal power she desired.' ('Placidia tandem potato illata regno.') See Thomas Christopher Lawrence, 'Crisis of Legitimacy: Honorius, Galla Placidia, and the Struggles for Control of the Western Roman Empire, 405-425 C.E.', dissertation, p.266.

20. See *Orientalism and the Reception of Powerful Women from the Ancient World*, ed. Filippo Carlà-Uhink, Anja Wieber, pp.152-153.

21. Galla Placidia's church of St Paul outside the Walls in Rome was badly damaged by fire in the 19th century.

22. Description of Theodoric by the historian Procopius, an official in the army of the Eastern Empire, *Gothic Wars*, Book I, 24, Penelope.uchicago.edu

23. Procopius *Wars*, V, 1.26, quoted from Kaelyn McAdams, 'Western Perceptions of Eastern Romans', Undergraduate Research Thesis, Ohio State University, April 2017, p.23.

24. John Moorhead is among those who consider that the charges against Theodoric of illiteracy were mistaken.

25. See Jonathan J. Arnold, *Theoderic and the Roman Imperial Restoration*, p.110 and John Moorhead, *Theoderic in Italy*, note 200, p.108.

26. 'Romanus miser imitatur Gothum et utilis Gothus imitatur Romanum.' Anonymus Val. 61, cf. Thomas S. Burns, 118, translation quoted from J.C. Rolfe, 547; also cf. John Moorhead, *Theoderic in Italy*, p. 103.

27. Several historians have pointed to how those Romans who chose to have a moustache always seem to have worn a beard as well. Questioning the importance often placed on this matter by many critics who have defined a moustache as a characteristic that was particular to the Goths, Jonathan J. Arnold argues that 'thorough examination of literary and artistic evidence demonstrates that lone mustaches were rare among

Goths and, moreover, not unique to their culture. A number of ancient and early medieval peoples were mustachioed, and despite scholarly claims to the contrary, many Romans, including certain emperors, were as well.' 'Theoderic's Invincible Mustache', in *Journal of Late Antiquity*, p.152, muse.jhu.edu

28. Jonathan J. Arnold, *Theoderic and the Roman Imperial Restoration*, p.74.

29. Procopius, quoted by John Moorhead, see *Theoderic in Italy*, p.221.

30. See Philip Ward, *The Aeolian Islands*, pp.30-32.

31. Totila never took Ravenna.

32. The Visigoths would only finally convert to Catholicism in 589, and the Lombards a century later.

33. Description of 'the Guiscard' by Anna Comnena, in the *Alexiad* Book VI.

34. Charlemagne had been crowned the first new Emperor of the Romans by the pope in 800, and over the following centuries the standing of the subsequent Holy Roman Emperors had grown, their influence gradually extending over much of central Europe.

35. There is a proposed programme to carry out further analysis on these remains.

36. Doubt is thrown on the real reasons for the divorce by the fact of Alberada's later marriage to Robert's nephew, the son of his half-brother Drogo.

37. Quoted from Anna Komnena, *Alexiad*, IV.6, by Patricia Skinner, 'Halt! Be Men', *Gendering the Middle Ages*, p.93.

38. Doubt remains over the precise year he died, some suggesting 1109, others 1111. The confusion possibly arose from the various calendar systems with different dates for the new year. Gadolin suggests the separate dates might refer to Bohemund's death and later interment. See A. R. Gadolin, 'Prince Bohemund's death and the Apotheosis in the Church of San Sabino, Canosa di Puglia', p.127.

39. There is debate as to the date of the cathedral's construction, one theory suggesting this to have taken place around 1040.

40. Early pictures show that for a time the dome was covered or replaced by a pointed roof.

41. Ernst Kantorowicz *Frederick the Second 1194-1250*, p.353.

42. See John Gillingham, Review of *The Emperor Frederick 1 / of Hohenstaufen. Immutator Mundi*, by Thomas Van Cleve, *The English Historical Review*, April 1976, Vol. 91, No. 359, p. 358, quoted from Daniel Lauri, 'Fredrick II: Anti-Papal or Papal Manipulator? A study into the Cause of Conflict Between Emperor Frederick II and Pope Gregory IX', p.10.

43. The definition of tolerance is tricky, the interpretation having changed over the centuries, particularly from the time of the Enlightenment. Voltaire in the 18th century is credited with moving it from a mere acceptance of the other, to a more positive determination to assure the rights of someone or something whose views one might not like. In this early context, I have used the term in the more general sense.

44. To avoid confusion with Frederick's third wife, here she is referred to by her alternative name Yolande.

45. The campaign was dubbed the War of the Keys after the papal insignia.

46. When he became the King of Jerusalem he was given a less flattering description, being said to be red faced, balding, and with 'weak eyes'. See Daniel Lauri, 'Fredrick II [*sic.*]: Anti-Papal or Papal Manipulator? A study into the Cause of Conflict Between Emperor Frederick II and Pope Gregory IX', p.55.

47. See Alexander Gillespie, The *causes of war*, Vol. II, note 80

48. Louis Green, *Chronicle into History*, p.22.

49. Brunetto Latini: *The Book of the Treasure (Li Livres dou Tresor)*, Vol. 90, p.57.

50. When William of Holland was killed nine years later, the crown was offered to Richard Duke of Cornwall, younger brother of Henry III of England.

51. Jean de Meun in the *Romance of the Rose* also claimed that Manfred held his lands by 'force' and 'guile'. See Alexander Gillespie, *The causes of war*, note 83.

52. Brunetto Latini, *The Book of the Treasure*, p.54.

53. Manfred's second wife and two of their children died in captivity.

54. Louis Green, *Chronicle into History*, p.24.

55. Lord Byron, *The Giaour* (IV.13-18)

56. *A History of Venice*, John Julius Norwich, p.6.

57. The *Commune* was replaced by the Signoria in 1423.

58. See Richard John Goy, *Building Renaissance Venice: Patrons, Architects and Builders, c. 1430-1500* (Yale, New Haven and London, 2006)

59. When Enrico Dandolo was later engaged in the Fourth Crusade, his son, who was left in Venice, would only be the acting *vice*-doge until his father's return.

60. A few years earlier, Coloman had married the daughter of Count Roger I of Sicily.

61. 'Inferno' translation ccel.org.

62. Biograd was renamed as Zara Antica by the Italians, and once reconstructed it would become a refuge for those fleeing in 1202 from the siege of present-day Zadar that lies around 30 kilometres to the north.

63. Alexios's sister Irene, who was now married to Philip, had been previously intended to be the wife of Tancred's oldest son, the heir to the Sicilian throne.

64. Alexios V Ducas would also later be blinded by the former emperor Alexios III, and then he, too, was put to death when the Franks brought him back to Constantinople and threw him off the top of Theodosius' column.

65. Henry Wotton, 16 January 1608 (quoted from Marie-José *Gransard, Venice: A Literary Guide for Travellers*, p.33).

66. While this was the contemporary Cronaca Caroldo's version of events, over time a different interpretation had been put on things; Francesco Sansovino, for one, would portray the 'circumspect' and 'prudent' doge as responsible for the secure base on which the 16th-century Republic of his own day rested. According to Sansovino, Gradenigo had achieved this through 'his excellent ordering of the elements [*cose*] of government'. See Debra Pincus, 'Hard Times and Ducal Radiance: Andrea Dandolo and the Construction of the Ruler in Fourteenth-Century Venice', in *Venice Reconsidered: The History and Civilization of an Italian City-State, 1297-1797*, p.91.

67. Ragusa and Venice are credited with first initiating the practice of 'quarantine'.

68. Marino Faliero had been governor of San Lorenzo del Pasenatico (Sveti Lovreč) near Pola, *podestà* of Chiogga, Padua and Treviso, and more than once been a member of the Council of Ten. He had also played an important role in the earlier defeat of the Hungarians at Zara.

69. Roger, Crowley, *City of Fortune*, p.192.

70. Roger Crowley, *City of Fortune*, p.314.

71. It would seem that the authorities may have more than once glossed over uncomfortable truths that could upset Venice's peace and security. As John Julius Norwich suggests, Doge Celsi's death in 1365 may have been opportune, as the Council of Ten had immediately ordered the destruction of all evidence relating to charges against him.

72. Roger Crowley, *City of Fortune*, p.368.

73. Roger Crowley, *City of Fortune*, p.282.

74. Roger Crowley, *City of Fortune*, p.369.

75. Harry Hodgkinson, *Scanderbeg* (Centre for Albanian Studies, 1999), p.164.

76. Mary, like her younger sister Jadwiga in Poland, was crowned with the honorary title of king.

77. At this time the Serenissima's territory of Venetian Albania stretched from Ragusa to Durazzo, reducing in size after 1573 when it was centred around Cattaro (Kotor).

78. Gjon became eventually Count of Soleto, Duke of San Pietro in Galatina, and eventually Signore of Gagliano del Capo and Oria.

79. Orville Prescot, *Princes of the Renaissance*, p.68.

80. Sigismondo Pandolfo di Malatesta to Federico da Montefeltro, 21 February 1445. Quoted from Hugh Biceno, *Vendetta*, p.155.

81. Vespasiano da Bistici, Le Vite, in Cecil H. Clough, 'Federigo da Montefeltro: The Good Christian Prince', warwick.ac.uk, p.331.

82. The couple appear in the 'Inferno', Canto V, the circle of the lustful.

83. 'Romagna tua non e, et non fu mai, / sanza Guerra n' cuor de' suoi tiranni.' ('Inferno', 27. ll.37-38).

84. At the time Guelf and Ghibelline were terms used only in relation to Florentine affairs. See Richard Lansing (ed.) *Dante, the Critical Complex: Dante and Interpretation*, note 40, p.109.

85. Quoted from Helen S. Ettlinger, 'The Sepulchre on the Façade: A Re-evaluation of Sigismondo Malatesta's Rebuilding of San Francesco in Rimini', p.138.

86. Although it was centuries before Italy became a united country, as a concept it had long existed, Petrarch for one speaking of 'Italia mia'. See Anthony F. D'Elia, *Pagan Virtue in a Christian World*, p.117.

87. See Helen S. Ettlinger, 'The Sepulchre on the Façade: A Re-evaluation of Sigismondo Malatesta's Rebuilding of San Francesco in Rimini', in *Journal of the Warburg and Courtauld Institutes*, Vol. 53, jstor.org.

88. Some have noted how the likeness of the saint to the Emperor Sigismund. See Marilyn Aronberg Lavin, 'Piero della Francesca's Fresco of Sigismondo Pandolfo Malatesta before St Sigismund', in *The Art Bulletin*, Vol.51, p.354, jstor.org.

89. See Franz Babinger, *Mehmed the Conqueror and His Time*, (Princeton University, 1978), p.201.

90. Kenneth Meyer Setton, *The Papacy and the Levant*, p.246.

91. See Miranda B. Hickman, *One Must Not Go Altogether with the Tide: The Letters of Ezra Pound and Stanley Nott*, p.280.

92. Guido's son, another Bonconte, would be more fortunate, he being relegated to *Purgatorio*.

93. Giovanni Santi *Cronaca*, quoted from Cecil H. Clough, 'Federico da Montefeltro: the good Christian prince', p.328, warwick.ac.uk.

94. Quoted from Cecil H. Clough, 'Federico da Montefeltro: the good Christian prince', p.343. His 'brother', Ottoviano's child, also died in this same plague.

95. An exception to this is found among his manuscripts which shows him represented from the other side. See Heinz Hofmann, 'Literary Culture at the Court of Urbino during the Reign of Federico da Montefeltro', p.42.

96. Besides suggesting that Roberto was poisoned, Hugh Bicheno proposes that it was 'even likely' that Federico 'was also a party to the Rovere plot to kill' him. See *Vendetta*, p.222 and p.225.

97. Cecil H. Clough, 'Federigo da Montefeltro: the good Christian prince', p.317.

98. In 1939 the *studiolo* in Gubbio was moved to the Metropolitan Museum of Art, in New York.

99. John Knox, 'The Empire of Women is Repugnant to Nature' in *The First Blast of the Trumpet Against the Monstrous Regiment of Women*.

100. See Elizabeth McGrath, 'Ludovico Il Moro and his Moors', jstor.org.

101. Quoted from Elizabeth Lev, *Tigress of Forlì: The Life of Caterina Sforza*, p.18.

102. Quoted from Elizabeth Lev, *Tigress of Forlì: The Life of Caterina Sforza*, p.32.

103. Quoted from Miles Unger, *Magnifico: The Brilliant Life and Violent Times of Lorenzo De' Medici*, p.360.

104. Quoted from Elizabeth Lev, *Tigress of Forlì: The Life of Caterina Sforza*, p.231.

105. Joyce de Vries, *Caterina Sforza and the Art of Appearances, Gender, Art, and Culture in Early Modern Italy*, p.60.

106. As Antonia Fraser has pointed out, Isabella of Castile's draconian measures, backed by her husband Ferdinand, have been partly excused on grounds of their being in keeping with the policies directed by the Church.

107. See Elizabeth Lev, *Tigress of Forlì: The Life of Caterina Sforza*, p.191.

108. Psalm 44, 11-12, referenced by the bishop on Bona's arrival in Poland.

109. See Jerzy K. Kulski, 'The *Mona Lisa* Portrait: Leonardo's Personal and Political Tribute to Isabella Aragon Sforza, the Duchess of Milan', researchgate.net.

110. Quoted from Elizabeth Lev, *Tigress of Forlì: The Life of Caterina Sforza*, p.172.

111. Isabella d'Este, famous for her highly cultured court in Mantua, has been suggested as another possible subject of the *Mona Lisa*.

112. It is interesting that in this period when many were said to be unwashed, there were those for whom this was not true. Lucrezia Borgia washed her hair on an almost daily basis.

113. The nobility in Poland was unlike those found abroad, the *szlachta* being made up of individuals who, despite their differing social and financial backgrounds, believed themselves to be united by a common ancestry among the ancient Sarmatians. See Boggis-Rolfe, *The Baltic Story*, p.108.

114. See Wojciech Szymon Rothbard, 'The cultural influence and artistic patronage of Queen Bona Sforza in early 16th-century Poland-Lithuania' p.72 and note 170, etd.ceu.edu.

115. Pietro Aretino to the doge in 1530. Quoted from William T. Rossiter, '"Lingua Eius Loquetur Mendacium": Pietro Aretino and the Margins of Reformation Diplomacy', in *Huntington Library Quarterly*, Volume 82, Number 4, Winter 2019, p.525, ueaeprints.uea.ac.uk

116. It was at this time, while Clement was feeling threatened by the Emperor – the nephew of Catherine of Aragon – that Henry VIII made his request for an annulment of the marriage. This would persuade the pope to refuse the demand, a refusal that unintentionally put in train the process that ended with the English king's break from the Catholic Church.

117. Although originally restricted to just one individual at a time, around 1570, at a moment of high tension, their number was increased to nine.

118. See Stanko Guldescu, *The Croatian-Slavonian Kingdom: 1526-1792*, p.102.

119. Among other things, the Peace of Cateau-Cambresis saw the division of the Romagna between the Papal States, Ferrara and the city states of Parma-Piacenza and Modena-Reggio.

120. This was the backdrop to Shakespeare's *Othello*.

121. In 1714 Peter the Great would use galleys to great effect to win the Battle of Gangut against the Swedish, but in that case the battle was fought between different types of craft. The Swedes had large sailing ships, less manoeuvrable in the shallow and sheltered waters.

122. On the death of Bona Sforza's son, Sigismund II Augustus, the Poles had elected the son of Henri II of France to be their new king and the Grand Duke of

Adriatic

Lithuania. But a year later on the death of his older brother Charles IX, he raced home to claim his throne as Henri III, leaving the way open for Bona's daughter Anna to replace him in Poland.

123. Richard Knolles, *The Generall Historie of the Turkes* (London, 1603, p.1), quoted from G. E. Rothenberg, Christian Insurrections in Turkish Dalmatia 1580-96', in *The Slavonic and East European Review*, Vol. 40, No. 94, p.136, jstor.org

124. Ferdinand's younger son Archduke Charles now ruled the semi-independent Inner-Austria from Graz. Despite being a devout Catholic, he showed tolerance towards Protestants, and also earned a reputation for promoting the arts. Today, he is probably better remembered for the stud he founded at Lipica (Lipizza) about ten miles east of Trieste. From its initial breeding stock imported from Spain, this would become the stable of famous Lipizzana horses, whose dressage skills of *haute école* are still performed at the Spanish Riding School in Vienna. Besides suffering the effects of earthquake, war and other hardship, the stud would also undergo repeated moves to various new locations, but it has now returned to where it was founded.

125. Because of his good relations with the Venetians, Count Joseph de Rabatta had offered such good terms that his own unpopularity was increased at home. Already loathed for his brutality, two years later he was assassinated.

126. Gunther E. Rothenberg, 'Venice and the Uskoks of Senj: 1537-1618', p.153, jstor.org.

127. While Rothenberg explains that the heads of the 60 prisoners were returned to Venice for display, Bracewell mentions that some Albanians, working for the Venetians, took about the same number of heads to be put on show in Split. See Catherine Wendy Bracewell, *The Uskoks of Senj: Piracy, Banditry, and Holy War in the Sixteenth-Century*, p.286.

128. Voltaire, *Le Mondain*.

129. The final treaty gave Sardinia to the Emperor, and Sicily to the House of Savoy, but these islands were exchanged in 1720.

130. Today the number of permanent residents has dropped from this figure by more than 100,000.

131. 'Un paese, in cui tutti vivono bene, tutti godono la libertà, la pace, il divertimento, quando sanno essere prudenti, cauti ed onorati.'*La Bottega del Caffé*, scena ultima, p.98, letteraturaitaliana.net

132. Il n'y a pas de lieu au monde où la liberté et la licence règnent plus souverainement qu'ici. Ne vous mêlez pas du gouvernement, et faites d'ailleurs tout ce que vous voudrez.' Charles de Brosses, *Lettres familières d'Italie: lettres écrites d'Italie en 1739 et 1740*, p.83.

133. 'Je vous jure qu'il n'y a rien de si plaisant que de voir une jeune et jolie religieuse, en habit blanc, avec un bouquet de grenades sur l'oreille, conduire l'orchestre et battre la mesure avec toute la grâce et la précision imaginables.' Charles de Brosses, *Lettres familières écrites d'Italie en 1739 et 1740*, p.97.

134. The carnival would also be banned by the Fascists in the 1930s, but it was revived 50 years later.

135. Montesquieu in the 1730s would remark that these things were not really a disguise. He claimed it was easy to recognise everyone since people did not change their clothes very often. See Léon Ollé-Laprune, 'Notes de Voyage de Montesquieu', *Le Correspondant: religion, philosophie, politique*, Vol 176, p.47.

136. *La Princesse de Babylone*: Texte entire, Chapitre XVIII, fr.wikisource.org.

137. Venetians were given to such superstitions and Casanova himself recalled being taken as a child to a witch to cure a nosebleed.

Endnotes

138. 'Le peuple de Venise est le meilleur peuple du monde: il n'y a point de gardes au spectacle et on n'y entend point de tumulte: on n'y voit point de rixes.' Léon Ollé-Laprune, *Le Correspondant: religion, philosophie, politique*, p.46.

139. See John Julius Norwich, *A History of Venice*, note, p.638; Peter Ackroyd, *Venice, Pure City*, pp.98-99.

140. 'Si canta per le piazze, per le strade, nei canali; cantano i mercanti smerciando le loro mercanzie, cantano i lavoranti nell'escire dai loro lavori, canta il gondolier stando ad aspettare il suo padrone. Il carattere della nazione è l'allegria.' Collezione complete delle Comedie di Carlo Goldoni, p.193.

141. See Margaret Plant, *Venice: Fragile City, 1797-1997*, p.187. It was equally detested by Ruskin.

142. 'Li pittore devono procurare di riuscire nelle opera grandi, cioè in quelle che possono piacere alli signori nobili, e ricchi perché questi fanno la fortuna de' professori, e non già l'altra gente, la quale non può comprare quadri di molto valore.' Flaminia Giorgi Rossi, 'Tiepolo, Giambattista', treccani.it.

143. Just two years later the century's third war of succession broke out over the Austrian throne.

144. This had to repeated by his son, as Trani harbour again became silted up.

145. This would burn down on 13 December 1836 but was reopened twelve months later.

146. Letter of Lippomano to A. Querini, quoted from Eric Dursteler, *A Companion to Venetian History, 1400-1797*, p.858.

147. '[Siamo] soppiantati da stranieri che penetrano fin nelle viscere della nostra città. Stiamo spogliati della nostra sostanza e non si trova l'ombra dei nostri antichi mercanti tra i nostri cittadini o tra nostri sudditi. Il capitale manca, non nella nazione, ma nel commercio. É usato per sostenere l'effeminatezza, la stravaganza eccessiva, gli spettacoli oziosi, I divertimenti pretenziosi e il vizio, invece di sostenere e aumentare l'industria che è la madre della buona morale, della virtù e del commercio nazionale essenziale.' Quoted from 'Storia della Repubblica di Venezia', it.techwikibd.com.

148. The Manins had bought their position in the patriciate in 1651.

149. The northern Italian regions had become Spanish possessions after the Battle of Pavia in 1525, and these were later passed from Charles V to his brother who succeeded him as Emperor. With the end of the War of the Spanish Succession in 1713, when the Habsburgs had to acknowledge the Bourbon royal dynasty in Spain, the Empire was given Sicily and Naples (which it held on to until 1738), and it retained its northern Italian possessions with a few changes until the time of Napoleon.

150. Mantua had been an Austrian possession since 1708.

151. '...détruire un gouvernement féroce et sanguinaire, defacer le nom vénitien de la surface du globe.' Louis Gabriel Michaud, *Vie publique et privée de Napoléon Bonaparte* digitilised 6 April 2010, p.37.

152. Others picked up this description of him. His arch rival, Maria Carolina of Naples, although strongly opposed to Napoleon, respected him for his achievements. She wrote to her ambassador in October: 'He is the Attila, the scourge of Italy, but I have a genuine esteem and deep admiration for him. He is the greatest man several centuries have produced.' Quoted from Waltraud Maierhofer, 'Maria Carolina, Queen of Naples: The "Devil's Grandmother" Fights Napoleon', in *Women against Napoleon*, p.67.

153. It was given its alternate name of Santa Maria dei Scalzi after its barefooted monks.

154. Giudichi il mio lettore della sorpresa e cordoglio mio, quando in quel vasto recinto, ove non solea vedersi a' felici tempi che il contento e la gioia dell'immenso concorso

del vasto popolo, non vidi, per volger gli occhi per ogni verso, che mestizia, silenzio, solitudine e desolazione. Non v'eran che sette persone, quando entrai in piazza.' Lorenzo Da Ponte, *Memorie*, pp. 1067-1068, quoted from Clara Allasia, 'Il "mio grand'Ugo Foscolo": Lorenzo Da Ponte "Esule Risorgimentale', p.241, core.ac.uk.

155. Lord Byron: *Childe Harold's Pilgrimage*, IV, 13.

156. '...esultante di gioia, penetrata dalla più viva riconoscenza verso il grande e magnanimo suo Liberatore, e tutta fremente nello sciogliere le prime sue voci per confessor a tutta l'Europa di essere debitrice della sua libertà alla gloriosa Nazione francese e all'immortal Bonaparte.' Antonio Spinosa, *Napoleone, il flagello d'Italia*, Kindle Loc 1952.

157. See Andrea di Robilant, *Lucia: In the Age of Napoleon*, p.110.

158. See Monique O'Connell & Eric R. Dursteler, *The Mediterranean World: From the Fall of Rome to the Rise of Napoleon*, p.285.

159. Jonathan North, 'Camillo Elefante's diary, detailing events in Barletta in 1799', jpnorth.co.uk.

160. Jeaffreson Miles, *Vindication of Admiral Lord Nelson's Proceeding in the Bay of Naples*, pp.13-14.

161. At the same time Napoleon officially recognised the sovereignty of the San Marino Republic, which had earlier refused his offer to expand its own territory to the sea.

162. These events form the backdrop to Verdi's opera, *Tosca*.

163. Lucio Ceva, "Napoleon's Grand Armée," *History 95* (May, 1976), p. 30-37, quoted from Dr. Ioannis-Dionysios Salavrakos, 'An Analysis of the French economic industrial and military mobilization in the Revolutionary and Napoleonic wars 1789-1815', in *Journal of Military and Strategic Studies*, jmss.org.

164. The foreign minister Adam Czartoryski declared: 'Whatever turn our relations with Turkey may take, it will always be in the interest of Russia to keep Cattaro... As long as we possess Cattaro, Turkey will be dependent on us.' Quoted from Tadusz Świetochowski, 'Czartoryski and Russia's Turkish Policy, 1804-1806', in *The Polish Review*, p.33, jstor.org.

165. Vivaldi had once studied theology at the church of San Geminiano.

166. See Ferdo Šišić, Hrvatska Povijest, Treći Dio, 1790 to 1847 (Zagreb: Matica Hrvatska, 1913), p. 104, quoted from George J. Prpic , *French Rule in Croatia: 1806-1813*, p.257.

167. Zara's governor at this time was Vicenzo Dandolo - a liberal member of the famous Venetian family - who was introducing his own reforms and improving the lives of the people.

168. 'Ce petit pays, qui jouissait du plus grand bonheur, dont les habitants sont doux, industrieux, intelligents; oasis de la civilization au milieu de la barbarie.' A. F. L. Marmont, Mémoires du Maréchal Marmont, Duc de Raguse (Paris: Perrotin, 1857), II, 375, quoted from George J. Prpic , *French Rule in Croatia: 1806-1813*, p.231.

169. Bizarrely, to this day Vis still has a cricket club, one established at this time.

170. Josip Bersa, Dubrovačke Slike i Prilike 1800-1880 (Zagreb: Matica Hrvatska, 1941), pp. 29-31; Petar Skok, "Dalmacija," in Hrvatska Enciklopedija (Zagreb: Hrvatski Izdavalački Bibliografski Zavod, 1942), IV, p.474, quoted from George J. Prpic, *French Rule in Croatia: 1806-1813*, p.259.

171. The republic's rights to independence had been guaranteed by the Habsburg rulers in 1684 and 1772.

172. 'Das war es, was mir in meinem Unglück noch gefehlt hat, des Teufels Großmutter zu werden', see *Women against Napoleon: Historical and Fictional*

Responses to his Rise and Legacy, Waltraud Maierhofer, Gertrud M. Rösch, Caroline Bland (eds.), p.58.

173. Because of damage from the weather, these were replaced by replicas in the 1980s, the originals now just inside the basilica.

174. Byron, *Childe Harold's Pilgrimage*, II, 62.

175. See K. E. Fleming, *The Muslim Bonaparte: Diplomacy and Orientalism in Ali Pasha's Greece*, p.116.

176. Quoted from K. E. Fleming, *The Muslim Bonaparte: Diplomacy and Orientalism in Ali Pasha's Greece*, p.44.

177. See Noel Malcolm, *Rebels, Believers, Survivors: Studies in the History of the Albanians*, p.174.

178. See K. E. Fleming, *The Muslim Bonaparte: Diplomacy and Orientalism in Ali Pasha's Greece*, p.182.

179. Quoted from Noel Malcolm, *Rebels, Believers, Survivors: Studies in the History of the Albanians*, pp.167-168.

180. To Spiridion Foresti, 22 October 1803, in 'The Letters and Dispatches of Vice Admiral Lord Viscount Nelson with Notes by Sir Nicholas Harris Nicolas', archive.org, p.270.

181. 'To the Right Honourable Earl Moira', 2 July 1803, in 'The Letters and Dispatches', archive.org, p.115.

182. Ibid.

183. 'To Right Honourable Henry Addington', 24 August 1803, in 'The Letters and Dispatches', p.173, archive.org

184. See 'To the Right Honourable Lord Hobart', 10 April 1804, in 'The Letters and Dispatches', archive.org, p.499.

185. Parga would remain in French hands until Napoleon's abdication, at which point its people, fearing they might fall into Ali's hands, surrendered to the British. The latter, however, let the citizens down five years later by selling the town to the hated pasha, after which it remained under the Ottomans until 1912.

186. Quoted from Peter Cochran, ed. *Byron and Women [and Men]*, p.xxviii.

187. Quoted from Peter Cochran, ed. *Byron and Women [and Men]*, p.xxiv.

188. Quoted from Ian Strathcarron, *Joy Unconfined*, p.105.

189. Byron's letter to his mother 12 November 1809, see Robert Elsie, 'Texts and Documents of Albanian History', quoted from Lord Byron, *Selected letters and journals in one volume*, edited by Leslie A. Marchand (London, 1982), albanianhistory.net

190. (194) Ibid.

191. Simon Bainbridge, *Napoleon and English Romanticism*, p.10.

192. Quoted from Peter Cochran, 'Byron's Boyfriends', in *Byron and Women [and Men]'s Letters and Journals, IV*, p.48.

193. *The Works of Thomas Moore*, Vol. XIV, p.441.

194. Lawrence Durrell, *The Greek Islands*, p.232.

195. (195) Byron, *Childe Harold*, II, 15.

196. Quoted from G. B. Rizzoli, 'Byron's Unacknowledged Armenian Grammar and a New Poem', p.5, jstor.org

197. Quoted from Giancarlo Bolognesi, 'Byron e l'Armeno', p.11, jstor.org

198. Byron, 'In the Wind's Eye', 1821-1822, in *Byron's Letters and Journals*, ed. Leslie A. Marchand, p.31.

199. Letters CCLXXXI, & CCLXXX to Mr Murray, *Letters and journals of lord Byron: with notices of his life*, by T. Moore, p.84-85. google.co.uk

200. To Thomas Love Peacock, December 1818, in 'The Correspondence between Byron and Percy and Mary Shelley', petercochran.files.wordpress.com.

201. Marie-José Gransard, *Venice: A Literary Guide for Travellers*, p.72.

202. Byron, *Don Juan*, V, 52.

203. See Jane Stabler, '"Something I have seen or think it possible to see": Byron and Italian art in Ravenna', in *Byron and Italy*, ed. Alan Rawes.

204. Letter CCLXXXI, in *Letters and journals of lord Byron*, p.86, google.co.uk

205. To Thomas Love Peacock 10 August 1821, quoted from Peter Cochran, petercochran.files.wordpress.com

206. Benita Eisler, *Byron: Child of Passion, Fool of Fame*, p.704.

207. Byron, *Childe Harold* IV, 145-153.

208. John Julius Norwich, *Paradise of Cities*, p.105.

209. Quoted from Daryl S. Ogden 'Byron, Italy, and the Poetics of Liberal Imperialism', p.121, jstor.org

210. Quoted from Wilfred J. Dowden, 'Byron and the Austrian Censorship', p.68, jstor.org

211. Byron, *Childe Harold*, IV, XII.

212. Quoted from Daryl S. Ogden, 'Byron, Italy, and the Poetics of Liberal Imperialism', p.136, jstor.org

213. Quoted from Peter Cochran, 'Byron and Shelley: Radical Incompatibles', p.11, érudit.org

214. Quoted from William St Clair, 'Lord Byron Joins the Cause', in *That Greece Might Still be Free: The Philhellenes in the War of Independence*, p.154, jstor.org

215. The island remained British until 1864.

216. Quoted from James A. Notopoulos, 'New Sources on Byron at Missolonghi', in *Keats-Shelley Journal*, p.45, jstor.org

217. Taken from *On this day I complete my thirty-sixth year*

218. Quoted from James A. Notopoulos, 'New Sources on Byron at Missolonghi', in *Keats-Shelley Journal*, p.44, jstor.org

219. Quoted from Johathan Keates, *The Siege of Venice*, p.404.

220. Jonathan Keates, *The Siege of Venice*, p.36.

221. See David Laven, *Venice and Venetia Under the Habsburgs: 1815-1835*.

222. In October 1851 Charles' daughter-in-law Marie-Thérèse – the only child of Louis XVI and Marie Antoinette to survive the 1789 revolution – was also buried here in Kostanjevica Monastery, outside Nova Gorica now just inside the Slovenian border.

223. Quoted from 'Bloody Glamour', Tim Parks, London Review of Books, *Giuseppe Mazzini and the Globalisation of Democratic Nationalism, 1830-1920*.

224. Quoted from Michael Huggins, 'The "Nation" and Giuseppe Mazzini, 1842-48', in *New Hibernia Review*, p.23, jstor.org

225. Quoted from 'Revolutionary turmoil: The Italian States in 1848', in *Italy Revolution 1848*, age-of-the-sage.org.

226. See Cohn Jr, S. K., 'Cholera revolts: a class struggle we may not like', in *Social History*, eprints.gla.uk.

227. Quoted from Jonathan Keates, *The Siege of Venice*, p.64.

228. John Julius Norwich, *Paradise of Cities*, p.98.

229. Quoted from R. J. B. Bosworth, *Italian Venice: A History*, p.9. For those wanting to try and imitate the experience of earlier travellers, from Marco Polo airport it is still possible to take a water taxi or the public water bus to arrive at the Riva degli Schiavoni close to the Piazzetta.

Endnotes

230. Quoted from Paul Ginsborg, 'Peasants and Revolutionaries in Venice and the Veneto, 1848', in *The Historical Journal*, p.510, jstor.org

231. The king fled in disguise to England, together with his wife Queen Maria Amalia, daughter of Ferdinand I and Queen Maria Carolina of Naples and niece of Marie Antoinette.

232. 'Onore a questi prodi! Onore a tutta l'Italia che in questo momento è veramente grande! L'ora è suonata [...] della sua liberazione.' Quoted from Philip Gossett, 'Giuseppe Verdi and the Italian Risorgimento', in *Studia Musicologica*, p.250, jstor. org

233. Having by now chosen Venice to be his place of exile, the 73-year-old Marshal Marmont, would die in the city four years later.

234. Quoted from Jonathan Keates, *The Siege of Venice*, p.101.

235. Palmanova (today a national monument) that was first built as a fortress town by the Venetians in the 1590s, was further strengthened by Napoleon.

236. Louis-Napoleon became Emperor Napoleon III three years later in 1852.

237. The revolution had been largely caused by Franz Josef revoking the March Laws granted to the Hungarians by Ferdinand. The Emperor was more successful at the end of the year when on 31 December he incorporated the Kingdom of Illyria into the Habsburg crownlands.

238. Gazzetta di Gaeta, 9 December 1860, number 21, p.1, quoted from 'HM Francis II, King of the Two Sicilies', in *Royal House of Bourbon Two Sicilies*, realcasadiborbone.it.

239. It was on this occasion that Garibaldi made his famous one-word reply, 'Obbedisco'.

240. Quoted from Tina Schwenk, 'A Habsburg on Monetzuma's Throne', p.235 (253).

241. Quoted from Joan Haslip, '*The Lonely Empress,* p.425.

242. David F. Marley, *Mexico at War: From the Struggle for Independence to the 21st-Century Drug Wars*, p.215.

243. Tina Schwenk, 'A Habsburg on Monetzuma's Throne', p.57 (75), Thesis.pdf.

244. Quoted from Tina Schwenk, 'A Habsburg on Monetzuma's Throne', p.80, Thesis.pdf.

245. Quoted from Tina Schwenk, 'A Habsburg on Monetzuma's Throne', p.87, Thesis.pdf.

246. *The Letters of Queen Victoria*, Vol. 3, ed. A. C. Benson, Reginald Brett, Viscount Esher, p.297.

247. Joan Haslip, *Imperial Adventurer*, p.98.

248. Joan Haslip, *The Lonely Empress*, p.125.

249. Tim Wooten, 'Letters from the Emperor', p.35, jstor.org

250. Tina Schwenk, 'A Habsburg on Monetzuma's Throne', p.199 (217),Thesis.pdf.

251. Kératry, *Rise and Fall of Maximilian, 1861-67* (Samson Low, London, 1868), p.9, tile.loc.gov

252. It is a poignant irony that while Maximilian would be executed as Emperor of Mexico, the Danish prince who took the Greek throne he had refused as King George of the Hellenes would also come to a violent end, assassinated in 1913.

253. John W. Foster, 'Maximilian and his Mexican Empire', p.202, jstor.org

254. Tim Wooten, 'Letters from the Emperor', p.35, jstor.org

255. Tina Schwenk, 'A Habsburg on Monetzuma's Throne', p.144, Thesis.pdf.

256. Archduke Maximilian, 1863, quoted from Tina Schwenk, 'A Habsburg on Monetzuma's Throne', p.110, Thesis.pdf.

257. Tina Schwenk, 'A Habsburg on Monetzuma's Throne', p.157, Thesis.pdf.

258. Three years later in 1867, the Austrian Empire became the Austro-Hungarian Empire.

259. Joan Haslip, *The Lonely Empress,* p.174.

260. Tina Schwenk, 'A Habsburg on Monetzuma's Throne', p.185 (203), Thesis.pdf.

261. Tina Schwenk, 'A Habsburg on Monetzuma's Throne', p.228 (246),Thesis.pdf.

262. Joan Haslip, *The Lonely Empress*, p.207 (original emphasis).

263. Tina Schwenk, 'A Habsburg on Monetzuma's Throne', p.259 (277), Thesis.pdf.

264. Joan Haslip, *The Lonely Empress*, p.125.

265. Quoted from J. Kemper, *Maximilian in Mexico: Life Stories for Young People*, trans. George P. Upton, p.125, gutenberg.org

266. Tina Schwenk, 'A Habsburg on Monetzuma's Throne', p.261, Thesis.pdf.

267. At the time of his birth there had been questions regarding his legitimacy, gossips hinting that he was a love-child. These unproven rumours were based on the considerable affection his mother had shown for her husband's nephew, the Duke of Reichstadt, Bonaparte's son, Napoleon II.

268. Manet would produce five compositions on the subject overall. These would be refused by the Salon who saw them as subversive, but the final painting would be put on show in the US in 1879 and be later bought in 1909 by Mannheim Museum at a period when French-German tensions were high.

269. Tim Wooten, 'Letters from the Emperor', p.35, jstor.org

270. Tim Wooten, 'Letters from the Emperor', p.38, jstor.org

271. In *Marie-Thérèse, Child of Terror*, Susan Nagel addresses the claim that Marie-Thérèse was replaced while she was still alive.

272. For details of these arguments, see Tina Schwenk, 'A Habsburg on Monetzuma's Throne', pp.265-66, Thesis.pdf.

273. Mathilde married the Count of Trani, the half-brother of her brother-in-law, Francis II of the Two Sicilies.

274. Joan Haslip, *The Lonely Empress*, p.440.

275. Joan Haslip, *The Lonely Empress*, p.246.

276. Quoted from Mark Mazower, *The Balkans*, p.110.

277. When in early 1527, after four centuries of personal union with Hungary, the old Kingdom of Croatia – today comprising just the north-western part of the country – had finally chosen to be ruled by the Emperor Ferdinand I, he wanted to create a buffer from the Ottomans and so established an adjacent military zone to protect his new borders. In 1699, this was extended into the Kingdom of Slavonia that had been created out of territory taken from the sultan.

278. The coastal town of Bar, which had been in Ottoman possession since 1571, had originally been named by the Venetians after the Pugliese city of Bari on the opposite shore.

279. Milan was reported to have had an affair with Winston Churchill's famously promiscuous mother.

280. Because so many of his children were married into the courts of Europe, like the Danish king Christian IX, Nikola would be dubbed the 'father-in-law of Europe'.

281. Pašić, who had earlier been sentenced to death, was one of those who received a pardon.

282. The later Italian prime minister, Giovanni Giolitti would insist that the ex-queen of Naples Maria Sofia, the Emperor's sister-in-law, was implicated in this assassination. She was openly opposed to the House of Savoy that had overthrown her husband, but there is no actual proof of her involvement in Umberto's murder.

283. Modern History Sourcebook: The Treaty of Berlin, 1848: Excerpts on the Balkans, sourcebooks.fordham.edu.

284. Quoted from Mark Mazower, *The Balkans: From the End of Byzantium to the Present Day*, p.102.

285. There is considerable discussion over the origin of Dimitrijević's nickname. Besides the suggestions that it came from either the ancient Egyptian bull-god or a mythological Greek king, a third option proposes it refers to a bee.

286. Quoted from Karen Owens, *Franz Joseph and Elizabeth: The last Great Monarchs of Austria-Hungary*, p.160.

287. Still called Cattaro while it was under the Austrians, the town would not officially become Kotor until 1929 and the establishment of Yugoslavia.

288. Jovan Jovanović to the regent Alexander, quoted from Dragoljub R. Živojinović, 'King Nikola and the Territorial Expansion of Montenegro, 1914-1920', p.364, doiserbia.nb.rs.

289. *History Today*: 'The Catastrophe at Caporetto'.

290. Hans Ulrich Gumbrecht, 'I redentori della vittoria: On Fiume's Place in the Genealogy of Fascism', in *Journal of Contemporary History*, p. 261, jstor.org.

291. Samuel Cohen, 'The "Politics of Poetry": the influence of Friedrich Nietzsche upon Gabriele D'Annunzio's Leadership of Fiume', p.8, bir.brandeis.edu.

292. Marja Härmänmaa, 'Gabriele D'Annunzio and War Rhetoric in the "Canti della Guerra Latina"', in *Annali d'Italianistica*, p. 31, jstor.org, and Samuel Cohen, 'The "Politics of Poetry": the influence of Friedrich Nietzsche upon Gabriele D'Annunzio's Leadership of Fiume', p.8, bir.brandeis.edu.

293. Samuel Cohen, 'The "Politics of Poetry": the influence of Friedrich Nietzsche upon Gabriele D'Annunzio's Leadership of Fiume', p.12, bir.brandeis.edu.

294. Ibid.

295. Italy would not declare war on Germany until August 1916.

296. Hans Ulrich Gumbrecht, 'I redentori della vittoria: On Fiume's Place in the Genealogy of Fascism', in *Journal of Contemporary History*, p. 265, jstor.org.

297. 'Per il largo e per il lungo/ torneremo in signoria / D'Istria, Fiume, di Dalmazia, di / Ragusa, Zara e Pola /Carne e sangue dell'Italia!'

298. Hans Ulrich Gumbrecht, 'I redentori della vittoria: On Fiume's Place in the Genealogy of Fascism', in *Journal of Contemporary History*, p. 261, jstor.org.

299. See Mark Phelan, 'D'Annunzio and the Irish Republic, 1919-21', in *History Ireland*, pp. 44-48, jstor.org.

300. Samuel Cohen, 'The "Politics of Poetry": the influence of Friedrich Nietzsche upon Gabriele D'Annunzio's Leadership of Fiume', p.9, bir.brandeis.edu.

301. Quoted from Samuel Cohen, 'The "Politics of Poetry": the influence of Friedrich Nietzsche upon Gabriele D'Annunzio's Leadership of Fiume', p.45, bir.brandeis.edu.

302. Hans Ulrich Gumbrecht, 'I redentori della vittoria: On Fiume's Place in the Genealogy of Fascism', in *Journal of Contemporary History*, p. 267, jstor.org.

303. Ibid.

304. Quoted from Osbert Sitwell, 'Gabriele D'Annunzio', in *Noble Essences or Courteous Revelations*, p.122, archive.org.

305. John Robert Woodhouse, *Gabriele D'Annunzio: Defiant Archangel*, p.334.

306. John Robert Woodhouse, *Gabriele D'Annunzio: Defiant Archangel*, p.362.

307. Quoted from Fred Licht, 'The Vittoriale degli Italiani', in *Journal of the Society of Architectural Historians*, p.318, jstor.org.

308. Quoted from Paolo Monelli, *Mussolini*, trans. Brigid Maxwell, p.96.

309. The liberal Giolitti, a man despised by D'Annunzio, would ironically be given the same nickname of St John the Baptist for the reason that he had tried for a time to find a way to work alongside the Italian Fascists.

310. Quoted from John Robert Woodhouse, *Gabriele D'Annunzio: Defiant Archangel*, p.365.

311. Quoted from Osbert Sitwell, 'Gabriele D'Annunzio', in *Noble Essences or Courteous Revelations*, p.122, archive.org.

312. During this period Italy also took from the Ottomans the Dodecanese islands, including Rhodes, but here the situation remained unresolved until 1923, when they were annexed by Mussolini, finally surrendered to Greece in 1947.

313. Quoted from Robert Soucy, 'Fascism': 'Conservative economic programs', in *Britannica*, britannica.com

314. Quoted from, 'Benito Mussolini's Rise to Power in Fascist Italy', in *Brewminate*, ed. Matthew A McIntosh, brewminate.com.

315. Quoted from Paolo Monelli, *Mussolini: An Intimate Life*, p.132.

316. Quoted from Peter Tase, 'Italy and Albania: The Political and Economic Alliance and the Italian Invasion of 1939', p.66, academicus.edu.al.

317. See 'The Battle of Taranto', in *Navy Wings*, navywings.org.uk.

318. See 'The rare testimony of the 90-year-old from the USA: "I gave Vasil Laçi the gun that shot King Victor Emmanuel III because..." The unknown story of the assassination...' memorie.al.

319. Quoted from Paolo Monelli, *Mussolini: An Intimate Life*, p.169.

320. 'Da questo porto la notte del 9 settembre 1943 l'ultimo re d'Italia fuggi con la corte e con Badoglio consegnando la martoriata patria alla tedesca rabbia. Ortona repubblicana dalle sue macerie e dalle sue ferite grida eterna maledizione alla monarchia dei tradimenti del fascismo e della rovina d'Italia anelando giustizia dal popolo e dalla storia nel nome santo di repubblica. 9-9-1945. Quoted from, 'Porto di Ortona -lapide', in *Associazione Nazionale Partigiani d'Italia*, anpi.it.

321. This atrocity is graphically described in Louis, de Bernières' novel, *Captain Corelli's Mandolin* (Vintage, London, 1998) Footnote p.276

322. Mussolini's mistress Claretta would stay at *Il Vittoriale* for a time.

323. Quoted from, 'Operation Eiche: the Rescue of Benito Mussolini', in *Sky History*, history.co.uk.

324. Quoted from Paolo Monelli, *Mussolini: An Intimate Life*, p.246.

325. I am grateful here for the information given by Paolo Heywood in 'Fascism, uncensored: Legalism and neo-fascist pilgrimage in Predappio, Italy', in *OpenEdition*, No. 72, 2019, journals.openedition.org.

326. Quoted from Paolo Monelli, *Mussolini: An Intimate Life*, p.176.

327. Quoted from Paolo Monelli, *Mussolini: An Intimate Life*, p.180.

328. Louis Adamic, *The Native's Return* (Harper, New York, 1934), p.188.

329. 'Bolje grob nego rob, bolje rat nego pakt'.

330. Sue Onslow, 'Britain and the Belgrade *Coup* of 27 March 1941 Revisited', p.54, sas-space.sas.ac.uk

331. Aaron Gillette, *Racial Theories in Fascist Italy*, p.59, tankona.free.fr.

332. See Daniel Carpi, 'The Rescue of Jews in the Italian Zone of Occupied Croatia', yadvashem.org.

333. 6 September 2003', *The Spectator*, spectator.co.uk.

334. Komunistička Partija Jugoslavije.

335. Bob Moore considers that this explains why, once the Russians had freed their own POWs from the east German prison camps, the Americans and British apparently became less concerned about the extremely harsh treatment of German prisoners by the Free French. See Sven Milekic, 'Croatia has Tarnished its Image Over the Bleiburg Mass', *Balkan Transitional Justice*, balkaninsight. com.

336. Harriman, Special Envoy, p.416, quoted from Lord Hankey, 'USSR and Exchange of Prisoners', House of Lords, 17 March 1976, Hansard, para.314, apl.parliament.uk.

337. Lord Campbell of Croy, House of Lords, 17 March 1976, Hansard, para. 321-23.

338. Arrigo Petacco, *A Tragedy Revealed: The Story of Italians from Istria, Dalmatia, and Venezia Giulia, 1943-1956*, trans. Konrad Eisenbichler, p.78.

339. Nasiha Alicic, 'Localizing the International: Yugoslavia and the Trieste Controversy, 1945-1954', p.20, scholarship.org.

340. Quoted from Arrigo Petacco, *A Tragedy Revealed: The Story of Italians from Istria, Dalmatia, and Venezia Giulia, 1943-1956*, trans. Konrad Eisenbichler, p.89.

341. These events are still a cause of tension today, the Croatian government having stirred up feelings in certain quarters with a commemoration service held in Sarajevo in May 2020, its aim being partly to attempt to rehabilitate Croatia's reputation. This had been stained by the activities of the *Ustaše*, in particular their murder of some 80,000 Serbs and others at Jasenovac concentration camp. For the same reason, the Far Right have held annual commemorations at Bleiburg. See Sven Milekic, 'Croatia has Tarnished its Image Over the Bleiburg Mass', *Balkan Transitional Justice*, balkaninsight.com

342. Quoted from 'Josef Stalin', in *World Heritage Encyclopedia*, Gutenberg Self-Publishing, self.gutenberg.org.

343. The exact number of these places is uncertain. Some claim there to have been as many as 100 available to Tito, but Donald Niebyl has found evidence of only 34 buildings that were actually used. See 'Examining the 34 Villas of Yugoslav President Josip Broz Tito', spomenikdatabase.org.

344. One particularly significant event for the people in the region of the Gargano at this time was the death in San Giovanni Rotondo in 1968 of Padre Pio, a simple local priest, who was canonised in 2002. World famous by the time he died, not just for his miracles and receipt of the stigmata but also for his spirituality, good works, and powers of healing, he was particularly loved in his small hometown for having founded a hospital. Already welcoming its first patients in 1954, thanks to generous global donations, it would become one of the country's top medical centres.

Bibliography

Abulafia, David, *Frederick II: A Medieval Emperor* (Oxford University, New York, Oxford, 1988)

Ackroyd, Peter, *Venice: Pure City* (Vintage Books, London, 2010)

Adamic, Louis, *The Native's Return* (Harper, New York, London, 1934)

Aiello, Alina Adamczyk, *Bona Sforza d'Aragona regina della Polonia*, in *Storia, La Rassegna d'Ischia*, 2/1995), ischialarassegna.com

Alicic, Nasiha, 'Localizing the International: Yugoslavia and the Trieste Controversy, 1945-1954', Master of Arts Thesis (March 2020), University of California Riverside, scholarship.org

Allasia, Clara, 'Il "mio grand'Ugo Foscolo": Lorenzo Da Ponte "Esule Risorgimentale', (Università di Torino), core.ac.uk

Armstrong, Edward, *The Emperor Charles V*, 2 vols, (London, Macmillan, 1910), archive.org

Arnold, Jonathan J., 'Theoderic's Invincible Mustache', in *Journal of Late Antiquity* 1.1 (spring), (John Hopkins University, 2013), muse.jhu.edu

Arnold, Jonathan J., *Theoderic and the Roman Imperial Restoration* (Cambridge University, New York, 2014)

Aronberg Lavin, Marilyn, 'Piero della Francesca's Montefeltro Altarpiece: A Pledge of Fidelity', in *The Art Bulletin*, Vol.51, No. 4 (Dec., 1969), pp.367-371, jstor.org

Babinger, Franz, *Mehmed the Conqueror and His Time*, (Princeton University, 1978)

Baddeley, W. St Clair, *Queen Joanna I. of Naples, Sicily and Jerusalem* (William Heinemann, London, 1893)

Baggally, John W., 'Russia, Great Britain and Ali Pasha', in *The Slavonic and East European Review*, Vol. 14, No.41 (Jan. 1936), pp.441-443, jstor.org

Bainbridge, Simon, *Napoleon and English Romanticism* (Cambridge University, 24 November, 1995)

Ballinger, Pamela, 'Rewriting the text of the nation: D'Annunzio at Fiume', in *Quaderni*, Vol. XI (1997), pp. 117-155, crsrv.org

Ballinger, Pamela, *History in Exile: Memory and Identity at the Borders of the Balkans* (Princeton University, 17 Nov 2002)

Barletta, Barbara, 'Giogio Castriota Scanderbeg', Personaggi del Medioevo, mondimedievali.net

Barolini, Teodolinda, 'Dante and Francesca da Rimini: Realpolitik, Romance, Gender', in *Speculum*, Vol. 75, No.1 (Jan., 2000), pp. 1-28, italian.columbia.edu

Bibliography

Batty, Peter, *Hoodwinking Churchill: Tito's Great Confidence Trick* (Shepheard-Walwyn, 2011)

Bazzoli, Luigi, 'La "Beffa di Buccari"', digilander.libero.it

Beard, Mary, *Women and Power: A Manifesto* (Profile, London, 2017)

Becker, Jared M., 'D'Annunzio, Socialism, and Poetry', in *MLN*, Vol. 105, No. 1, Italian Issue (Jan., 1990), pp. 74-86, jstor.org

Beem, Charles, *Queenship in Early Modern Europe* (Red Globe Press, 2020)

Bialasiewicz, Luiza, and Minca, Claudio, 'The "border within": inhabiting the border in Trieste', in *Environment and Planning D: Society and Space* (2010), Vol. 28, pp.1084-1105, pure.uva.nl

Bibb, Brian Robert, 'Dueling Eagles: Mihailovic, Tito, and the Western impact on World War II Yugoslavia', in *Trace: Tennessee Research and Creative Exchange*, Spring 5-2009, trace.tennessee.edu

Bicheno, Hugh, *Vendetta: High Art and Low Cunning at the Birth of the Renaissance* (Wiedenfeld & Nicholson, London, 2008)

Bjornlie, M. Shane, *Politics and Tradition Between Rome, Ravenna and Constantinople* (Cambridge University, 22 Nov 2012)

Boggis-Rolfe, Caroline, *The Baltic Story: A Thousand Year History of its lands, Sea and Peoples* (Amberley, reprint 2020)

Bogucka, Maria, 'The court of Anna Jagiellon: Size, Structure and Functions', *Acta Poloniae Historica* 99, 2009 rcin.org.pl

Bolognesi, Giancarlo, 'Byron e l'Armeno', in *Aevum*, Anno 71, 3, (Vita e Pensiero, Università Cattolica del Sacro Cuore, 1997), pp.755-768, jstor.org

Bornstein, Daniel, 'The Wedding Feast of Roberto Malatesta and Isabetta da Montefelto: Ceremony and Power', in *Renaissance and Reformation*, New Series, Vol. 12, No. 2, Spring, 1988), pp. 101-117, jstor.org

Bosworth, R. J. B., *Italian Venice: A History* (Yale, New Haven and London, 2014)

Bracewell, Catherine Wendy, *The Uskoks of Senj: Piracy, Banditry, and Holy War in the Sixteenth Century* (Cornell University, 20 Nov 2015)

Bradford, Ernle, *The Great Betrayal: Constantinople, 1204* (Hodder and Stoughton, London, 1967)

Brandt, Anthony, 'The Balkanized War', in *HistoryNet*, historynet.com

'Bucintaur (Bucintoro), The State Galley of the Doges of Venice', (July 06, 2007), istrianet.org

Burns, Thomas S., 'Theodoric the Great and the Concepts of Power in Late Antiquity', in *Acta Classica*, Vol. 25 (1982), pp. 99-118, jstor.org

Byron, Lord George Gordon, 'In the Wind's Eye', 1821-1822, in *Byron's Letters and Journals* (ed.) Leslie A. Marchand (John Murray, 1979)

Byron, Lord George Gordon, *Childe Harold's Pilgrimage* in *The Poetical Works of Lord Byron* (Ward, Lock & Co., London, Melbourne)

Cameron, Alan, 'Theodosius the Great and the Regency of Stilico', in *Harvard Studies in Classical Philology*, Vol. 73 (1969), (Department of the Classics, Harvard University), pp.247-280, jstor.org

'Captain William Hoste' in *Weapons and Warfare: History of Warfare* (May 28 2017) weaponsandwarfare.com

Carlà-Uhink, Filippo, and Wieber, Anja (eds), *Orientalism and the Reception of Powerful Women from the Ancient World* (Bloomsbury, 6 Feb 2020)

Carocci, Sandro, *Lordships of Southern Italy Rural Societies: Aristocratic Powers and Monarch in the 12th and 13th Centuries*, translated by Lucinda Byatt (Viella, 17 November 2018)

Adriatic

Carpi, Daniel, 'The Rescue of Jews in the Italian Zone of Occupied Croatia', yadvashem.org

Cassady, Richard F., *The Emperor and the Saint: Frederick II of Hohenstaufen, Francis of Assisi, and Journeys to Medieval Places* (DeKalb, Northern Illinois University, 2011)

Cassi, Gellio, *Il Mare Adriatico: Sua funzione attraverso i tempi* (Ulrico Hoepli, Milano, 1915)

Cattaruzza, Marina, 'The Making and Remaking of a Boundary – the Redrafting of the Eastern Border of Italy after the two World Wars', in *Journal of Modern European History*, Vol. 9, No. 1, Space Borderlands, Maps (2011), pp. 66-86, jstor.org

Cattaruzza, Marina, *Italy and its Eastern Border: 1866-2016* (Routledge, 2017)

'Cattaro and Ragusa (1813)' in *Weapons and Warfare: History of Warfare* (September 2 2017), weaponsandwarfare.com

Cavendish, Richard, 'Execution of Marin Falier, Doge of Venice', in *History Today*, Vol. 55, Issue 4 (April 2005), historytoday.com

Clarke, Peter D., *The Interdict in the Thirteenth Century: A Question of Collective Guilt* (Oxford University, 6 Sep 2007)

Clough, Cecil H., 'Federigo da Montefeltro: the good Christian prince', (University Library of Manchester, 1984), warwick.ac.uk

Cochran, Peter (ed.) *Byron and Women [and Men]* (Cambridge Scholars, Newcastle upon Tyne, 2010)

Cochran, Peter, 'Byron and Ali Pacha', The Newstead Abbey Byron Society, newsteadabbeybyronsociety.org

Cochran, Peter, 'The Correspondence between Byron and Percy and Mary Shelley,' petercochran.files.wordpress.com

Cochran, Peter, 'Byron and Shelley: Radical Incompatibles', érudit.org

Cohen, Samuel, 'The "Politics of Poetry": the influence of Friedrich Nietzsche upon Gabriele D'Annunzio's Leadership of Fiume', (April 2020), bir.brandeis.edu

Cohn Jr, S. K., 'Cholera revolts: a class struggle we may not like', in *Social History* (2017), 42(2), pp.162-180, eprints.gla.ac.uk

Collins, Joseph, *Idling in Italy: Studies of literature and life* (Scribner: New York, 1920), ebook (January 28, 2013), gutenberg.org

Connor, Carolyn L., *Women of Byzantium* (Yale, 2004)

Crowley, Roger, *City of Fortune: How Venice Won and Lost a Naval Empire* (Faber and Faber, London, 2012)

Curtis, Benjamin, *A Traveller's History of Croatia* (Interlink, Massachusetts, 2018)

Davis, John, *Venice: A History* (New World City, 2017)

Davis, John A., *Naples and Napoleon: Southern Italy and the European Revolutions, 1780-1860* (OUP, Oxford, 14 Sep 2006)

Davis-Weyer (red.), *Early Medieval Art, 300-1150*, Medieval Academy of America, (University of Toronto, 1986)

de Bernières, Louis, *Captain Corelli's Mandolin* (Vintage, London, 1998)

de Brosses, Charles, *Lettres familières d'Italie: lettres écrites d'Italie en 1739 et 1740* (Editions complexe, 1995)

D'Elia, Anthony F., *Pagan virtue in a Christian world: Sigismondo Malatesta and the Italian Renaissance* (Harvard University, Cambridge, Massachusetts, 2016)

Della Donna, Fulvio, *Federico II: la condanna della memoria* (Viella, Roma, 2012)

De Vries, Joyce, 'Caterina Sforza's Portrait Medals: Power, Gender, and Representation in The Italian Renaissance Court', in *Woman's Art Journal*, Vol. 24, No. 1 (Spring-Summer, 2003), pp. 23-28, jstor.org

418

Bibliography

De Vries, Joyce, *Caterina Sforza and the Art of Appearances: Gender, Art and Culture in Early Modern Italy* (Routledge, 2010)

Dinardo, Richard S., 'Glimpse of an Old World Order? Reconsidering the Trieste Crisis of 1945', in *Diplomatic History*, Vol. 21, No. 3 (Summer 1997), pp. 365-381, Oxford University, jstor.org

Di Robilant, Andrea, *Lucia in the Age of Napoleon* (Faber and Faber, 2007)

Djokić, Dejan, 'National Mobilisation in the 1930s: The Emergence of the "Serb Question" in the Kingdom of Yugoslavia' (2011), research.gold.ac.uk

Dowden, Wilfred J., 'Byron and the Austrian Censorship', in *Keats-Shelley Journal*, Vol. 4 (Winter, 1955), jstor.org

Drees. Clayton J., *The Late Medieval Age of Crisis and Renewal, 1300-1500: A Biographical Dictionary* (Greenwood, 2001)

Dunbabin, Jean, *The French in the Kingdom of Sicily, 1266-1305* (Cambridge University, 2011)

Durrell, Lawrence, *The Greek Islands* (Faber, 2002)

Dursteler, Eric (Contributor), *A Companion to Venetian History, 1400-1797* (BRILL, 2013)

Eisler, Benita, *Byron: Child of Passion, Fool of Fame* (Alfred A. Knopf, 1999)

Elsie, Robert, '1919 Essad Pasha Toptani: Memorandum on Albania', in *Texts and Documents of Albanian History*, albanianhistory.net

Elsie, Robert, Lord Byron's letter to his mother, 12 November, 1809, in *Texts and Documents of Albanian History*, albanianhistory.net

Emmerson, Charles, 'Gabriele D'Annunzio's Fiume Escapade', in *History Today* (12 Sept 2029), historytoday.com

Esposito, Walter, *La Dama Bianca* (Lampi di Stampa, 10 Dec 2018)

Ettlinger, Helen S., 'The Sepulchre on the Façade: A Re-Evaluation of Sigismondo Malatesta's Rebuilding of San Francesco in Rimini', in *Journal of the Warburg and Courtauld Institutes*, Vol.53 (1990), pp. 133-143, jstor.org

Facaros, Dana, and Pauls, Michael, *Northern Italy, Emilia-Romagna, including Bologna* (Bradt, UK, edition 1)

Farina, John, 'Caporetto: A Fresh Look', in *La Grande Guerra: The Italian Front 1915-1918*, worldwar1.com

Filippetti, Fabio, & Ravaglia, Elsa, *Alla scoperta dei segreti perduti delle Marche: curiosità, tradizioni e misteri* (Newton Compton, 7 Dec 2017)

Fitzlyon, April, *Lorenzo da Ponte* (Alma, UK, 1982)

Flavo, Joseph D., 'Urbino and the Apotheosis of Power', in *MLN*, Vol. 101, No. 1, Italian Issue (Jan., 1986), pp. 114-146, jstor.org

Fleming, K. E., *The Muslim Bonaparte: Diplomacy and Orientalism in Ali Pasha's Greece* (Princeton, New Jersey, 1965-), reprinted Amazon

Fletcher, Catherine, 'Murder at the Vatican', in *History Today* (2 Oct 2018), historytoday.com

Fornaciari, Antonio, 'L'esplorazione della tomba di Federico da Montefeltro (1422-1482)', Redazione, Università di Pisa, paleopatolgia.it

Foster, John W., 'Maximilian and his Mexican Empire', *Records of the Columbia Historical Society, Washington, D.C.*, Vol. 14 (1911), pp. 184-204, jstor.org

Fourdrinoy, Johan et al., 'The Naval Battle of Actium and the myth of the ship-holder: the effect of bathymetry' (2019), arxiv.org

Gabici, Franco, *Storia Illustrata di Ravenna* (Pacini, Pisa, reprinted 2018)

Gadolin, A. R., 'Prince Bohemund's death and apotheosis in the Church of San Sabino, Canosa di Puglia', in *Byzantion*, Vol.52 (1982), pp. 124-153 jstor.org

Gazzetta di Gaeta, 9 December 1860, number 21, quoted from 'HM Francis II, King of the Two Sicilies', in *Royal House of Bourbon Two Sicilies*, realcasadiborbone.it

Giannone, Pietro, *The Civil History of the Kingdom of Naples*, 2 vols (1731), trans. James Ogilvie (New York Public Library, digitized 7 Dec 2010)

Gilbert, Jane, Keen, Catherine, Williams, Ella, 'The Italian Angevins: Naples and Beyond, 1266-1343', in *Italian Studies*, 72: 2 (11 May 2017), tandfonline.com

Gillespie, Alexander, *The Causes of War: Volume II: 1000 CE to 1400 CE* (Bloomsbury, 1 Dec 2016)

Gillett, Andrew, 'Rome, Ravenna and the Last Western Emperors', *Papers of the British School at Rome*, Vol. 69, Centenary Volume (2001), (British School at Rome), pp. 131-167, jstor.org

Gillette, Aaron, *Racial Theories in Fascist Italy* (Routledge, London and New York, 2002), tankona.free.fr

Ginsborg, Paul. 'Peasants and Revolutionaries in Venice and the Veneto, 1848', in *The Historical Journal*, Vol. 17, No. 3 (Sept., 1974), pp. 503-550, jstor.org

Ginsborg, Paul, *Daniele Manin and the Venetian Revolution of 1848-49* (Cambridge, London, New York, Melbourne, 1979)

Giorgi Rossi, Flaminia, 'Tiepolo, Giambattista', in *Enciclopedia dei ragazzi* (2006), treccani.it

Glen, Diana, 'Francesca da Rimini', in *Dante's Reforming Mission and Women in the 'Comedy'* (Troubador, Leicester, 2008)

Glover, Gareth, *Fighting Napoleon: The Recollections of Lieutenant John Hildebrand 35th Foot in the Mediterranean and Waterloo Campaigns* (Grub Street, London, 2017)

Goldoni, Carlo, *Collezione complete delle Comedie di Carlo Goldoni* (Giachetti, 1828)

Goldoni, Carlo, *La Bottega del Caffé*, letteraturaitaliana.net

Gossett, Philip, 'Giuseppe Verdi and the Italian Risorgimento', in *Studia Musicologica*, Vol.52, No.1/4, (December 2011), pp.241-257, jstor.org

Gourdin, Henri, *Galla Placidia: Impératrice romaine, reine des Goths (388-450)* (L'oeuvre, Paris, 2008)

Goy, Richard John, *Building Renaissance Venice: Patrons, Architects and Builders, c. 1430- 1500* (Yale, New Haven and London, 2006)

Grady, Ellen, *The Marche and San Marino* (Blue Guide, Somerset, 2015)

Gransard, Marie-José, *Venice: A Literary Guide for Travellers* (Tauris Parke, London, 2016)

Green, Louis, 'Historical Interpretation in Fourteenth-Century Florentine Chronicles', in *Journal of the History of Ideas*, Vol. 28, No. 2 (Apr.-Jun., 1967), (University of Pennsylvania), pp. 161-178, jstor.org

Green, Louis, *Chronicle into History: An Essay on the Interpretation of History in Florentine Fourteenth-century Chronicles* (Cambridge University, 2008)

Gregson, H., 'Buffer states of the Balkans', macedonia.kroraina.com

Gumbrecht, Hans Ulrich, 'I redentori della vittoria: On Fiume's Place in the Genealogy of Fascism', in *Journal of Contemporary History*, Vol. 31, No. 2 (Apr. 1996), pp. 253-272, jstor.org

Hairston, Julia L., 'Skirting the Issue: Machiavelli's Caterina Sforza', in *Renaissance Quarterly*, Vol. 53, No. 3 (Autumn, 2000), pp. 687-712, jstor.org

Hametz, Maura E., 'Uncertain States: Repatriation and Citizenship in the Northeastern Adriatic, 1918-1921', Old Dominion University, ODU Digital Commons, digitalcommons.odu.edu

Hamilton Jackson, F., R.B.A., *The Shores of the Adriatic: The Austrian Side, the K˘stenlande, Istria, and Dalmatia* (John Murray, London, 1908), gutenberg.org

Härmänmaa. Marja, 'Gabriele D'Annunzio and War Rhetoric in the "Canti della Guerra Latina"', in *Annali d'Italianistica*, Vol. 33, The Great War and the Modernist Imagination in Italy, pp. 31-51, jstor.org

Haslip, Joan, The Lonely Empress (Weidenfeld and Nicolson, London, 1965)

Haslip, J., *Imperial Adventurer: Emperor Maximilian of Mexico and his Empress* (Littlehampton Book Services, London, 1971)

Hatcher, Anna, 'Dante's Ulysses and Guido da Montefeltro', in *Dante Studies, with the Annual Report of the Dante Society*, No. 88 (1970), (John Hopkins University), pp. 109-117, jstor.org

Heywood, Paolo, in 'Fascism, uncensored: Legalism and neo-fascist pilgrimage in Predappio, Italy', in *OpenEdition*, No. 72 (2019), journals.openedition.org

Hibbert, Christopher, *The Borgias* (republished Constable, London, 2011)

Hickman, Miranda B., *One Must Not Go Altogether with the Tide: The Letters of Ezra Pound and Stanley Nott* (McGill-Queen's, 2011)

Hofmann, Heinz, 'Literary Culture at the Court of Urbino during the Reign of Federico da Montefeltro', in *Humanistica Lovaniensia*, Vol. 57 (2008), (Leuven University), pp. 5-59, jstor.org

Holland, Henry, *Travels in the Ionian Isles: During the years 1812 and 1813* (Longman, London,1815), albanianhistory.net

Horodowich, Elizabeth, *A Brief History of Venice: A New History of the City and Its People* (Hachette, UK, 7 Feb 2013)

House of Lords, 17 March 1976, Hansard, para.314, apl.parliament.uk

Howard-Johnston, James, 'Bilingual Reading, the *Alexiad* and the *Gesta Roberti Wiscardi*', in *Reading the Byzantine Empire and Beyond* (eds) Teresa Shawcross, Ida Toth (Cambridge University, 4 Oct 2018)

Huggins, Michael, 'The "Nation" and Giuseppe Mazzini, 1842-48', in *New Hibernia Review*, Iris Éireannach Nua, Vol. 17, No. 3 (FÓMHAR/ AUTUMN 2013), pp.15-33, jstor.org

Hughes-Hallett, Lucy, *The Pike: Gabriele D'Annunzio, Poet, Seducer and Preacher of War* (Fourth Estate, London, 2013)

'I Francesi a Trieste: Il occupazione francese', in *Destini Imperiali: Dinastie Reali in Friuli Venezia Giulia*, destini-imperiali.com

'Italian Unification: Cavour, Garibaldi and the Making of Italy', age-of-sage.org

Jansen, Sharon L., *The Monstrous Regiment of Women: Female Rulers in Early Modern Europe* (Springer Palgrave Macmillan, Oct 17 2002)

Johnson, Mark J., 'The Mausoleum of Bohemund in Canosa and the Architectural Setting of Ruler Tombs in Norman Italy', in *Romanesque and the Mediterranean: Patterns of Exchange Across the Latin, Greek and Islamic Worlds c.1000-c.1250* (ed.) Rosa Bacile (Routledge, 2 Dec 2017)

Jones, P. J., *The Malatesta of Rimini and the Papal State*, reprint (Cambridge University, 2005) Jonker, Marijke, 'Crowned, and Discrowned and Decapitated: Delacroix's *Th Execution of the Doge Marino Faliero and its Critics*', in *Nineteenth-Century Art Worldwide*, Volume 9, Issue 2 (Autumn 2010), 19thc-artworldwide.org

'Josef Stalin', in *World Heritage Encyclopedia*, Gutenberg Self-Publishing, self. gutenberg.org

Kaegi, Walter Emil, 'Arianism and the Byzantine Army in Africa 533-546', *Traditio*, Vol. 21 (1965) (Cambridge University), pp. 23-53, jstor.org

Kantorowicz, Ernst, *Frederick the Second, 1194-1250*, first published 1931 (republished Frederick Ungar, New York, 1957)

Kasmi, Marenglen, 'Scutari crisis', in *International Encyclopedia of the First World War*, encyclopedia.1914-1918-online.net

Keates, Jonathan, *The Siege of Venice* (Pimlico, London, 2006)

Kemper, J., *Maximilian in Mexico: Life Stories for Young People*, trans. George P. Upton, (McClurg, Chicago, 1911), gutenberg.org

Knight, Roger, *The Pursuit of Victory: The Life and Achievement of Horatio Nelson* (Penguin, 2006)

Knolles, Richard, *The Generall Historie of the Turkes* (London, 1603)

Komnena, Anna, *Alexiad*, trans. E. R. A. Sewter (Penguin, London, 1969)

Ković, Miloš, 'The British Adriatic Squadron and the evacuation of Serbs from the Albanian Coast 1915-1916' (January 2018), in *Balcanica* 2018 (49), pp. 29-41, researchgate.net

Kulski, Jerzy K., 'The *Mona Lisa* Portrait: Leonardo's Personal and Political Tribute to Isabella Aragon Sforza, the Duchess of Milan', in *International Journal of Art and Art History* (December 2018), Vol. 6, No. 2, pp. 31-50, researchgate.net

Laddaga, Reinaldo, 'A City for Poets and Pirates: Gabriele D'Annunzio and the Fiume adventure', in *Cabinet* (Summer 2015), cabinetmagazine.org

Lane, Frederic, *Venice, A Maritime Republic* (John Hopkins University, Baltimore and London,1973)

Lansing, Richard (ed.) *Dante, the Critical Complex: Dante and Interpretation*, Vol. 7 (Routledge, New York & London, 2003)

Larner, John, *Lords of Romagna* (Springer, 18 July 1965)

Latini, Brunetto, *The Book of the Treasure*, trans. Paul Barrette, Spurgeon Baldwin, Vol. 90, Series B, Garland Library Medieval Literature, reprint (Routledge, 2013)

Lauri, Daniel, 'Fredrick II: Anti-Papal or Papal Manipulator? A study into the Cause of Conflict Between Emperor Frederick II and Pope Gregory IX' (2011), scholarship.shu.edu/theses/198

Laven, David, *Venice and Venetia Under the Habsburgs: 1815-1835* (Oxford University, 2002)

Lawrence, Thomas Christopher, 'Crisis of Legitimacy: Honorius, Galla Placidia, and the Struggles for Control of the Western Roman Empire, 405-425 C.E.', Doctoral Dissertation (University of Tennessee, May 2013), trace.tennessee.edu

Ledeen, Michael A., *The First Duce: D'Annunzio at Fiume* (John Hopkins University, Baltimore and London, 1977)

Lendering, Jona, 'Siege of Dyrrhachium (49/48 BCE)', livius.org

Letters and journals of lord Byron: with notices of his life, by T. Moore, Vol. 2 (Harper, 1831), books.google.co.uk

Lev, Elizabeth, *Tigress of Forli: The Life of Caterina Sforza* (republished Head Zeus, London, 2012)

Licht, Fred, 'The Vittoriale degli Italiani', in *Journal of the Society of Architectural Historians*, Vol. 41, No. 4 (Dec., 1982), pp. 318-324, jstor.org

Linsenmeyer, William S., 'Italian Peace Feelers before the Fall of Mussolini', in *Journal of Contemporary History,* Vol. 16, No. 4 (Oct., 1981), pp.649-662, jstor.org

'Lodovico Manin, ultimo doge', enricodavenezia.it

LoPrete, Kimberley, 'How was Bohemond of Taranto viewed as a first crusader by his contemporaries?' (17 January 2014), Bohemond of Taranto First Crusade |Eoghan Fallon-Academia.edu

Luscombe, David, and Riley-Smith, Jonathan (eds), *The New Cambridge Medieval History IV, c.1024-c.1198 Part II* (Cambridge University, 1995)

Bibliography

Maierhofer, Waltraud, Rösch, Gertrud M, Bland, Caroline (eds), 'Maria Carolina, Queen of Naples: The "Devil's Grandmother" Fights Napoleon', in *Women against Napoleon*, (Campus Verlag, Franfurt/New York, 2007)

Mainati, Giuseppe, *Croniche ossia memorie storiche sacro-profane di Trieste, cominciando dall'XI secolo sino a nostri giorni. Coll'aggiunta della relazione dei vescovi dal primo sino al decimo secolo*, (Picotti, 1818) (digitized 12 March 2018), books.google.co.uk

Malcolm, Noel, *Rebels, Believers, Survivors: Studies in the History of the Albanians: Studies in the History of the Albanians* (Oxford University, 8 July 2020)

Marley, David F., *Mexico at War: From the Struggle for Independence to the 21st-Century Drug Wars* (ABC-CLO, 11 Aug 2014)

Martin, Brian Joseph, 'Napoleonic Friendship at the Top: Marsal Lannes, General Duroc, General Junot' in *Napoleonic Friendship: Military Fraternity, Intimacy, and Sexuality in Nineteenth-century France* (UPNE, 2011)

Martin, John Jeffries, and Romano, Dennis, *Venice Reconsidered: The History and Civilization of an Italian City-State, 1297-1797* (John Hopkins University, Baltimore and London, 2003)

Martinez, H. Salvador, *Alfonso X, the Learned: A Biography* (BRILL, 210)

Mazower, Mark, *The Balkans: From the End of Byzantium to the Present Day* (Phoenix, London, 2000)

McGrath, Elizabeth, 'Ludovico Il Moro and his Moors', in *Journal of the Warburg and Courtauld Institutes*, Vol. 65 (2002), jstor.org

McIntosh, Matthew A. (ed.) 'Benito Mussolini's Rise to Power in Fascist Italy', in *Brewminate* (May 31 2019), brewminate.com

McLees, Mother Nectaria, 'The Prophet and Ali Pasha, the Lion of Ioannina', in *Road to Emmaus*, roadtoemmaus.net/back_issue_articles/RTE_06/The_Prophet_and_the_Pasha.pdf

Metcalfe, Alex, *The Muslims of Medieval Italy* (Edinburg University, 2009)

Meyer Setton, Kenneth, *The Papacy and the Levant (1204-1571)*, Vol. III, the Sixteenth Century (American Philosophical Society, 1976)

Michaud, Louis Gabriel, *Vie publique et privée de Napoléon Bonaparte* (Michaud, 1844), (digitilised 6 April 2010), google.co.uk

Milekic, Sven, 'Croatia has Tarnished its Image Over the Bleiburg Mass', in *Balkan Transitional Justice*, balkaninsight.com

Miles, Jeaffreson, *Vindication of Admiral Lord Nelson's Proceeding in the Bay of Naples* (A. H. Baily, Great Britain, 1843)

Modern History Sourcebook: 'The Treaty of Berlin, 1848: Excerpts on the Balkans', Fordham University, sourcebooks.fordham.edu

Mombauer, Annika, 'July Crisis 1914', International Encyclopedia of the First World War, encyclopedia.1914-1915-online.net

Mondschein, Ken, 'The Wager of Battle, Duels and Tournaments', in *Game of Thrones and The Medieval Art of War* (MacFarland, 2017)

Monelli, Paolo, *Mussolini: An Intimate Life*, trans. Brigid Maxwell (Thames and Hudson, London, 1953)

Moore, Bob, 'Unruly Allies: British Problems with the French Treatment of Axis Prisoners of War, 1943-1945', in *War in History*, Vol.7, No.2 (April 2000), pp.180-198, jstor.org

Moore, Thomas, *The Works of Thomas Moore*, Vol. XIV (Galignani, Paris)

Moorhead, John, *Theoderic in Italy* (Clarendon, Oxford, 1992)

Morier, J. P., and Baggally, John W., 'Russia, Great Britain and Ali Pasha', in *The Slavonic And East European Review*, Vol. 14, No. 41 (Jan., 1936), pp. 441-443, jstor.org

Morris, Jan, *Trieste and the Meaning of Nowhere* (Faber and Faber, London, 2002)

Morrissey, Thomas E., 'Padua in Crisis and Transition around 1400', oslo2000.uio.no

Morton, H.V., *A Traveller in Southern Italy*, first published 1983 (Methuen, London, 1986)

Muehlberger, Ellen, 'The Legend of Arius' Death: Imagination, Space and Filth in Late Ancient Historiography', in *Past & Present*, Vol. 227, Issue 1 (May 2015), pp.3-29, academic.oup.com

Musto, Roald G., *Writing Southern Italy before the Renaissance: Trecento Historians of the Mezzogiorno* (Routledge, 4 December 2018)

Nelson, Admiral Horatio, 'The Letters and Dispatches of Vice Admiral Lord Viscount Nelson with Notes by Sir Nicholas Harris Nicolas', archive.org

Newby, Eric, *On the Shores of the Mediterranean* (Harper, London, republished 2011)

Niebyl, Donald, 'Examining the 34 Villas of Yugoslav President Josip Broz Tito', spomenikdatabase.org

North, Jonathan, 'Camillo Elefante's diary, detailing events in Barletta in 1799', jpnorth.co.uk

Norwich, John Julius, *Paradise of Cities* (Doubleday, New York, London, 2003)

Norwich, John Julius, *A History of Venice* (Penguin, republished 2003)

Norwich, John Julius, *The Middle Sea: A History of the Mediterranean* (Vintage, 2007)

Norwich, John Julius, *The Normans in the South, 1016-1130* (Faber & Faber, London, republished 2018)

Notopoulos, James A., 'New Sources on Byron at Missolonghi', in *Keats-Shelley Journal*, Vol. 4 (Winter 1955), jstor.org

O'Connell, Monique, & Dursteler, Eric R., *The Mediterranean World: From the Fall of Rome to the Rise of Napoleon*, (JHU, 23 May 2016)

Ogden, Daryl S., 'Byron, Italy, and the Poetics of Liberal Imperialism', *Keats-Shelley Journal*, Vol.49 (2000), jstor.org

Oke, Richard, *The Boy from Apulia* (Arthur Barker, London, 1936)

Okey, Thomas, *Venice and its Story*, first edition October 1903, third edition 1910 (A Public Domain Book, e-book)

Oliphant, Mrs, *The Makers of Venice: Doges, Conquerors, Painters* (Macmillan, London and New York, 1891)

Ollé-Laprune, Léon, 'Notes de Voyage de Montesquieu', in *Le Correspondant: religion, philosophie, politique*, Vol 176 (V.-A. Waille, 14 February 2013)

Onslow, Sue, 'Britain and the Belgrade *Coup* of 27 March 1941 Revisited', in *Electronic Journal of International History* (2005), Institute of Historical Research, University of London, core.ac.uk

Owens, Karen, *Franz Joseph and Elizabeth: The last Great Monarchs of Austria-Hungary* (McFarland, 8 Nov 2013)

Oxenberg, Catherine, 'My mother's triumph – exhumation and burial of Prince Paul of Yugoslavia' (October 30, 2012), catherineoxenberg.wordpress.com

Papa, Emilio R., 'Discorrendo di D'Annunzio Politico', in *Studi Novecenteschi*, Vol.26, No. 58, (dicembre 1999), pp. 275-293, jstor.org

Parks, Tim, 'Bloody Glamour', London Review of Books, *Giuseppe Mazzini and theGlobalisation of Democratic Nationalism, 1830-1920* (eds) C. A. Bayly and Eugenio Biagini, (Oxford, September 2008)

Bibliography

Parla, Jale, 'From Byron's *Giaour* to Jezernik's *Wild Europe*: Theory or *History?*', in *Imagining the Turk* (ed.) Božidar Jezernik (Cambridge Scholars, Newcastle upon Tyne, 2010)

Pastrnak, Patrik, 'A Bridal Journey: The Case of Bona Sforza', MA Thesis in *Medieval Studies*, Central European University, Budapest (May 2017), etd.ceu.edu

Paunović, Jelena, 'The Deaths of the Obrenović family in Serbian History and Remembrance', in *Istrazivanja Journal of Historical Researches* 29 (2018), pdf online

Penn, Imma, *Dogma Evolution and Papal Fallacies* (AuthorHouse, 30 May 2007)

Perrottet, Tony, 'Who Was Casanova?', in *Smithsonian Magazine* (April 2012), smithsonianmag.com

Petacco, Arrigo, *A Tragedy Revealed: the Story of the Italian Population of Istria, DalmatiaAnd Venezia Giulia, 1943-1956*, trans. Konrad Eisenbichler (University of Toronto, Toronto, Buffalo, London, 2005)

Peterson, Thomas E., 'Schismogenesis and National Character: The D'Annunzio-Mussolini Correspondence', in *Italica*, Vol. 81, No. 1 (Spring, 2004), pp. 44-64, jstor.org

Phelan, Mark, 'Gabriele D'Annunzio and the Irish Republic, 1919-21', in *History Ireland*, Vol. 21, No. 5 (September/October 2013), pp. 44-48, jstor.org

Pilato, Francesca, '"En mille endroits charmants". L'incontro tra d'Annunzio e Debussy', in *Studi Francesi*, 172 (LVIII I I) 1, 2014, pp. 100-107, journals.openedition.org

Pincus, Debra, 'Hard Times and Ducal Radiance: Andrea Dandolo and the Construction of The Ruler in Fourteenth-Century Venice', in *Venice Reconsidered: The History and Civilization of an Italian City-State, 1297-1797* (eds) John Martin and Dennis Romano (John Hopkins, Baltimore and London, 2000)

Pirro, Deidre, 'Prince Paul of Yugoslavia: Avid art collector and owner of Villa Demidoff at Pratolino', in *The Florentine* (May 20, 2020), theflorentine.net

Plant, Margaret, *Venice, Fragile City: 1797-1997* (Yale University, 2002)

'Pope Alexander VI', *Catholic Encyclopedia*, newadvent,org

'Porto di Ortona-lapide', in *Associazione Nazionale Partigiani d'Italia*, anpi.it

Pozza, Marco, 'Michiel, Domenico', in *Dizionario Biografico degli Italiani*, Vol, 74 (2010), treccani.it

Prescott, Orville, *Princes of the Renaissance* (Routledge, reprint 2019)

Preveden, Francis R., *A History of the Croatian People*, Vol. I, Prehistory and Early Period until 1397 A.D. (Philosophical Library, New York, 1955)

Preveden, Francis R., *A History of the Croatian People*, Vol. II, 'from their arrival on the shores of the Adriatic to the present day' (Philosophical Library, New York, 1962)

Prokopios, *The Wars of Justinian*, trans. H. B. Dewing, Contributors Anthony Kaldellis, Ian Mladjov (Hackett, 3 Sep 2014)

Prpic, George J., 'French rule in Croatia: 1806-1813', in *Balkan Studies*, 1964, ojs.lib. uom.gr

Queen Victoria, *The Letters of Queen Victoria*, Vol. 3 (eds) A. C. Benson, Reginald Brett, Viscount Esher (Cambridge University, 2014)

Rajić, Suzana, 'The Russian Secret Service and King Alexander Obrenović of Serbia (1900- 1903)', Faculty of Philosophy, University of Belgrade, doiserbia.nb.rs

Raspopović, Radoslav, 'Montenegro', International Encyclopedia of the First World War, encyclopedia.1914-1918-online.net

Rebenich, Stefan, 'Gratian, a Son of Theodosius, and the Birth of Galla Placidia', in *Historia: Zeitschrift für Alte Geschichte*, Bd. 34, H. 3 (3rd Qtr., 1985), pp. 372-385, jstor.org

Rickard, J. (15 September 2016), *Battles of the Great Roman Civil War, 49-45 BC*, historyofwar.org

Rizzoli, G. B., 'Byron's Unacknowledged Armenian Grammar and a New Poem', jstor.org

Romano, Dennis, *The Likeness of Venice: a life of Doge Francesco Foscari, 1373-1457* (Yale University, New Haven, Conn., c.2007)

Rothbard, Wojciech Szymon, 'The cultural influence and artistic patronage of Queen Bona Sforza in early 16th-century Poland-Lithuania', MA thesis, Central European University (Budapest, Hungary, 2010), etd.ceu.edu

Rothenberg, G. E., 'Venice and the Uskoks of Senj: 1537-1618', in *The Journal of Modern History*, Vol. 33, No. 2 (Jun., 1961), pp. 148-156, jstor.org

Rothenberg, G. E., 'Christian Insurrections in Turkish Dalmatia 1580-96', in *The Slavonic and East European Review*, Vol. 40, No. 94 (Dec., 1961), pp.136-147, jstor.org

Russell, Eugenia, and Russell, Quentin, *Ali Pasha, Lion of Ioannina: The Remarkable Life of The Balkan Napoleon* (Pen and Sword, 30 Sep 2017)

Saho, Margaret Ann, *Imago Triumphalis: The Function of Triumphal Imagery for Renaissance Rulers* (Peter Lang, New York, 2004)

Salavrakos, Dr. Ioannis-Dionysios, 'An Analysis of the French economic industrial and Military mobilization in the Revolutionary and Napoleonic wars 1789-1815', in *Journal of Military and Strategic Studies*, Vol. 18, Issue 3, jmss.org

Salisbury, Joyce E., *Rome's Christian Empress* (John Hopkins University, USA, 2015)

Sass, Erik, 'WWI Centennial: Archduke Ferdinand is Murdered in Sarajevo' (June 28, 2014), mentalfloss.com

Schaff, Philip and Wallace, Rev. Henry (eds), *Nicene and Post-Nicene Fathers*: Second Series, Volume X, Chapter XIX (Cosimo Classics, New York, 1 June 2007)

Scheltema, J. F., 'Venice Delivered', in *The Sewanee Review*, Vol. 27, No. 4 (Oct., 1919), pp.423-437, (John Hopkins), jstor.org

Schwarcz, Andreas, 'Marriage and Power Politics in the Fifth Century', in *Medieval Prosopography*, Vol. 24 (2003), pp. 35-43, jstor.org

Schwenk, Tina, 'A Habsburg on Monetzuma's Throne', University of Stirling, 2010, Thesis.pdf

Setton, Kenneth Meyer, *The Papacy and the Levant, 1204-1571: The fifteenth century* (American Philosophical Society, 1976)

Seward, Desmond, and Mountgarret, Susan, *Old Puglia: A Cultural Companion to South- Eastern Italy* (ArmchairTraveller, London, 2006)

Shiver, Conelia, 'The Carbonari', in *Social Science*, Vol. 39, No. 4 (Oct., 1964), pp. 234-241, jstor.org

Sims, Josh, 'A Man of Many Parts: Gabriele D'Annunzio', in *The Rake*, therake.com

Sirvan, Hagith, *Galla Placidia: The Last Roman Empress* (Oxford University, 2011)

Sitwell, Osbert, 'D'Annunzio' in *Noble Essences, or Courteous Revelations*, (Macmillan, London, 1950), archive.org

Skinner, Patricia, 'Halt! Be Men!': Sikelgaita of Salerno, Gender and the Norman Conquest of Southern Italy', in *Gendering the Middle Ages* (eds) Pauline Stafford, Anneke B. Mulder-Bakker (Blackwell, Oxford, 2001)

Smith, Captain John, *The generall historie of Virginia, New England and the Summer Isles, together with the true travels, adventures and observations, and A sea grammar – Volume 1, Chapter XII. The Arrivall of the third Supply*, published 1624 (Library of Congress), virginiaplaces.org

Soucy, Robert, 'Fascism': 'Conservative economic programs', in *Britannica* (4 Nov, 2020), britannica.com

Sowards, Steven W., 'The Balkan Causes of World War One' (1996), firstworldwar.com

Spinosa, Antonio, *Napoleone, il flagello d'Italia* (Mondadori, Milan, 7 October, 2010), ebook

Stabler, Jane, '"Something I have seen or think it possible to see": Byron and Italian art in Ravenna', in *Byron and Italy* (eds) Alan Rawes, Diego Saglia (Manchester University, Dec 2017)

Stafford, David A. T., 'SOE and British Involvement in the Belgrade Coup d'État of March 1941', in *Slavic Review*, Vol.36, No. 3 (Sep. 1977) (Cambridge University), pp. 399-419, jstor.org

Strathcarron, Ian, *Joy Unconfined: Lord Byron's Grand Tour Re-toured* (Signal, Oxford, 2010)

Stuart Williams, Michael, *The Politics of Heresy in Ambrose of Milan: Community and Consensus in Late Antique Christianity* (Cambridge University, 2017)

Świetochowski, Tadusz,'Czartoryski and Russia's Turkish Policy, 1804-1806', in *The Polish Review*, Vol. 12, No. 4, (Autumn, 1967), pp. 30-36, jstor.org

Tallon, James, 'Albania's Long World War I (1912-1925)', Albania in WWI, ResearchGate, January 2014, researchgate.net

Tase, Peter, 'Italy and Albania: The Political and Economic Alliance and the Italian Invasion of 1939', academicus.edu.al

'The Battle of Taranto', in *Navy Wings*, navywings.org.uk

'The Corfu Declaration, 20 July 1917', Primary Documents, firstworldwar.com

'The Letters and Dispatches of Vice Admiral Lord Viscount Nelson with Notes by Sir Nicholas Harris Nicolas', January 1802 to April 1804, Vol.5, archive.org

'The Scuole', in *The Churches of Venice*, churchesofvenice.co.uk

The Spectator (6 September 2003), spectator.co.uk

The Spirit of the Pilgrims, Vol. 4 (University of California, 1831: digitized 1 Nov 2007), books.google.co.uk

Theotokis, G., 'Bohemond of Taranto's 1107-8 campaign in Byzantine Illyria – can it be viewed as a Crusade?' (2012), rosetta.bham,ac.uk/Issue_11/theotokis.pdf

'The Story of Gjergj Kastrioti Skanderbeg – A True Enemy to the Sultan', Medieval History, about-history.com

Tolstoy Nikolai, 'Close Designs and Crooked Purposes: Forced Repatriation of Cossacks and Yugoslav Nationals in 1945', Introduction by Charles Crawford, *CRCE Centre for Research into Post-Communist Economies*, May 2012, crce.org.uk

Unger, Miles, *Magnifico: The Brilliant Life and Violent Times of Lorenzo De' Medici* (Simon and Schuster, 2008)

Van-Houts, Elizabeth, *Medieval Memories: Men, Women and the Past, 700-1300* (Routledge, 13 Sep 2013)

Voltaire, *La Princesse de Babylone*: Texte entire, Chapitre XVIII, fr.wikisource.org

von Redlich, Marvellus Donald A. R., 'Montenegro an Independent State and King Nicholas a Sovereign?', in *Social Science*, Vol. 6, No. 3 (Jul., 1931), pp. 231-243, jstor.org

Vryonis, Speros, Jr., *Byzantium and Europe* (Thames and Hudson, London, 1967)

Waltré, Mats, 'When did Diocletian die? Ancient Evidence for an Old Problem' (March 2011), www.matswaltre.se/pdf/Diocletian.pdf

Ward, Phillip, *The Aeolian Islands* (Oleander, 1974)

Ward-Perkins, Bryan, *The Fall of Rome and the End of Civilization* (Oxford University, 2005)

Weltecke, Dorothea, 'Emperor Frederick II, "Sultan of Lucera", "Friend of the Muslims", Promoter of Cultural Transfer: Controversies and Suggestions', in

Cultural transfers in dispute: representations in Asia, Europe and the Arab World since the Middle Ages (ed.) Jörg Feuchter (Frankfurt: Campus-Verl., 2011), pdfs. semanticscholar.org

West, Rebecca, *Black Lamb and Grey Falcon: A journey through Yugoslavia*, first published 1942 (Canongate, Edinburgh, London, 1993)

'What was the relationship (if there as one) between the various Norman states of the 11-12th Centuries?', reddit.com

Wiegler, Paul, *The Infidel Emperor, and his struggles against the Pope* (Routledge, London, 1930)

Wilcox, Vanda, 'The Catastrophe at Caporetto', in *History Today* (24 October 2017), historytoday.com

Wilkinson, Sir John Gardner, *Dalmatia and Montenegro: With a Journey to Mostar in Herzegovina*, Vol. 1 (John Murray, London, 1848)

Williams, Stephen, and Friell, Gerard, *Theodosius: The Empire at Bay* (B T Batsford Ltd, London, 1994)

Williamson, Samuel R. Jr, 'Influence, Power, and the Policy Process: The Case of Franz Ferdinand, 1906-1914', in *The Historical Journal*, Vol. 17, No. 2 (Jun., 1974), pp.417-434, jstor.org

Winder, Simon, *Danubia: A Personal History of Habsburg Europe* (Picador, London, 2013)

Winfield, Rif, *French Warships in the Age of Sail, 1786–1861: Design, Construction, Careers and Fates* (Casemate, 16 Sep 2015)

Wiseman, James, 'Insight: Encounters with Ali Pasha', in *Archaeology*, Vol. 52, No. 4 (July/August,1999), pp. 10-15, jstor.org

Wood, Ian, and F.A. Loud, F.A. (eds), *Church and Chronicle in the Middle Ages: Essays Presented to John Taylor* (A&C Black, 1991)

Wood, Ian, 'Theoderic's Monuments in Ravenna', in *The Ostrogoths: From the Migration Period to the Sixth Century: An Ethnographic Perspective* (eds) Sam J. Barnish and Federico Marazzi (Boydell, San Marino, 2007)

Woodhouse, J. R., 'Gabriele d'Annunzio's Reputation and Critical Fortune in Britain', in *Annali d'Italianistica*, Vol. 5 (1987), pp. 245-258, jstor.org

Woodhouse, John Robert, *Gabriele D'Annunzio: Defiant Archangel* (Oxford University, 2001)

Woolridge, Dorothy Elizabeth, 'Yugoslav-United States Relations, 1946-1947, Stemming from the Shooting of U.S. Planes over Yugoslavia, August 9 and 19, 1946', MA Thesis, Houston, Texas (May 1971), scholarship.rice.edu

Wooten, Tim, 'Letters from the Emperor', in *The North American Review*, Vol. 278, No. 3 (May-Jun., 1993), pp. 35-39, jstor.org

Wright, D. R. Edward, 'Ludovico Il Moro, Duke of Milan, and the Sforziada by Giovanni Simonetta in Warsaw', bbc.ac.uk/hosted/Leonardo/Wright_Sforziad.pdf

Zaccaria, Benedetto, 'Yugoslavia, Italy, and European integration: was Osimo 1975 a Pyrrhic victory?', in *Cold War History* (27 Sep 2029) (Taylor & Francis Online), tandfonline.com

Zanlorenzi, Silvia, 'The Scuola Dalmata di San Giorgio e Trifone: A Place for the Dalmatian Community in Venice' (Università degli Studi di Padova), edizionicafoscari. unive.it

Živojinović, Dragoljub R., 'King Nikola and the Territorial Expansion of Montenegro, 1914-1920', in *Balcanica* XV (2014), doiserbia.nb.rs

Index

Index

Index

Index

Index

Index